Upstream Metropolis

[An Urban Biography of Omaha and Council Bluffs]

LAWRENCE H. LARSEN

BARBARA J. COTTRELL

HARL A. DALSTROM

& KAY CALAMÉ DALSTROM

D1124702

University of Nebraska Press
Lincoln and London

Library of Congress
Cataloging-in-Publication Data
Upstream metropolis : an urban biography of Omaha and Council Bluffs /
Lawrence H. Larsen . . . [et al.].
p. cm.
"A Bison original"—T.p. verso.
Includes bibliographical references and
index.
ISBN-13: 978-0-8032-8002-1 (pbk. : alk.
paper)
ISBN-10: 0-8032-8002-5 (pbk. : alk.
paper)
1. Omaha (Neb.)—History. 2. Council
Bluffs (Iowa)—History. 3. City and
town life—Nebraska—Omaha—History.
4. City and town life—Iowa—Council
Bluffs—History. 5. Urbanization—Nebraska—Omaha—History. 6. Urbanization—Iowa—Council Bluffs—History.
7. Omaha (Neb.)—Social conditions.
8. Council Bluffs (Iowa)—Social conditions. I. Larsen, Lawrence Harold, 1931–
F674.O5U675 2007
978.2—dc22
2006051062

Set in Minion by Kim Essman.
Designed by A. Shahan.

To the memory of
James C. Olson (1917–2005),
teacher, friend, colleague,
and distinguished scholar.

[Contents]

[Illustrations]

[Preface]

In 2006 a number of municipalities of all sizes, both very small and quite large, made up what is formally called the "Omaha–Council Bluffs, NE-IA Metropolitan Statistical Area" (MSA). MSA is an artificial term used by the census to delineate the nation's most populous urban concentrations. The census normally defines an MSA as a central city or neighboring cities of fifty thousand or more, plus their surrounding counties. In 2005, the Omaha–Council Bluffs MSA ranked sixtieth among the 370 such metropolitan areas in the United States and Puerto Rico.

The territory of the Omaha–Council Bluffs MSA is divided roughly in half by the Missouri River. Many of the communities in the MSA are small; some have grown into large suburbs. Omaha, with more than four hundred thousand people, is the central city, sometimes called a core city, of the MSA which has over eight hundred thousand inhabitants. The second-largest community in the MSA is Council Bluffs, Iowa, with a population approaching sixty thousand. Originally called Kanesville, it was an early portal to the West, used by the Mormons as a staging point for their trek to Utah. In 1854 promoters from Council Bluffs founded Omaha directly across the Missouri River from Council Bluffs. River bottoms and a large floodplain separated the two cities, rivals that developed somewhat independently of each other but with some recognition that their fates were joined. Some observers considered the two communities at a divide between the eastern and western portions of the United States.

Adjoining modern Omaha on the south is Bellevue, once a trading post and government Indian agency that was Nebraska's first settlement. Outside decision makers had stymied Bellevue's ambitions in Nebraska's early development, but with the coming of World War II and the Cold War, a new set of outside decision makers brought a huge war industry and later a big military base to the community, ending its eighty-year experience as a small town with a seemingly limited future. Rapid growth ensued, and by 2000 Bellevue, with a population of more than forty-four thousand, was Nebraska's third-largest city.

Before white settlement, native people in the Omaha–Council Bluffs area had recognized the importance of the region. In the mid-nineteenth century, the Omaha Indians—the "upstream people," according to their tribal name—and other aboriginals were removed to reservations. What determined the ascendancy of the new town of Omaha was the decision during the Civil War to build the eastern half of the first transcontinental railroad, the Union Pacific Railroad, out of what was then a small community with uncertain prospects. The coming of the railroad cemented Omaha's position as the most important place in Nebraska, dashing the hopes of Nebraska City, another Missouri River city. But eastern transportation connections were basic to Omaha's growth, and even before the rails linking Omaha to California were completed in 1869, a railroad tied Council Bluffs to Chicago and points east. Other lines soon added to the importance of Omaha and Council Bluffs as railroad centers. Whether they were pursuing development of railroads or other entrepreneurial activity, Omaha's leaders consistently welcomed outside money, both private and public, while at the same time seeking to achieve freedom of action. This became a hallmark of the city.

Upstream Metropolis: An Urban Biography of Omaha and Council Bluffs is not an old-fashioned traditional local history, with facts laid end-to-end without an apparent purpose. Since the birth of the Republic over one hundred thousand local histories have been produced in America that are valuable factually and chronologically but that contain little in the way of critical analysis or interpretation. Nor is *Upstream Metropolis* a modern "social history" that deemphasizes economics and politics and attempts to explain the history of a city by telling the stories of urban people, especially minorities. *Upstream Metropolis* does not have an agenda. Through extensive research in economic, social, and political material, the book explains historically how Council Bluffs and Omaha developed from their early to present days. Given that the book uses traditional means to tell how the Omaha–Council Bluffs area developed, with conclusions being drawn when appropriate as the story unfolds, there are no lists of incorporation dates of places, or lists of mayors, or chronologies of events. *Upstream Metropolis* provides a framework that concentrates on delineating the process of urbanization. The purpose is to use only necessary and representative information to build an argument illustrating, for instance, the importance of outside decisions.

Upstream Metropolis, while urban history, concentrates on urbanization, a concept narrower than the current definition of urban history, which in a general sense is all inclusive, covering everything that happens in a city. Urbanization is an independent variable, but everything that happens in a city is not necessarily urbanization history unless it is put in context and relates to city building. For example, the construction of the Union Pacific was a great engineering project that helped bind the nation together. Considered in that way, it is unimportant that the railroad happened to have an Omaha terminal. But, in *Upstream Metropolis*, the Union Pacific is considered in terms of its impact on the urbanization of the Omaha area, setting patterns that have affected Omaha's development for over 140 years, ensuring it and Council Bluffs of central-city status in a modern regional metropolis.

All cities inside a MSA have their historical pasts, so considering them as a whole is very difficult. For example, St. Louis County in the St. Louis Metropolitan Area has some ninety-three different incorporations. The Milwaukee–Waukesha MSA includes the big city of Milwaukee plus the old important cities of industrial Racine and commercial Waukesha, both of which continue to have strong identities. As another example, Leavenworth, Kansas, an important military town since frontier days with a solid identity of its own, is part of the Kansas City, Missouri, MSA.

Because of research limitations and other restraints imposed on a given project, almost all urban biographies concern a single city. This is illustrated by Pulitzer Prize–winning biographies of Washington and New York. The scope of the research is simply too broad in most cases to consider their suburban components. The few exceptions are rather broad accounts of very large urban areas, such as those for New York and Los Angeles, which have for obvious and urgent reasons attracted the interest of urbanologists from many different disciplines. Hardly any scholarly studies exist for the nation's MSAS.

This book makes no attempt to treat every community in what now constitutes the Omaha–Council Bluffs MSA, which by governmental redefinition grew from five to eight counties as the project neared completion. Of necessity, it gives prime attention to the core cities of Omaha and Council Bluffs.

Bellevue is problematic. Its peculiar history with a significant early period, a long, fairly somnolent middle era, and a dynamic recent past is reflected in the narrative. Outlying towns and suburban counties are treated only insofar as their development reflects the growth of the metropolitan area. There are some good studies on the histories of these communities, and as the case with the core cities, much remains to be written about them.

Of the many different kinds of primary and secondary sources that are used in writing about cities, newspapers are among the most rewarding and, at the same time difficult to use. Newspapers are the "manuscripts of the city" and researching them over a long period of time is daunting and tedious. Except for newspapers from recent years, the Internet is usually of no help because back runs of newspapers are not available through this medium. As a result, in researching years before the 1990s, microfilm at appropriate depositories is the only alternative. Although *Upstream Metropolis* relied upon years of work by many scholars doing research in Omaha newspapers and other materials, when the project was started, little had been done on the development of Council Bluffs after the frontier period. Hence, doing research on Council Bluffs for *Upstream Metropolis* required the reading of a good bit of microfilm, primarily searching for information on topics not treated in the Council Bluffs Public Library's extensive clipping files. For some time we have maintained our own clipping file of the *Omaha World-Herald*, which proved invaluable for writing about the metropolitan area's recent period. Much additional research by the present authors and other scholars, especially for the 1982 and 1997 editions of *The Gate City: A History of Omaha* has made *Upstream Metropolis* possible. In any event, this book is a pioneering effort in the urbanization history of the nation's sixtieth-largest metropolitan area.

So many people have given help and encouragement over the years in writing about Omaha and the surrounding area that all of them can not be acknowledged. Of special help were the late A. Theodore Brown, Lyle W. Dorsett, Fredrick M. Spletstoser, Niel M. Johnson, Garneth Oldenkamp Peterson, Ann Diffendal, James E. Potter, Donald Snoddy, the late Jean Dunbar, Richard Overfield, William Pratt, William Petrowski, Roger T. Johnson, and Charles N. Glaab.

Lawrence H. Larsen thanks appropriate officials of the University of Missouri–Kansas City for their aid. Harl Dalstrom is especially indebted to the

College of Arts and Sciences of the University of Nebraska at Omaha for released time to conduct research. All the authors owe a particular debt of thanks to the work of UNO graduate students whose masters of arts theses provide important information on the history of Omaha and the surrounding area. Orville D. Menard, professor emeritus of political science, UNO, whose scholarly writings and hundreds of public programs have done much to advance the understanding of Omaha's history, has been a source of encouragement. James C. Olson, president emeritus of the University of Missouri and a distinguished historian of Nebraska, provided valuable background information. Mark Norman of the Council Bluffs Chamber of Commerce; the staffs of the Greater Omaha Chamber of Commerce; Karen Klein, Planning Department, city of Omaha; Gayle Malmquist, Department of Community Development, city of Council Bluffs; and Paul Mullen and Pat Jesse of the Metropolitan Area Planning Agency afforded timely assistance. The staffs of the Council Bluffs Public Library, the Omaha Public Library, and the University Library, UNO, helped make research a pleasure. Thanks for help on the photographs goes especially to Timothy M. Fitzgerald, manager, photography, University Affairs, UNO; Lynn Friesner, Reference Department, Council Bluffs Public Library; Terri Raburn, Nebraska State Historical Society; and David Boutros, associate director in Kansas City of the Western Manuscript Collection, a joint collection of the University of Missouri and the State Historical Society of Missouri. Significant research on Omaha was done in Lincoln at the Nebraska State Historical Society.

As custom and prudence demand, the authors of *Upstream Metropolis* are responsible for any errors.

[UPSTREAM METROPOLIS]

[Part 1] The Beginning to 1854

[1] The Council Bluffs

Saturday, August 21, 1999, was a typical sunny summer day as people gathered at a construction site at Sixty-seventh and Pacific streets in central Omaha to witness the dedication of a new building. The structure, housing the Peter Kiewit Institute of Information Science, Technology and Engineering, was a $70 million project combining private and public funds to ensure that Omaha and the state of Nebraska would be in the vanguard of the information age. U.S. secretary of education Richard Riley told the crowd that the institute, which would be operated by the University of Nebraska–Lincoln and the University of Nebraska at Omaha, would help the nation meet its needs in information technology education. Walter Scott Jr., a business and civic leader who had done much to make the Kiewit Institute a reality, said that the next challenge was to make the institute one of the best such learning centers in the nation. In a high-tech version of the traditional ribbon-cutting, Scott activated a robot that cut a fiberoptic cable. The robot then bowed to Scott and University of Nebraska president L. Dennis Smith.

The Peter Kiewit Institute was part of an information technology complex rising on property formerly belonging to the civic organization, the Knights of Ak-Sar-Ben (reverse spelling of "Nebraska"), which had operated a horse racetrack not far south of the new structure. On a day during racing season in 1979—like many other days in other years—the voices of upwards of thirty thousand racing fans had sounded across this flat stretch of land. In less than a generation, the heyday of racing gave way to casino gambling on the Iowa side of the metropolitan area, the track closed, and the horse barns were razed. In 1999 the old Ak-Sar-Ben land was passing to uses that scarcely could have been imagined twenty years earlier.

A few miles away in south Omaha, another big event was going on this Saturday, but no civic or educational leaders marked the occasion. In the lobby of the seventy-three-year-old Livestock Exchange Building, people from many places in Nebraska and Iowa had gathered for the second day of an auction of an array of items from the stockyards, which after existing 116 years were soon to close. On the surface the atmosphere was cheerful, but many of the people who were present knew that an institution and a process that had linked Omaha to the Corn Belt and Great Plains for five generations were passing. Probably like others at the auction, Betty Votaw, from a Nebraska ranch over three hundred miles west of Omaha, had a longstanding family tie to the south Omaha yards. Her father-in-law, Eli Votaw, had sold cattle at this market for over half a century, and she declared, "Eli would turn over in his grave if he knew this place was closing." Just over two months later, the stockyards closed.

The two events of August 21, 1999, appropriately reported on the same pages of the *Omaha Sunday World-Herald*, illustrate the process of evolution and adaptation that characterized the first century and a half of the history of a metropolitan area that had emerged on both sides of the Missouri River. People attending one of the two symbolic events on that August day in what most of them deemed the final year of the twentieth century would have agreed that the capacity to adjust successfully, if not easily, to changing times is the hallmark of any dynamic urban center.

A CHANGING LANDSCAPE

Many of the people at the old Ak-Sar-Ben grounds or the stockyards probably reflected upon the impermanence of many human institutions, but probably few if any of them could have imagined the landscape before development. Through the geologic eras extending over hundreds of millions of years, the environment of what is now the Greater Omaha area, as elsewhere in the evolution of the planet, underwent tremendous changes.

From the standpoint of Omaha's origins, a good period of time in which to look at the physical setting is the early to mid-nineteenth century—the period just before beginning of European settlement of the area and region. In short, what did the land look like? This is not an easy question to answer for four major reasons. First, urban development literally reshaped the landscape. For example, in what became downtown Omaha, massive excavation projects in the late nineteenth and early twentieth centuries reduced street grades to levels more manageable for transportation, just as contemporary highway and real-estate projects cut through hills, create embankments, and alter the course of streams. Second, the settlement process radically altered the flora and fauna of the area. Third, the Missouri River and its valley, which would be basic to the development of the metro area, have changed tremendously in character and appearance since settlement began. Finally, metropolitan Omaha is located in the western portion of the tallgrass prairie, an environment typical of eastern Nebraska, most of Iowa, and extensive areas of other Midwestern states. Unlike the nation's deserts, mountains, high-plains grasslands, and forest areas, only small remnants of the tallgrass prairie remain. For this reason, it is difficult to contemplate a landscape of grass standing six feet or higher and reaching almost treeless to the horizon. In the area where the south Omaha stockyards would be built, tallgrass prairie probably predominated, and in what would become the Ak-Sar-Ben area, trees along a branch of the Papillion Creek probably shared the setting with waving grass. Certainly the latter was the view that greeted Erastus Beadle, who resided briefly in Omaha in 1857 and contemplated developing a farm west of the three-year-old town. Near what is now the busy intersection of 102nd Street and West Center Road in the total quiet of a summer evening, Beadle looked across "a wide expanse of rolling prairie" broken only by trees along the Big Papillion Creek. Looking to the northwest, up the Papillion (now commonly called the "Papio"), he estimated that he could see for twenty miles.

The bluffs rising upwards of two hundred feet from the Missouri River floodplain composed the signature landform of the Council Bluffs–Omaha area. These hills are a product of the region's most recent geological era. A series of glaciers reached into what became the Omaha area, but the last two glacial thrusts, the Illinoisan and the Wisconsinan, did not extend that far south. As these glaciers advanced, they ground rock to a powderlike consistency, and when they melted, the runoff carried this fine-textured material onward. In time, the land dried, and winds blew away the particles. This windborne soil, known by the German word *loess*, was deposited in central and eastern Nebraska, much of Iowa, and adjacent states. The Missouri River valley, along what is now the border of Iowa and Nebraska, was a rich source of such soil, and winds lifted the loess particles, depositing them to such depths as to form the adjoining hills. Because the prevailing winds were westerly, the loess bluffs are most pronounced on the east side, but the winds were sufficiently variable so as to create parallel hills across the approximately five-mile-wide valley. The loess bluffs adjoining the Missouri valley were not formed in one single time period but developed at intervals during the lengthy conclusion of the ice age. Over the course of about the last twelve thousand years, water eroded the bluffs to approximately their present condition. The dry, rugged western slopes of the Iowa loess hills sustain yucca plants and some other species that are not otherwise found in the wild, east of the Great Plains. For persons arriving in Omaha via the Missouri River valley, these bluffs are the most beautiful feature of the landscape.

The Missouri River floodplain was a place of tall grass, rushes, and marshes. In May 1843 John James Audubon, famous naturalist and painter of birds, made a trek on horseback from the river across the floodplain in the area of modern Council Bluffs, Iowa. He recalled, "My guide was anxious to take a short cut, and took me across several bayous, one of which was really up to the saddle; but we crossed that, and coming to another we found it so miry, that his horse wheeled after two or three steps." The floodplain was a fine habitat for waterfowl, but as was often the case with other such lowlands, it gained a reputation as a malarial environment. Early European American occupants would find the bottoms good for grazing livestock, although in time the wetlands would be drained and the floodplain transformed into high-quality farmland and commercial, industrial, and residential properties. The flat terrain would be ideal for the development of railroad lines, marshalling yards, and in later times, highways and a major airport.

This transformation made the river bottomland an integral and highly valuable part of the twin cities of Council Bluffs and Omaha, but it was a risky undertaking. For generations after settlement, the Missouri was a wild river whose channel frequently shifted during floods. To live on the floodplain was to tempt fate. Not until the mid-twentieth century, when the U.S. Army Corps of Engineers built six huge dams and reservoirs from the Nebraska–South Dakota border upstream through North Dakota to Montana, was the flow of the Missouri River past the Omaha area regulated. The corps also developed a navigation channel from the Missouri's mouth upstream almost one thousand river miles to Sioux City, Iowa, and the agency's bank stabilization work straitjacketed the river below the dams. In April 1952 residents of Council Bluffs and Omaha withstood what would be the old Missouri's final challenge as it carried water from parts of seven states and two Canadian provinces past dikes maintained only by Herculean efforts.

A silent witness to the life of the once wild Missouri River greets every person who makes the short trek via Abbott Drive from Eppley Airfield to downtown Omaha. As one exits the airport, on the Nebraska side of the river, one sees Carter Lake, a horseshoe-shaped body of water. Someone unfamiliar with the area would have no reason to know that the land immediately west of the lake from the airport is part of the town of Carter Lake, Iowa, and that the lake itself was once the Missouri River channel. Shortly after the lake disappears on the right, and with the downtown Omaha skyline looming larger, the visitor may be puzzled to read a sign proclaiming "The People of Iowa Welcome You." After less than half a mile, one is back in Nebraska and is soon downtown. The anomaly of a sliver of Iowa being on the Nebraska side of the river dates from an 1877 flood in which the Missouri River cut a channel across the base of the horseshoe bend, leaving the land inside the horseshoe as an Iowa enclave in Nebraska. Carter Lake, the old river channel, was for many years appropriately named Cut-Off Lake and is one of many oxbow lakes formed when the Missouri went on a rampage.

Today, gambling casino vessels implicitly romanticize nineteenth-century steamboat travel, but a journey on the untamed Missouri could be a daunting experience. Venturing into shallow water, running aground on sandbars, and hitting submerged trees (snags) that had tumbled into the water from flooding or bank erosion made travel a challenge. Among the most notable early travelers on the river were Maximilian of Wied-Neu Wied, a German prince and scholar, and Karl Bodmer, a Swiss artist who accompanied the prince. Traveling up the river on the steamboat *Yellowstone* in the spring of 1833, Prince Maximilian recorded numerous occasions in which these navigational challenges impeded the vessel's progress, and Bodmer made a watercolor painting of snags downstream from modern Omaha. Five years later, a Belgian-born Jesuit priest, Father Pierre Jean De Smet, traveling up the Missouri aboard the steamboat *Wilmington* to the area that would become Council Bluffs, Iowa, observed similar menaces, plus the nagging but reasonable prospect of death from an exploding boiler:

At the same time the weather was excessively hot: the warm, muddy water of the Missouri was our only drink, and the myriads of mosquitoes, fleas, and other insects were our traveling companions. Still everyone spoke of the beautiful fortunate voyage we had made. I fear the sea, I will admit, but all the storms and other unpleasant things I have experienced in four different voyages did not inspire so much terror in me as the navigation of the somber, treacherous, and muddy Missouri.

Early travelers left attractive written and visual images of the country along the Missouri River near what would become the Greater Omaha area. Prince Maximilian noted the "pleasantly green, densely forested hills" at Bellevue, just downstream from modern Omaha, and at this remote trading post and government Indian agency, he was impressed by "the layout of the place and its lovely view of the river." He was a knowledgeable naturalist and added, "On the hill blue phlox and the *Staphylea trifoliate*, also the red *Aquilegia*, bloomed in mass." A short distance upstream he saw "a picturesquely wild forest." His frequent references to the beauty of the redbud trees ring true to anyone who has spent a spring in the area.

By contrast, Father De Smet would see a dangerous, pest-ridden environment when he began his missionary work a short distance to the northeast. As he wrote in July 1838,

> It is not uncommon to meet bears in our neighborhood; but this animal will seldom attack a man first, though he will defend himself when wounded. Wolves come very often to our very doors; quite lately they have carried off all our chickens. They are of all kinds; prairie-wolves, small and timid; black mountain wolves, large and dangerous. We are obliged to be continuously on our guard against these bad neighbors, and so I never go out without a good knife, a tomahawk or a sword-cane. There are snakes too, among which I might name the copper-head, the garter-snake [?couleuvre], blacksnake and rattlesnake. Field, forest and cabin swarm with mice, which gnaw and devour the few fruits that we possess. Insects, butterflies especially, are very numerous here, and very variegated and very large. Night-moths are of all colors and of a prodigious size; they are no less than eight inches in length. We also live in the midst of horse-flies and mosquitoes; they come upon us by thousands and give us no rest day nor night.

Settlement would bring an end to bears and wolves in the region, and the problems of venomous snakes and massive numbers of mice did not endure.

In an area in which prairie was the norm, local woodlands could not ultimately sustain the pressures of building Omaha, Council Bluffs, other towns, and the surrounding farmsteads. Moreover, many of the trees adjacent to the river were cottonwoods, a species ill suited for construction use. Photographs of Omaha in the 1860s contrast with the sylvan image that Prince Maximilian described some three decades earlier, for they show buildings standing starkly on essentially barren hills. To what extent early urban development denuded local woodlands is uncertain, but in the long run it was essential that an external supply of lumber be available. For Council Bluffs, Omaha, and communities across the region, timber from the white pine forests of the upper Great Lakes country, marketed through lumber companies in Chicago, supplied the essential lumber.

Looking from an upper floor of a tall building on a summer day across modern Omaha, one sees the maze of concrete and asphalt that typifies urban development. But equally prominent, if not more, is the panorama of green that reaches across much of the skyline. The Omaha skyline, and probably the skyline of every other Midwestern and Great Plains city, reveals an urban forest. However much early settlers cut timber, permanent settlement in the region brought human intervention on the side of trees. In the tallgrass-prairie region, settlers replaced the grassland with fields of corn and other crops. In rural areas, including the loess hills along the Missouri, human influence in the generations since settlement has facilitated the advance of trees and shrubs into the remaining prairie.

PREHISTORIC AND HISTORIC NATIVE PEOPLE

Neither of the symbolic events on that Saturday in August 1999 would have called upon those in attendance to ponder the questions of why and how, less than a century and a half earlier, a town called Omaha had arisen on the west bank of the Missouri River. Even more remote in the minds of those who attended were the topics of who had occupied this land prior to the coming of European Americans and how these people had lived.

Just as change would mark the experience of Omaha's residents through the generations since the American settlement of the area began in the mid-nineteenth century, impermanence characterized the experiences of the prehistoric and historic Native peoples of the mid-Missouri River valley. Current archeological knowledge suggests human habitation of the middle Missouri region dates to at least about 8000 BC—typical for the midcontinent area. A drought extending over several millennia after circa 6000 BC probably brought an end to this early activity. In the first millennium AD what is known as the Early Ceramic (Plains Woodland) Culture prevailed in the region. Evidence of the Woodland Culture has been found in the Ponca Creek area just beyond Omaha's northern boundary. The Woodland people made conical-shaped pottery, and there is evidence that they domesticated plants, if not in Nebraska, at least at some places within the region. The Plains Woodland people were deer hunters and may have eventually used the bow and arrow.

The plight of the Plains Woodland people after about 800 AD is a mystery, but from about 900 to the middle centuries of the second millennium AD, which archeologists term the Middle Ceramic (Plains Village) Period, a people known as the Nebraska Culture resided in the Missouri valley bluffs along the modern Iowa-Nebraska border. The Nebraska people, like others of the Middle Ceramic Period, lived by hunting, gathering, and horticulture, the last including growing beans, maize, and squash on lowland plots. They hunted with bows and arrows, and bison were their primary prey. In contrast to the conical pottery of their Woodland predecessors, Middle Ceramic people produced globe-shaped ware. On the Iowa side of the river, from modern Council Bluffs southward, lived the Glenwood people, who were part of the Nebraska Culture. They also grew crops, hunted deer and elk, and fished in the Missouri River. Their pottery suggests a connection with the Mississippian Culture and perhaps that society's great center at Cahokia, on the Illinois side of the Mississippi River near modern St. Louis.

Both Early and Middle Ceramic people excavated earth in the floor area of their dwellings, but the circular structures of the Early Ceramic Period gave way to more rectangular structures by Middle Ceramic times. Support timbers, poles, and a covering of grass, earth, and sod characterized such a home, which had a vestibule entry and a midstructure smoke hole. A few shallow excavations marking Nebraska Culture dwellings are preserved in forested river bluffs in the Omaha area. Archeological data suggests that a long drought in the mid-Plains region in the fourteenth and fifteenth centuries may have forced migrations that ended the Middle Ceramic Period.

If our knowledge of people of the Nebraska Culture is scant, the early history of the Native people whom Omaha was named after is also obscure. In the half-century prior to the founding of the town in 1854, the homeland of the Omaha Indians might be described as what became northeastern and east-central Nebraska from about modern-day South Sioux City in the north, one hundred miles southward to the Bellevue-Omaha area. In short, the city that bears the name of the tribe was at the southern end of the home area of the Omaha people. The word "Omaha" means "against the current," "those [people] going against the wind or current" or "upstream," and apparently dates from sometime before 1541. No one knows the exact area of origin of the Omaha people who spoke a Siouan language of the Dhegiha branch, but tribal lore suggests a background in the Great Lakes region, the Ohio River valley, or the Appalachian Mountains. Despite this seeming incongruity, these are adjoining areas and make up a comparatively small part of the continent. According to Omaha tradition, at some unknown time the tribe moved west or southwest in the Ohio valley region and crossed the Mississippi River. In the process, the tribe was accidentally divided, with the Omahas moving up the Mississippi valley, while the other part, which became known as the Quapaws, meaning "downstream," remained in what would become the state of Missouri.

After crossing the Mississippi, the Omahas migrated northward to Minnesota and eventually to eastern and then central South Dakota. Parallel with the long migration of the Omahas, the Teton Dakotas, more commonly called the Sioux, migrated out of the forest region west of Lake Superior and gradually built a power base on the northern Plains. In the Big Sioux River valley region of eastern South Dakota, the Omahas may have come into conflict with the Sioux, a situation that boded ill for their future. Through the eighteenth century, the Omahas seemed to have moved down the Missouri River valley until by 1775 they were at their Large Village in what became Dakota County in northeastern Nebraska.

By the early eighteenth century, the Otoe Indians, who spoke the Chiwere branch of the Siouan languages, had emigrated from the Great Lakes region into southeastern Nebraska and the adjoining parts of Iowa, Missouri, and Kansas. Just as the modern Omaha area became the southern extremity of the homeland of the Omaha people, it became the northern limit of the Otoe people and the related Missouria. In the early nineteenth century, another Siouan people, the Iowa (Ioway), longtime residents of various areas of the state bearing their name and linguistically akin to the Otoe-Missouria, briefly occupied the country between the Des Moines River in Iowa and the Missouri River, sometimes crossing the latter stream into the lower Platte River valley. A common reason why all of these Native peoples established a significant presence in what is now the Omaha area was to escape dangerous exposure to other tribes. In case of the Omahas and Otoes, the Teton Dakota were the key menace; for the Missouria and the Iowa, conflict with the Sauk (Sac) and Mesquakie (Fox) in eastern Iowa made migration a wise decision.

These tribes living in or around what would become the Council Bluffs–Omaha area shared a lifestyle that combined agriculture and hunting. For example, Omaha villages were composed of circular-shaped earth lodges built over slightly excavated floors. Vertical timbers supported beams over which a roof was made of willow branches and a heavy grass cover overlaid with sod. A smoke hole permitted the use of a firepit, and the earth floors were carefully hardened to facilitate cleaning. The entry was through a vestibule that normally faced east. Bulb-shaped cache pits for the storage of food and other items were excavated to a depth of some eight feet and were located adjacent to the entry. While on the hunt, lodging consisted of highly portable bison hide tepees.

Corn raising and bison hunting were at the heart of the livelihood and spirituality of these Siouan people near the Missouri River as was the case with Nebraska's largest tribe, the Pawnee, a Caddoan people, who lived farther west. Women planted and tended crops on lowland plots that in addition to corn included beans, squash, and pumpkins. In the case of the Omahas, bison hunting westward on the Great Plains meant that most people able to travel would be away from the village for as long as nine months a year. The Omahas and the Otoes had obtained horses from the Pawnee, who in turn had acquired the animals from the Spanish at Santa Fe. For these tribes and other Native people who gained their livelihood on the Plains, horses were crucial to the bison hunt.

A NEW ERA BEGINS

A vastly more powerful influence upon the Native people would be the growing European presence in the region. By the early 1700s, the area that is now modern Iowa and Nebraska was on the peripheries of the French and Spanish empires. In the 1750s a French and British dispute over which country would control the Ohio River valley led to the Seven Years' War, a conflict that came to include other European powers and reached from America's back country to points around the world. Part of the peace settlement in 1762–63 transferred the Louisiana region at the mouth of the Mississippi from France to Spain and recognized Spain as the ruler of the more northerly areas west of that river. For the first time from the European viewpoint, sovereignty was established over the area that now includes metropolitan Omaha and the Missouri valley. Before the end of French rule, the governor had given some entrepreneurs a monopoly on trade around the confluence of the Missouri and Mississippi rivers, resulting in the founding in 1764 of a settlement called St. Louis. In time, this community would nurture the development of the entire Missouri valley, including early Omaha and its neighbors.

Not until the 1790s did St. Louis businessmen, with the blessing of the Spanish authorities, make a serious effort to develop the upper-Missouri fur trade. To accomplish this, they had to deal with Native leaders, especially Black Bird, an able but ruthless Omaha chief. Traditionally the Omaha people had no chiefs, although white traders chose to bestow this honor upon certain persons, one of whom was Black Bird. He inspired awe among his people in part because of his ability to predict when certain persons would die, a talent for prognostication enhanced by his timely use of arsenic, which he obtained from the Europeans. Ironically in light of the role of commerce in his rise to power, Black Bird made the St. Louis traders pay a heavy tribute. A strategic purpose underlay this approach, for the Omahas had established trade interests with other Native peoples farther up the Missouri and wished to be middlemen in any European commerce within their reach. At the same time and despite Spanish notions of sovereignty, the Omahas maintained important trade connections with the British at Green Bay and later at the Des Moines River.

The 1790s, perhaps the heyday in the known history of the Omaha Nation, gave way to the first years of the nineteenth century during which three events heralded disaster for the Omahas and other nearby tribes. First, the years 1800–1801 brought a smallpox epidemic that apparently claimed over half the Omaha population. Within twenty years the tribes of the area would recover their numbers, but smallpox epidemics in the 1830s again devastated the Missouri River tribes and cholera brought added losses. Second, war and international diplomacy dramatically altered the future of the trans-Mississippi region. Although the British continued to occupy some points in what is now the Midwest for many years after the United States formally gained its independence in 1783, the peace settlement that year extended American sovereignty westward to the Mississippi River.

In 1800 Spain secretly ceded the Louisiana region to France, but after President Thomas Jefferson learned about this change, he undertook the negotiations that led to the Louisiana Purchase of 1803 by which the United States acquired the enormous, but then undelineated, region west of the Mississippi, including Iowa and Nebraska. In July 1804 Meriwether Lewis and William Clark led their famed Corps of Discovery up the Missouri past what would become metropolitan Omaha as they studied America's new possession and showed the flag to the Native people. That summer also brought the third symbolic development, albeit far more obscure than the first two, when the Brule Dakota mounted a significant assault upon the Omahas. Continuing trouble from the Dakotas to the northwest, the devastation of disease, and a growing American impact would show that the river bluffs and tallgrass-prairie homeland of the Omaha Nation and its neighbors was a most insecure environment.

Although the Omahas were usually at peace with the Pawnees, sporadic intertribal conflicts with and among their other neighbors occurred. Much more important was the increasing threat that the Teton Dakotas (Plains Sioux) posed to Omaha and Otoe-Missouria people along the Missouri River and the Pawnees in Nebraska's interior. With a rising population and the expansion of their power southward, the Dakotas made it ever more hazardous for the river tribes and the Pawnees to conduct bison hunts on the central Plains. This limitation upon hunting over a wide range, plus the arrival of some whites, fostered a depletion of game animals in the eastern Nebraska homeland.

The Sauk and Fox expelled the Omahas from Large Village in 1820 and may have continued to prevent their return through the decade, but it was the eventual Dakota ascendancy that thwarted Omaha attempts to regain their home site. Pushed southward, they lived for a time in the lower Elkhorn River valley and by 1845 were residing in a village on the lower Papillion Creek in what is now the area around Thirty-sixth Street and State Highway 370 in the southern portion of the metropolitan area. By the 1840s the Otoe-Missouria were residing just to the south, near the mouth of the Platte River.

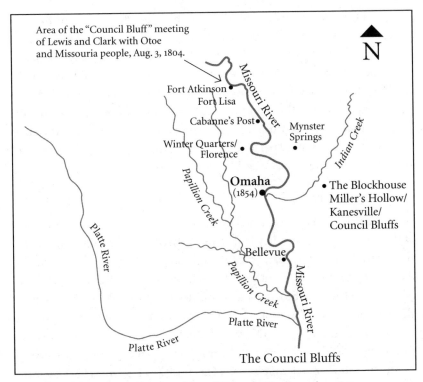

Area of the "Council Bluff" meeting of Lewis and Clark with Otoe and Missouria people, Aug. 3, 1804.

N

Missouri River

Fort Atkinson
Fort Lisa
Cabanne's Post
Mynster Springs
Winter Quarters/ Florence

Indian Creek

Papillion Creek

Omaha
(1854)

The Blockhouse
Miller's Hollow/
Kanesville/
Council Bluffs

Bellevue

Platte River

Papillion Creek

Missouri River

Platte River

Platte River

The Council Bluffs

Map adapted from Henry Chapman, Map of Nebraska Territory, circa 1857. In possession of Harl A. Dalstrom.

When Lewis and Clark came up the Missouri River in August 1804, they met with a group of Missouria and Otoe Indians somewhere near modern Fort Calhoun, Nebraska, about fifteen miles north of today's downtown Omaha. William Clark called this meeting place the "Councill Bluff." Even though the meeting of Lewis and Clark with the Missourias and Otoes was essentially ceremonial, Meriwether Lewis promised that a trading post would be established in the area if the Indians maintained intertribal peace and did not interfere with white travel on the river. He gave a strong warning that the United States would not tolerate misbehavior. Perhaps the most enduring outcome of the meeting was the name bestowed upon the site where the Otoes and Missourias met with Lewis and Clark. Within a few years after the journey of the Corps of Discovery, travelers along the Missouri River were speaking of "the Council Bluffs." This plural reference came to be a designation for not one specific point, but for the entire area along both sides of the

Missouri northward from about the mouth of the Platte River or the Bellevue area to "the Council Bluff" (singular) of the Lewis and Clark meeting, a stretch of some thirty miles. "Council Bluffs" would be a general label lasting until 1853 when residents of the Iowa community that would become the nucleus of urban development in the area adopted the name. Although the singular and plural distinctions produced enduring confusion, the name "the Council Bluffs" proved durable enough to draw the attention of travelers, entrepreneurs, and other persons interested in the West to the area north of the intersection of the Platte and Missouri rivers.

THE FUR TRADE

In 1806 Lewis and Clark returned from their great journey to the Northwest with news that the lands they had visited offered abundant opportunity for the fur trade. The next year, St. Louis entrepreneur Manuel Lisa established a company to trade with tribes in the Yellowstone and Big Horn valleys of what would become the eastern part of Montana. Troubles with Indians in this part of the upper Missouri basin, coupled with the outbreak of war between the United States and Great Britain, led Lisa in 1812 or 1813 to establish his base far downstream in the same locale as the Corps of Discovery's "Councill Bluff" of a decade earlier. This post was known as Fort Lisa, and although its exact location has not been discovered and little is known about the Missouri Fur Company's specific operations from this site, Lisa's firm apparently had satisfactory relations with the Indians. Lisa's contacts with the Natives had potential military and political significance. From Prairie du Chien, across the Mississippi from what is now northeastern Iowa, the British exercised much influence with the Indians of the midcontinent. Accordingly, William Clark (of Lewis and Clark fame), governor of Missouri Territory, in August 1814 appointed Lisa to be sub-agent for Indian affairs. His job was to keep the Native people friendly to the United States; and to aid him in accomplishing this task, the government provided him with gifts to be distributed. Lisa held this position until 1817 and apparently succeeded in building pro-American feelings in the region. In keeping with a common fur-trade practice, Lisa married into the Omaha tribe, something that he handled adroitly when his St. Louis wife came upriver to the post.

Manuel Lisa's long-term perspective was that the far reaches of the upper Missouri were the prime fur-trading area, but to maintain free passage to that region, it was essential to keep the friendship of the tribes in the lower reaches of the river, including the Council Bluffs area. The troubles of the second decade of the nineteenth century had temporarily disrupted the trade in what is now Montana, and as historical geographer David Wishart has said, "Fort Lisa at the Council Bluffs became the focal point of a retrenched trading area from 1812 to 1819."

When Lisa died in 1820, Joshua Pilcher, an experienced trader, emerged as the leading figure in the Missouri Fur Company, but by this time the U.S. Army had established a presence in the area. Following the War of 1812, the Monroe administration decided to fortify key places in the upper Mississippi and Missouri valleys. In partial implementation of this plan, the Yellowstone Expedition, composed of two army regiments under Col. Henry M. Atkinson, reached the Council Bluffs area in the autumn of 1819 where on the river bottoms, probably not far from Fort Lisa, they established their quarters, known as Cantonment Missouri. The entourage included Maj. Stephen H. Long, commanding an engineer group that would engage in scientific work. Indicative of the fast-emerging impact of technology upon America's westward expansion was the arrival of Long's men aboard the *Western Engineer,* the first steamboat to reach the area. In any event, the military failed to properly provision over 1,100 men on this remote frontier. As the winter wore on, scurvy claimed many lives at the bottomland quarters.

In June 1820 Long's group, which had wintered just downstream, headed west to the Rocky Mountains on an expedition that resulted in a report that did much to label the Plains region as the "Great American Desert." That month, a flood wiped out the buildings at Colonel Atkinson's camp. After a budgetary reduction, the army gave up plans for a post farther up the Missouri River, and the recently-dislodged troops of Cantonment Missouri erected Fort Atkinson on the safety of a bluff. Fort Atkinson, located at the eastern edge of the modern town of Fort Calhoun and now restored, was the most westerly U.S. military post during its seven-year existence. Here was stationed an agent to attend to the government's relations with the local Indian tribes. A post surgeon kept Nebraska's first weather records—data that showed the climatic extremes that remain typical of the Omaha area. More importantly, the highly successful crop and livestock raising at the post suggests the role agriculture would play in the evolution of the economy of the urban area. However, as a military establishment Fort Atkinson soon proved to have little value, and in 1827 it was abandoned in favor of the development of Fort Leavenworth, some two hundred miles to the south. This post was well positioned to protect the developing trade on the nearby the Santa Fe Trail.

For its first few years, Fort Atkinson was a neighbor to Fort Lisa, but Joshua Pilcher decided to move the Missouri Fur Company post some twenty-five miles south to a location not far above the confluence of the Missouri and Platte rivers. Why he did so is unclear. The fact that Lisa's family, rather than the company partners, owned Fort Lisa may have been an incentive as would a possible change in the Missouri River's channel. A more plausible situation was that Pilcher, needing to rebuild the post, found that the recent construction of Fort Atkinson had left an inadequate supply of timber for this work. Circumstantial evidence suggests that initial construction of this new post—which came to be known as Bellevue—occurred in the autumn of 1822. It is certain that the post, which would become Nebraska's oldest community, was in operation by the next summer. Although travelers on the Missouri River had various terms for the place, Pilcher probably originated the name "Bellevue." This name, implying a beautiful view of the river valley, became, as did the nearby Papillion (meaning "butterfly") Creek, a remnant of the French and French Canadian fur-trade connection to the region's early development.

The next few years brought success to the Missouri Fur Company in its operations in the upper Missouri River and Yellowstone River areas, but in 1823 the firm lost key personnel and an investment in trade goods in an attack by a group of Blackfeet Indians. Further troubles that year between traders and the Arikara Indians in modern South Dakota were answered by an unsuccessful punitive military expedition mounted from Fort Atkinson. In the middle of these hard times the Missouri Fur Company partnership was terminated in 1824. Pilcher, continuing at Bellevue, now faced competition from a trader named John Pierre Cabanne, who in 1822 or 1823 had established a post a few miles south of old Fort Lisa. Cabanne's Post was built just south of the mouth of Ponca Creek, adjacent to what is now Hummel Park at Omaha's northeastern extremity. Cabanne, who had been associated with Manuel Lisa, was a partner in a St. Louis group called the French Fur Company. Working with Cabanne in the operation of this post was another St. Louis trader, Joseph Robidoux. The competition between Pilcher and

Cabanne became so fierce that the two men worked out a truce in which they would share the trade. To assure compliance, Cabanne stationed a representative at Bellevue while Pilcher sent an agent to Ponca Creek, but because of superior financial backing, Cabanne held the upper hand.

The 1823 troubles on the upper Missouri were instrumental in partially reorienting the fur trade toward beaver trapping in the central Rocky Mountains. The Platte River valley was an excellent route to that area, and Bellevue was well located to serve as a jumping-off point. In 1827 Pilcher and his partners, finding themselves unable to survive in the Missouri River fur trade, mounted an expedition to the Rockies. When this endeavor did not prove to be as lucrative as anticipated, Pilcher dropped out of the partnership and turned his attention to the Pacific Northwest, while his associates, William H. Vanderburgh, Charles Bent, and Lucien Fontenelle, returned to Bellevue to carry on as best they could.

Some time after this venture into the Rockies, Lucien Fontenelle purchased the Bellevue post. Fontenelle, born in 1800 in the New Orleans area, had gone to work for the Missouri Fur Company in about 1819. He had been the key figure in the operations at Bellevue from the founding of the post and had taken an Omaha woman as his wife. Probably because Fontenelle lacked the capital to return immediately to the Rockies, he and a longtime associate, Andrew Drips, entered a business relationship with John Pierre Cabanne. Because Cabanne's operations had become part of the vast American Fur Company domain, this relationship brought Drips, Fontenelle, and the Bellevue post largely into the company's fold.

Posts such as Cabanne's became regional centers of commercial outreach to the Native people. In the autumn, traders from Cabanne's Post transported wares to the villages or encampments of the Omahas, Otoes, Pawnees, and more distant peoples where they established residence for winter commerce. Because it was impractical to bring bulky foodstuffs from St. Louis, the residents at Bellevue and Cabanne's, like their counterparts at posts farther up the river, raised crops and livestock. A summer visitor to Bellevue in the 1830s would have found a number of good-yielding corn fields and, continuing upstream through the Council Bluffs, might have seen fifteen acres of corn growing adjacent to Cabanne's Post. At Bellevue, Lucien Fontenelle, seeing Indians and Rocky Mountain–bound trappers as potential consumers, enthusiastically embarked upon a hog-raising enterprise.

When artist George Catlin visited Bellevue in 1832, he was pleasantly surprised to see cattle, poultry, potatoes, and abundantly bearing fruit trees as well as cornfields and hogs. Archeological evidence suggests that at least some of the people living at Bellevue and Cabanne's Post enjoyed amenities not usually associated with the remote frontier. These included good dining utensils, decorated china dinnerware, furniture and doors with proper fittings, glass-paned windows, wine, and brandy. According to Presbyterian missionary Samuel Allis, Cabanne "was a very kind and polite gentleman and quite an epicure. . . . Whatever was served on the table was always in the best style, and he was very attentive to his guests at table and elsewhere."

Although livestock, cornfields, and domestic household items linked the two posts at the Council Bluffs to civilization, the dark sides of life were never remote. At Bellevue, two homicides resulted when Fontenelle and his wife in separate episodes settled standing grievances, while at the Ponca Creek post too much whiskey probably contributed to a fatal shooting on December 25, 1833. The specter of death from cholera visited the people at the Council Bluffs posts in 1833 and 1835; and in 1837 the American Fur Company steamboat *St. Peter's* carried smallpox infection and death to Bellevue. From there, the vessel went on to what are now South Dakota and North Dakota, and at each stop its passengers further spread the disease, which wrought devastation to the Native people.

THE 1830S AND 1840S: NEW DIRECTIONS

The 1830s brought important changes to the Council Bluffs country that illustrated the continuing white American impact upon the West. The first was the establishment in 1832 of a federal Indian agency at Bellevue. Here, the United States government would attempt to carry out its basic Indian policy: get the Native people to adopt the values and lifestyle of white civilization, particularly the settled routine of farming as distinguished from their traditional combination of small-scale agriculture or horticulture with hunting. Farmers, employed by the agency, would give instruction in agricultural techniques; teachers, blacksmiths, and blacksmiths' assistants, known as "strikers," would help in this instruction. Fostering intertribal peace was another government objective, and like other agencies, Bellevue would be a center for the distribution of annuity payments made in compensation for Indian land cessions. After the closing of Fort Atkinson in 1827, Indian agent John

Dougherty, a former employee of the Missouri Fur Company, had tried to handle relations with the Omaha, Otoe, and Pawnee tribes from Fort Leavenworth. From time to time he visited the Council Bluffs region, sometimes making Cabanne's Post his temporary headquarters, but western superintendent of Indian affairs William Clark felt that Dougherty should be situated closer to the tribes within his jurisdiction. No longer able to resist pressure to move upstream, Dougherty in 1832 purchased Lucien Fontenelle's Bellevue property for use as the Council Bluffs Indian agency. Fontenelle relocated his operations less than one-half mile to the south, thus continuing Bellevue's function as a trade center. Because the Pawnee villages were some distance west of Bellevue, it was necessary to locate some agency personnel at these points. By the 1840s the agency would have upwards of two dozen employees, about half of whom were stationed among the Pawnees.

In 1833 the arrival at Bellevue of Baptist missionary Moses P. Merrill, his wife, Eliza, and two other persons, who soon began educational work among the Otoes marked another new dimension of white activity. The following year, Presbyterian missionaries Samuel Allis and John Dunbar used Bellevue as a jumping-off point in their work with the Pawnee people to the west. In the next decade, Bellevue was the temporary home for the Allis and Dunbar families in their sincere but unsuccessful efforts to encourage the Pawnees to adopt a settled way of life and to accept Christianity. In 1846 after squabbles at the mission and Sioux attacks, Allis moved to Bellevue where he instructed Pawnee children at an agency school.

In the Council Bluffs country as elsewhere on the frontier, whites used alcohol in trade with the Native people despite a federal law prohibiting it. When in 1832 J. P. Cabanne learned that another trader had sent alcohol up the Missouri, he sent a subordinate, Peter Sarpy, to intercept this shipment and eliminate the competitor's trade advantage. Sarpy succeeded, but his approach brought legal action by which he and Cabanne were temporarily ousted from the Indian trade. In 1833 Joshua Pilcher, after ventures outside the area, replaced Cabanne at the American Fur Company post on Ponca Creek. Pilcher came up from St. Louis aboard the company steamboat *Yellowstone.* He immediately directed the refurbishing of the post and enlarged its agricultural production. Pilcher imposed a constructive discipline at the Ponca Creek post—sometimes called "the Otto [Otoe] Outfit"—where a number of *engagés,* men hired to work in the fur trade, lived with their

Native families. Samuel Allis later described Pilcher as "one of the most prompt, candid, and reliable gentlemen [he had] met with in the Indian country. He was well informed on almost any subject, especially respecting Indians, for he had great experience and was free to give any information that was interesting and reliable."

Although population figures are uncertain, it seems likely that twenty-five or more people normally were present at this post with similar numbers at Bellevue. They included trading personnel, Indian agency employees at Bellevue, and visiting missionaries. Cabanne's gourmet cook and a few other blacks, perhaps slaves, were among the residents at Ponca Creek. Other traders and their Native families also resided near the posts. Artist Karl Bodmer, who accompanied Prince Maximilian up the Missouri in 1833, left a painting that provides a valuable image of Bellevue.

In 1835 Joshua Pilcher left the Otto Outfit post and returned to government service as an Indian sub-agent on the upper Missouri and from 1839 to 1841 served as St. Louis superintendent of Indian affairs. In the meantime, he made a brief return to the Council Bluffs country in October 1836 when he assisted Indian agent John Dougherty in an important action that demonstrated Bellevue's regional significance. This was the negotiation of a treaty in which the Omaha, Otoe-Missouria, Santee Sioux, and Yankton Sioux nations gave up their hunting rights in the land between what was then the northwestern border of Missouri and the Missouri River. This area, called the "Platte Purchase," was soon added to Missouri and became the six counties north and west of modern Kansas City. In return, the tribes would share $4,420 in goods, plus lesser benefits.

Given the dominant position of the American Fur Company, it seems to have become evident that two posts were not needed at the Council Bluffs, and between the autumn of 1838 and the spring of 1839, the establishment at Ponca Creek was abandoned. During this period Lucien Fontenelle and his partners in Fontenelle, Fitzpatrick and Company had seemingly attained supremacy in the Rocky Mountain beaver traffic, but through their St. Louis financiers, they were under the control of the American Fur Company. In the Rocky Mountain fur business, trappers harvested furs that they traded to the company at an annual rendezvous, normally held on the Green River in what is now western Wyoming. Bellevue functioned as a transfer point from steamboats to wagons in the movement of supplies for the trappers.

However, by the mid-1830s overtrapping and a declining national and European market marked the passing of the brief heyday of Rocky Mountain beaver trapping. In about 1839, Lucien Fontenelle, though less than forty years of age, died at Bellevue, his last years plagued by debt, and his health apparently undermined by alcohol. The death of this man who symbolized the linkage of Bellevue to the Rocky Mountains via the Platte valley paralleled the virtual end of the Rocky Mountain fur business.

PETER SARPY: ENTREPRENEUR

Following Fontenelle's death, operation of the Bellevue trading post passed to Peter Sarpy, who at some thirty-four years of age was a veteran of the fur trade and had spent a few years in the Rocky Mountains. Although there is dispute as to Sarpy's earliest association with Bellevue, he brought familiarity with the Council Bluffs area and solid St. Louis financial connections to his work. When Fontenelle died, the buildings at the adjoining Indian agency were dilapidated, but the government contracted with Sarpy to reconstruct its facilities, a task completed in 1841.

Amid the relative quiet of life at Bellevue in the first half of the 1840s, Sarpy's trade among the Pawnee and other tribes of the region illustrated the continuing significance of the post. Probably the biggest event was the arrival on October 1, 1842, of 2nd Lt. John C. Frémont of the U.S. Army's Corps of Topographical Engineers and his detachment at Bellevue on their way back to St. Louis from a study mission to the upper Platte country. A few days before his party's arrival, Lieutenant Frémont had sent word ahead that he would need a boat built for travel down the Missouri. Sarpy immediately ordered the construction of the craft and also sent supplies back to Frémont. Charles Preuss, the Frémont expedition's German-born cartographer, noted in his diary on October 2, "we are again in a somewhat civilized country." Bellevue was a place where two cultures met, and Preuss went on to reveal his mixed sentiments:

> We found to our pleasure that the Indians living around here went on a hunt several days ago. Peace and cleanliness return as soon as these disagreeable guests are out of the atmosphere.
>
> This town consists of a half-dozen widely separated trading posts. We put up in that of the American Fur Company. To be able to again sit on

a chair, at a table, to eat with a fork instead of using one's fingers—those are luxuries which only a few people will recognize as such.

The period from the mid-1840s to the Civil War would bring a great American immigration overland to Oregon, Utah, California, and Colorado. The Platte River valley was the logical route to these destinations. Accordingly, Sarpy would provision travelers, operate ferryboats, and provide other services that would help transform the Council Bluffs area from a remote fringe of American civilization to an important gathering place for the onslaught of that civilization upon the half of the continent beyond the Missouri. Sarpy was one of the area's first resident entrepreneurs. His career would bridge the watershed year of 1854 that separated the era of the wilderness trader from the opening of Nebraska to settlement and the advent of urban development on the west bank of the Missouri. Although traders and missionaries had different lifestyles and perspectives on the West, Samuel Allis left an interesting and probably accurate commentary upon Peter Sarpy:

> He possessed some excellent qualities and traits of character; although sometimes rough and uncouth, was a high-toned gentleman, who exerted a great influence among the whites as well as the Indians. He was particularly generous to white men of distinction and wealth, also to the Indians when it paid well, but exacted every penny of his hired men and others who earned their living by labor. Still he was generous to the needy. He was active and persevering in his transactions of various kinds of business; employed considerable capital in Indian and other trade; but was often wronged by his clerks, which vexed him as he was very excitable. For a business man with a large capital he was rather a poor financier. Toward the latter part of his life he became addicted to intemperance—a habit of seven-tenths of the Indian traders. During my acquaintance with him of thirty years he was always kind to me and would accommodate me in every way he could. He was all that could be wished for a man of the world, except the habit of intemperance.

Today's urban Americans understandably may see the fur trade as a symbol of wilderness, scantly related to modern life. Nonetheless, at the Council Bluffs and many other places in North America that would evolve into urban centers, the fur trade was far in the vanguard of capitalistic enterprise. Fort Lisa, Cabanne's Post, and Bellevue were conduits that linked Native people and a vast western landscape and its animal population via St. Louis to the markets and financial and material resources of eastern America and Europe. In overexploiting and sometimes even plundering animal life, in unwittingly spreading disease, and in its profit-driven degradation of Native people, the fur trade brought varying degrees of tragedy to large areas of the continent, including the Missouri valley. Nevertheless, the traders with their wealth of knowledge of the wilderness were valued guides to those who would come to the Council Bluffs or other frontier places.

THE POTAWATOMI INTERLUDE

Meanwhile, there had been significant activity on the east side of the Missouri in the Council Bluffs. Sometime around 1820 a man named Heart or Hart may have operated a trading post near the Mynster Springs area, north of what became the city of Council Bluffs. Some navigational maps labeled the area as "Hart's Bluffs," and a new river channel, created by a flood in 1832, was named "Hart's Cut-Off." Francois Guittar traded in the area and remained after settlement to become a store proprietor in the early days of the town of Council Bluffs. In September 1833 a treaty signed in Chicago with the Potawatomi tribe, plus some Chippewas and Ottawas, provided for the relocation of these peoples from their lands in the lower Great Lakes region to territory adjoining the east bank of the Missouri River. In 1835 they were moved to the east bank of the Missouri across from Fort Leavenworth, but this land would soon be part of the Platte Purchase, and they were not able to stay. Finally, in July and August 1837, steamboats brought the first of them to the Council Bluffs area, approximately opposite Bellevue. Others, escorted by troops from Fort Leavenworth, followed overland. These Potawatomis at the Council Bluffs were recognized as the United Bands, a name distinguishing them from other Potawatomi people who took up residence in what became Kansas. The government's sub-agent for the newcomers at the Council Bluffs was Edwin James, MD, who had been on Maj. Stephen Long's trek through the region in 1819–20. Perhaps because he reported to the Council Bluffs Indian agency at Bellevue, Dr. James located his sub-agency on the east side of the Missouri, at Trader's Point (Pointe aux Poules) close to that site.

Although some of the Indians in Dr. James's charge headed inland, a band that may have eventually totaled some five hundred persons, following their chief, Billy Caldwell, a man of Irish and Indian extraction who was recognized as a Potawatomi chief, occupied the area near the intersection of the river bluffs and floodplain where downtown Council Bluffs later developed. By the time the first Potawatomis reached the Council Bluffs, a company of dragoons from Fort Leavenworth also arrived. The assignment of the soldiers, under the command of Capt. D. B. Moore, was to construct a blockhouse for the protection of the relocated Indians from possible Sioux attack. The structure, apparently twenty-four feet on each side, erected at Caldwell's settlement, was completed by the start of November when the troops returned to Fort Leavenworth. In the long run, the blockhouse may have attracted other Indians to follow the initial group to Caldwell's site.

By 1838 the last of what government records showed to be a total of 2,734 Potawatomi, Chippewa, and Ottawa Indians had been resettled in what is now southwestern Iowa. The Council Bluffs sub-agency for a time employed a farmer who was supposed to teach agriculture to the resettled people. Likewise, the government built a mill to serve the Indians, but such efforts to help them lacked continuity, perhaps in part because of frequent turnover in the office of sub-agent. Moreover, Billy Caldwell, described by anthropologist James Clifton as an "intercultural broker," died in 1841, rendering the Potowatomis' future in Iowa less secure. Another serious problem was that even before their westward move, the Potawatomis had developed a taste for alcohol that would bedevil them in their new homeland.

On May 31, 1838, the steamboat *Wilmington* arrived at the Council Bluffs. Aboard the vessel were three Catholic priests from St. Louis who had come to minister to the relocated Indians. One of them was Father Pierre Jean De Smet, who would become one of the most prominent figures in the nineteenth-century American West. The military gave the blockhouse to Father De Smet to use as a mission, and Billy Caldwell provided the priests with three nearby cabins. They soon discovered that their task of meeting the spiritual needs of the Indians would be far greater than they had imagined. As Father De Smet ruefully informed his father superior, "We were far from finding here the four or five hundred fervent Catholics we had been told of at the College of St. Louis."

Soon after his arrival, Father De Smet noted the evil impact of alcohol upon the Indians. Such a problem, along with cultural differences including the language barrier, led him to remark, "This portion of the divine Master's vineyard requires from those who tend it, a life of crosses, privations and patience." In the spring of 1839, De Smet journeyed to what is now southeastern South Dakota where he met with members of the Yankton and Santee Sioux tribes in order to foster better relations between these peoples and the Potawatomis. Although this trip seemed fruitful, the "crosses and privations" in his ministry to the Potawatomis did not abate. Through the summer of 1839, he recorded frequent alcohol-induced fights, drownings, and homicides—situations no less appalling than one might find in the hardest modern urban environment. Mustering his patience, he remarked in December, "our endeavors have not been altogether fruitless and unavailing," but he soon left the Council Bluffs mission. His colleagues would continue the mission until July 1841, but Father De Smet's obvious pessimism suggested not only the mission's failure but the broader tragedy of the Potawatomi experience. The problems facing the Catholic priests differed significantly from those that would bring failure to the Presbyterians' work with the Pawnee, but both experiences demonstrated the enormous cultural gap between the whites and Indians who met in or near the Council Bluffs.

In order to abate the alcohol problem among the Indians along the Missouri, the commissioner of Indian affairs in 1842 appointed a special agent to patrol the river upstream from the Council Bluffs. Holding the job until 1846 was Andrew Drips, a former partner of Lucien Fontenelle. Because Drips was well disposed to the American Fur Company, he advised traders on how to circumvent government whiskey inspections. In 1844 a group of 396 Potawatomis, recognizing that the easy availability of alcohol had rendered their future at the Council Bluffs hopeless, moved to what is now northeastern Kansas. This action and the thinking behind it, including a recognition that white settlement would soon come to western Iowa, seemed to signal the complete exodus of the remaining Potawatomis, Chippewas, and Ottawas from the area, for in the summer of 1846 a treaty providing for their removal to Kansas was signed and ratified. The move began in the autumn of 1847 and was completed within a year. The departure was uneventful, and from St. Louis, the superintendent of Indian affairs reported that the removal had come to pass "without the slightest embarrassment to the government."

These were desperate years for the Native peoples on the west bank of the Missouri in the Council Bluffs area. Teton Dakota aggression kept the Omahas from returning to their former home at Large Village in northeastern Nebraska, and this same menace continued to severely curtail their bison hunting on the Plains. This threat also kept the Otoe-Missouria from hunting very far to the west, while the Potawatomi occupation of what is now southwestern Iowa precluded both west-bank tribes from hunting in that area. Smallpox and cholera took many Omaha lives in the 1830s, and chronic ailments and alcohol continued to debilitate them. Getting food became a challenge, and at times in the 1840s they often ate roots. For years the Omahas sought annuity payments from the U.S. government to ease their situation, but such money was not forthcoming until 1853. The peak population of the Omaha Nation had been about two thousand prior to the smallpox devastation at the turn of the century, and it subsequently recovered to this approximate figure; by 1855, the hardships of the past generation reduced their total to eight hundred persons. Perhaps their only good fortune was to have two able chiefs, a father and a son both named Big Elk. These leaders fostered unity within the tribe and encouraged adaptation to what the younger Big Elk termed the "coming flood" of white Americans.

The Otoe-Missouria, living in villages along the lower reaches of the Platte at the southern extremity of what is now the modern metropolitan area, were worse off than the Omahas. In the 1820s their population was about 1,200, but problems similar to those endured by their Omaha neighbors reduced them to 943 persons by 1840, a figure that might have been even lower without smallpox vaccinations. In contrast to the Omahas, the Otoe-Missouria lacked good leadership. In 1837 the tribe was seriously divided as a result of internal fighting. More stress arose from increasing ill feelings between the Otoes and the Missourias, and in 1839 the Missourias established a separate village.

Early in 1841, reportedly the result of alcohol, the Otoes burned their own village, causing a four-way split of the tribe. Ever mindful of the evil influence of whiskey, Samuel Allis emphasized that Bellevue-area trader Baptiste Roy was especially flagrant in dispensing alcohol to the Otoes. Poor crops in 1842 aggravated existing food problems, and starvation was common despite the government's emergency distribution of rations from the Council

Bluffs Indian agency at Bellevue. The Missourias and some Otoes now lived in villages on the south side of the Platte River near its mouth, while the remaining Otoes inhabited a settlement on the north bank, but in 1847 Dakota warriors destroyed the north side village and slew twenty-eight of its inhabitants. The survivors withdrew to the south bank where they were just before white settlement. If these difficulties were not enough, Otoe-Missouria relations with whites were significantly less cordial than those between the Omahas and Americans.

DECISION AT LOCUST CREEK

Some years stand out as landmarks or watersheds of time. In the history of North America, 1846 was what historian Bernard De Voto called "The Year of Decision." In 1846 a war between the United States and Mexico began that would end two years later in a peace extending U.S. sovereignty from the Rocky Mountains to the California coast. An 1846 settlement between Washington and London over the ownership of the Oregon country established the northwestern border of what became the lower forty-eight states. Early in this exceptional year, a chapter in one of nineteenth-century America's most unusual episodes began to unfold when a large group of whites started across the ice-laden waters of the Mississippi River from Nauvoo, Illinois, into Iowa Territory. They were members of the Camp of Israel—the initial group of members of the Church of Jesus Christ of Latter-Day Saints, better known as the Mormons, en route from Nauvoo, Illinois, to a then unknown haven beyond the Rockies.

Indeed, the Mormons had been on the move since the founding of their church in Fayette, New York, in 1830 under the leadership of Joseph Smith. Their cohesiveness made them targets of intolerance, and after settling briefly in Ohio, they went on to Missouri. By 1838 their plight in Missouri was so perilous that they fled northeastward to a point on the Illinois side of the Mississippi where beginning in 1839 they built the community of Nauvoo. Even there, the Mormons came to believe that their faith could flourish only at a place well removed from what they deemed to be an unregenerate society. The murder of their prophet Joseph Smith and his brother by a mob in 1844 heralded the end of their Nauvoo sojourn. Divisiveness over the issue of who would succeed Smith added to their trials, but Brigham Young soon established his leadership over the main body of the church. In early February 1846 the Camp of Israel, numbering some three thousand people, began its exodus across the Mississippi from Nauvoo, although it would not be until March 1 that the westward trek would proceed from the Iowa shore.

At first, Young and the other leaders planned a course toward the Council Bluffs. While they were still in southeastern Iowa, they decided to take a more southerly route to Banks Ferry, near present-day Oregon in northwestern Missouri. Whatever their past troubles in Missouri, they believed that supplies could be more readily procured downstream. At this time, Young hoped to travel far beyond the Missouri River before the next winter. Then, March and April brought wearisome cold, seemingly unending rain, and swollen streams. With the Camp of Israel mired in what Young called "a great mud hole," the Mormons stopped at Locust Creek just north of the Missouri border in modern Wayne County, Iowa, where they reconsidered their plans. They now decided that in sticking close to settled areas they were being subjected to price gouging. If they went back to their initial plan and proceeded toward the Council Bluffs, they could obtain land along the way and develop farms that would serve as supply points for later emigrants from Nauvoo. Accordingly, upon leaving Locust Creek, the Camp of Israel headed northwest, then west, and along the way developed two farm settlements. By early June, improved weather enabled the Mormons to move quickly along an Indian path westward, and on June 13 their first units reached Indian and Mosquito creeks along what is now the south edge of Council Bluffs. The next day, the main group of the Camp of Israel reached the point where the river bluffs opened onto the Missouri valley.

REGROUPING AT THE COUNCIL BLUFFS

Given their harsh experiences, many Mormons were not well disposed toward their fellow Americans. But Brigham Young was a practical man who recognized the value of friendship with the U.S. government, and as the Camp of Israel moved through western Iowa, two men, Jesse Little and Thomas L. Kane, represented Mormon interests in Washington. Kane, a non-Mormon Philadelphian with good political connections, advised President James K. Polk to cultivate positive relations with the Mormons lest they complicate the Oregon boundary question by seeking British help in settling in the far northwest. With war between the United States and Mexico imminent, the president asked Little and Kane if the Mormons would be willing to commit some five hundred men to American military service in California.

After news of the proposal reached Fort Leavenworth, an officer from that post journeyed to the Council Bluffs and presented the president's proposal to Young, who immediately agreed to allow the raising of a Mormon battalion. Young clearly saw the advantages that would accrue from the successful recruitment of the battalion: permission for the Mormons to spend the next winter on Indian lands, some of the soldiers' pay coming to the larger group, and a positive public image for his people. Although recruiting was a challenge, by mid-July the Mormon Battalion was raised and departed a few days later.

In the meantime, the Mormons had constructed a Missouri River ferry a short distance upstream from a ferry that Peter Sarpy operated from near Bellevue to Trader's Point on the Iowa side. Using their own vessel, and perhaps Sarpy's, many Mormons crossed the river in July and encamped at a site known as Cold Springs, near what is now Sixty-first and Hascall streets in south-central Omaha. When this location became overly congested, they relocated to the north at Cutler's Park, west of what is now the Florence section in far north Omaha. Here, the Mormons, or Saints as they were sometimes called, gained permission from the Omahas and Otoes to camp on the west side of the river for up to two years. Earlier, government officials had allowed them to reside on what was still the Potawatomi domain in Iowa. Indeed, many Saints remained on the Iowa side of the river, and in 1846 two more large groups of the faithful set out from Nauvoo. At any given moment, there were significant numbers of Mormons on the trail of more than three hundred miles between Nauvoo and the Council Bluffs, including many temporary residents of two way stations in south-central Iowa.

Until well into July, Brigham Young had hoped to lead a large contingent of the Saints to the Grand Island of the Platte River in what is now central Nebraska where they would spend the winter. However, such considerations as the fine Missouri River bottom pasturage for their livestock, trade, and temporary employment opportunities in the relatively nearby settlements in northwest Missouri, and the insecurity of the Mormons still at Nauvoo led him to abandon hope of moving on from the Council Bluffs in 1846. On September 11 the Mormon leaders selected a new site east of Cutler's Park, on a bench of land between the west bank of the Missouri and its bluffs which would be known as Winter Quarters. The place was platted in the rectangular pattern typical of American frontier communities, and by the last week of September, the first of the Saints were moving there. By year's end, 3,483 people resided at Winter Quarters, and eventually the place had some eight hundred dwellings, ranging from relatively well-built structures to rude dugouts in the bluffs. Some 2,500 of the faithful were at the Council Bluffs on the east side of the river, and perhaps some 2,300 more were at points along the trail in Iowa.

Illness and death were common features of the Mormon experience on the west bank from the summer of 1846 through the spring of 1847. Afflictions such as malaria and pneumonia probably explain many of the early fatalities, but as winter wore on, scurvy appeared in the camp with debilitating and often fatal effects. Infants apparently had a particularly high mortality rate. One scholar has estimated that there were some four hundred Mormon deaths on the west bank from June 1846 through May 1847, with far fewer total fatalities at the encampments of the Saints on the east side. Perhaps the less compact settlement on the east side produced a healthier environment.

Brigham Young and other church leaders continued to consider where the Mormons would eventually settle in the country beyond the Rockies. Peter Sarpy provided helpful information and Father De Smet, whose missionary career had carried him into that region, seems to have been instrumental in focusing their attention on the Great Basin. Late in 1846 discussion of the route west produced a modest challenge to Young's leadership, although he readily prevailed and made plans for an initial group of Saints to head west through the Platte valley in a quest for a new homeland. On April 16, 1847, this group of 148 departed from a point west of Winter Quarters and reached the Great Salt Lake valley on July 24, a trek of over one thousand miles. Here the Saints would settle and some two thousand additional Mormons would make this journey in 1847.

Meanwhile, the Mormons remaining along both sides of the river at the Council Bluffs carried on extensive farming. On Turkey Creek, at the north edge of Winter Quarters, Young built a mill that failed as a business enterprise but provided employment. Despite their bitter memories of persecution in Missouri in the 1830s, the nearby inhabitants of that state were critical to the Saints' survival. As Young had hoped, the farms and settlements of northwestern Missouri provided some Mormons with temporary employment; vendors from Missouri brought goods to Winter Quarters; and St. Louis was a key supply point for the encampment's store. Because of the absence of men serving in the U.S. Army's Mormon Battalion or holding jobs in Missouri, women at Winter Quarters at one point outnumbered men by two and one-half to one. On the Iowa side of the river, a number of Mormons settled just west of the former blockhouse, buying dwellings from the Indians who had followed Billy Caldwell. This area, called Miller's Hollow in recognition of Mormon storekeeper Henry Miller, became their principal east-bank encampment. However, as they continued to arrive in the area from 1846 to 1852, they also established almost ninety small hamlets to the north, south, and east.

Although the Mormons had negotiated agreements with the Omahas and Otoes to reside temporarily on their lands, government officials responsible for Indian relations grew increasingly troubled over the continuing Mormon presence on the west bank. Moreover, although Young worked to maintain proper relations with the Native people on the west bank, Indian theft of Mormon-owned livestock was nettlesome. After returning to Winter Quarters in the autumn of 1847, Young announced that Winter Quarters would be abandoned the coming spring. Given the vigorous Mormon proselytizing in Great Britain and other missionary efforts, it was essential that the church have guidelines for those converts wishing to join its main body in western America. Accordingly, on December 21, at Winter Quarters, the church leaders, known as the Quorum of the Twelve Apostles, issued a "General Epistle to the Saints Throughout the World," urging them to come to the Great Salt Lake valley. The document added, "We have named the Pottawattamie lands as the best place for the brethren to assemble on the route."

In the meantime, on December 5 most members of the Quorum of Twelve met at Miller's Hollow where they decided that Brigham Young should be formally designated as Joseph Smith's successor. A conference of church members would have to ratify this action and about two hundred men took three weeks to build the Log Tabernacle at Miller's Hollow where the assembly would be held. On December 27, some one thousand of the faithful gathered at the Log Tabernacle and confirmed Young as First President of the Church of Jesus Christ of Latter-Day Saints.

KANESVILLE

By the summer of 1848, the last of the Mormons at Winter Quarters had moved on to the Great Salt Lake, to Miller's Hollow, or one of the outlying east-side settlements. In March 1848 apparently as a result of Thomas L. Kane's influence in Washington, a post office was established at Miller's

Hollow. Recognizing Kane's services to the Mormons, a church conference at Miller's Hollow in April changed the name of that settlement to Kanesville. Orson Hyde, one of the members of the Quorum of the Twelve Apostles, had made the motion to so honor Kane, and the same conference designated Hyde to have prime responsibility for church matters on the east side of the Missouri, including supervision of Mormon emigration from the Council Bluffs to the Great Salt Lake. Despite the fact that the Mormons did not intend to remain at Kanesville, the settlement grew markedly in 1848. One resident established a school, and another developed a combination gristmill and sawmill, which he powered by harnessing the water of Indian Creek. Heralding the community's future was the arrival of Jonathan B. Stutsman and Cornelius Voorhis, both non-Mormons, who established stores primarily intended to outfit overland travelers.

In the absence of organized civil authority, secular as well as spiritual power in the east-bank Mormon settlements rested with a Pottawattamie high council, led by Orson Hyde. Following the Louisiana Purchase, the area between the Mississippi and Missouri rivers that is now Iowa was part of the District of Louisiana and then the Territory of Louisiana. It became part of Missouri Territory in 1812, but when Missouri achieved statehood in 1821, the area we know as Iowa reverted to unorganized status. From 1834 to 1836, it was part of Michigan Territory and from 1836 to 1838, it was included in the Territory of Wisconsin. By the 1830s American settlement was spreading along the west bank of the Mississippi River, and in 1838 Congress established the Territory of Iowa. On December 28, 1846, Iowa became the twenty-ninth state in the rapidly expanding American Union. Although Pottawattamie County was formed in September 1848, no county officers were in place, and the Kanesville voting precinct remained under the jurisdiction of Monroe County, which was far to the east. As initially established, Pottawattamie County replicated the ill-defined bounds of the 1833 grant to the Potawatomi Indians that included much of southwestern Iowa.

With the help of Orson Hyde, the Whig Party won the overwhelming vote of the Mormons in 1848, but the Democrats, in control of Monroe County, ignored the Kanesville tally. This Democratic fear that the Mormon area would be a Whig bastion may have stymied the implementation of Pottawattamie County government until 1851 when voters elected county officers and designated Kanesville as the county seat. Mormons, including Brigham

Young's nephew, were elected to all offices. By this time, the Iowa legislature had reduced the size of the county and defined its boundaries as they remain to this day.

The years between 1846 and 1850 brought changes in the remote West that would highlight the potential role of the Council Bluffs as a gateway for national expansion. The 1848 peace settlement in the Mexican War extended the sovereignty of the United States from New Mexico and the central Rocky Mountains to California. That same year brought the discovery of gold in California and the establishment of territorial government in Oregon. In the nation's capital, the political dynamics of the slavery issue and western expansion produced that famous package of federal laws known as the Compromise of 1850, which among other things admitted California to the Union and created the territories of New Mexico and Utah.

The 1850 census showed that Utah had 11,380 residents and the Council Bluffs remained the great turnstile through which the Saints moved west. However, the rush of gold seekers headed to California in 1849 via the Platte valley started a vast change at Kanesville. First, the forty-niners greatly stimulated the growth of business in the community, where they could obtain supplies for the trip west. The accompanying boom in Kanesville's economy brought inflated prices, and some Mormons, particularly newcomers from Britain, suffered as a result. Nevertheless, the Saints generally probably prospered from transactions with the California-bound. Second, unlike the family-oriented Mormons, the gold seekers were typically single men, and their gambling, drinking, and sometimes rough conduct suggested that they were not seeking the Kingdom of God. Horse races disrupted the town streets even on the Sabbath, and the Ocean Wave Saloon, prominently located on Broadway, earned a reputation in keeping with the town's new diversity. As historian Richard Bennett put it, there was a "clash of values" at Kanesville where the Saints and the gold seekers "eyed one another with idle curiosity at a respectable distance."

On February 7, 1849, Orson Hyde published the first issue of the *Frontier Guardian,* the pioneer newspaper at the Council Bluffs. Because the paper carried a great deal of church news, it had a readership that extended far beyond that of a typical biweekly paper. As a church leader, Hyde knew that Kanesville would not be the permanent abode of the Saints, but like other frontier newspapermen, he boosted his community and chronicled its development.

In October 1849 he noted that Kanesville had six big stores for supplying travelers, ten mills, two ferries, and a variety of wagon shops, public houses, and other providers of goods and services. Hyde provided guidance to west-bound Mormons and was a source of information for other travelers.

The *Guardian*'s reports show how Kanesville had joined Independence and St. Joseph, Missouri, and other downstream communities as an important jumping-off point. For example, some 574 persons, all but twenty of whom were apparently adult males, departed Kanesville for California in May 1849, while a freight wagon train carrying over 60,000 pounds of cargo and employing about thirty drivers hired locally left for Salt Lake. On June 12, 1850, the *Guardian* noted that 13,500 men and 4,500 wagons, drawn by some 22,000 animals had come through Kanesville en route to California that travel season. Additionally, about 700 wagons had departed for Utah, accompanied by some 9,000 head of horses, mules, sheep, and cattle. The *Guardian* was a persistent advocate of better mail service over the routes serving Kanesville via Missouri and Fort Des Moines. Sometimes private persons carried mail, and in September 1849 the *Guardian* proclaimed "A Day of Rejoicing" when such a service linked Kanesville and Salt Lake City. That same month, stage service was inaugurated between Kanesville and St. Joseph, Missouri.

The 1850 U.S. Census showed that 7,828 persons were residing in Pottawattamie County. Of Iowa's forty-nine organized counties, Pottawattamie ranked eighth in population. Its status as the only western county with a relatively large number of people suggests its importance as a jumping-off point. Indicative of the county's recent settlement and its highly transient population was the absence of communities with formally organized town governments; accordingly, the census did not give a population for Kanesville. In any event, by 1850, the Log Tabernacle was near the physical center of the settlement of some 350 dwellings along Indian Creek in what remains the heart of downtown Council Bluffs.

A herald of change came in May 1851 when the *Guardian* published the Fifth General Epistle from Salt Lake City, declaring that North American Mormons should immigrate to Utah by the end of the coming year. Soon, the Saints in the Kanesville area were selling their property, and non-Mormons obtained property cheaply as the exodus to Zion grew enormously. In the first months of 1852, Kanesville may have had five thousand residents, but its status as a predominantly Mormon community would end that year.

Between 1848 and 1852, about 6,400 Mormons from Britain bound for the Great Salt Lake valley had entered the United States at New Orleans and journeyed to Kanesville by steamboat. These British and other European converts were frequently from cities and often lacked the skills necessary for routine rural life that Saints from the United States and Canada typically possessed. Their stay at Kanesville or the surrounding settlements was probably a time when they learned about building cabins, harnessing draft animals, and many farming practices. At least 12,000 and perhaps as many as 25,000 or more Mormons passed through Kanesville between 1848 and 1852 en route to Zion, traveling as part of at least forty-four wagon trains. All told, these trains included 2,817 or more wagons. In early June 1852 amid the Mormons exodus, Almon Babbitt's *Western Bugle* reported that 15,000 persons had left Kanesville that spring, headed for California or Oregon. The passing of the Mormon heyday brought a brief drop in the town's population to about 2,000, and the *Frontier Guardian* did not survive long after Orson Hyde's departure. However, in a rapidly developing West, opportunities for persons who would settle on the east side of the river at the Council Bluffs were abundant.

COUNCIL BLUFFS: BUILDING UPON A NAME

As early as 1849, Orson Hyde had boosted Kanesville as a prospective rail center, and in the next few years the idea of a railroad to California, if still far from realization, was becoming less of a fantasy. But one must also look east in considering the possible role of the Council Bluffs area as a rail center in national expansion. Almost five hundred miles across the Iowa and Illinois prairies, Chicago had risen from a swampy outpost of forty-two people in 1834 to a city of 29,963 in 1850. Its growth would be intimately associated with its development as a railroad hub where lines from the East ended and routes west began. Railroad building westward from Chicago commenced in 1848, and in a few years this work began to focus clearly upon the Council Bluffs area.

In 1852 as the builders of the Chicago and Rock Island Railroad laid tracks toward the Mississippi River, they organized the Mississippi and Missouri Railroad to continue the Rock Island line route westward from Davenport, Iowa. The M and M charter from the Iowa legislature provided that the line would extend to "Council Bluffs," which still could be taken to include various points between the juncture of the Platte and the Missouri and the area of Lewis and Clark's meeting with the Indians. In January 1853 the Iowa legislature enacted bills providing for changing the name of Kanesville to Council Bluffs and incorporating the community as a city. The name change, effective February 19, may well have reflected a strategy of Kanesville boosters to secure the western terminus of the M and M by preempting other communities from choosing the name "Council Bluffs."

Whether such a timely idea influenced events is uncertain, but in May 1853 Peter A. Dey, chief engineer for the M and M, and his assistant engineer, twenty-two-year-old Grenville M. Dodge, began to survey a railroad route across Iowa, and on November 22 they entered the recently named city of Council Bluffs. Townspeople gave the M and M surveyors a warm reception as they did a short time later when surveyors for a line that later became part of the Chicago and North Western Railroad arrived. In an action that suggested Council Bluffs' potential as a gateway community, Dodge soon ran a preliminary survey beyond the west bank of the Missouri to the Platte River.

For Council Bluffs the years 1853 and 1854 symbolized that interesting mixture of eastern civilization, violence, tragedy, hope, and progress that typified an up-and-coming western town. In 1853 the Reverend George G. Rice completed construction of a Congregational Church, a log structure that for a time also served as the Methodists' place of worship. A robbery and murder in the transient population led to a lynching that May. In another case, a man accused of murder fled town after being granted bail. Two fires in one November day destroyed many businesses along Broadway; nevertheless, Christmas night 1853 brought a gala event when S. S. Bayliss, a local entrepreneur, opened the Pacific House, a fine three-story brick hotel. Indeed, brick construction symbolized a second stage of development on the urban frontier, and in 1854 a number of such buildings replaced structures on Broadway that had gone up in flames.

The opening of a United States land office in March 1853 and the beginning of sales from the public domain in June inevitably brought land speculators to town, but it helped make possible the establishment of clear real-estate titles. An act of Congress in April 1854 provided a town-site land grant for Council Bluffs that led to the survey of lots and the resolution of property ownership disputes. The absence of land titles had severely impaired municipal government because it was impossible to levy property taxes, and city officials were now freed from having to rely upon the pittance of revenue obtained from the annual licensing of gambling places and saloons.

By this time, the nation's attention was about to focus upon the huge unorganized region west of the mid-Missouri River and east of the Rocky Mountains called "Nebraska." Along the east bank of the Missouri River, frontier entrepreneurs pushed for the opening of the Nebraska country to settlement, for only then would it be possible for towns to be developed on the opposite shore, any one of which might become the eastern terminus of a Pacific railroad. Such planning was a huge gamble, for American history is full of names of "paper towns" that never progressed beyond plat maps and "ghost towns" that flourished briefly and perished. Few locations were naturally destined to become cities, and this was just as true in the middle Missouri valley as elsewhere. The uncertain results of their decisions have always shaped the fortunes of urban dreamers, and in the decade before the Civil War it was by no means certain that the rails that would eventually link California to the rest of the Union would go west from the Missouri River. Still, optimism was a driving force in the age of Manifest Destiny, and by 1853 the city of Council Bluffs, with its population now estimated at three thousand, had its share of boosters dreaming of a city on the west bank. Their aspirations would result in what would become the nucleus of Omaha.

[Part II] 1854–1870

[2] The Lone Tree Ferry and the Founding of Omaha

One William D. Brown, a former county sheriff and brickyard operator from southeastern Iowa, was the original Omaha pioneer. He had started west during the California gold rush, getting only as far as Kanesville. There, seeing the thousands of persons waiting to leave in the spring of 1850 for California, he decided that he could make more money by staying than by moving on. He started a Missouri River ferry, first near the old Winter Quarters and then a few miles farther south. He called his operation the Lone Tree Ferry, naming it after some scattered trees on both sides of the river. Brown, whose ferry was an oar-propelled flatboat, soon became half owner of the Bluff House, a small hotel in Council Bluffs. He sought broader horizons and in the summer of 1853 helped organize a steam-ferry company, the Council Bluffs and Nebraska Ferry Company. Brown, with little money of his own, was not even the president of the enterprise. What he did have was vision. He wanted to found a town across from Council Bluffs. While the company did buy and operate a steam ferry, the *General Marion,* it remained interested in town promotion. Secrecy cloaked this intent for an obvious reason: the Omaha Indians still owned the land.

In the fall of 1853, members of the ferry company undertook informal surveys of the site; in later years several of them took credit for staking the first claim. Three men crossed over from Council Bluffs in a leaky scow after the ferry captain refused to go over through some ice floes. One pioneer bailed, one rowed, and one acted as helmsman. They waded ashore and spent a miserable night huddled by a flickering fire. Every waving tree appeared a band of tomahawk-wielding natives, and at first dawn the intrepid pioneers hastily undertook the quick and rudimentary work. "With a hatchet," one wrote, "I blazed a corner tree near our camp, and stamped the initials of my name

42

therein with a survey-making iron. . . . I claim that this was probably the first survey ever made in Douglas County." Following such work, and after seeing an Indian some distance away on a bluff, the men pushed their boat through an ice-cold marsh and made an unpleasant and wet crossing, landing far downstream from their original starting point. Of such stuff were cities built. It was hardly a Roman triumph; even so, the men were the vanguard of settlement. All along the Middle Border, speculators, land sharks, and settlers studied the bluffs across the wide Missouri. All were caught by a combination of greed, ambition, and idealism—the concept of "Westward the Star of Empire." Here was a story of the American experience, one that went beyond the undertakings of underfinanced Iowa frontier speculators that would unfold with the rise of a Midwestern metropolis.

For nearly a decade, politicians and frontier boosters in Illinois, Iowa, and Missouri had been pushing to open the Nebraska country to settlement, and it was clear that they were on the verge of success. Mindful of this reality, commissioner of Indian affairs George Manypenny in the autumn of 1853 traveled west where he met with representatives of the Omaha and Otoe-Missouria tribes and convinced them that the white advance was inevitable. On March 15, 1854, representatives of the Otoe-Missouria people signed a treaty in Washington surrendering their existing land claims and agreeing to move to a reservation along what became the Kansas-Nebraska border. They stayed on this land south of Beatrice, Nebraska, and north of Marysville, Kansas, until the period between 1876 and 1881 when they moved to what is now Oklahoma where they remain. Another crucial step toward opening the eastern part of the Nebraska country to settlement came in Washington on March 16, 1854, when Omaha tribal representatives signed a treaty that would place their people on a reservation in their old home area in northeastern Nebraska. In 1865 the Omahas ceded the northern part of their reservation to Winnebago Indians who had come from Wisconsin after a sojourn in Dakota Territory, but to this day the Omaha Nation remains on land some sixty-five miles north of the area where the city bearing their name arose.

The first organized activity in Omaha occurred on a clear and hot Fourth of July in 1854. A group of men and women crossed over on the ferry from Council Bluffs to hold a picnic on newly named Capitol Hill, high above the surrounding pastoral countryside. The owners of the town company wanted the celebration to have symbolic significance as well as to stimulate future real-estate sales. All of those present felt part of great events. The United States was at a watershed. The month of May had seen the passage and signing of the Kansas-Nebraska Act. This controversial legislation reopened the slavery issue, split the Democratic Party of President Franklin Pierce, tore the opposition Whig Party apart, and led to the formation of the Republican Party, which opposed the extension of slavery.

The measure was part of a political power play engineered by Senator Stephen A. Douglas of Illinois, a railroad advocate and a Democratic presidential hopeful whom his supporters praised as the choice of "Young America," shorthand for the West. Douglas, in what opponents claimed was a ploy to quickly people the central Great Plains so that a federally subsidized transcontinental railroad benefited Chicago rather than a southern terminal, had introduced a bill in 1853 to create a gigantic new territory opposite Missouri and Iowa. When the measure failed, he returned the next session with a compromise that held out to the South the prospect of a new slave state in exchange for a northern transcontinental railroad. His plan called for the creation of two new territories, Kansas and Nebraska. It necessitated the repeal of the Compromise of 1820 that had kept slavery, except in Missouri, out of the northern parts of the Louisiana Purchase. Voters in the two new territories would decide whether they wanted slavery. The phrase coined by the politicians was "Popular Sovereignty," which sounded good but left fundamental questions unresolved. A basic assumption was that the bulk of Kansas residents would come from the slave state of Missouri, while Nebraska would be settled by Iowa free staters. Kansas settlement because of interference by pro and antislavery forces, was a catastrophe. President Pierce had to send federal troops into "Bleeding Kansas" to restore order. Meanwhile few, except those directly involved, paid much attention to Nebraska. There were no reporters present to record the excursionists' activities on Capitol Hill. If there had been, they might have caught the optimism, warranted or otherwise, that was so much a part of the American frontier experience.

A presidential proclamation of June 24, 1854, enhanced Omaha's chances to survive and prosper. It announced the ratification of a treaty with the Omaha Indians that ended tribal claims in the area. The promoters, disregarding the niceties of federal land laws, quickly hired a surveying party. Carrying chains and driving stakes, the surveyors platted 320 blocks, each 264 feet square, plus streets of 100 to 120 feet in width. Why boosters took the

Indian name "Omaha" for their prospective town is unclear. Although tribal tradition held the word to mean "against the current" or "upstream people," an alternative translation was "Above all others upon the stream!" The last may have implicitly caught the sense of rivalry that drove the town's founders as they contemplated the challenges of other urban promoters in the valley. Another account contended that the speculators thought "Omaha" sounded pretty. Whatever the reason for the name, the people at the Fourth of July picnic tried to think in larger terms. They had lunch, started to build a log cabin, and listened to a toast: "Nebraska—May her gentle zephyrs and rolling prairies invite pioneers from beyond the muddy Missouri river to happy homes within her borders, and may her lands ever be dedicated to free soil, free labor, and free men." Afterwards a politician started a speech. Suddenly Indians appeared and frightened the audience. Everyone climbed on the wagon that had brought provisions across, returned to the ferry, and went back to Council Bluffs. Over thirty years later, an old settler recalled, "I remember that some resolutions were adopted and a few speeches made. The stand on which the speakers stood was a common wagon owned by my old friend Harrison Johnson, who, with some of the members of his family, constituted a portion of the party." Yet the picnic had accomplished a significant purpose. It provided Omaha with an official founding date.

Exuberant visions of urban destiny often accompanied city building in the American West. Jeffersonian ideas, which envisioned an agrarian society, were only of importance to urban promoters so far as farms might result in prosperous hinterlands that they could exploit. Predictions of material success—great moneyed operations and gargantuan transportation systems—sustained settlers, created a sense of pride, and provided a framework for defining aspirations.

Omaha had a booster before it had a street map. He was J. W. Pattison, a lawyer, business agent, and coeditor of the first newspaper published under an Omaha dateline. He had come west as a correspondent for the *New York Herald*. His paper, the *Arrow,* published in Council Bluffs, appeared on June 28, 1854. While the masthead proclaimed it "a family newspaper devoted to the arts, sciences, general literature, agriculture, and politics," the *Arrow* was strictly a promotional sheet. In his first editorial, "A Night in Our Sanctum," Pattison discussed the possibility of Omaha becoming a commercial metropolis. He claimed that he had dreamed of a great future for the new city as he lay beneath buffalo robes on Nebraska soil, listening to the howl of wolves and knowing that not far away glimmered the crackling campfires of the Pawnees and Omahas.

Pattison said that after he went to sleep, the busy hum of industrial and commercial activities reached his ears and the ears of those around him, all of whom had spent a hard day cutting logs for cabin claims.

> The incessant rattle of innumerable drays over the paved streets, the steady tramp of ten thousand of an animated, enterprising population, the hoarse orders fast issued from the crowd of steamers upon the levee loading with the rich products of the state of Nebraska and unloading the fruits, species and products of other climes and soils greeted our ears. Far away from toward the setting sun came telegraphic dispatches of improvements, progress and moral advancement upon the Pacific coast. Cars full freighted with teas, silks, etc., were arriving from thence and passing across the stationary channel of the Missouri river with lightning speed hurrying on to the Atlantic seaboard. The third express train on the Council Bluffs and Galveston R. R. came thundering close by us with a shrill whistle that brought us to our feet with knife in hand. We rubbed our eyes, looked into the darkness beyond to see the flying train. They had vanished and the shrill second neigh of our lariated horses gave indication of the danger near. The hum of business, in and around the city, and the same rude camp-fires were before us.

Many images had more substance in flickering fires than in the cold light of dawn. Pattison must have thought so. The *Arrow* suspended publication in November of 1854 after only twelve intermittent issues, and he left for Missouri. He never returned to Omaha to see his dream come true.

THOMAS B. CUMING: THE POLITICS OF TOWN BUILDING

The first objective of the members of the Council Bluffs and Nebraska Ferry Company was for Omaha to become the territorial capital. They wanted to fix or at the very least influence the race for urban power in Nebraska before it started. Otherwise, many distinctive duly chronicled events—first religious service, first actual settlers, first forge, first white child, and first hotel—would probably mean nothing. In September 1854 a map appeared that showed

Omaha the location of a territorial meeting place. To buttress the claim, the diagram called the place "Omaha City." It was an attempt to convince potential investors of its supposed significant urban dimensions, but the ploy failed and "City" was soon dropped from the name.

Omaha was only one of several "paper towns" on the Nebraska side of the Missouri River. Below Omaha, excitement ran high in places like Bellevue, Plattsmouth, Nebraska City, and Brownville, at least during daylight hours when entrepreneurs crossed over from Iowa and Missouri to improve their property. A few miles north of Omaha, on the site of the old Mormon Winter Quarters, James C. Mitchell and others had founded Florence, but Omaha and Bellevue had the best chances. Both had the backing of different combinations of Iowa Democratic politicians, and Bellevue had the advantage of three decades of existence. The law establishing Nebraska Territory specified that the territorial governor would designate the initial meeting site of the legislature. President Pierce appointed Francis Burt, an obscure South Carolina Democrat. The forty-seven-year-old Burt, who held a patronage job in the Department of Treasury at the time of his selection, had previously been a state legislator for almost twenty years. The son of a slaveholder, he was a former newspaper editor. As a delegate at the 1832 South Carolina nullification convention, he had supported an ordinance that opposed a federally enacted tariff.

Burt hardly seemed the right choice to launch a free state, and he never had the opportunity. On October 7, 1854, he reached Bellevue, suffering from an undiagnosed illness. Hospitalized at the local Presbyterian mission, his condition steadily worsened, and he died on October 16, two days after taking the oath of office. Various town delegations had visited his sickbed, pressing their claims. He may have favored Bellevue as the first territorial meeting place, but he never issued an official proclamation. His death placed the decision in the hands of the territorial secretary, Thomas B. Cuming, who became acting governor. Cuming, a rising young Iowa Democratic politician, was a short and swarthy man with raven-black hair and eyes set deep in bushy eyebrows. He claimed to have been born in New York in 1828, but he was probably older. He had worked as a geologist and had served in the army during the Mexican War. Following hostilities he had moved to Keokuk, Iowa, where he became first a telegrapher and then a newspaper editor. Cuming wanted to further his political ambitions in western Iowa by helping Council Bluffs, and he had landholdings in Omaha. According to opponents, he demanded and received bribes from the Council Bluffs and Nebraska Ferry Company.

Cuming moved swiftly to establish civil government and to advance Omaha's fortunes. He divided Nebraska Territory into eight counties, with an equal number north and south of the Platte River. The wide, shallow, and sandy Platte, which was very difficult to ford and had few ferry sites, acted as a natural division, cutting the territory in half and promoting competing political interests. He placed Omaha and Bellevue in Douglas County and appointed Omahans to county offices. Although a census showed more people south than north of the Platte, he apportioned the territorial legislature in favor of the north bank. Then in December 1854 after an election held posthaste, Cuming announced that the first legislative session would convene in Omaha. His critics, just about everyone in Nebraska outside of Omaha, assumed a fix. Mass meetings denounced him, and a convention in Nebraska City, fifty miles south of Omaha, approved a resolution that called him an "unprincipled knave." The participants in these assemblies had been in Nebraska Territory only a short time. J. Sterling Morton, the author of the Nebraska City resolution, had arrived a month earlier from Michigan. The whole controversy was typical of the frontier. Crucial decisions were made with no knowledge of the land.

The first Nebraska territorial legislature assembled in Omaha on January 16, 1855, in a meeting house provided for "public purposes" by the Council Bluffs and Nebraska Ferry Company. The thirty-by-forty-five-foot, two-story structure stood out from the surrounding twenty or so shacks, houses, saloons, and stores; it was the only brick building in town. The editor of the *Bellevue Palladium* claimed that it was too small: "We were struck with the singularity of taste displayed in the curtain furniture of the different rooms, which consisted of two folds of plain calico, the one green and the other red, which we took to be symbolic of jealousy and war—which monsters we fear, will make their appearance before right is enthroned and peace established." During the initial meeting the delegates from Bellevue and from south of the Platte wore red blankets to indicate their "savage" intentions toward Cuming. Few of the members had spent more than a night in their districts. After each day's business, they took the ferry to Council Bluffs. A saloon, adjacent to the assembly chamber, set the tone for riotous proceedings. Members, some moving back and forth from their seats to the bar, gave impassioned speeches. There were numerous hot verbal exchanges and threats of physical violence. The acrimonious session had a major accomplishment: the new territorial governor, Mark W. Izard of Arkansas, arrived in time to persuade the body to establish a framework of government by adopting in toto the laws of Iowa. That took half an hour.

Much of the time featured public debates and private manipulations over the location of the territorial capital. Omaha promoters took precautionary measures, bribing members—"inducing" was the word used—with money, land, and promises. Some received "sugar," while others got "salt" in what sarcastic observers called "Scrip Town," a half-mile wide stretch of property on Omaha's north and west sides. A joint resolution of February 22, 1855, placed the capitol building in Omaha. The representative from Florence switched his support to Omaha at the last minute after receiving sixty lots, which he soon sold for sixty dollars each. Two Glenwood, Iowa, residents initially committed to Plattsmouth voted for Omaha. One had to move to Council Bluffs to escape a lynching; the other barely avoided a public beating. A Glenwood mass meeting denounced the two for misrepresentation in "the Nebraska legislature." The question of whether the territorial government should remain in Omaha occupied every Nebraska territorial assembly, inflamed by the indignation of people outside the city and prolonged by the precedent of rewards for votes. Once, a rump group attempted to move the body to Florence. Another time, opposing forces brandished knives and guns at each other. By hook or crook, the territorial government remained in Omaha until statehood.

VISIONS AND REALITIES: 1855–1863

During the bitterest moments of the capital fight, acting governor Cuming had struck a responsive chord among even his most vehement legislative foes by calling upon them to petition Congress to build a Pacific railroad through Nebraska.

Many reasons lead to the conclusion that such a memorial from you will be of practical efficacy in contributing to the speedy consummation of such an enterprise—an enterprise of such absolute necessity as a means of inter-communication between the Atlantic and Pacific states, and as a purveyor of a lucrative commerce with India, China and the Pacific islands. Among these are the facts that the valley of the Platte is on the nearest and most direct continuous line from the commercial metropolis of the east, by railroad and the great lakes, through the most practical mountain passes, to the metropolis of the west; that it is fitted by nature for an easy grade; and that it is central and convenient to a great majority of grain-growing states.

Almost everyone in Nebraska who heard or read his address agreed. After all, that was why they had come to the territory—to take advantage of its potential as a highway across the upper Plains to the Rocky Mountains and the Pacific slope. Nor was railway boosting being neglected in Council Bluffs where Grenville Dodge, a Massachusetts native and graduate of Norwich University in Vermont who been a key figure in the survey of the Mississippi and Missouri Railroad, had made his home by 1856. Dodge strongly believed that the best rail route west lay through Council Bluffs. He backed his belief by extensive land acquisitions and thwarted efforts by a faction of M and M directors to adopt a more northerly route to Florence.

The transcontinental railroad, after two decades of research and development, appeared on the verge of realization. In the middle of the 1850s a survey of five possible routes by the United States Corps of Topographical Engineers indicated that a railroad could be built over a "Central Route" from Council Bluffs to California. However, the estimated cost of $131 million was prohibitive, and the maps that were produced were too general for construction purposes. Survey parties representing Chicago lines and headed by Dodge, one of the nation's first railroad civil engineers, started detailed studies of a route through Nebraska. Dodge wanted to apply a "commercial point of view" to the federal reports and to find the gentlest grades and easiest curves, never previously investigated or reported. He later wrote, "Private enterprise explored and developed that line along the forty-second parallel of latitude. This route was made by the buffalo, next used by Indians, then by the fur traders, next by the Mormons, and then by the overland immigration to California and Oregon. It is known at the 'Great Platte River Route.'" If either public or private interest built a railroad through the valley, its Missouri River terminal would be of crucial importance; the technology did not exist to bridge the stream. So, all concerned with urban developments in Nebraska concentrated on obtaining communication connections. Entrepreneurial decisions, rather than theories of urban dominance or political intrigue, would determine the winner. Or was that the case? Had Omaha's political ties given it an overwhelming advantage, predetermining the victor, no matter what other places did? This was the claim of the critics in rival communities.

During the steamboat era, Omaha had trouble competing with other river towns. By 1854 Council Bluffs had regular service, which soon extended to the settlements in Nebraska. Omaha's steamboat connections developed gradually; with the impetus of the Colorado gold rush, 268 boats arrived between March and November of 1859. A few side-wheelers ran over a thousand miles above Omaha to Fort Benton in Montana. There were triweekly runs between Omaha and St. Joseph, Missouri, the western terminal of the Hannibal and St. Joseph Railroad. A passenger line operated on regular schedules from St. Louis to Omaha.

The steamboats used on the lower Missouri were as elegant as any on the Mississippi. The largest were 250 feet long, carried 400 passengers, and had a freight capacity of 700 tons. Arrivals in Omaha were community events. One traveler reported 1,500 persons at the landing to welcome his boat. Captains frequently allowed visitors aboard for a formal dance in the grand salon. The great white steamboats with their enormous paddle wheels, and tall black stacks—the *Spread Eagle*, the *Florilda*, the *Alonzo Child*, and the *Platte Valley*—signaled community progress in the America of their day. With two to seven arrivals weekly during the spring-to-autumn shipping season, Omaha in time surpassed Florence and the inland community of Council Bluffs as a steamboat port. The editor of the *Omaha Nebraskian* crowed, "Of all the would-be towns in Nebraska, Florence has received the most puffing and blowing. . . . So blow away ye Florenceites . . . your town is but a sickly 'Infant mewing and [puking] in its nurse's arms.'" What the journalist failed to mention was that Nebraska City had eclipsed Omaha as a steamboat and trading center.

Omaha interests emphasized the virtues of a 180-mile-long trail, called either the North Platte Trail or the Mormon Trail. It ran from the city to Fort Kearny. "Mormons, like buffalo and Indians, always choose the shortest and best routes," the editor of the *Omaha Times* claimed. The trail, improved between 1856 and 1858 by the federal government, had good and bad points. For the first twenty-five miles out of Omaha it passed through fairly settled areas;

users had little trouble obtaining provisions and usually made steady progress. Then came muddy sloughs, expensive ferries, and hazardous crossings, especially over the Loup Fork and Platte rivers. The Platte sometimes took several days to cross, usually at much risk to wagons and supplies. Guidebooks issued in Omaha claimed the route was seventy-five miles shorter than the one along the south side of the Platte from Nebraska City. This was untrue. In 1857 when the Leavenworth freighting firm of Russell, Majors and Waddell, which handled most of the army's freighting business in the West, established an up-river headquarters, it never seriously considered Omaha, deciding instead on Nebraska City. The concern bought 138 town lots and spent $300,000 on facilities. It also built a new road that shortened the distance between Nebraska City and Fort Kearny. Russell, Majors and Waddell turned Nebraska City into a roaring camp. Every month thousands of wagons rolled through the streets as bullwhackers cracked whips over the plodding teams of oxen. Riverboats lined the waterfront. Other western freighting concerns moved to the town, which soon became the second most important settlement in the territory. It easily eclipsed Brownville and Plattsmouth and threatened Omaha. By the end of the 1850s there were sixty-four freighters in Nebraska City and twenty-four in Omaha. And, to make matters worse for Omaha, none of its firms were comparable to Russell, Majors and Waddell.

Freighters operating out of Omaha traded in Colorado, Utah, and California. Early ties built up with Mormon interests and gold seekers paid handsome dividends. Local merchants handled the buffalo hide business, a colorful but relatively insignificant activity. More materially, the freighters' wagons carried a wide variety of items from foodstuffs to mining machinery, both of which were essential to western development. Some concerns had only one wagon, capable of hauling three to five tons of freight, and six to twelve yoke of oxen. Large operations that relied on government contracts and bulk shipments frequently had hundreds of wagons and thousands of oxen. Profits and risks were high.

Omaha freighting firms incurred serious losses in the national depression that followed the Panic of 1857. "Wild Cat" banks, which issued their own paper currency, failed. The bottom dropped out of the real-estate market; fifty thousand dollars in scrip issued by the city to help pay for a capitol building lost all value, and jobs were scarce. An 1858 arrival in the settlement, which then had approximately two thousand inhabitants, wrote, "And, as I soon learned, not one in twenty of these had any visible means of support, any faith in the country, or any expectation whatever, other than to leave as soon as he could sell his lot in town, or his pre-emption in the country, which, quite likely he had acquired, not by an investment of hard-earned money, but by certain circumlocutory processes—the inventions of speculators of inventive genius." This was a dark hour for Omaha. After a successful start, it appeared on the verge of oblivion, relegated to a ferry station opposite Council Bluffs, overshadowed on the Missouri's west bank by Nebraska City. Then came the 1859 Pike's Peak gold rush. It happened so suddenly, and at such a fortuitous moment, that some conspiracy-minded observers charged that reports of gold came in advance of actual discovery. Omahans could hardly believe their good fortune; the city went from bust to boom within a few months.

Omaha was in an ideal position to serve Colorado gold seekers. Because Nebraska City was a freighting center geared to supporting military posts, it was not prepared to meet the needs of thousands of emigrants, nor were Omaha's other rivals. Bellevue had no facilities, and although Florence had been a jumping-off place for Mormons from 1856 to 1863, the town had such poor accommodations that travelers were diverted to Omaha. The steamboats that operated from St. Louis and St. Joseph to Omaha took on new significance, as did the steam ferry between Council Bluffs and Omaha along with previously minor express, mail, and stage routes. The Western Stage Line ran through Omaha from the end of the track in eastern Iowa to Fort Kearny and other points. Omaha merchants quickly recouped their losses incurred in the depression. In 1859 it cost a person over five hundred dollars for outfitting and travel from Omaha to Colorado. Adventurers crowded the new four-story Herndon House, which boasted over one hundred rooms. White-topped wagons, handcarts, and men on foot filled the streets. Outfitters made tremendous profits; freighters received or initiated large orders. One small carrier transported apples to the gold fields and another, a load of domestic cats. The return of prosperity bolstered the spirits of Omaha's entrepreneurs, several of whom were Council Bluffs merchants who had opened branches in the village. By the spring of 1859, grocery and hardware stores had daily sales over three thousand dollars. Without exaggeration, a writer in the *Omaha Nebraskian and Times* wrote, "No one can fail to note the rapid increase of business in our city, and each succeeding day adds to our commercial operations, in an arithmetical ratio."

In the meantime, Council Bluffs shared in this dynamism. One of the most notable figures in the early history of Council Bluffs was Amelia Jenks Bloomer, who with her husband, attorney Dexter Bloomer, settled there in 1855. Before moving west after a year in Ohio, the Bloomers had lived in Seneca Falls, New York, acclaimed as the birthplace of the women's rights movement. There, Amelia came under the influence of Elizabeth Cady Stanton, a leading advocate of voting rights for women. Bloomer championed reform in women's dress, and by 1851 had made the wearing of "bloomers"—pantaloons that were worn with a skirt shorter than the ground-sweeping dresses then the norm—a daring, but short-lived challenge to Victorian orthodoxy. In 1856 Amelia Bloomer crossed the river to Omaha where she convinced the lower house of Nebraska's territorial legislature to adopt women's suffrage, but the upper house failed to act upon the measure. Bloomer would continue to work for women's suffrage and the closely related effort to prohibit alcoholic beverages, but she preferred writing rather than speaking in support of these causes.

Like Omaha, Council Bluffs also suffered from the depression after the Panic of 1857, and Nebraska paper money was part of the problem. On May 2, 1857, a few months before the economic collapse, William Wirt Maynard, with financial help from Grenville Dodge and banker John T. Baldwin, published the first issue of a weekly newspaper, the *Council Bluffs Nonpareil*, which became the principal voice in southwestern Iowa of the new Republican Party. When the depression hit, Maynard took various economies, including the acceptance of wood to fire his steam press in lieu of money owed him. As in Omaha, the Rocky Mountain gold rush brought a resurgence of economic vitality to Council Bluffs. Despite the timing of its founding, the *Nonpareil* survived the hard times to become a daily in 1862, outlast its rivals in later years, and continue to the present, the area's oldest newspaper.

Aside from Dodge, no person thrived more upon the dynamics of time and place that marked Council Bluffs in the late 1850s and early 1860s than William H. Kinsman, a twenty-four-year-old Nova Scotia native who arrived in town in 1858. A Victorian romantic with a taste for adventure cultivated in his maritime background, his buoyant personality, ambition, writing talent, and social graces were particularly valuable qualities in an up-and-coming frontier community. Kinsman quickly established a good rapport with

Dodge, Maynard, and other community leaders. He studied law, wrote for the *Nonpareil*, served as secretary of the Pottawattamie County Agricultural Society and the Teacher's Institute, and was active in boosting Abraham Lincoln and the early Republican Party in western Iowa. In the spring of 1859, he traveled to the Colorado gold-mining region, and his reports to the *Nonpareil* served Council Bluffs' interests as an outfitting center. Returning to Council Bluffs, he was active in the political swirl, and by December he was off to Washington where he spent the next four months as a man about town, reporting on doings in the capital to the *Nonpareil*. By the spring of 1860, he was back in Council Bluffs where he became a law partner of Dexter Bloomer.

With the outbreak of the Civil War, Kinsman commanded a company in Dodge's Fourth Regiment of Iowa Volunteers. He reported to the *Nonpareil* on the activity of the Fourth Iowa in Arkansas and Missouri and eventually became commander of the Twenty-third Iowa Infantry. Impetuous and restless, he was court-martialed for disobeying a superior officer, but he was soon restored to his command. Not surprisingly, in May 1863 Kinsman died from a wound he received while leading a charge at the Big Black River Bridge, Mississippi, on the road to Vicksburg. His combat death would be his primary memorial. His brief and intense association with the development of Council Bluffs symbolized the best traits of the urban West.

In the meantime, the sudden prosperity in 1859 did not immediately lead to the formation of a cohesive Omaha business community. Omaha was new, and it had experienced enough problems to deter some investors. The Council Bluffs and Nebraska Ferry Company lost importance once it sold most of its lots. Ferry operator Brown, eventually killed in a street brawl, was never a town leader; former acting governor Cuming died suddenly in 1858. Some investors moved on after the Panic of 1857, seeking places with better prospects. It was a common practice on the frontier. The emerging leaders in Omaha were men who arrived during the first years of settlement and who had enough faith to stay during the short period of financial adversity. While they engaged in a variety of business pursuits, everything from banking to lumbering, they all had freighting and outfitting connections.

The enterprises formed by the Kountze and the Creighton families were the most visible. Both groups, made up of Ohio natives, started their Omaha operations in 1856. The four Kountze brothers, Augustus, Charles, Herman, and Luther, were sons of a German immigrant from Saxony. After making money carrying freight for the federal government, they founded the Kountze Brothers Bank, one of Omaha's first successful banks. Luther moved to Denver, where he established a financial institution, giving the family an impressive regional base. Charles soon followed. Augustus and Herman remained in Omaha to consolidate and coordinate activities. The Kountzes called themselves "Bankers and Collectors" dealing in "Gold Dust and Land Warrants." They reorganized their bank in 1863 as the First National Bank of Omaha. Later they broadened their holdings still more by establishing a bank in New York City and by buying property in Texas and Chicago.

The three Creighton brothers, Edward, John, and Joseph, plus a cousin, James, were among the first suppliers to Colorado miners. Edward Creighton, born in 1820, was the most important member of the family. He started out in Omaha as the owner of a lumberyard, a business he soon abandoned. It was far removed from the area that became the core of his business—building telegraph lines, the "singing wires" that in the mid-nineteenth century were bringing an amazing transformation in communication. In the late 1850s he supervised the construction of a line from Jefferson City, Missouri, to Fort Smith, Arkansas. He met in Cleveland, Ohio, with powerful Western Union capitalists and became the company's general agent. After Western Union persuaded the last Congress prior to the Civil War to award a forty-thousand-dollar annual subsidy for ten years to the builder of a system from the Missouri border to California, Creighton completed the Missouri and Western line from St. Louis to Omaha in the early fall of 1860, pushing on before winter to Fort Kearny. He then undertook a hazardous survey trip to California, stopping for several days in Salt Lake City to cultivate a friendship with Brigham Young. Following negotiations in San Francisco in which Creighton arranged for telegraph connections to be built east from California, he returned east by ocean steamer. Despite the Civil War, he hurried west to direct construction. Overcoming logistical problems through a series of brilliant decisions, among them dividing his construction parties into eastern and western units, he linked up with the California line at Salt Lake City on October 20, 1862, many months ahead of schedule. Stock issues enabled Creighton to make several hundred thousand dollars, which he parlayed into a considerable fortune. He invested in many enterprises and joined with the Kountze interests in establishing the First National Bank of Omaha. One of the richest men in Nebraska when he died in 1874, Creighton gave Omaha needed direction, pointing it on a course of destiny as a communications center.

FROM THE PACIFIC HOUSE TO PROMONTORY SUMMIT

On an afternoon in August 1859, Abraham Lincoln, standing on an Iowa bluff, looked across the Missouri River at Omaha. Lincoln, an unannounced candidate for the 1860 Republican presidential nomination, was in the midst of a business, political, and pleasure trip. He had made public appearances in Kansas before taking a steamboat from St. Joseph to Council Bluffs. Whenever Lincoln went on deck, a crowd surrounded him, charmed by his interesting comments and distinctive manner of speech. In Council Bluffs he checked into the Pacific House. His presence attracted a delegation of civic leaders who persuaded him to give a speech at the Concert Hall. The next day he transacted private business. He carefully studied ten acres on the west side of Council Bluffs that he had received as collateral for a defaulted $3,500 loan. After determining the land was worth at least that much, he decided to take it as payment in full. He returned to Pacific House, where he met Grenville Dodge, whom he had learned was an expert on railroads. In what proved to be a two-hour conversation on the hotel porch, Dodge found that Lincoln's "kindly ways" drew from him all he knew about the western country. "As the saying is," Dodge recalled, "he completely 'shelled my woods,' getting all the secrets that were later to go to my employers." Nevertheless, Dodge had taken the opportunity to impress upon Lincoln the merits of Council Bluffs as the eastern terminus of a railroad extending to the Pacific via the Platte valley. The next day, Lincoln went east by stage, albeit without having visited Omaha.

The key to the future of Omaha was the Pacific Railroad Act approved by President Abraham Lincoln on July 1, 1862, which provided for construction with federal help of a transcontinental railroad. With southern interests out of Congress, a road over a northern route had become a foregone conclusion. Under the act the Central Pacific Railroad received federal help to build east from Sacramento, California. In addition, the measure chartered a new corporation, the Union Pacific Railroad. It was authorized to construct a single line west from an "initial point" 247 miles west of Omaha. Surveyors were to fix the exact location on the one hundredth meridian. Four branch lines would radiate eastward from the initial point to Omaha, Sioux City, Kansas City, and Atchison. Of special importance was the Iowa Branch running through Nebraska from the initial point to the Missouri River. It was to become part of the Union Pacific's main line, connecting with eastern roads at a point on the western boundary determined by the president of the United States. The Sioux City and Atchison spurs, included to satisfy parochial interests and to cloak actual intentions, were of no real importance. The Kansas City Branch was to run no further than the one hundredth meridian. On the surface, the legislation seemed to favor Omaha.

Chicago railroad interests, in league with powerful eastern capitalists and Iowa promoters, were instrumental in helping to secure passage of the act. The plan, sold in part as a war measure, tied in with Chicago's emerging railroad strategy. It ignored two St. Louis–controlled roads: the Hannibal and St. Joseph Railroad, which had been completed to the Missouri River in 1859, and the line that would later be known as the Missouri Pacific, which had a railhead in Sedalia, Missouri, two-thirds of the way across the state. Three Chicago lines that had already penetrated eastern Iowa planned to build on to Council Bluffs as soon as hostilities ended. Indeed, most of the survey work had already been completed. Omaha leaders were jubilant: "We have an abiding faith that if our people prove true to themselves, there is a prosperous future for Omaha," the editor of the *Omaha Nebraska Republican* wrote on March 11, 1863. "The prospect that the Pacific Rail Road is to have its eastern terminus here—the fact that the Iowa system of Railroads is to terminate in Council Bluffs, or rather on the river's edge, opposite this city—the certainty that the Platte River and the Loup Fork are to be speedily bridged—our rapidly growing trade with the Western Mines—all point to such a consummation."

The original leaders of the Union Pacific were not satisfied with the act, because they thought it failed to provide large enough government subsidies. This was particularly true of the road's first promoter, Thomas C. Durant, a physician turned financier who had a reputation for "sharp" dealings. Stock subscriptions went slowly, although Omahans subscribed for the amount of twelve thousand dollars. In the spring of 1863, Lincoln summoned Dodge to Washington from the battlefields of northern Mississippi; Dodge had left surveying work to become a major general in the Union Army. The president, despite the war, was anxious for the Union Pacific to start construction.

He understood the complicated nature of the whole Pacific railroad strategy. During the 1850s he had worked as a lawyer for Chicago lines, most notably the Rock Island and Illinois Central railroads. When Lincoln asked Dodge about the problem, he replied that he thought the project of such great magnitude that it should be undertaken entirely by the federal government. "He objected to this," Dodge recalled, "saying the Government would give the project all possible aid and support, but could not build the road; that it had all it could handle in the conflict now going on. But the Government would make any change in the law or give any reasonable aid to insure the building of the road by private enterprise."

This was exactly what Dodge had wanted to hear. Before returning to the field, he went to New York City to convey the news to Durant. The railroad leader knew what to do. He went back to Congress, spending money lavishly in the right places. He received the aid of powerful Massachusetts Republican congressman Oakes Ames, who along with his brother Oliver Ames, would later enter the Union Pacific management group. As a result of Durant's manipulations, an amendment to the original act became law in the summer of 1864. The measure, which among other things doubled the size of the land grant (part of the subsidy package to encourage construction), pleased the owners and encouraged them to quickly go ahead with plans to sell bonds and start construction.

Meanwhile, Lincoln had designated the eastern terminal. John P. Usher, the secretary of the interior, related a conversation that he said took place between Durant and the president. "Now the natural place for this terminal point is at the mouth of the Platte River," Durant explained, "but Omaha is the principal town in Nebraska . . . the best thing is to start it from Omaha." Lincoln, after studying a map of the region, replied, "I have got a quarter section of land right across there, and if I fix it there they will say that I have done it to benefit my land. But, I will fix it there, anyhow." At the time of his meeting with Durant on November 17, 1863, Lincoln hastily issued an executive order describing the terminus as "so much of the western boundary of the State of Iowa as lies between the north and south boundaries of the United States township within which the city of Omaha is situate." Because Iowa's western boundary was the Missouri River channel, this order and a subsequent one issued on March 7, 1864, were ambiguous enough to set the stage for a legal wrangle a decade later between Omaha and Council Bluffs as to which city should be the eastern terminus of the Union Pacific.

Durant decided that Lincoln meant for the Union Pacific to start from Omaha. To dramatize the occasion and to impress investors with the Union Pacific's determination, he orchestrated a gala celebration in Omaha. On December 2, 1863, he flashed the word of the presidential order in a telegram from his New York headquarters, directing the Union Pacific engineer in Omaha to "break ground." In midafternoon, a thousand persons assembled near the north end of the levee, a short distance from where the Pacific Telegraph crossed the Missouri River. While a large American flag flapped in the breeze, and after a clergyman "invoked the blessing of Divine Providence upon the Great Work about to be inaugurated," officials turned the first shovels of earth. The crowd cheered and dignitaries from Omaha and Council Bluffs made speeches.

The orators stressed the importance of the Union Pacific in saving the Union and altering false geographical notions. Addressing the latter point, a leader proclaimed, "The region of the Rocky Mountains and the great plains beyond, once regarded by geographers and geologists as a wild waste of volcanic desolation, has unbosomed unknown wealth, of which this road is now to be the outlet. . . . Nebraska, the great American desert, as it was then called, will, under the influence of this road, be revealed to the world as the great American garden."

After closing remarks, ceremonial guns boomed on both sides of the river. On the same day, Federal troops fought and died in the South. The theme of the day, on a wintry mud flat far removed from the fighting, was peace, progress, and prosperity. Perhaps this was not inappropriate. Those present were also a long way from the board rooms of greedy New York speculators or the congressional haunts of grasping politicians. Almost all of those assembled felt that they bore witness to the start of a great enterprise and a watershed that ushered in a new industrial era in America, one that would totally change the country after the Civil War. That was the result desired by George Francis Train, the chief publicist for the Union Pacific Railroad. Things went about as planned.

Train came and left just as fast. The five-foot-ten-inch-tall Train had a corpulent build, blue eyes, a prominent nose, and dark curly hair streaked with grey. He said he was born in Boston in 1829 and that he earned ninety-five thousand dollars at the age of twenty-one while running a shipping firm in Melbourne, Australia, and establishing stage coach service between that town and Sydney. Shortly before the Civil War, he promoted street railroads in the United Kingdom and the Atlantic and Great Western Railroad in Ohio. An accomplished lecturer on his own activities and an inspirational speaker, his stirring speeches on behalf of the Union cause and his experience in railroad work attracted the interest of Union Pacific leaders. He seemed an excellent choice to head their advertising campaign despite an 1862 arrest in Boston for disrupting a public meeting. People who came in close contact with Train thought his ideas "extravagant," at the same time finding him likable; he did not seem to take life all that seriously and he liked practical jokes. A friend called him, "A locomotive that has run off the track, turned upside down with its cowcatcher buried in a stump and the wheels making a thousand revolutions in a minute—a kite in the air which has lost its tail.... A noonday mystery, a solved conundrum—a practical joke in earnest—a cipher wanting a figure to pass for something; with the brains of twenty men in his head all pulling in different ways."

When called upon to make remarks at the end of the Union Pacific groundbreaking ceremony, Train asserted that Omaha was at the starting point of the grandest undertaking God ever witnessed in the history of the world. At first, he had demurred to speak, pleading that the effects of three nights in a stage across Iowa had "done him up." But, when the crowd refused to leave, he climbed upon a buggy, removed his overcoat, rolled up his sleeves, and launched into an address. Speaking rapidly and without notes, he demonstrated why he had a reputation as a spellbinder. Applause greeted Train's assertions about Omaha's future role in America: "The Great *Pacific Railway is commenced.* . . . The President has shown his good judgment in locating the road where the Almighty has placed the signal station at the entrance of a garden seven hundred miles in length and twenty broad. Look at the face of nature here—study the map, and point out, if you can, another place for the central station of the *World's Highway.* The enterprise is national— 'tis the *People's* road." In the words of the *Council Bluffs Nonpareil,* Train's address was "the raciest, liveliest, and best-natured and most tip-top speech ever delivered west of the Missouri river." That night he was the center of attention at a railroad banquet; he had become an instant community hero.

Train founded Credit Foncier of America to develop communities along the Union Pacific route. "One of my plans," he recorded, "was the creation of a chain of great towns across the continent, connecting Boston with San Francisco by a magnificent highway of cities." He bought five thousand lots in Omaha, helped erect the forty-thousand-dollar Cozzen's House Hotel and purchased ten other buildings. His holdings in other places were equally impressive—seven thousand lots and a hotel in Columbus, Nebraska, plus one thousand lots in Council Bluffs. He was eased out as an important Union Pacific official after a number of congressmen contended he was mentally unbalanced and proof that the Union Pacific would never be completed. Train's town promotions went sour; he failed to recoup by making heavy investments in Denver. Going into politics, he supported radical causes but continued to enjoy a good press in Omaha. In 1872 when he ran unsuccessfully for president on a third-party ticket, an Omahan called him a "Man of Destiny and the People's Candidate."

After that, Train's career took erratic turns; he served time in prison for circulating obscene literature and was declared legally insane. His Omaha fortunes waned and the original owners foreclosed on his property. Train, who always said he owned $30 million in Omaha land, drifted on to new promotions and controversies before his death in 1904. As one historian said, "Train was a real showman—a combination of Liberace and Billy Graham." In his prime years, he was an Omaha prophet of destiny, and as another scholar has written, "He made the future look bright to the citizens of the young commonwealth of Nebraska."

Train was also responsible for naming what became one of the most controversial American corporations of the nineteenth century—Credit Mobilier of America, the construction company set up by the owners of the Union Pacific to build the railroad. The initial activities of Credit Mobilier had caused anxiety in Omaha. Except for preliminary work, very little happened until after the war. For a time it appeared that Omaha might lose the terminal. To keep its charter, the Union Pacific had to finish much of the stretch between the Missouri River and the initial point by June 27, 1866. In addition, to earn the right to build on west it had to beat any other road to the one hundredth meridian.

After spending one hundred thousand dollars on an unsatisfactory due-west course, Durant ordered new surveys, one to the north at Florence and the other to the south at Bellevue. He selected the so-called ox-bow route, which dipped south from Omaha for a distance of nine miles, before turning west at the northern environs of Bellevue. Leaders in Omaha who had not considered Bellevue a rival since the capital fight were, to say the least, very upset. They feared that the Union Pacific would build a bridge and shops at Bellevue, making their city on an insignificant spur. They did not trust Durant, with reason. In February of 1865, he issued a statement: "The line has been changed to avoid heavy grades, not with the intention of interfering with the terminus." Soon afterwards, however, he secretly wired his engineers: "Make surveys immediately from river at Bellevue to the nearest point on the line and report probable cost of right of way. Also best location for shops at Bellevue or Fremont."

After threats and counterthreats, the Union Pacific built over the ox-bow route, but the terminal stayed in Omaha. Durant owned 4,360 acres in Omaha and 951 acres in Council Bluffs. He feared that a blatant change might upset delicate political relationships already complicated by Lincoln's assassination. The new president, Andrew Johnson, was unenthusiastic about government participation in the transcontinental out of Omaha. Anyway, Durant, whose critics implied that his only purpose was to shake down Omaha interests for more money, acted in character. To maximize government subsidies, he ordered the maps used for such payments adjusted so that the Omaha terminal would start two miles north of the station.

The positive outcome notwithstanding, the Bellevue episode illustrated that Omaha's future was largely dependent upon external forces, including decision makers with questionable motives. Joseph Barker Jr., an Omaha resident who managed substantial local real-estate holdings for his family in England, had brooded over the Bellevue threat, an anxiety mitigated by the fact that the U.S. Army was increasingly using Omaha as a supply and operational center for its activities on the Plains. Finally in October 1866, he wrote home, saying, "I begin to feel satisfied and I think People generally feel satisfied that we have nothing—or at best very little, to fear from Bellview."

The Union Pacific had to overcome great difficulties. Stock issues did badly despite fanfare. Durant had a bad commercial reputation, and businessmen considered the Union Pacific a premature enterprise thrust into empty country. Under the circumstances, the subsidies—the greatest ever granted a railroad—were unattractive. In 1866 the participation of New England investors headed by the Ames brothers improved confidence and guaranteed a major construction effort. The new group planned to take advantage of the company's role as its own chief contractor through Credit Mobilier. Using railroad construction companies to ensure profits from high-risk lines was a common business device. However, there had never before been so much federal money involved, and Oakes Ames apparently saw nothing wrong in using his congressional position to ensure success. When questions rose about the inflated size of construction contracts, he gave Credit Mobilier stock to prominent politicians. Insiders knew how to conduct business in Congress. The public morality of the Gilded Age was fast and loose, and, after all, he was not handing out flat cash payments as the Union Pacific–Eastern Division Railroad did to get a charter to build across Kansas beyond the initial point. In 1872 *New York Sun* reporters exposed Ames, then a member of the Union Pacific executive committee, calling him "The King of Frauds" and detailing his Credit Mobilier stock transactions. Censured in 1873 by the House of Representatives, he died a few months later, leaving an estate of several million dollars.

Congressional hearings showed that Credit Mobilier charged $92 million for a road that cost $40 million to build. Those connected with the enterprise argued that the profit margin was reasonable under the circumstances. Few agreed. Credit Mobilier—a nineteenth-century Teapot Dome and Enron—ultimately cast a pall over the whole Pacific Railroad project, causing long-run problems for both the Union Pacific and Omaha. These difficulties lay ahead when the Union Pacific mounted a gigantic construction effort out of Omaha in the spring of 1866.

It was important that the Union Pacific build through the Platte valley, reaching the one hundredth meridian and beyond as quickly as possible. What became the Union Pacific–Eastern Division Railroad, which had no business connections with the Union Pacific, had already started building toward central Kansas. The Pacific Railroad Act of 1866 authorized the Central Pacific to continue eastward from Nevada, where the road was originally to stop. Durant came to Omaha to deal with mounting problems. The tall, thin, and sharp-featured financier dressed in the style of a frontier dandy, wearing a costly slouch hat, velvet sack coat and vest, corduroy breeches, and high-top boots. "Durant was of a nervous temperament—all nerve—quick in motion and speech, and decisive in character, sometimes rather imperious," an Omahan remembered. Accompanied by a beautiful blond woman, Durant resided for six months in a Lutheran parsonage; rumors spread that he had bought his companion a twenty-five-thousand-dollar gown. Real railroad-building work languished until Grenville Dodge returned from the army on May 6, 1866, to assume duties as the Union Pacific's chief engineer. Wounded three times in action, he left service a hero. Dodge, small in stature, had what a friend called a "modest demeanor" and an even disposition. He quickly organized survey, construction, and supply operations along military lines and hired a firm run by former Union general John (Jack) Casement and his brother Daniel to lay track and keep discipline in the work force.

Building proceeded rapidly, saving the charter by reaching the one hundredth meridian on October 6, 1866, well ahead of the opposition. Over the next three years, Union Pacific rails drove west, overcoming Indians, rivers, financial problems, and internal bickering. The Casements kept one thousand men employed at the head of the track. Thousands of others worked on other aspects of the tremendous undertaking. It required forty carloads of material and supplies to lay one mile of track, all of which had to be transported from the Missouri River. Every mile the railroad moved westward complicated supply considerations.

Omaha reaped rewards beyond expectations from the building of the great railroad. The Union Pacific made the city its base of operations, leasing the Herndon House as a headquarters. Crews laid out a large yard and erected massive shops. The company employed six Missouri River steamboats. Hundreds of teams and wagons operated between Iowa railheads and Omaha. Oliver Ames bought five thousand dollars in shares in an Omaha bank; other railroad officials poured in money, hoping to capitalize on a boom that they had initiated. Speculators arrived from across the country; in fact, when Omaha's first city directory was published in 1866, George F. Train and eight other persons simply gave "speculator" as their occupation. Several businesses in Council Bluffs and rival Nebraska communities relocated in Omaha. The city became a roaring camp that handled every conceivable need of the Union Pacific. Thousands of workers came through town. So did gamblers, prostitutes, thieves, and bunko artists. They were interested in a share of the action at the Hell-on-Wheels, the colorful tent-city gambling and recreational center that moved west with the tracks. In Omaha gigantic piles of tracks and stacks of ties awaited shipment from the waterfront to distant plains and mountains. Because cottonwood, a poor building material, was the principal timber available during the early construction phase, the railroad operated a plant at Omaha that used a preservation technique called "burnettizing" that replaced natural moisture with a fluid containing zinc to render cottonwood ties more durable. Merchants and jobbers received railroad orders, and business further increased as the first small towns sprang up along the line.

Conditions were so good that in 1867, Omaha interests acquiesced at the time of Nebraska statehood to the moving of the government to Lincoln, sixty miles to the southwest. What had been considered a prize fifteen years earlier no longer seemed so important. The state government's importance hardly compared with the fulfillment of railroad destiny. On May 10, 1869, the last spike, a gold one, welded the Union Pacific and Central Pacific together at Promontory Summit in western Utah. The word "Done," transmitted to Omaha over a thousand miles of wire, touched off a prearranged celebration. A thousand-gun salute boomed out, bells rang, whistles blew, and fire wagons paraded through the streets. A leader said, "Westward the Star of Empire Has Found Its Way," closing the first chapter in the history of Omaha.

In a sense an age had passed between August 13, 1859, when Abraham Lincoln visited with Grenville Dodge in Council Bluffs about a transcontinental railroad and the ceremony at Promontory Summit on May 10, 1869. Lincoln had been elected president, led the nation to victory in the Civil War, and had become a martyr to the Union cause, all while supporting the transcontinental railroad. Dodge, badly wounded in the Battle of Atlanta in 1864, would stand at Promontory at the western end of 1,086 miles of track that were in no small measure the fruit of his work as the Union Pacific's chief engineer. Although the world had entered the age of steam power and telegraphic communication, building the Union Pacific and the Central Pacific over the 1,876 miles of plains, deserts, and mountains between Omaha and Sacramento had taken the muscular strength of thousands of men and beasts—the same energy sources that had been basic to the human experience for thousands of years past. Amazingly, less than ten years had elapsed since that conversation on the porch of the Pacific House.

THE GATHERING OF THE LINES

Council Bluffs also celebrated the event at Promontory Summit, but the linking of Sacramento and Omaha would have been almost pointless without railroads tying the eastern terminus of the Union Pacific to the rest of the na-

1. Grenville M. Dodge. *Courtesy Council Bluffs Public Library, Council Bluffs, Iowa.*

tion. Railroad construction from the Mississippi River across Iowa had begun in the mid-1850s. The depression triggered by the Panic of 1857, and then the Civil War brought almost a complete stop to construction. By late in 1864, the Cedar Rapids and Missouri River Railroad, a subsidiary of the Chicago and North Western line, had reached Boone in central Iowa, the closest rail link to Council Bluffs. Freight lines and stagecoaches bridged this gap while stages ran between Council Bluffs and Kellogg, Iowa, connecting with the Chicago, Rock Island and Pacific Railroad, successor to the bankrupt Mississippi and Missouri line.

Connection with the Union Pacific was an obvious incentive for railroad entrepreneurs to build to Council Bluffs, but that community's civic leaders did not take such construction for granted. As the local paper, the *Nonpareil*, remarked in September 1865, "a reasonable inducement" from Pottawattamie County would help in securing the line from Boone. At a festive public meeting in Burhop's Hall on July 9, 1866, Maj. M. Turley contributed eighty acres of land for a depot and other railroad facilities, and other boosters pledged some thirty-six thousand dollars. Under the guidance of John I. Blair, a key builder of the Chicago and North Western system, the Cedar Rapids and Missouri pushed on rapidly, and that autumn, construction crews laid track southwestward through the Boyer River valley. On January 22, 1867, a big civic celebration at the Council Bluffs depot marked the completion of the line. Among the speakers that night at a board of trade gathering was Gen. Grenville Dodge who noted that the completion of the line meant that Council Bluffs now had "the only all rail route from the Missouri River to the Atlantic coast." Getting to one of his basic beliefs, Dodge said, "Nature has been lavish in concentrating here in this valley and around this city advantages for a commercial and railroad centre, possessed by no other point between St. Louis and the head of the Missouri River." He predicted that if local people focused their energy and resources properly over the coming two years, Council Bluffs could have "five great trunk railroads" and become "the metropolis of the Missouri Valley." On February 8, 1867, Council Bluffs residents, amid the thunder of cannon, a procession to the depot, more speeches, and the presence of Leland Stanford, the leading figure in the building of the Central Pacific eastward from California, celebrated the arrival of a passenger train from Chicago over the North Western system. However, problems including a hard winter delayed scheduled passenger service on the 488-mile route until June 5.

Pre–Civil War work on a Council Bluffs and St. Joseph Rail Road was restarted late in 1865, in part with assistance from Pottawattamie County residents who donated land for its right of way. Because the Union Pacific had devoured the local timber supply, the Council Bluffs and St. Joseph contractor had to acquire wood for ties and bridges in Mills County, Iowa, south of town. On January 9, 1867, a number of local residents rode an excursion train from Council Bluffs to the end of track, over halfway to the Missouri border, the first passengers in the city's long odyssey as a rail center. Soon,

James F. Joy, president of the Burlington and Missouri River Railroad, became a large investor in the line, which eventually became part of the Burlington system. On August 19, 1868, the first train from St. Joseph pulled into Council Bluffs.

About one hundred miles up the Missouri valley from Council Bluffs, Sioux City began to emerge as a significant community after 1858. From California Junction, north of Council Bluffs, the Sioux City and Pacific Railroad began building northward in September 1867 and in March 1868 was completed to Sioux City. The line used the Cedar Rapids and Missouri to reach Council Bluffs from California Junction, and both roads eventually became part of the Chicago and North Western system.

The completion of the Union Pacific–Central Pacific line was not the only major event in 1869 to shape the evolution of Council Bluffs and Omaha as a great rail center. By the final months of 1867, the Rock Island Railroad was pushing westward, and by the close of the following year some six thousand laborers had built the line seventy-six miles beyond Des Moines toward Council Bluffs. The Rock Island reached Council Bluffs on May 12, 1869, two days after the golden spike was driven in Utah, and regular service began the following month. This was a hard-won triumph for the people of Council Bluffs who in 1857 had approved a three-hundred-thousand-dollar bond issue for the Rock Island's forerunner, the Mississippi and Missouri. In an age of minimal accountability in railroad financing, the bond issue brought a mere four thousand dollars' worth of grading.

Meanwhile, the Burlington and Missouri River Railroad, through the leadership of Charles E. Perkins and with financial help from the Chicago, Burlington and Quincy Railroad, had resumed construction westward from Ottumwa towards the Missouri River, about 180 miles distant. On November 26, 1869, the B and M was completed to East Plattsmouth on the Missouri River. At nearby Pacific Junction in Mills County, the B and M joined the Council Bluffs and St. Joseph line and used that road for its connection north to Council Bluffs. The arrival of a Burlington train at Council Bluffs on December 4, 1869, marked the fifth railroad to reach the city in less than three years.

Like the Union Pacific and Central Pacific, the three railroads that crossed Iowa received land grants as construction incentives. The Cedar Rapids and Missouri River line—in essence, the Chicago and North Western Railroad—as the first line to reach Council Bluffs and a potential link to the Union Pacific was a challenge to the Rock Island and the Burlington to attain the same objective. While the Burlington was the last of these three lines to reach Council Bluffs, it was the only one to avoid bankruptcy in the turbulent times after 1857. On a more positive note, by 1869 all three roads had bridged the Mississippi River, leaving the Missouri River in the Council Bluffs–Omaha area as the sole barrier to the completion of transcontinental rail service. Dodge's hope for "five great trunk railroads" at Council Bluffs by 1869 had not been met, but three such roads, and counting the Union Pacific, a fourth, plus two regional lines had set his hometown and its western neighbor on course to become one of the world's great rail centers. Rails west to the Pacific were fundamental to the urban aspirations of Omaha and Council Bluffs, but rails in other directions—especially east to Chicago, the lower Great Lakes area, and the Atlantic—were essential in their evolution into gateway cities. At the start of the twenty-first century, Council Bluffs boosters would describe their community as "Iowa's leading edge," a slogan that conjures the idea of the city as a gateway to the East. Such a concept is helpful in understanding the importance of the years 1867 to 1869 as a decisive period in shaping both Council Bluffs and Omaha.

LOOKING BACK

In retrospect, observers claimed Omaha's success was easily explained. They cited a number of geographic factors, such as "river lines" and "breaking points," as proof of the inevitability of Omaha's role as a "Gate City." By applying the theories commonly used by nineteenth-century urban developers, a tremendously complex chain of events became predestined. This reduced to little consequence the hopes and aspirations of the participants in the story of Omaha and the continued development of its parent, Council Bluffs. Nature's favors are undeniable, but it would take William D. Brown and his hope of a town at the western terminal of his ferry, J. W. Pattison and his dream of greatness as described in the *Arrow,* and Thomas B. Cuming and his stake in selecting a territorial capital to bring them to fruition. The future of the upstream cities also depended upon individuals who worked on grander scales: Augustus Kountze and his plan for regional banking, Edward Creighton and his knowledge of telegraphy, Grenville Dodge and his surveys of railroad routes, George Francis Train and his extravagant plans, and Abraham Lincoln and his strategy for nation building. Although they were hardly community builders, Thomas Durant and his design of a railroad empire and Oakes Ames and his desire to build a gigantic fortune were important in shaping Omaha. Of course, the success of Omaha and Council Bluffs were intertwined. Dodge was also in the vanguard of building Council Bluffs, which would be his home for the rest of his long life. Nevertheless, just as such key Union Pacific figures as Ames and Durant did not reside in Omaha, the entrepreneurs and railroad men who brought the five lines to Council Bluffs were outsiders. These persons and others made the decisions that helped Omaha and Council Bluffs grow. They formulated the programs and marshaled the resources. It remained to be seen what lay ahead. Would these cities go on to other triumphs, becoming "the metropolis of the Missouri Valley" that Dodge hoped for? Or would Omaha or Council Bluffs—or both together—become just another provincial center of medium stature? The answer depended on new considerations, not the least being the fortunes of the Union Pacific and the future of Nebraska.

[3] Goddess and Harlot

At the beginning of her carefully crafted historical novel, *The Lieutenant's Lady*, Bess Streeter Aldrich portrayed the mixed impressions that the twelve-year-old place called Omaha conveyed to residents and travelers in 1866. She wrote,

> An orator of the day said the young city stood there on the Missouri River like a goddess lighting the way to the territory's hospitable borders to the great west beyond. A disgruntled investor said the town wallowed in the mud like a harlot plucking at travelers' sleeves and begging them to stay with her.
>
> Whatever the interpretation of it, Omaha sprawled over the Missouri flats and the river bluffs, muddy or dusty, sun-browned or snow-packed, but always lustily noisy with the vehemence of youth and growth.

The Omaha of 1866 was a dynamic mixture of the civilized and the uncouth. Nevertheless, the town had an aura of permanence that it lacked a decade earlier and was a better place to live than the uglier and more unpleasant place it had been in the mid- to late- 1850s. The town's original plat was a conventional grid. Farnam, the main street, ran west from near the river. For a couple of blocks, saloons, hotels, banks, mercantile houses, and other commercial establishments lined the thoroughfare. Behind it were other buildings, scattered across the landscape in no particular order. The first permanent structure in town was a sixteen-by-sixteen-foot log cabin that the Council Bluffs and Omaha Ferry Company erected to house employees. Identified as the St. Nicholas Hotel on promotional maps, it was better known locally as "The Claim House." Omaha pioneers lived in log cabins, dugouts, and sod houses. One settler resided in a thatched hut of "luxuriant" slough grass. The first baby was born in a squatter's log cabin. A large sod house, the Big 6, was a combination grocery and saloon. Throughout the village, tallow candles provided illumination; fireplaces were used for cooking and heat. Territorial governor Mark W. Izard shivered noticeably in a cold room at a ball in his honor. Water for domestic purposes came from wells lined with brick, stone, or wood, except during droughts when most went dry. Then people depended upon muddy Missouri River water. Debris of all kinds piled up in yards, and during the summer tall weeds were everywhere. Neighbors laughed at a Michigan man who planted some ornamental shrubs on his property. As long as Omaha was a frontier camp, few persons, despite the promoters' lavish claims for the future, were willing to invest in long-range projects. They wanted to wait and see if Omaha would last and grow. This was in the tradition of town building in America.

Indeed, observers viewed Omaha from different perspectives. The Reverend Joseph Barker, an English immigrant who arrived with his family on April 2, 1856, found little that impressed him: "At that time the city consisted of a few huts, two or three decent houses, a bank, the State House, a saw mill, and a few stores," he recalled. "The population would be about three or four hundred. The country round was one vast wild. The prairie fires had passed over it, as far as your eye could reach. The surface was black as coal. To us it had a somewhat hideous appearance. It looked anything but inviting to the eye." A few days earlier, on March 26 the editor of the *Omaha Nebraskian* had described the scene more positively: "Every thing about our city, gives promise of unparalleled improvement and prosperity. Settlers are constantly arriving and sales in real estate are going as briskly as ever. Persons are much more eager to purchase than to sell. Several new frames have already been put up and enclosed this season." It was a familiar story on the frontier and was repeated time and time again as settlement moved across the continent. There was a wide difference between what boosters claimed and what settlers found.

In Omaha as all along the Middle Border, everyone, no matter what their goals or impressions, wanted to believe in the inevitability of success. J. Sterling Morton, a Nebraska City promoter and politician, caught the spirit of town building. He admitted, "We all felt, as they used to print in large letters on every new town plat, that we were 'located adjacent to the very finest groves of timber, surrounded by a very rich agricultural country, in prospective, abundantly supplied with building rock of the finest description, beautifully watered, and possessing very fine indications of lead, iron, coal and salt in great abundance.' In my opinion we felt richer, better and more millionarish than any poor deluded mortals ever did on the same amount of moonshine and pluck."

Frontier communities attracted a wide variety of people, and Omaha was no exception. The village was a transfer point and jumping-off place for thousands of emigrants—Mormons, fur traders, freighters, soldiers, gold seekers, and adventurers. There was no civilization for thousands of square miles to the west. Over six thousand western pilgrims, most bound for Colorado, passed through during the spring and early summer of 1859. Emigrants, frequently dressed in the style favored by veteran mountaineers—red shirts, high-topped boots, and slouched hats—roamed the streets, affecting a rollicking, independent air. During the Pike's Peak rush, the town's stores and saloons operated around the clock. Bullwhackers could be heard at all hours cursing and cracking whips. Plainsmen from the West frequently remained a few days to "rest up" from their sojourns in the trackless wilderness. According to a local expression, they made "Rome howl." An early wholesaler explained, "After having thoroughly 'rested,' the freighters would put in an appearance, and then all would be rush and bustle, to get their trains in order, and they generally wanted this done on Sunday, the day of rest."

A large floating population remained a characteristic of Omaha; the construction of the Union Pacific Railroad in the 1860s brought more wayfarers through town than the mineral rushes of the 1850s. Although of crucial importance in building an economy, voyagers did not form the nucleus of a permanent citizenry. All promotional tub thumping to the contrary, few looked around and decided they wanted to remain. If anything, most carried away negative impressions, believing that storekeepers had overcharged them. Reactions to Omaha were typical of attitudes held toward other towns along the eastern edge of the Great Plains. Permanent settlers had to come from other sources.

Many of Omaha's pioneers were from right across the river in Council Bluffs, although a few came from farther away. There were the officials of the founding land company, plus the usual quota of land sharks and unsavory characters drawn to any highly touted new community. A large number claimed to be lawyers. All hoped to make quick fortunes or gain political advantages. A couple of merchants and physicians drifted in, as did some skilled and unskilled workers. Few families came; the early Omahans included many ambitious young men. In the beginning, not as many settlers arrived as the promoters had hoped. Confident accounts in the *Omaha Arrow* about tremendous progress were not substantiated by statistics. By June of 1855, a little less than a year after initial settlement, there were only between 250 and 300 inhabitants. The population increased slowly and then spurted in 1856 during a premature boom. Between June and October of that year, the number of Omahans climbed from 800 to 1,500. This rise, hardly comparable to San Francisco swelling from 100 to 10,000 people in one year during the 1849 gold rush, caused an Omaha newspaper editor to proclaim: "The growth of Omaha astonishes—is a fact few can comprehend." After that, many people left, their spirits crushed by the adversity that followed the Panic of 1857.

At the start of the Civil War, Omaha had fewer than two thousand residents, but thousands more had passed through the town on the way to more promising destinations. William N. Byers, born in Ohio in 1831, was one of many settlers who made an imprint on early Omaha and then moved on. As the town company's surveyor, he produced the first map of the city. After serving in the first territorial legislature and the first Omaha City Council, he struck out for Denver in 1859, taking a printing press with him. In the Queen City he founded the *Rocky Mountain News*. William Clancy was another member of the first territorial legislature who emigrated to Colorado. The owner of the Big 6, he became embittered when authorities cracked down on his business. In retaliation he made himself unpopular by supporting a "manifesto" to remove the capital to Florence. When he pulled up stakes, he left behind few friends and many enemies. Another man who came in the founding year and who was in the first assembly, Thomas Davis, was a Welsh immigrant. He owned a sawmill for many years and was active in local politics before returning east in 1870 to Indianapolis, Indiana. Such men were not unusual in mid-nineteenth-century America. They were but one part of a vast reservoir of restless people who went to the frontier to seek a better life. The superintendent of the 1850 census had discussed the "roving tendency" of the nation's people, a turn of phrase that described Omahans of the 1850s and subsequent decades.

Some other pioneers remained despite the community's inauspicious beginnings. They came for a variety of reasons and stayed because they eventually did well. George R. Armstrong, born in Maryland in 1819, was a printer in Ohio when he decided to "go west and grow up with the country." Following visits to several localities, he settled in Omaha in 1854. He made money as a construction contractor and enjoyed a successful career as a local and territorial politician. Elected mayor in 1862, he resigned to lead the Second Nebraska Cavalry against the Indians. He then returned to Omaha where for many years he worked for the Union Pacific Railroad and ran an agricultural-implement business. Charles W. Hamilton, a New York native, reached Omaha in 1856. He worked for a time as a hotel clerk but soon went into banking. He became a prominent citizen, serving in many religious, civic, and fraternal offices prior to his death in 1906. A physician turned politician, Enos Lowe, was an organizer of the Council Bluffs and Nebraska Ferry Company. Lowe, born in 1804 in North Carolina, had served as president of the second Iowa constitutional convention. He expected to make money in Omaha and he did. He joined in building a gas works, engaged in railroad speculation, incorporated a bank, and invested in a hotel. In 1866 he helped establish the Old Settlers Association, composed of "Builders of Omaha" who had arrived before 1858.

No one saw anything wrong with creating a society to honor the founding fathers of a community only twelve years old. The frontiersmen of Omaha were well aware that the town had succeeded, and they were proud of their own accomplishments. They thought it important to record that O. B. Seldon fired the first forge, that William Snowden conducted the first auction, and that John Withnell laid the first brick. A list of settlers had another effect; it placed everyone on the same level, acknowledging contributions and lending a degree of human dignity to those who did not achieve positions of high responsibility.

Many of the pioneers had experienced hard times. One young German immigrant, Vincent Burkley, who had anglicized his name, came to Omaha with his wife and children. He started a small clothing store that failed in 1857 and for a while eked out a meager living selling vegetables from his garden door-to-door. He went to Colorado to make a quick fortune in the gold fields but returned empty-handed. For the next year he husked corn in the fall, cut and sold hardwood in the winter, and operated his small produce business in the spring and summer. Although he had little money, his family had plenty to eat. His few cows and chickens assured a ready supply of milk, cheese, butter, and eggs. He bought, slaughtered, and dressed an occasional pig or calf.

A nephew in St. Joseph, Missouri, sent apples every year from his orchard. Burkley's son wrote,

> Mother's cellar would be considered comfortably stocked in the fall when she had a hundred pounds of lard, three or four hams and shoulders, a half barrel of sauerkraut, a large crock of mince meat, and the safe or cupboard well filled with pickles, preserves, cheese, etc., also a liberal quantity of sausage meat cut fine and seasoned to our own taste which certainly went well with homemade buckwheat cakes on a cold wintry morning. Besides these we had wild gooseberries, currants, grapes, strawberries, raspberries, plums, haws, elderberries, chokecherries, and quantities of hazel nuts, walnuts and hickory nuts which we would gather in the fall.

After business conditions improved, Burkley worked as a clerk in a general store. He renewed ties with his wholesalers in the East, many of whom were reluctant to do business until wartime prosperity led them to resume operations on the frontier. Early in the Civil War he again opened his own store and went on to a successful career, first in business and then in journalism. His experience of frequently shifting occupations was characteristic of the frontier. Few persons enjoyed immediate success.

SEEKING STABILITY

An early problem that confronted the Omaha founders involved federal land laws that they considered unfair and unenforceable. Critics—most people in the West—argued that the government's policy of selling land impeded rather than promoted progress. They ignored the fact that land sales represented a major source of federal revenue; they believed sinister elements responsible. Some imagined a plot by southern planters to curtail free homesteading; others thought industrialists in the Northeast wanted to hold up settlement to prevent drains on populations in the older states. Almost all thought that the land policy favored wealthy speculators. There was a growing conviction that the government should give land away to encourage western settlement. The Free Soil party of Martin Van Buren, which ran third in the 1848 presidential election, advocated such a course. The clamor increased the next year when the Illinois Central Railroad received a gigantic land grant. Free land became a tenet of the Republican Party, culminating in the passage of the Homestead

Act of 1862, under which an individual could obtain 160 acres for a small fee. Arrangements were different in 1854 before the change in policy. Land-office clerks continued to take in money and to go through the motions of pretending to enforce an unpopular system that had severe operational defects.

Supposedly, at least on paper, the first Omahans could obtain land under the Pre-emption Act of 1841. An individual marked out a claim to a 160-acre quarter section, made certain improvements, waited for the official survey and obtained a clear title by paying $1.25 an acre on the date that the government put the property up for sale. Payment could be in cash or military land warrants. Special provisions covered some potentially serious problems. Survey crews were responsible for making minor adjustments in property lines to ensure equity; titles could be conveyed by quitclaim deeds. Another law, the Federal Townsite Act, allowed a town company to stake out 320 acres. The proprietors, acting on their own, had the right to claim their 160-acre tracts to which the Pre-emption Act entitled them from adjoining land. These were the general ground rules. The problem was that what looked clear on paper failed to work in practice. The land office did not officially begin survey work around Omaha until 1856, two years after the ending of Indian claims and the start of settlement. An office, authorized for Omaha in 1854, opened three years later. The land sale, scheduled for 1857 but held up for political and economic reasons, finally occurred in July 1859, five years after settlement. With the prospect of homestead legislation, Nebraska settlers fought to put the sale date off as long as possible.

The Omaha investors, almost all members of the Council Bluffs and Nebraska Ferry Company, acted on their own and on the side of what a local historian and early resident, Alfred Sorenson, claimed was human greed. He said the company "accordingly undertook to secure the lion's share of the plunder." First, it took more land than it was entitled to by the law, grabbing at least six sections. Members of the enterprise and other favored persons each claimed an additional quarter section. This effectively tied up roughly sixty square miles of the public domain. The participants saw nothing wrong with their actions. They had no respect for the federal land laws, and at the very least they hoped to use proceeds from sale of the added acres to pay for the land to which they were legally entitled. All involved took a calculated risk. If the project failed, as did most town speculations, the legal essentials lost meaning. At any rate, they wanted to protect their interests. So they turned to a common frontier extralegal device, a claim association. Indeed, rival town promotions in Nebraska all formed similar organizations.

On July 22, 1854, persons who "got in on the ground floor" crossed the river from Council Bluffs and founded what became the Omaha Township Claim Association. Assembled under the "lone tree," the company quickly ratified claim laws characteristically used as the frontier moved westward through the Northwest Territory to the Middle Border. The rules provided for the protection of all holdings up to 320 acres, with the understanding that no member could own more than 80 acres of timber. There were a number of detailed provisions, including one requiring a claimant to erect a house within thirty days. This was cynical to say the least; the moving of a mobile dwelling from place to place satisfied the requirement. More importantly, the organizers made provisions for enforcement. Elected officers included a "judge" and a "sheriff." Serving under their jurisdiction were "regulators" from the ranks of association members. The motto was the same as elsewhere: "An injury to one is the concern of all." To remain in good standing, members were required to spend fifty dollars annually to improve their claims.

At first, the Omaha club functioned much like others along the eastern border of Nebraska. It dissuaded land sharks and other unsavory elements from taking advantage of the drifting nature of a weak central government by intruding on what should have been an orderly procedure. However, regulators chased away some legitimate settlers who were in full compliance with federal law, setting precedents for later actions. On one occasion a hundred armed men destroyed a shack. They scattered the lumber to the four winds before allowing a terrified owner to flee back to Iowa. The first territorial legislature, oblivious to the Constitution, passed a bill recognizing the activities of claim clubs. This was only natural. Most members belonged to one, as did the signer of the measure, acting governor Thomas Cuming.

Sporadic violence occurred in the Omaha area in 1856 and 1857 when regulators dealt harshly with suspected or actual claim jumpers. That was at the height of the first Omaha land boom, when choice river lots sold for as much as $2,500. At a mass meeting of the Omaha club, a member who recently had been acquitted of murder made a choking noise and thrust his hand in the air, yelling: "Instead of letting them prove up we'll send them up." His colleagues, while having no intention of going that far, were ready to intimidate people.

A most highly publicized incident concerned a man named Callahan. In the winter of 1857, he claimed a piece of land on Omaha's west side. Officers from the Omaha Township Claim Association arraigned him and forced him to stand at a mock trial. The verdict was that he renounce the claim or face drowning. Given thirty minutes to decide, he refused to relinquish his holdings. Led onto the Missouri River ice, he remained obstinate as regulators chopped a hole big enough for a man. He held out through three lengthy dunkings before capitulating, convinced that his tormentors intended to let go the next time they pushed him under. He was nearly frozen stiff. Following a cursory medical examination, Callahan, wrapped in heavy blankets and fortified with three doses of whisky, signed a document of relinquishment. That affair convinced most other potential claim jumpers to stay away. In the few cases where the association lost, challengers defended claims by brandishing rifles and shotguns, touching off feuds and generating ill will that lasted for years. On the whole, however, the claim association, according to one of its members, functioned as an omnipotent force.

The Omaha Township Claim Association disbanded following the official government land sale. There was no further need for the body. Almost all claimants who filed for additional land gained permanent titles through false entries, and the original speculators succeeded in protecting their holdings. In a later decision, the United States Supreme Court refused to overrule the actions of frontier claim associations. The Omaha club contributed stability to a chaotic process. The club's main function had been to preserve what members saw as legitimate rights of property. It had the usual contradictions of frontier voluntary societies. They protected members from illegal actions, at the same time guarding their acquisitions of more land than allowed by law. As it was, claim associations were only a part of an intricate structure of informal control mechanisms.

If examples for the rule of law were needed, Council Bluffs did not provide them, even though a district court session had convened there as early as 1851. Although Iowa had entered the Union over seven years before the creation of Nebraska Territory, early frontier conditions prevailed in the western half of the state, and institutional development in Council Bluffs reflected this reality. In May 1853 a mob lynched a man who had allegedly robbed and killed a California-bound traveler. The next month, Mayor Cornelius Voorhis established a vigilance committee. In 1860 Philip McGuire, according to a message left by the vigilantes in 1860, was "[h]ung for all manner of rascality." There was another lynching in 1865, but the plight of Union Army veterans William and Patrick Lawn was especially shocking. On a night in June 1867, a mob seized the men from their Council Bluffs hotel room and took them south over the county line and hanged them.

In Omaha, vigilante committees, disorderly throngs, and extralegal tribunals meted out punishment for criminal acts. This approach to law and order related directly to the inability of the federal government to develop machinery to protect citizens from criminal elements—horse thieves, rapists, murderers, and robbers—common to the frontier. Incompetence, delays, and technicalities made it easy for law violators to go free without standing trial. Federal judges concentrated on civil cases. It made little difference that the first territorial legislature in Nebraska had adopted the criminal laws of Iowa; there were not enough officials to run the system. As late as 1857, the only regular judicial authority in Omaha was the mayor sitting as a police judge. The Nebraska federal marshals were not of the same vibrant stripe as those who later tamed the Kansas cattle towns. There were no Wyatt Earps or "Wild Bill" Hickocks. Rather, they were nondescript political appointees. U.S. marshal B. P. Rankin, ordered by the chief justice of the territorial court to disperse a mob, delivered the command in a stage whisper, knowing full well that no one would pay attention. Nor was the federal attorney of any help in prosecuting offenders; he concentrated on personal pursuits. In essence there was no federal legal presence in Nebraska Territory. Given the mess in Kansas, Nebraska had a low priority and seemed far away from the thoughts of embattled national politicians trying to contain the explosive issue of slavery in the territories. Against the backdrop of "Bleeding Kansas," the thirteen slaves reported in the first Nebraska territorial census virtually assured a policy of statutory neglect; slaveholders and abolitionists knew the latter would win. The first wave of Nebraska settlers took advantage of the opportunity to take the law into their own hands.

Frontier Nebraska was probably not as violent as several previous pioneer settlements. The federal court records for the Additional Court for Michigan Territory, which in the 1820s and 1830s had jurisdiction over the future states of Wisconsin, Minnesota, and Iowa, indicated a high incidence of violence among lead miners and fur traders, attributed directly to the heavy use of hard liquor. Few criminal actions ever went to trial. The court left the punishment up to local citizens, concentrating instead on civil land and personal-property suits. During the 1849 gold rush, when there was no legal structure in California, law and order broke down completely. Only a quick institution of harsh vigilante justice stopped the outrages. Over fifty thousand persons had swarmed into California from all across the country. The situation in Nebraska was much different. A few thousand settlers arrived in the first couple of years, and almost all lived along an eighty-mile stretch of the Missouri River. Moreover, while freebooters did go to the new territory, more went to Kansas, attracted by the possibility of quick plunder under the guise of serving the causes of slavery or freedom. Naturally, the criminals in Nebraska caused serious concern. In Omaha, citizens attempted to stop nefarious practices, moving from informal mob action to sophisticated vigilante activities. The progression illustrated an aspect of community building, showing how Omaha passed through an important part of the frontier experience.

In 1856 two bungling offenders were the first to feel the brunt of Omaha frontier justice. They stole two horses in Omaha, selling them to nearby Pawnee Indians, who traditionally had good relations with whites. The horses escaped and galloped home. The Indians followed, learned they had been duped, and promised to provide what help they could. Not long afterwards, the thieves appeared at the Pawnee village trying to sell two mules. The Indians grabbed the men and took them to Omaha. The surprised residents could hardly believe their good fortune; horse thieves, unless captured at the scene of the crime, almost always escaped punishment.

Omaha did not have a jail, and a mob gathered around the hapless prisoners. Following a discussion, a consensus developed: the prisoners would have their heads shaved and be given thirty-nine lashes. After a barber shaved the right side of one man's head and the left of the other, they were led to a "liberty pole" across from the Apex Saloon. Members of the mob tied the first thief to the pole. Next, there was a slight delay. No one volunteered to apply a rawhide horsewhip. After a discussion, those assembled decided that the Indians should do the work on the grounds that they were the main victims. They readily assented, but when one of their number applied the lash with killing strokes, the mob decided that something else would have to be done. The job fell to the owners of the horses, who carried out the punishment. One man seemed to enjoy the work. He counted each lash and after the last stroke shouted, "That's all." The Indians whooped and yelled. Many whites watched in a solemn mood, feeling the affair necessary but regrettable. The only person opposed to the punishment, the chief justice of the territorial court, had to watch helplessly. When it was over, escorts took the two victims to the steam ferry and ushered them out of the territory. Nebraska Territory's criminal code provided for jail terms for convicted horse thieves. The penalty for armed robbery was ten to twenty years and for other robbery two to ten years. The usual punishment handed out by a frontier mob was lynching. The Omahans had acted with restraint. The next time would be much different.

In March 1858 a posse chased and apprehended two Iowans, Harvey Braden and John Daley, accused of stealing horses near Florence. Both men, known desperadoes, had the horses in their possession. In Omaha, Braden and Daley had a preliminary hearing before a magistrate. In default of bail, he committed them for trial. Early in the evening a few days later, a small group appeared at the jail. The sheriff was away, and there were no pedestrians in the streets. Only the sheriff's wife was in the building, and she offered no resistance as men took the key, opened the cell, led Braden and Daley outside, tied them up, dumped them on a wagon, and drove away. The vigilantes, followed by a large crowd of onlookers, took their captives north of town. The procession stopped by a stout oak tree with a large protruding branch. Men threw a single rope over the limb, tying one end around Braden's neck and the other Daley's as they stood huddled together on the wagon. A whip cracked and the vehicle moved away, leaving the horse thieves, dangling in the air back-to-back. The mob quickly dispersed; the two men swung freely through the night. A coroner's jury examined twenty to thirty hostile witnesses who, while they admitted being present, contended they had not participated and were unable to identify any of the perpetrators. The jury brought four bills, but no one was ever convicted. The cases, tried in another county after a change of venue, ended in acquittal.

A brutal incident marked the final series of actions that moved Omaha in the direction of law and order. George Taylor, a construction engineer, and his wife lived ten miles out of Omaha on the military road. Taylor was away on business in the spring of 1861 when two men, James Bouve and John S. Ilher, appeared at his isolated homestead. They tied his wife to the bed, assaulted her, and absconded with valuables, including the silverware. Ilher had to restrain his accomplice, Bouve, when he threatened Mrs. Taylor with a gun and said he wanted to burn her alive in her own bed. The two men fled to Omaha, where they buried their loot on the river front and went to a saloon. There, they drank, played cards, and attracted attention by freely spending money. They expected no trouble; rape was a crime that usually went unreported. Furthermore, itinerant big spenders were frequent in Omaha. They reckoned without George Taylor. He returned home, heard his wife out, went to Omaha, and swore out a robbery complaint. Ilher and Bouve, arrested on suspicion, protested their innocence, claiming they had just come in from the west to seek employment as laborers. Released for lack of evidence, they returned to the saloon, playing innocent. Not realizing they were under surveillance, the two eventually left the tavern. At that point, the city marshal placed them under arrest.

The victim identified the two men at a hastily held arraignment. Described as a tall, slim, and stately woman, she answered a judge's question about her assailants by screaming, "Yes, I could tell them among ten thousand people!" She picked both men out of an identification line. Stopping before Bouve, she exclaimed, "You are the man. I know you even if you have shaved off your whiskers, for I never can forget those eyes!" Walking a few steps further, she halted before Ilher, stating, "And you are the other man; you saved my life. It was you who said, 'Jim, don't shoot the old woman!'" That night, after intensive questioning, Ilher confessed and led authorities to the bottoms, where they found the loot from the Taylor cottage. The next day, five hundred men assembled, selected a "jury," appointed managers, and tried the two men in a kangaroo court. Two lawyers represented them, arguing that the law should be allowed to take its course. The so-called jury brought in a verdict of guilty, recommended clemency for Ilher, and left the crowd to decide whether or not to turn the two over to the vigilance committee for a "neck-tie sociable." Following pro and con speeches, the throng, voting by walking across a line, turned the affair over to the vigilantes. At midnight, a mob appeared at the jail and overpowered the marshal. Ilher was set free and allowed to run off into the darkness as revolvers cracked, sending bullets whistling past his ears. Bouve, a professional gambler and criminal reported to have killed many men in Colorado, suffered a different fate. He died, strung up on a hall beam in the jail, the tip of his toes touching the floor. A coroner's jury, possibly consisting of some of the lynching party, attributed his death to hanging by persons unknown.

Vigilante action failed to end crime in Omaha. There were several sensational murders in the sixties. In 1863 Cyrus Tator, a former member of the Kansas territorial legislature, went to the gallows for killing a business associate. There was a difference between his case and others: he received a trial before a legally constituted jury that declared him guilty and a higher court denied his appeal. On April 23, 1863, after he gave an hour-long speech stating his innocence, officials tied a rope around his neck, drew a black hood over his head, and dropped him into eternity. That concluded the first legal civilian execution in Nebraska and with it the activities of the Omaha vigilantes. There was no longer a need for such a practice. A lawful hanging—hardly an event that a community wanted to commemorate—signified a fundamental change in standards. The city had crossed an invisible line. The normal administration of justice in Omaha seemingly had passed out of the frontier period. This and other signs seemed to indicate a new era.

"THE REFINEMENT . . . OF OUR PEOPLE"

The settlement slowly evolved into an established community; the goal of all western town promoters. As quickly as possible they wanted to re-create the institutions associated with civilization in the eastern portions of the United States. What they wanted was hardly unique, merely an extension of the experiences of city builders in the more established parts of the country. The decisions of individual entrepreneurs, who had little vision beyond their own experiences, were crucial in determining urban contours. During the first years environmental factors, so important after a place started to show significant growth, had little if any impact. No one in early Omaha worried about industrial pollution or grasshopper infestations; it was a case of one thing at a time. Omaha's promoters were aware that most town sites never had the opportunity to grow. Cut off in infancy, they at best were relegated to the role of country crossings, marked only by a roadhouse and a few houses. Moreover, a large population by western standards did not always result in the creation of an established social order. Many mining camps, which at the height of their glory had several thousand inhabitants, never had schools or churches. Conversely, carefully planned small Puritan communities in colonial New England quickly acquired religious and educational institutions.

Creating a city that mirrored eastern norms was somewhat like constructing a house. Although there was already a generally understood blueprint, much needed to be done from the laying of the foundations to completion. Sometimes building went forward at a rapid rate; at other times there were long delays because of a lack of materials. The speed of the accomplishment depended upon the ingredients that went into the initial years of organization. Omaha was never a pastoral village or a mining camp. It was a communications point nurtured by speculation and, from its inception, by corrupt politics. The territorial government had little positive influence on the cultural scene. If anything, considering the antics of members of the territorial legislature—they frequently adjourned so that the proceedings would not affect their alcoholic consumption, brawls occurred with regularity on the floor, and debates had juvenile attributes—their presence retarded the establishment of conventional practices. The work fell to a few dedicated individuals who felt it was important to bring stability to the Nebraska frontier.

One of these men was attorney James M. Woolworth. Speaking of Omaha in his 1857 book promoting settlement in Nebraska, Woolworth said, "The population of this place is made up of intelligent and enterprising men. They are generally from the cultivated and educated classes of the East. In the character of its society, as regards intelligence and culture, genteel, and even fashionable life, Omaha City rivals [the] best towns of twice her population which can be named in New York or New England."

This boosterism notwithstanding, Omaha from its very early years had residents who worked to establish the cultural institutions that they had known in their places of origin. In 1857 a group of businessmen and lawyers founded the Omaha Library Association. Motives varied but included the education of future generations, the desire to promote adult education, the wish to copy eastern practices, the aim to further reform, and the plan to sell Omaha as a cultural center. The organizers rented a room, charged a nominal fee to join and soon acquired over a hundred different publications, including many current newspapers and periodicals. The Nebraska delegate to Congress sent the *Congressional Globe* and various printed compilations of federal documents.

Within short order, the Library Association decided to hold a lecture series, a device widely used in other parts of the country to cultivate the arts. There was no way to obtain top talent from the East; Omaha was too far off the beaten path for such luminaries as Henry David Thoreau and Ralph Waldo Emerson. Instead, the association relied on area residents. Speakers gave formal talks on "Our Constitution and the Laws," "Progress," "Emigration," "Free Thought," and "Labor." While the lecturers were admonished to avoid religion and politics, Council Bluffs feminist Amelia Bloomer gave a controversial presentation, claiming women were intellectual equals of men. Between 250 and 400 persons, close to a third of the population, attended at least one session during the 1857 season, encouraging organizers to offer programs the next year.

The editor of the *Omaha Times* gave extensive coverage, claiming the lectures afforded "positive evidence" that there were people on the frontier "capable of delivering good lectures." Contradictions existed between the goals of the Library Association and reality. The Claim Association continued to drive off land claimants; the vigilantes were at the apex of their power. Some of the same individuals probably belonged to all three groups. Be that as it may, a few Omahans saw the value of bringing intellectual pursuits to the village. Their contributions loomed large in creating a community. Without articulating a viewpoint, they realized that there was more to forming a city than protecting property and taking a harsh position on law and order.

There was a gradual building up of religious institutions. In August 1854 a Methodist, Peter Cooper, an English immigrant and quarry operator, gave the first-known sermon in Omaha in a private home. The sixteen worshippers entered through a kitchen shed. The service was symbolic; at that time almost all the Omaha pioneers lived in Iowa. Next spring, the Methodists sent a circuit rider. He conducted services in the territorial capitol and started a six-member congregation, hardly an auspicious beginning. The town company donated two lots to the new organization, which sold them for $1,500, using the proceeds to erect a church. Baptists, Presbyterians, Congregationalists, Episcopalians, and Roman Catholics followed, enjoying various degrees of success. The Roman Catholics dedicated St. Philomena's Cathedral in 1856, a plain structure that within three years became the seat of the Nebraska See. The wife of Edward Creighton strongly supported the Catholic Church, which grew into one of the most affluent religious bodies in the region. The Episcopalians in Omaha counted many local leaders among their membership. Baptists, Congregationalists, and Presbyterians had trouble getting established; a pioneer Baptist preacher commented that religion "met only a left-handed favor." A succession of study groups, storefront churches, and itinerant ministers failed before permanent congregations were finally created.

Nevertheless, by the late 1860s religious institutions appeared on the way to being solidly established. While Omaha was hardly a city of churches, and attendance was not as good as leaders desired, steeples that rose toward the heavens were further indications that Omaha neared the end of the frontier experience. In 1866 Omaha's first city directory—itself a milestone of civic progress—observed that "the towering steeples of our different places of worship bespeaks [sic]the refinement, liberality, and morality of our people."

Education gained a footing. In the earliest days there was more interest in promoting higher education than primary or secondary schools. Omaha merely copied earlier urban experiences in the older sections of the country. The desire to first stress higher learning characterized early American settlements from colonial times onward. The Council Bluffs and Nebraska Ferry Company persuaded the territorial legislature to charter a "paper university" and claimed to set aside a thousand acres to further development. The institution, named Simpson University, had a governing board. Announcements proclaimed the start of classes, but none were ever held, and the school died stillborn. It was simply a promotional device, as were several other colleges founded in Nebraska during the fifties.

The first schools in Omaha were subscription schools, where patrons paid set student fees directly to teachers. Again, this was a common part of the nation's educational experience. There was no public system until 1859. The curriculum emphasized the three R's, "Readin', Ritin', and 'Rithmetic." Discipline was harsh. Teachers generally accepted the adage "No lickin', no larnin'," and kept switches on prominent display. The board of education, beset with financial problems, established a tuition structure based on matriculation levels for individual courses; arithmetic cost one dollar per quarter and algebra three dollars. Even though almost five hundred students enrolled, exigencies forced the schools to close for two years during the Civil War. Private schools filled the void. S. D. Beals started what he called a high school, which soon had almost three hundred pupils. For a time, the institution aroused suspicion and hostility; supposedly it instilled "highfalutin" elitist concepts. Despite criticism, a realization dawned that Omaha needed good primary and secondary schools; it was part of the coming of civilization. The public schools reopened. The board erected three frame primary-school buildings and made a commitment to run a high school. In 1871 the state legislature created a consolidated school board in Omaha. Although a great deal remained to be done, public education, nonexistent in the community's formative years, had become a reality.

In 1857 the third Nebraska territorial legislature granted Omaha a city charter providing for a mayor and council. This was the standard form of local government used in the United States. The legislature kept certain powers over financial matters and the police. Imprecise wording over technical issues and partisan politics resulted in drawn-out controversies. There were several other charters before one in 1873 increased the role of the mayor and allowed a measure of home rule. The original charter had left the mayor without veto power and made him just another member of the city council. While the charter provided the machinery for the first election, it gave no guidance on council procedures. The new government met daily for a couple of months to determine routine business practices. The city recorder obtained copies of the ordinances for Iowa City, Iowa, which became the basis for those written for Omaha.

The elected officials had little previous experience in government. Proceedings were very informal with the tone set by the first mayor, Jesse Lowe, a forty-three-year-old former North Carolinian and one of the first settlers. The brother of Council Bluffs and Nebraska Ferry Company leader Enos Lowe, Jesse was a combination Indian trader, banker, and real-estate man, with a colorful and sinister past. "He was a strange man," an Omaha minister said. "I suppose in his younger days he was Captain of a robber band in Texas where he made a great deal of money. . . . They say he was a very dangerous man. His body, I suppose, has numerous cuts & scars & gunshot wounds, and a Bowie knife, was once pushed through his body. . . . They say he has four wives living." Lowe presided over a council that local residents called the "city circus." As the territorial legislature demonstrated, parliamentary procedure and decorum were not strong points of the governmental process in Nebraska Territory.

The territorial city government hired officials, established departments, passed ordinances, and strongly supported spending money on projects designed to help Omaha. The first city councils appointed municipal officers: a collector, a treasurer, a marshal, a clerk, and a few others such as election judges on a temporary basis. An important item of concern was fire protection. The first council rejected a plan to buy a $1,500 engine. Instead, they purchased hooks and ladders. In 1860 after an insurance company contributed $75 toward the formation of Pioneer Hook and Ladder Co. No. 1," the council purchased a fire engine. From then on, expenditure increased in relation to growth; in 1865, at the organization of "Fire King Engine Co. No. 1," the aldermen authorized another engine, plus 1,500 feet of hose.

Ordinances covered everything from animal control to the regulation of bowling alleys. One statute encouraged citizens to plant shade trees; another allowed the stacking of hay on designated streets. In early actions, the council committed the city to spending $50,000 to finish the territorial capitol and extended aid for the construction of the Herndon House Hotel, the owners receiving land originally set aside for park purposes. The council's attempt to finance the capitol with $50,000 in scrip ended disastrously in the wake of the Panic of 1857, contributing to a city debt in 1858 of $60,000. This brought a sense of false economy. Reflecting the need for sound fiscal management, the city printer presented a bill for $110 and received $70, and the election clerks had three-dollar bills cut in half. In 1868 after threats from Union Pacific leaders, the council floated a $200,000 bond issue to help the railroad build a Missouri River bridge at Omaha. A decade later, city debts totaled close to $288,000; only $28,000 of the Union Pacific bonds had been redeemed and canceled. The first political leaders, all of whom had close ties to business, took such a policy for granted.

SHARP CONTRASTS

Omaha advanced in many ways through its first two decades. There was no longer a need for a claim association; the vigilante committee had outlived its usefulness. The Omaha Library Association signified a move in the direction of a developed society. This meant some social stratification as suggested in Bess Streeter Aldrich's fictional re-creation of a typical 1866 Omaha street scene. She said, "Dressed in eastern styles, the wives and daughters of the leading citizenry picked their way daintily through slush, mud, or dust, while at their elbows calico-clad women in sunbonnets went in and out of the stores, all alike averting their eyes when the orange-haired 'other kind' went by."

Rev. Joseph Barker's son Joseph, who had just returned to Omaha from England after an absence of almost six years, observed in May 1866, "All West-

ern people are on a common level and have a common interest." Still, his letters to his family suggest that Omaha was developing a social structure that
was eroding this equality. Joseph Barker Jr. circulated with Omaha's upper
crust, and he left vivid images of their social life. Describing a party at the
new home of banker and real-estate investor Herman Kountze in December
1866, he noted that there was "A large room up stairs to Dance in . . . A Fine
Band & Gentlemen's smoking room & Ladies room[.] There was a splendid Company [—] all the elite. All the officials & every body well & often
splendedily dressed. There was a splendid Supper, and Coloured servants
to attend and Lamps enough to make it like day." Although such events on
successive nights were probably exceptional, the next evening found Barker
at a gathering in honor of the visiting commissioner of Indian affairs. As he
told his family, "The Regular Army officers allways appear in their Uniforms
which gives quite a stylish appearance to partys. And people are much more
exclusive than they used to be and particular to keep out strangers who are
not well introduced."

By the 1870s Omaha had taken on the physical attributes of eastern cities
in which buildings were jammed together, business streets were crowded, and
a smoky haze rose from hundreds of chimneys. Still, it remained a frontier
community. Josie McCague McCulloch remembered, "Omaha at this time
. . . was a little pioneer town, with streets deep in mud or dust. Tiny cottages
of frame were the rule, with occasional two-story houses and a very few
brick ones. The Kountze home . . . seemed palatial. It was surrounded by a
few acres of ground and had a fence and gate around it. But this was exceptional." Photographs of early Omaha reveal buildings set in a stark landscape,
but as early as 1866 Joseph Barker Jr. noted "the flourishing trees round many
Houses . . . help to fill up and give body to the City."

A young journalist, Henry M. Stanley, who would attain renown in Africa,
was in Omaha in 1867 and portrayed the strongly contrasting images of the
community. In February he wrote,

> Omaha City . . . is beautifully located on a high, level plateau, forty feet
> above the highest water mark, on the west bank of the Missouri. A low
> range of hills, gradually rising to an elevation of eighty to one hundred
> feet above this plateau and about one mile from the river, affords fine
> locations for private residences. . . . The panoramic view from these

2. Byron Reed Real Estate on Fourteenth Street, between Douglas and Farnam streets, Omaha, 1862. *Courtesy NSHS, RG2341 PH O 1135.*

hills, and especially from Capitol Hill, is rarely if ever surpassed in picturesque beauty, and even grandeur.

That September, he again noted the city's "beautiful location," and he commended Omaha as a "wide-awake, energetic town." But, he added,

> truth compels me to say . . . that no town on the Missouri River is more annoyed, even afflicted, by moving clouds of dust and sand—when the wind is up—than Omaha. It is absolutely terrific. The lower terrace along the river is a waste of fine sand, which is blown about in drifts, and banked up against houses, like snow in a wintry storm. For two or three days people have been obliged to shut themselves up in their houses for protection from the sand.

ON THE EAST SIDE OF THE RIVER

In 1866 Joseph Barker Jr., near the end of his trip from England back to Omaha, was taken by how much Council Bluffs had changed since he left the area in 1860: "It is twice the size it was when we left. There are many good stores and it has a prosperous thriving looke." Council Bluffs, along with its established retail and service enterprises and its emerging importance as a rail center, was developing other urban features. Pork packing, then a winter industry, began in 1859 and became a more durable feature of the community the following year when John W. Ross constructed a brick packing plant. In 1860 Charles Hendrie from Burlington, Iowa, established the Council Bluffs Iron Works on Main Street. Conrad Geise in 1869 opened a brewery on Broadway that became a sizeable operation producing a large amount of malted barley as well as beer. As in Omaha, real-estate speculation, commonly involving the most prominent residents, attested to the recentness of settlement and the availability of good land in southwestern Iowa. In 1857 the city's boundaries had been vastly extended in order to better serve the interests of speculators in town land. Although the Panic of 1857 briefly put a damper on this activity, speculators soon snapped up some eight hundred thousand acres through the Council Bluffs land office. In 1859 voters approved the establishment of a school district, and for many years attorney Dexter Bloomer guided the district as its president. Bloomer was among the civic leaders who worked to establish a free public library. Other notable steps in Council Bluffs' development between 1866 and 1868 included the construction of a Pottawattamie County courthouse, the city's purchase of a steam fire engine and the building of a fire house, and designation as the site for a state school for the deaf. In making their pitch for the school to the Iowa legislature, the champions of Council Bluffs successfully contended that western Iowa lacked state institutions.

The sordid aspects of life were not confined to the newer town on the west bank of the Missouri. Probably as an effort at cosmetic cleanup, the Council Bluffs city council in 1865 directed the marshal to "abate" the brothels. However in 1869, a young man returning from the West with a large sum of money stopped at the bordello in Council Bluffs operated by a madam known as "French Moll." One of the women at her place was "Indian Moll," and the two decided to relieve the young traveler of his money. They got him drunk, and with the help of a "notorious scamp" named Bill Strope, hauled their victim off to a magistrate and had the young man married to Indian Moll. When the hapless fellow regained his sobriety and recognized what had happened, he became so distraught that he shut himself in his hotel room and committed suicide by ingesting strychnine.

On the other hand, some residents took comfort in 1861 when a lightning strike caused the Ocean Wave Saloon to go up in flames. Six years later, a large Methodist Episcopal church was completed on this location where Broadway Methodist Church now stands. When local businessmen raised ten thousand dollars to assist in building a new hotel, the result was the construction of the Ogden House in 1869, appropriately named after William B. Ogden, Chicago's first mayor and a pioneer in railroad development west of his city. An early historian touted the Ogden House as "the handsomest and most complete hotel between San Francisco and Chicago."

LOOKING BACK

Aspirations and achievements stood in bold contrast on the American frontier, a reality symbolized by two plat maps of Omaha—one from 1856 and the other from a decade later. The earlier map shows a pretentious array of streets and blocks that existed only in the minds of Omaha's boosters. By contrast, the 1866 map shows far fewer streets and blocks and is much closer to reality. Surrounding the city, beyond the area platted into streets and blocks, the 1866 map shows the land holdings of "ground floor men" like Jesse Lowe; George

F. Train; Byron Reed, who founded a real-estate firm that exists to the present; and the Kountze and Millard families who established national banks that became foundations of Omaha's financial structure.

The 1870 U.S. Census indicated that Council Bluffs had 10,020 residents while Omaha had 16,083 inhabitants. Neither city—or both together—could as yet properly claim to have become "the metropolis of the Missouri valley" that Grenville Dodge had projected as a short-term goal in 1867, because Kansas City, Missouri, now had 32,260 inhabitants and St. Joseph had a population of 19,565. But together they occupied a strategic position in the national transportation network and were becoming important urban centers. The diverse values characteristic of American society were abundantly apparent in Omaha and Council Bluffs as gateway cities. Omaha had surpassed Council Bluffs in growth, but both places were fertile seedbeds for human aspirations ranging from the noble to the base. Omaha, and by projection, Council Bluffs, was at once goddess and harlot, a mixture fundamental to the urban experience.

In describing Kansas City's pioneer leaders, historian Charles N. Glaab could have been portraying many upstream city builders and other nineteenth-century boosters of urban America when he wrote, "Their lives do not provide object lessons that illustrate fine American traditions or even the professed ethical principles of capitalism. They simply took society as they found it and unreflectively got things done." As the 1866 plat map of Omaha implied, those persons who followed the early pioneers of the upstream cities could build upon what a local historian called "[a] record of settlement, organization, progress and achievement."

[Part III] 1870-1900

[4] From Small Town to Gateway City

Between 1870 and 1900 Omaha grew from a frontier railroad center into a regional metropolis despite recurring economic troubles. The Panic of 1873 and the ensuing national depression halted several years of prosperity. Hard times set in, and recovery failed to come until near the decade's end. Tremendous progress followed in the eighties. Transportation, commerce, and industry flourished. Rapid settlement of the upper Great Plains created the opportunity for vast hinterlands for Omaha business. Omaha developed a clearly defined business community. During the nineties, drought conditions in Nebraska and the Panic of 1893 once more brought severe adversity. Thousands of persons left Omaha during the economic decline before the city and the rest of the country regained a solid financial footing. By the turn of the century, prosperity had returned, and Omahans believed their community on the threshold of a golden age. "Few, if any, were idle, and the busy hum of industry was heard and could be seen on every hand," a local leader remembered. "Immigration was fast pouring into our state, wholesale houses were being established here, parks and boulevards were improved or constructed. . . . In short, not a cloud appeared upon the horizon without its silver lining." Whether or not Omaha had achieved its highest potential, the city had secured a place in the American urban mosaic.

Omaha had to operate within the context of an emerging urban system. The large outfitting trade in the 1850s and the location of the Union Pacific Railroad ensured survival and dominance in Nebraska. Freighters in Nebraska City could not compete, and the town's prospects fell accordingly. Success, though, brought new obligations and problems. As it tried to move ahead, Omaha had to challenge other new western cities. When the frontier drew to a close, several places had already hewed out regional empires that affected Omaha's aspirations. San Francisco, created in the frenzy of a great gold rush, was among the top cities in the nation. Its aggressive business-men had extended their interests far beyond California, throughout the gold fields of Nevada and Colorado, challenging Omaha interests. Salt Lake City, a unique community, its policy determined by Mormon leaders before the arrival of overland railroads or gold discoveries, had a firm grasp over the economy in the Salt Lake Basin. The best Omahans could hope for was to improve upon established relations. The same was true in regard to Denver. The Queen City had created the "Rocky Mountain Empire" and had excel-lent ties with Omaha.

Closer to home, Omaha had to contend with other regional forces. Less than two hundred miles to the south, Kansas City had achieved part of the promise predicted by earlier experts. It outdistanced several neighboring towns. Then, in the competition to win regional prominence it contested successfully with Leavenworth, Atchison, and St. Joseph for the first railroad bridge over the Missouri River. The span opened on July 3, 1869, and Kan-sas City quickly gained connections into the Southwest. In addition, the old Union Pacific–Eastern Division Railroad, renamed the Kansas Pacific Rail-road, joined the Union Pacific at Cheyenne, providing a transcontinental route. Kansas City capitalists wanted to extend their interests into Nebraska, thus competing directly with their Omaha counterparts. Members of the Kansas City Board of Trade hoped to make their town the country's prime livestock and packing center, building on a profitable and growing agricul-tural base in Kansas. On the northern Plains, other cities threatened Omaha. At the Falls of St. Anthony in Minnesota, the old lumber town of Minne-apolis, helped by a massive influx of outside capital, moved ahead in the first years following the Civil War to corner the flour-milling industry. The mill owners, operating in concert, plotted to control sources of supply. Their strategy involved dominating grain supplies in the Dakotas, which Omaha merchants had taken for granted as part of their natural marketing area. St. Paul, headquarters of James J. Hill's rail transportation empire, added to the growing preeminence of the Twin Cities. Other places gained regional promi-nence. Sioux City enjoyed a short-lived promotional boom. Rapid City and Sioux Falls were possible competitors, but Omaha had nothing to fear from them; they lacked metropolitan dimensions. Of more real danger to Omaha was another place, one that had played a part in its rise—Chicago.

Chicago prospered initially because of the Illinois and Michigan Canal, but its leaders soon formulated a successful railroad strategy based on the assumption that "natural channels" had had their day. The first Chicago line, the Galena and Chicago Union Railroad, garnered an impressive amount of upper–Mississippi River trade and paid large dividends. As a result, northeastern capitalists eagerly invested the millions of dollars that Chicago railroaders needed to construct massive systems. In the fifties several new railroads helped the Windy City take trade away from its major challenger in the Midwest, the Mississippi River city of St. Louis. First overconfidence and then recognition that it had no way of countering Chicago's railroad strategy changed the objectives of St. Louis. Enriched by the fruits of Midwest commerce and industry, Chicago surged to hegemony over a vast section of the upper–Mississippi River valley. An important aspect of Chicago's drive had involved, in addition to a Pacific railroad out of Omaha, the building of railroads across Iowa to Council Bluffs.

In their first years of settlement, Council Bluffs and Omaha had been nurtured by steamboat ties to St. Louis, but after the Civil War this changed as railroads linked them to Chicago. An example of this reorientation came on March 11, 1884, when the Burlington Railroad, under contract with the Post Office, began its six-day-per-week *Fast Mail* train between Chicago and Council Bluffs. The first edition of a Chicago daily paper aboard the train when it departed the Windy City at 3:00 a.m. would reach Council Bluffs that evening, fifteen hours and fifty minutes later.

BRIDGE, TERMINUS, AND "OMAHA GATEWAY"

None of Omaha's first business leaders had a grand railroad strategy. They left matters up to the Union Pacific Railroad. There were no local railroad programs at the time of the decision to build the Union Pacific out of Omaha. The city could not even boast a railroad messiah until George Francis Train proclaimed, "The Pacific railroad is the nation and the nation is the Pacific railway." Omahans welcomed the Union Pacific with open arms, extended favors, and went on the company payroll. It ended there. The Omaha capitalists had no way of controlling the broad contours of their own destiny. They lost that opportunity with the driving of the first Union Pacific spike. Of course, there is no reason to assume they would have been able to build a great city if they had unlimited funds and decision-making powers. They were mainly men of small vision. Anyway, the great capitalists who started the Union Pacific had no intention of letting Omaha entrepreneurs have a significant say in affairs. Telegraph executive Edward Creighton fell out with railroad officials; banker Augustus Kountze served as window dressing on the railroad's board of directors. At the dawn of the Gilded Age, the future of Omaha was in the hands of the railroad's executive group, which included some of the most buccaneering capitalists in all of American business history.

Although tradition holds that the first transcontinental railroad was completed with the driving of the golden spike at Promontory Summit, the task would not be truly finished until a Union Pacific bridge extended across the Missouri River. The truism that location is everything in urban development was well illustrated in a controversy that arose as to the precise place where the bridge would be built. There were three prospective sites: a point on Omaha's north side, one near the city's southern edge, and a third at Childs Mill, near Bellevue in what is now the Fontenelle Forest area. The final choice of the Union Pacific's directors involved engineering questions; differing interests in Omaha, Council Bluffs, and Bellevue; and the diverse desires of the officials of the connecting railroads. A directors' committee recommended the Childs Mill site, and in March 1868 the full board tentatively approved this location that would have entirely bypassed Omaha.

One more consideration entered the decision-making process; as Union Pacific scholar Mavvy Klein put it, "the directors resolved the location question by simply throwing it up for auction." Strong backing for the Childs Mill location came from the Burlington Railroad and initially from Grenville Dodge and Council Bluffs interests. Dodge switched his position to support the site just south of the heart of Omaha, despite Childs Mill's superiority from an engineering standpoint and the fact that a bridge there would benefit his real-estate investments. Aware of the danger that a Childs Mill crossing posed to the future of their city, the Omaha business community responded by sending a delegation that included former territorial governor Alvin Saunders to New York to negotiate with Thomas C. Durant and other Union Pacific leaders.

At first a solution favorable to Omaha had appeared impossible. The delegation received a cool reception; the members had to sit for a day in the railroad's offices before Union Pacific leaders would receive them. Eventually, a "compromise" provided for an Omaha bridge. On March 26, 1868, the delegation's chairman sent a telegram home that contained news of the

3. Council Bluffs Business District, circa 1875. *Courtesy Council Bluffs Public Library, Council Bluffs, Iowa.*

agreement: "The bridge is located at Train table. Omaha pledges the depot grounds and $250,000; Council Bluffs pledges $200,000; ground and right of way will be condemned." The message started a spontaneous community celebration, and people set bonfires in the streets. The delegates returned in triumph. The rejection of the Childs Mill bridge removed the last obstacle during the frontier era to Omaha's emergence as an important city, but it meant that Bellevue would remain a small town until the 1940s.

Building the "High Bridge" was a major engineering and financial challenge for the Union Pacific. Deep quicksand at the Omaha site precluded the use of pilings; hence Dodge investigated an alternative technique that had been used in constructing a bridge over New York's Harlem River. Accordingly, the Union Pacific entrusted the bridge's construction to Theodore E. Sickels, a key figure in the New York project. Eight-and-one-half-foot-diameter iron cylinders sunk into the river would compose all but one of the twelve piers supporting the bridge. Pressurized air would be used to remove the water from the cylinders, and after workmen removed the sand from the piers, they would be partly filled with concrete atop which masonry was placed. The excavation work was dangerous, and men working in the piers routinely experienced the bends. For a time, construction halted because of the precarious condition of the Union Pacific's finances, a situation complicated by a change of contractors, but in February 1871 Congress authorized the company to issue bonds for the project and, upon completion, to impose bridge tolls. On March 14, 1872, two years and ten months after the ceremony at Promontory Summit, a locomotive with Sickels aboard pushed two flatcars laden with six hundred thousand pounds of stone across the 2,700-foot-long bridge, marking its completion.

Acting in concert, the railroads reaching Council Bluffs from the east and south did not use the bridge in part because charter limitations and land-grant terms may have prevented them from extending beyond Iowa and perhaps because of the prospect of high tolls. Certainly, persons championing the growth of Council Bluffs had no desire to see their community become a mere station on the route to Omaha. Accordingly, the Union Pacific established a subsidiary railroad company to operate the bridge. It transferred freight cars and ran a Dummy Train—so named because of its special oddly configured locomotive—for through passengers. For shippers and through travelers the necessity of using this bridge line meant an additional transfer that could be avoided if there were a direct connection between the Union Pacific and the railroads entering Council Bluffs.

While the Union Pacific regarded Omaha as its eastern terminus, Council Bluffs boosters believed that federal legislation had set the terminus in Iowa. In 1875 a federal circuit court ruled that the Union Pacific's eastern terminus was on the Iowa side of the Missouri River, a decision that the U.S. Supreme Court upheld on February 28, 1876. Both rulings seemed to herald a bright future for Council Bluffs. Upon receiving a telegraph report of the final decision, the *Daily Nonpareil* ran an extra edition, while cannonading by the Bluff City Battery let townspeople know that it was no ordinary afternoon. In the evening there were celebratory speeches at Dohany's Opera Hall. Despite the fact that Omaha was the offspring of Council Bluffs, there was much rivalry between the cities, at least in the newspapers. The *Nonpareil* boasted of the triumph over the "Omahogs," while the *Omaha Republican* proclaimed that the decision's impact would "not hurt Omaha in her business and values" and spoke of the "superfluity of zeal" in Council Bluffs. For Omaha, words of reassurance came from Union Pacific superintendent S. H. H. Clark and chief counsel Andrew J. Poppleton, who deemed it unlikely that the company would move its headquarters and shops to Council Bluffs. Soon, the Union Pacific built a large depot and transfer building in Council Bluffs and rented space to the other railroads, which used the structure. The Transfer included a hotel, restaurant, bar, ballroom, and offices for express companies, and for a time its amenities made it a local attraction. The construction of the Transfer stimulated home and business construction in the adjoining area.

Such development encouraged Council Bluffs to spread westward across the flood plain to the Missouri River. Before the completion of the Union Pacific bridge, the area along the Iowa side of the river west of Council Bluffs was the site of railroad depots and adjoining housing. In 1929 Andrew McMillen, who had spent his childhood in the area and had gone on to serve as a local Union Pacific official, left an interesting portrait of the land between Council Bluffs and the river circa 1870:

Along the river front between the Union Pacific bridge and Broadway [Council Bluffs' primary east-west thoroughfare] was quite a settlement consisting of some fifty or more houses [elsewhere McMillen said "about forty houses"] and a store and a boarding house. Nearly all of the men living in the locality were employed on the ferry boat, on the bridge work or by the railroads.

The banks of the river were covered by a very dense growth of willows and cotton wood trees. The timber was full of wild grapes and wild plums as well as wild game such as turkey, prairie chicken and rabbits. In the summer the prairie was covered with wild strawberries. The people did not lack food.

Steamboats made regular trips up and down the river and there were three ferry boats operating between Council Bluffs and Omaha as all passengers arriving on the trains either into Omaha or Council Bluffs had to cross the river on the ferry. The territory lying between the river and what is now Eighth Street was commonly known as the bottoms and was covered by a dense growth of sunflowers that grew so high they would strike the face of a person riding on horseback.

Every year the natives were affected with what as known as the "fever and ague," which was believed to be caused by the presence of the sunflowers. The favorite remedy was Smith's ague tonic and there was enough of that remedy used to have floated a battleship.

I can recall having the fever that one day I would go to school and the next day I would stay at home and nearly shiver myself to pieces.

After the bridge was completed most of the people living at the river moved their homes to the location of the transfer depot. About this time a Mr. Street, who had visions of the town growing toward the river, started a small settlement and built a number of houses in the vicinity of what is now Broadway and Twenty-second street. The settlement was known as "Streetsville" and that portion of town is still referred to by that name.

Sunflowers were not the cause of ague, a malarial affliction common to pioneers in interior lowlands. Flooding would be a more durable problem, but the critical challenge facing Council Bluffs would continue to be sharing economic growth with the city on the west bank.

The emergence of Council Bluffs as a rail center rested upon the fact that the city was part of the "Omaha gateway," and developments following its official recognition as the Union Pacific's eastern terminus would not bring the Iowa community out of the shadow of its western neighbor. Nevertheless,

Council Bluffs continued to prosper as a railroad center. In 1879 the completion of a rail line to the southeast, which became part of the Wabash system, gave the city a second connection to Missouri. Three years later, the Chicago, Milwaukee, St. Paul and Pacific (the Milwaukee Road) reached Council Bluffs. The Illinois Central Railroad reached across northern Iowa from Dubuque to Sioux City, but its leaders decided that the road needed a line to Omaha. Reversing traditional practice, the company drove a golden spike to begin construction in May 1899 of a line running from Tara, near Fort Dodge, which was completed to Council Bluffs, 131 miles to the southwest, in December. Building to Council Bluffs was a wise decision, for as railroad historian John F. Stover said, "The importance of the traffic through to the Omaha gateway soon almost made the new line the main line, with the road to Sioux City becoming the branch route." Between August 1902 and July 1903, the Chicago Great Western laid 133 miles of track from Fort Dodge to Council Bluffs, paralleling the Illinois Central route about one county distant. Omaha businessmen assisted Great Western president A. B. Stickney in financing this project, and soon the line entered Omaha through an agreement with the Union Pacific.

The Great Western's agreement with the Union Pacific reflected a reality that prevented Council Bluffs from realizing the high hopes that the terminus ruling had given the city. In 1890 the Milwaukee and the Rock Island railroads entered Omaha after negotiating agreements to run their trains over the Union Pacific bridge. What had emerged was an integrated transportation complex that was the principal driving force in the development of both Omaha and Council Bluffs. Although railroads loomed large in the lives of Omahans at the beginning of the twentieth century, they probably were even more central to the experience of Council Bluffs residents. The 1900 census showed that 1,410 persons in Omaha and 1,294 in Council Bluffs were "Steam railway employees." With a population of just over one-fourth that of its west-bank neighbor, Council Bluffs' railroad workers proportionately far exceeded Omaha's. The claims of city boosters are suspect, but one such pronouncement in 1900 was on the mark when it said, "[I]t is as a great railroad center that Council Bluffs has gained her chief distinction."

FROM PANIC TO BOOM

The completion of the Union Pacific left open the possibility that Omaha would stagnate as a division point. Despite grim predictions, the local economy flourished in the early seventies. Immigration into Nebraska generated new business. The whole decade saw considerable construction in Omaha; the erection of several large structures lent a more cosmopolitan flavor to Farnam Street and its environs in the downtown district. Union Pacific shops employed over six hundred workers. Hotels reported good and improving business. The work of developing the hinterland went ahead. At least fifty-six commercial travelers operated out of Omaha. Then came the Panic of 1873, which ushered in a national depression that lasted several years. By early 1874 Omaha's economy had taken a sharp downturn. Conditions were so bad that the local press felt compelled to take note. On January 17, 1874, the *Omaha Bee* obliquely acknowledged, "Several business failures have occurred in this city within the past few days but not as many as were expected by the knowing ones." The downturn continued during the next four years. Prices dropped for Nebraska farm produce, while locusts ravaged crops, at times plaguing Omaha.

On May 8, 1874, Edward Rosewater, a rising figure in Omaha life and the editor of the *Bee*, took local businessmen to task for following what he considered a policy of complacency. He accused them of sitting around "like so many opium eating Turks, enveloped in the illusive but enchanting cloud land, where magic air castles are built and precious gifts abound." Meanwhile, "wide-awake and energetic rivals, without natural advantages" had industriously applied artificial resources in building up profitable commerce, using the profits to develop home manufacturing. He said that Omaha had allowed Kansas City, St. Joseph, and Sioux City to garner Nebraska trade. Instead of fighting, he claimed, Omaha capitalists had invested their money and time in "wildcat speculations" in Texas, Utah, and Colorado, inaugurating "a system of public stagnation on the do-nothing plan." Rosewater contended that it was "no wonder" that retail trade had stagnated and unemployment increased. He called upon the city to shake off the "blightening role of old foggies," and to renew its advance. "She cannot afford to remain contented with mere transfer pickings, and roads from nowhere to nowhere," he concluded. "We must have railroad outlets to the northern and southern borders, and we must open an outlet to the vast granaries in Central Nebraska."

Omaha had powerful allies in exhorting settlers to come to Nebraska. The Union Pacific wanted people along its line. Land companies, some under railroad ownership, wanted to sell real estate. Early in statehood, Nebraska established an immigration board. Pamphlets were a favorite promotional device. In 1878 L. D. Burch, the western correspondent for a Chicago newspaper, wrote *Nebraska as It Is: A Comprehensive Summary of the Resources, Advantages and Drawbacks of the Great Prairie State.* As might have been expected, Burch found the region had few drawbacks. He attacked "grumblers" and "nomads" interested in "howling" about droughts, hot winds, Indians, and grasshoppers. He condemned "lazy, thriftless, shiftless, improvident fellows who never struck a sturdy blow," whose incompetence in dealing with what should have been a minor problem gave the state a bad name during the 1874 grasshopper infestation.

Conversely, Burch found much to praise in what he called "an empire, almost as fair as the fabled Eden, and as rich in productive resource as the historic valleys of the older lands." He called Nebraska "THE GARDEN LAND," where a farmer, rarely "driven with his work," could easily grow anything from peanuts to wheat without even having to use fertilizer. That was the siren call of the Plains.

Of more interest than the lay of the land to potential immigrants was the problem of rain. Burch, stressing that Nebraska in Indian dialect signified "wide flowing water," argued that scientific meteorological studies conducted by University of Nebraska professors indicated that rainfall in the state increased between 1867 and 1877. "A gradual change," he claimed, "had come over the State, which is still going on, and this change is indicated by an increasing moisture of the atmosphere and rainfall. . . . From the increasing rainfall of the State, it is also evident that at no distant day the whole State as far as its western limits, will have an abundant rainfall for all the needs of the agriculturist." Burch did not explain the reasons for the startling change, but several self-proclaimed experts presented what they considered plausible reasons. A favored theory held that rain followed the plow. Supposedly, moisture that fell on broken ground recirculated into the atmosphere, automatically increasing the rain supply. Other postulates emphasized the influence of modern technology in bringing rain. Humming telegraph wires created an electric quality in the sky, causing electric storms. Smoke from belching locomotives made rain clouds. If all else failed, the setting off of explosive charges and the firing of artillery pieces brought rain. The message was clear: irrigation was unnecessary in even the most subhumid parts of Nebraska. Farmers could succeed by using the same methods used back east.

In the eighties Nebraska enjoyed spectacular growth. The state shared in the movement of hundreds of thousands of people to the arid sections of the Plains. Settlers lured by easy land and lavish promotional claims flocked to "banana belts" and "silk growing regions." During the decade enough rain to grow grain fell just about every year, even on the western edges of the Plains, lending substance to claims of gradually increasing rainfall. The pioneers came from many places—the steppes of Russia, the lowlands of Denmark, the fjords of Norway, the green fields of England, the hills of Germany, and the fruited plains of America. According to official statistics, Nebraska had 452,402 inhabitants at the start of the 1880s and 1,058,910 at the end, an increase of more than 600,000. This represented a growth rate of 134 percent, far above the national average. Even previously remote areas registered substantial gains. Custer County, in the rolling treeless hills of central Nebraska, jumped from 2,211 people in 1880 to 21,677 in 1890. Sheridan County in the Sandhills of western Nebraska, one of twenty-six counties organized in the eighties, reported 8,687 residents in 1890. Several farming counties experienced growth rates in excess of 1,000 percent. Some observers later questioned the validity of the census totals, but there was no doubt of significant progress. Nebraska had become a key cattle- and grain-producing state. The sod houses on the "Farmers' Last Frontier" had tremendous significance for Omaha. Almost overnight, the city had gained an agricultural hinterland.

THE MAGIC CITY

Stockyards were the cornerstone of a new economic policy for Omaha. Agitation for one had started back in the 1870s with insignificant results. However, there were few cattle herds on the upper Plains, and the main goal of local business interests had been to ride out the depression. A leader had set the tone in a rousing 1876 Fourth of July oration when he said, "As the fabled Minerva came full-fledged from the brain of Jupiter, so was Omaha born with her fighting garments upon her. . . . If she seems weary with her duties today, she goes forth to-morrow to encounter and overcome new and greater obstacles with the strength of inspiration."

By 1871 pork packing was beginning in Omaha, but in this time before refrigeration the activity was limited to the winter months. James E. Boyd emerged as the most prominent of the early packers, and in 1878–79 his firm processed some sixty thousand hogs. Nevertheless, if Omaha were to become a large marketing and packing center for hogs, beef, and sheep, stock-yards where animals could be fed, watered, and sold would have to be built. In 1876 John A. Smiley organized the Union Stock Yards Company, but he soon abandoned his efforts to develop facilities north of the city limits when Chicago investors could not obtain the assistance they desired in Omaha. In any event, with the railroad bridge on the south side of town, it was logical that any significant stockyard development would be close to the Union Pacific's juncture with the lines crossing Iowa. An area on what was then Omaha's southwestern fringe, near Twenty-fourth and Martha streets, became the next focal point of stockyard development in 1878 when A. P. Nicholas and four other persons established the Omaha Stock Yards Company on land leased from the Union Pacific Railroad. Soon, the Union Pacific induced a group of investors led by William Paxton to develop a stockyard on another portion of the same tract. His yards, named the Union Stock Yards Company, began operation in May 1879. The following winter, the Union Pacific made another "lucrative arrangement" with Paxton to move his operations to Council Bluffs. Other investors in this Council Bluffs enterprise included Wyoming cattleman Alexander Swan as well as some Chicagoans prominent in the packing industry.

The other yard, the Omaha Stock Yards Company, had trouble from the start. The Union Pacific refused to give it shipping advantages and levied a heavy toll on cattle crossing the bridge. Cries of the existence of a "Bridge Moloch" had no effect on the railroad. Soon, the Omaha Stock Yards Company sold out at a 60 percent loss. The lesson seemed clear. No stockyards could succeed in Omaha without the cooperation and participation of the Union Pacific Railroad. That meant doing business with Jay Gould, the brilliant investor who had become the railroad's dominant figure. William A. Paxton did just that, and three years later he would be a prime mover in setting Omaha on the way to becoming a major livestock center.

Paxton was a classic rugged individualist of the Horatio Alger mold. Born on a Kentucky farm in 1837, he grew up in Missouri. He first came to Omaha in 1857 to build bridges along the military road that extended from the city to Fort Kearny. After that he drifted back and forth between Missouri and Nebraska, working on construction projects. He married a Missouri woman and made Omaha his home. In 1860 he worked as a foreman for Edward Creighton on the Pacific telegraph. Next, Paxton ran a livery stable in Omaha, earning twenty dollars a month. Dissatisfied with that position, he became a mule skinner and started a small freighting business. He carried freight between Omaha and Denver and for the Union Pacific, which was then under construction. He quickly put to good use $14,500 that he made on Union Pacific contracts. During 1869, he went to Abilene, Kansas, where he bought cattle from Texas, brought them to Omaha, and sold them on the hoof for a $12,000 profit. After that he engaged in new speculations. He bought stock in the local Omaha and Northwestern Railroad and directed construction of the first twenty miles of the line. More importantly, he became a partner in a firm that won a lucrative government contract to supply the beef allotment for Indian agencies, furnishing from twenty-five to seventy-five thousand head of cattle annually.

By the middle of the 1870s, Paxton was a big plunger. Taking advantage of rock-bottom depression prices, he invested heavily in Omaha real estate. Branching out into other activities, he bought stock in local banks, started a wholesale grocery, and acquired an interest in the Council Bluffs stockyard. Paxton proceeded quietly, and his activities went relatively unnoticed, receiving much less publicity than other Omaha entrepreneurs had. Many thought Paxton another mule skinner who had made some money. He soon acquired a much different image.

Paxton, as any successful speculator must do, anticipated a trend: the coming of fundamental changes in the range cattle industry. By the Civil War, an estimated four million longhorn cattle roamed the Texas plains. Worth a dollar a head in their native habitat, they had the potential to bring as much as forty dollars each on the eastern market. The problem was how to get them there; no through railroads ran into Texas. The end of the war saw the initiation of the famous long drives, first to Sedalia in Missouri and then to a series of Kansas cattle towns. Paxton was among those who saw a way around the expensive drives and—once lines were built into Texas—the long rail trips. The solution was relatively simple: stock upper plains ranges with beef cattle.

In 1873 Paxton started a cattle ranch some three hundred miles west of Omaha near Ogallala, Nebraska, on the Union Pacific main line. He was extremely successful, receiving more than the 40 percent annual return customary in the greatest days of the range cattle industry. As he rose to power, Paxton, a hulking man seldom seen without a pipe between his clenched teeth, became increasingly ruthless. Speaking about a competitor who sought an accommodation, Paxton loudly proclaimed, "Who in the hell wants to go into partnership with a fool, the best way is to freeze out the son-of-a-bitch."

In the early 1880s the Union Stock Yards in Council Bluffs functioned as a transfer point where animals were unloaded and watered en route to Chicago. However, from Alexander Swan's perspective as a rancher and the leading figure in the Wyoming Stockmen's Association, a terminal market at Omaha would offer lower freight rates and yardage fees. Unlike earlier Omaha entrepreneurs, he devised a stockyards scheme in 1882 in which the real-estate development package would not be under railroad control. The challenge was accumulating funds to obtain a large tract of land adjoining Omaha to the south. Swan's brother-in-law, Leverett M. Anderson, and Cornelius Schaller quietly invested ten thousand dollars in real-estate purchases to begin the process. Because significant capital for American ranching came from Scotland, Swan made a trip to that country to raise money for his own operations and also tried to interest investors in his Omaha project. Scottish investors did not warm to the proposal. Swan now brought Paxton into the project, and other prominent Omahans invested. Some of these men—including John McShane, John Creighton, and distillery owner Peter Iler—had ranching or other livestock interests. Among the key investors were Chicago packers who had joined Paxton in the Council Bluffs enterprise. Paxton helped organize two concerns—the Union Stock Yards Company of Omaha (Limited) and the South Omaha Land Company. Both were controlled by the "Syndicate," which included investors in the overall project as well as the Ogallala Land and Cattle Company, which Paxton had helped to found.

Alexander Swan later took credit for organizing the Omaha stockyards. In fact, there had been much prior interest in such an enterprise. He was never more than a minority stockholder in any of the Syndicate's three companies. Of more importance was the role of the Union Pacific. Jay Gould, the railroad's dominant figure, desperate for traffic to solve his railroad's increasingly serious financial difficulties, made an arrangement with the Syndicate. In doing so he abandoned plans to put the railroad into the stockyard business in a big way. The Syndicate received favorable shipping rates, assuring a corner on all livestock trade handled by the Union Pacific. Some of the Syndicate's members worked for the Union Pacific, and the first stockyard went up on land purchased from the railroad by the South Omaha Land Company. It was a convenient arrangement for all concerned.

Of course, the resulting demise of the Council Bluffs stockyards was further evidence of the ascendancy of Omaha in the emerging metropolitan area. In retrospect, Council Bluffs resident Andrew McMillen said, "Through the indifference of our citizens and because of the big flood of 1881 and the generous offers of the citizens of Omaha we lost the stock yards. On account of being unable to furnish suitable sewer facilities and good roads leading to the yards, the Omaha people easily convinced the stock yards management that South Omaha was the logical and ideal location for them."

The Union Stock Yards Company of Omaha (Limited) had an initial capital of $1 million. A total of $700,000 was subscribed at the time of establishment. Paxton, who held four hundred shares with an opening book value of $40,000, became president. In an early order of business, the firm bought his holdings in the small Council Bluffs "transfer yard" for $100,000. Next, the Union Stock Yards Company of Omaha (Limited) bought 156.5 acres of land from its companion South Omaha Land Company and started construction. The yard opened in August 1884. The first shipment consisted of 531 longhorns from Medicine Bow, Wyoming. The cattle, after feeding and watering, were transshipped east within twenty-four hours to Chicago packing plants. Receipts of livestock for 1885, the first full year of operations, totaled 117,000 head of cattle, 153,000 hogs, 19,000 sheep, and 2,000 horses and mules. "It was slow work at first; the market did not build in a day, and for a considerable time the yards remained merely a feeding station for stock en route to the eastern markets," an official contended. "Being located on the natural route from the West to the East, the beaten trail so to speak, of the stockmen going to and from market, Omaha's natural advantages were easily advertised, and as the volume of stock which stopped at the Union Stock Yards for rest and feed increased, it at length began to draw buyers and dealers as honey draws bees." It also helped to have a monopoly. In 1890 the yards handled 615,000 head of cattle, 1,700,000 hogs, 154,000 sheep, and 5,000 horses and mules. The stockyards, by then worth over $4 million, paid handsome dividends to the investors. The yards, capable of handling over 10,000 cattle alone daily, had within a few years become the heart of a gigantic livestock-producing complex.

A whole new town, South Omaha, developed in the vicinity of the stockyards on property originally owned by the South Omaha Land Company. It was a fantastic success story made possible by the policies of the Syndicate and far-reaching changes in meat packing. The perfection of refrigerated boxcars, the creation of fast through-freight service, and hauling agreements favorable to packers eliminated the need to process meat in distribution centers. In the 1870s Chicago houses had established Kansas City plants that handled southwestern livestock for the national market. The spreading of cattle to the northern Plains, coupled with the dramatic increase in Nebraska livestock production, made similar plants economically feasible for the Omaha area. Still, the great Chicago packers had no intention of coming to Omaha of their own volition; they demanded inducements and the laying of the necessary groundwork. It was not enough for the South Omaha Land Company to build packing houses and to lease them at very liberal terms. Those considerations persuaded Geo. H. Hammond and Company of Detroit to open a slaughterhouse that began operating in January 1885. Even so, many farmers sold their hogs at a stockyard next to the Union Pacific bridge because it did not levy fees, an advantageous arrangement for Omaha's James E. Boyd packing firm. Through undisclosed means, John A. McShane, a major stockholder in the Syndicate and president of the Union Stock Yards Company, forced Boyd to buy at the new yards, and the movement of hogs to the Union Stock Yards rose to a volume favorable to Hammond's needs. Other actions typical of Gilded Age morality needed to be undertaken in order to make the new packing center viable.

John A. McShane, a prime stockholder in the three Syndicate companies, had the task of carrying on negotiations. At first, he faced problems from Chicago railroads that operated in Iowa. When the Chicago and North Western placed an embargo on livestock shipments to Omaha, McShane went to the railroad's main office. He threatened to have a bill passed by the Nebraska legislature prohibiting the shipping of livestock from the state to Chicago. When a railroad executive asked him in a matter of fact way if he could do it, McShane replied, "I know I can do it." Two weeks later the railroad lifted the embargo. It was just a routine shakedown that had failed because of counterthreats.

Dealing with the giants in the packing industry was another matter for McShane. They were not about to be intimidated by the possibility of action by the Nebraska state government. More tangible and lucrative incentives attracted them. The Union Stock Yards drew Fowler Brothers, a Chicago packer with strong business ties to the United Kingdom, to South Omaha by providing one hundred thousand dollars for plant construction and other inducements that created an economic package worth over two hundred thousand dollars. The firm began operations as the Anglo-American Packing Company in November 1886, but when P. L. Underwood of Chicago gained half ownership in 1888, it became the Omaha Packing Company.

Sir Thomas Lipton, the English tea merchant and yachtsman, promised to open a hog slaughterhouse in exchange for a free five-year lease. After the completion of the building, he pulled out of the deal because he could not obtain the kind of "light hogs" he desired. McShane used the facility as part of an offer to lure the Armours and Cudahys. Philip Armour, at first rejecting overtures, telegraphed McShane to come to Chicago for an interview. McShane recounted their conversation:

> He referred to his former statement that he had declined to consider any Omaha project owing to the fact that he had all the business he desired, and he then said that he had a boy in his employ to whom he was paying a salary of $25,000 a year, and was willing to pay him $50,000 if he could stay with him. But the boy wanted an interest in the Armour business. "I can't give him that as I want the business to go to my sons," said Armour, "but I stand ready to finance this boy—Ed Cudahy—to any extent necessary to establish a packing house in Omaha." I then suggested that he buy the Lipton equipment, and he acted almost at once on the proposition. Terms were soon arranged. We gave Armour the Lipton house and $350,000 of stock in the stockyards company, and the contract was signed by myself. Within less than eighty days Michael Cudahy had the beef house completed and was killing cattle and sheep.

Armour-Cudahy took over the Lipton property in the summer of 1887, a transaction that the Union Stock Yards Company facilitated with large subsidies for plant expansion, Stock Yards Company shares, and a stock option. In December 1890 the Armour-Cudahy partnership was terminated, and the Cudahy Packing Company was sole owner of the South Omaha plant. In the meantime, in February 1887, there was euphoria in South Omaha when another large packer, Swift and Company, declared that it was coming to town. Although reports differ as to the specific details of the inducements given to Gustavus F. Swift, John McShane said, "We handed him $100,000 in cash and $100,000 in stock." In April 1888 Swift began regular operations in its recently completed South Omaha plant. The next significant development was the return of Armour to South Omaha. Construction of a plant that would comprise five buildings began in November 1897, and by July 1898 it was in operation. At this time, Cudahy and Swift also expanded their plants.

The packing plants all had their killing areas, fertilizing departments, bone yards, and gut departments. Worth millions of dollars, the plants employed thousands of men who yearly slaughtered and dressed millions of animals. Among the by-products were butterine, oleomargarine, lard, soap, glue, and pepsin. Support facilities such as a Livestock Exchange Building, Cudahy's large tin shop for fabricating containers, and twenty miles of rail line serving the stockyards and packing houses were essential to operations. Electric power was a recent innovation that was critical to the new plants. The rapid growth of the stockyards and packing industry outgrew the local water supply, and South Omaha soon arranged a connection with Omaha's provider, the American Water Works Corporation. Although the various packers harvested ice from Cut-Off Lake and other points in the area, the plants installed Arctic Ice machines, a recent advance in refrigeration. Beginning in September 1891, the postslaughter inspection of pork assured that the meat of each animal destined for export was free from the parasite that caused the disease trichinosis. Most of the inspectors were women who used microscopes to examine two samples of meat from each carcass. While meat inspection for the home market was a decade and a half in the future, the inspection of pork for export, stemming from French and German insistence, was an early demonstration of the relationship of international commerce to the livelihood of South Omaha and the region.

The results of what McShane called "promoting the stockyard enterprise" satisfactorily to all parties directly involved represented a triumph for Omaha. It was on a par with obtaining the Union Pacific Railroad; Omaha assured itself of becoming the dominant city in an emerging region. In a single stroke, its capitalists enriched themselves, lessened the domination of the Union Pacific (and created a strong friend out of a potential enemy), garnered millions of dollars in packing plants, and assured a large working population. No longer did Omaha interests need to respond to threats to move bridge or stockyard locations. They could now start to think in different terms.

The Chicago packers were components of great regional combinations involved in a wide variety of activities including railroading and banking. They had gained a foothold in Nebraska and the West with what they considered advantageous terms. In effect, the move into Omaha increased the size of Chicago's Midwestern empire, further incorporating Nebraska into the new region.

South Omaha developed into what its promoters called the "Magic City," but its early years were reminiscent of the frontier that had passed in the rest of the urban area. By 1886 some 1,500 persons lived in the new settlement that as yet had not been organized as a municipality. That July a group of citizens asked the Douglas County Board of Commissioners to incorporate South Omaha as a village. Their petition said the county board already knew "how . . . exposed [they were] without any protection against tramps and murderers—having no jail, no church, one school house (and that falling to decay)[,] one saloon for every twenty inhabitants, one gambling house, two houses of ill-fame, one justice of the peace, one deputy sheriff . . . , one post office, [and] no constable proper here." Two groups objected to the petition: one claimed that many of its signers were nonresidents and that most residents did not want incorporation; the other, coming from the Syndicate, expressed a need for clarification of the boundaries of the proposed village. By autumn, the problems were apparently resolved, and on October 16 the county commissioners, responding to a new petition, established the village of South Omaha. South Omaha soon advanced its status to that of a city of the second class under Nebraska law, but a police force brought no quick achievement of decorum. In keeping with state law, each saloon now paid a five-hundred-dollar annual license fee, money that went to the operation of schools.

In 1890 the new community reported 8,062 inhabitants and claimed to have 327 businesses, among them three banks and thirty-seven cattle companies. South Omaha was the nation's third-largest packing center, ranking behind only Chicago and Kansas City. The plants in those cities and South Omaha were part of a single monopolistic system. As a municipality, South Omaha was not a true suburban area; there was no open ground separating it from Omaha. What incorporation did was to provide the founders of the Syndicate with their own private town. In May 1890 Omaha voters approved the annexation of South Omaha, but a modest majority of South Omaha's electorate rejected the measure, and the Magic City would maintain its political autonomy from its big neighbor for another generation. South Omaha's link to Omaha was symbolized by the continuing interest of William Paxton in its economy. Paxton was not content to rest on his reputation as a town builder. He became an official of the Union Stock Yards Bank and, along with his other holdings, continued to make money in South Omaha.

FROM BOOM TO PANIC AND RECOVERY

During the 1880s manufacturing moved ahead in Omaha as part of the original boom. A Missouri River flood that inundated the industrial districts in 1881 caused only short-term disruptions. The $2.5 million Union Pacific machine and car shops were the biggest concern. It covered fifty acres and employed 1,600 men, many of whom were skilled mechanics and engineers. In an average year, the facility repaired or rebuilt seven thousand cars and two hundred locomotives. Another large company, the Omaha and Grant Smelting and Refining Works, which had 600 workers, processed a significant amount of the lead, gold, and silver produced by western mines. In 1890 it smelted over sixty-five thousand tons of ore valued at $14 million. The firm, in which Union Pacific officials had large holdings, was worth $3 million. No other Omaha factory had a capitalization approaching $1 million. There was a wide variety of different industries, including basket manufacturers, foundries, carriage works, and syrup refiners, among the more than 150 ventures. Most were small operations. Metz Brothers' Brewery employed 40 men, the Woodman Linseed Oil Works an average of 75. Despite promotional claims, Omaha was not a major industrial center.

In a more immediate sense, Omaha experienced a great boost in trade and commerce. By the end of the 1880s, there were more than five thousand miles of railroad track in Nebraska. The Union Pacific main line was the spine of a gigantic network that covered the center of the state from east to west. The Chicago, Burlington and Quincy Railroad entered Omaha in 1871 by buying a short line, then crossed the Platte south of the city, and built through Lincoln and on to Kearney in central Nebraska, where it joined the Union Pacific. Omaha gained a direct link to Denver when the Burlington completed a line to that city in 1882. Other roads, among them the Missouri Pacific Railroad; the Chicago, St. Paul, Minneapolis and Omaha Railroad; and the Fremont, Elkhorn and Missouri Valley Railroad (ultimately part of the Chicago and North Western system) added further luster to Omaha's railroad web. In 1886 the Missouri Pacific completed construction of the Belt Line Railway, an oblong route around the city. In time, businesses needing easy rail access built up along the Belt Line in a pattern that later would be replicated by interstate highways on the outskirts of urban areas. In fostering industrial development along its right of way, the Belt Line stimulated housing construction in nearby areas.

In 1887 a group of businessmen including Burlington Railroad officials established the East Omaha Land Company with plans for industrial development on the river bottoms northeast of downtown. Their plans included the development of streetcar and railroad lines that would integrate the area with Omaha, South Omaha, and Council Bluffs. A major part of this undertaking would be the construction of a vehicular traffic, streetcar, and railroad bridge over the Missouri River, and to accomplish this goal they established the Omaha Bridge and Terminal Railway. In 1891 the project received congressional approval, and despite problems with quicksand and high water, the structure was finished late in 1893. Unlike the earlier bridges at Omaha that were built high above the water, this structure was so low that it included a draw span to permit the passage of vessels.

The bridge did not develop as a streetcar or traffic artery, but after the Illinois Central Railroad reached Council Bluffs, it acquired its own route into Omaha by leasing the structure from the Bridge and Terminal Railway. East Omaha did not become a second South Omaha as an industrial center, although one important firm, the Carter White Lead Company, operated there after its initial plant on South Twentieth Street burned in 1890. The Carter Company processed pig lead from the Omaha and Grant smelter into lead carbonate used in paint manufacture. Its owner, Levi Carter died in 1903, but the Carter White Lead Company plant continued to operate in East Omaha until a merger brought its closing in 1907. The following year, Selena Carter Cornish, Levi Carter's widow, funded land acquisition for an Omaha city park adjoining Cut-Off Lake in East Omaha. Accordingly, that body of water was soon renamed Carter Lake.

Omaha's jobbing trade grew with its industrial and transportation development. An 1890 credit report listed 207 retail and jobbing firms with aggregate sales of $50.2 million. They dealt in just about every conceivable product: groceries and provisions, dry goods, toys, drugs, millinery, lumber, oysters and fish, notions, twines and cordage, books and stationery, and il-luminating oils. A considerable warehouse district developed. Downtown department stores, notably one owned by Jonas L. Brandeis, did a flourish-ing business. The New York Life Insurance Company and other eastern busi-nesses established regional headquarters in Omaha. The seven national, seven private, and four savings banks underwent healthy expansions. Private banks were very important in cementing ties to the hinterlands. They bought and sold land, made farm loans, wrote insurance, and dealt in grain and livestock. Over six hundred commercial travelers scoured Nebraska and neighboring states for new business. Omaha was in motion. Tens of thousands of new res-idents arrived every year. The city received national attention; some observ-ers predicted it would be the next Chicago, a true "Wonder City of the West." Then came the fall. Omaha's commercial economy collapsed like a house of cards.

It all started with a bad crop year. In 1890 Nebraska's average rainfall of seventeen inches was the lowest since 1864. This had an immediate impact on Omaha. "The short crops in 1890 caused a heavy falling off in business dur-ing the first half of the year," the Board of Trade's fiscal 1891 report admitted. "The retail dealers found it difficult to meet obligations, men were forced to sell goods on long credit. The money stringency further complicated the matter producing a feeling of insecurity."

The adverse conditions touched off a political explosion in Nebraska. Rail-roads were special targets of collective wrath. Almost every farmer in the state accused the railroad leaders of taking the best soil under their land grants, bribing all levels of government by giving out free passes, charging exces-sive rates, engaging in monopolistic business policies, fixing prices, and lur-ing settlers with false claims. The practices of the Union Pacific added fuel to the fire. It openly falsified prices. A general freight agent in Omaha, when asked by a reporter about rates, replied, "Certainly, which side do you want to prove? I can give you figures for either." Other aspects of Nebraska life ran-kled the agrarians almost as much. Farm machinery cost so much that they sensed a conspiracy. Produce prices seemed exorbitantly low, reflecting col-lusion. Town dwellers appeared eager to gouge farmers at every turn. Mort-gage rates rose so sharply that debtors believed bankers to be parasites who wanted to live off honest labor. As a bleak year drew to a close, an Omaha businessman cheerily prophesied, "To truly present the possibilities in store for Nebraska, one would need the pen of inspiration. . . . There is yet room for millions more upon our vast prairies and fertile fields. . . . It is the favored country, the modern Eden." Few people on the sod house frontier agreed.

Nebraska farmers turned to politics. While the revolt against the established order seemed sudden, agrarian discontent had roots that extended back into the early days of statehood. The Patrons of Husbandry, commonly called the Grange, gained control of several Midwestern legislatures in the 1870s. Its platform called for state regulation of railroads and an end to alleged exploitation of farmers by middlemen and manufacturers. In Nebraska, the Grange enrolled an estimated twenty-thousand members. The fraternal body, never strong enough to take over the statehouse, did start cooperatives and two farm-implement factories. When these enterprises failed, the Nebraska Grange went into decline. The organization left two legacies: a provision in a new state constitution requiring railroad regulation and a precedent for political action by farmers.

During the 1880s another protest movement, the Farmers' Alliance, gained a foothold in Nebraska. Its leaders called for laws designed to enforce the constitutional provision regulating railroads and for a general war against the excesses of capitalists. There was little interest until the end of the decade; as late as 1889, a state meeting of the Alliance attracted only a hundred delegates from fourteen counties. The next year was different; the bad crop conditions brought thousands to the Alliance's banner. Former Republicans sang rousing songs: "Goodbye, Old Party, Goodbye" and "A Mortgage Has Taken the Farm, Mary." Democrats and Republicans combined to denounce "Popocrats" as "hogs in the parlor" and "political thugs." In the fall, the Alliance, having evolved into the Populist or People's Party, gained control of both houses of the legislature, almost beat the Republican nominee for governor, and helped elect a young Democrat from Lincoln, William Jennings Bryan, to Congress. The Alliance triumphed in other parts of the country. Its candidates, running under a variety of labels, won offices at all levels throughout the northern Plains. In the South men favorable to the Alliance principles captured many Democratic primaries, assuring victory in the general election. Alliance candidates did so well that there was soon a call for a national party.

In early July 1892 over ten thousand persons assembled in Omaha to nominate the People's Party's first candidate for president of the United

States. They selected an aging former northern Civil War general from Iowa, James B. Weaver, whose choice seemed incidental to the proceedings; he had changed sides so frequently that friend and foe alike called him "Jumping Jim." But the convention did call attention to agrarian demands. Colorful and extravagant oratory dominated the proceedings: "And now for the first time the classes in these United States are marshaling their armies for the greatest struggle the world ever saw," a speaker proclaimed. "A mortal combat is on, and the ballot will be the weapon of the war."

Ignatius Donnelly of Minnesota, Paul Vanderford of Nebraska, Mary Lease of Kansas, and other orators flayed the nation's financiers and called upon producers to rise. An hour-long demonstration followed Mrs. Lease's speech. "It had the appearance of pandemonium turned loose," an alternate delegate claimed, "a parade that will pale into insignificance any ever witnessed in Omaha—banners waved, drums beat, flutes and fifes without number played." The Populist Party platform called for nationalization of railroads, government ownership of communication systems, reform of the monetary system, change in election practices, establishment of postal savings banks, and the end of subsidies to private corporations. Critics denounced the goals as socialistic, even though many Populists were small capitalists. What they wanted to do was to improve their position in the system by socializing enemies. This was not exactly what the Omaha businessmen had in mind when they had constructed the huge arena to attract conventions. They much preferred the patronage of the General Methodist Episcopal Conference or the Human Freedom League. Yet the great Populist meeting, held in the midst of another year of drought as a hot July sun streamed through the windows of the auditorium, was but a portent of things to come for Omaha. Grim events lay ahead.

In the spring of 1893, a great depression swept across the United States. The economic misfortune wrought havoc upon Nebraska farmers, already hard-pressed by low rainfall, rising costs, and falling prices. The state received 16.24 inches of rain in 1893 and 13.54 the next year, far from enough to successfully raise crops. Days with high temperatures and desiccating south winds hastened the devastation. On July 26, 1894, a wind that seemed to have come from a blast furnace drove the mercury at Omaha to 106 degrees by 2:30 p.m. As it lashed the Great Plains and Midwest, it finished the destruction of corn crops, forcing farmers into ruinous livestock sales, and struck a blow at Omaha's economy and the livelihood of scores of other communities. However, 1892 had brought a resurgence of Republican strength, and it became evident that the Populists could not triumph over the two traditional parties. The result was Populist "fusion" with the Democrats, an action that brought the election and reelection of a Populist governor in 1894 and 1896 and his successor in 1898. Fusion and other political and economic realities ultimately subordinated the zeal and objectives that had marked the birth of Nebraska Populism. Although the Populist movement produced some modest reforms, countless thousands of people had no choice except to give up the struggle of eking out a living on the arid plains of western Nebraska.

Omaha's economy was nearly paralyzed. Factories and stores closed. The city, which had gained an estimated sixty-thousand residents in the late 1880s, at best held its own in the 1890s. For many people, soup kitchens and charity houses seemed the only flourishing establishments. Construction stopped; over five thousand homes stood empty. There was no money available. The depression brought bankruptcy to some of the nation's most important railroads, including the Union Pacific. For years, the Union Pacific had struggled with debt, and rate wars with competing lines compounded the company's troubles. Finally, in October 1893 the road went into receivership. Edward Morearty, an Omaha lawyer and politician, thought his fellow citizens were in "anguish and despair" during 1895, the worst year of the depression. He declared,

> Times were growing harder and men and women were out of employment, with no ray of hope in sight. Raids by the depositors were made on many of our strongest financial institutions, some of whom were fortunate enough to meet the demands made on them, thereby restoring confidence to the depositors, who in most cases re-deposited. Others were not so able to weather the storm and were forced to close their doors. . . . Those failures worked additional hardship and suffering on the public and the depositors, many of whom were forced to wait for years the report of the receivers, then receiving but a few cents on the dollar.

The depression that began in 1893 produced an episode that highlighted the problems of a society that was increasingly urban and capitalistic while illustrating the importance of the Omaha Gateway. On Sunday, April 15, 1894, a Union Pacific freight train pulled into Council Bluffs, its boxcars laden with a group of some 1,400 unemployed men called "Kelly's Army," most from the San Francisco Bay and Sacramento areas of California. Led by "General" Charles T. Kelly, a printer by trade, the group was en route to Washington where it would presumably join "General" Jacob Coxey's legion of unemployed men. Together they would implore the United States Government to take the dramatic and unprecedented action of creating a public-works program to counter the depression. The trek of Kelly's Army had begun in Oakland with the seizure of an east-bound Southern Pacific freight train, a process repeated with the Union Pacific train near Ogden. The Union Pacific had taken no action in order to minimize service problems.

Following the leadership of the Chicago and North Western Railroad, the lines reaching east from Council Bluffs refused to haul Kelly's Army. Gov. Frank D. Jackson and Iowa National Guard troops were in Council Bluffs when Kelly and his men arrived, but it soon became apparent that Kelly was maintaining close discipline and that his followers desired good relations with the people along their route. An atmosphere of patriotic and religious fervor surrounded Kelly and his followers. Thousands of people from both sides of the river flocked to the Council Bluffs rail yards to see the Washington-bound contingent and while there donated money, food, and supplies to the travelers. Local newspapers were cordial to Kelly's Army, and in coming days the people of Council Bluffs and Omaha continued to provide sustenance. In Omaha, merchant Emil Brandeis, who had sent a large load of pies to the men upon their arrival, and Mayor George P. Bemis urged businessmen to aid Kelly's men. The outspoken hostility of Nat M. Hubbard, counsel for the Chicago and North Western, and other railroad leaders toward Kelly's Army did much to fuel public support. But no one, including Council Bluffs civic leaders and Governor Jackson, could induce the railroad leaders to help move the group eastward.

The day following its arrival, Kelly's Army moved to the Chautauqua grounds near Council Bluffs and after a wet sojourn moved a short distance to Weston. With the men still close to the urban area, excitement about their plight continued and animosity toward the recalcitrant railroads mounted. In one ominous gesture, Union Pacific shop men from Omaha carried bread loaves impaled on spikes across the Missouri River bridge as part of their ongoing support for Kelly's men. By Friday, April 20, sentiment in behalf of Kelly's Army was especially intense. The Knights of Labor union staged a big rally, and many people proceeded as a group to Council Bluffs. Some of the demonstrators, including women, took control of a Union Pacific bridge train, added cars, and ran it out to Weston where Kelly's Army was encamped. Kelly, not wishing to engage in any further unlawful actions, declined use of the train, which was returned to Council Bluffs.

On Sunday, April 22, Kelly's Army began a hard march to Des Moines, and its ranks now included writer Jack London who had followed the army from California to Council Bluffs. At Des Moines, shallow-draft scows were built, and the group floated down the Des Moines River to the Mississippi, up the Ohio, and overland to Washington. The amazing trek of Kelly's Army, like that of Jacob Coxey's group, did not convince federal authorities to create jobs to combat the depression. Nonetheless, the support for Kelly's Army in Council Bluffs and Omaha illustrated the tensions in the industrial capitalism of late-nineteenth-century America. Beyond the excitement of the moment, the army's quixotic trek suggested a changing attitude of the American people toward the role of government in the economy.

Hard times continued into 1896 when the Democratic Party nominated Bryan for president. He embraced Populist doctrines, and the party, with no real alternatives available, made him their candidate as well. At the Democratic National Convention, Bryan gave his famous "Cross of Gold" speech, claiming that the nation would prosper only if agriculture prospered. His panacea for recovery was the creation of inflation through a pat formula: the free coinage of silver at a ratio of sixteen ounces to one ounce of gold, taking the United States off the gold standard. In Omaha advocates of "16 to 1" harangued the unemployed, claiming that adoption of the policy would pay off the entire national debt within a year. On election day, Bryan lost Omaha by 1,000 out of 18,000 votes cast. He carried Nebraska, most of the rest of the Plains, and the silver-producing states of the West. He suffered defeat after defeat in the remainder of the country, running poorly in eastern urban centers. William McKinley, the Republican victor, represented conservative eastern interests of the same type that had long dominated Omaha. Still, the election settled vexing national monetary questions.

Business, which had started to recover shortly before the election, continued to register gains following McKinley's inauguration. Industries reopened, and the real-estate market improved. Charitable organizations closed. And,

4. Omaha in the late nineteenth century, looking north and northwest from South Ninth Street. Large building is Union Pacific Freight Depot. *Courtesy NSHS, RG2341 PH O 786.*

rain fell again on Nebraska. The farmers who had survived knew much more about Plains agriculture than before the debacle, particularly the folly of planting crops on grazing land. The claims of early propagandists only had substance in that they applied to good cycles; inevitably, farmers would have to plan for prolonged dry periods, taking them as a matter of course. In addition to such fluctuations, they had to reconcile themselves to varying prices and monopolistic practices. Few people pondered those kinds of basic considerations for very long; they enjoyed the return of prosperity. Old Populists welcomed the improvements. Edward Morearty, active in the movement, exclaimed, "In 1898 the joy bells began to ring . . . nature seemed to have removed that staring, dejected and melancholy look from the faces of the people, and in its stead left a look of joy, hope, confidence and contentment. A smile like unto that which spread upon the faces of the children of Israel when led out of the land of Egypt and the house of bondage."

THE UNION PACIFIC: A NEW ERA

On November 1, 1897, some five hundred people came to the Union Pacific's Omaha freight depot to witness the receivership sale of the railroad. The matter-of-fact proceedings bore no resemblance to the railroad's groundbreaking ceremony that had taken place on December 2, 1863, not over a mile away. There was no George Francis Train to exclaim that Omaha was the divinely designated "signal station at the entrance of a garden seven hundred miles in length and twenty broad." But as unpromising as the day seemed, the receivership sale would be a new start for the Union Pacific that under the leadership of Edward Henry Harriman would find a financial strength and stability that it had not known in its early years.

Even before Harriman commenced a massive modernization of the road, the Union Pacific shops in Omaha were in the vanguard of railroad technology. In 1889 they received electric lighting, and the following year they began to use pneumatic equipment. Within the next few years the Omaha shops were designing and building machinery. In the meantime, the railroad and the city had engaged in a dispute over paying for the construction of viaducts to eliminate grade crossings over the many tracks that intersected South Tenth and South Eleventh streets. Under a cost-sharing agreement between the Union Pacific and Burlington railroads and the city, an Eleventh Street viaduct was erected in 1886–87. A Union Pacific subsidiary paid for the construction of the 1,520-foot-long Tenth Street viaduct that was built in 1890 and opened on New Year's Day 1891. The latter thoroughfare would be an important north-south streetcar and vehicular-traffic route and would provide public access to the rail terminals.

In 1889 the Union Pacific had promised the city of Omaha that it would build a new passenger station. Although litigation and the financial collapse of the railroad brought a halt to this project, work on the Union Station resumed in 1898, and the Neoclassical structure on the east side of the Tenth Street viaduct began serving the Union Pacific and other roads in December 1899. Across the tracks at the south end of the viaduct, the Burlington had completed a Classical-style depot that opened in June 1898. In addition to freight traffic, by 1903 ninety-nine passenger trains served Union Station daily. Accordingly, along with building Union Station, the Union Pacific equipped the terminal area with interlocking switches and yard towers to improve safety and efficiency.

COUNCIL BLUFFS: CANDY, FLOWERS, GRAPES, & GREASE

Despite the depression of the mid-1890s, Council Bluffs had a promising economy at the end of the century. Aside from the city's exceptional stature as a rail center, its promoters claimed, "Council Bluffs is the second distributing point of importance in the world for farm implements and vehicles." However grandiose this contention, in 1900 the city had about thirty-nine jobbers and transfer firms, such as Peru Plow and Implement Company, Pioneer Implement Company, Union Transfer Company, and Deere, Wells and Company, which represented some 125 manufacturers of implements, wagons, and buggies. Their inventories were stored in large warehouses and distributed not only to Council Bluffs' immediate trade area in southwestern Iowa and adjacent states but to more distant points. While Council Bluffs was not a big industrial center, the Superior Scale Works produced weighing devices, while the Kimball Brothers manufactured elevators and scales. The Sprague Iron Works made such products as boilers, engines, smokestacks, grates, and kettles for canneries. Mindful that creative packaging might help sell even the least attractive products, the Monarch Manufacturing Company marketed axle grease "in fine lithographed tin boxes and pails" across the trans-Mississippi West. John G. Woodward and Company, a Council Bluffs candy manufacturer, marketed its products internationally.

5. Grand Court, Trans-Mississippi Exposition, Omaha, 1898.
Courtesy NSHS, RG2752 PH O 56.

Pottawattamie County was in the heart of the western Corn Belt, but by 1900 the loess hills soil made the Council Bluffs area a significant producer of apples, grapes, and other produce. With his greenhouses on East Pierce Street and operations in the nearby countryside, J. F. Wilcox was the leading figure in making Council Bluffs a major producer and shipper of cut flowers and plants to distant points. Eventually over one million square feet of glass would cover the city's major greenhouses, and the Wilcox firm had about three-quarters of this space. The shipment of flowers, disc harrows, and wagons reflected the centrality of railroads to Council Bluffs' livelihood and economy.

"THE NEW WHITE CITY"

The symbol of Omaha's rebirth was the Trans-Mississippi and International Exposition of 1898. Conceived as a means of promoting the city, it had the strong backing of all major civic groups. Omaha obtained the exposition after complex negotiations with the Trans-Mississippi Commercial Congress. Central to success was the active participation in 1895 of William Jennings Bryan, then editor of the *Omaha World-Herald*. He gave a rousing presentation, claiming that Omaha was an ideal place to display the products of the West. It was the center of a region with 16.5 million persons who had an aggregate wealth of $20 billion. Bryan's blatant urban boosterism, far different from his position toward cities in his unsuccessful presidential campaign, demonstrated the importance of the exposition to Omahans.

The driving force in making the exposition a success was Gurdon W. Wattles, president of the corporation established to operate the extravaganza. Wattles was a relative newcomer to the Omaha scene. He had arrived in town in 1892 at age thirty-six. Born in New York, he had grown up in Iowa, attended college, and taught school. Making considerable money in small-town banking in Iowa, he had sought new horizons, coming to Omaha as the vice president of the Union National Bank. Wattles appeared almost a stereotypical village banker. Yet he was more than that. He was an intelligent and calculating man with a driving ambition underscored by an ability to develop a successful and deliberate plan to rise rapidly in Omaha business. The Panic of 1893 helped him to achieve his goals; it created opportunities for new men. Wattles joined all the right clubs. He said in his memoirs that he "sought every available means to make new acquaintances and friends and to serve the people of [his] new home." Undertaking the task of running the Trans-Mississippi and International Exposition was a risk on Wattle's part. If he failed, he could be discredited; and at first, his prospects did not appear bright. "It quickly became evident," he recalled, "that we had undertaken a Herculean task at a time when it seemed absolutely impossible to secure the money for its completion." Of course he had immense faith, not misplaced, in his own ability and a belief that the economy would improve.

Wattles did an excellent job of raising money from a wide variety of public and private sources. He accomplished his objectives by adroit lobbying, the use of delegations of businessmen, and appeals to self-interest. The Nebraska legislature contributed $100,000; other states and territories gave $138,000 for buildings and exhibits. Congress appropriated $250,000 on the condition of matching funds. Omaha business interests made generous contributions. In all, Wattles raised a total of $600,000. To ensure favorable press, he dispensed liberal printing contracts to Omaha newspapers. His gamble was an outstanding success. Between the spring and fall of 1898, despite the Spanish-American War, over 2.6 million persons attended the fair. Visitors included President McKinley who, from his temporary residence at the Omaha Club, remained in contact with Washington by telephone. Wattles took justifiable pride in the Trans-Mississippi Exhibition, seeing it as the start of an era. In opening day ceremonies, he proclaimed, "This exposition . . . opens new fields to the investor, inspires the ambition of genius, incites the emulation of states and stands the crowning glory in the history of the West."

The Omaha exhibition had no relationship to the sod houses of western Nebraska or the modest houses of South Omaha's packing-house workers. Inspired in part by the Chicago World's Columbian Exposition of 1893–94, the Omaha exposition represented an attempt to be as up-to-date as the Illinois metropolis. At the center of the Omaha showcase for the West was a Venetian lagoon, complete with small craft and gondoliers. The eclectic plaster of Paris structures around the Grand Court were, according to an observer, "freely inspired by the classical and the renaissance." The Fine Arts Building had a statue of a young girl surrounded by cupids; seminaked nymphs adorned the grounds. A huge plaster of Paris warrior, *Omaha*, drawn in a chariot pulled by four lions occupied a conspicuous place. Behind the main buildings was a wide midway where the main attraction was a group of dancing girls who performed in the Streets of Cairo concession—until they were forced to change their act. Off to one side was an Indian powwow grounds, where several hundred native people displayed wares, danced, and lost mock battles to whites.

The exposition gave the boosters of Council Bluffs an opportunity to highlight their city and county. Donations from businesses and individuals, supplemented by a contribution from the county, funded the construction of the Pottawattamie County Wigwam near the Iowa Building on the fairgrounds. This large teepee-shaped structure had four floors with windows. The first two levels housed exhibits, the third floor was a parlor for women and children, and the top floor was a men's smoking lounge that offered a fine view of the exposition grounds.

Over twenty thousand incandescent electric lights illuminated the exposition buildings and grounds, gently creating a dreamlike aura that symbolized past achievements and heralded the unknown wonders of a new century. Indeed, to many Omahans, the exhibition represented a release from a long period of black nights. The fair raised hope and lifted up hearts even before the first visitor passed through the gates. "After so many years of financial depression, it was a joy to the heart and souls of us all to hear the pleasing sound of hundreds of hammers and saws and the presentment of so many beautiful buildings in course of construction," an old resident recalled. "The new white city seemed magic, rising Phoenix-like from clay—nay, like reading a chapter from Arabian Nights." And so, after a decade of shattered ambitions, Omaha and its people moved confidently into the twentieth century. Few doubted that untold triumphs lay ahead. The Omaha story was just beginning.

[5] Growing Pains and Public Improvements

The Trans-Mississippi Exposition celebrated the march of American civilization: "Within the memory of men now living almost every foot of the great trans-Mississippi country was the habitat of Indian tribes," Albert Shaw wrote in an 1898 article in a national magazine. "The Omaha Exposition signalizes the triumph of the Anglo-Saxon pioneers, first over the aborigines, and second, over the forces of nature." According to the director of the 1890 census, the frontier was over. In 1893 historian Frederick Jackson Turner had analyzed the meaning of the change. He said that America's democratic institutions owed much to the frontier and that its closing had ended the first chapter in the nation's history. Omaha was no longer a city in the wilderness. At some point after 1870, it had entered a new era, acquiring the settled characteristics of places in the eastern United States. Social and political institutions had matured and stabilized. Visions of metropolis that had helped sustain the early builders of Omaha had taken on substance. Many of the pioneers were active participants in the transformation, taking satisfaction in contributing to the construction of a great regional center.

This accomplishment had involved overcoming Omaha's image as a wild and wide-open town. Its role as a transfer terminal automatically attracted numerous undesirable elements. The Third Ward was the center of vice. The tenderloin district, in the vicinity of Ninth and Douglas streets, a short distance from the Union Pacific station, operated around the clock. There was a great deal of truth in the poem "Hast Ever Been In Omaha," which appeared in an 1869 issue of *Harper's Magazine*:

Hast ever been in Omaha,
Where rolls the dark Missouri down,

And four strong horses scarce can draw
An empty wagon through the town?

Where sand is blown from every mound
To fill your eyes and ears and throat—
Where all the steamers are aground
And all the shanties are afloat?

Where whiskey shops the livelong night
Are vending out their poison juice;
Where men are often very tight
And women deemed a trifle loose?

Where taverns have an anxious guest
For every corner, shelf and crack;
With half the people going west,
And all the others going back?

Where theaters are all the run,
And bloody scalpers come to trade;
Where everything is overdone
And everybody underpaid?

If not, take heed to what I say:
You'll find it just as I have found it;
And if it lies upon your way,
For God's sake, reader, *go around it!*

The author was probably itinerant journalist Frank Streamer, who worked in various capacities for local papers. Said to have had a severe drinking problem, he had firsthand knowledge of the dives of Omaha. After a few years he drifted on to the Pacific coast to try his luck there.

Rotten politics was the rule in Omaha. During the 1870s and 1880s, the First Ward frequently decided the outcome of local elections. An often heard expression was, "As goes the First Ward, so goes the city." There was no corrupt practices act. Votes, in a day before the Australian ballot, sold for one dollar; election judges, all in league with criminal elements, did not challenge the many "repeaters" escorted to cast votes by their handlers from one polling station to another. Saloonkeepers represented the First Ward on the council. An Omaha editor who regularly attended meetings called the body a haven for rogues. Champion S. Chase, the mayor of Omaha in the late 1870s, ran a free and easy city. He was impeached following disclosures that his appointee as city marshal had pocketed fines collected from inmates of houses of prostitution. There was an unofficial license system that avoided police-court coffers. A designated city official received ten dollars a month from madams and five dollars from inmates, which supposedly went to the city treasury.

Police judges were part of the corruption system. Judge Patrick O. Hawes, a genial man who always wore a silk vest and a white stiff-bosom shirt, carried on business in a casual manner, making a living from court costs. "It was no unusual thing for him," an acquaintance recalled, "to fine a prisoner while sitting at a beer table, on the statement of a friend who related the facts to him, sticking the fine in one pocket and the costs in the other." After a police raid resulted in the arrest of several men and netted a large "haul," another police judge, hastily summoned at midnight, fixed bail at five dollars. He then adjourned with the accused men and the city marshal to the notorious Crystal Saloon to negotiate the fines. It was no wonder that prostitution, gambling, and saloons flourished, with all their attendant violence and social evils.

It was easy to get a drink throughout the town at any time of the day or night. All the grocery stores, including those patronized by the town's leading citizens, kept a keg of whiskey on tap as a regular service. Customers imbibed while shopping, charging the costs of shots on their pass books just the same as sugar or potatoes. Saloons had no closing times; some of the busier establishments never locked their front doors. Between 130 and 140 saloons operated in Omaha, roughly one for every 110 men, women, and children. The Crystal Saloon, a haunt of gamblers and politicians, was one of the more luxurious places. On New Year's Eve in 1875, the owner held a formal masquerade ball for the sporting crowd. All the leading madams and their prettiest and most sought-after charges attended, dressed in evening gowns and wearing expensive jewelry. Less ornate but still well patronized was the large Central Beer Garden near the railroad station. Professional gamblers owned the garden, using it as a front for their activities. A saloon run by Fatty Flynn, a 425-pound former circus clown and fat man, catered to "visiting sports" interested in a quick game of cards for high stakes between trains. Of lower repute were a series of "colored dens," notorious gambling houses presided over by black managers and owned by white criminals. Near Fort Omaha, a small military post north of town, a dozen unsavory dives, few of which bothered to pay license fees, stayed open only until soldiers had spent their monthly pay. These rough places palled when compared with a Third Ward dance hall, the St. Elmo Theatre. Billed as a "variety show," it had a reputation locally as the toughest joint between Chicago and Leadville. A week seldom passed without a murder or barroom brawl.

In 1881 much to the surprise of the liquor interests, the state legislature enacted the Slocumb local option law, requiring a one-thousand-dollar license fee—it was one hundred dollars in Omaha at the time—and providing for compulsory closings on Sundays and election days. When Col. Watson B. Smith, a federal court official in Omaha, advocated strict enforcement of the legislation, unknown assailants shot him to death in his office. Despite moves toward regulation, saloons remained a major feature of Omaha.

Violence was accepted as part of the everyday routine. Typical incidents of the 1870s epitomized conditions. One afternoon, a drunk caused a disturbance in the Variety Bazaar. Bouncers beat him and tossed him into the street. Passing policemen, called "stars," picked up the unfortunate man and carried him off to jail. This was an accepted procedure. Men found in gutters accounted for a high percentage of all arrests. Many disturbances never appeared on police blotters. Violence aroused public ire only when local citizens got in trouble. After a popular Union Pacific railroad worker was stabbed in the stomach during a barroom brawl, his colleagues threatened those responsible, hanging one in effigy. Fights occurred every Saturday night. Once a crowd of over a hundred spectators gathered at the main intersection to watch two men, both crazed by hard drink, flail away at each other. In a larger confrontation, soldiers and townsmen exchanged shots. In the most disturbing affair of all, toughs beat the Omaha police chief senseless at the Crystal Saloon with no resulting convictions. With some relish, a Kansas City newspaper reporter wrote,

It requires but little, if any, stretch of the imagination to regard Omaha as a very cesspool of iniquity, for it is given up to lawlessness and is overrun with a horde of fugitives from justice and dangerous men of all kinds who carry things with a high hand and a loose rein. . . . Mobs of monte men, pickpockets, brace faro dealers, criminal fugitives of every class find congenial companions in Omaha, and a comparative safe retreat from the officers of the law. . . . If you want to find a rogue's rookery, go to Omaha.

The high license fee imposed by the Slocumb law did little, if anything, to reduce either the presence or the negative impact of saloons. Evidence of this may be found in an unusual source. Like their neighbors to the south, Canadians in the late nineteenth century were debating the issue of prohibiting or more strictly regulating the manufacture and sale of alcoholic beverages. As a result of parliamentary action in Ottawa, the governor general of Canada in 1892 created the five-member Royal Commission on the Liquor Traffic to study liquor laws at home and abroad in order ascertain the impact of such measures. Part of the commission visited Omaha and Council Bluffs, and their final report in March 1895 included some noteworthy observations about those cities.

The commissioners were hardly neutral on the subject of their inquiry. Of the five members of the commission, only the Reverend Doctor Joseph Mac-Leod supported prohibition and judged liquor laws in terms of their capacity to diminish or eliminate saloons. The clergyman was one of the commissioners to visit Nebraska, and he concluded that the high license fee imposed by the Slocumb Act had not brought any positive impact in Omaha. In fact, he argued that the law encouraged other vices:

The logical outcome of deriving large revenues in license fees from the liquor traffic is the demand made, and practically conceded, that prostitution and gambling be also licensed. In Omaha, Neb., and other places in which the high license system is in operation, gambling is practically recognized as a legitimate business by the payment of a monthly fee (nominally a fine) into the city's treasury. . . .

The social evil [prostitution] is recognized and authorized in the same way. Once a month the wretched women who live by sin pay a fee, and are not interfered with so long as they make payments promptly. Many thousand[s] of dollars are received by the city, annually, for the authorization of these two evils. The effect of all this is to obliterate moral distinctions and to debauch the public conscience. Rev. B. Fay Mills, an eminent religious teacher and leader, after spending several weeks in Omaha, said in a public meeting: "I have been in nearly every city in the United States, but nowhere have I found vice so open and without shame upon its countenance as in this promising city of yours. Nowhere have I seen the gambling hells run so openly and defiantly as here. Licensed by the city to carry on their damnable work, they run openly and without fear of molestation. Nowhere have I seen the social evil so prominent. . . . There is no other city in the United States that will compare with yours in open temples of depravity."

Dr. MacLeod also declared that Omaha's saloons sold alcoholic beverages to minors and remained open on Sundays. As he put it, "[O]n the Sunday the commissioners were in Omaha, a man was nearly murdered in one of the saloons."

Commission data showed that in 1894, Omaha had 219 saloons, or one for every 685 residents. Compared to other cities functioning under high license fees, Omaha's number of saloons in relation to its population was middling. However, the commission's figure was based upon what seems to have been a major overestimation of Omaha's population and a more accurate ratio may have been about one saloon for every 468 inhabitants. Even using this latter figure, fourteen of the thirty-eight U.S. cities with high license fees had more saloons per capita than Omaha. Moreover, although the number of saloons had increased as the city's population had grown, the per capita figure had fallen, a point that was not in the commission's data. Of Omaha's 6,246 reported arrests, 2,049 were for drunken and disorderly conduct, and the per capita number of arrests on this charge was in the middle range for cities with high license fees.

Iowa had banned alcoholic beverages in 1884, but enforcement of the statute was spotty. As Dr. MacLeod said, "The testimony is uniform that the lax enforcement of the law is in the border cities and towns, and in those in which the foreign population is dominant." In Council Bluffs, liquor was served in seventy-eight "disorderly houses," which functioned with the knowledge of the police. Each month, the proprietors of these establishments were formally charged with violation of the liquor law. The saloon operator went to the police, posted $50.00 in "security" and $2.10 in costs to assure a court appearance and simply forfeited the money by not appearing for adjudication of the charges. Hence, for $52.10 monthly, the saloon-keepers were permitted to violate Iowa's prohibition law.

In the meantime, Iowa's prohibition law had become a political burden for the long dominant Republican Party. As elsewhere, the Democrats opposed such legislation, and in 1889 Horace Boies, their gubernatorial candidate, triumphed in part because of his antiprohibition stand. In becoming the first Democratic governor in more than three decades, the politically moderate Boies was victorious in Iowa's nine largest cities, which included Council Bluffs. Voters of German background, especially prominent in cities such as Council Bluffs, opposed prohibition. Perhaps businessmen tended to see a hard line on prohibition as troublesome; in any event, after Boies's reelection in 1891, moderation on the prohibition question gained ascendancy in Iowa's Republican Party. When Council Bluffs business leader E. F. Test purchased the *Nonpareil* in 1891, he placed that Republican paper on the side of legalizing alcoholic beverages under local option and a high license fee. Even though the *Nonpareil*'s circulation shot up, the paper soon plummeted into temporary bankruptcy, possibly as a partial result of the wrath of prohibition advocates. In 1893 a Republican returned to the governor's office, and the following year, the legislature enacted the Mulct Law, a weird measure that allowed counties to permit saloons to operate if such establishments paid yearly fines of six hundred dollars for violating the 1884 prohibition statute. The new law in effect sanctioned existing practice.

Although Omaha was not exceptional among urban centers for arrests for drunk and disorderly conduct, prostitution indeed flourished in the city. "Many immoral women inhabited the tenderloin district in the vicinity of Ninth and Douglas streets," Alfred Sorenson, the Omaha journalist, reported. "Police raids on the disorderly houses were of rare occurrence, no arrests being made unless some serious disturbance required the presence of the officers of the law." Once in a while, the police staged a raid to appease public opinion. In 1873 they temporarily incarcerated fifty-six members of the "frail sisterhood" for "social eviliance." When the police made arrests, there were frequently no convictions. One of the few actual closings of a disorderly house came when a police judge ordered the notorious Red Light shut down and fined the owner twenty-five dollars. While some practitioners of the "oldest profession" freelanced, the majority worked out of saloons or bawdy houses. A beautiful woman, Anna Wilson, the companion of a handsome gambler Dan Allen, became queen of the underworld. She lived lavishly and once had $10,000 in diamonds stolen from her person after she drank too much champagne. Rumors claimed that she was a member of a respectable southern family. A shrewd businesswoman, at her death in 1911 she left an estate of $250,000 to charitable and public causes in Omaha.

Prostitution was also a well-established vice in Council Bluffs. In 1875 despite police crackdowns on prostitution near the intersection of Washington Avenue and Market Street, the *Nonpareil* observed, "[T]he residents of that section now loudly complain of the presence there of harlots and their abettors in numbers altogether too numerous." Two decades later, the report of the Canadian commissioners who visited Council Bluffs to study Iowa's prohibition law noted that, like saloons, other vices were allowed to continue in the city by what amounted to routine forfeiting of posted bonds.

In Omaha, gambling was the mainspring of the corruption system. Faro banks, keno games, and poker houses ran around the clock, seven days a week. "Evenings I sauntered leisurely around the city," Edward F. Morearty said, recounting what it was like in Omaha during the summer of 1880, "and in so sauntering, curiosity prompted me to follow a crowd of men going up the steps of a two-story brick building located on the southwest corner of Twelfth and Douglas streets. . . . The crowd that was surging in there were gamblers, eager to get in on the game run by Dan Allen; Gotley Brooker was dealing the cards." Many visitors found it surprising to see keno and poker rooms operating in broad daylight. Every saloon had gambling tables. Curses rang out as cards turned. At one place, an old "moocher" and self-styled frontier bully scared tenderfeet by pretending to draw a revolver and yelling, "You super-annuated son of a sea cook," or words to that effect.

Many big rollers preferred different surroundings. One maintained a genteel room for high-class players; another conducted a game that featured sumptuous lunches. The leading gamblers of Omaha customarily played every afternoon in a room over a Twelfth Street saloon. In 1887 "a Big Four" combination opened the Diamond in a two-story building on Douglas Street. The ground floor had an expensively furnished bar, a pool room, and a horse-betting parlor; the second, faro, hazard, roulette, poker, and other games. There were many more losers than winners in the wagering rooms of Omaha, and pawnbrokers did a good business. Tales of unsuccessful plungers abounded. In a much publicized incident, a deacon tried to explain his gambling away of church funds by claiming that he hoped to win money to buy books for a Sunday-school library.

Losses from chicanery tarnished the name of Omaha gambling. Complaints by honest gamblers led to the closing of "Dollar Stores," which operated around the railroad stations. For one dollar a customer drew an envelope from a box, hoping to win a prize of from one dollar to fifty dollars. Of course, the Dollar Stores were pure bunko games, and patrons had no chance of winning. More sophisticated were the activities of a gang headed by Canada Bill, a former riverboat gambler capable of numerous ruses. His criminal band consisted of a clever crew of card artists, cappers, and confidence men. Their nefarious exploits received a great deal of attention. They followed their trade in the vicinity of the stations and in nearby saloons. Their favorite and most successful swindle was the three-card monte trap. Once in while, members branched out into other areas: fixing horse races, rolling drunks, and plotting armed robberies. The Omaha police generally left them alone; most of their problems came from railroad detectives. The Canada Bill gang broke up in 1876. The members moved west to the gold fields but not before establishing precedents for illegal activities that continued in Omaha for many more years.

Aside from the social cost of crime and the bad image of the city that it fostered, most violations of the law were relatively minor. There was a routine character to law breaking evident in a report by Council Bluffs chief of police H. H. Field from March 1883 to March 16, 1884, indicating a total of 1,157 arrests. Of these, 386 were for drunkenness, 155 for disturbing the peace, and 151 for prostitution. There were 96 charges of larceny, 75 of vagrancy, 53 for assault and battery, and 34 for "keeping [a] gaming house." Field added that the total number of arrests "does not include station lodgers of whom there has [sic] probably been 1,000." The problem of transients remained, and in 1889 Council Bluffs police chief O. H. Lucas recommended a mandatory work program to abate a "tramp nuisance."

POLITICS AND JOURNALISTS

During the Gilded Age, there was no major call for political reform in Omaha. The closest the city came to having a crusader was Mayor William J. Broatch, and he had suspect motives. He arrested saloon owners who stayed open beyond the never previously enforced 1:00 a.m. closing time, double-crossing elements that had helped him get elected. Most politicos left well enough alone. They generally avoided the issues, although at times they had to take stands on questions that stirred the electorate: the condition of the streets, the need for a better water supply, the level of protective services, and the awarding of traction franchises. When possible, they concentrated on state and national matters. Both Omaha Republicans and Democrats combined to help defeat proposed amendments to the Nebraska constitution that would have allowed women to vote and ushered in prohibition. Even Omaha Populists avoided calling for reform in local affairs; rather, they advocated national change.

Perfidy and vote buying were accepted as matters of course. Opponents denounced members of one council as "Corporation Cormorants and Venal Vampires." The 1887 Republican primary pitted privately owned public utilities against the liquor interests. "Such a disgraceful primary was never held in any republic; men voted from three to five times and often ten times that day; wagons and all kinds of vehicles were used to carry men from one voting place to another, and there voted regardless of residence or political affiliations," a participant declared. "Every ward heeler was liberally supplied with money, whiskey and streetcar tickets; the voting places were amply guarded by the right kind of police officer whose chief duty was to obey orders from the ward boss." Liquor was an accepted part of politics. In 1890 when William Jennings Bryan ran for Congress, he made an evening canvass of the saloons, sipping soda as an aide set each house up with a free round of beer. Those tactics helped Bryan, a "dry" but not yet a prohibitionist, carry a predominantly Republican district by ten thousand votes.

Throughout the 1870s a small group of railroad executives controlled the dominant Republican Party's organization in Omaha. Ward heelers who attempted to follow an independent course ran the risk of having their names listed in the black books used for hiring and firing and kept by every corporation in town. In the 1880s there was a quiet revolt against what rank-and-file Republicans called King Caucus. After every national convention, local Republicans formed clubs to carry on the campaign. The dissidents, working through corporations interested in breaking railroad dominance, put forward successful slates of businessmen that had been decided on in advance. Despite the breaking of the more oppressive aspects of the old system, the Union Pacific in particular remained an important force in the Omaha GOP. The Democrats did not have an organization until 1884, when they established the Samoset Club patterned after Tammany Hall in New York City.

Members of the Samoset Club had stylish uniforms for use in frequently held political parades. The society, which succeeded in reviving interest in the Democratic Party in Omaha, disbanded in 1890 following the formation of a broader-based organization called the Jacksonian Club. The Populists worked through temporary organizations during their greatest days. In 1898 after the party had gone into decline, they formed the short-lived Peter Cooper Club. If nothing else, the Omaha politicians put on good shows in public, complete with monster rallies, uniformed men on foot and horseback, marching bands, and torchlight parades.

Three of the most important Omaha political leaders of the period were all newspaper editors: Edward Rosewater, George L. Miller, and Gilbert M. Hitchcock. Of the group, Rosewater was the most colorful and controversial. A Bohemian Jew, he had immigrated to the United States with his parents in 1854 when he was thirteen years old. During the Civil War he was a telegrapher in the U.S. Army Telegraph Corps. In 1863 he came to Omaha to work in the Pacific telegraph office where he soon became the local manager, holding the position for seven years. In the course of his duties, he acted as an agent for the Associated Press and as a correspondent for several eastern newspapers. He resigned from the telegraph company in 1870 to found the *Omaha Tribune*, but he soon sold out after winning election to the state legislature as a Republican. He served only one term, receiving considerable publicity for successfully sponsoring a bill providing for an Omaha school board and for taking an active lead in helping to impeach the governor for misappropriation of state funds. To promote his political views, he started the *Omaha Bee*. Conceived of as a temporary sheet, it flourished, soon becoming one of the leading newspapers in Nebraska. Ultimately it made Rosewater a wealthy man. At the time of his death in 1906, he was one of Omaha's most important citizens.

Rosewater's strong views, not always consistent, made him many enemies. Late in his career, vindictive state legislators denied him election to the U.S. Senate. Although a partisan Republican, Rosewater opposed monopolies, frequently attacking the policies of the Union Pacific Railroad. Yet his opposition to power by the few did not extend to his own self-interest. Along with other Omaha publishers, he bitterly criticized printers when they struck for higher wages. Rosewater was a careful writer and a good debater. His debates with national figures drew large crowds. In 1881 he outpointed Susan B. Anthony on the question of whether women should be granted the vote. During the 1896 presidential campaign, neutral observers thought he bested Bryan in a debate on financial questions.

Over the course of a long career, Rosewater attacked thousands of persons in print. It was not unusual for him to break with associates, on occasion, leading to trouble. When he started to horsewhip the editor of the *Omaha Republican* following an exchange of insulting articles, his larger opponent slammed him to the ground and sat on him. Another editor accosted Rosewater on the street and hit him on the head with a billy club. A saloonkeeper, Dick Curry, enraged when the *Bee* called his place of business, "A squalid place of resort; a wretched dwelling place; a haunt; as a den of business," received a four-year prison sentence for having a henchman beat Rosewater senseless. Rosewater was fortunate no one ever shot him; irate subscribers killed several frontier editors.

George L. Miller became a journalist after working as a physician, politician, and army sutler. Born in upstate New York in 1831, he studied medicine and opened a practice in Syracuse. He immigrated to Omaha in 1854, entered political life and twice won election to the territorial council. During his second term he was president of the body. In 1860 he moved to St. Joseph, Missouri, where he submitted articles to local papers. By this time, he had decided to give up his medical pursuits. At the start of the Civil War, he received an appointment as post sutler at Fort Kearny. In 1864 he returned to Omaha and stood unsuccessfully as a Democratic candidate for Congress. The next year he and another man, whom he bought out within three years, founded the *Omaha Herald*. He ardently championed the Democratic cause and rose into a position of leadership in Nebraska. For several years, Miller and J. Sterling Morton carried on a feud within the Democratic Party. Miller increasingly combined his political fortunes with the promotion of Omaha and Nebraska. He was a member of the delegation that negotiated with Union Pacific leaders for a bridge at Omaha, and he invested heavily in real estate. He became a wealthy man and had lost much of his crusading zeal when he relinquished his editor's chair in 1887. Miller hoped for a cabinet position that never came, so he devoted the remainder of his life to his Omaha business interests.

Gilbert M. Hitchcock, born in Omaha in 1856, was the son of an early Nebraska political leader. His father, Phineas Hitchcock, was first a territorial delegate and after that a U.S. senator. Gilbert received his higher education

6. An Omaha home circa 1870s: David and Amanda Harpster residence 402 North Fourteenth Street. Note wooden sidewalks. Site now under I-480 overpass. *Courtesy Mrs. Louise Baumann.*

outside of Nebraska. He attended school in Germany for two years and after that obtained a law degree from the University of Michigan. He burst upon the Omaha scene in 1882 when he debated feminist, Phoebe Cousins, before a large crowd. Edward Morearty, a spectator, remembered:

> I will confess it was the first time I had ever seen or heard of him; yet I am free to say that as the debate progressed he proved to be an agreeable surprise to the audience and to me. During the debate he became so enthused in his subject that he invoked the wrath of his opponent to such an extent that she arose from her seat to attract his attention, and pointing her long bony forefinger at him menacingly, exclaimed: "Mr. Hitchcock, you are a disgrace to the mother who bore you." He was applauded to the echo and won the debate on its merits.

In 1885 Hitchcock helped found the *Omaha Evening World.* Four years later he purchased Miller's old *Herald* and merged the two papers into the *Omaha World-Herald.* Overnight, Hitchcock, the principal owner in the new morning and evening paper, became a major figure in Nebraska journalism. The *World-Herald* supported the Democratic Party; Bryan was editor at the time of his 1896 presidential nomination. Hitchcock subsequently entered politics and served three terms in the House of Representatives and two in the Senate. He capped his activities by being the first Omaha newspaper publisher to make a mark in national political and international affairs.

THE DEVELOPMENT OF URBAN SERVICES

Throughout the frontier period in Omaha, the bad condition of the streets caused many residents to experience lingering doubts about the idea of progress. Even though grading operations started at an early date, thoroughfares remained in terrible shape. For several decades the city council did little. It bowed to strenuous opposition from the property owners who did not want to pay for improvements. During rainy periods wagons sank up to their hubs on main roads, and residents wore knee-high boots to wade through the ruts and potholes. At times the streets became rivers. "Streets are in bad condition, and are daily getting worse," a reporter warned in 1876. "The water is ploughing them out right smart, leaving deep furrows here and there." Trying to use the wooden sidewalks was a frustrating undertaking; during the winter people used the planks for firewood. In 1880 only a quarter mile of Omaha's estimated 118 miles of streets had paving. The city, which spent approximately $11,500 annually on road work under an inefficient contract system, owned neither a stone crusher nor a roller. Downtown Farnam Street was one continuous mudhole until the laying down of what was known as a Sioux Falls granite surface in 1883. Makeshift repairs and general inefficiency continued to frustrate Omahans until well after the end of the frontier.

Poor municipal sanitation contributed to inconveniences experienced by pedestrians. The streets were a dumping ground for waste paper, ashes, garbage, and other items. Beasts lay where they expired. "The dead mule, which was lying a short distance northeast from the Union Depot, for several days, and from which a thousand double stinks was emanated every second, has been removed much to the relief of the offended First Ward nostrils, but greatly to the regret of the dogs, cats and rats who were taking their regular square meals off the deceased animal in delightful harmony," Edward Rosewater wrote in 1872. For many years, only a good strong wind improved matters. Authorities gave up; until the 1880s they never attempted to clean the streets. They justified inaction by pointing out that few other western cities bothered with the problem. This failed to impress outsiders, and Omaha gained a reputation as a dirty and unkempt town.

Information provided by the city to the 1880 census—the last taken by the federal government prior to the frontier's official close—indicated that Omaha had many sanitary problems. Omaha had no system of sewerage, while Council Bluffs had a mere 1,600 feet of lines that discharged into river-bottom sloughs. Human excreta accumulated in privy vaults, hardly any of which were watertight. Chamber, laundry, and kitchen slops normally went into dry wells or cesspools, mostly porous and without overflows. Omaha had no regulations governing the disposal of manufacturing by-products. Householders had the sole responsibility of removing garbage and ashes. No uniform way existed of disposing of ashes, and garbage piled up on the banks of the Missouri River. "All these things will be speedily changed," an Omaha judge contended. "Thus far the city has grown too fast for public improvements to keep up."

Many Omahans believed a waterworks the solution. As late as the 1870s, water for domestic use came from wells. Firefighters depended on water pumped from the river into cisterns located at intervals throughout town. For many years the city council declined to take any action, citing high costs. Bids submitted by outside interests were allegedly far too high; the project became bogged down in politics. By the late 1870s, public sentiment, as expressed in mass meetings, seemed to favor a reservoir and gravity system proposed by the Holly Company that had built similar waterworks for many other towns. A controversy evolved over ownership; Rosewater and other leaders charged that the "solid eight" on the council had received bribes to grant a franchise to the Holly Company. After sensational charges, judicial actions, disputed ordinances, and a hotly contested election, a group of local businessmen won a twenty-five year franchise. In September of 1881 the City Waterworks Company went into operation, solving a vexing difficulty. Whether it led to a cleaner city remained open to question.

Serious problems plagued the new works, even as local boosters praised the combination direct pressure and gravity system, which featured a powerful pumping engine that brought up water from the Missouri River to a ten-million-gallon-capacity reservoir on Walnut Hill. The water distributed through the mains contained too many dead fish and too much raw sewage to satisfy customers. To compound matters, there were no meters, resulting in an enormous waste of water. During 1886, the original owners, unable to capitalize on their monopoly, sold out to a Boston syndicate. A year later, a

Chicago group acquired the works and constructed at a cost of $1.5 million a new pumping house and reservoir at Florence, north of Omaha. The new facilities did not lead to better management; people remained bitter about service. In 1891 New Jersey interests bought the firm and renamed it the American Waterworks Corporation. The company's unsuccessful attempts to gain a franchise extension in 1896 touched off a bitter political battle over public ownership that eventually involved the Nebraska state government and federal courts. The conflict extended into the twentieth century and did not end until the city purchased the works for $6.5 million in 1912.

During the 1880s and 1890s Omaha had increasingly required more efficient and comprehensive urban services. It was no longer enough to have a few jerry-built sewers, wooden pipes, or hastily dug ditches that carried everything from street runoff to human excrement. Nor could Omaha function effectively with impassable streets during much of the year. As the town expanded in physical size and the first of many suburban components appeared, there was a need for different kinds of transportation. Growth and change came too fast for long-range planning and careful deliberations, but it was no longer possible or fashionable to blame inaction on rapid growth. Real problems, not abstractions, confronted those responsible for setting policy. While franchises became local footballs and many citizens grumbled over the level of services, Omaha—like other new western cities—overcame the worst of its problems, generally providing citizens with services comparable to those in the older portions of the land.

Andrew Rosewater, brother of *Bee* editor Edward Rosewater, was the most influential of Omaha's late-nineteenth-century city engineers. He played a major role in determining the quality of life in the community, representing the city in the building of the first waterworks and, starting in 1881, supervising construction of a sewage system. Rosewater followed plans—with some modifications—for "separate systems," intended to separate sewage from storm runoff. George Waring Jr., the leading American sanitary expert of the day, advocated this approach. Rosewater supervised the construction of a $1 million system of sixty-nine miles of storm and sanitary sewers. When rapid growth overwhelmed the sanitary parts of the system, Rosewater changed the basic design, adopting a plan of building large trunk sewers with lateral branches. Abandoning separate systems worked reasonably well, solving Omaha's sewage problems until well into the twentieth century.

Unlike many contemporaries, Rosewater saw a direct connection between sewers and streets. Following 1883, he directed a comprehensive program of street improvements. Within a few years, Omaha had forty-four miles of pavement, mainly asphaltum, Colorado sandstone, Sioux Falls granite, and wooden blocks. Even though a local leader exaggerated in claiming that by 1889 Omaha had a reputation as having some of the better thoroughfares in the United States, there had been a considerable improvement over the previous sorry state of affairs. Rosewater was in the vanguard of a nation-wide movement that saw sanitary engineers take the lead in the professionalization of city management. He followed the policies and practices advocated by early national organizations in the field. This led to a somewhat uniform approach: a faith that technology would solve the problems associated with urban growth. The efforts of Rosewater and his colleagues generally went unrecognized; politicians took credit for the improvements and blamed bureaucrats for mistakes. Few Omahans thought of Rosewater when they flushed toilets or drove down paved streets, unaware of his considerable contribution.

In Council Bluffs, the development of water service by 1883 followed a pattern similar to that in Omaha. Water was drawn from the Missouri River into two settling basins, after which it was pumped to a Fairmount Park reservoir. From this high elevation, it was distributed through mains that by 1889 totaled over thirty miles. By then, 252 hydrants were at the disposal of a fire department that in 1883 had passed from volunteer to professional status.

Council Bluffs began paving its main streets in 1884 and within five years had completed some fifteen miles of such work. A booster book in 1889 declared, "In Broadway, which is paved to the Missouri river, we have one of the finest drives in the United States." Granite blocks composed some of the surfacing, but cedar blocks, which did not prove durable, were more commonly used. Additional improvements included extensive street grading and the installation of curbing, but rain sometimes carried heavy deposits of silt from the bluffs onto the paved streets.

Omaha's street railway system developed without a master plan. In 1867 the territorial legislature granted a fifty-year franchise to the Omaha Horse Railway Company, incorporated by a large number of local businessmen. The firm, prohibited from using steam power, soon had two miles of track in operation, all along a main street. From the first, the line barely made operating expenses. The cars, which ran every twenty-eight minutes when on schedule, were very slow owing to the poor condition of the roadway. Potential patrons found it easier to walk. The bulk of riders were stockholders and politicians, all of whom rode free. A drop in the fare from ten to five cents failed to attract new customers. To compound matters, the horse-car drivers, described as deaf and nearsighted by the press, passed by many potential users. The concern underwent several ownership changes and finally in 1878 was sold to the highest bidder for twenty-five thousand dollars at a sheriff's auction. The new owner extended the line, regularly cleaned the notoriously dirty cars and laid wooden planking between the tracks to improve the speed of service. In 1880 the line boasted impressive dimensions: five miles of tracks, ten cars, seventy horses, twenty employees, and 495,000 passengers annually. These statistics tended to hide the company's poor reputation, which would shortly result in drastic changes in transit services.

Public transportation was essential to the integration of the growing urban centers on both sides of the Missouri, and in 1868 the Council Bluffs city council granted a twenty-five-year franchise to seven local businessmen to operate the Broadway Street Railway. In 1870 the line commenced horse-car service from downtown along the city's principal thoroughfare, Broadway, to the Chicago and North Western depot and on to the river. At the last point, a ferry, the *H. C. Nutt*, provided transportation to Omaha, while during winter one could reach Omaha by crossing the ice or using a temporary pile bridge. Transitional weather made cross-river travel precarious. In 1872 the Council Bluffs horse-car line was extended southward from downtown to the Transfer Grounds where it connected to the Union Pacific's Dummy Train that ran over the Missouri River bridge to the Omaha depot. The Dummy Trains not only handled transfers of through passengers between railroads; they greatly facilitated routine travel between Council Bluffs and Omaha. This travel became easier in 1883 when the Union Pacific extended its dummy route to downtown Council Bluffs. In the meantime, another extension of the Council Bluffs horse-car line provided service between downtown and other railroad depots. The advent of these transportation innovations did not spell the immediate end of the use of horse-drawn omnibuses and ferry service.

An increase in the size of Omaha from twelve to twenty-four square miles in 1887, as a result of the first annexation since 1869, created opportunities for the expansions of transit lines. The Omaha Horse Railway Company added routes that for a time were identified by the red, green, and yellow color of their cars. Mules were added as motive power. In 1882 service intervals varied from ten to twenty minutes, depending upon the route, but horse cars sometimes served the railroad station every two and one-half minutes.

In 1884 city voters approved a franchise for the Cable Tramway Company, which began operation in December 1887. The Omaha Horse Railway refused to cooperate with its new rival, but when both firms were confronted with the prospect of competition from electric streetcars, they merged in January 1889 to form the Omaha Street Railway. The new company operated twenty-seven miles of horse-car lines and nine miles of cable-car routes. Although cable cars were popular, the combination wire and hemp cables that pulled them were costly and wore out quickly. Cable-car service proved short-lived, ending in January 1895.

A huge step toward further cross-river integration began in 1886 with the incorporation of the Omaha and Council Bluffs Bridge Company. The firm contemplated building a street-traffic bridge and establishing electric streetcar service between the cities. With the blessing of the Council Bluffs city council and federal approval of the interstate bridge, the company went forward. Although Council Bluffs residents approved a tax levy for the project and local entrepreneurs invested in it, a large portion of the capital came from Britain. Progress in building the bridge linking Douglas Street in Omaha and Broadway in Council Bluffs was rapid and electric illumination enabled workers to continue work at night. On October 30, 1888, with much festivity, the toll bridge was opened, having a span of 3,200 feet and approaches totaling 2,500 feet. As the bridge neared completion, the Omaha and Council Bluffs Bridge Company purchased the Council Bluffs horse-car line and converted it to an electric system. After start-up problems, the company began regular operation in December 1888, including service to the end of the bridge in Omaha. In a situation that would be characteristic of the long-term relationship between Council Bluffs and its offspring on the west bank, Council Bluffs businesses soon lamented the loss of trade to Omaha.

Electric streetcar service in Omaha was the outgrowth of the incorporation in 1887 of the Omaha Motor Railway. The firm struggled with the Omaha Street Railway Company for the use of public thoroughfares. Under the leadership of Dr. Samuel D. Mercer, Omaha Motor Railway developed its initial system. Service on two lines began in late July 1889, and by this time cars from Council Bluffs were making a loop through downtown Omaha. The Omaha Motor Company and the Omaha Street Railway, which was starting electric streetcar operations, soon merged, taking the name of the latter firm. The last horse-car route in the city ceased operations in June 1895.

Public transportation was at once a response to and a stimulus for urban and suburban development. In 1887 a real-estate boom highlighted Omaha's rapid growth and also marked the beginnings of suburban development with Erastus Benson's projection of a community northwest of the city that would bear his name. Lots in Benson sold quickly, and Benson and his associates planned a street railway linking the new town to Omaha via the old Military Road.

The proliferation of transit lines in the Council Bluffs–Omaha area, either real or projected, was chaotic. The whole business greatly confused and frustrated passengers. Doubtless many hoped that someone would take advantage of an 1889 measure passed by the Nebraska legislature providing for consolidation. Nothing happened until Gurdon W. Wattles in the late 1890s purchased controlling interests in the Omaha Street Railway and a new line that was developing on both sides of the river. In December 1902 the various lines in the two cities were consolidated under the Omaha and Council Bluffs Street Railway Company in a transaction that brought the firm under eastern financial control. From 1906, until his retirement as its president in 1919, Wattles would be the key figure in the traction company's operation. He later wrote that he pushed for consolidation after making a bad business decision. He said he bought a street railway on the assumption that he would make a fortune in real estate by laying tracks into developing parts of town where he already owned property. Wattles soon realized that he should have put his money into depressed downtown real estate. However, once committed, and faced with the drain of running a street railway upon which he had never expected to make money, he reluctantly promoted the creation of a single system, hoping to salvage something out of his investment. There were no politics involved; the legislative groundwork had been laid over a decade earlier.

Indeed, Wattles, whatever his actual motives, found himself hailed as a community benefactor. Few persons in Omaha paid much attention to the ramifications of the gigantic local traction merger; all they wanted was better service, which was what they received. The new company gave Greater

Omaha a comprehensive transportation system that comprised 140 miles of track and over 1,500 employees. The importance of streetcar transportation is found in the fact that in 1907 the Omaha and Council Bluffs Street Railway Company collected fares for 40,400,744 passenger trips and issued 10,865,585 transfers. At the time of its inception, it seemed to be a model of free enterprise and a public-spirited solution to a serious problem—a view that would change markedly in later years.

In many parts of the country, the early years of the twentieth century brought a wave of construction of interurban electric streetcar lines. Residents of South Omaha, East Omaha, Benson, and the new western suburb of Dundee traveled by trolley cars to and from Omaha. Northward extension of the streetcar system helped make the old town of Florence part of the greater urban area. Then, in 1909, came the opening of a line running south from Council Bluffs to the Iowa School for the Deaf. In 1906 a subsidiary of the Omaha and Council Bluffs Street Railway linked Bellevue and the adjoining army post, Fort Crook, to South Omaha and Omaha. Although more ambitious interurban routes were projected, the only other line to be built in the Greater Omaha area was that of the Nebraska Traction and Power Company, which connected Omaha and South Omaha to the southwestern towns of Ralston and Papillion in 1911.

As was true in other urban areas, the streetcar system expanded the recreational horizons of the residents of Council Bluffs and Omaha. A Missouri River flood in the spring of 1881 formed an oxbow lake south of Council Bluffs. Eventually, local people recognized the recreational potential of this body of water, known as Lake Manawa, and a few built homes nearby. In 1888 a steam rail line began service between Council Bluffs and the lake. Over the years small steamboats and other craft transported visitors across the lake to the Manhattan Beach, and the owner of the rail line developed other entertainment facilities. Following the bankruptcy of the steam line, electric trolley service to Lake Manawa started in 1900, a change that helped make the lake an easier destination for Omahans. In the meantime, a trolley line to Courtland Beach on Cut-Off Lake (Carter Lake) did much to make it a summertime recreational option for thousands of people. By 1901 streetcars were carrying crowds to Krug Park, an amusement park on the east side of Benson, but persons who favored more serene and sylvan settings could travel by streetcar to various city parks, such as Omaha's Hanscom Park or

Fairmount Park in Council Bluffs. Almost one-half of the streetcars were open-sided, providing fresh air during the summer, while the rest of the cars had some form of heating.

Obtaining adequate lighting was complicated by rapid technological change. The Omaha Gas Manufacturing Company, granted a fifty-year franchise by the city council, started operations in November 1869. In the spring of 1870, the Council Bluffs city council granted permission to the Council Bluffs Gas Company to install mains to distribute gas for business, residential, and street lighting. The firm was authorized to charge up to $4.50 per one thousand cubic feet for its product made from British coal. In Omaha the gas company soon gained a reputation for terrible service. It used such cheap coal that one year the gas gave out at dusk an average of three times a week. This enraged Omahans, and at one time the works had less than two hundred commercial and residential customers. Only the supplying of gas to a hundred street lamps (a status symbol among growing cities of the time) prevented bankruptcy. Conditions gradually improved; by 1880 the plant produced thirty thousand cubic feet daily, charging consumers $3.50 per one thousand cubic feet, which was in line with national averages for cities in Omaha's class. The firm's retorts produced nine hundred thousand cubic feet every day in the 1890s and more than double that amount by World War I; but by then, the gas works sold hardly any illuminating gas.

On January 26, 1883, Omaha began to enter the age of electrical lighting when a number of businesses in the heart of the city were illuminated, initially from 6:00 to 10:00 p.m. In Council Bluffs, the Pilcher Electric Light Company began tentative operations late in 1883, but it was four years before the city inaugurated electric lighting of streets. Initially arc lamps on seven high towers illuminated key areas of the city. By 1900 the Council Bluffs Gas and Electric Company also provided power for another 125 arc lamps for this purpose. Businesses used 25 more arc lights while 2,500 incandescent bulbs exorcised darkness. Frisby L. Rasp, a Nebraska farm youth studying at the Omaha Business College in 1888, probably captured the sense of awe that anyone from the countryside would have experienced in a city during this time of rapid technological change. Writing home, he said, "I was down to the eclectric [*sic*] light plant and saw the largest engine I ever saw in my life. The balance wheel was half under the floor and what stuck up was over 10 feet high. 16 motors were running. The eclectric lights are the nicest I ever saw. I went up in an elevator this evening, the first thing of the kind I ever saw."

Indeed, during the 1880s Omaha acquired a number of electric plants. The Union Pacific electrified its station; a hotel had its own generating plant. The gas company built a power station, converting the street lights from gas to electricity. In 1903 after the perfection of dynamos and distributing systems, the Thomson-Houston Company, an early Omaha electricity producer, gained control of all the small competing companies in Omaha. Monopoly had become an accepted practice in the industry; and Omahans took that and electric lights for granted, as indications of continued progress.

The telephone added a new dimension to Omaha's role as a communication center. The first phone call in Nebraska came in 1877 when two telephone pioneers, L. H. Korty and J. J. Dickey, spoke to each other over a line between Omaha and Council Bluffs. The two men strung a number of private lines in Omaha before the establishment of an exchange. In 1880 the Omaha Electric Company had 179 miles of wire and an estimated annual net income of four thousand dollars. Many problems needed solving. Early switchboards were large and cumbersome, and transmission lines frequently broke. As with most innovations, initial costs to consumers were quite high. The first subscribers were professional persons, commercial establishments, and a few wealthy individuals. Frequently, physicians had direct lines to drugstores. During the 1890s, when the initial patents expired, the telephone business temporarily became more competitive. Some people in Omaha believed that telephones would never have anything more than specialized purposes. After a successful Omaha storekeeper sold his establishment to work for a phone company, friends said he had made a serious error, arguing that the bulk of commercial pursuits would always be carried by mail or word of mouth. Thirty years later he headed the Northwestern Bell Telephone Company, which served 640,000 patrons and had 11,000 employees.

The evolution of protective services represented another important element in the rise of Omaha. The fire department moved rapidly from a volunteer to professional status following a disaster. On September 4, 1878, the five-story Grand Central Hotel, a symbol of community aspirations, caught fire in the early evening hours. A workman apparently had kicked over a candle on an upper floor during a renovation project. After the ringing of the fire bell, tragic errors followed. Five firemen died when they went onto upper floors that were obviously in danger of collapse. Only the arrival of firefighters from Council Bluffs prevented the burning of Omaha's downtown. After the catastrophe, viewed by thousands of persons, the fire chief lost his job. By 1880 Omaha had phased out all except one of its volunteer units. The backbone of the reorganized force consisted of an authorized unit of sixteen professional firemen, who manned four engines, including a hook and ladder. From the 1880s onward, despite an occasional terrible fire, the Omaha Fire Department enjoyed a good local reputation.

The police department had trouble overcoming the taint of corruption. By the 1880s, Omaha's force consisted of eighteen patrolmen and a chief called a city marshal. "All policemen, including the marshal," an observer claimed, "were appointed by the mayor, subject to confirmation by the city council, and it being no unusual thing to have an entire new police force following the election of a new mayor and council, as the police force was the reward of the faithful ward heelers, regardless of physical, intellectual or moral fitness for the position; in fact, it was but a political football." In 1887 the state, in a controversial move that ran counter to prevailing national trends toward home rule, took control of the Omaha police, establishing a police board appointed by the governor. This brief innovation resulted for a short time in better police, but frequent changes in the state-appointed board led to demoralization inside the department. Most appointees were political discards or businessmen interested only in the title of commissioner. Favoritism and political regularity rather than competence became the criteria for hirings, promotions, and dismissals. The "moral squad" decided what was corrupt and what was not. The only consolation was a general belief that circumstances were probably about the same in other emerging cities.

The motto of the Omaha Board of Health, "In time of peace prepare for war," had little relationship to reality. A formally constituted board, which had been created by the council in 1871, had minimal authority. An 1878 reorganization made the board more efficient on paper. It included the mayor, the president of the council, and the city marshal. Annual expenditures totaled $240, hardly enough to carry on a comprehensive program. There was no full-time investigator. The only board member with police powers was the mayor. There was no special program concerning the inspection and correction of nuisances. The city did not own an isolation hospital. Except for minor outbreaks of smallpox, cholera, diphtheria, and malaria, Omaha remained relatively free of epidemic disease in the nineteenth century. This was more good luck than anything else. In the 1880s even after authorities devoted more attention to cleaning streets, heaps of decaying vegetation and large ponds of stagnant water accumulated in the river bottoms during summer months. About the best that could be said was that most other communities in the country were equally negligent in spending money on public health.

Omaha did not have a coordinated welfare system. The city ran a poor farm, and occasionally, the council appropriated small amounts of money for relief. Church and voluntary organizations aided their needy members. Several hospitals maintained charity wards. Some factory owners, during periods of layoffs, felt an obligation to provide food baskets for loyal employees. Various private agencies augmented the welfare picture. Three national societies that operated in Omaha, the Young Men's Christian Association, the Young Women's Christian Association, and the Salvation Army, carried on a wide variety of activities. Several local groups had specialized functions. For example, the Omaha City Mission and the Nebraska Society for the Prevention of Cruelty to Children and Animals concentrated on helping abused and underprivileged children. Unwed mothers received aid from the Child Saving Institute and the Home of the Good Shepherd. The Rescue Home Association attempted to reform prostitutes. While in some instances wealthy citizens accepted welfare obligations—the Omaha Women's Club played an important role in founding the Visiting Nurses Association of Omaha—there was no general outpouring of support for welfare causes. Most unfortunates were left to fend for themselves. During the depression years of the 1890s, countless thousands took the clearest course open to them. They moved away from Omaha.

EDUCATION

Omaha schools received considerably more attention. The rapid growth of the city necessitated an almost yearly expansion of the public-school system, and voters responded by passing the bond issues to finance school construction. A harbinger of progress was a $250,000 high school completed in 1872 on Capitol Hill, the former site of the old state house. The four-story building contained seventeen classrooms, four large recitation halls, small offices, commodious library facilities, four apparatus rooms, and quarters for a janitor. Each of the classrooms had a capacity of fifty-five students. The spire was

390 feet above the Missouri River, making the school easily the most visible landmark in Omaha. In 1883 five full-time instructors had the responsibility of teaching 140 students, the vast majority of them males. Few students were diligent about pursuing a curriculum that had little relevance to life on the Middle Border; it included physiology, astronomy, Latin, and moral philosophy. Sometimes there was retribution for a lack of studiousness, as a girl who neglected her lessons discovered. "Yes, I did have a jolly time skating and playing and thinking my wits would carry me through," she wrote. "They didn't, and I paid for my fun by making up my lessons so I could go on to graduate with my class." Part of the problem with a lax attitude toward schoolwork lay at the primary level. Overworked and undertrained teachers in the elementary schools frequently had to instruct several grades in the same room. Small Roman Catholic and Episcopalian primary schools augmented the public system.

Only one of several plans to establish a university succeeded. In 1878 a fifty-thousand-dollar bequest from the will of Mary Creighton, widow of telegraph builder Edward Creighton, led to the establishment of Creighton College. Under the leadership of Father Michael Dowling the Jesuit institution, originally a preparatory school, admitted its first college class in 1887. Philanthropist John Creighton, brother of Edward, placed the school on a firm financial foundation by giving $2 million in cash, donating land, and building a medical school. The state of education, after a sorry start in the early years, was a further indication of Omaha's modernization.

In 1870 the opening of a high school in Council Bluffs marked an advance for that city's eleven-year-old public-school system. By 1900 the system had eighteen schools with an average attendance of 4,132 students taught by 125 teachers. As a booster supplement to the *Nonpareil* noted that year, "the average compensation of teachers per month is: males, $110.91; females, $54.62," a disparity hardly limited to its time and place. Two Catholic academies added to the educational options, while the Iowa School for the Deaf was a notable landmark on the city's southern outskirts.

CITY AND REGION: AK-SAR-BEN

As in any city, a host of organizations, ranging from national groups such as the Masons, the Moose, the Elks, the Grand Army of the Republic, and the Women's Christian Temperance Union to local organizations like the Commercial Club and the Omaha Club reflected the diverse interests of Omaha's residents. Ethnic organizations such as the Danish Brotherhood, the Hibernians, the Czech Sokols, and the German Turnverein showed the cosmopolitan character of the city. A fraternal insurance group, the Woodmen of the World, was founded in Omaha in 1890.

The society that had the most lasting impact was the Knights of Ak-Sar-Ben. Founded in 1895, it had both economic and social purposes. An Ak-Sar-Ben secretary wrote,

> The organization was the result of an admitted need of stimulus and was designed to promote patriotism among the citizens, advertise the city and create a friendly feeling among neighbors. At the annual ball, the crowning social event of the year, one of the members of the board of governors is crowned "King" and a young society woman "Queen." . . . During carnival week. . . . one hundred thousand people or more come to Omaha to witness the gorgeous parades and partake in the festivities.

Ak-Sar-Ben epitomized the booster spirit that infected the Midwest after the end of the frontier. It also was an indication of a growing stability and recognition of Omaha's interdependence with its trade area.

TOWARD THE "CITY BEAUTIFUL"

Parks served as another sign of progress. Omaha was fortunate that in 1872 two civic leaders, Andrew J. Hanscom and James G. Megeath, donated seventy-three acres for a park. Hanscom Park became a showpiece: "The circular drives, the shady nooks, the tables and seats, and the dancing platform, large enough to accommodate about twelve sets, combine to make it the largest picnic ground anywhere to be found in this vicinity," a reporter for the *Omaha Bee* claimed in 1874. Numerous improvements made over the following decade and a half, some supervised by city engineer Rosewater, enhanced the park's beauty and usefulness. There were two lakes, a waterfall, extensive flower beds, macadamized roadways, fountains, and magnificent stands of trees, plus a pavilion, bandstand, and greenhouse. In 1891 a four-hundred-thousand-dollar bond issue enabled the city to purchase more park land. Much of it, along with other parks acquired through the years remained unimproved, although one, Riverside Park, had a small zoo.

While Omaha did not have a comprehensive beautification plan, the board of park commissioners managed to acquire jurisdiction over a couple of boulevard streets. The board hired H. W. S. Cleveland, a prominent Minneapolis landscape architect, who devised a system of connected parks and boulevards that was partially implemented. In their 1898 report, the commissioners claimed that they needed more money to create systems on a par with those in other cities in the vanguard of the national "City Beautiful" movement. The commissioners believed that recent enthusiastic support for parks by property owners and improvement clubs bode well for the future: "We believe our work is generally approved. Those who criticize it will be found to be those who would have no parks at all, who never visit parks, and who really have the most need for the revivifying influence of a day in the parks." Certainly, there were firm foundations upon which to build.

Architecturally, Omaha experienced a boom that lasted from the late 1870s until the Panic of 1893. At the start of the upsurge, the *Bee* interviewed local architects about construction trends. One saw things from a narrow perspective, predicting that in order to remain competitive, store owners would have to pay more attention to the interiors of their establishments. Another, A. R. Dufrene, made thoughtful and broader observations: "There has been too much sameness. People would insist on having a house just like some other one. Now, although there is a decided tendency towards better styles, such as the Queen Anne and the Gothic, there is more room for good effects in these styles. . . . And this demand is not alone for dwellings, but also for stores. Patterned and colored bricks are now used in fronts with good effect." His statement applied to the homes of the affluent. His firm of Dufrene and Mendelsohn designed the three-story Fred Drexel residence built in 1884 at a commanding point above the Missouri River. The twenty-seven-thousand-dollar mansion was of English Gothic design. The exterior featured ornamental stone carvings and a porch running around the sides. The interior plan made elaborate use of wood finishings. In 1889 F. M. Ellis of Omaha designed the forty-thousand-dollar, twenty-five-room Henry W. Yates home, a three-story dwelling with a stone exterior and a slate roof. All the interior woodwork was solid with no veneer. It had four bathrooms and nine fireplaces. Few persons in Omaha could afford such opulent domiciles. Most of the thousands of homes built in the 1880s were the work of tract developers. The dwellings had the monotonous sameness that Dufrene hoped was past. They were wooden one- and two-story square or rectangular boxes of five to six rooms. Usually, carpenters planned them on the spot. It was small solace to professional architects that they resembled houses throughout the region.

DOWNTOWN

The large downtown buildings built during the time of expansion shaped Omaha's urban design for many decades to come. Public buildings, banking houses, business blocks, hotels, theaters, and offices showed architectural forms characteristic of Midwestern cities. The conspicuous new Douglas County Courthouse, built in 1882, was 140 feet from base to dome. Fireproof, it had dark marble-bordered corridors and elaborately finished iron stairways. The rectangular seven-story First National Bank of Omaha had a solid look that featured relatively clean lines. Boyd's Opera House seated 1,700 persons. Constructed in the Modern Renaissance style, it had a large stage capable of holding up to twenty sets of scenery. The regional headquarters of a prestigious eastern insurance company, the New York Life Building, was among the most imposing edifices in Omaha. A striking feature of the ten-story building, which had nearly four hundred rooms, was the entrance and rotunda. Two polished Norfolk pink granite pillars guarded the vestibule, which had floors of Lake Champlain marble, walls of Tennessee and French marble, and ceilings of gold and silver leaf. None of the hundreds of buildings in the central business district won any architectural prizes; but taken together, and lining the streets wall-to-wall, they gave Omaha a metropolitan appearance.

An important aspect of the construction activities involved the erection of jobbing houses in a five-block area on the east side of the downtown. The numerous warehouses in the area were great brooding beasts of buildings dedicated to commerce. A wide variety of items passed through them on the way to stores and dealers throughout a wide expanse of the country. The warehouses stood as monuments to the success of objectives stated in the 1881 report of the Omaha Board of Trade: "We are endeavoring to make Omaha the great distributing point of the extreme west, and as far as possible the depot of purchases of the northwest and southwest sections." By the nineties, this vision had become reality. Hundreds of "Knights of the grip"—salesmen—sold the products that served as the warehouse district's reason for being. Although the Panic of 1893 had dropped the annual value of sales by Omaha jobbers below the 1890 figure of $47,200,000, the economic recovery of the late nineties brought total sales of $62,500,000 in 1900. In many ways, the gray buildings helped to explain why Omaha experienced such rapid growth in a short span of time.

THE PEOPLE

One characteristic of Omaha in the last half of the nineteenth century was that it had a large floating and rapidly changing population. In 1860 it had an enumeration of 1,883, including 985 white males, 876 white females, 20 free colored, and 2 Indians. The number of persons in 1870 stood at 16,083. Of these, 9,763 were natives and 6,320 foreign born. Blacks totaled 446. Census figures for 1880 showed 30,518 inhabitants of Omaha. Females made up 44 percent, foreign born 33 percent, and blacks 3 percent. These percentages were in line with those for other communities in the urban West at the end of the frontier.

Omaha's listed population in 1890 was 140,452. Critics later claimed this represented a gigantic overenumeration of close to 38,000 people. They based their case on other indices such as school returns and tax rolls. The official returns cut two ways. In 1890 it suited the purposes of Omaha leaders to inflate returns; in 1900 following drastic losses—the census listed a populace of 102,555—it was in the interests of promoters to minimize losses by claiming mistakes had been made a decade earlier. A similar point has been made with respect to the populations of Lincoln and some smaller Nebraska cities.

Many factors besides the possibility of improperly conducted enumerations complicated conclusions in Omaha about the population. By law, census takers counted individuals in places where they were domiciled on the day of the enumeration. This meant missing thousands of railroad workers and drummers. No one systematically tallied inmates of saloons and houses of ill fame nor those in the hundreds of rooming houses near the railroad tracks. At any given time, there were thousands of transients in the city. The best that could be said was that the "official" population was mobile and volatile.

The attitude of ethnic and religious groups toward each other changed markedly as Omaha moved through the frontier period. In the beginning, there was considerable cooperation and an acceptance of the "meting pot."

Josie McCulloch, who grew up in Omaha in the 1870s and 1880s, had vivid memories of the early days: "In that neighborhood Swedish, Bohemian, Italian, Irish, and Negro children all contributed to the process of Americanization," she recalled.

By the 1890s things were different as local ethnic tensions rose in keeping with a national trend. The American Protective Association (APA), a national organization that was anti-Catholic and opposed certain forms of immigration, appeared in Omaha. Edward F. Morearty, a member of the city council, felt that the local APA was primarily a device to get individuals of Irish descent out of politics.

Whatever the tribulations of some Irish politicians, their plight hardly compared with that of George Smith, a black man. The 1880 census counted 881 African Americans in Omaha, but according to the 1890 enumeration, the city's black population had risen to 4,665. Although this figure was perhaps inflated, the number of blacks residing in Omaha had at least kept pace with the growth of the white population. On October 9, 1891, Smith was in jail, accused of the assault two days earlier of five-year-old Lizzie Yeates. The press assumed Smith's guilt, and stories suggested that lynching would be appropriate.

At noon on October 9, a convicted murderer was legally hanged inside walls erected adjacent to the Douglas County courthouse and jail. Anticipation of this event added to the excitement and seems to have inflamed the passion for revenge. Making matters worse, that evening the *Omaha Bee* reported that Lizzie had died, a story that proved untrue. As the evening wore on, a crowd gathered around the courthouse, but police efforts to avert mob action were minimal. Despite pleas from past and future governor James E. Boyd and other officials, the mob broke into the courthouse and with cold chisels and sledge hammers gained entrance to the maximum-security cell to which Smith had been taken. Outside, the fire department's efforts to disburse the mob, which may have numbered at least eight thousand persons, resulted only in slashed hoses. After midnight, Smith was dragged from the courthouse and was probably dead before he was hanged from a trolley wire. The electric arc street lamps, symbolic of nineteenth-century technological progress, ironically illuminated the barbarism of the autumn evening.

The next day, on orders from county attorney T. J. Mahoney, nine of the mob leaders were arrested and charged with first-degree murder. At this time, two men, one black, the other white, were in custody on separate murder charges. That night, a crowd again gathered around the courthouse, demanding freedom for the nine alleged leaders in the Smith lynching and the handing over of the black man. What the mob of some four thousand persons did not know was that a judge had already ordered the release of the nine individuals charged in the Smith case and that the authorities had quietly sent the two other men to the state penitentiary in Lincoln. When the jailer allowed a delegation of sober members of the gathering to enter the courthouse and verify that no one of interest to the mob was being detained, the crowd disbursed. Likewise, Mahoney's efforts in bringing those responsible for Smith's lynching to justice came to naught. As an early history of Omaha, published three years after the episode, declared, "The better element of the community deplored the resort to violence, but very few felt otherwise than that Smith was justly dealt with."

In Council Bluffs in January 1894, Leon W. Lozier, a white man, was accused of a crime similar to that which had doomed George Smith. Arrested in Omaha aboard a train, he was returned to Council Bluffs where the police, anticipating trouble, took him from the city lockup to the very durably built county jail. Still, a crowd estimated at two thousand persons assembled during the evening, with some members of the throng shouting their desire to lynch Lozier. One of the agitators was an African American man who exclaimed that if Lozier were black, he would have already been hanged. However, the sheriff and his deputies and the city police augmented by a military unit, the Dodge Light Guard, stood their ground, and the next morning the authorities quietly took Lozier off to safety. Perhaps more determined law enforcement and a smaller, less-determined mob standing outside on a January night contemplating the lynching of a white man saved Leon Lozier and Council Bluffs from the mob action that had occurred in Omaha just over two years earlier. Whatever the differing circumstances, both episodes demonstrated the volatile passions that could surface in the two cities and in other parts of the nation at the end of the nineteenth century.

Typical of cities outside the South in 1900, Omaha, South Omaha, and Council Bluffs all had large numbers of persons who were either foreign born or were first-generation Americans. Of Omaha's 102,555 residents, 23,552 were foreign born. The "Magic City" of South Omaha had grown from a reported population of 8,062 in 1890 to 26,001 in 1900, and in the latter year was home to 5,607 persons of foreign birth. Council Bluffs had grown steadily from 18,063 residents in 1880 to 21,474 in 1890 and 25,802 in 1900. According to the 1900 count, 3,723 foreign-born persons lived there. Typical of the Midwest, Germans were pervasive in all three communities, constituting the leading foreign-born group in Omaha (5,522) and South Omaha (1,228) and the number-two group in Council Bluffs (889). Austrians, Germans from Russia, and a few German Swiss enhanced the German cultural presence. The many Danes and Swedes, plus some Norwegians, gave Scandinavians as a group a high profile in Omaha (6,710 persons) and Council Bluffs (1,502) but relatively less prominence in South Omaha (811). Swedes were the second-ranking foreign-born group in Omaha (3,968) and ranked fourth and fifth in South Omaha (469) and Council Bluffs (314) respectively. Danes were the third most numerous foreign-born people in Omaha (2,430), but they easily outnumbered the Germans as the top group (1,109 persons) in Council Bluffs. However, comparatively few people (280) of Danish origin lived in South Omaha. Bohemians, the number-four group in Omaha (2,170), were the second-ranking group in South Omaha (1,113) but numbered only 17 persons in Council Bluffs. Fifth place in Omaha went to the Irish (2,164), who ranked third in both South Omaha (1,073) and Council Bluffs (386). Omaha and South Omaha had 595 and 323 Poles respectively, but Council Bluffs had only 4 persons of Polish birth. Despite their differences, the English-speaking people from Britain, Ireland, and Anglo-Canada, plus a handful of Australians, with a total of 5,480 persons, constituted nearly one-fourth of Omaha's foreign born in 1900 and more than one-fourth of the total in South Omaha (1,592) and Council Bluffs (1,023).

A further sense of ethnicity may also be gained by considering the numbers of persons born in the United States and having one or both parents born in another country. First-generation Americans, particularly from non–English-speaking backgrounds, probably reflected their parents' origins. Adding the numbers of foreign-born and first-generation Americans gives an overall sense of the ethnicity of a community. By this measure, the 1900 census revealed that 56,430 people in Omaha—55 percent of the city's population—were either foreign-born or one generation removed from another country. In South Omaha, 13,847 persons, or 53.3 percent of the city's population fit this category. Council Bluffs, less ethnically diverse than the neighboring Nebraska cities, still had 10,580 persons—41 percent of the total census count—who were foreign-born or first-generation Americans. Even though such nearby places as Lincoln; St. Joseph; and Kansas City, Missouri, and Kansas, had lower figures than Council Bluffs, the figures for Minneapolis, St. Paul, and Chicago were much higher than those for Omaha and South Omaha. In some New England mill towns, between 83 and 86 percent of the residents were immigrants or first-generation Americans. By contrast, immigration had generally bypassed the South. Fewer than 9 percent of the people in Atlanta, Knoxville, and Montgomery were in the combined category of foreign-born and first-generation American, while Nashville and Memphis had totals of 12.7 and 15.5 percent respectively.

Census takers in 1900 found 3,443 black persons living in Omaha, a figure that amounted to 3.35 percent of the city's population. Nearly 42 percent of them were concentrated in the downtown Third Ward, an area of inexpensive lodging. Almost 20 percent of Omaha's African Americans resided in what was then the Sixth Ward, an area north of downtown that later became the heart of the city's black population. Of the 571 blacks in South Omaha who composed 2.19 percent of that city's residents, males heavily outnumbered females, a fact that may have reflected the recent packing-house boom. In keeping with its tendency to less ethnic diversity, Council Bluffs had only 240 blacks, or less than 1 percent of the total population.

Religious affiliations in the three cities mirrored ethnic patterns. Persons of British American and Scandinavian origin were normally affiliated with Protestant denominations, while Germans might be either Protestant or Roman Catholic. With some exceptions, such as a minority of Czechs, people of central and eastern European origin were Catholic as was the growing number of Italians. The 1906 U.S. Census of Religious Bodies showed that 15,053 of Omaha's residents were communicants of the Roman Catholic Church. This figure, far and away the highest total for any denomination, was consistent with figures elsewhere, particularly in growing places that required unskilled laborers who were often part of the so-called new immigration from eastern and southern Europe. The largest Protestant denominations in Omaha were the Methodists (3,230), Presbyterians (3,205), Episcopalians (2,094), and Northern Baptists (1,923), churches that reflected the old-stock Anglo American heritage. The various Lutheran churches had a total of 2,235 members, organizations that had many communicants of German and Scandinavian background. The years around the turn of the century brought an increasing number of people from southeastern Europe to Omaha, as seen in the 1,500 Greek Orthodox communicants reported in 1906. Jewish congregations reported a membership of 335 heads of families, a total in keeping with the 1890 enumeration. Over the years, both orthodox and reform leaders worked to establish strong Hebrew assemblies, despite the relative small number of Omaha Jews.

South Omaha's religious pattern clearly reflected the fact that its labor-oriented economy attracted workers of Irish and eastern European origin and a significant number of blacks. The Roman Catholic Church had 5,684 communicants in South Omaha in 1906, while the principal Protestant denominations were the Presbyterians (728), Methodists (457, plus 71 members of the African Methodist Episcopal Church), the several Lutheran groups (410), Episcopalians (258), and Northern Baptists (249). There were also 400 members of the Greek Orthodox Church in the Magic City.

The lesser degree of ethnic diversity of Council Bluffs was reflected in the 1906 religious census. There, Roman Catholics numbered 2,162, followed by 998 Methodists, 749 Northern Baptists, 663 Presbyterians, 571 members of Lutheran congregations, 561 Disciples of Christ, 400 Episcopalians, and 353 Congregationalists. A comparison of the number of Roman Catholics to the total number of Protestants in Council Bluffs, Omaha, and South Omaha suggests striking cultural variations among the three cities. In Council Bluffs, Roman Catholics numbered over 31 percent, while in Omaha the figure was over 47 percent, and in South Omaha it was nearly 72 percent.

The ethnic diversity within the Roman Catholic Church became evident in the last decades of the nineteenth century. The downtown cathedral church of St. Philomena's reflected the strong position of the Irish in American Catholicism as did Holy Family Parish, established in 1876 to serve the many people of Irish background who lived north of downtown Omaha near the Union Pacific shops. Although the Irish were the dominant force within American Catholicism, the church was forced to address the needs of the large influx of Catholics from central, eastern, and southern Europe. The desire of German immigrants for their own parishes led to the creation of St. Mary Magdalene Church in 1868 and St. Joseph's Church in 1887. St. Wenceslaus Church was formed in 1877 to serve the Czech people who resided in the "Bohemian Town" or "Prague" area around South Thirteenth Street. In 1894 Assumption Church was established in South Omaha for Czechs who had previously worshipped at St. Agnes Church, an Irish parish. By this time, the Catholic Church was well along with a policy of establishing "national" parishes, a practice that would continue in later years.

In 1890 the first year that the federal government took what its experts considered a successful religious census, figures revealed that only 13 percent of Omaha's people were communicants of any faith. This was the lowest figure for any city west of the Mississippi River. By contrast, the total for San Francisco was 31 percent, for Kansas City 24 percent, and for Denver 31 percent. As in many other growing metropolises, the floating nature of Omaha's population obviously was part of the reason. Probably more important was the apparent padding of city's 1890 census, a figure that would have produced a significantly lower percentage of residents who were affiliated with a religious body. By comparison, the 1906 religious census, when compared to population estimates for that year, showed that some 27 percent of Omahans had a religious affiliation, compared to 34 percent for Kansas City, and 39 percent for Denver. A Council Bluffs figure above 28 percent in 1906 was probably high when taken as a percentage of the official 1910 census of population. By contrast, the 1906 religious census for South Omaha, compared to that city's population estimate, implied that fewer than 23 percent of the Magic City's people were church members. This probably understated the proportion of church members to South Omaha's actual population as indicated in the 1910 census. Given the time discrepancy between the population counts and the religious census, it is impossible to know exactly what proportion of the people of Greater Omaha were members of religious groups in any given year around the beginning of the twentieth century. Probably just over one-quarter of the total population held such affiliation, with minor variations among the three cities.

At the close of the nineteenth century, Omaha, South Omaha, and Council Bluffs composed one of the trans-Mississippi West's key urban areas. The rise of South Omaha in less than two decades justified the "Magic City" booster label, while during these years Omaha and Council Bluffs had grown dramatically in population and other indicators of development. To some extent, each community had, and would retain, its own identity; but railroads, other industrial and commercial interests, and a public-transportation system assured that Omaha, South Omaha, and Council Bluffs would continue to evolve as one urban area. The tangible signs of modernization and urban prominence were at every hand. Day and night in Omaha, huge presses spewed forth thousands of newspapers all destined for local and regional distribution. The sound of the printing machines competed with that of the streetcars that rumbled down the paved streets. Large buildings dominated the downtown landscape; throughout town church spires rose toward the heavens. Warehouses held goods and produce scheduled for distribution throughout the vast expanse of the American West. Thousands of houses stood on property that had been a few years earlier open country. Across the urban area, water and sewer lines, gas service, telephones, and electricity were further indications that the frontier had passed. Parks and boulevards attested to a growing interest in esthetic values and were tools of boosters who desired further urban growth. Of course, as the frontier ended, old problems remained unresolved and new ones appeared. Omaha was still a wide-open town by any definition, while South Omaha and Council Bluffs were hardly citadels of virtue. And, in Omaha there were the vexing issues raised by the activities of the APA and the vicious lynching of a black man. Some experts believed that the massive influx of foreigners created "Social Dynamite." As a new century dawned, that was a problem for people of all stations.

[Part IV] 1900-1930

[6] The Country's Center

Omaha entered the twentieth century as an important part of the American urban mosaic. A key gate of entry into the West, its packing plants served a national market. Behind lay the milestones that shaped the city: the capital fight, the quest to obtain the Union Pacific terminal, the machinations involved in gaining the Missouri River bridge, the manipulations that brought in the Chicago packers, and the glories of the Trans-Mississippi Exposition. The city had survived depressions, dry weather, population losses, and insect infestations. Every setback had been followed by a sudden advance, and Omaha emerged as a regional metropolis.

Council Bluffs was part of Omaha's suburban ring, which included the factory center of South Omaha, the residential community of Benson, the old Mormon camp of Florence, and the fashionable village of Dundee. Former challengers—Bellevue, Plattsmouth, and Nebraska City—had lost in significance. Bellevue's most notable features were a small college and a new army post, Fort Crook. Although Plattsmouth, a county seat, prospered from its Burlington Railroad shops, it had lost the Burlington headquarters for the trans-Missouri region to Omaha. Nebraska City was a county seat with some industry and a good agricultural base. The rapid growth of Lincoln as a prosperous capital and university city of over forty thousand by 1900 afforded Omaha excellent commercial and cultural opportunities. Other Nebraska cities added luster to Omaha's urban crown: Grand Island, North Platte, and Columbus. Omaha continued to enjoy a special relationship with Denver and to exploit connections in Sioux City, Sioux Falls, and Rapid City. The opening of the Northwest held promise of new ties. "Omaha is awake, alert and reaching out eagerly for new business," a report by a local commercial organization declared. "The businessmen of the city are heartily co-operating in efforts to extend Omaha's trade and to make this city the most important commercial and industrial center of the west."

Indeed, as the twentieth century began, Omaha, excluding the separate municipality of South Omaha, was the fourth-largest city in the trans-Missouri West. Omaha's population of 102,555 trailed far behind that of the West's largest city, San Francisco, which counted 342,782 persons in 1900, and Kansas City, Missouri (163,752), but compared more favorably with Denver (133,859). Although the 1900 census showed Los Angeles trailing Omaha by only 76 persons, Omaha had far more residents than Houston (44,633), and over twice the number of people in Dallas (42,638) and Fort Worth (26,688) combined. In fact, Council Bluffs and South Omaha with populations of 25,802 and 26,001 respectively, were each well ahead of such places as San Jose (21,500), San Diego (17,700), Tucson (7,531), and Phoenix (5,544). Los Angeles would surge far past Omaha by 1910, heralding the rise of the "Sun Belt" cities, but the burgeoning of population of much of the Sun Belt east to Florida would come later. With some reason Omaha boosters in the early twentieth century Omaha touted their city's regional importance.

Between 1900 and 1910, a "Golden Age" of agriculture in Nebraska boded well for Omaha. The years of trial that accompanied early settlement appeared over, but not all indicators reflected the optimistic aspect of the changed conditions. Nebraska's population only advanced from 1.1 million to 1.2 million, almost all as a result of urban growth. The most significant agricultural increase came in the northwestern Sandhills after federal legislation enlarged homestead land grants. Throughout the state, mortgage debts and farm tenancy rose sharply. Even so, changing production patterns, coupled with growing knowledge about the capability of Nebraska farming, led to an era of progress and prosperity. The initial phase of agricultural experimentation had ended on the northern Plains.

Steady agrarian progress characterized the first decade of the new century in the Cornhusker State. The listed value of farm property jumped from $748 million to $2.1 billion. Farm buildings and land per acre rose in value from $19.31 to $49.95. Livestock valuations enlarged from $145 million to $222 million. Increased mechanization, labor-saving techniques, and the introduction of new crops helped improve productivity and profits. Development of a serum for hog cholera helped to almost double swine production. The introduction of alfalfa as a major forage crop and a rapid move to winter wheat production were crucial developments. These and other advances came during a lucky ten years. Adequate rainfalls—except for 1907 the annual mean was 22.84 inches—led to a succession of good crop yields, coming when the market was in a generally upward spiral. Wheat prices went up 67 percent, corn 140 percent, and hogs 133 percent. In keeping with the high returns, cattle on the Nebraska plains peaked at over three million.

Good times in agriculture spelled opportunity for Omaha and Council Bluffs. Omaha interests sought new gains through the organization of the Omaha Grain Exchange. As the largest city in southwestern Iowa, Council Bluffs was an important trade and service center for the surrounding farms and small communities.

THE NEW UNION PACIFIC

The resurgence of the Union Pacific Railroad was a primary cause of optimism. The railroad fell into desperate straits following exposures of corruption and the administration of Jay Gould. The reform-minded president of the railroad, Charles Francis Adams Jr., told congressional investigators that speculators intended to loot the road and leave behind "two rusty streaks of iron on an old roadbed." After a period of receivership, a brilliant capitalist picked up the road and made it not only an integral but a successful part of the American economic system. The person responsible for the change was a man few except insiders noticed before he acquired the Union Pacific. He was E. H. Harriman, a small and unobtrusive individual with a moustache. There was a temptation to write him off as just another office clerk, which was what he had been at the start of his career in Hempstead, New York. Such a view would have ignored his ability to evaluate and acquire railroad properties. Without fanfare, he had made a fortune dealing in railroad stocks and gained the backing of powerful New York banking interests. In 1900 after two years of purchasing common issues in the Union Pacific at relatively low prices, he acquired control of the railroad. Given the road's history, there was a tendency to equate Harriman with the previous management—either as a "crooked renegade" or a "do good reformer"; he was much more. He wanted to consolidate western roads into vast monopolistic combinations, and he thought of improving service. His policies, which challenged those of the federal government, directly aided the Omaha business community.

Harriman's first step in his campaign to create a western railroad empire was to revive the moribund Union Pacific. Through his financial connections, he had the necessary money to make extensive physical improvements.

Furthermore, he determined to plow any initial profits back into the railroad, a policy that in the long term served stockholder interests. His engineers replaced light rails, widened embankments, rebuilt roadbeds, reduced grades and curves, and improved trestles. To upgrade passenger service, Harriman built dozens of new stations, including Omaha's new depot, added modern rolling stock, and ran trains on time. Double tracks and the institution of block signals improved safety standards. The changes allowed for the introduction of heavier and more powerful locomotives, greatly improving hauling capacities per unit. As these policies went ahead, Harriman set about reacquiring auxiliary lines, many of which were still in receivership. When he took control of the Union Pacific, the former eight-thousand-mile system had been reduced to the main line from Omaha to Ogden, the division from Kansas City to Cheyenne, and three hundred miles of branches. In a short time Harriman regained the suddenly profitable agricultural feeders, leaving old Colorado mining roads, called "suckers," to fend for themselves.

With the Union Pacific secure, Harriman quickly broadened his horizons by buying the six-thousand-mile Southern Pacific Railroad. In a single stroke he became one of America's men of power. Through complicated manipulations, Harriman also moved into the Northwest, taking over the Oregon Short Line and the Oregon Railroad and Navigation Company. He operated these roads, plus the Southern Pacific and the Union Pacific, as a single unified line: the closest thing yet to a western railroad monopoly. Even though Harriman was temporarily checked by the famous antitrust case, *Northern Securities Co. v. United States* (1904), he remained the nation's greatest railroad baron. Undismayed by the setback, he went right on acquiring railroad stock, gaining a dominant voice in the management of the Illinois Central Railroad. His rise had great implications for Omaha. The Union Pacific had achieved its promise, emerging as a significant force in American economic life.

Harriman's critics argued that he used unscrupulous tactics in the daily operations of the Union Pacific Railroad. Just as other railroad owners did, he gave free passes to politicians, rebates to favored shippers, and freight differentials to large producers. He continued the policy of long and short hauls, under which big interests received lower rates for thousand-mile hauls than individual farmers did for ones of a hundred miles. When pressed he retorted with a standard line followed by his colleagues; he did not like discriminatory practices but had to resort to them in order to compete. People who had no choice except to ship on his tracks found it very difficult to accept such a rationalization.

Dislike of the Union Pacific throughout Nebraska continued well after the death of the Populist movement. About the only place in the state where the road had any support was in Omaha. Even though competition continued between the Union Pacific and the Southern Pacific in regional parts of the system, more through business went via Omaha than ever before. Certain railroads in which Harriman had holdings, notably the Illinois Central, stopped soliciting transcontinental business from other routes. This helped Omaha, as did increased activities in the shops and the headquarters. Then, too, Omaha business leaders ultimately made money from the road's increased profitability. When Harriman died suddenly in 1909, he was in the eyes of many Americans a malefactor of great wealth. He was a transitional figure in railroading and a bridge between rugged individuals like Jay Gould and such corporate bankers as J. P. Morgan.

AFTER THE PIONEER LEADERS

Omaha's business leadership also underwent a transition. Two towering figures, William A. Paxton and John A. Creighton, passed away in 1907. Paxton was a prime example of the unbridled self-determination that helped to build the city in its first half century. The muleskinner turned capitalist had been involved in everything from wholesale groceries to real estate. A mover in the establishment of the stockyards and of South Omaha, he was essentially his own man in spite of a talent for organizing syndicates. He was not averse to taking unfair advantage of business opponents, and he knew how to drive hard bargains. A rough-talking man, he was willing to use whatever tactics necessary to achieve his ends.

Creighton, honored as a papal count, was a former overland freighter turned financier. For over twenty-five years he managed extensive family properties and made a great deal of money through his own business affairs. His Montana mining holdings brought large returns, as did his Omaha real-estate investments and speculations. His principal position was that of president of the First National Bank of Omaha. Like Paxton, he helped make Omaha a livestock and packing center. Unlike his colleague, he was a devout Roman Catholic with a social conscience. He gave liberal portions of his fortune to Omaha institutions. Of particular note were donations of hundreds of thousands of dollars to St. Joseph's Hospital and to Creighton University. Privately, he assisted numerous worthy charities and individuals. He received many honors from Catholic organizations, including a Laetare medal awarded by Notre Dame University. When the white-bearded Creighton died at age seventy-five in 1907, he was among the most revered men in town. He and Paxton represented contrasting styles of business leadership. One, a hard driver of the William Rockefeller mold, saw no reason to share his money with anyone. The other, like Andrew Carnegie, believed that he had an obligation to use wealth to advance society. Whether the two Omaha business pioneers were "Industrial Statesmen" or "Robber Barons" remained a moot question, although no one disputed their contribution to the raising up of the city.

As Omaha historian Garneth Peterson has said, these pioneer leaders were "Omaha's ground floor men." By contrast, she described their successors as "Organization Men" who represented changing local and national realities:

> The 1890s and the turn of the century made way for a new, twentieth century leader who reflected the increasing organization of American life. These new leaders recognized by the community were men who assumed civic responsibility with a sense of "noblesse oblige"—who offered their superior leadership skills to boost their personal images along with that of their community.

Gurdon W. Wattles typified the organization man. The former Iowa banker, who did such a successful job of running the Trans-Mississippi Exposition, was a leader for the twentieth century. He had all the right credentials to direct Omaha's fortunes in the postfrontier era: humble beginnings, outstanding ability, a fine intellect, impeccable manners, driving ambition, and a ruthless streak. Wattles had the skill of being able to define complex problems, to reach solutions, to organize the means to carry things out, and to bring affairs through to a satisfactory conclusion. He enjoyed reading books and had a more scholarly bent than many of his contemporaries. His second wife was a professor of home economics at the University of Nebraska, and he considered it a great honor that Iowa State College awarded him an honorary degree. Wattles belonged to just about every social organization in

Omaha; he saw the value of such connections in building a career. In 1905 in an elaborate ritual viewed by thousands of fellow townspeople, he was crowned King of Ak-Sar-Ben. Prior recipients of the annual award received their titles in recognition of civic contributions and social connections. In Wattles's case, it seemed an official coronation.

Wattles was head of the state commission that had responsibility over the Nebraska exhibition at the 1904 World's Fair in St. Louis; a moving picture he commissioned extolling the state's economic development received wide acclaim. A few years later, in 1908 and 1909, Wattles was president of the National Corn Exposition, a regional show designed to publicize the role of Omaha as a grain center. Serving as a delegate to the 1904 Republican National Convention, he was not an extreme partisan. During World War I he served a Democratic president, Woodrow Wilson, as food administrator of Nebraska. Promotional and political activities advanced Wattles's business fortunes. His growing banking interests allowed him to branch out in other directions. In 1913 he built the Fontenelle Hotel, which quickly became an Omaha landmark. His skill at consolidating businesses had served him well when he organized the Omaha and Council Bluffs Street Railway Company. Included in the responsibility of running a transportation monopoly was the task of dealing with labor. Here, Wattles refused to compromise. Indeed, he took such a hard line in favor of the rights of management that it hurt his standing in Omaha.

Labor troubles had steadily increased as the city became more industrialized. In the 1880s and 1890s the governor had sent militia into Omaha during smelting, railroad, and packing-house labor disputes. Sometimes the workers won limited victories. Employees of the Omaha and Grant Smelting and Refining Works gained an eight-hour day and higher wages as a result of the 1891 walkout. More often the strikers lost. In 1894 the packing companies, helped by six companies of militia and by strikebreakers, swiftly broke a strike by beef butchers. By the early twentieth century packing workers had unionized, greatly furthering their bargaining position. They won pay increases during an 1898 stoppage and achieved another round of raises five years later through strike threats. By 1903 unions had made much headway in Omaha, especially in the buildings trades, and the future of local collective bargaining seemed bright.

The formation in 1903 of an Omaha Business Men's Association (BMA) marked the start of a collective effort to maintain the open shop as a counterweight to unionization. It is unclear who took the initiative in forming the BMA, and its full membership remained a well-kept secret. However, that spring, the organization stymied strike efforts by at least fourteen unions, most notably the teamsters, to impose the closed shop or make other gains.

A test between management and labor came in September 1909, when the Amalgamated Association of Street and Electric Railway Employees made another attempt to organize the traction workers. Wattles secured a unanimous resolution from the BMA executive committee approving any "attitude" he decided to take, and he made a contingency arrangement with Waddel and Mahan, a New York firm that engaged in strikebreaking. After that, Wattles refused a demand by the streetcar men for recognition and a contract, adamantly rejecting arbitration. He said, "There are some things in this world that you cannot arbitrate." Following a discussion of several hours with labor representatives, he issued a statement clearly expressing what he intended to do if his workers walked out. "Now," he declared, "I am not a timid man either . . . I say to the Union men, if they quit the employ of this company, there will never be another union man employed by this company. . . . I have prepared this company for a strike, and I have men employed waiting to take the place of every man who quits . . . this company will go right along and operate its cars; if *necessary under the protection of the government itself.*" Wattles proved a man of his word.

When the streetcar men struck, he acted swiftly and with characteristic resolution. On September 19, 1909, the first strikebreakers arrived. Over five hundred armed men established headquarters in the car barns that had been equipped with barricades, cots, and commissaries. The hardened veterans of numerous labor disturbances disdainfully ignored police deployed to protect them. Few who saw the men believed company claims that they were motormen and conductors recruited from the ranks of the Brooklyn Rapid Transit Company. Wattles called them a "jolly lot of disreputables. . . . always ready for a fight." The strike was marked by occasional damage to streetcars and some personal injuries, but the public sided with the strikers and remained off the cars when they occasionally rolled. Wattles, undismayed by the violence, brushed aside attempts at negotiation.

The strikers refused Wattles's offer to return to work without penalty if they would agree not to belong to a union; so he went ahead with the process of breaking the strike. In the middle of October he won the inevitable victory. He took back only the men he wanted, providing they signed "yellow dog" contracts. The strikebreakers moved on to other centers of labor unrest. "No compromise was made, and the strikers were defeated," Wattles proclaimed. "The union was destroyed." He proposed a national "standing army" to break traction strikes and violently attacked unions in a privately printed publication, *A Crime against Labor: A Brief History of the Omaha and Council Bluffs Street Railway Strike,* 1909.

The traction strike showed the strength of the Omaha Business Men's Association. In the course of the strike, the BMA published the names of the members of its executive committee. In addition to these twenty-six men, the names of seven other BMA leaders had been published since the founding of the organization. If these persons were representative of the total membership of the Business Men's Association, this anti–organized-labor group was composed primarily of leaders of local enterprises. These men were linked to one another through their membership in a host of social and civic organizations. Interestingly, businesses of national scope, such as the Union Pacific and the large meat packers, were not represented in the BMA leadership, nor were Omaha's daily newspapers, breweries, or Jewish-operated firms. This suggests that Omaha's business elite was not a monolithic group of persons with a single perspective on society; nevertheless, as labor historian William C. Pratt has said, the BMA "pretty much established Omaha as an open-shop town for a generation."

The following years would bring violent strikes in the meat-packing industry; 4,500 men left their jobs in 1917 and 6,000 in 1921. Strikebreaking became an accepted way of life in Omaha; management broke several strikes including a short 1918 traction work stoppage and a 1919 walkout by teamsters. During a lengthy labor dispute in the building trades, the governor of Nebraska actually appointed a member of the BMA to investigate the situation. Such favoritism was a symptom of a carefully nurtured antiunion attitude in Nebraska that, reflecting the work of the BMA, produced a 1921 antipicketing law. This statute was retained easily in a referendum held the following year. The provision had the desired effect. It completed what Wattles started: the shattering of the union movement in Omaha for many years to come.

Wattles dealt with other aspects of economic life. He took advantage of the agricultural boom to strengthen hinterland ties in Nebraska, and he extended his city's influence in other directions. These activities also countered efforts by increasingly aggressive Kansas City businessmen. The Missouri city, which had enjoyed a development similar to Omaha's, wanted to broaden its markets from Kansas to other parts of the Plains. Wattles needed a defensive strategy to keep the Kansas City Board of Trade, which had operated a grain futures market since 1877, out of Nebraska. This was no mean task given the power of the organization. Wattles had little chance of making inroads into North and South Dakota. The powerful Minneapolis Chamber of Commerce—a combination of great flour mills—controlled sources of supply, working in league with railroads and grain elevator companies. Chances for Omaha seemed better in Iowa. Wattles believed that excellent opportunities existed to compete successfully with Cedar Rapids, Des Moines, Ottumwa, and Sioux City for livestock and grain. The National Corn Exposition, in addition to promoting the growing of corn, demonstrated Omaha's interest in Iowa markets. Wattles had no illusions about breaking the hold of Chicago capitalists over Iowa's economy. He did see commercial opportunities, if they were orchestrated correctly.

The extension into Omaha of the Chicago Great Western Railroad in 1903 helped to improve Omaha's fortunes as a grain market. This gave the CGW a direct route between the city and Chicago, and more importantly, it touched off a violent rate war. Prior to the coming of the Great Western, the railroads serving Omaha had their price structures so arranged that the city had no profitable way of handling grain destined for distribution outside Nebraska. Rates from interior points to distant markets were far less than those from the same points to Omaha.

Great Western president A. B. Stickney changed this long-haul arrangement. He worked out a plan under which the through rates were made equal to the sum of the local rate in and the proportional rate out. In short, he charged what the traffic would bear. The other roads had no choice except to compete if they wanted traffic. Stickney received very strong support from Wattles and Omaha business interests that did not have direct ties either with the Union Pacific or the Burlington. The railroads, which had compromised earlier over Kansas City rates when faced with competition from Stickney, did so again. A general agreement overhauled the rates in and out of Omaha, making it feasible for Omaha to function competitively with older grain centers.

In November 1903 Wattles had taken the lead in organizing the Omaha Grain Exchange. Receipts in the first year amounted to 16 million bushels, an unimpressive total by national standards. Poor area elevator facilities hampered the new exchange. The one-million-bushel Union Elevator burned to the ground, leaving storage space for only 2.3 million bushels. New construction improved matters, but it was several years before local elevators came close to meeting demand. They had a capacity of 6 million bushels in 1906 and almost 7 million in 1909, and in the same span receipts advanced from 35 million to 50 million bushels. By the end of the decade, Omaha ranked overall as the nation's fourth largest grain market. Totals for corn were especially impressive; over 20 million bushels annually made Omaha the world's second-largest handler of the commodity. Wattles, then president of the Omaha Grain Exchange, boasted in 1909:

> These results have been obtained because of the enterprise and business acumen displayed by the grain men who comprise the Omaha Grain Exchange. The market has been, from the start, an active and open market. . . . It is pleasant to reflect that this growth and development has been based upon Nebraska and Iowa grain only, and that a large field outside of the territory we have reached in these two states still remains to be invaded by the Omaha dealers if only the transportation charges can be adjusted to a proper basis.

Wattles failed in his primary goal of making Omaha the nation's second-greatest grain market. The Omaha Grain Exchange never traded in futures. Instead, it bought and sold grain shipped to the city. Still, Wattles had created an economic institution that added a new and profitable dimension to Omaha's economy.

Wattles made a mark on Omaha. His civic activities enhanced the city's image. He fought hard to establish its economic independence. On one hand, he successfully challenged unions. On the other, he maneuvered to free Omaha from domination by the railroad companies. He placed the men who used their monopolistic position to fix rates in the same category as labor agitators. Unlike the packing-house owners, who brought money and jobs, they took without giving much in return. Thus he opposed what he believed unfair designs by both outside capital and labor. Of course, he saw nothing wrong with pushing an aggressive strategy of creating a larger and more secure productive and distributive region for Omaha. Wattles was neither a philanthropist like Creighton nor a rough-and-tough capitalist like Paxton. He confided to a friend in 1918, "I don't enjoy being the target for attack by all socialistic and anarchistic elements, but when attacked there is only one road to follow, and that is the road that leads to justice and honest dealings." In the early 1920s he moved to a large mansion in Hollywood, California, where he continued to tend his extensive interests until his death in 1932. No one raised any statues or named parks in his memory. Still, he had convinced some Omahans of their city's greatness.

Edward F. Morearty, explaining why he wrote *Omaha Memories: Recollections of Events, Men and Affairs in Omaha*, articulated the sense of purpose that Wattles gave the city:

> Because it is in the geographical center of the United States through which passes the channels of commerce from the rock-bound coast of Maine to the Golden Gate of California, and from the snow-capped mountains of Canada to the pleasant glades of Florida; because it has the most even and healthful climate of any spot in the United States; because it is the second primary livestock market of the world; because it is the fourth primary grain market of the world; because its jobbing trade in 1916 was $188,000,000; because its factory output for 1916 was $219,000,000; because it is the greatest creamery producing city in the world. Because in 1999 it will have a population of 1,000,000 people; because it is the greatest lead ore reducing city in the world; because it is the second primary corn market in the world; because it is the greatest sheep feeding market in the world; because it has the broadest streets and best kept of any city of her size in the United States; because it has more palatial residences and the greatest number of home owners in proportion to population than any other city in the world; because it has the most extensive, best equipped, best service street car system in the world; because it has the most schools and most efficient teachers in this nation.

This kind of extravagant exaggeration was more than boosterism. It represented an attempt to articulate aspirations in a context that would gain widespread community support and spur city building for the furthering of common goals.

The numerous salesmen based in Omaha were an important element in promoting the city's future. The best drummers met the challenge—holding old territory and pioneering new—in the face of growing competition. Selling a tractor in Ankeny, Iowa; negotiating an agreement to supply shirts in Hastings, Nebraska; and writing an order for tacks in Mitchell, South Dakota—these meant the difference between success and failure. The salesmen acted as spearheads of commerce that brought gigantic amounts of money into the city. They covered areas well beyond the 150-mile radius considered by business experts as standard territory for convenient sales operations, making it possible for the hundreds of wholesale and jobbing houses in Omaha, such as M. E. Smith and Company in wholesale dry goods, the Omaha Baum Iron Store in hardware, and the Carpenter Paper Company in paper to do immense amounts of business. During the 1910s and 1920s aggregate annual sales rose from $100 million with the way led by automobiles and accessories, groceries, building materials, and agricultural implements. In 1929 an Omaha promotional pamphlet claimed that a tradition of service and aggressive marketing had combined to make the city "the logical jobbing capital of the central United States." A generation of salesmen working the Plains gave a semblance of reality to that conclusion. They were the unsung heroes of the Omaha story.

The livestock market remained one of Omaha's greatest strengths. In 1915 South Omaha became part of Omaha, adding over twenty-five thousand persons to the city. Most laborers in South Omaha worked in the livestock yards or the packing houses. The Big Four packers—different than that of earlier days because of name changes and mergers—were Armour, Cudahy, Swift, and Morris. There were also a number of smaller plants. Cumulatively, the big and small companies employed over thirteen thousand people, with an annual payroll of $13 million. The slaughterhouses needed large facilities. Armour's buildings sprawled over several acres. A new structure erected in 1915 was one of the largest in the region. The building contained a sheep killing and cooling department, an engine room, a machine shop, and a car shop, all prerequisites for improved operations. The yards were equally impressive. They covered 200 acres of which 175 had a paved surface. There were 4,298 pens all equipped with concrete watering troughs supplied by the stockyards' own water department. In 1920 Skinner Packing Company opened a new plant that it soon leased to Dold and Company. Wilson and Company—one of a later Big Four—purchased this plant in 1938. Annual receipts for livestock traded rose in 1900 from 830,000 cattle, 2.2 million hogs, and 1.3 million sheep to 1.2 million cattle, 1.9 million hogs, and 3 million sheep in 1910. There was a gradual upturn; in 1925 receipts were 1.6 million cattle, 3.4 million hogs, and 2.4 million sheep. By that time, freight charges on Omaha livestock and packing products totaled over $17 million yearly. The dominant symbol of the city's packing industry was the new Livestock Exchange Building, completed in 1926, which towered eleven stories above the stockyards.

The Omaha Livestock Exchange, which had about 250 members, handled almost all the necessary transactions. The Union Stock Yards Company of Omaha continued to have significant responsibilities. Its general manager from 1907 until 1923 was Everett Buckingham, who previously had been a high official of the Union Pacific Railroad. His presence suggested continuing railroad involvement in Omaha business undertakings. Another indication of outside influence was that a large minority of shares in the Stock Yards Company were in the hands of the Armour family of Chicago. Economic relationships were such that no one in Omaha, Wattles included, could obtain complete fiscal independence.

In 1916 the Ford Motor Company opened an assembly plant just north of downtown. Over the next sixteen years the plant, which at one time employed 1,200 persons, turned out 408,682 automobiles and 45,031 trucks. The operation of Ford's Omaha plant illustrated that the new automotive age was not a complete misfortune for the nation's railroads. In 1924 the *Benson Times*, using data for the previous year, described the plant as "Omaha's second biggest shipper, having absorbed 3,468 carloads of materials and shipped out 5,420 carloads of finished products, in addition to the thousands of cars and trucks driven overland from the factory by dealers."

Other manufacturing pursuits moved forward in Omaha, as indicated by figures for 1915, a representative year. The Union Pacific shops employed over 1,500. Another large concern, the American Smelting and Refining Company, operated a thirty-one-acre smelter, which refined metals and by-products with an estimated annual value of $39 million. Aside from a few other foundries—the Paxton and Vierling Iron Works and the Omaha General Iron Works—plus the Bemis Omaha Bag Company that produced burlap and cotton bags for the grain industry, most industrial activities were extractive. Five breweries had an output valued at $3 million, almost all for the local market. All were owned by Omaha interests unlike another firm in the liquor business, the Willow Springs Distilling Company, which was part of a national distilling group. The five large creameries had a product in excess of $7 million, most of which was "process butter." Two plants mixed alfalfa and molasses to make stock food sold throughout the Plains. Other important business lines were flour and mill products ($3.2 million), bakery products ($2.4 million), grocery specialty items ($2.3 million), and clothing goods ($1.3 million). School children in Omaha learned a litany: "Omaha macaroni is sold in Italy! . . . Omaha pig lead is sold all over the world!" Still, the words failed to hide the reality that Omaha had not developed much in the way of manufacturing outside of the agricultural sphere.

"OVER THERE . . ."

World War I was an interlude that had little immediate impact on Omaha. Given the nature of the local industrial system, there were no munitions plants. Hostilities lasted too short a time, from April of 1917 to November of 1918, to cause significant changes. The establishment of an army balloon school at Fort Omaha elicited much comment resulting from the novelty of manned balloons drifting over the city but generated little money for the economy. While close to twenty thousand Omahans served in the armed forces, creating local labor shortages, the most serious hardships experienced on the home front were "wheatless" and "meatless" days. A sharp increase in railroad passenger traffic brought some new business; many soldiers and civilians had to lay over for several hours between trains. The livestock and packing industries were already operating at around full capacity when America became involved in the war. Receipts remained at high levels, with livestock that could not be handled diverted to other markets.

During and immediately after hostilities there was a massive expansion of agriculture throughout the Great Plains. Cultivated land in Nebraska rose by three million acres, with most going into wheat and corn. The vast enlargement, which related to good crop yields, high prices, and patriotism, greatly increased the grain trade in Omaha. At the same time, it stimulated commercial and jobbing pursuits. Few persons seemed concerned that much of the new farmland was in areas that defeated farmers had left late in the previous century. Wartime demands and prosperity took precedence. Omaha businessmen held their own, maintaining their city's prewar position against rivals. No place in the region gained any appreciable advantage over another because of the war. The Plains were prosperous at the conflict's end and so was Omaha. Its leaders looked ahead to further prosperity in the 1920s.

A PROBLEMATIC NECESSITY

A recently developed industry, electric power, led Omaha into what many believed the climax of the machine age. By the postwar period, electricity was taken for granted as a source of light. More importantly, generators no longer had to be constructed close to users. Technological advances enabled the transmission of electricity through power grids over long distances. Indeed, it was possible to transfer electricity from one grid to another, and a whole new national industry arose. Those in on the ground floor, such as capitalist Samuel Insull of Chicago, who developed large holdings throughout the Midwest in the twenties, wanted neither government handouts nor interference. The power interests argued that federal involvement would lead to higher rates. Critics claimed that it was the other way around; increased governmental regulation would lead to lower rates because power monopolists gouged consumers. One of the shrillest critics was a Nebraska progressive Republican, Senator George W. Norris of McCook, a community in the southwestern part of the state. He championed public power for reclamation projects and argued in favor of the "yardstick" principle under which pilot federal projects would be used to measure power costs. Norris was particularly incensed by the practices of the new darling of Omaha's business constellation, the Nebraska Power Company.

Reformers found it easy to dislike the Nebraska Power Company. They did not even approve of its slogan, "Electric Service Is Cheap." To them, the firm embodied objectionable business practices. In 1917 a powerful national holding company, the Electric Bond and Share Company, had acquired an Omaha power producer and changed the name to the Nebraska Power Company. As a result of this transaction, Electric Bond upped the fixed capital in Nebraska Power from $6.4 million to $13.5 million. Some $5 million of a resulting common-stock issue went directly to another Electric Bond subsidiary, the American Power and Light Company. This stock transition, worthy of any undertaken by Jay Gould in Union Pacific issues, paid handsome dividends. According to an investigation by the Federal Trade Commission, the rate of return on ledger value was 96.8 percent over the ensuing ten years. Dividends for one year amounted to 160 percent. Following a rate cut and in a year of depression, 1930, dividends reached $1.2 million.

Nebraska Power added local businessmen to its executive group. At one point, nine out of fifteen members of the board of directors were Omahans. Nebraska Power produced roughly 60 percent of the electricity in the state. Its Omaha power stations had key responsibilities in the operation of the national transmission network. Such considerations guaranteed criticism under the best of circumstances. Nebraska Power reacted by mounting a massive advertising campaign to counter the view that it was an insensitive monopoly run by outside forces only concerned with taking profits out of Nebraska.

The person responsible for improving Nebraska Power's image was James E. Davidson. A pioneer in the industry, he was the firm's vice president and general manager. Born in 1879, he grew up in Port Huron, Michigan, quitting high school to take a job at the Port Huron Light and Power Company. He became superintendent at the age of twenty-one, starting an executive career. He moved up rapidly and soon headed an American Power and Light Company subsidiary in Portland, Oregon. Davidson assumed his Omaha responsibilities in 1917 and quickly became a prominent local figure. In addition to gaining respect as an able manager, he was a likeable man with a genial personality. He gave a great deal of time to civic activities and belonged to the leading social clubs and service organizations. Twice he directed community chest drives, which unified charitable fund-raising efforts. His adopted city gratefully appreciated such altruism and, accordingly, honored him. He was King of Ak-Sar-Ben in 1923 and named the outstanding Omaha citizen of the year in 1929.

Although he held several local directorships, Davidson devoted most of his business activities to Nebraska Power. Unlike Wattles at an earlier date, Davidson had little interest in using civic connections to gain footholds in a variety of Omaha businesses with the purpose of achieving community power. Rather, he did it for enjoyment and self-fulfillment, at the same time helping Nebraska Power. It served the monopoly well to have a highly visible public-spirited leader. After all, during the dark winter months, Nebraska Power occasionally turned off the power for the nonpayment of bills at the homes of widows and orphans. And almost every storm brought breaks in lines, frequently throwing whole towns into darkness. Davidson was aware

of the general reaction to such circumstances; every session of the state legislature saw the introduction of bills, defeated or swiftly tabled through intensive lobbying, calling for municipal ownership.

Davidson's specialty was public relations. He was instrumental in establishing the Nebraska Committee of Public Utility Information. This organization did such a successful job of improving the image of private power in
Nebraska—it produced a textbook glorifying the community contributions
of private electric companies and equating foes with the "Red Menace"—that
Davidson received national recognition. He remained in the electric business
in Omaha for many more years, gaining a reputation as the "Number One"
power salesman in the country. Davidson was cognizant of the means of promoting consumer products in a hostile environment.

COUNCIL BLUFFS

Probably the greatest symbol of the passing of the pioneer builders of Council Bluffs and Omaha was the military funeral of Maj. Gen. Grenville M.
Dodge in Council Bluffs on a cloudy bitter cold day in January 1916. The military ceremonies were a tribute to Dodge's stature as a Union commander,
and he was unexcelled as a leader in making his home city and its offspring,
Omaha, a major urban center in the middle of the continent.

Fifteen months after General Dodge was laid to rest, a new generation of
Americans set off to war. Two surgeon-soldiers, Donald Macrae Jr., MD and
Mathew A. Tinley, MD achieved distinguished records in World War I and
symbolized a new age of professional and civic leaders in Council Bluffs.
Dr. Macrae, son of a pioneer Council Bluffs physician and a University of
Michigan medical graduate, served as a surgeon during the Spanish-American War, returned to his medical practice in Council Bluffs and was mayor
from 1904 to 1907. For a decade he was professor of anatomy at the University of Nebraska College of Medicine. When the country entered World War
I, he organized and commanded Unit K, Mobile Hospital 1, which with its
contingent of doctors and nurses from Council Bluffs served in France. In
1923 he was a key figure in opening a Council Bluffs clinic, and after a fire destroyed the Grand Hotel in 1925, Macrae was a leader in a fund-raising drive
that induced Omaha hotel man Eugene C. Eppley to erect the Hotel Chieftain. Completed in 1927, the Chieftain, adorned with Grant Wood murals,
functioned for many years as a center of community activity. Dr. Tinley, a

native of Council Bluffs and an anatomy student of Dr. Macrae's, served in the Spanish-American War and in World War I commanded a unit of the Forty-second Rainbow Division. Resuming his medical practice after the war and remaining active in the National Guard, Dr. Tinley attained the rank of lieutenant general and was the Thirty-fourth Division commander from 1924 until he retired from military service in 1940.

During the first three decades of the twentieth century, Council Bluffs continued to develop upon its existing economic base. Each day in 1920 more than eighty passenger trains and two thousand cars of freight rumbled through the city. In 1921 Pacific Fruit Express opened a plant at Council Bluffs for icing some eight to nine hundred rail cars each day during a shipping season between July and November. Just as the Omaha–Council Bluffs rail gateway was a funnel in the movement of people and goods, it was fundamental to the flow of mail. As a Chamber of Commerce publication noted in 1920, "The Transfer post-office at Council Bluffs is the largest mail distributing point in the United States for the handling of through mail. East and West mail, as well as all Oriental mail, is transferred at this point."

With the passage of time, Council Bluffs gradually lost most of its farm-implement dealers to Omaha following fires in 1900 and 1906. Andrew McMillen, longtime resident and amateur historian, attributed the departure of these firms to inadequate fire protection and suggested that Council Bluffs lacked a constructive business environment. Whatever the merits of his latter point, these fires highlighted the deficiencies of the city's privately owned water system that dated from 1881–82. Not only was water pressure inadequate for fire hydrants, the untreated water was ill-suited for domestic use. As public-school librarian Helen Ruth Montague noted, "It was possible to draw a tumbler of water from the tap, let it stand for a short time, and have from an eighth to one-fourth of an inch of mud in the bottom of the glass." In 1909 the Iowa legislature passed a bill that enabled the city to purchase the water system, and following a judicially imposed valuation of the property, the municipal government assumed ownership and operation of the facilities in 1910. This change brought modernization of the system, including water treatment, extension of mains, and a level of service that brought low fire-insurance rates.

Despite the decline of the implement business, other established facets of the economy remained vital: in 1920 some 450 to 500 persons were employed

7. John G. Woodward and Company Candy Factory, Council Bluffs. *Courtesy Council Bluffs Public Library, Council Bluffs, Iowa.*

in Council Bluffs candy factories, most notably the John G. Woodward firm, while the 1,825,000 square feet of glass in local greenhouses gave evidence to the continuing importance of the distant marketing of cut flowers. As in the past, this Corn Belt city's boosters emphasized local grape production, claiming that only Germany's Rhine River valley and China's Yellow River valley equaled the suitability of the surrounding area for viticulture. In 1931 members of the Council Bluffs Grape Growers' Association shipped the equivalent of about 125 carloads of grapes to Midwestern destinations. The storage of eggs and locally grown fruit and the processing of dairy products were significant activities. Two hospitals and a sanitarium, grain elevators, retail stores, and farm credit through local mortgage bankers and insurance company representatives tied Council Bluffs to its hinterland.

One notable addition to Council Bluffs industry was intimately connected to the city's stature as a rail center. In September 1921 the Griffin Wheel Company, a national firm, opened a 160,000-square-foot plant for the manufacture of railroad car wheels. This foundry, located in the western part of the city near the Union Pacific terminal and employing between seventy-five and one hundred persons, made some 300 to 360 new freight car wheels daily by recycling the metal from worn out wheels. In any event, transportation and services remained at the heart of Council Bluffs' livelihood. In 1930 Council Bluffs was Iowa's sixth-largest city, but 1929 data showed that the community ranked thirteenth in both value of manufactured products and value added by manufacture.

SPEEDING CHANGE: THE MOTOR AGE

Although an automobile had been featured at the Trans-Mississippi and International Exposition in 1898 and Council Bluffs resident Maurice Woolman soon built an auto, such self-propelled vehicles remained a curiosity in the first few years of the twentieth century. In 1902 motor enthusiasts formed the Omaha Automobile Club, which included members from Council Bluffs; and two years later, Omaha adopted an ordinance to register and regulate the speed of the new devices. As early as 1904, Iowa established speed limits. The year 1905 brought Nebraska's first motor-vehicle registration law and Omaha's first automobile death, although a coroner's jury found that the deceased, suffering from cancer, committed suicide by jumping in the path of a car. In 1910 and 1911 mounting evidence of irresponsible driving brought more regulatory measures, including a ban on persons under age sixteen operating motor vehicles. Initially, automobiles were often perceived as the toys of the wealthy, but practical use of motorized vehicles including trucks and taxis was becoming evident.

The second decade of the twentieth century brought dramatic increases in the numbers of motor-vehicle registrations. In 1913 Nebraska had 25,617 registered vehicles, but by 1920 the figure was 100,534. Iowa's registration totals rose from 147,078 in 1915 to 437,378 in 1920. These figures meant that by 1920 there was one motor vehicle for every 6.3 Nebraskans and one for every 5.5 Iowans. In the early automobile age, proportionately fewer Omahans owned cars as compared to the residents of many Nebraska rural counties probably because the city had a good streetcar system. In 1913 the Omaha and Council Bluffs Street Railway Company counted 55,030,000 paid riders, a figure that rose to 61,650,839 passengers in 1920.

Aside from the increasing number of autos on the streets of Council Bluffs and Omaha, the post–World War I years brought further evidence of the implications of motor-vehicles for the metro area. A *Council Bluffs Nonpareil* editorial in January 1919 urging highway development noted, "A shrewd business man standing on Broadway Tuesday observed one after another a dozen auto trucks headed for South Omaha with loads of cattle and hogs. He observed that 'the age of the auto truck is here.'" As the paper said, "He was correct." In fact, in the first three months of 1919, a season of difficult travel on unpaved roads in Iowa and Nebraska, some 100 to 125 trucks brought a daily average exceeding 900 head of livestock to the South Omaha stockyards. Favorable road conditions on April 1 brought the arrival of 2,734 head. Given the primitive state of the country's roads, trucking livestock or other products was limited to a radius of forty to fifty miles from the metro area, but trucklines reaching nearby communities heralded the rise of a new transportation business. The Omaha Chamber of Commerce and the Bureau of Markets of the U.S. Department of Agriculture supported the Firestone Tire and Rubber Company's "Ship by Truck" campaign. In 1920 the Council Bluffs Chamber of Commerce boasted, "There are over 3,400 trucks in Pottawattamie County alone," and, "Council Bluffs is located on fifteen marked highways, four of them being transcontinental."

Another sign of a new age in transportation came in 1922 when Boulevard Transit Company began motor-bus service five times each day covering the thirty-six miles between Omaha and Fremont, Nebraska. The Council Bluffs Chamber of Commerce's suggestion that its community was a highway hub was premature, but *Nonpareil* editor William R. Orchard was an important promoter of the "get Iowa out of the mud" movement for better roads. In fact, state and federal spending for highways foretold the evolution of a road network that would link the lives of the farm and townspeople of eastern Nebraska and southwestern Iowa ever more intimately to Omaha and Council Bluffs.

By 1933 motorists from Omaha and Council Bluffs could reach such places as Lincoln, Sioux City, Kansas City, and St. Louis without leaving pavement. In addition to injuries and fatalities arising from such traffic, the automobile fostered criminal links between metropolitan Omaha and the surrounding area, particularly during the prohibition years. The 1920s brought a sharp increase in crime in Iowa, and robbers of small-town banks or perpetrators of other crimes occasionally fled to Omaha.

More important in the long run, improved highways and the magnet of shopping opportunities in Omaha would erode the economic base of the small towns. During the 1920s Omaha businessmen used advertising to further the fortunes of the city. On one level, there was a need to uphold the community image as a growing regional metropolis. This involved boosterism emphasizing statistical virtues: thirty-sixth in area, thirty-fourth in population, fourth-largest railroad center, first in home ownership, second-largest livestock market, and $2.3 billion in bank clearings. Of more immediate economic consequence were efforts to call attention to Omaha's standing as a place to shop or find entertainment. The quick adoption of the automobile made it practical for farmers in eastern Nebraska and western Iowa to reach Omaha and return home the same day. Symbolic of the role of autos in forming stronger ties of the metro to its trade area was the fact that in 1931 the RKO-Orpheum Theatre in Omaha started running movie ads in the newspaper in Logan, Iowa, a county seat northeast of the city. Adroit publicity proclaimed the wonders of the downtown district:

> Omaha's main retail market covers an area of a little more than two square miles. Here are the department stores and exclusive shops, to be counted by the hundreds, where all the latest merchandise gathered from the marts of the world is offered to the thousands of daily buyers.

The last word in styles and merchandise from Paris, Vienna, London and other world markets in as great variety, and at prices commensurate with those to be found in any other of America's great metropolitan retail markets, are stocked by these Omaha stores to meet the demands of a prosperous and discriminating customer clientele.

For many persons who grew up in the Omaha region in the first quarter of the twentieth century, their first lasting memory of the city was going with their parents to the Brandeis Store. It was the successor to the Boston Store, started in the late nineteenth century by pioneer merchant Jonas Brandeis. His three sons, Arthur, Hugo, and Emil, all of whom played important roles in Omaha commercial real-estate development, erected the huge emporium in the heart of downtown, making it the apex of their extensive holdings. "Brandeis" as it was called locally, was the finest department store on the northern Plains. The seven-story establishment covered an entire block. From the bargain basement to rooftop restaurant, there was a dazzling array of merchandise. The three restaurants suited the needs of tired shoppers and were relaxing places to spend an hour. The main floor, with its high ceilings, white fluted Corinthian columns, broad aisles, large potted ferns, and unobstructed sight lines, created a pleasing atmosphere for the displays of high-class merchandise. The escalator system, the only one in the area, attracted considerable attention. The store offered a free area telephone service, a post office branch, a checkroom for packages, and a cashier's desk. Brandeis acted as a magnet that brought buyers to the city in droves. It was common practice when meeting someone downtown to "meet under the clock" just inside the store's front door. Brandeis was a community institution that helped the whole downtown, contributing in many ways to furthering Omaha's annual retail trade of several hundred million dollars. The department store was a local version of Marshall Field's in Chicago and Macy's in New York City.

Through the 1920s, motor vehicles were bringing changes in public transportation within the urban area. In August 1925 the Omaha and Council Bluffs Street Railway began running buses on four routes to link the end of trolley lines to more distant areas of the city. However, competition with automobiles contributed to the demise in 1926 of the interurban trolley line to Ralston and Papillion. Five years later, buses replaced trolleys to Bellevue, and the street railway began retrenchment of its trolley service to outlying points in the Council Bluffs area. During the 1920s, automobiles had taken about one-third of the Omaha and Council Bluffs Street Railway's customers as the number of passengers fell from 61,650,839 to 41,426,482 with the decline in Council Bluffs especially dramatic. Illustrating the public's interest in motorcars was the fact that some ten thousand people packed Ak-Sar-Ben Coliseum on the evening of February 17, 1930, for the start of the Aero-Auto Show. To counter the trend, the street railway company hired Ross W. Harris, a Madison, Wisconsin, transportation consultant, who in 1929 devised a plan for restructured streetcar routes and the creation of crosstown bus lines. The latter broke with the traditional pattern of lines running from outlying parts of the city to or through downtown. The streetcar route restructuring did not gain public acceptance and had to be reconsidered, but the crosstown bus routes proved popular. Henceforth, buses would play a vital part in the city's public transportation, and one authority, G. Mac Sebree, has called Ross Harris "the father of Omaha's bus system."

KEEPING PACE BY RAIL AND AIR

Even as automobiles and trucks were starting to challenge the primacy of the railroads, it became clear that the Union Station completed in 1899 was inadequate. In 1924 the Omaha Chamber of Commerce established a New Union Station Committee. After studying the city's rail terminal needs, the committee worked with the Union Pacific and other lines on this question. The result was an agreement that the Burlington Railroad would retain its separate station, which would be remodeled and linked to the new Union Station by an enclosed passageway above the terminal tracks. The architect for the Union Station, Gilbert S. Underwood of Los Angeles, had designed many stations for the Union Pacific Railroad and would later become the supervising architect for the U.S. government. Some forty thousand people visited the new Omaha Union Station on January 15, 1931, the day the art deco structure was dedicated. Omaha was fortunate in that the terminal modernization was undertaken before the start of the Great Depression; moreover, in 1920 tickets sold for trains using the former Union Station had peaked at 754,369 and then declined to 352,945 in 1926. Nevertheless, impressive railroad stations remained a mark of urban stature, and the new Union Station heralded Omaha's prominence and its status as operating headquarters of the Union Pacific Railroad.

By the 1920s, Omahans were starting to develop a municipal airport. In May 1920 airmail service to the city had begun with planes using Ak-Sar-Ben Field in what was then the southwestern part of town. Four years later, airmail operations were moved to Fort Crook at Bellevue. In 1925 the city of Omaha purchased Missouri River bottomland northeast of downtown for subsequent airport development. The American Legion raised money to build a hangar, and the Aerial Transportation Committee of the Omaha Chamber of Commerce worked to build public interest in aviation. The city's aviation advocates also faced a tough challenge in convincing Boeing Air Transport, the forerunner of United Air Lines, that the prospective airport site was suitable. In 1928 Omaha voters narrowly approved a bond issue for airport development, and subsequent favorable votes in 1930 made its development possible. Mail flights could now be transferred from Fort Crook. In November 1930 with the completion of a hangar-terminal building, field lighting, the clearing of nearby trees, and assurance that fog would not be a major problem, the Municipal Airfield welcomed the start of Boeing Air Transport service.

THE CITY EXPANDS

Omaha experienced a building boom in west-side districts annexed earlier in anticipation of future development. A master plan produced in 1919 by the Omaha City Planning Commission called for widening heavily traveled streets to carry increased automobile traffic. The following year Omaha's first zoning ordinance contained stipulations designed to prevent commercial and industrial encroachments on land designated for residential purposes. A zone of apartments and duplexes separated downtown from the west-side housing tracts. Several thoroughfares, among them Dodge, Harney, and Leavenworth, provided arterial connections with the central core. West-side subdivisions catered to the wealthy. Builders, emphasizing the advantages of the automobile and the prospects of a cycle of rising land prices, lured rich Omahans away from the older north-side enclaves of Kountze Place and Miller Park to Fairacres and other western areas. Developers sought to construct self-contained garden suburbs patterned after those in Chicago and elsewhere. Happy Hollow, near the site of a former country club, contained rolling hills, lush shrubbery, manicured lawns, numerous trees, Tudor-style homes, and winding streets. In one year alone, 1922, over 1,500 new homes appeared in west-side neighborhoods. West Dodge Acres, Bensonville Place, Beverly Hills, and Elmwood Gardens attracted buyers. So did the older suburban towns of Dundee and Benson. American intellectuals found little to praise about the housing trends; Sinclair Lewis attacked suburban values in *Babbitt*. Nevertheless, Happy Hollow and other sections exemplified how many Americans wanted to live in the 1920s, a decade of urban prosperity.

The annexation of South Omaha in 1915 was the highlight of Omaha's expansion in the first half of the twentieth century, but at the same time the city annexed Dundee, a western suburb. In 1917 Omaha annexed Benson to the northwest and Florence to the north. Despite their loss of self-governance, all four communities, especially South Omaha, retained their identities, including their business districts. Such growth necessitated more public services; for example, the Omaha Public School system built four new high schools in the 1920s while Council Bluffs added a second.

EDUCATION: NEW DIRECTIONS

Through the last two decades of the nineteenth century the Omaha Medical College gave evidence of the professionalism that marked urban growth, but funding was a challenge. An attempt in the 1880s to develop a medical school at the University of Nebraska in Lincoln soon failed, and in 1902 the university began to absorb the Omaha Medical College. In 1913 the first building of the University of Nebraska College of Medicine opened at Forty-second and Dewey streets, and four years later a University Hospital was added. The beginning of the medical campus was early evidence of Omaha's westward expansion. Additionally, Omaha's specialized medical services were an increasingly important link between the city and its hinterland. A 1921 Chamber of Commerce ad proclaimed, "Omaha is one of the leading hospital centers west of the Mississippi" and that its "fifteen modern hospitals" each year cared for "more than 70,000 patients from Nebraska, Iowa, South Dakota, Wyoming, and surrounding states."

In 1908 a group of Presbyterians, joined by some other Protestants, founded the University of Omaha as a nonsectarian alternative to the Jesuit-operated Creighton University. Despite a few generous grants and the persistent labor of the school's first president, Dr. Daniel E. Jenkins, a Presbyterian clergyman who was on the faculty of the Omaha Theological Seminary, the University of Omaha led a precarious existence for its first generation. A way out of the dilemma came in 1929 when the school's supporters got the Nebraska Legislature to enact a law permitting the voters of Omaha to decide if their city should operate a tax-supported municipal university. The following year, the electorate narrowly approved this proposal, and the privately operated institution became the Municipal University of Omaha, which now developed with a much better, albeit far from a lavish, financial base.

ON THE BRINK OF DISASTER

The problems that increasingly afflicted Plains agriculture in the 1920s—overproduction, adverse climatic conditions, shrinking overseas markets, increased costs, and downward prices—caused little concern in Omaha. Those involved in making economic decisions rode the trend of general prosperity, risking that periodic adjustments, realignments, and reallocations would straighten things out. Enormous purchases of material items by hinterland residents—everything from automobiles to radios—more than compensated for lower quotations for livestock and commodities on the exchanges. Studies of previous achievements convinced Omahans that the past was prologue. Seventy-five years after the formation of Nebraska and the founding of Omaha, at the time of the diamond jubilee for state and city, the slogan adopted by the Chamber of Commerce, "Onward Omaha," summed up the objectives of the business community. A promotional publication asserted:

Omaha faces a future rich with promise of continued domination in field, garden, and stock-yard. Omaha faces a future in which the great economic battles will be fought and won by cities with transportation facilities and quick contacts. Omaha is the country's center. Already it is the fourth railroad center; already it commands the highways; but now commerce is to travel by water and air. A navigable channel, down the Missouri and Mississippi to the Gulf of Mexico, will be the gift of the next few years, and when it comes, it will open a new avenue to the markets of the world. Omaha, according to aviation experts, is ideally situated to become the capital of the skyways. In the geographical center of the United States, Omaha is built on level, rockless and comparatively treeless land which lends itself naturally to flying fields. No mists, little smoke, and rare fogs hinder the free movement of airplanes in the Midwest. Omaha leaders have been quick to grasp their opportunity, and the city is riding the rising tide of aviation. Omaha faces the future backed by all of her old allies, and fortified with the strength of two new ones—water and air!

Then the New York stock market collapsed, starting a tidal wave of adversity that swept over the United States. Omahans in all walks of life had more to worry about than the advance of air and water transportation. A network of bankrupt railroads, idle factories, and empty stores stood as testimony of what befell the Plains. As in the 1890s, abandoned farms were the rule rather than the exception. The ruin of agriculture seemed to spell an end to glory for Omaha. The metropolitan area, in lieu of prosperity, faced instead the onslaught of depression. The fabric woven over many years faced severe testing. Under these circumstances the people of Omaha and their social institutions took on new a significance that transcended the standards advocated by the business community.

[7] Urban Crosscurrents

Omaha underwent numerous changes in the first thirty years of the twentieth century. Many decades later, experts, after studying technological trends, would describe the process as "modernization." At the time, people equated developments with normal community progress or else took them for granted. As it was, changes in Omaha as throughout the United States related to several considerations: the transformations wrought by the machine age, the positive attitude of the voters toward improvements, the growing professionalism among those responsible for urban services, and the evolution of social and cultural institutions.

The success of bond issues at the polls, always in the face of charges that the increased costs would ruin the city, facilitated the implementation of vast improvements that Omaha needed as it increased in physical size. By 1929 the community covered twenty-five thousand acres. It had seven hundred miles of streets and six hundred miles of sewers. The Omaha Fire Department met the challenge of community enlargement with mechanized equipment, outlying stations, and better training methods. The police also became more efficient, adding motor traffic control to their responsibilities. The public schools added many teachers, and Omahans had established a municipal university. Religious bodies enjoyed membership increases, and a number of new churches and synagogues graced the skyline. There was interest in providing adequate public funding for a library and for furthering the arts in general. Several cultural institutions elicited favorable comment. "The cultural future of Omaha," an *Omaha Bee* staff writer wrote on the eve of the Great Depression, "seems as certain of greatness as the commercial future. . . . The symphony orchestra, the Art institute, the Community Playhouse and other organizations are on firm foundations and Omaha is destined to be not only a bigger, but a better city, both financially and culturally."

Underlying the quest for refinement were four concerns that threatened and ran counter to the quest for stability. Sometimes, they shaped policies in fundamental ways; at other times they were more subtle. Some had deep roots in the past; a few were of relatively recent origin. The first prolonged query involved the character of the population. The mixing of ethnic groups, in addition to giving the city a diversified cultural heritage, caused numerous tensions. A second serious matter, which evolved from the first, was interracial violence that twice in ten years shook the town to its foundations. Third was Omaha's enduring and well-deserved reputation as a wide-open town, a stigma that increasingly disturbed citizens in other parts of Nebraska and culminated in political action. The fourth question centered around the nature of the political system. Omaha had acquired a boss whose political machine controlled local politics for close to three decades. Supporters argued that the machine ameliorated pressures toward community disintegration by creating a consensus and giving people in the lower strata of society a voice. Critics viewed it as a disgrace that prevented solutions to ethnic, racial, and vice problems. In any event, the boss system touched upon many aspects of the body politic in Omaha, either directly or indirectly. Whether this was for good or bad remained in dispute.

"HELP WANTED—FEMALE"

Whatever the big questions about the future of their community and society were, the people of Greater Omaha faced the reality of earning their livelihoods. The 1900 U.S. Census revealed that about one-fifth of the country's women ages sixteen and older were "breadwinners." The Omaha figure was higher, but as was the case nationally, women's employment levels reflected age and ethnicity. Foreign-born white women and white women whose parents were born in this country were less likely to be gainfully employed than American-born white women with one or both of their parents born in another country. By contrast, proportionately far more of Omaha's African American women were breadwinners. Employment of Caucasian women peaked among those from twenty to twenty-four years old and fell sharply between the ages of twenty-five and thirty-four and older. The pattern for black women was very different: the employment level remained high and peaked for those in the thirty-five to forty-four age bracket. It stayed comparatively high for the age forty-five and older category. This reality, an ominous indicator for the black family, undoubtedly reflected racially based hardships.

"Help Wanted—Female" advertisements reflected a narrow range of employment opportunities for Omaha women in 1900. Ads for "general housework" and related domestic employment were common, and there were openings for cooks and waitresses. However, there were emerging opportunities in business: J. L. Brandeis's Boston Store, one of the city's premier retailers, sought "an experienced lady stenographer"; another ad sought "A young lady to keep books," albeit with the caveat that she should be "willing to start with small wages."

By 1910 women constituted just over 20 percent of the gainfully employed work force in Omaha, South Omaha, and Council Bluffs. Reflecting traditional gender roles, women often found employment as cooks and housekeepers or in domestic positions that the census described as "other servants." Many women were employed as laundresses; others worked as dressmakers, seamstresses, and milliners. Reflecting a growing urban economy, many women held jobs as store clerks, salespersons, stenographers, typists, and bookkeepers. The importance of women in the daily functioning of businesses was suggested in the fact that over 80 percent of the stenographers and typists in Greater Omaha were female. Likewise, 91 percent of the schoolteachers in the three cities were women. Although there was only one woman in the legal profession in the three cities, over 8 percent of the physicians were female. The overwhelming majority of the 488 trained nurses and most of the telephone operators in the cities were women as were a significant number of the telegraph operators.

Many jobs were the absolute domain of males. Nevertheless, there was a noteworthy presence of women in other largely male occupations. Of the eighty-nine persons in Omaha who were listed in the 1910 census as "bankers and bank officials," six were women as were five of the city's forty-five persons in the "chemists, assayers and metallurgists" category. In a study of women and organized labor in Omaha, William Pratt noted that "as early as the 1890s" the ranks of the Omaha Typographical Union included women and that after 1900 women worked as printers for local newspapers. Four of the ten individuals in Omaha who gave their profession as authors were women, and there were nine women among the 108 persons designated as "editors and reporters."

An interesting figure in Omaha's publishing business was Rose Rosicky. Born in Crete, Nebraska, to Czech immigrants, Rosicky's family moved to Omaha in 1876, where her father operated the National Printing Company, which published *Hospodar*, a Bohemian newspaper. At her father's death in 1910, she assumed managerial and editorial responsibility for National Printing Company's periodicals. She became a skilled Czech-English translator and wrote a book, *History of Czechs in Nebraska* in both languages, a key work on the immigrant experience.

Omaha was important in the career of a prominent journalist, Bess Furman Armstrong. The daughter of a newspaper publisher in Danbury, Nebraska, she edited the Kearney State Normal School *Antelope* during her college days. After working for the *Kearney Daily Hub*, Furman was a reporter with the *Omaha Daily News* and the *Omaha Bee-News* through the 1920s. In 1929 she left for Washington, DC, where she spent the balance of her career, principally as a correspondent for the Associated Press and later for the *New York Times*.

The packing industry in Omaha reflected the national scope of labor-management relations. Some women, especially those employed in sausage production, participated in the ill-fated 1904 packing strike and again in the 1917 action that brought a modest wage hike for packing-house workers. In December 1921 a wage cut in the packing industry precipitated another strike, and once more women were picketers. On December 21, strike-related matters led some three hundred women to protest at Omaha's city hall, but the strike ended in a severe setback for organized labor in the meat-packing industry.

As would be the case through the twentieth century, employed women in the Greater Omaha area in 1910 were much more likely to find themselves in subordinate, lower-status, and lower-paying positions than were men. However, business, professional, and technological advances in the context of urbanization were gradually expanding their employment horizons. Unfortunately, this clearly did not apply to African American women. The 1910 census found only four black women in Omaha who were bookkeepers or in similar positions; four were trained nurses; three were stenographers or typists; one was a schoolteacher; and none were telephone operators.

Omaha's ethnic mix seemed to many observers a key to understanding the nature of the city. Evaluations were not always positive. When Rudyard Kipling passed through the town in 1889, he concluded that it "seemed to be populated entirely by Germans, Poles, Slavs, Hungarians, Croats, Magyars, and all the scum of the Eastern European States." Between 1900 and 1910, Omaha's population rose from 102,555 to 124,096 persons. Of the latter figure, 27,179 or 22 percent, were from overseas. The larger numbers came from Germany (4,861), Sweden (3,805), Austria-Hungary (3,414), Denmark (2,652), Russia (2,592), and Italy (2,361). The most dramatic change was the rising number of Italians. Many of those from central Europe were Bohemians but were listed by the census as Austrians or Germans. South Omaha in the last count prior to its 1915 annexation by Omaha had 26,259 people. The Magic City had grown by only 258 inhabitants in the first decade of the century. After construction of the packing plants and the establishment of levels of production, there was little need for additional workers. Even so, the numbers and percentages of foreigners moved upward markedly: 8,021 accounting for 31 percent of the total, with 3,551 individuals hailing from Russia constituting the largest single block.

After 1910, Omaha's demographic characteristics started to stabilize. In 1920 there were 191,601 inhabitants of whom 35,385, or fewer than 19 percent, were foreign born. However, changes in countries of origin showed up in the census despite little new immigration. Many persons formerly listed as coming from Germany or Austria-Hungary now claimed to be from the new nations created because of World War I, particularly Czechoslovakia and Poland. Three other countries each contributed over 10 percent of Omaha's immigrants: Germany, 4,270; Russia, 3,825; and Sweden, 3,708.

Both numbers and percentages fell in the 1920s, when the United States government enacted measures that drastically curtailed immigration. The 1930 population of Omaha was 214,066; and the foreign-born percentage had declined to 14 percent, the lowest figure in the century. By nationality the largest aggregates were Czechoslovakians (3,946), Germans (3,700), Italians (3,221), Swedes (2,977), Danes (2,561), Poles (2,546), and Russians (2,084). The statistics presented a general picture of Omaha's primary population trends. There were things that they failed to show. Estimates placed the number of persons of Danish extraction at 10,000 and of Bohemian at 7,000. Many of the Russians were Jews who had fled the country to escape religious persecution. The Italians were primarily from southern Italy and Sicily. A majority of immigrants of all nationalities were males. Throughout the period 1900–30 Omaha's foreign-born percentage was larger than that of the nation as a whole and much larger than that of other cities in the Missouri River valley and watershed. There was no doubt that Omaha qualified as an immigrant city.

In the 1920s, when roughly 50 percent of the population was immigrants or their children, Omaha reached the zenith of its ethnic diversity. There were numerous ethnic neighborhoods, all in older sections near downtown and in South Omaha. Most Germans, Swedes, Danes, and Irish had dispersed throughout town, but some other groups had clustered in their own areas. In turn, Irish, Germans, and Italians had lived in an uninviting area of several blocks on the flood plain just to the southeast of downtown near the factory and warehouse districts. Some Italians had already left Little Sicily, southeast of the business district. Rigid segregation patterns restricted blacks to two ghettos, a small one next to the stockyards and a larger one on the Near North Side close to the Union Pacific shops. The original Bohemian district was along South Thirteenth Street, a north-south thoroughfare. Newer Czech districts were on South Omaha's east side. Sheeley Town, on Omaha's southwest outskirts, was the first Polish district, although it did have a significant Czech presence. Poles soon spilled over into South Omaha, creating a Little Poland. Greek immigrants had dwelled near the packing plants in a district later inhabited by African Americans and Hispanics.

Another neighborhood on South Omaha's south side, directly in the path of prevailing winds from the stockyards and packing plants, was a "zebra striped" dumping ground for poor immigrants from eastern Europe. Serbs, Croatians, Lithuanians, and others all endured the squalid rooming houses of the polyglot precinct before moving away as quickly as possible. Even so, other immigrant sections with their ethnic churches and distinctive architectural forms acted as forces of stability in Omaha. Symbolic of the city's diversity and the economic reality that drew so many nationalities was the smelter on the river near the Douglas Street bridge. There, employees spoke a total of fourteen languages, and sometimes persons in need of a translator came to this place of roaring furnaces that produced copper, gold, and silver and was reputed to be the nation's largest lead refinery.

8. American Smelting and Refining Company, Omaha. *Courtesy NSHS RG2341 PH O 379.*

Some of Omaha's foreign-born groups moved without much trouble into the mainstream, the Germans serving as a case in point. They started coming early in Omaha's history, and their transition to American life was eased by the presence of thousands of other residents of German extraction. German immigrants settled in the older parts of Omaha and in the suburbs of South Omaha, Benson, and Florence. Many acquired their own homes and businesses, rising quickly to important positions in the community. They generally tried to keep Germanic customs, teaching their children the German language, worshiping in German churches, reading German papers, and keeping traditional German mores. On Sunday afternoons they liked to go in family groups to beer gardens to socialize and listen to brass bands. Among their organizations were the Platt-Deutschen Verein, Omaha Musik Verein, and German Turnverein.

Efforts to keep Teutonic cultural forms alive in Omaha, while at the same time embracing American economic and political values, gradually broke down. World War I was a contributing factor. Unknown parties defaced a statue of Johann von Schiller. Federal legislation required Germans who were not American citizens to register as "Alien Enemies." State-encouraged patriotic organizations placed them under observation. To prove loyalty to their adopted land, many Germans abandoned the old ways, going out of their way to oppose the Kaiser. The *Omaha Tribune*, a German language journal, ardently championed the Allied war effort. Prohibition brought another blow, forcing the closing of beer gardens. Immigration fell off sharply, and older people passed away. By the end of the 1920s there was little outward evidence of German culture in Omaha.

Bohemians too arrived in Omaha when it was a young community. In Civil War days, a small party came to the city from Cedar Rapids, Iowa. Throughout the 1870s controversial newspaper editor Edward Rosewater, who put forward an unverified claim as Omaha's first Czech immigrant, helped advertise the virtues of Nebraska among Bohemians. During the last twenty years of the nineteenth century, many Bohemians moved into South Omaha. Some came directly from abroad; others had given up trying to farm in Nebraska. While a majority never advanced beyond the packing houses, fully three-fourths owned homes, and a few rose in professional and business fields. They were one of the best-organized nationalities in Omaha. Of special importance were Sokols, societies that promoted gymnastic and cultural activities. Even so, their social activities became increasingly American. Many second- and third-generation Bohemians continued to take pride in their roots, but so did the members of other immigrant groups. Among Czechs, the assimilation process was virtually complete by the Great Depression.

Swedes and Danes, the chief Scandinavian elements in Omaha, quickly Americanized. The first Swedes arrived in the late 1860s at the start of large-scale emigration from Sweden into the United States. Many who came to Omaha found employment in the Union Pacific shops. When they emigrated, they had little education and few skills. They worked hard, but having little money to start with, they had trouble getting ahead, and the vast majority remained unskilled workers. The Swedes had ethnic lodges, notably the Independent Order of the Vikings and the Order of Vara, but they showed little interest in preserving former customs. The same was true of the Danes. Their clubs were almost entirely social. The major one was the Danish Brotherhood, a national organization founded in Omaha to sell insurance. Economically, they did about as well as the Swedes, advancing slowly. The Danes had come to the United States in immediate post–Civil War times to escape the

German military occupation of their native provinces. In the United States few of these Scandinavians made an effort to teach their children the rudiments of Swedish or Danish. This resulted in almost complete acculturation by the second and third generations.

The Irish constituted another component of Omaha's foreign-born community. The largest single body came originally to help build the Union Pacific. Those who stayed in Omaha went to work in the railroad shops or secured jobs as common laborers. Very few, almost all of whom were men, had come directly to Omaha from the Old Sod. By the 1890s, when the American Protective Association singled them out as targets in an unsuccessful attempt to drive immigrants and their children out of Omaha, the Irish lived throughout town. They had intermarried and adopted American ways to the extent that they had virtually lost identity as a separate ethnic group. Even though they observed St. Patrick's Day, they showed little positive interest in the bitter fight over home rule for Ireland. In Omaha they moved into all levels of society, being particularly influential in politics and city government. They greatly strengthened the Roman Catholic Church; indeed, in the period from 1859 to 1916, the first three bishops in Omaha were natives of Ireland. Many early church benefactors were Irish immigrants or their sons and daughters.

Omaha had a significant Polish community before many other American cities. Early in the 1870s the first Poles came to Sheeley Town to work in a small packing house. More Poles came in the 1880s and 1890s. Few spoke English or had skilled occupations. They toiled in the packing plants and stockyards or worked on the railroads. They were hard-working people with strong family ties. They owned small homes and raised many children. Polish social life revolved around the Roman Catholic Church and fraternal organizations. There were Polish schools and recreation centers sponsored by a number of societies: the Polish Roman Catholic Union, the Polish Union of the United States, the National Alliance, the Pulaski Club, the Polish Welfare Club, and the Polish Citizens' Club. The Poles, as other central Europeans, enjoyed music and dancing. A prime event was the wedding dance, a festive affair open to the public. Older Poles were clannish and showed little inclination to learn more than the rudiments of English or to make drastic changes in their lifestyles. The younger Poles reacted in an opposite manner. They eagerly adopted American values, showing a great interest in sports. During the 1920s Sheeley Town produced powerful amateur baseball teams, affording ample evidence of the acceptance by Poles of America's national pastime.

In the early 1880s there was an influx of Russian Jews into Omaha as part of a general immigration. In Omaha many started anew as peddlers and small shop owners. Some went on to become outstanding merchants. Initially, most Russian Jews settled in a few neighborhoods in the older sections, but they never lived in ghettos. They had a strong tradition of education and had a reputation as being keenly intellectual. Their cultural life centered on the Jewish Community Center, which had a library, gymnasium, auditorium, and Talmud Torah. The Hebrew religion remained a strong force among them, but they showed no interest in preserving Russian customs. After all, pogroms—the organized massacre of helpless people promoted by the authorities—had prompted the Jews to leave Russia.

The Italians, who did not start arriving in large numbers until after 1900, were very individualistic. Fears of restrictions on immigration helped to spur the immigration of thousands of uneducated and unskilled Italians into the United States; a number who moved to Omaha were from what were essentially feudal southern estates and villages. Many were young men who lived together in crowded rooming houses. Most had temporarily left their families behind in Italy. They gained employment almost exclusively as day laborers and showed little interest in American customs. Their ways brought recriminations from older residents who called them "dagos," "guineas," and "wops." A leadership group, mainly from the ranks of the few Italians who had lived in Omaha prior to rapid immigration, gradually emerged. Their influence, along with that of the Roman Catholic Church and the arrival of Italian women and children, added stability. By the 1920s almost all the Italians in Omaha belonged to one or more of twenty-four societies. Predominantly Italian Roman Catholic churches held large festivals, including the annual summer feast of St. Lucia. Most of the stresses and strains related to a desire of Italian immigrants to keep old ties while at the same time becoming loyal Americans: "Though America must be first does not mean that we cannot cherish a love for our mother country," Giulio Agazzoni, a patriarch of the community, said.

There were numerous other immigrant groups in Omaha. Several hundred English and Canadian immigrants lived throughout town, as did those from Norway, Wales, France, and Belgium. Other nationalities were in small colonies in South Omaha. Lithuanians, Serbs, and Croatians resided within the shadow of the packing plants, where almost all of them worked as common laborers. The same part of town contained Romanians, Hungarians, and Austrians. They were too few in number to have much in the way of an impact on the city. Several hundred Syrians, the first arriving in 1890, occupied a tightly packed South Omaha neighborhood. Few Syrians worked in the livestock district. The men started as street merchants, hawking shawls, carpets, and clothing, after a time acquiring small shops. The Syrians clung tenaciously to their old customs with their community concerns centering around two fraternal orders, the Knights of Furzol and the Syrian-American Club.

Shortly after World War I, the packing houses brought in Mexican strikebreakers during a labor dispute. After helping to break the strike, a couple of hundred stayed on in Omaha. Some continued to work in the packing industry. Others sought employment on the railroads and during summer months in Nebraska beet fields. The Mexicans had a strong sense of unity, and they soon had their own Roman Catholic Church, the Nuestra Senora de Guadalupe. Immigrants of all nationalities worked together on the job and then went their own ways after quitting time. Usually they got along well, but there were barroom brawls or shouting matches. The possibility of a major clash was always present, and a sign of the brewing trouble came in a short-lived anti-Japanese outburst.

"THE UNIVERSALITY OF THE PRINCIPLE OF RACE ANTIPATHY"

While the 1900 census showed only two persons born in Japan living in the metropolitan area, Japanese laborers were employed as packing industry strikebreakers in South Omaha in 1904. The strike was a defeat for organized labor, and the Japanese inhabitants, many of whom continued to work at the Cudahy plant, were the focus of lingering bitterness. On the morning of April 17, 1905, some two hundred pupils at South Omaha's Lowell School staged a protest against the attendance of two Japanese male students, aged twenty and twenty-one. Some residents petitioned the school board to bar the enrollment of Japanese pupils, and some parents egged on the striking students, but a level-headed principal and the police kept order. In this time of the Russo-Japanese War, an added complication may have been the presence of the children of South Omaha's Russian community at Lowell School. The following day the situation calmed, although many children remained absent. The president of the South Omaha school board declared that the board could not bar Japanese students, and he added that if all of the white youths studied as diligently and behaved as well as the two Japanese students, "our schools would be materially improved." After a one-day absence, the Japanese students returned, and according to the *Omaha Bee*, many of the petitioners opposing the presence of the Japanese claimed that they had been pressured to sign the document. Whatever the case, the incident reflected the ethnic tensions of the era.

Less than four years later, South Omaha would be the scene of violent ethnic confrontation. Large numbers of Greeks had moved into the Omaha area during the first decade of the twentieth century. The packing houses hired some to break a strike; the railroad brought in others as contract laborers. While contract labor was illegal in the United States, there was no serious attempt to enforce the law. By 1909 Greeks constituted a significant ethnic group. Some lived in a small area in Omaha as permanent residents. They owned shops, had regular jobs, and congregated at a combination tavern and pool room. Most Greeks resided in crowded rooming houses in South Omaha in a district originally called "Indian Hill" that quickly acquired the new designation of "Greek Town." The section's population doubled to approximately two thousand persons in the winter months when the railroads laid off section hands.

Almost all the temporary residents of Greek Town were men aged fifteen to thirty-five. They intended to return to their native land at a future date, so they made no pretense of adopting American ways. Having nothing to do, they spent their days in coffeehouses, drinking thick Turkish coffee, arguing Greek politics, and playing cards. Other workingmen in South Omaha resented their apparent indolence, not stopping to consider the long and hard hours that the Greeks toiled in the summer on remote stretches of railroad track. Adding to resentment of Greeks was the fear that they corrupted South Omaha women. The Greeks did not help matters by making lewd remarks to passing females. Moreover, at least forty Greeks lived openly with American women. The Greeks, hardly any of whom spoke English, rapidly gained the status of unwelcome intruders. These proudly nationalistic people, who traced their heritage back to classical times, never realized that trouble was brewing until it was too late to reverse the tide.

In February 1909 two Omaha newspapers launched bitter attacks against the Greeks of South Omaha. An article in the *Omaha Bee* declared, "The thing that sticks in the craw of the anti-Greek element is that they work cheap; live even more cheaply, in groups, are careless of many of the little details that Americans set much store by; once in a while are imprudent, ignore the restrictions of American law that lay heavily on the true patriot—in short, do not mix, are not 'good fellows' like the citizens we get from northern Europe, for instance." Joseph Pulcar, the editor of the *Omaha Daily News*, was even more explicit in discussing the habits of the Greeks: "Their quarters have been unsanitary; they have insulted women; in many ways they have made themselves offensive in the eyes of the great majority of the people of South Omaha, too." After that denunciation, Pulcar called the Greeks threats to the workers of Omaha. "Herded together in lodging houses and living cheaply," he stressed, "Greeks are a menace to the American laboring man— just as the Japs, Italians, and other similar laborers are." All that was needed was an incident, and that soon came.

A popular South Omaha police officer met a violent death in the course of apprehending a Greek. Patrolman Edward Lowery was forty-two when he died in the line of duty. He left a wife and two children, one a University of Nebraska student. Lowery and his wife were both Irish immigrants. He was a foreman in the Cudahy Company's lard department for several years until he walked off the job in sympathy with strikers in 1904. Summarily fired, he experienced a lengthy period of unemployment before securing an appointment in the South Omaha Police Department. He soon gained a reputation as a respected and understanding officer, frequently helping drunks home instead of arresting them. He was a rising and respected member of the Irish community when he acted on a complaint to arrest John Masourides for vagrancy on January 19, 1909. Masourides was already under police surveillance because of an arrest for gambling. His new troubles stemmed from information that he possibly had an illicit relationship with a seventeen-year-old minor, Lillian Breese. She was a Grand Island, Nebraska, girl who claimed to make a living teaching English to immigrants. Lowery surprised the couple in a rented room and apprehended Masourides. The circumstances enraged Masourides, and there was an altercation. In front of witnesses Masourides pulled a gun; he later claimed he intended to throw it away to avoid charges of having a concealed weapon. Lowery drew his service revolver and both men fired. Lowery fell, fatally hurt; Masourides, slightly wounded, was easily subdued by bystanders. Word of the incident spread quickly. The South Omaha police had to transfer Masourides to an Omaha jail to prevent a lynching. The ambulance carrying him ran a gauntlet of five hundred enraged persons. Shots rang out as horses, running hard, pulled the vehicle out of town. It was a portent of things to come.

On Saturday, the *Omaha World-Herald* carried a banner headline: "ED LOWERY, SOUTH OMAHA POLICEMAN, IS SHOT AND KILLED BY GREEK." The story of the incident contained the text of a petition hastily drafted by Joseph Murphy, an Irish leader in South Omaha:

> Whereas, Many instances of their flagrant disregard and insolence of our laws and ordinances of this city have occurred during the past years, and Whereas, The so-called quarters of the Greeks are infested by a vile bunch of filthy Greeks who have attacked our women, insulted pedestrians upon the street, openly maintained gambling dens and many other forms of viciousness . . . Therefore be it resolved, That we the undersigned citizens and taxpayers of the city hereby believe that a mass meeting should be held on Sunday afternoon, February 21, 1909, at the city hall to take such steps and to adopt such measures as will eventually rid the city of Greeks, and thereby remove the menacing conditions that threaten the very life and welfare of South Omaha.

As if this were not provocative enough, the Sunday-morning edition of the *World-Herald* carried a "proclamation of Mourning" issued by Mayor Frank Koutsky of South Omaha. "Grief unspeakable watches the bier of the martyred hero today," it began. "A Greek, one who in his own native land was never accorded the privilege of lifting his head and looking outward and upward, murdered Officer Lowery."

The thousand men who assembled on Sunday afternoon on a vacant lot near Greek Town turned into a mob. They passed resolutions directed against the "outlawry and viciousness of Greeks," and the "scurvy Greek assassin." In addition, they heard speeches eulogizing the fallen officer and condemning Greeks. An Irish politician said, "It is about time for the citizens to take steps to rid the city of this menace." Thus prompted, the crowd stormed Greek Town. As if under orders, the howling horde systematically looted and burned buildings, beating senseless any Greeks in their way. During the worst of the rioting, the South Omaha police mobilized but stayed at their headquarters. Mayor Koutsky informed the governor of Nebraska but requested no troops. Authorities in Omaha declined to intervene. In the wake of the rampage, the South Omaha Greeks left town as quickly as they could. Many went over the bridge into Iowa, carrying belongings on their backs.

In Council Bluffs, some of the refugees found lodging with fellow Greeks who lived in the Union Pacific Transfer area. However, on Monday afternoon, chief of police George H. Richmond ordered the detention of the uprooted men found on the streets or in business places. Men with weapons were disarmed, while those with train tickets were escorted to the depots. The rest were lodged for part of the evening at the Council Bluffs auditorium but quickly went to local hotels or boarding houses. Explaining his dragnet operation, Chief Richmond remarked, "I simply desired to prevent the possibility of trouble here, and to see that these men were taken care of properly. I could not permit them to congregate in this city, many of them armed, all homeless and most of them frightened and desperate. There has not been any intention to prefer charges against them."

There was a national reaction to the disturbance. Newspapers around the country tended to view the Omaha Greeks as victims. Closer to home, the *Omaha World-Herald* said that the rioters were the "dregs" of South Omaha. Masourides, after two trials, received a fourteen-year sentence for second-degree murder. He served five and a half years before being furloughed and deported. The U.S. Justice Department carried on an investigation of the events in South Omaha. No indictments resulted, but the government paid over eighty thousand dollars in indemnities to Turkey, Greece, and Austria-Hungary.

Three days after the South Omaha riot, the *Council Bluffs Nonpareil* declared that the local authorities should have suppressed the "foul mass meeting" that led to the violence but concluded that there was a strong possibility that such an episode may have been inevitable. In an editorial that both reflected and condemned the ethnic and racial prejudices of the day, the paper concluded, "The South Omaha occurrence has again indicated the universality of the principle of race antipathy." Although the *Nonpareil* said that such problems could be averted if newcomers such as the Greeks and Japanese did not concentrate in significant numbers, it said that the feelings against them stemmed from their "rigid frugality" and related traits that set them apart from the established American population. As the paper said, "The American is the spendthrift of the globe. Frugality is his natural enemy." Over a year after the upheaval, the 1910 census counted only fifty-nine persons born in Greece who resided in South Omaha. Nevertheless, small Greek communities survived in Omaha and Council Bluffs.

"LOOK AT WHAT HAPPENED IN OMAHA"

The blacks of Omaha had deeper roots than those of many of the immigrant groups. Early in Omaha's history, blacks found employment on the railroads and in the hotels. Dining-car personnel, chair-car attendants, mail-car workers, and Pullman conductors made their homes in Omaha. They had steady jobs and a generally good family life. The railroad employees were often respected members of the Greater Omaha society, despite having little say in public affairs and little material wealth. The census listed the black population of Omaha at 3,443 in 1900 and 4,425 in 1910. These figures were probably a little low. People were counted in place at the time of the enumeration; so some Omaha blacks, on trains across the region, showed up in the returns as residents of towns, usually division points, far away from Omaha.

On the surface, African American life appeared quite stable. Harry Haywood, a black born with the name Haywood Hall in South Omaha in 1898, had many pleasant childhood memories of life in the Brown Park area, home to many Bohemians. As he remembered, members of the small black community in South Omaha got along well with their Bohemian and other neighbors. Haywood attributed the good relations to the small number of African Americans, but in 1913 his father, a packing-house worker, was beaten up by a white gang and threatened with death if he did not leave South Omaha. The elder Hall said that gang included Irish youths from Indian Hill and some adults. The Hall family quickly moved to Minneapolis, and Haywood continued on an odyssey of experiences that would eventually lead him to prominence in the Communist Party U.S.A.

The center of Omaha's black community was a several-block district north of the downtown. There were over a hundred black-owned businesses, and there were a number of black physicians, dentists, and attorneys. Over twenty fraternal organizations and clubs flourished and the National Association for the Advancement of Colored People had a strong chapter. Church life was diverse. Of more than forty denominations, Methodists and Baptists predominated. Of course, outward appearances of solidity failed to hide a number of depressing realities: white resentment, unofficially segregated facilities, low levels of education, marginal housing, abject living standards, poor salaries, and few opportunities. Prejudice over color negated any initial advantage that blacks had over other elements in the Omaha melting pot.

Confrontation sometimes arose from interracial contacts. Many of Omaha's saloons were in or around the red-light district that in the early twentieth century was located between Davenport Street on the north, Douglas Street on the south, reaching westward from Eighth to Twelfth Street and sometimes Fourteenth Street. Many blacks resided in this old downtown area near the emerging ghetto to the north. During these years racial discrimination was emerging in Omaha in employment and housing, and some saloons made it clear that they did not want black patrons. In other drinking establishments blacks and whites mingled, and sometimes alcohol brought underlying racial feelings to the surface. Because inexpensive easily concealed handguns were abundantly available, such saloon encounters were sometimes deadly.

Law enforcement in Omaha in the years 1880 to 1920 clearly discriminated against blacks. By 1920 the number of blacks in Omaha had risen to 5.38 percent of the city's total population, but for the four decades ending that year, they accounted for 24 percent of Douglas County's homicide indictments. Blacks were found guilty in 85 percent of these cases, while 34 percent of the white defendants were found guilty. Black defendants, normally lacking good legal defense, were far more prone than whites to accept plea bargains that might lead to easy convictions.

The Omaha African American community experienced dramatic changes in the World War I decade. Of great significance was the loss of political influence. During previous years, black leaders had made certain small but significant advances. An Omaha black served as a justice of the peace in the 1880s; in the 1890s another, M. O. Ricketts, MD, was a two-term member of the state legislature. Ricketts was an adroit politician, and he succeeded in gaining a number of patronage positions for blacks. In the 1900s he moved to Missouri, and saloonkeeper Jack Broomfield emerged as the leading black political leader in Omaha. Critics charged that he displayed more interest in promoting and protecting gambling enterprises than in furthering the status of his race. He acquiesced to the replacement of blacks on public bodies, and before long they had almost entirely disappeared from places of influence; there were, for example, no black teachers by the second decade of the century. Concurrently, there was a large influx of blacks into Omaha. They came as part of a World War I migration of rural southern blacks to northern cities. In Omaha many of the newcomers obtained employment in the packing houses. They performed a variety of tasks including those of skilled butchers and trimmers. The 1920 census reported that Omaha had 10,315 blacks: 5,598 males and 4,717 females. The number of African Americans in the city had doubled in ten years.

The pressures created by the influx gradually moved toward a disastrous confrontation. Since the lynching of George Smith in 1891, there had been two incidents that could have produced a similar outcome. In March 1906 police thwarted a mob outside the county courthouse that tried to seize three blacks in custody following a robbery and murder, and in August 1917 authorities eluded a Florence mob bent upon lynching a black who had been apprehended after a murder. Whites returning from service sometimes found their jobs taken by blacks. This automatically caused tensions. Complicating matters was the breakdown of local black political influence. Recent migrants had little respect for the older leadership. At the same time, a new reform government in Omaha had few lines of communication beyond the business community. The administration's enemies, especially those associated with vice, sought incidents to discredit it. Conditions started to deteriorate in the summer of 1919—a Red Summer in American race relations. Blacks died in violent disturbances from the crowded tenements of the South Side of Chicago to the shantytowns of East St. Louis. Through the summer, Omaha's three daily newspapers carried reports about alleged assaults upon white women by black men and other racially related troubles, but the *Bee* played up these stories. Even though cases collapsed under investigation—one man was over a hundred miles away when an attack on a white woman occurred—the newspapers continued to make sensational charges. The Reverend John Williams, the editor of the weekly *Monitor*, Omaha's only black-owned paper, tried to calm fears. He contended that what happened elsewhere could not possibly happen in Omaha. Events proved him wrong.

Early on Friday, September 26, 1919, nineteen-year-old Agnes Loeback reported a serious incident. Her story was as follows: while out walking with a "crippled" acquaintance, Milton Hoffman, a black man suddenly leaped out of the bushes. After slugging Hoffman senseless, he assaulted her and ran off into the night. What followed was a disturbing event in the history of Omaha. Decades later it still remained a source of controversy. On the day after the alleged crime the police arrested a suspect, William Brown, an itinerant packing-house laborer from Cairo, Illinois. Detectives took him to Miss Loeback's house, where from a sick bed she identified him as her assailant. A crowd gathered, and the officers had trouble getting Brown away to a jail cell on the upper floors of the Douglas County court house, located in the heart of the business district. H. J. Pinkett, a black lawyer, talked to Brown and observed his physical condition: Brown had severe rheumatism and moved with great effort. It seemed hard to believe that he had either the dexterity or energy to stage a mugging and rape. If anything, he seemed an innocent victim.

The Omaha papers did not bother with such particulars. Extra editions reported that still another assault had occurred and that the culprit was under lock and key in the courthouse. By Saturday night the city seethed with self-righteous indignation, and Brown was the talk of the town. Afterwards, an official report noted, "It is known that at least one party on Saturday night went about to the various pool halls in the south part of the city and announced that a crowd would gather at Bancroft School and from there would march to the courthouse for the purpose of lynching the colored man." Those responsible for these activities were never identified.

On Sunday afternoon several hundred teenage whites assembled on a South Omaha school grounds. Goaded on by Milton Hoffman, Loeback's companion at the time of the alleged attack, the crowd marched on the courthouse. Their purpose, according to a participant, was "to get the Nigger." They were led by two students beating on drums. A squad of police who tried to stop the march were cursed and brushed aside. When the marchers reached the courthouse, they found it protected by thirty police officers.

For an hour nothing much happened, except officials ordered a black detective inside after he infuriated the throng by drawing his revolver in response to a racial slur. After that there were friendly exchanges between police and demonstrators. It looked as if there would be no serious trouble.

The four-story courthouse, built in 1912, was one of the sturdiest buildings in town. Supposedly the imposing structure was both "mob proof" and "fire proof." Brown, housed with 120 other prisoners on the top floor, appeared in no danger. The police chief was not even present; nor had he seen fit to take any extra precautions such as securing gun shops in the downtown district. Some fifty policemen standing by at the central station downtown were released from duty. The chief assumed that the crowd would disperse and go home at the supper hour. It did not.

Things started to get out of hand shortly after 5:00 p.m. News of the trouble at the courthouse quickly spread throughout Omaha. At 6:20 p.m., Lt. Col. Jacob Wuest, U.S. Army commander at Fort Omaha, received a phone call from an Omaha police captain, seeking military aid to restore order. Colonel Wuest, unaware of a 1917 relaxation of War Department regulations governing the use of federal troops in civil disturbances, spent four hours seeking approval from Washington. In the meantime, swarms of people, estimated in excess of five thousand, converged on the building. Leaders began to emerge. Older and more determined men, identified as from the "vicious elements," took the place of the boys. They seemed to know exactly what to do. Some looted sporting goods stores and pawnshops for guns and ammunition. Others ordered people to get gasoline to burn the building. A young man on horseback appeared, brandishing a heavy rope. Two girls distributed stones out of tin buckets. The police, showered by rocks, withdrew inside the building.

An assault party stormed the south entrance; the police beat it back by using two powerful streams of water from fire hoses. Bricks crashed through the courthouse windows, and random gunfire echoed in the streets, the crowd continuing to grow by the minute. The chief of police and two commissioners had trouble getting into the building, even though escorted by twenty officers. When the chief tried to make an appeal from an upstairs window he reeled back, hit on the head and slightly injured by a stone. The new reform mayor of Omaha, Edward Smith, arrived, making an unobtrusive entrance. Not long after that, fire bombs started to crash through the windows, setting fire to county offices on the first floor. The mob overpowered firemen and took their ladders, preparing to use them to storm to upper floors. As smoke poured into the jail, guards took the prisoners to the roof, where they lay flat to avoid gunfire. A more desperate situation could hardly be imagined for the city government of Omaha. Over a thousand active rioters surrounded the courthouse, screaming, "Give us the Nigger." Spectators blocked all the streets in the business district, making immediate police reinforcement impossible. The mayor and key safety officials were trapped in the burning building. Discipline disintegrated around them. Officers became passive; and some, reconciled to disaster, made farewell telephone calls to their families.

Mayor Smith was running out of options. His "law and order" government was in a shambles. His personal popularity had fallen since earlier in the year, when he had apparently condoned the use of strikebreakers. He was a short, stocky man with strong ties to the business community. He was also a man of courage. He walked out of the courthouse to face the mob but never had a chance to speak. A man cried, "He can give us the nigger if he will and save the courthouse." A youth yelled something about a gun. Several thugs assaulted Smith, knocking him to the ground. When some horrified spectators tried to help him, a husky youth yelled, "Don't let them get Mayor Smith away. Let's string him up. Shoot him. He's a negro-lover. They elected him. He's not better than they are!" The mayor, covered with blood, shouted, "No, I won't give up this man. I'm going to enforce the law, even with my own life." That further enraged mob members. They set fire to a car sent to help him escape and pushed and shoved him through the main streets of his city. At an electric pole, men dropped a noose around his neck and threw the end of the rope over a beam. An unidentified man cut the rope as it was being drawn tight and ran back into the crowd. Another person pleaded, "He's a white man. For God's sake, use a little judgment. Don't do something you'll be sorry for. Don't be a bolsheviki." The vigilantes listened for a moment and then resumed the work of lynching the mayor. Thousands of spectators looked on. At that point, police appeared with drawn pistols. They formed a ring around the mayor and took him away to a hospital, where he was to undergo a lengthy recovery. The mayor's rescue happened so quickly that he was gone into the night before his attackers had time to react. After realizing what had happened, they retaliated by burning a police car and launching a violent attack on the courthouse.

The mob went from room to room in the unburned parts of the large structure, smashing furniture and starting small fires. The chief and the commissioners stood aside and watched helplessly. The sheriff defended a stairway, which the mob bypassed and cordoned off. A group of prisoners took

9. Burning of William Brown's body, 1919 Omaha courthouse riot. *Courtesy NSHS, RG2281 PH O 69.*

Brown, clad in blue prison overalls, and pushed him down a flight of stairs into the arms of the mob. Reports said he went willingly, realizing that there was no hope. Men passed Brown head over head to the outside of the building as police watched, their attempts to save him defeated. By the time Brown reached the ground, he had been beaten unconscious, castrated, and stripped. Someone threw a rope around his neck, and men attached the other end to an auto bumper. As the vehicle dragged Brown through the crowd, persons fired bullets into him. At a major intersection, Eighteenth and Harney streets, Brown's battered and bleeding remains were hanged from an electric light pole. Crazed white men fired hundreds of bullets into the body before it was cut down. Then it was pulled behind an auto to another crossing. While a news camera flashed and thousands watched, boys poured oil out of street lanterns stolen from a construction project onto the remains, which were then ignited as those present roared approval. Incredibly, the horrifying events had not yet ended. Men tossed a rope around the heap of charred flesh and bones and dragged what was left through the streets for close to two hours while spectators hooted and cheered. Before the riot ran its course, a white boy died, killed by a stray bullet; and many other persons received injuries. By dawn, Omaha was peaceful, its night of shame over.

As with the anti-Greek riot of the previous decade, Council Bluffs experienced reverberations from the upheaval across the river. A number of blacks crossed to Council Bluffs, taking refuge in and around the rail yards as they made plans to catch south-bound trains. On Monday, a brakeman on a north-bound Burlington train approaching town, saw a coal car on a freight train headed south crowded with blacks. An Iowa National Guard unit was quickly called into service to assist the Council Bluffs police in the event of any problems. On Monday night, there was potential racial trouble on the south side of the city. As the *Nonpareil* reported, "In the Sixteenth avenue district there was some disposition among the rougher element to congregate and mutter against the Negroes, but these little gatherings were broken up by the officers." A heavy rain also helped to preserve order. The following night, Guardsmen "with guns loaded and bayonets fixed" were on duty in black neighborhoods. The authorities took other precautions such as detaining blacks or seizing ammunition from them. More evidence of the tension in Council Bluffs after the Omaha riot was found in a sharp increase in gun purchases.

The aftermath of the "Court House Riot" was predictable. Too late to do any good, authorities dispatched 1,600 heavily armed federal troops into the city. Gen. Leonard Wood, commander of the soldiers, initially blamed the disturbance on the newspapers. "One of the first steps toward the preservation of law and order should be the suppression of a rotten press where there is one," he announced. "I am strong for the freedom of the press where it is honest and fearless; gives facts, not lies." A few days later, he reached another conclusion. After praising local unions for their support of the legal process, he turned to the lynching, stating, "[J]ust one agency was to blame for this—that was the I. W. W. and its red flag, the Soviet organization of this country." Eventually, the troops left and conditions returned to normal. The county spent five hundred thousand dollars repairing the courthouse, and soon no outward trace of the riot remained. Loeback recovered in time to marry Milton Hoffman. Rumors circulated that the mob action was planned in advance, that the assault was a hoax, and that Brown was the victim of a sinister conspiracy either plotted by the mayor to make himself appear a hero or by his political enemies to discredit him and all his works. Formal investigations collected data that failed to prove any conspiracy existed. A number of suspects arrested for participating in the riot eventually went free.

Newspaper editorials tried to explain what had happened and to analyze its significance. Under the heading, "Omaha Bows in Shame," the black editor of the *Monitor* wrote, "It all seems as though it were a hideous nightmare, a disturbing dream that must vanish when one awakens. And would be to God that this were true! But, unfortunately, it is no dream, but an awful reality that has horrified and stunned the community." He concluded that Brown's lynching was an isolated incident and not a race riot. An editorial in the *World-Herald* attacked "jungle rule" and the "mob spirit" of the "wolf pack." It intoned, "It is over now, thank God! Omaha henceforth will be safe for its citizens, and as safe for the citizens within its gate, as any city in the land. Its respectable and law-abiding people, comprising 99 per cent of the population, will see to that." After denouncing "red handed criminals," the editorialist warned Omaha blacks to obey the law. The *World-Herald*, which had attacked black lawbreakers prior to the riot, received a Pulitzer Prize for the editorial. The paper's publisher, Gilbert Hitchcock, was minority leader of the U. S. Senate. And so the incident ended with the mutual consent of most concerned. Few remembered the name of the victim in the racial tragedy.

Almost nine months later, on June 15, 1920, one person had urgent reason to recall Omaha's riot and lynching. In Duluth, Minnesota, district court judge William Cant stood before a mob that had assembled downtown near the police headquarters and jail. Inside the jail were young black men from a traveling circus who were suspects in the alleged rape of a young white woman the previous night. Facing what was obviously a crowd contemplating lynching, Judge Cant exclaimed, "This is wrong. Look at what happened in Omaha. The riot there disgraced that city. The honor of Duluth is at stake. Most of you are all law-abiding citizens, and if you do this terrible thing, you will never live it down and neither will Duluth." The judge's plea briefly brought calm, but before midnight, in scenes starkly reminiscent of what had happened in Omaha, three young black men hung from a lamppost.

COUNCIL BLUFFS: GROWTH AND SOCIAL STRESS

Population changes in Council Bluffs during the early twentieth century followed the trend toward stabilization and the slow fading of Old World identities evident on the west side of the river. Between 1900 and 1910, the population of Council Bluffs rose from 25,802 to 29,292, and the census of the latter year counted a record number of 4,268 of foreign-born white persons or 14.57 percent of the city's population. The 1920 census showed that the population of Council Bluffs had risen to 36,162, but the number of foreign-born whites had fallen to 3,988 or slightly over 11 percent of the city's residents. This trend continued in 1930 as Council Bluffs' population reached 42,048, and the number of foreign-born white persons dropped to 3,036 or 7.22 percent of the total. The 1930 census counted 906 persons in Council Bluffs who were born in Denmark and 585 who gave Germany as their birthplace. As in 1900, Danes and Germans ranked first and second respectively among the city's foreign born. Persons born in Sweden (231), Russia (206), Italy (200), England (184), the Irish Free State (163), Canada (131), Greece (114), and a smattering of other nations gave Council Bluffs a measure of ethnic diversity as did 305 Mexicans. While the number of blacks in Council Bluffs had more than doubled from 320 in 1910 to 669 in 1930, this increase brought the total to just under 1.6 percent of the total population.

Although the population of Council Bluffs was somewhat less diverse than that of Omaha and South Omaha, the city was not spared the ethnic tensions that afflicted its Nebraska neighbors. Around Christmas 1903, reports of black men robbing and assaulting white women led to the arrest of two African Americans who were incarcerated in the county jail. A mob gathered on the night of December 28, and a few agitators tried to rile the crowd. However, well-armed police aided by a local National Guard unit kept control, and the next day the prisoners were taken to the state penitentiary for their own security.

Much more serious was an episode nearly a decade later. Just before 11:00 p.m. on the night of May 27, 1913, a person slashed the throat of Howard Jones, a young railroad fireman, at the Chicago and North Western roundhouse. Jones died soon, and his alleged assailant, Francesco Guidice (sometimes spelled "Giudice"), who used the name Henry Wiley, was arrested. Revenge may have been the motive for the slaying because Jones had reportedly complained that Guidice had not properly serviced the firemen's locomotive, a complaint that had cost Guidice his job.

The police and sheriff's officers took particular care to guard the accused man at the county jail. They were correct in anticipating trouble because on the night of Thursday, May 29, the eve of the Memorial Day holiday, a mob assembled at the jail and called upon the jailor to hand over Guidice. By this time, the prisoner had been removed from the city, and representatives of the mob were shown through the county and city jails to gain assurance that Guidice was not present. Apparently angered that they could not get their man and not dissuaded by his use of the Anglo name "Wiley," the mob of about two hundred surged through the downtown area around Pearl Street and Broadway, breaking windows and doing other damage to businesses operated by Italians and Greeks. The rioters then headed for the Chicago and North Western roundhouse, their objectives being to "Drive the dagoes out of town." They pelted the homes of Italians with bricks and chased away men of Italian background from railroad bunk cars and the roundhouse.

Before the night was over, the local militia unit, the Dodge Light Guards, was mobilized to help restore order. There was no further trouble. Council Bluffs mayor Thomas Maloney, lamely seeking a scapegoat in reports that some of the troublemakers had come from South Omaha, asserted, "Our city will not be over run again by a bunch of Nebraska hoodlums." However, a *Nonpareil* editorial said, "We are scathing in our denunciation of Russian treatment of Jews. And yet the Russians are simply doing to the Jews what was done to the Italians and Greeks in Council Bluffs Thursday night, May 29. We denounce Mexican government as altogether bad, but here is a sample right in our own midst."

Barely a month after the riot, Francesco Guidice, following a change of venue of his trial to Glenwood, Mills County, was convicted of the murder of Howard Jones and received a sentence of life imprisonment. The verdict was overturned, but Guidice was later retried and again convicted. In the meantime, the services of the Italian workers who had fled Council Bluffs in terror were missed. Some five weeks after the upheaval, the *Nonpareil* reported that approximately one-half of their number had gone back to their roundhouse jobs cleaning locomotive fireboxes and performing hard tasks that other persons would not do.

FAILED REFORMERS

The courthouse riot in Omaha finished the ruin of Mayor Smith's hapless administration, and he declined to seek reelection. He had been elected in 1918 under a unique commission plan adopted six years earlier. In a nonpartisan general ballot, the voters elected seven commissioners. Once installed, the commissioners selected a mayor and department heads from their own ranks. Candidates normally ran on slates and announced beforehand what functions they wanted to fill if elected, be it mayor or fire commissioner. Smith had headed a divided Allied Slate. One wing, consisting of the Committee of Five Thousand, favored prohibition and a crusade for moral purity. Another had a strong business orientation. The members considered themselves "moderate progressives." They stood for changes in the structure of government and for efficiency and economy. The Good Government group, sponsored by the Omaha and the Douglas County Dry League, supported the Allied slate, with the exception of one Jewish candidate. A Good Government official explained, "The state must stand for Christianity." Smith was the only Democrat on the Allied Slate; the rest were Republicans. Smith had a reputation as a progressive reformer and had much support among the "better elements." Smith and four other members of his slate, including the man not endorsed by the Good Government group, swept to victory on election day. The Allied Slate ran best among "old stock" whites and worst among blacks and newer immigrants. The victory was very popular with commercial interests. The *Omaha Trade Exhibit* explained the reform victory by saying, "the business men of this city, the big men who are responsible for the city's rapid growth and wonderful progress determined to have a four-square city, a well regulated and well balanced city, and one whose political machinery and city government would be a true representation of the place in business and social affairs in this great trade territory that Omaha now holds."

The new city government experienced serious problems almost from the beginning. The commissioners had differing social and economic philosophies, and they soon fell out over a wide variety of issues. They failed to agree about the location of a settlement house, schemes to catch bootleggers, and whether or not to keep a women's detention hospital. A commissioner opposed the settlement house as an unwarranted interference with immigrants' control over their children; another claimed that the strict enforcement of prohibition would give Omaha a bad name. Police commissioner J. Dean Ringer, a member of the Committee of Five Thousand, opposed the hospital: "I don't want Omaha advertised as a place where prostitutes can be cured." Ringer hoped to use the police department as a vehicle for a moral crusade. As for Mayor Smith, it turned out that he had a limited view of his duties. He told an assembly of clergy, "I have no desire or ambition to have my administration known as a 'reform' administration. . . . My role is to sit on the lid of expenditures."

Controversies ended with the September 1919 disaster. After that, the commissioners, reconciled to the impossibility of consensus and demoralized by Mayor Smith's refusal or inability to exercise further leadership, concentrated on staking out positions for the 1921 election. When it came, the reformers' choice for mayor was prohibitionist Abraham L. Sutton, who had been defeated for governor on the Republican ticket in 1916. The campaign of the "Progressive Seven" concentrated on saving Omaha from sin. Ringer, candidate for reelection and leader of the slate, said the "morals of the youth of the city are at stake" and contended, "In my mind the moral issue in the city is the greatest of them all." Other appeals, such as one entitled "To the Mothers of Omaha," failed to have an impact. The voters threw out the reformers in favor of the United Seven, headed by former mayor James C. Dahlman. Reform government ended, foundering over ideological differences and an inability to develop a workable program.

OMAHA'S "PERPETUAL MAYOR"

James C. Dahlman, except for Smith's tenure, was mayor of Omaha from his initial election in 1906 until his death in 1930, winning seven out of eight mayoral campaigns. He sought to obtain home rule and to control the excesses of private utility interests. The first campaign platform he ran on called for the reduction of gas prices. He was later a key figure in the city's acquisition of the waterworks. A slender and brown-eyed man, he brought an unusual style to the mayor's office. He lived without ostentation with his wife and daughter and refused an official car, preferring to use public transportation. When he needed an automobile for official functions, particularly the entertaining of visiting dignitaries, he rented one out of his own pocket. He ate sparingly; his favorite meal was a sandwich, milk, and a piece of pie. Almost always he wore cowboy boots, putting the right one on first out of superstition. Routine administration bored him, and he turned most paperwork over to his secretary. During office hours he talked to anyone who came by, holding what one observer called a sort of open house. He regularly saw from ten to a hundred constituents a day and talked to many more over the telephone. He took cranks in stride, calling them "enthusiasts."

Dahlman strongly favored family life. He frequently pardoned husbands in jail for drinking or minor offenses if their wives explained what had happened. "If it was the man alone who paid the penalty for the offense I would let him stay in jail," Dahlman often commented. "I cannot see a mother and children suffer because the husband and father drank a little too much." People contacted him about all sorts of matters, all of which he handled himself. He saw nothing wrong with attending to complaints about potholes, chickens running wild, and uncut weeds. Critics argued that there was little substance to his administration and that he had little control over the machinery of government. Nor could he have, for under Omaha's commission system of government implemented in 1912, voters elected a seven-member city council/commission that combined legislative and executive power. Following its election, this body divided administrative duties and chose one of its number to be what amounted to a weak mayor. As the people expected, Dahlman's colleagues faithfully elected him to this office, and he continued to enjoy direct contacts with constituents. He went about his tasks, earning the title of "the perpetual mayor of Omaha" and keeping an earlier sobriquet, that of "Cowboy Jim." Few mayors of major cities served longer or were closer to the people.

Dahlman had an extraordinary career. Born on a Texas ranch in 1856, he had little formal education. At age seventeen, he won a statewide riding tournament in Texas. He became a cowhand, earning a reputation as an expert with the lariat. When he was twenty-two, he fled to Nebraska after killing his brother-in-law during a confrontation. Dahlman, who used an alias until he learned a judge ruled the killing self-defense, went to work punching cows on the large N-Bar Ranch. He was proud of his occupation and critical of the popular view of cowboy, which depicted them as swaggering, hard-riding men who spent their free time drinking, gambling, wenching, and fighting. "The cowboy is of entirely different makeup," he claimed. "His business is the expert handling of cattle—this is what is expected and demanded by his employer."

In the 1880s Dahlman married a refined eastern woman who had come west to teach and settled down in the remote western community of Chadron, Nebraska. He worked as a brand inspector for the Wyoming Stockmen's Association and entered Democratic politics. For several years he was on the Chadron city council. After that he was first sheriff and then mayor. During the 1890s he embraced Populist doctrines, but although a delegate to the 1892

Populist convention, he remained a Democrat. He supported William Jennings Bryan and ran the Democratic statewide campaign of 1896 in Nebraska. Following the election, Dahlman left Chadron, living for a short while in Lincoln, where he was secretary of the state transportation board. In 1898 he moved to Omaha and worked in the livestock commission business prior to running for mayor. He had statewide aspirations and in 1910 ran unsuccessfully for governor. A contributing factor to his defeat was his stand against prohibition. Bryan, by then an avowed dry, opposed him. Even so, Dahlman and Bryan remained the best of friends and continued to cooperate on other matters. Dahlman seemed to get along with just about everyone. His acquaintances included such diverse personalities as Theodore Roosevelt, William "Buffalo Bill" Cody, and Sioux chieftain Red Cloud. Several times Dahlman was a delegate to national conventions of the Democratic Party.

No one ever questioned Mayor Dahlman's integrity, though there were charges that he was a frontman for sinister elements. His critics said that he performed routine and ceremonial functions and in exchange for support at the polls allowed a crooked machine to dominate local politics. In 1911 the editor of the *Omaha News* charged that Dahlman's backers were "crooks, bums, outcast negroes, gamblers, frequenters of dives and pool halls, parasites on fallen women, and other men of that stripe." Such charges implied a continuance under Dahlman of a traditional relationship that had existed in the nineteenth century between politicians and vice elements. Dahlman felt comfortable with a wide-open Omaha: there was no doubt that he accepted machine help. The question, never answered, was to what extent it influenced his performance as mayor. It could be argued that he simply took support where he found it and that he looked upon the dives of Omaha as business operations that contributed to the city's economy in much the same way as Gurdon W. Wattles's transit line and James E. Davidson's power company. Yet it was probably more complex. He appeared to have a mutually advantageous relationship with a man he never associated with in public, Thomas Dennison, Omaha's political boss.

THE "BOSS" AND HIS ASSOCIATES

Thomas Dennison, sometimes labeled the "Old Man" in his later years, was a shadowy figure in the life of the city. Physically, he was a large and powerful man with a weatherbeaten face and a cauliflower ear. At the height of his power he dressed immaculately and wore large diamond rings. He had steely eyes and a narrow smile. Born in Iowa, he grew up on farms there and in Nebraska. As a teenager, he toiled for several years as a farm laborer. He went west at age twenty and worked as a blacksmith, a railroad section hand, and a prospector. After a time, he gravitated to Leadville, Colorado, one of the roughest towns in the country. In 1880 the city of fourteen thousand perched high in the Rocky Mountain mining district had over a hundred dance halls. Dennison started as a bouncer in the large and notorious Texas Saloon, advancing within a short time to a quarter-owner.

He became a professional gambler and ran dance houses in several mining towns before moving to Omaha in 1892. He arrived with a great deal of money and may have represented a gambling syndicate. After running a profitable policy game, he invested in several "dens," including the Budweiser Saloon, which he used as a headquarters. When some leading gamblers left town near the turn of the century after police harassment, which Dennison may have instigated, he emerged as leader of the Third Ward. It was in that part of town, the old First Ward, where vice activities centered. Quickly solidifying power he served as middleman between gamblers and saloonkeepers, established a satisfactory arrangement with the police force, developed ties with *Omaha Bee* owner Edward Rosewater and dealt through intermediaries with important businessmen. Dennison also funded a "charitable organization," financed with money he collected in the Third Ward from fellow gamblers and others and through which he regularly distributed clothing, food, and other goods to the needy. In return, he "expected value received" at the polls, and he usually got it. Grateful recipients voted for his ticket; and that, plus ballot stuffing and intimidation, enabled him to influence city elections. He never held office, but police officers chauffeured him about town and few doubted that he was the "Boss."

Dennison preferred to stay in the background, particularly after he won acquittal on two charges in the early 1900s. He was accused of stealing jewelry and of trying to dynamite an enemy. A teetotaler, he lived quietly with a wife and daughter. As a hobby, he raised champion wire-haired terriers. "I like dogs," he said. "They're honest and don't try to double-cross you." He believed that legislation had no effect on human conduct. He explained: "Some people are good and some are bad. Laws can't change them. Laws that people don't believe in can't be enforced if whole armies tried it. There are so many laws that lawyers are either lawbreakers or hypocrites. For my part, I hate a damn hypocrite." As for gambling, he compared it to accepted business practices and minor law violations, stating, "People are always getting excited about little things, like minor lawbreaking and misdemeanors. Take gambling, for example. A dinky crap game or penny-ante poker causes a hell of a racket. But the stock market gambling was all right." Dennison took a practical approach toward politics. Talking about the possibility of a reform government in 1918, he supposedly ruminated, "I think we better let the bastards have it their way for awhile. Let's just lie low for the next election . . . they'll be glad to see us back."

For many years an Omaha printing company president, Frank B. Johnson, supposedly acted as Dennison's conduit to the business community. Some persons thought Johnson the boss, speculating that he gave Dennison "daily marching orders." Probably it was the other way around. Dennison received considerable publicity from time to time, particularly in 1930 when, following the death of his wife, he married seventeen-year-old Nevajo Truman. By this time, the fortunes of his organization were declining. In January 1930 the death of Mayor Dahlman spelled uncertainty for Dennison's relations with city hall. The subsequent murders of two bootleggers highlighted underworld rivalry in Omaha, but when Harry Lapidus, a respected businessman, was gunned down in his car in December 1931, a furor was unleashed which contributed to the demise of Dennison's organization.

Leading the charge was city commissioner Roy N. Towl, abetted by a defector from the Dennision machine. In October 1932 Dennison and fifty-eight other persons were brought to trial in federal court, charged with violation of the prohibition law. Although the trial ended in a hung jury, the apparent purpose of the prosecution succeeded—the public discrediting of the Dennison organization. By now, seventy-four-year-old Tom Dennison was in declining health, and in May 1933 his ticket went down to defeat in a local election. In 1934 he died in California of a cerebral hemorrhage. Over one thousand persons attended his interment in Omaha's Forest Lawn Cemetery. An editorial in the *Omaha World-Herald*, which consistently opposed his machine, concluded on February 16, 1934, "There were quite the makings of another sort of man in Tom Dennison. . . . He had . . . . the qualities of natural leadership, of the fighter, and he was industrious and persevering. . . . Suppose he had been directed into a better path for a better end. . . . Our guess is that he would have gone far and won for himself a deservedly honored name."

The Omaha of the Dennison-Dahlman era was wide open. Gambling, though outlawed, continued to flourish throughout the Third Ward. Police raids occurred only when an establishment's owners had run afoul of the organization. An illicit drug traffic existed; its scope a carefully kept secret. Professional criminals frequented the vice district, using it as a haven and base of operations. Saloons increased markedly in number during the ten years before World War I. Opponents considered them the cornerstone of vice in Omaha, and a state-enacted 8:00 p.m. closing law had little effect. Juries refused to convict alleged violators. A 1916 state constitutional amendment authorizing prohibition contained no provision for implementation. National prohibition flopped in Omaha, owing to Dennison's satisfactory relationship with the police department and the business community's total disinterest in pushing for energetic enforcement. A survey made in 1929 claimed that at least 1,500 places, including many drug stores, sold liquor. Nebraska attorney general Christian A. Sorensen prepared a report on vice in Omaha and told city officials, "Clean up Omaha or I'll come and do it for you." His campaign resulted in some well-publicized raids and forced many liquor interests under cover. Vice activities dispersed throughout town, ending the heyday of the Third Ward. The saloon vanished, replaced at the end of prohibition by cocktail lounges and taverns. Still, despite cosmetic changes, Omaha remained a boisterous town.

Prostitution remained a reality of Omaha life. However, things were not as open as earlier in the century when a huge resort, the Arcade, a four-block area of brick houses and paper shacks, operated in the Third Ward. Three hundred women paid two dollars a day for "cribs" in surroundings protected by security men, bright lights, and iron fences. By 1910 Omaha had 2,600 professional ladies of the night, plus many more irregular freelancers in the "army of vice." Most of the latter had no connections with houses and worked out of dance halls. "Few of these girls are bad, they are simply inexperienced," a reformed prostitute explained. "These unsophisticated girls do not realize the danger they encounter. . . . The dance hall, or Sunday dance, where a promiscuous collection of people meet, where drink is dispensed and dope used as a refreshment and stimulant to the dancers cannot but bring about new recruits to the district." Some of these amateurs graduated to professional status, acquiring pimps or ending up in one of the hundred or so major houses. Estimates claimed that collectively these places had average annual incomes from 1905 to 1911 of $17.5 million, a portion of it generated by liquor business. In 1911 legislators in Lincoln passed the Albert Law closing the houses. The only effect was to disperse the harlots throughout Omaha to rooming houses and hotels. One streetwalker told a reporter, "It's a poor girl on the street who can't make at least five dollars a night in Omaha."

Sharing power with Dennison was Billy Nesselhous, a former jockey, coal hauler, and street gambler, usually accompanied in public by a beautiful call girl or actress. Upon his death in 1937, he left a huge estate that apparently was much larger than that of Dennison who gave much money away. The contrasting personalities of Dennison and Nesselhous had served the organization well. As Orville D. Menard, the authority on bossism in Omaha has said, "Dennison . . . had in Nesselhous a colleague who delighted in nights devoted to partying with individuals who warranted entertaining. The taciturn and reserved political boss was balanced by his outgoing associate, Nesselhous playing the role of genial diplomat to the blunt and frank Dennison."

By the end of the 1920s, Omaha was a cosmopolitan city with a violent and bawdy reputation. The specter of machine rule hung over the community. Outstate politicians railed against vice and crime in Omaha, contending that the existing conditions gave Nebraska a bad name. Some concluded that a tornado that had smashed through Omaha in 1913, killing 140 persons and causing $5 million in damage, was an indication of God's displeasure. The town's ethnic heritage came under attack. Racial purists believed that immigration had made Omaha a cauldron of discontent, contributing to a host of problems. Some observers perceived a direct connection between corrupt politics and immigrant groups, arguing that the foreigners provided the votes that kept the machine in power. Omaha leaders objected, claiming that the existence of vice was much overemphasized and that most residents were law-abiding persons living and working together with minimal friction. They said that the city was no different from other metropolises and better than most. After all, Omaha had no Al Capone; and many more people had died in other racial disturbances than in the Court House Riot. Civic image builders dwelt on the stability of family life and talked about the contribution of religion, the richness of numerous ethnic celebrations, and the enlightened influence of education.

In the meantime, righteousness had not reigned unchallenged in Omaha's parent city. About 1900, John C. Mabray moved from Webb City, Missouri, to Council Bluffs, where he made the downtown Merriam Block headquarters for an intricate swindling operation. Relying on greed as a common human foible, Mabray used many "steerers" or agents to lead moneyed persons to wager on unlawful horse races, conducted in the sporting environment south of town around Lake Manawa. The victim would bet on a seemingly invincible horse in a two-horse contest, but lost his money when its jockey flew from the saddle and feigned death. In some cases, Mabray used boxing matches or other rigged contests that may have bilked his suckers of upwards of $5 million prior to state and federal authorities breaking his racket. In 1909 a steerer was convicted of larceny in state court, and in 1910 a federal judge in Council Bluffs fined Mabray ten thousand dollars for mail fraud and sentenced him to two years in prison.

Ben Marks, a native of Waukegan, Illinois, who had entered the Union Army at age thirteen and who had settled in Council Bluffs after the Civil War, had a gambling operation at Lake Manawa. After the Trans-Mississippi and International Exposition, Marks purchased and disassembled the log structure that had been the Minnesota pavilion at the exposition. He rebuilt and enlarged the building south of Council Bluffs, which he used as a resort known as the Hog Ranch for gambling and prostitution. The location of the Hog Ranch astride the boundary of Pottawattamie and Mills counties served the interests of its patrons in the event of an unfriendly sheriff's visit. Marks, affiliated with John C. Mabray in racing at Lake Manawa, faced federal indictment after a jockey was shot. This situation, along with declining health, brought the end of his career. Aside from his illicit enterprises, Marks raised livestock and reportedly had significant land holdings in Nebraska and South Dakota as well as extensive property around Lake Manawa. When Grenville Dodge donated land for a city park near the river, Marks also contributed property for such use. Before his death in April 1919, he had as his obituary said, "formally embraced christianity." Paradoxically, like Dennison, he was a well-known local figure whose activities were necessarily in the shadows. In the laconic words of the *Nonpareil*, "During the palmy days of gambling in Council Bluffs, Marks . . . was reputed to control the business of this character in the city. He was a power in politics at one time."

In the meantime, law enforcement in Council Bluffs had been tainted with corruption. In 1910 a district court ordered the suspension from office of chief of police and city marshal George H. Richmond on grounds that he had permitted gambling, prostitution, and unlawful liquor sales. Nothing in the ensuing trial showed that Richmond had a stake in the activity, and he contended that he was merely following established practice. Indeed, allegations that the city relied on pro forma fines collected for liquor and other violations had some credibility. Nevertheless, Richmond was removed from his offices.

THE JOSLYN MEMORIAL: HERALDING THE VIRTUES

The Joslyn Memorial, a magnificent Omaha art gallery, served as a positive symbol of community. The $3.5 million structure opened in 1931 after almost a decade of planning and construction. It was a gift of Sarah Joslyn, intended as a memorial to her late husband, George Joslyn, who had made a large fortune in a variety of businesses. As a young man, Joslyn, disenchanted with the prospects of life on the family farm in Vermont, went to Montreal, where he worked first as a bookkeeper and later as a printer in businesses owned by his uncles. With his Vermont-born wife Sarah, family connections took him in 1879 to a job with the Iowa Printing Company in Des Moines, a firm that produced preprinted news and feature material for insertion in weekly newspapers. Such "auxiliary printing" had tremendous growth potential, given the proliferation of small town papers in the Great Plains and elsewhere. In 1880 Joslyn established an Iowa Printing Company office in Omaha, and following a merger, the firm was renamed the Western Newspaper Union. By 1890 Joslyn was president of the Western Newspaper Union, and he continued to build it into what his critics deemed a quest for monopoly. In 1915, the year before he died, the Western Newspaper Union furnished ready-prints and ready-to-print plates to some twelve thousand weekly newspapers. By then, the firm had thirty-one printing plants and Joslyn's Western Paper Company, a wholesaler of paper and printing materials, was also a large operation. A symbol of both Joslyn's entrepreneurial success and Omaha's coming of age was the completion in 1903 of what local people would simply call the "Castle," George and Sarah's thirty-four-room Scottish baronial home.

The huge gallery of the Joslyn Memorial had proportions and features befitting a paper king. Its Georgia marble exterior had a modified classic de-

10. Joslyn Memorial Art Museum, Omaha. *Courtesy NSHS, RG2096 PH O 25, Condra Collection.*

sign, unrelieved by wall openings. The focal point in the interior was a floral court complete with fountains and a blue-green tiled octagonal pool. A concert hall, decorated in soft shades of rose and gray, had a seating capacity of 1,200 persons. The Joslyn contained many permanent collections, including those of the Art Institute of Omaha and the Helen Wells Seymour collection of oriental textiles.

Numerous lectures, concerts, demonstrations, and traveling art shows made the Joslyn, from its opening day, a cultural center. The memorial was what Omahans wanted visitors and others to remember; it provided a much more desirable cultural image than gambling dens, speakeasies, and whorehouses. And so almost four decades after the official closing of the frontier, Omaha leaders felt compelled to reemphasize that their city was not a roaring camp but a place of high culture. Their efforts harked back to early attempts to establish a genteel identity, particularly those of the Omaha Library Association of the 1850s. In the 1920s a successful community playhouse and a poorly financed symphony that died at the end of the decade received publicity out of proportion to their actual contributions. The whole process related to a development unclear at the time; Omaha had become a mature community.

Council Bluffs had followed a similar path, building on the foundations established by the start of the twentieth century. Although Council Bluffs was far smaller than Omaha and somewhat less culturally diverse than the west bank of the urban area, it experienced much of the same social friction. The fact that Council Bluffs had to cope with the aftermaths of the 1909 and 1919 riots was further evidence of its shared destiny with Omaha. The vice that flourished on the east side of the river revealed another facet of urban life that transcended the river and the state line.

Somewhat embarrassed by a stormy past, Omaha's boosters reacted defensively to criticism. There was a groping for a set of values that could bring together second- and third-generation Omahans. The metropolitan area remained on the move; hardly anyone thought of a decline. The way things transpired, it would have been a good idea to have considered that possibility.

[Part v]　1930–1960

[8] Into the Great Depression

One reason for the success of Omaha was the positive attitude of the business community toward newcomers. The first promoters, the Creightons and Kountzes, had worked together to gain the Union Pacific terminal. A generation later, William A. Paxton and his associates had gone to considerable lengths to bring in the packing plants. In the 1890s Gurdon W. Wattles had quickly gained entrance into Omaha's economic life, soon rising to the top. James E. Davidson had a similar experience in the late teens and early twenties of the twentieth century. If either Wattles or Davidson had gone to one of the many smaller thriving towns of the region, they might have encountered serious problems trying to break into the dominant groups. Established interests tended to discourage outsiders from coming in even if they had ability and money. Critics in the 1920s believed that the approach stifled small-town social development, but many small-town capitalists felt comfortable with existing patterns. The Omaha entrepreneurs never felt threatened nor had they been content to accept a settled state of affairs in part because Omaha was not a front-office town; executives from the outside were always coming and going. So Omahans welcomed new blood and money.

William Randolph Hearst's purchase of a daily Omaha newspaper was a continuation of the process. No one in power in the city expressed concern about a nonresident controlling an organ of public opinion. What they wanted was his money and support. In 1928 Hearst bought the *Bee-News*, which had combined the old *Bee* with the *Omaha Daily News*, a politically independent paper dating from 1899. In 1920 the Rosewater interests had sold the *Bee* to Nelson B. Updike, a local grain dealer. He acquired the *News* in 1927, only to sell his holdings the next year to Hearst's empire. Peter Hamilton of the *Bee-News* told the public that the change of ownership demonstrated Hearst's faith in Omaha. Hamilton declared, "Mr. Hearst shares with the people who preceded him to Omaha optimism for the future and commends to persons elsewhere seeking a place to live happily and prosper in, this city in the heart of the United States which so typically personifies the heart, mind and body of our country." This was certainly what the Omaha business leaders wanted to hear. A fanatical booster could hardly have said it better.

The problem was Hearst soon decided that he had made a bad investment. In 1937 he sold the *Bee-News* for $750,000 to the *World-Herald*. The new owners promptly folded the *Bee-News*, bringing an end to an era in Omaha journalism. Edward Rosewater's old *Bee*, Nebraska's first regional paper, had played an important part in building the city. The journal's rise had coincided with that of the town. Demise of the newspaper had grim implications. Hearst, cutting his losses, had become one of the first well-known American capitalists to invest heavily in Omaha and then pull out. To make matters worse, he destroyed a regional institution. After professing faith in Omaha, he left town.

Hearst's decision came after the euphoria of the 1920s had given way to the despair of the 1930s. The Great Depression shattered confidence. Tub-thumping statements of a few years before about a grand future based on land and sea transportation suddenly appeared classic examples of probusiness Babbittry rather than attempts to articulate community aspirations in modern advertising jargon. None of this boded well. Had Omaha reached the limits of its success? Was it experiencing an inevitable decline? Would industries leave in droves? The answers to these and other questions—all reflections of past queries—rested, as before, on the ability of the hinterland to sustain Omaha's transportation, commercial, and industrial operations.

During the first years of depression, the agricultural economy of Nebraska collapsed. There was a temptation to blame the disaster on the materialism of the 1920s and to conclude that automobiles, radios, and telephones had corrupted a generation of young Nebraskans. The opening in 1923 of a thirty-five-thousand-seat football stadium on the University of Nebraska campus in Lincoln epitomized a changing value structure. Instead of working in the fields on Saturdays in the fall, many farm families concentrated on following the fortunes of the Nebraska football team. It somehow did not seem right to numerous oldsters who had sacrificed to build a state. Willa Cather, author of the pioneer epic *My Ántonia*, wrote,

Too much prosperity, too many moving picture shows, too much gaudy fiction have colored the taste and manners of so many of these Nebraskans of the future. There, as elsewhere, one finds the frenzy to be showy; farmer boys who wish to be spenders before they are earners, girls who try to look like the heroines of the cinema screen; a coming generation which tries to cheat its aesthetic sense by buying things instead of making anything. There is even the danger that that fine institution, the University of Nebraska, may become a gigantic trade school.

There was no denying that most Nebraska farmers enjoyed a higher standard of living than their forefathers, but the economic adversity that befell the state had deeper causes than a desire to see football games or to go to town in cars on Saturday night.

Overproduction and rising costs were two fundamental causes of Nebraska's agricultural failures. Farming's "Golden Age" had come to an abrupt end. Wheat prices had fallen from $2.02 per bushel on December 1, 1919, to $1.31 per bushel a year later. The problem was that grain was a renewable resource. Production gradually returned to normal in areas of the world affected by hostilities, and trade patterns resumed their former characteristics. Foreign demands gradually declined, falling off sharply after the middle of the 1920s. Wartime prices made it difficult to assess what was going on; in terms of the prewar market, Nebraska farmers appeared to be doing well. The average state farm-price index from 1922 to 1929 was almost 35 percent higher than before the war. The figures were deceptive; they did not take in larger operating expenses, the loss of federal wartime price guarantees, or higher taxes. Despite a rise in gross farm income near the end of the decade, net income per farm had declined to an annual average of $1,795, compared with $3,087 during the period from 1914 to 1919. Throughout the 1920s land values fell. Farmers with mortgages had trouble making payments, and refinancing proved difficult.

A state bank guaranty fund could not meet the demands wrought by a massive failure of state-chartered banks, and the legislature was unable to save this protection for depositors. These considerations, part of a larger problem, caused national concern. The McNary-Haugen bill, designed to subsidize grain farmers, passed Congress on three occasions, falling victim each time to a presidential veto. A farm marketing measure enacted under

Herbert Hoover was not a workable remedy. Although some had believed that the prosperity of the Roaring Twenties was permanent, the Crash of 1929 showed otherwise.

Early in the Great Depression, already deflated farm prices plummeted to the lowest levels in Nebraska history. Between December of 1929 and the same month in 1932, corn dropped from $0.67 to $0.13 per bushel, wheat from $1.00 to $0.27, oats from $0.38 to $0.10, and barley from $0.49 to $0.13. By the hundredweight, beef cattle went from $10.50 to $4.10, and hogs from $8.20 to $2.30. Using 1914 to 1919 as base years, with a parity of 100, the purchasing power of Nebraska agriculture products averaged 87.22 throughout the 1920s and then dropped all the way to 54 in 1932. On top of this collapse came several drought years. Especially poor were 1934 and 1936, when rainfall fell below fifteen inches. The lack of rain affected the whole Great Plains, and great dust storms swept over the Nebraska prairies. Even in a year of normal rainfall, 1935, growing conditions were not good, and yields were much smaller than usual.

Some farmers left, but there was no exodus on the scale of the 1870s and 1890s. New Deal programs saved the day. From 1933 through 1940, Franklin Roosevelt's administration pumped more than $200 million into Nebraska agriculture. The Farm Credit Administration alone advanced $185 million to the state's farmers. Over 80 percent of all the farms in Nebraska profited from the first and second Agricultural Adjustment acts. In 1939 over 129,000 farms received $20 million. Even so, the agricultural aspects of the Great Depression were devastating. As the authors of *Nebraska: A Guide to the Cornhusker State* (1939) said, "The condition of the farmers affected Nebraska merchants, lumber dealers, realtors, school teachers, laborers, and artisans. Housewives stocked their pantry shelves with the simplest essentials; construction lagged; school administrators curtailed their programs as tax receipts went down; day laborers, formerly sure enough of a place on Nebraska farms and in Nebraska industries, began the long trek of the unemployed."

Omaha's business community first assumed that the Depression would not have a serious impact on the city. At the time of the 1929 crash, the Omaha newspapers had not headlined the debacle, placing detailed stories on the business pages. There was unjustified faith that agriculture would hold up, enabling Omaha to ride out the storm. When the crisis became prolonged, Omaha began to suffer severely. Bank clearances fell from $2.9 billion in 1929 to $997 million in 1933. In the same period, deposits dropped from $115 million to $83 million. While no Omaha area banks failed in the 1920s, four state banks that combined held 6 percent of all deposits in the city went under in August 1931. The three largest Omaha banks—First National, Omaha National, and U.S. National—remained open. Total grain receipts for 1930 were 78 million bushels, the highest ever. Then they plunged to 57 million bushels in 1931 and cascaded to 26 million in 1932, before starting back upward to 45 million in 1936. At the bottom, in 1932, it was unprofitable for farmers to market their crops. Wheat receipts only amounted to 17.5 million bushels, as opposed to 44.6 million bushels three years earlier. For corn, the figures were 6 million bushels against 24 million bushels, and for barley 133,000 bushels against 1.3 million bushels. Livestock receipts also dropped and so did production. From 1929 to 1933, cattle moved downward from 1.4 million to 1.3 million, hogs from 3.7 million to 3.1 million, and sheep from 3 million to 2.4 million.

Reminiscent of the visit of Kelly's Army in the depression year of 1894 was the arrival in Council Bluffs on May 18, 1932, of over three hundred World War I veterans from Portland, Oregon, aboard boxcars on a Union Pacific train. A contingent of the famed "Bonus Army," they were en route to Washington where they would join veterans from across the nation in seeking early payment of their military service benefits. They stayed only a day in Council Bluffs, for arrangements were quickly made for a Wabash freight train to take them, along with local recruits, to St. Louis. As in 1894, Council Bluffs residents treated the visitors well, providing them with places to clean up and with a good supply of food.

TEAR GAS AND MACHINE GUNS

In July 1929 the *Council Bluffs Nonpareil* had remarked, "Money invested in Iowa land is safer than money in a bank." In the 1920s, Iowa had experienced problems similar to those in Nebraska, but few if any persons could have foreseen that in just over three years Council Bluffs and Omaha would gain national attention when farmers confronted law officers in a desperate effort to improve their economic plight. In May 1932 a Farmers' Holiday Association was formed in Des Moines with the goal of attaining a monetary return to farmers that would equal their production costs. On the premise that keeping farm produce off the market would boost agricultural prices, a withholding action was scheduled to start on July 4. This came to naught, but in August the efforts of Sioux City–area dairy farmers became entwined with the Farmers' Holiday effort. On August 11, farmers on a picket line blocked trucks hauling milk into Sioux City. A subsequent milk-price settlement in Sioux City did not immediately end protest activity.

A similar milk-price grievance existed in the Greater Omaha area, and by August 23 pickets were on the highways on the outskirts of Council Bluffs. That night, some one thousand persons, including curious townspeople, lined Highway 34 where sheriff's deputies used tear gas to clear the way. The following day, pickets blocked milk trucks on two of the four highways entering town. Forty-nine persons, almost all from north of the immediate area, were arrested. Pottawattamie County sheriff P. A. Lainson, although sympathetic to the plight of the farmers, labeled the pickets as "hoodlums." With ninety-eight deputies sworn for the emergency, he declared, "I'm going to fight it out if it takes 5,000 deputies and $50,000." On Thursday, August 25, amid reports that one thousand men were driving in from northwestern Iowa to force the release of their jailed compatriots, a special deputy was fatally wounded while a regular deputy was demonstrating the use of a riot gun. To help preserve order, the Omaha Police Department provided two detectives and two machine guns. A submachine gun at the Pottawattamie County courthouse was aimed at the jail to prevent an assault. Anticipating a showdown, upwards of five thousand people assembled in the vicinity of the courthouse. On Thursday afternoon, the protesters from the north reached town, but a violent confrontation at the jail may have been avoided when fifty-five incarcerated men were released on bond. Through the initiative of the Council Bluffs Chamber of Commerce, a "peace conference" convened that evening at the Hotel Chieftain. The three-and-one-half-hour meeting resulted in Sheriff Lainson agreeing to allow his deputies to aid in nonviolent picketing if the Iowa attorney general held this to be legal. The attorney general's office held that this would be unlawful, but the negotiation helped reduce tension.

Lainson kept his deputies on duty, and the picketing settled into a routine made uncomfortable by rains, chill, and nighttime mosquitoes described as "large enough to harness and put on a plow." Milk still reached town, some of it by rail, but strike activity shifted to Nebraska roads leading into Omaha. Despite efforts by Omaha mayor Richard L. Metcalfe to bring a settlement between milk producers and dairies, there were clashes between picketers and sheriff's deputies on three nights on the city's outskirts. On September 1, one thousand persons watched picketers pitch rocks and logs at deputies escorting trucks into the city from the west along Dodge Street. It was now clear that such disorder would not help farmers, and Farmers' Holiday Association leaders—never in control of these events in western Iowa and eastern Nebraska—announced a suspension of market withholding actions. What had taken place in a week in the late summer of 1932 was only an event that drew newsmen and motion-picture crews to Council Bluffs and Omaha, not a harbinger of imminent revolution or massive social disorder. Aside from the excitement, life went on as usual, yet law-enforcement officers armed with riot guns and machine guns showed that the people of the Midwest were not living in normal times.

AFTER THE PICKETS LEFT

Illustrating the growing challenge of funding unemployment assistance was the proposal of a Council Bluffs city councilman in November 1932 that the city issue one hundred thousand dollars in scrip for partial payment to workers on relief projects. The city solicitor soon ruled that such action was beyond municipal authority, but in 1933 the *Nonpareil* paid its employees partly in scrip that businesses could redeem in advertising. The advent of the winter of 1932–33 highlighted the hardships of the Depression. People in the Carter Lake area dug oil-saturated soil from around a refinery and used the peat-like material for home heating. Some idea of the shared plight of urban and rural dwellers could be seen in the publication in mid-December of the delinquent-property tax list for Pottawattamie County. There were multiple entries for many persons, but the fact that it took twenty-four full newspaper pages to publish the list was perhaps more staggering evidence of the scope of the economic collapse than the episode of the late-summer milk strike.

Low farm prices persisted until the impact of federal price-support programs. To their sorrow, the leaders of Omaha business discovered that regional agriculture proved unable to withstand the onslaught of a national economic debacle. There was the expected search for scapegoats and a longing for older, more prosperous times. An elderly capitalist, discussing the days when the railroad companies made many decisions in Omaha, much to the profit of certain interest groups, recalled, "We were like an army; we obeyed orders and got in on the gravy. I used to wear a uniform and I wish to God I was wearing a uniform now." He could only watch in dismay as railroads throughout the middle of the United States fell into receivership.

When this had happened in the 1880s and 1890s, it had been a combination of unscrupulous or inept managerial practices and a building of tracks into unsettled areas. Now, it was different; railroads running through what only a few years before had been prosperous farming territory lost business and fell into bankruptcy. Under the circumstances, Omaha's great transportation network became a liability rather than a strength. It served a collapsing hinterland. This was even more the case in Council Bluffs, the quintessential railroad town. In January 1940 a *Nonpareil* editorial entitled "All Eggs in One Basket" noted that Pottawattamie County payrolls had fallen from $3,003,800 in 1929 to $651,209 in 1937, while highly rural Fremont County in Iowa's southwestern corner had shown significant payroll recovery after 1933. The paper attributed the lethargic recovery of Council Bluffs and Pottawattamie County in large measure to a heavy reliance upon railroad employment. The *Nonpareil* had faith that better days were ahead for the railroads but concluded that diversification of the local economy was essential.

Unemployment in Omaha mounted steadily in the early years of the Great Depression. Industrial and commercial establishments laid off large numbers of workers. In November 1932 assembly work ended at the Ford Motor Company plant, although Ford continued to use the property as a parts and accessories distribution center until 1954. There was a corresponding loss of public jobs. New entrants into the work force found few available positions. Employed men and women faced dismissals, severe pay cuts, and deteriorating conditions. Under the weight of prolonged mass unemployment, private, local, and state relief broke down. A five-hundred-thousand-dollar expansion project at the municipal airport, authorized by a 1930 bond election, made only a small dent in overall employment.

THE NEW DEAL

In the first three years of the Depression, President Herbert Hoover opposed direct federal relief, but the New Deal quickly abandoned the outmoded policy. The Federal Emergency Relief Act and the measure establishing the Civil Works Administration provided temporary help for millions of Americans, including 1,771 men in Council Bluffs by December 1933. During the first months of Roosevelt's presidency, over 11,000 unemployed Omahans registered for federal relief. This was a high total for a community that had had 94,000 gainfully employed persons in 1930. As the New Deal progressed, many federal relief functions fell under two more permanent agencies, the Public Works Administration (PWA) and the Works Progress Administration (WPA), both of which provided employment for thousands locally, having an important effect on the economy prior to the upturn caused by World War II.

Despite the Depression, census statistics indicated that Omaha gained 9,838 residents in the 1930s. The increase came even with a steady drop in manufacturing jobs from sixteen thousand in 1929 to eleven thousand in 1939. Other areas—transportation, wholesale, retail, and personal service occupations—held up, with significant losses in industry compensated for by federal employment. The government expended several million dollars in Omaha. The funds went for various projects, most of which contributed to cultural, beautification, and urban services concerns. Matching PWA monies helped construct a 360-room building for the Municipal University of Omaha. Other large undertakings included erecting a bridge over the Missouri River at South Omaha and changing the river's channel. Additional appropriations went to landscape parks, lay sewers, and improve streets. In the late 1930s the United States Housing Authority sponsored construction of the Logan-Fontenelle Homes in North Omaha and the South Side Terrace Homes in South Omaha. By 1940 roughly sixteen thousand people over fourteen years of age in Omaha either received unemployment benefits or engaged in emergency work.

After seven decades of steady growth, Council Bluffs in the 1930s lost 609 persons, or just over 1.44 percent of its population. This slight decline probably reflected the less-diversified character of the city's economy as compared to Omaha's. Nevertheless, New Deal programs, similar to those in Omaha, did much to help Council Bluffs and its southwestern Iowa trade area get through the depression. A full-page advertisement in the *Nonpareil* in January 1934 touted "2,767,815.46 [in] CORN LOAN MONEY had been recorded in southwestern Iowa by Tuesday, January 3." The ad also noted that this area, shown in a map of nine Iowa counties, would get an additional $230,000 for "governmental projects." Unintentionally evoking the image of a person whistling while scurrying past a cemetery at night, the ad concluded "Business Is Fine In Council Bluffs Stores."

11. Club House, Lake Manawa, Iowa, 1931. *Courtesy Council Bluffs Public Library, Council Bluffs, Iowa.*

Such declarations could not drive away the Depression, and early in 1935 some 2,500 Council Bluffs families were receiving some form of public assistance. New Deal work programs were essential in meeting the relief burden in Pottawattamie County. Three years later, about 1,000 families in the county received a distribution of surplus food from the federal government. Seasonal considerations and funding realities brought significant variations in WPA employment levels. For example, the average number of persons on relief in Pottawattamie County remained steady in 1938 and 1939—2,880 and 2,882 persons respectively. Nevertheless, in 1938 the WPA employed an average of 1,643 people, but only 1,392 the following year. As elsewhere, WPA projects varied widely, from street, sidewalk, and sewer work to flood-control and water-works improvements. Another New Deal agency, the Civilian Conservation Corps, worked to restore Lake Manawa, and the WPA helped improve that important recreational site.

Three New Deal projects not only contributed to the local economy but provided lasting improvements. The previously mentioned South Omaha bridge, completed in 1936 with PWA funding, was linked to Highway 34 on the southern outskirts of Council Bluffs. The bridge facilitated the movement of livestock from southwestern Iowa to the South Omaha stockyards, contributing in the long run to the development of the southern portion of Council Bluffs. In 1936 work began on a flood-control project on Indian Creek, a stream that rose in the bluffs north of town and flowed through heavily developed parts of the city before discharging into the Missouri River. Although Indian Creek was short, between 1883 and 1935 it inflicted six large flash floods and five lesser floods upon Council Bluffs. The project was funded with a city bond issue and a PWA grant. Its completion did not end the flooding, but it was a key remedial step. In 1939 work began on a new city hall, partly financed from revenue from the municipal water system with the majority of the funds coming from the WPA. When it was dedicated in January 1941, the *Nonpareil* said, "For many years the affairs of the city have been carried on in an old rookery of which everybody was ashamed but now we have a building of which every citizen may well be proud." For later generations, the city hall's architecture heralded its New Deal origin; for Council Bluffs residents in 1941, its modern appearance must have suggested the passing of the Depression and a brighter future.

Omaha businessmen, like their counterparts elsewhere, first became displeased with Roosevelt's vehicle for a business revival, the National Recovery

Administration (NRA), in the spring of 1934. Conditions had started to improve, and they saw no further need for government controls. Soon after the death of its founder, former senator Gilbert M. Hitchcock, the *World-Herald*, long a Democratic journal, denounced FDR. The NRA's blue eagle emblem, displayed to show compliance, became a target of scorn. Inconsistencies and piles of regulations involved in attempts to regiment business under "codes of fair competition" led to widespread opposition to the agency long before a 1935 Supreme Court decision declared it unconstitutional. In Omaha, employer condemnation of Roosevelt and all his works failed to hide the obvious: they had lost control over a measure of their own affairs.

THE "WHITE SPOT OF THE NATION"

To bolster the economy, Omaha business leaders preached a gospel of tax restraint. In 1932 Walter L. Pierpoint was a key figure in establishing the Association of Omaha Taxpayers, a watchdog group that eventually gained national publicity. By the mid-thirties, Democratic governor Robert L. Cochran was touting Nebraska's lack of state income and sales taxes and state bond debt. In 1937 *World-Herald* publisher Henry Doorly took the initiative in forming the Associated Industries of Nebraska that would use the theme of minimal taxation to encourage businesses to relocate to the state. With the help of the Omaha Chamber of Commerce, the association raised funds for a series of advertisements in *Time* magazine that described Nebraska as the "White Spot of the Nation." The ads included an all-white map of Nebraska surrounded by an all-black map of the rest of the United States. Newspapers within the state also ran these ads. Many civic organizations produced a variety of promotional gimmicks, such as milk-bottle tops, bumper stickers, pins, and stationery emblazoned with the White Spot slogan. The White Spot campaign, at its peak in 1938, reportedly led five businesses to settle in Omaha, but critics of the initiative saw it as fostering inequitable taxation and parsimony in meeting public needs. In any event, the White Spot campaign, largely inspired by Omaha businessmen, helped earn Nebraska a reputation for tight-fisted public spending.

1935: AN ESPECIALLY NASTY YEAR

In Omaha new villains appeared in the form of government officials, "brain truster" Rexford Tugwell and WPA head Harry Hopkins. They personified all the vexations of Omaha's dominant group. High-ranking bureaucrats were hard to oppose. They were difficult to see and issued countless regulations, many contradictory or hard to understand. It was all very frustrating. Even so, a common resolve existed to keep alive the boast of the Omaha Business Men's Association, "Omaha is the best open-shop city of its size in the United States."

The battlefield was an old one: the Omaha traction lines. Here Gurdon W. Wattles had smashed unionization activities in 1909. Now buttressed by Section 7A of the National Industrial Recovery Act, which recognized the right of workers to organize, the Amalgamated Association of Street and Electric Railway Employees decided to force the Omaha and Council Bluffs Street Railway Company to grant recognition and other demands. These included a pay increase for operators from fifty-two cents to sixty-eight cents an hour. A strike in April of 1934 ended after a few days when sides agreed to federal arbitration. The arbitrator, Richard L. Blume of the National Labor Board's Kansas City office, wrote a report granting a five-cent retroactive pay increase. Nothing was said about union recognition. In July the workers rejected the settlement by a vote of 359 to 1 and walked out again. Their spokesman attributed the cause to "continued discrimination against members of the union by officials of the company." Blume hurried to Omaha and soon effected an uneasy peace. The men returned to work in exchange for minor wage concessions, promises of a board to settle grievances, and assurances that further arbitration would solve other outstanding issues. Implicit in the settlement was the possibility of an election on collective bargaining. Organized labor appeared on the verge of sweeping away the open shop in Omaha. Unfortunately for unions, the old ways of management did not die easily.

The Street Railway Company had no intention of giving in; it merely wanted to buy time and to solidify support from Omaha businessmen and politicians. Through its new cocounsel, Richard L. Blume—the arbitrator for the National Labor Board in the previous two strikes—the company contended that no election was necessary, arguing that it had negotiated with the union during the previous two strikes. In the spring of 1935, the National Labor Board agreed, saying that there was no need for an election. Buttressed by the ruling and with its advance planning completed, the Street Railway Company took a hard line. It broke off all negotiations with the union, refusing further arbitration of demands for union recognition, seniority rights, a six-day week, and new wage increases. On April 20, 1935, the streetcar and bus drivers went on strike, assuring a serious confrontation with their employers. There would be no industrial peace in Omaha.

A long and bloody strike ensued. The Street Railway Company fired all the men who walked out, adopting what it called "Our New Plan." Advertisements announced the retention of an Omaha private-detective bureau, the Midwest Adjustment Company, to "protect the company's property." Midwest Adjustment, backed by an arsenal of submachine guns and sawed-off shotguns, provided a force of one hundred men. The agency's director, Benjamin Danbaum, a former state law-enforcement official, had a close working relationship with the Omaha police; during the strike he helped them obtain a consignment of tear gas from an Ohio chemical company. It was a situation reminiscent of 1909 except that this time the traction line employed local instead of outside strikebreakers. As before, many persons in Omaha sympathized with the strikers.

When the Street Railway Company asked Mayor Roy Towl, a civil engineer elected on a "reform" ticket, to guarantee adequate protection to cars put back into operation, he replied that the decision to resume service rested solely with the company. This was a course that the company was ready to follow. The first streetcars, screened by heavy wire, rolled on the morning of April 24. Heavily armed police and company guards were on board. Armed automobiles preceded and followed each car. The trams, which attracted few passengers, negotiated their routes without opposition. Following this elaborate show of force, the company rejected a city council resolution calling for arbitration. It gradually resumed spasmodic day and night service over most lines, employing 250 strikebreakers, all protected by Midwest Adjustment Company personnel. Violence soon occurred. A striker fired on a car; others beat up a strikebreaker. Bombs damaged the home of a Street Railway Company official and blasted two streetcars. These incidents were almost innocent precursors to what lay ahead.

Council Bluffs temporarily averted trouble by banning streetcar operations, but in the middle of June heavy rioting swept across the south side of Omaha. For three straight nights mobs roamed the streets burning streetcars, causing an estimated four hundred thousand dollars in damage and looting a grocery store owned by a man suspected of riding on a trolley. There were two deaths and a hundred injuries. The city council voted a fifty-thousand-dollar emergency fund for added law enforcement; but before anything further could be done, the police lost control of the situation. On the morning of June 15 as gutted streetcars smoldered in the streets, Mayor Towl and the sheriff reluctantly sent a joint wire to the governor's office to request troops. Gov. Robert L. Cochran was out of the state, but the acting governor swiftly complied with the request. He declared martial law in Omaha, rushed in 1,800 National Guardsmen and ordered the traction company to stop running streetcars. Cochran, a New Deal Democrat with prolabor leanings, rushed to Omaha, where he took charge of the city. The newspapers called him the "Dictator of Omaha."

Cochran called for an "immediate settlement" and asked the union and the company to name representatives to an arbitration board. The company said it would agree to arbitrate "all but three points": the rehiring of strikers, the closed shop, and the question of seniority. Because these were fundamental points, the company really had not altered its previous stand. The governor reacted by telling the company that no streetcars would run until the company complied. At that point, the company gave in and agreed to the governor's demands. Arbitration began on June 19, the same day that the city finance commissioner released a report disclosing that the company had a net profit over the previous four years of $1.5 million, far more than its officials had claimed. There was what appeared to be a swift settlement, virtually dictated by the governor's representative on the arbitration panel. The strikers were to return to work at their old pay, and the strikebreakers were to be fired. At an unspecified future date the arbitrators were to consider the possibility of a pay increase. A special two-man board was to decide the seniority question. Cochran ended martial law and withdrew the National Guard.

The agreement quickly disintegrated. The strikebreakers with help from the company obtained a court injunction preventing implementation of the understanding on the grounds that the governor had exceeded his authority. When the two-man board voted full seniority rights to all strikers, the company rejected the decision. The streetcars returned to the streets, manned as before by strikebreakers and armed guards. This time there was little violence; the union wrote the strike off as lost. Governor Cochran claimed "the tram company broke faith immediately after the national guardsmen left Omaha."

Council Bluffs was the scene of an anticlimax to the 1935 streetcar strike. After a decorous meeting of strikers in Bayliss Park, near the heart of the city, on the night of July 19, a small group of men pelted a nearby streetcar with bricks and set it ablaze. That night Mayor Hugh P. Finerty implored a mob not to damage the Street Railway Company's Council Bluffs carbarn. Soon a gun-toting strikebreaker rolled up in his automobile, leaped out, and ran toward the carbarn, firing shots into a throng of strikers. He wounded one man, but the police quickly arrived and took him to jail in a neighboring county where he would be safe. Meanwhile, the strikers turned the strikebreaker's car over and torched it, blocking firemen from extinguishing the blaze. This ended the tentative restoration of trolley service in Council Bluffs. Because about two thousand residents of the city who worked in Omaha relied upon public transportation, Mayor Finerty pushed the traction firm to restore service across the bridge. Not until August 1 did the Street Railway Company begin to resume Council Bluffs operations.

Like Mayor Finerty and Gov. Clyde Herring of Iowa, Governor Cochran and Mayor Towl recognized that the Street Railway Company's ownership of the bridge linking downtown Omaha and Council Bluffs was a rich source of tolls that had enabled the traction firm to withstand the strike. Such recognition stimulated a movement to establish a free intercity traffic link. Another positive result of the strike came in 1938 when the National Labor Relations Board cited the traction firm for unfair labor practices on the seniority issue. The latter was a Pyrrhic victory for the strikers who had long since gone on to other jobs.

In the meantime, the new role of the federal government and other perceived challenges to the traditional economic system made 1935 an especially nasty year on another front. In 1931 the board of regents of the Municipal University of Omaha named Dr. William E. Sealock to be the first president of the institution following the end of the school's private status. Sealock, who had been dean of the Teachers' College at the University of Nebraska, quickly moved to improve the faculty and took other steps toward achieving accreditation for the University of Omaha. By the autumn of 1934, there were allegations of radicalism on campus, and by the following spring divisiveness had spread to the faculty and board of regents amid rumors that a campus spy network was seeking to ferret out subversives. The conservative animus was eventually directed against President Sealock. The resignation of regent

Paul L. Martin, a Sealock supporter and a critic of the witch hunting, precipitated a showdown. The battle lines became clearer when Dr. Sealock declared that board of regents president James E. Davidson, president of the Nebraska Power Company, was disgruntled over reports that faculty members had praised the New Deal's Tennessee Valley Authority as a good alternative to private enterprise power systems. He also said that Davidson had objected to his service as chair of the state NRA Adjustment Board on grounds that affiliation with the NRA was tantamount to communist affiliation or sympathy. Davidson staunchly contended that he had not meddled with teaching at the university. On June 27, 1935, the regents voted to discharge Sealock, then on a faculty recruitment trip. He gained much support, and Martin tried to arrange for him to meet with Davidson. A tragedy resulted from this plan. On Sunday evening, July 7, Martin phoned Dr. Sealock at his home and told him that Davidson had backed out of a conference. Sealock then took poison and died that night.

Just as the community moved beyond the tumult of the streetcar strike, the university soon moved on from this tragedy. Even before the University of Omaha had become a municipal institution, its leaders had recognized the need to obtain a more spacious campus than its quarters on the north side. President Sealock had worked toward this objective that reached fruition in 1938 when the university under the presidency of Rowland Haynes moved to a new campus on the city's western outskirts. Ironically, given the anti–New Deal perspective of Sealock's critics, President Haynes had served as Nebraska director of the Federal Emergency Relief Administration, and much of the money for the large Georgian-design university building completed in 1938 came from Washington. The development of the new campus led to accreditation in 1939.

FROM DEPRESSION TO WAR

The influence of Washington was also evident on the organized labor front. In 1938 the National Labor Relations Board cited the Omaha and Council Bluffs Street Railway Company for unfair labor practices over the seniority question. By winning the streetcar strike, the Street Railway Company achieved what first appeared a victory for the Omaha Business Men's Association. Journalist George R. Leighton, who wrote an interpretive history of Omaha in 1939, summed up the situation when he concluded that the cars were running and Wattles's precepts had been upheld. Still, the success was only short term; in retrospect it was more of a dramatic last stand than anything else. The Congress of Industrial Organizations made inroads in the packing houses and other industries. Surveys indicated that the vast majority of nonunion laborers in Omaha wanted to organize. Federal legislation and rulings provided the basis for Omaha becoming a union town. Omaha businessmen reluctantly acquiesced, learning how to adjust to the changed conditions. Developments on the labor front in the Great Depression resulted in a lessening of the Omaha business community's power over its working force. The Wagner Labor Relations Act of 1935, which created the Nation Labor Relations Board, became a hated entity in Omaha board rooms. Businessmen viewed it as a further indication of Roosevelt's supposed plot to "socialize America" and to centralize all power in the hands of New Deal planners in Washington. This position, of course, did not preclude accepting various forms of federal largesse. After all, a goal had always been to lure capital into Omaha. So, after World War II broke out in Europe in 1939, Omaha manufacturers competed with other cities for government defense contracts.

By this time, the economy was better than it had been in the mid-1930s. Unfortunately, the Depression was not over. Data on retail and wholesale activity in Council Bluffs and Omaha in 1939 compared to 1929 illustrates this point. In 1939 both cities had more retail firms than they had in 1929 and more employees, but total payrolls and sales were markedly lower in 1939 compared to 1929. Both cities also had more wholesale firms in 1939 than a decade earlier, but fewer employees and drastically lower total payrolls and sales.

Wholesale sales figures for Omaha are one measure of the course of the Depression. In 1929 the city did wholesale business worth $703,465,000, but the value fell to $344,525,000 in 1935 before recovering to $390,754,000 in 1939. Omaha's plight reflected that of the Census Bureau's seven-state West North Central Region which included Kansas, Nebraska, South Dakota, North Dakota, Missouri, Iowa, and Minnesota. Wholesale sales in the region in 1939 were 31.3 percent below their 1929 level, well below the figures from the bureau's eight other areas. Nevertheless, even in 1935 Omaha ranked twenty-fourth in the nation in wholesale sales, ranking ahead of Indianapolis, Washington, DC, Denver, and Portland.

It became conventional wisdom in Omaha to claim that the war and not the New Deal got the city out of the Depression. Actually, there was no abrupt departure from the New Deal philosophy that government spending would bring about a return to prosperity. The biggest change was that the expenditures went for the war effort rather than for WPA and PWA programs. Despite motives framed in patriotism and the necessity of quick action to ensure national survival, the results were the same—the pumping of massive amounts of federal money into the economy. There was more government money going daily into the economic system than any New Dealer had envisioned back in 1933. Wartime controls led to a tremendous expansion of government power in many walks of life. By the time the conflict ended, government involvement in Omaha had become accepted and institutionalized. Prosperity depended upon federal funds flowing into town. Curtailment of federal activities in Omaha and its region would have had disastrous consequences. There was a price to pay to keep the money coming; and it was an ever-increasing federal say over all levels of affairs in Omaha. The dreams of Wattles for the business community to obtain a free hand in setting policy had ended.

The first war contracts won by Omaha firms had little impact on the economy. Many of the early orders, gained through competitive bidding, helped small and already established concerns. The S and L Neckware Company received one for $1,150 to produce ten thousand field caps; the Omaha Seat Cover Company agreed to furnish twenty-five thousand half-shelter tents for $9,000. More substantial were two contracts for a total of $5.5 million obtained by the Omaha Steel Works to produce artillery ammunition components. These developments had little impact on the unemployment problem, and in January 1941 the Nebraska State Employment Service clearance supervisor confidentially told federal authorities that he anticipated no serious labor shortages in Omaha. Four months later, a federal study on Nebraska's economy admitted, "To date, direct defense orders have had little effect on employment. We estimate that at this time no more than 1,300 workers are being employed directly as a result of the defense program. . . . One steel plant has had substantial orders for material, but employment has been held back because of a lack of machine equipment." The situation changed overnight after America went to war. Omaha, as other cities, soon needed manpower, particularly skilled workers in all industrial classifications. Relief programs ended, and the vexing problems created by wartime needs were for many persons a welcome change from the 1930s.

The economic expansion took different forms. Of minor value were activities such as gathering scrap iron and planting Victory Gardens, which were encouraged by the authorities to give the public a feeling of participation in the war effort. Other developments were more substantial. The Omaha area gained many new factories, almost all of which owed their being to the war. In Council Bluffs, Leo Meyerson and his associates transformed a radio-parts business into the Scientific Radio Production Company that gained large military contracts for the production of quartz crystals used in transmitter frequency control. For many years after the war, Meyerson's firm, subsequently known as World Radio Laboratories, would be a national marketer of amateur radio equipment.

Senator George W. Norris used his prestige and Washington connections to help gain vast facilities for the Omaha area. Norris argued that not putting plants in Nebraska would be "injurious to this long-suffering part of the country." He reached Roosevelt through Chester C. Davis, the head of the Advisory Commission to the Council on National Defense. While the primary function of Davis's section was to offer advice on farm matters, it also dealt with industrial plant locations and the expediting of war production priorities. Norris wrote Davis on November 27, 1940, calling attention to proposals for a powder plant between Lincoln and Omaha, a military cantonment south of Hastings, and an "aircraft engine research laboratory" at Omaha. The senator noted Nebraska's PWA Tri-County Power project, stating that the government should "patronize one of its own children." This letter sent on to the White House brought a direct reply to Norris from Roosevelt in early December. The president said that one of several large Midwestern aircraft plants had been recommended for Nebraska and that he hoped it was the forerunner of other developments. More projects followed: one of the most important was an ordnance plant near Wahoo, which employed thousands of commuters from Omaha. Norris felt that Nebraska defense plants resulted from his long fight for public power. He saw cheap electricity as the key to the state's wartime prosperity.

THE MARTIN BOMBER PLANT AND THE NEW BELLEVUE

Exactly a year before the attack at Pearl Harbor, Omahans read a big newspaper story announcing that a massive aircraft plant would be built just south of the city. What would become the state's largest war establishment was the Glenn L. Martin–Nebraska Company bomber plant. The concern was a subsidiary of the Glenn L. Martin Company of Baltimore, Maryland, a leading producer of military aircraft. Martin leased the government-built-and-owned facility as part of the plan to place a large aircraft assembly plant in Nebraska. The bomber plant, located near Bellevue, was at Fort Crook. This was a small post that continued to operate throughout the war primarily as a supply depot, training school, and reception center. The fort was also the site of Offutt Field, which was greatly expanded during the course of hostilities. It handled the planes produced by Glenn L. Martin–Nebraska. One of the prime contractors for the construction of the bomber plant was Peter Kiewit Sons Company of Omaha. The plant, mostly built in 1941, had 1,200,000 square feet of floor space; among its nine large structures was a 600-by-900-foot assembly building. At its peak of production the plant employed 14,500 people. In terms of numbers of employees at a single site, the bomber factory was one of the country's largest war plants. It modified over 1,000 planes; made 1,585 B-26 Martin Marauders, two-engine medium attack bombers; and 531 B-29 Superfortresses, four-engine planes that carried the air war to Japan. The two B-29s that dropped atomic bombs on Hiroshima and Nagasaki were both made and modified at the plant.

The construction and operation of the Martin bomber plant began the modern development of Bellevue. With a population of 1,184 in 1940, the town that had once aspired to be Nebraska's capital was not even the seat of Sarpy County. Although it had few sewers and no streetlights or pavement, Bellevue remained the pleasant location that had evoked favorable comments from early travelers. For some of its residents, it was a suburban haven from their jobs in Omaha. Following the announcement that the Martin bomber plant would be built adjacent to their town, Bellevue's officials recognized that the imminent arrival of some three thousand people made land-use planning urgent. Although jurisdictional squabbles confused the question of zoning jurisdiction around Fort Crook in early 1941, Bellevue's village board adopted its own zoning measure. Aside from meeting local apprehension about the possible proliferation of trailer dwellings, this action was necessary if the Federal Housing Administration were to guarantee loans for housing construction.

A legacy of Bellevue's urban ambitions in the territorial period was the continued existence of a large number of unused town lots. The taxes on

many of these parcels were long delinquent, and in a series of auctions between January and September 1941, real-estate developers acquired these
properties cheaply. Rapid construction of hundreds of relatively inexpensive houses followed. As historian Jerold Simmons has said, there was "a bellowing sense of optimism" in the town. The housing boom lasted until October 1942 when the Federal Housing Authority, apparently responding to
shortages of building supplies, greatly curtailed its underwriting. Despite
Bellevue's boom, perhaps three-quarters or more of the Martin plant workers resided elsewhere in the Omaha–Council Bluffs area, many of them car-
pooling to and from work.

As Bellevue's boom began, the town quickly obtained federal funds, including PWA and WPA money, for sewers and sewage treatment, a water system, schools, and other improvements. The construction of the Martin plant
brought a rapid increase in traffic, and in 1941 the road from Fort Crook to
Omaha became the state's first divided highway. Within Bellevue, street paving did not keep pace with other construction, and residents were bedeviled with mud and related inconveniences. The problem was more attributable to growing pains than poor leadership. Even so, in the town elections
in April 1944, the mayor and two council members, all prewar residents, lost
to write-in candidates who were newcomers employed at the Martin plant.
Fortunately, Bellevue apparently escaped polarization between old and new
residents, perhaps because newcomers bought homes, thereby establishing
themselves as part of the community.

ADJUSTING TO POSTWAR REALITIES

Less dramatic, but of fundamental significance, were advances in areas that
had long been important. Omaha's railroads prospered as a result of war
traffic and booming agricultural production. Stockyard receipts rose to the
greatest heights ever, and Omaha boosters again talked confidently about
possibly surpassing Chicago as the world's largest livestock market. Then
came the end of the war and a flurry of telegrams terminating government
contracts: Martin-Nebraska stopped production on September 30, 1945. The
return of peace raised an important question. Would prosperity last?

In 1945 the Omaha City Planning Commission issued a cautiously optimistic report. Avoiding the florid language of the booster literature of the

1920s, it stressed that Omaha had gained in population during the 1930s, contending that this and wartime changes seemed to indicate future progress. The planning commission envisioned a bright future for the food-processing industry and in addition noted that workers in defense plants had developed a variety of skills in new areas of fabrication. The prospect of increased air and barge transportation also seemed to favor Omaha. Questions of economic and political perspectives aside, there was a growing accommodation with the realities of the changes wrought by the Great Depression, the New Deal, and World War II. Omaha had entered a transitional period.

The electrical and traction industries reflected the changes in the wind. The Nebraska Power Company and the Omaha and Council Bluffs Street Railway Company had led the fight in prewar times for free enterprise and internal direction of affairs by the business community. Nebraska Power Company's president James E. Davidson surrendered quietly to the public power interests, doing so adroitly and with considerable grace. Indeed, he took the lead in going public. In 1944 he helped a state-authorized Electric Committee buy Nebraska Power from its parent company, the American Power and Light Company. Two years later, the state created the Omaha Public Power District, the first head of which was Davidson. He easily made the transition from private to public power, citing changing times and conditions. His pleasing personality and public-relations skills tended to cloud a fundamental change.

The Street Railway Company did not surrender as easily or gracefully, battling until the end to continue the policies that Wattles had articulated many years earlier. The war years brought a great increase in the use of public transportation. In the postwar years, Americans resumed their craze for automobiles, and in Omaha the number of public transit riders fell from 52,600,000 in 1948 to 44,800,000 in 1949 and 25,100,000 in 1954. In 1954 the company employed 480 workers, only about half the 1941 figure. For years, the firm had not improved its Council Bluffs service. Although the streetcar line to Omaha ran at a profit, the three trolley lines within Council Bluffs did not, and the company was unwilling to establish bus service. In 1947 the Street Railway Company's Council Bluffs franchise expired. Public sentiment favored buses, and a vote on a new franchise was scheduled for August 1948. Voters would decide between the Omaha-based Street Railway Company and a new Council Bluffs–based firm. Only belatedly did the Street Railway Company clearly commit itself to buses and make other concessions. At the same time, the firm noted that a defeat in the franchise vote would end the jobs of over one hundred of its Council Bluffs employees. Nevertheless, a majority of the voters, perhaps inspired by resentment against high-handedness from Omaha, decided in favor of the rival Council Bluffs Transit Company. In September 1948 after legal maneuvering by the Street Railway Company, the mayor of Council Bluffs ordered the trolley cars removed from his city's streets, ending a sixty-year streetcar era. The Council Bluffs Transit Company had prevailed, although both firms would run intercity buses.

In the late 1940s and into the 1950s, frequent strikes continued to characterize the Street Railway Company's labor relations. While the traction leaders gradually adopted the then-current national practice of phasing out streetcars in favor of buses, they seemed incapable of adopting a new approach to employer-employee relations. The firm's rigid stand came just as automobiles made transit strikes more of an inconvenience to users than anything more. Shortly after streetcar service ended in Omaha in March 1955, the Street Railway Company was renamed the Omaha Transit Company. A franchise change added public appointees to the company's board, paving the way for municipal control.

By midcentury, the fight against unions in Omaha assumed different, albeit not very effective, forms. After World War II, the Omaha Business Men's Association, dating from 1903, was in its waning days. In 1946 the Omaha-based Nebraska Small Business Men's Association emerged as an energetic successor to the BMA and spearheaded a campaign for a right-to-work amendment to the state constitution. With the support of agricultural organizations, the amendment was adopted that autumn. Voter approval of this measure, which banned the closed shop or compulsory union membership in the workplace, was part of a national backlash against perceived abuses by organized labor. The 1947 session of the state legislature passed laws implementing the amendment.

A strike of more than eight thousand Omaha packing-house workers in 1948, part of a national work stoppage in the meat processing industry, kept public attention on organized labor. Acting police chief Henry Boesen did not enforce restrictions on picketing to the satisfaction of the packers. When he joined fire- and police-union representatives in publicly presenting a check to the strike committee of the United Packinghouse Workers of America, the

World-Herald and the packing companies called for his dismissal. Elected officials, probably mindful of the labor vote, left Boesen alone. After more than two months the strike ended without the union achieving its objectives, but the presence of blacks and women on picket lines and broad support in South Omaha attested to the union's strength. In November conservative Republican congressman Howard Buffett lost to Democrat Eugene O'Sullivan who had supported the packing-house workers' cause. This proved to be only a two-year hiatus in the Republican domination that characterized the city and state in the generation after the Depression.

The packing-house strike encouraged the 1949 session of the state legislature to enact a new antipicketing law. The 1946 right-to-work amendment hurt unions, but in the long run these measures did not determine the plight of organized labor. By 1960 roughly 50,000 of 150,000 gainfully employed workers in Omaha belonged to labor organizations, and national unions wielded growing political power. While many of the same business leaders who had fought for the older goals remained in key positions, attitudes had changed. Despite continued rhetoric about the virtues of capitalism—an uninhibited kind in which entrepreneurs would have a free hand in the marketplace—in practice Omaha's dominant economic groups accepted a new age.

Omaha continued to enjoy prosperity throughout most of the postwar era. The general upward economic movement came despite serious inflation in the years immediately after the war, severe drought conditions on the Great Plains in the early 1950s, and periodic recessions in 1949, 1954, and 1958. Federal money never stopped coming into Omaha and its hinterland. Irrigation projects improved hundreds of thousands of acres of the agricultural base. Farm-price support and commodity programs, which especially worked to the advantage of grain farmers and cattle ranchers, helped bring a much-needed element of stability to Nebraska farming. Disaster relief and farm-loan legislation lessened the impact of the drought and recession times. Foreign-aid programs such as the Marshall Plan furnished ready overseas markets.

Closer to home, the Veterans Administration opened a large regional hospital in Omaha, constructed between 1946 and 1951 by local contractors. In addition, the Korean War led to increased military demands for produce. The Corps of Engineers stepped up its traditional functions along the Missouri

River. The Pick-Sloan engineering plan for the Missouri River basin, which called for construction of a series of dams and other public works, added another dimension to the economic picture. Lewis A. Pick, best known for his role in building the Ledo Road in Burma during World War II, headed the Corps of Engineer's Omaha office. He had good connections in Washington, ensuring careful congressional consideration of his proposals, even though he never realized his dream of a full-scale Missouri Valley Authority. Another federal program, the Interstate Highway Act of 1956, brought millions of dollars for freeway construction. Many Omaha and other Nebraska politicians rode to power by denouncing government spending and raising the twin specters of inflation and high taxes. Their declarations found a responsive audience, but big government played an essential role in keeping Omaha's economy healthy.

SAC

Of great importance was the moving of the headquarters of the Strategic Air Command (SAC) to Offutt Air Force Base, the site of the former Glenn L. Martin–Nebraska Company bomber plant. The massive facility had reverted to the government after the war. It had one of the few midcontinent runways capable of handling fully loaded B-29s, which required over ten thousand feet to take off. Although SAC commander Curtis LeMay complained about having to operate a global air force out of an old factory building, the bringing of SAC to Omaha guaranteed a share of postwar defense spending.

The decision was a complex one that related to a combination of military and political considerations. Nebraska's two Republican senators, Hugh Butler and Kenneth Wherry, wanted postwar defense bases for the state. In 1946 Butler had sought unsuccessfully to get Fifth Army headquarters located in Omaha. A supporter of military-spending programs and an opponent of New Deal measures, he was a resident of Omaha. Wherry, Republican Senate whip in the Eightieth Congress, exerted behind-the-scenes pressure. The Omaha Chamber of Commerce and other local groups also provided enthusiastic support. While this helped, congressional action loomed as far more important. No one at the local level had the power to decide events.

In July 1946 Lt. Gen. Ira C. Eaker, deputy commander of the United States Army Air Forces, decided that SAC headquarters should be moved from Andrews Air Force Base near Washington to "a station in the mid-West." He thought the capital too crowded with military personnel and airbases and believed a large continued military presence undesirable. Colorado Springs was the first choice, but orders moving SAC there were countermanded after air force representatives determined that a serious housing shortage existed in the area. In February 1947 Lowry Field near Denver came under serious consideration. However, Gen. Carl A. Spaatz, the commanding general of the Army Air Force, ruled that Lowry would remain an air-training command base. There matters stood until December 1947, when another survey ruled SAC had to relocate in the Midwest. Early in 1948, representatives of the new United States Air Force recommended four sites, including Offutt Air Force Base.

The SAC commander, George C. Kenney, strenuously objected to the first choice, Topeka Air Force Base, because he wanted SAC headquarters to stay in Washington. If SAC absolutely had to move, he felt it should be no further from Washington than Mitchell Field, New York. Kenney's superiors, including Hoyt S. Vandenberg, the air force chief of staff, and William Stuart Symington, the secretary of the air force, overruled him. During the deliberations, Wherry had promised Symington that Omaha business interests would provide adequate housing for base personnel. In late May 1948 Symington informed Wherry's office that SAC headquarters would move to Omaha, and on June 3 General Vandenberg signed an official order to that effect. Without much public fanfare, Omaha had obtained what had the potential to develop into a major defense installation.

Wherry's next goal was to ensure that SAC headquarters would remain permanently at Offutt Air Force Base. Omaha builders gave little sign of providing the estimated two thousand housing units that the SAC base required. Secretary Symington did not help matters when he responded to an inquiry by a prominent Omaha realtor by stating, "present Air Force plans contemplate the indefinite utilization of this base." Under the circumstances, no developer wanted to take the risk, especially when LeMay hinted that Omaha had military and administrative drawbacks. Wherry, who had promised that Omaha interests would provide housing units, sought a solution. To begin with, he blamed the military rather than Omaha builders. On December 28, 1948, he wrote Secretary of Defense James Forrestal, "I know from personal contacts that if home builders in Omaha were sure that the SAC or a similar installation were to be permanently headquartered at Offutt Field, the builders would solve the housing shortage at Offutt within the year." Next, Wherry introduced legislation under which the Federal Housing Administration would guarantee mortgages for housing units built on military bases designated as "permanent." He told the Senate Banking and Currency Committee that his purpose was to keep existing military bases in Nebraska. The Wherry housing bill, which received strong backing from the armed forces, easily passed Congress and became law in August of 1949. While it required technical changes, the legislation led to a solution of Offutt housing problems. Omaha civic leaders donated fifty acres adjacent to the base to the government; and a local builder, the Carl C. Wilson Offutt Housing Corporation, started a housing project after receiving a $5 million FHA loan. A measure designed to solve a specific problem that had national implications helped keep SAC headquarters at Offutt Air Force Base. In the process, Bellevue's continued growth was assured.

In its early Offutt days SAC had only a small number of B-29s modified to carry nuclear weapons. But, as the Cold War progressed, SAC became one of the West's chief weapons. In deciding how to counter the Russians, contingency planners ruled out a preemptive strike and developed a system to protect North America against a surprise attack from over the North Pole. Offutt Field was at the heart of these plans. It lay behind four lines of defense: an early warning system in the Arctic, two other lines to the south across Canada, and finally short-range missile batteries around population centers. If Russian bombers should come, the scheme called for SAC officers at Offutt to coordinate worldwide retaliatory strikes against targets in the Soviet Union. Large sums flowed into Offutt for runways, buildings, and underground fortifications. Omaha contracting and engineering firms received lucrative contracts. By the late 1950s the base was already a city in itself with over twenty thousand servicemen and dependents. Again, outside factors—these related to the prospects of global war—had advanced Omaha's economic fortunes.

BUSINESS, INDUSTRY, AND POPULATION GROWTH

The Omaha Chamber of Commerce claimed that the postwar progress resulted from the pluck and spirit of private enterprise, plus the attractions of the area. "Omaha has enjoyed a steady, healthy growth during the past several years," a 1958 promotional booklet indicated. "Because of its abundant water supply, natural resources, friendliness of its people, geographical

12. Omaha Stockyards, circa 1954. *Courtesy NSHS, 054-412.*

location, unexcelled transportation facilities and because Omahans are united as a civic team, our community has prospered." A number of indicators buttressed the assertion. Aggressive promotion brought new industrial concerns into Greater Omaha, including the Continental Can Company, the Allied Chemical and Dye Corporation, and the Omaha Production Company, a division of the Sperry Corporation. In 1956 Western Electric announced that it would construct a huge plant near the southwestern suburb of Millard. By the fall of 1959, the new plant employed more than four thousand persons. C. A. Swanson and Sons won renown as a pioneer mass producer of frozen "convenience" meals, first with chicken pot pie in 1951, then with turkey and beef pies, and in December 1953 with its famous "TV Dinner." Frozen fried chicken soon followed, and through a television advertising jingle, the firm told Americans that "C. A. Swanson and Sons present the kind of chicken that is Heaven-sent."

Manufacturing and other employment lines stabilized so that throughout the 1950s Omaha's workforce stood between 140,000 and 150,000, far above Depression-era levels. Livestock receipts increased from 5.3 million in 1948 to 5.9 million in 1958 with the number of animals slaughtered locally rising from 3.3 million to 4.3 million. Changing industry practices brought decline to the Chicago and Kansas City markets, giving Omaha its long-sought goal of becoming the nation's leading meat supplier with an annual business in excess of $5 billion.

Equally impressive was the rise of the insurance industry. The fraternal Woodmen of the World moved to Omaha in 1895. After changing the age of those eligible from fifty-one to forty-five, altering membership qualifications to exclude blacks, and adding a hazardous-occupation clause, the Woodmen prospered. By 1912 the nineteen-story Woodmen of the World Building stood as Omaha's first skyscraper, and in 1933 the Woodmen claimed assets of more than $26 million and a membership of 134,000. The fraternal insurance society survived the Depression and in the immediate postwar era claimed to be the largest insurance organization of its kind in the country. By then another Omaha insurance company was better-known and more successful. Mutual of Omaha, founded in 1909 as the Mutual Benefit Health and Accident Association, after a slow start did well over the years under the leadership of Dr. Clair C. and Mabel L. Criss. The firm and a subsidiary had over six hundred employees in 1939. During the 1950s Mutual of Omaha, helped by aggressive selling and nationwide advertising, became the nation's leading accident insurance company. By 1960 Omaha was the home of thirty-eight insurance companies, many subsidiaries or spin-offs of the original concerns. The industry employed eight thousand persons and had a premium income of $325 million. Like other Midwest financial hubs—Chicago, Milwaukee, Kansas City, and Des Moines—Omaha developed an insurance industry of impressive proportions. Because of the complexities of coverage warranties and estates, banking and insurance many times developed in the same centers. Moreover, Nebraska had some of the most lenient insurance laws and probusiness regulatory agencies in the United States. Indeed, another Cornhusker city, Lincoln, rivaled Omaha as an insurance center.

Not all growth came from big corporations. One entrepreneur built a business that became a local, and later, a regional landmark. Rose Gorelick Blumkin, a Russian immigrant born in 1893, arrived in Omaha with her husband in 1919. In 1937 she opened a furniture store at Thirteenth and Farnam streets. Through her hard work, ingenuity, and business honesty, the Nebraska Furniture Mart after occupying two more locations on Farnam moved in 1970 to a huge store on South Seventy-second Street. Nebraska Furniture Mart eventually became the nation's largest furniture and carpet retailer. "Mrs. B," as she was known, continued to work in the business until she was 103. In 1983 she sold controlling interest to Warren Buffett's Berkshire Hathaway. As Buffett said, "We gave Mrs. B a check for $55 million, and she gave us her word. That made for an even exchange."

Omaha's diverse economy spelled prosperity. The population increased from 251,117 in 1950 to 301,598 in 1960. Grain receipts rose to over sixty million bushels and shipments to fifty million bushels. Omaha remained an important wholesaling and warehouse center. From 1947 to 1957, the annual wholesale volume increased to slightly over $2 billion. In the same period retail sales jumped by 51 percent, with 1957 totals of $421 million. At that time, the city had an estimated 3,500 retail establishments. Combined deposits in Omaha's ten major banks advanced accordingly, crossing the $500 million mark late in the decade. As had been the case for decades, Omaha continued to serve as a transportation hub. Nearly two hundred freight and over seventy passenger trains entered and left Omaha every day. Thirty-five major trucklines and another 120 franchised motor carriers had headquarters in the city. Five airlines afforded fast national and regional transportation. More advances seemed in the offing, and there was a general uplift in the community spirit. In 1954 a hundred years after initial settlement, Prof. Walter H. Rawley Jr., of the University of Nebraska history department, viewing construction activities as a unifying theme, commented in the Omaha *World-Herald* on what he believed to be the prevailing mood:

> Gratifying evidence of civic achievement surrounds Omahans in their Centennial Year. There is the City-Wide Planning Commission; the building of the Outer Drive, with massive reinforced concrete piers waiting to support a massive viaduct over the Union Pacific Shops along the new arterial linking the Municipal Airport with downtown Omaha; construction of a Belt Line Highway; plans for increased parking facilities in downtown Omaha; remodeled and modernized department stores; a small but firm step toward solving the city's slum problem, and the long stride toward easing the community's traffic congestion by the adoption of an engineer's report calling for a one-way street plan. . . . So post-war progress—in business, transportation, education, art and

private housing—is Omaha's tribute to its founders on its one hundredth birthday.

This period also brought impressive growth to the other communities in the metropolitan area. The years of the Martin bomber plant and the coming of the Strategic Air Command to Offutt Air Force Base drove the population of Bellevue from 1,184 in 1940, to 3,858 in 1950, and 8,831 by 1960. Just as the rapid growth of Bellevue heralded the development of Sarpy County, the completion of the Western Electric plant pushed Millard's population from 391 in 1950 to 1,014 in 1960, starting a southwestward urban thrust. To the northeast of downtown Omaha, the blue-collar community of Carter Lake, Iowa, grew from 1,183 in 1950 to 2,287 in 1960. After a slight population dip during the Depression, Council Bluffs grew from 41,439 in 1940 to 45,429 in 1950. In the next decade the city gained over 10,000 residents, reaching a population of 55,641 in 1960. Lewis Township, just south of Council Bluffs and close to Bellevue and Omaha, grew from 2,189 residents in 1950 to 3,736 in 1960.

Home to some 7,000 union members, organized labor was a strong force in Council Bluffs. Like Omaha, Council Bluffs remained a rail center. Noting the typical dress of a railroad worker, a 1953 magazine article described Council Bluffs as "The Blue Denim City." That Council Bluffs was a railroad town was evident to motorists on Broadway, the city's main thoroughfare, stoically waiting for a slow train to pass. While Omaha in 1960 had 5,517 railroad and railroad express employees compared to 2,600 in Council Bluffs, as in the past, railroad employment was proportionately far larger in Council Bluffs. In fact, Council Bluffs, Iowa's seventh-largest city, had well over twice the number of railroad employees as did Des Moines, the state's principal urban center, which ranked second in the number of such workers. Still, a troubling sign of change could be found in the fact that the number of railroad workers in Council Bluffs had declined by over 23 percent between 1950 and 1960. Whatever the future held for the city as a rail center, in August 1955 the completion of a long viaduct carrying Broadway traffic over the tracks eliminated a great traffic impediment. Along with the Broadway Viaduct, planned since the latter part of the Depression, came more sewer construction and the paving of unsurfaced streets.

Omahans and their neighbors in the urban area took pride in what had been accomplished in a relatively short period. The making of the city had involved overcoming numerous challenges. In that context, the Great Depression was just one in a series of problems that confronted Omahans. Yet the economic disaster defied simple quantification, given its indispensable role in first raising questions about the possible boundaries of aspirations and then setting the course of events for ensuing decades. As it turned out, the questions had affirmative answers. Omaha had not reached the limits. There was no inevitable decline. Industries stayed. The hinterland recovered faster than expected. While all this was for the good, the reasons for the return to prosperity were somewhat disturbing.

Council Bluffs residents with memories reaching the 1930s could recall the excitement of the Farmers' Holiday episode while taking pleasure in the better times that followed the Depression. Like Omaha, their city remained a great rail center into the postwar years, and probably few people had taken to heart the 1940 contention of the *Nonpareil* that Council Bluffs was too reliant upon railroad employment. Whether business and political leaders could have more markedly reshaped the city's economy in the midcentury years is uncertain, but the validity of the newspaper's judgment would be gradually revealed in the generation after 1960.

Through the three decades of the New Deal, World War II, and the Cold War, federal money was the key to putting the Omaha area back on a positive course. The emergence of Bellevue and its continuing development in the Cold War era would be the biggest local monument to this truism. Washington's largesse came at a high price: ever greater federal interference in local affairs and a long and ominous inflationary cycle characterized by a gigantic increase in the national debt.

Further questions intruded upon the Omaha scene and shadowed rosy economic predictions. The bottom line remained the same as always; there was no easy way to build a city in the United States. For every success and difficulty overcome, there were new challenges to confront. In attempting to maintain and expand the position of Omaha, its leaders would have to continue to respond to outside forces, both public and private, while developing innovative ways to counter aggressive rivals. It was a price that came with the responsibility of metropolitan advance and one that Omaha's business leaders believed worth paying. A strong spirit of enterprise continued to exist.

[9] Riding Out the Storm

On the upper Plains, many small towns that flourished at the end of the 1920s were in serious decline thirty years later. They were victims of the Depression, the changes in agricultural marketing patterns, and the ability of larger and more powerful rivals to hold, maintain, and expand their hinterland empires. Omaha survived because of the position it had achieved prior to the crash. Its role as a transportation, financial, and agricultural center was of such regional importance that it had to figure in plans for recovery and then in those for the war and postwar economy.

According to the Omaha Chamber of Commerce, the city made dramatic strides between 1945 and 1960. As proof, the chamber in addition to citing all sorts of statistical evidence, called attention to the construction of freeways, the erection of large buildings, the development of numerous subdivisions, and the modernization of city government. Despite assertions of great progress, there was much about the Omaha of 1960 that resembled the Omaha of 1930. There had been little in the way of new downtown construction; so the skyline looked the same. New buildings such as the headquarters of Mutual of Omaha were west of the business district. The Union Pacific Railroad still played a crucial role in the life of the community; the operating headquarters was in the city. The stockyards and packing plants remained important, enhanced by Omaha's advance to the world's number-one livestock center. Hinterland boundaries set by the 1920s were about as before. The public schools were a source of local pride, and the Joslyn Memorial afforded a sense of culture. The Knights of Ak-Sar-Ben carried out a variety of activities. The outward changes had not been as obvious as claimed by boosters. About the best that could be said was that Omaha had succeeded in accomplishing what its business leaders had hoped for in the depths of Depression: to ride out the storm and to maintain the city's hard-earned position in the American urban system.

There was a price to pay, and those who bore it were the people of Omaha. In the harsh realities of the moment, it was all too common to not think of them individually. Rather, taken as a whole they served as the basis for the statistical data used in the formulas that determined relief expenditures, war contracts, and urban housing programs. From the 1930s through the 1950s the faith of Omahans in the future of the city was first shattered and then gradually restored. Restoration did bring new conceptions about the nature of the city. By the 1950s many Omahans felt that they lived in an increasingly cosmopolitan community that had evolved into a typical American regional metropolis. This was far different from the prevailing view back during the 1930s. Works Progress Administration writers analyzing Omaha in those years caught the prevailing mood when they wrote in 1939,

> Omaha has not yet lost a sense of surprise over becoming a big town: at heart it is still a city in the making, with Saturday night brawls, "drugstore cowboys" and packing-house workers on parade. Overalls and straw hats are not out of place in the marble lobby of the Livestock Exchange, and an occasional Indian is seen on the streets. The city has the small town's interest in local boys who made good; the front page always has space for the doings of any "former Omahan," whether he wrote a script for Hollywood or was arrested for theft in Denver. . . . Life here has more variety than is usual in Nebraska: gambling halls, dime-a-drink girls, formal banquets, a community art museum, conventions, folk festivals of European tradition, and the annual crowning of a King and Queen of Ak-Sar-Ben. . . . Notwithstanding the soot in the air and the odor of the stockyards that pervades South Omaha, the people are practically convinced that although Omaha could be improved upon, it is better than any other town within a thousand miles.

Even as the WPA writers drew their conclusions, forces of change were at work, which were rooted in the Great Depression and which had a fundamental effect upon community ideology.

The economic collapse had an impact on every person in Omaha. As might have been expected, vantage points differed. The wealthy saw it mainly in terms of paper losses and the threat of a loss in social status; membership in Ak-Sar-Ben dropped markedly. Even so, the lifestyles of local business leaders—merchant George Brandeis, hotel owner Eugene Chase Eppley, railroad executive William M. Jeffers, and electric power official James E. Davidson—remained much as before. The prestigious Omaha Club was still a citadel of privilege, and the coronation of the King and Queen of Ak-Sar-Ben remained the social event of the year. Things were much different for the middle and lower classes of Omaha. They experienced anguish and suffering: wage cuts, pink slips, loss of savings, debilitation caused by long-term unemployment, and the sickening feeling of downward mobility. They were the unfortunates in a generation of Americans who had had an unwanted rendezvous with destiny.

Omaha's black population was especially hard-hit. Historically, blacks had occupied the lower economic rungs, excluded from skilled blue-collar positions and white-collar office work. Generally, blacks were the last hired and the first fired. They performed tasks that whites did not want to do when better alternatives existed. Packing-house labor, including skilled positions such as butchers and trimmers, provided opportunities for blacks disproportionate to their share of the city's population. In 1931 major Omaha industrial firms employed 1,800 blacks out of a total working force of 16,000. A year later these same concerns had 14,750 operatives, but only 600 were black. Opportunities for blacks dried up in direct relationship to rising white unemployment. "We have used a few Negroes as porters and in the stables but there is no opportunity open now in either place," the manager of a large dairy reported. "The men we have in these departments are sticking rather close to their jobs." Sometimes, ethnic clannishness was an employment factor. In an extreme case early in the Depression, a new Bohemian foreman in a large downtown office building arbitrarily discharged thirty-two black cleaning women and replaced them with Bohemians.

Although black students composed over 5 percent of the city's population and 6 percent of the Omaha Public Schools' 1930 enrollment, there had been only two black elementary teachers in the system since 1901. Indeed, black students in teacher education at the University of Omaha could practice teach only at the black St. Benedict the Moor Catholic school. With the exception of the public schools, African Americans did hold public-sector jobs, albeit not in numbers reflective of their local presence. A pessimistic and discouraged J. Harvey Kerns, executive secretary of the Omaha Urban League, concluded in 1932, "[T]he inferior economic status of the Negro in

Omaha, involving as it does, irregular employment and low wages of men and women and limited opportunities for economic advancement, is one of the most serious problems confronting the race." Kerns described a situation that in its worst forms was to exist the rest of the decade throughout all of black America.

Social problems were inseparable from these economic difficulties for the city's black community that numbered 11,123 persons in 1930. The illiteracy rate for Omaha's African Americans was over twice the black community's proportion of the population. What later came to be called "de facto segregation"—informal but effective racial segregation that existed despite an 1893 state civil-rights law—governed much of the black experience in Omaha. In 1930 two public schools were over 70 percent black. Churches were focal points in the lives of many Near North Side residents, but membership was spread over many congregations. As a result, resources were fragmented, weakening religion as an effective force in the community. Despite the efforts of the Young Women's Christian Association and the Urban League, constructive recreational opportunities for young people were limited, and the numerous pool halls were undesirable options.

Health and crime problems loomed proportionately much larger in black Omaha than in the white community. While the Visiting Nurses Association and the Urban League worked to improve health, the percentage of Omaha blacks dying from tuberculosis and coronary disease far exceeded that of whites. A relatively high mortality of black infants reflected child-care problems arising from the necessity of mothers working outside the home and other poverty-related issues. This absence of parental supervision may have contributed to a proportionately high rate of black juvenile delinquency. Arrest rates for vagrancy, intoxication, and prostitution were also far higher for African Americans than for white Omahans.

Despite these problems, which were hardly the result of the Depression, the black community was a dynamic place. Paradoxically the color line in housing fostered the continuing development of the Near North Side with its own business and professional people; fraternal, religious, and social organizations; and places of entertainment. As had been the case since 1889, black newspapers promoted a sense of community. Founded in 1927 by B. V. Galloway and C. C. Galloway, the *Omaha Guide* attained a circulation of more than twenty-five thousand within a decade. In 1938 Mildred Brown and another former *Guide* employee established the *Omaha Star*, which continues to the present. Until the demise of the *Guide* in 1958, the black community had two papers. North Twenty-fourth Street was the heart of this community, and from the 1920s to the 1960s James Jewell Jr.'s Dreamland Ballroom featured such famous musicians as Louis Armstrong, Count Basie, Duke Ellington, and Lionel Hampton. Black music flourished at the Dreamland, the Club Harlem, and other Near North Side nightspots. Preston Love, a local youth who became enamored with Count Basie's band in the 1930s, went on to play with that orchestra in the 1940s as part of a long and distinguished musical career. By the 1940s and 1950s Omaha was a booking center and headquarters for both black and white "territory bands" that performed throughout the region. Dance advertisements in Plains towns might herald the coming of "Preston Love and His Popular Colored Band" or Ted Schroeder's "Big Colored Band Direct From Omaha, Nebraska." In 1936 Nat Towles Orchestra relocated to Omaha from Texas and emerged as one of Omaha's most prominent black bands, performing in places as diverse as New York City and Madison, South Dakota.

In 1941 researchers for the Federal Writers Project of the Works Progress Administration for Nebraska interviewed several dozen Omahans about their experiences during the Depression. Few cared to discuss in detail the hardships that they endured. Rather, they tended to recall happy moments and to talk about their lives in general. The Life History Project, an early experiment in oral history, was somewhat unstructured. The participants were not asked many specific questions but were encouraged to talk about themselves. This methodology, considered imperfect by later standards, had an unintended dividend. Their observations provided a unique record of what average Americans thought of when they tried to recall and explain what the cruel decade had meant in human terms.

Peter Christensen, seventy-four years old at the time of his interview in his modest home, was far from bitter about his Depression experiences. He had no formal schooling, but through self-study he had attained a third-grade level of competency. Born in Denmark in 1867, he immigrated to the United States in 1881. After living for short periods in Ohio and Massachusetts, he moved to the Great Plains. He settled in South Dakota, married, and fathered fifteen children. During most of his life he was either a farmer or grain elevator manager, but like countless others, he fell victim to the Depression. Forced out of work in 1932, he immigrated to Omaha two years later, where he eventually eked out a meager living peddling eggs. He was six feet tall, weighed 185 pounds, had iron-grey hair, a moustache, and blue eyes. Musing over his daily routine, he viewed his state of affairs with a certain degree of optimism, claiming it did not bother him to have customers slam doors in his face.

Christensen placed his hopes for the future in the Townsend Plan. Referring to the controversial proposal advanced by a retired Californian, he said,

> It would take care of us oldsters—make us feel secure. That's about the worst trouble with getting old—the insecurity—we can't get jobs. We've put our lives into doing our share for the country, and now, when we are old, the security we'd get from the Townsend Plan would allow us to live our last days happily. The money we'd receive would have to go right back into circulation and it would leave profits to people all the way down the line, from raw material to delivery-boy. I'm for it—even though my own needs are well taken care of. Just think of being forced to spend $200 a month!

Sam Piccinoni, born in Sicily in 1894, was of medium height, rather heavy-set, and partly bald. He had a round face, dark eyes, and a pleasant disposition. He had a wife and one child. Educated in common schools in Italy, he was a businessman in Omaha until ruined by the Depression. He said that he had few regrets about his experiences in Omaha and America, even though he failed three times in the restaurant business in the 1930s. After that he was unemployed until his wife gave birth to a baby girl, and he decided to swallow his pride and go to work for the WPA:

> I thinks this WPA work is ver' good to help people without anything. This people who work for WPA, they need money. They have to support their families. Many people criticize this government, but, from my estimation, they are wrong. The people who criticize this WPA, they are the people who never had to work hard in their lives, or people who are mean and never have any love for poor people. . . . Cold weather, hot weather, rain or storm, I know [no] mind. I am living very happy.

At the time of his interview, Piccinoni was a sewer department foreman.

Another subject of a Life History Project, James Breezee, born in Wisconsin in 1917, had had an unpleasant childhood. His mother died, and his stepfather committed him to a home for the feebleminded. He escaped after completing fourth grade and became a drifter. Breezee, who made a living selling trinkets on street corners, had lost a leg while trying to catch a freight train in Council Bluffs. He had no permanent address when a WPA worker asked him about his experiences as a youthful runaway:

> I usually eat at some of those beaneries down on lower skid-row. What is skid-row? Well, in Omaha that's Douglas Street. There are some pretty rotten dumps down there too, while some of them are not so bad for the money. Sometimes I sleep at the Salvation Army but a lot of times I just sleep out doors. Last night I slept out doors all night; no it wasn't cold. Starting early in the fall, it makes one tough to stand the winters. Sometimes I sleep out doors all winter. The toughest thing is not to be able to get a bath whenever you want it. They stick you from twenty cents to thirty-five cents for a bath down there, and a fellow has got to clean up once in a while.

In a 1933 Hollywood movie, *Wild Boys of the Road*, a young runaway lost a leg while riding the rails. The film was a significant social document that called attention to the hundreds of thousands of teenage Americans put on the move during the Great Depression. James Breezee was one of those persons. Glimpses of similar stories could be had on a bitter day in the winter of 1933–34 amid the dried reeds on the shore of frozen Big Lake, north of Council Bluffs, where transients huddled about a campfire. At the same time the Union City Mission in downtown Council Bluffs would have provided another vignette of wandering Americans. Some of the transients were confirmed hobos who had been on the road long before the Depression, but others were victims of the hard times. The government was building facilities to accommodate transients, but veteran hobos disdained what they perceived to be the regulated environment of what they called "concentration camps." Younger men may have had a different attitude. Without such camps, transients were a burden to communities, and one option was to dispatch wanderers to the next place. A terse editorial in the *Nonpareil* in February 1934 gave more insight into the plight of men like James Breezee: "They have a transient camp in Omaha. One day during the week our police department headed thirteen transients in that direction. The next day no transients appeared at our department. The code applying to transients seems to be working." Despite the initial objections of some residents, Council Bluffs soon had such a camp.

Photographs as well as fiction convey a feeling for the hard times. John Vachon, a photographer for the Farm Security Administration, traveled the country catching many images of life in America. His photos taken in Omaha in November 1938 form an invaluable perspective. A fictional portrait of the starker aspects of life in South Omaha in the Depression era is found in Tillie Lerner Olsen's novel, *Yonnondio: From the Thirties.* Olsen's parents, who left Russia after that country's 1905 revolution and eventually settled in Omaha, were committed socialists; and about the time Tillie Lerner left Omaha in her late teens, she joined the Young Communist League. Although she spent much of her subsequent years in California, *Yonnondio,* written in the 1930s but not published until 1974—and then with an incomplete but forceful narrative—depicts the hardships of a poor family that had moved from a Wyoming mining settlement to a South Dakota farm and on to South Omaha in a failing quest to eke out a livelihood. Especially graphic—and transcending the Depression—is Olsen's description of the hard working conditions in the packing houses.

THE WPA: LOOKING BEYOND RELIEF

In Omaha as throughout the nation, the wpa tried to combine relief activities with social reconstruction. Activities ranging from Sunday concerts in city parks to sewing bees represented an attempt by a president of the United States to use federal agencies as a means of standardizing life in the country. Typical of the New Deal efforts to progress beyond economic recovery were several programs in Douglas County sponsored by the wpa Division of Women's and Professional Projects. In 1938 the division employed over 1,600 persons on sixteen different projects, several of which had been in operation for more than four years. Usually the sponsors were city or county agencies that sometimes had contributed money toward operational expenses. The idea was that all those employed in the programs would have something to show for their efforts. There was a conscious effort to avoid patterns set by a few of the more controversial early New Deal relief programs. In some places unemployed workers dug ditches in the morning and then refilled them in the afternoon, leaned on shovels, or raked and reraked leaves. Community action was at the core of WPA efforts in Omaha: the needy would help the needy. The objective was to develop a collective solution to community problems far transcending immediate economic needs—a response that would break down ethnic, racial, and parochial barriers and give rise to a new and more united American society.

Working for the good of the individual and of the state took many forms. A thousand women participated in a sewing project sponsored by Douglas County that provided $2,000 for space, equipment, and materials. Pleased bureaucrats noted that after three years the WPA workers had produced 245,000 garments, repaired 2,300 pairs of shoes, and made 2,000 burlap rugs. City agencies in Omaha used WPA personnel in a number of ways. Seventy-five men enumerated over seventy thousand dwellings as part of a comprehensive real property survey. The library board employed twelve people to repair and bind books. A daycare nursery for children between the ages of two and six had a staff of twelve and enrolled over 8,400 youngsters. Throughout the Omaha school system, twenty-four clerical assistants handled routine office tasks, allowing administrators more time for educational duties. The health department contributed $2,200 to start a disease prevention and treatment service. Six nurses spent most of their time in a new program of home visitations and examinations. An adult education project that initially cost $13,000 had seventy-seven teachers. WPA statistics claimed that classes had attracted 19,000 participants. Another success was a park department recreational scheme. The department received a very good return on its contribution of $35,000, most of which went for space and equipment. In 1938, a total of 222 recreational leaders staffed twenty-six centers. In its first four years of operation, close to 950,000 persons visited the facilities. A WPA official reported, "The community cooperation . . . is wonderful."

In Omaha highly qualified WPA employees worked for several years to write a comprehensive survey of the city for the American Guide Series. Their goal was to produce a descriptive history, to identify and discuss important points of interest, and to analyze the social fabric. Ethnic and religious groups received prime consideration. The Life History Project of Omahans was a small portion of the many cubic feet of collected and codified research material. The project died just short of publication. The Nebraska

State Historical Society gained custody of the manuscript drafts and raw research, which constituted for future generations an indispensable, unique, and informative source about Omaha.

Two cultural uplift programs, the Dramatic Unit and Children's Theatre and the Music Project, highlighted the WPA's role in the life of Omaha. During the first two years of operation, an estimated 70,000 people witnessed theater productions. More than twice that number attended symphonies conducted under the direction of the Music Project. The Omaha Urban League helped organize sixty-five musicians into "colored and white symphonies." Audiences totaled 178,465 over a two-year period.

Council Bluffs also had a WPA program that sought to enhance the quality of life of children and adults. Under the direction of the Reverend Edwin H. Berger with the city park department as local sponsor, the WPA recreational program began in January 1936 using churches and other existing buildings. By June the program was functioning at nine sites, "including one for Negroes." By the following January there were twenty-four centers, and an average of 1,645 persons per month used each of these recreational sites. The Republican *Nonpareil*, often critical of the Roosevelt administration, strongly praised this program. The paper said that although WPA projects had done much to improve local streets, alleys, and highways, the less-publicized recreational program possibly had greater value than these material achievements. Underlying this conclusion was the argument that how Americans used their leisure time would do much to shape their nation's future. Leisure time, said the *Nonpareil*, "must become an integral part of our educational system." In extolling the practical value of the WPA recreational program, the paper remarked, "Many of us have noticed that acts of vandalism in the parks and elsewhere have well nigh disappeared. In these supervised recreational centers the minds of youngsters have been concentrated on their work. This has prevented concentration on acts of vandalism." In stressing that constructive use of children's leisure time was a part of education, the *Nonpareil* implicitly recognized that the WPA recreation program had an importance that transcended the Depression.

AFTER TOM DENNISON

Unlike the situation in some other large Midwestern cities, relief programs in Omaha generally did not become entangled in politics. The lack of political interference in the city's New Deal programs related directly to two deaths, those of Mayor James C. Dahlman in 1930 and "Boss" Thomas Dennison in 1934. Without their dominating personalities, Omaha's commission form of government was too ineffective and divided to determine relief policies despite apparent efforts to do so. The business community, accustomed to dealing through Dennison, had not developed an alternative way to exercise power.

Dahlman's successor, Richard L. Metcalfe, a veteran Democratic politician, had been a *World-Herald* editor and civil governor of the Panama Canal Zone. As mayor, he was associated with the Dennison faction in its waning days and, perhaps sensing political change, withdrew from the 1933 municipal general election campaign.

The next mayor, Roy Towl, was a professional engineer who was initially elected to the city commission in 1918 in the first triumph of the reformers. As commissioner of public improvements, he was active in early zoning development, the paving of residential streets, and other traffic improvements. When the Dennison-Dahlman group regained city hall in 1921, Towl was defeated for reelection, but he was reelected to the city commission in 1930. Because responsibility for law enforcement had inevitable political perils, the pro-Dennison majority soon switched Towl from the office of commissioner of fire protection and water supply to that of commissioner of police. This plan to make him the scapegoat for police malfeasance backfired, and his colleagues moved him back to his old job. As a key figure in the declining days of the Dennison organization, Towl won reelection to the city commission in the Independent Voters' League victory in 1933. His new colleagues chose him to be mayor, but the limited powers of his office under the commission system of government may explain his failure to take the leadership in dealing with the traction strike of 1935. Towl turned the city over to Gov. Robert Cochran without making a major effort to restore order.

Dan Butler, mayor from 1936 to 1945, was a portly bachelor whose appearance, if not his temperament, fit the caricature of the urban politician. As a young man he had played and coached football at Creighton University. As coach, a 103 to 0 home defeat in October 1905 at the hands of the University of Nebraska may have encouraged him to reflect upon other career options. He won election as city clerk in 1906 and in 1912 began the first of five consecutive terms as a city commissioner. He had a falling-out with the Dennison organization and was finally defeated in 1927, but the reform vote in 1933 brought him back to city hall. Like Dahlman, he was a Democrat, enjoyed the limelight of office, and was honest. He had a commanding presence among his fellow commissioners, but as he aged he gained a reputation for bluntness and irascibility. In a draft of Butler's obituary—prepared thirteen years before his death—a newsman wrote, "He never went around shaking hands and slapping backs. 'Why should I?' he once asked. 'If I grab somebody's hand and say how glad I am to see him, he may be thinking, "Who the hell is this bird, anyway?!"'"

Butler's efforts to protect public morality added color to his reputation. In 1937 he barred a performance of *Tobacco Road*, and a short time later he tried unsuccessfully to force the theatrical couple Alfred Lunt and Lynne Fontanne to delete some lines from their Omaha performance of the play, *Idiot's Delight*. The following year, in announcing that Omaha was off-limits for stripteaser Gypsy Rose Lee, he proclaimed, "She won't even get to unpack her bags." He also directed that Mari Sandoz's novel *Slogum House* be removed from the public library. Even though he had progressive inclinations in his earlier career, Butler's tenure as mayor reflected an increasingly sclerotic aura of Omaha's commission form of government.

Despite the passing of the Dennison organization and notwithstanding Butler's moralistic efforts, the old vices, especially gambling, could still to be found. In the summer of 1936, soon after Butler took office, a *World-Herald* reporter interviewed some bookies, tavern keepers, a proprietor of a "dime-a-dance place," and "Queenie, the faded lady who has three girls in her second floor flat." Although there was apprehension about a change in police administration, most persons questioned took the change in stride and did not seem especially worried about efforts to root out the demimonde or police shakedowns as the price of continuing in business. Queenie claimed that latter practice had been a problem. Perhaps yearning for the measure of certainty that seemed to protect such entrepreneurs in Dennison's era, she remarked, "I'd rather pay a hundred dollars a month and know what's what than 10 dollars a month and not know what it's all about."

Whatever the plight of prostitution, it was the bookies or operators of "wire joints" who would be in the limelight. Bookies conducted horse-race betting through a subscription wire service connection to distant tracks. Typically bookmaking was done in cigar stores and bars and, except for the larger wire joints, was a supplemental source of income for the owners of these businesses. By 1936 illegal off-track gambling places were well established in Omaha. Their patrons included women as well as men, and the fact that that bets as small as fifteen cents could be placed probably enhanced their popularity. Such public support undoubtedly made law enforcement difficult. As a bar owner said, "They have never run the wire joints out of business and they couldn't close them up with less than the standing army. People are going to bet on the ponies and somebody is going to take their bets."

In the 1920s a subsidiary of Omaha's premier civic organization, the Knights of Ak-Sar-Ben, sponsored horse racing at its track just to the southwest of the city. Then in 1929, the Nebraska Supreme Court ended such racing meets on grounds that they violated the state's law against lotteries. In 1934 Ak-Sar-Ben succeeded in a drive to amend the state constitution to permit pari-mutuel horse-race betting, and the following year the legislature adopted a law implementing this change. Because the law stipulated that betting was to be confined to the premises where authorized racing was conducted, bookie operations presumably remained unlawful. Curiously, Ak-Sar-Ben, the hallmark of civic leadership and respectability, reached accommodations with the Independent Bookmakers Association, a body representing sixty-three bookies, in which the latter agreed that its members would not operate during the local racing meet. This, according to Ak-Sar-Ben executive secretary J. J. Isaacson, was "a courtesy usually accorded in cities where tracks are located."

The unimpeded operation of wire joints obviously sent a mixed message to the people of Omaha. The message became even more dubious when, in the wake of failed efforts to obtain convictions against bookmakers, the city council decided that if bookies were to flourish, the municipal government should get revenue from them. Accordingly, the council passed an ordinance requiring bookmakers to pay a five-hundred-dollar annual occupation tax. Even though council members declared that their action did not legalize off-track betting, the operators of the wire joints who paid the tax naturally assumed that they were free to carry on business.

That gambling in Omaha was part of a far-flung web of activity was evident when Nationwide News Service and its local subsidiary sought to establish a monopoly in wire service to bookies, a situation that divided local operators. Further evidence of outside interest in local gambling came when police reported that twenty Chicago men came to Omaha following the 1938

Ak-Sar-Ben racing meet for the purpose of "taking over" bookmaking operations in the city. The *World-Herald* joined local clergymen in denouncing what it termed "the 'bookie' evil" that "reache[d] its greedy pilfering hand down into the pockets of the very poor, taking from them the two-bit pieces that [were] desperately needed for the bare necessities of life." The paper also feared that the widespread bookmaking activity could lead to the creation "of a new political machine, financed by the underworld, feeding the underworld, with all honest persons its victims." Lending credence to this concern was the fact that some leading gamblers in the gambling business, such as Edward Barrick and Sam Ziegman, had been prominent in the business in the Dennison era.

In February 1938 Richard C. Hunter, attorney general of Nebraska, launched a campaign to shut down seventy bookie establishments in Omaha, which had a daily "handle" or business volume estimated to be from $75,000 to $100,000. When the attorney general persuaded the city council to repeal the occupation tax, lawyers for the bookies impeded the campaign by various maneuvers, including what the *World-Herald* called the "legal legerdemain" of convincing a judge that bets placed with bookies were lawfully executed at race tracks. Another complication was the fact that gambling flourished outside the city limits. Mayor Butler and Douglas County sheriff John Hopkins blamed each other for failing to suppress gambling within their respective jurisdictions. Continued prosecution of bookies, the election of a new sheriff, and the dissolution of the Nation Wide News Service when its owner was indicted in federal court on charges of income-tax evasion assisted in the battle against gambling in the Omaha area. Even so, despite police raids it was possible in the 1940s to find a bookie in Omaha.

For gambling operators and their patrons, the state line was a source of comfort. Omahans wishing to bet on races or play slot machines simply had to cross the river to Council Bluffs where gambling flourished despite desultory efforts to eliminate it. In January 1939 a *Nonpareil* editorial, noting almost daily "reports of flagrant law violations," declared, "We have reason to think that conditions in Council Bluffs are getting worse all the time." The battle against off-track betting in Omaha was the apparent reason for a huge increase in such activity in Council Bluffs, prompting the paper to recall an occasion when inadequate local law enforcement had led to state intervention: "This occurrence brought Council Bluffs into bad repute and we do not want it to happen again."

There were other Iowa options for local gamblers. In March 1938 shortly after Attorney General Hunter began his offensive, the proprietors of the Chez Paree on the river bottoms northeast of downtown Omaha moved a short distance to a log building just over the state line in Carter Lake. Here, entertainment seekers could indulge in blackjack, craps, and roulette, "out of reach of Nebraska's gentlemen of the law." The Chez Paree soon won the favor of Carter Lake residents, donating generously to such local causes as helping purchase Sunday-school books and providing Christmas baskets for the needy. Delegations of Carter Lake citizens asked Pottawattamie County sheriff Riley Nelson not to trouble the Chez Paree and Mayor Wilson Mabrey declared, "I don't know whether they gamble there. . . . But I do know that they run a quiet place. We never have any trouble with them." For the next decade, despite a 1942 fire, the Chez Paree and its patrons would take advantage of the enclave of Iowa that was physically detached from the rest of that state. Almost a half-century after his cordial comments about the Chez Paree, Mabrey would recall having seen a governor and an attorney general of Nebraska as well as a mayor of Omaha at the place, "And I was proud to meet them there."

Between 1941 and 1943, William J. Syms and notorious crime figure Meyer Lansky were partners in the Dodge Park Kennel Club, a dog-racing track near the Council Bluffs end of the bridge from downtown Omaha. The track circumvented Iowa's antigambling statutes through the device of selling "options" in lieu of taking bets on racing dogs. The holders of options on dogs finishing first, second, or third in races received payouts similar to what winning ticket holders would receive in a pari-mutuel contest. Because the Kennel Club operated on city park land, it paid a weekly fee of one thousand dollars to the Council Bluffs Board of Park Commissioners that enabled that body to make a corresponding reduction in the tax levy. This revenue also helped the city pay debts from its centennial celebration. The Dodge Park Kennel Club was popular and a one-time police officer recalled, "They had a very clean operation." Lansky was sociable and made charitable donations, but Mayor William A. Byers blocked the opening of the 1944 racing season on grounds that the track was a "gambling operation" and hence unlawful. By contrast, one person came close to what would be a major justification for gambling in the city two generations later when he remarked, "I don't understand why a man would stop about the only paying thing in Council

Bluffs. At least three out of five of the people at the track were from Omaha. It wasn't our money." In 1946 the Kennel Club was about to reopen, but when an Iowa Bureau of Criminal Investigation agent threatened antigambling prosecutions, Syms declared, "We have finally made up our minds to pull out of Council Bluffs forever."

On the South Omaha Bridge Road, outside of Council Bluffs, one could still gamble at the Riviera Club or the larger Stork Club. The Stork Club went into business in 1942 and was very profitable—so profitable that men associated with Charles Binaggio, a Kansas City crime figure, may have used a more proactive mode of persuasion than normal in real-estate transactions to convince its Omaha and Minneapolis owners to part with their property. As the 1940s ended, both Iowa and Nebraska were again fighting crime, and these places closed. Clearly, unlawful gambling was common in the Omaha–Council Bluffs area in the 1930s and 1940s. Senator Estes Kefauver's committee studying organized crime in the United States in 1951 reported the ties that had existed between Kansas City and Council Bluffs.

Meyer Lansky and some leading gambling operators in Omaha such as Edward Barrick and Sam Ziegman became prominent figures in the early development of Las Vegas. So, too, did John D. "Jackie" Gaughan, who learned the rudiments of the gambling business as a teenager in Omaha in the 1930s from Barrick and his uncle Casey Gaughan also a leading bookmaker. After running a cigar store–bookmaking place in Omaha and graduating with a business degree from Creighton University, Jackie Gaughan moved to Las Vegas in 1951 where he obtained an interest in the Flamingo Club. He sometimes employed dealers who had worked at the Chez Paree and Stork Club. In a long career Gaughan acquired seven of the smaller casino hotels in Las Vegas. Indeed, at one time Las Vegas was occasionally called "Little Omaha."

The persistence of illegal gambling in Omaha was trumpeted in a 1952 exposé, *U.S.A. Confidential.* The authors, Jack Lait and Lee Mortimer, followed in the tradition of the sensationalists who produced "Sins of the City" literature in the late nineteenth century. Together, Lait and Mortimer had coauthored "confidential" studies of the underworld in New York, Chicago, and Washington. They gathered material on Omaha during a short visit. According to them, they almost left immediately upon arrival when they noticed that all the taxicabs carried advertisements on the rear reading, "Visit your church on Sunday." They stayed after a "hackman" asked them, "Whatta you wanna do? Places to bet? Just go to Chet's cigar store across the street from the Burlington bus terminal. Or try the Rocket on Farnam St." The result was an uncomplimentary short section in *U.S.A. Confidential* entitled "Omaha— Beef and Bookies," which raised questions about how some aspects of life in Omaha had changed since its days as a wide-open town.

Lait and Mortimer offered little new about conditions in Omaha beyond undocumented comments, derogatory statements, and a few street addresses. They demonstrated no knowledge about the history of the city, and their information about geography and sectional mores appeared muddled. The response in Omaha was one of rage, a response that was part of an attempt to create new images and to articulate different goals.

SOCIETY AT MID-CENTURY

Meanwhile, World War II had roughly the same effect on Omaha as on other parts of the country. Dislocations and separations were common. The great number of women drawn into manufacturing forced adjustments, as did increased shift work. As elsewhere, war-labor needs heralded social changes. Of 13,217 persons employed at the Glenn L. Martin–Nebraska bomber plant, 5,306 were women. Traditional commercial business habits changed; many stores remained open during evening hours. More money went for recreation than at any time since the Depression. Omaha's entertainment district, its wide-open tradition curtailed in the 1930s by pressure from state authorities, regained some of its former luster. "Gin mills" located near the stations competed with the Red Cross and separate black and white United Service Organizations for the patronage of the thousands of military personnel who daily changed trains in Omaha. While the war brought a temporary end to horse racing at Ak-Sar-Ben, other gambling outlets continued to operate. Such activities constituted only a small part of the city at war. Citizens took their home-front duties seriously. They bought war bonds, endured rationing, and served in civilian defense groups.

A combination of a patriotic war supported by almost all citizens, coupled with the success of New Deal programs in making people accustomed to following the lead of the federal government, helped assure unified response to the emergency. Perhaps the New Deal and World War II made Americans of all races and creeds more alike and more aware than ever before that they shared a similar experience. This seemed especially true of the nation's larger cities. Key elements tended to come closer and closer together as they were pressured by an ever more powerful national government to move in the direction of common problem solving. Cities increasingly had less local or individual authority over their own affairs.

In 1946 an extensive program report prepared by the Young Men's Christian Association and the Young Women's Christian Association analyzed the needs and problems of Omaha's youth. The study was another indication of the growing acceptance of social planning as an important element in solving local problems. The authors believed that an outmoded conservative economic and social outlook gripped Omaha; as a result the community trailed other cities in recreation, school, and social programs. The survey collected data on youth "behavior problems." Indices showed that juvenile delinquency was more than just a wartime problem, as some persons had thought. The Omaha juvenile court, with a caseload of about five thousand per year and no real way to deal effectively with habitual offenders, was "under-staffed and under-served." Many truants from the commercial and industrial districts were another cause of concern. Because of lax enforcement of the Nebraska child-labor laws, many fourteen year olds who obtained legal summer work permits violated the conditions by continuing to work into the school year. Frequently, they found it hard to hold jobs and attend school at the same time. Juvenile deaths in street accidents added another dimension. Most occurred on service roads in black districts on the Near North Side that had few playgrounds. Just as disturbing were a series of drownings in suburban Carter Lake that were attributed to poor supervision.

Teenage drinking was a serious problem. Omaha had 752 liquor stores and drinking places, far more than other cities in the same population class. Oklahoma City had 610, Syracuse 488. The report contended, "With the poverty of public recreational facilities and social programs it is not surprising that Omaha leads cities of comparable size in the number of drinking places to total stores, and in the percent of total retail sales spent in drinking places." The general conclusion was that the girls and boys of Omaha could be best served by greater public expenditures for recreation. With the curtailment of federal funding, privately supported agencies were unable to meet the needs of the city. Still, there was increased public involvement in youth programs and political considerations evolved around how much money should be spent rather than about whether it should be spent. This was another legacy of the New Deal, one not as obvious and publicized as others, but it was a legacy just the same.

By early in the twentieth century it was clear that changing technology and urban growth brought more employment opportunities for women. In 1910 women had composed just over 20 percent of the Omaha area's work force, but a half-century later, the figure had grown to almost 34.7 percent. However, allowing for differences in reporting basic job descriptions, the 1960 U.S. Census showed scant progress in raising the stature of women's jobs. "Clerical and kindred workers" was by far the largest employment category for women, while many women were "service workers," which included restaurant employees. Employment in retailing and as domestics remained common, and women often worked in hospitals. Teaching was still a female bailiwick. Government employment of whatever classification had brought significant opportunities to women: just over 40 percent of the people holding such jobs in Greater Omaha were female. However, taken as a whole, women still occupied lower-status positions than men, a reality suggested in the fact that in 1959 the median income for males in the Omaha area was $5,027 compared to $2,307 for females.

The character of Omaha's population underwent significant changes from 1930 to 1960. By the 1940s many immigrants from Europe had died, and Omaha exhibited an increasingly American character. The total population rose from 223,844 in 1940 to 251,117 in 1950 and in the next decade jumped to 301,598. By contrast, the city's foreign-born population, which had declined sharply in the 1930s, continued to drop. At the start of the 1940s there were 23,311 foreign-born white persons representing slightly under 10 percent of Omaha's population, down by over 7,000 from ten years earlier. The decline continued in the next two decades, and in 1960 the city had only 14,185 foreign-born whites or just over 4.7 percent of the total number of residents. Persons of Italian, Czech, German, and Swedish birth in that order were the most numerous of Omaha's foreign-born residents in 1940, and twenty years later, Germany, Italy, Czechoslovakia, and Poland respectively were the principal birthplaces of Omahans from abroad. As in the past, there were very few non-European persons of foreign birth.

The decline in the number of Omaha's foreign-born residents would have been even more precipitous had it not been for the arrival of significant numbers of displaced persons from central and eastern Europe from 1949 into the 1950s. Omaha, already the home of many people who traced their ancestry to that region, became the destination for numerous refugees from lands under control of the Soviet Union, particularly East Germany, Latvia, Lithuania, and the western Ukraine. Among the displaced persons the Lithuanians were especially prominent. In 1949 and 1950 an estimated 655 Lithuanians arrived in Omaha, and by 1951 the figure reached about 1,000. In South Omaha they augmented a small Lithuanian community that dated from the early twentieth century, its people drawn to the area by packing-house jobs. At its heart was St. Anthony Catholic Church and parochial school. The veteran priest, the Reverend Joseph Jusevicius, himself a native of Lithuania, did much to bring about the mid-twentieth-century influx of people from his homeland.

South Omaha also attracted displaced people from Latvia who often found packing-house work. The nucleus of their small community was the Lutheran church they established in the early 1950s, about the same time the Ukrainians founded a Byzantine Rite Catholic parish in South Omaha. Whatever comfort they found in replicating their native cultures, the newcomers like immigrants of other generations found adjustment to life in Omaha challenging. Probably typical was the experience of a man who had been a lawyer in Latvia. Mindful of the problems of restarting his profession in the United States, he was happy to work in a packing house.

As in the past, ethnic diversity was more muted in Council Bluffs. While the city's population increased from 41,439 in 1940 to 45,429 in 1950 and 55,641 in 1960, the numbers of foreign-born residents dropped steadily. The 2,335 foreign-born white residents in 1940 represented a drop of 701 persons from the 1930 total. By 1960 Council Bluffs was home to only 1,111 foreign-born white persons. Danes and Germans remained the most numerous of the city's foreign born.

At midcentury the communities that Omaha had annexed between 1915 and 1917 all kept—and would continue to keep—their identities. In 1955 when Omaha surpassed Chicago as the world's premier packing center, South Omaha was the focal point of an industry that visibly linked the city to a hinterland extending from the Corn Belt to the Rockies. Although the heyday of immigration was two generations in the past, South Omaha retained a strong ethnic heritage, giving the industrial and residential suburb an identity and consciousness that set it apart from the rest of the city. Far smaller and less distinctive than South Omaha, the suburb of Dundee and the former country villages of Benson and Florence that had become residential suburbs kept their identities. Especially important, all four places retained distinct business districts that were the historic signatures of their once separate status.

In 1944 approximately 78 percent of all Omahans lived in single-family dwellings, making the city a "front porch town," in the terminology of the day. Community spokesmen found this desirable, equating it without substantial evidence with the promise of American life. They did not emphasize that enrollment in the public schools dropped between 1930 and 1944. The best available statistics on religion came from the 1936 federally conducted religious census released in 1941 that showed that fewer than 47 percent of all Omahans had a church affiliation. Of those who did, Protestants were in the majority, with Lutherans the largest body. Council Bluffs showed a similar denominational pattern but with a total church membership that was fewer than 37 percent of the city's population. Early in 1941, the Council Bluffs Ministerial Association ran a large newspaper ad encouraging attendance at worship services. The ad said that there were "TEN THOUSAND Unchurched Men, Women and Children in This City." A private religious census in 1950 indicated that church membership in both cities had increased in relation to their total populations. The Omaha survey counted 79,111 Protestants, 51,954 Catholics, and 3,990 Jews, a total of 53.78 percent of the city's residents. The enumeration in Council Bluffs showed that about 45 percent of the city's residents had "an active, live relationship to the Christian church or synagogue," a figure that the Nonpareil saw as "not good." All in all the various social statistics taken at different intervals and circumstances provided an important insight into the Omaha area in the immediate postwar years. So many changes had occurred that social trends seemed impossible to predict. As it turned out, the 1950s in metropolitan Omaha meant much the same as elsewhere: a false sense of stability.

World War II heralded a new age for African Americans in Omaha and elsewhere. Inevitably, the struggle against fascism abroad highlighted denials of equality at home; moreover, the war brought a labor shortage that meant employment opportunities for blacks. The war years brought the start of significant growth in the city's black population that increasingly illustrated the inadequacies of segregated housing. Until the early 1940s, the Omaha Urban League, while seeking better employment opportunities for blacks, had focused much attention upon adult education, health, youth recreation, and other community services, sometimes in conjunction with New Deal agencies. During the war, the Urban League gave greater emphasis to promoting employment opportunities for blacks, working with state and federal agencies to achieve its objectives. The league joined other organizations to improve race relations and cooperated with the local chapter of the National Association for the Advancement of Colored People (NAACP) in handling complaints of racial discrimination in public places. The war gave rise to what social historian Dennis Mihelich has called "a new militancy" among blacks that changed the work of the Omaha Urban League. As he said, the league made a transition from being "a dispenser of social services" to "a mediator for social justice."

In the decade after the war, three groups were especially active in promoting respect for blacks' civil rights. Once the Omaha Urban League made clear its basic change in direction, it became a strong force on behalf of fair treatment of African Americans. Somewhat later, a revitalized local NAACP followed suit. Peculiar to the city was the Omaha De Porres Club that between 1949 and 1954 was an especially persistent and significant advocate of fair-employment and fair-housing practices. All three groups had interracial memberships.

Father John Markoe, a Creighton University professor, founded the De Porres Club in 1947. The stated purpose of the organization, named after a black churchman, was to promote racial equality and integration. In order to work effectively with the black community and ease the university administration's anxiety over a controversial group on campus, the De Porres Club soon established its office on the Near North Side. Some of the most flagrant cases of employment discrimination against blacks were found in white-owned businesses within the black community. In 1950 the De Porres Club and its white president, Creighton student Charles "Denny" Holland, led a boycott against a Near North Side laundry, a majority of whose patrons were blacks. The *Star* backed this effort, but the laundry's owner, who expressed the old fear that white patrons would not care to deal with black employees, closed rather change the policy. The following year, the De Porres Club circulated thousands of flyers urging Omahans not to purchase Coca Cola until the local bottling plant, located near the western edge of the black community, agreed to hire African Americans. De Porres Club members also picketed the plant. After a month, the plant manager agreed to a nondiscriminatory employment policy. When Reed's Ice Cream declined to employ blacks at its Near North Side outlet, the club in January 1953 began a boycott. The firm was unyielding, and during the summer the club, with the *Star's* backing, picketed. Finally, a year after the boycott began, Reed's ended hiring discrimination.

In 1950 Whitney Young became executive secretary of the Omaha Urban League after service with the Urban League in St. Paul where he had worked effectively with both whites and blacks. Indeed, this became the hallmark of his three years of leadership of the Omaha Urban League before he left the city to become dean of the Atlanta University School of Social Work. The white presidents of the league, especially realtor Nathan Phillips Dodge, facilitated Young's access to business leaders. The league had varied success in eroding employment barriers, but Young stressed the value of keeping educated and talented blacks in the city. The Urban League received a sharp increase in Community Chest aid in the early 1950s that along with a great increase in membership facilitated its work. Although the Urban League did not resort to picketing as did the De Porres Club, the two organizations maintained a good relationship. As circumstances warranted, the conciliatory Young could point to the more direct and public methods that the De Porres Club might use.

In the immediate postwar years Omaha's NAACP chapter, which dated from 1914, lacked vigorous and effective leadership. In keeping with the conservatism of the national organization, the local NAACP eschewed the more activist methods of the De Porres Club and even the Urban League in favor of what one scholar has called "a legalistic approach." Although the *Star* pushed a NAACP membership drive, it was not until 1954 when under the presidency of the Reverend Emmett T. Streeter that the local organization reemerged as a strong force in Omaha's civil-rights movement. When the management of Peony Park, a popular commercial amusement center, refused to allow two black students to use its pool in a swimming meet, the NAACP successfully represented their parents in litigation. The next year the NAACP pressed charges against the American Legion Club, which refused to permit a visiting black veteran to use its advertised accommodations.

Probably no business was more resistant to pressure to end racial discrimination in employment than was the reactionary management of the Omaha and Council Bluffs Street Railway. After failing in 1949 to get the firm to change its policy, the De Porres Club tried again in 1951 and 1952, distributing flyers across the city and urging all persons who could do so to boycott the company. Other civil-rights groups and social-justice advocates joined in the effort, and *Omaha Star* proprietor Mildred Brown put her paper behind the cause. The company responded to the argument that there were black bus drivers in some other cities including Denver and Tulsa by saying that the public would not accept blacks as bus drivers or streetcar operators. Finally, a settlement came in 1954 as the transit company sought a franchise extension. When the firm employed three black drivers, civil-rights groups, unconvinced that the company had made a real commitment to end discrimination, successfully pressured the Omaha City Council to add a fair-employment-practices provision to the renewed franchise.

Getting any positive civil-rights action from city government or the Nebraska legislature in the decade after World War II proved nearly fruitless. In 1949 Mayor Glen Cunningham established a Human Relations Committee to study allegations of discrimination and recommend remedies. This device proved to be ineffective. Under the commission form of government, the mayor had little executive authority, and the members of the city commission showed scant inclination to challenge the status quo in race relations. Likewise, fair-employment-practices bills repeatedly failed in the legislature.

The "new militancy" confronted not only the opposition of whites who wished to maintain the status quo but also the problems of apathy and division within the black community. In 1941 the *Star* noted the low voter turnout among blacks and declared that poor public services were the result of such disinterest. Five years later in 1946, the paper denounced what it called "a staggering lack of colored leadership." The apathy remained evident when some blacks continued to patronize Reed's Ice Cream store during the 1953 boycott or went to functions at Peony Park after the swimming meet episode. By contrast, some black clergy opposed demonstrations, probably fearing a white reaction. Such timidity may for a time have impaired the work of the NAACP, and in the 1940s there were divisions among the members of the board of directors of the Urban League. The most outspoken voice within the black community in the late 1940s came from Anita Hayes, president of the Omaha Council of the National Negro Congress. Hayes, a Georgia native who had a "direct and often abrasive approach" in dealing with civil-rights issues, was the subject of FBI surveillance for having reportedly joined a Communist group.

As in other northern cities, the main thrust of the black civil-rights movement in Omaha would come in the 1960s. Nevertheless, during the 1940s and 1950s significant inroads were made in breaching discriminatory employment practices and discrimination in public places. The De Porres Club challenged racial barriers in parochial schools and Catholic parishes. In 1953 Archbishop Gerald T. Bergan denounced racial discrimination in what would be an increasing commitment to social justice within the Archdiocese of Omaha. Slow advances were being made in placing black teachers in the Omaha public schools. In 1939 four black teachers were hired, but the unofficial segregation of black students in the increasingly crowded Near North Side schools remained in place. By 1950 there were twenty African American teachers, including the system's first black principal who was appointed in 1947. They were placed in largely black elementary schools. No black person would receive a regular appointment as a high-school teacher in the Omaha system until 1957. In the meantime, at least one University of Omaha professor advised black students who were pursuing secondary-school certification to apply for jobs in Minneapolis.

Even as civil-rights organizations attempted to break the color line in housing and a few blacks moved outside the crowded, run-down ghetto environment, making advances on this front was particularly difficult. Racial prejudice, including restrictive covenants, remained a barrier against blacks moving out of the Near North Side. Moreover, low income levels, unhelpful or discriminatory banks, and the problem of selling their current dwellings were daunting challenges for African Americans aspiring to better homes. A few houses were built in the black area shortly after the war, which represented the only new home construction in that part of the city in many years. Between 1951 and 1953, the Omaha Housing Authority provided a palliative when it completed three public-housing projects in the area. However, the fact that Omaha's black population had more than doubled between 1940 and 1960 produced a serious housing shortage on the Near North Side.

All during the 1950s a cautious hold-the-line attitude prevailed in Omaha. Despite the return of prosperity, fear persisted—fostered by memories of bad times and by recurrent recessions—that good times would fade away plunging the town back into the depths of economic decline. Omahans had experienced too much adversity for an optimistic attitude to last. Events kept people on edge: the Korean War, the rise and fall of Senator Joseph McCarthy, the threat of hot wars in Europe and Southeast Asia, the fear of a missile gap, and the possibility of atomic attack. The horror of an apocalypse seemed very real in Omaha, given its proximity to the headquarters of the Strategic Air Command. It was as if Omahans wanted a return of the 1920s. Yet any longing for the past missed an important trend. As a result of changing employment patterns, particularly in insurance as opposed to meat packing, Omaha was slowly shifting from a blue- to white-collar town. This would bring significant cultural and social changes in following decades. By contrast, Council Bluffs maintained its stronger blue-collar tradition. In 1960 the median level of education of males aged twenty-five or older was 11.8 years in Omaha and 10.5 years in Council Bluffs. For Omaha females in this age category the median was 12.1 years and for Council Bluffs women the figure was 11.7 years.

The Knights of Ak-Sar-Ben continued to exert important influence in Omaha. Critics charged that the organization had far too much power, pointing out that for a number of years it controlled automobile and truck access into the city from the east by operating a Missouri River toll bridge. Defenders responded by pointing out that Ak-Sar-Ben purchased the link from the Street Railway Company in the depths of the Depression as a public-spirited venture. Ak-Sar-Ben officials worked out a faster schedule of paying off the bonds and lowered tolls, making it easier for Council Bluffs residents to cross to Omaha to shop. This enhanced Ak-Sar-Ben's local image as did its race track that brought thousands of patrons into town every late spring and early summer. Some of the pari-mutuel profits went to all Nebraska counties for educational purposes. Of all Ak-Sar-Ben's activities, from circuses to auto shows, none approached the prestige of the annual coronation of a prominent civic leader and his consort. While groups in several American cities crowned kings and queens, there was no other place in the country where the recipients exercised social power comparable to those in Omaha. Ak-Sar-Ben provided definite indication of the role of the business community in upholding conventional standards, but for ordinary Omahans who were not part of the social elite, the coronation hoopla was at most a matter of passing curiosity.

The image that Omaha's leaders wanted to present to the world ignored the harsher realities of life. In contrast to the seamy portrait of the city in Jack Lait and Lee Mortimer's *U.S.A. Confidential*, a sanitized view in booster publications depicted Omaha as a city of homes, peaceful neighborhoods, and numerous churches. The citizens appeared as a law-abiding group dedicated to following the rule of law. Ethnic and racial harmony supposedly prevailed in a classic sense. Vibrant charitable institutions illustrated the responsible spirit of Omahans to work together to build an even more stable community than already existed. A history of Omaha published in the *World-Herald* in 1954 to celebrate the hundredth anniversary of the city made little mention of crime or vice. Rather, it concentrated on community building.

"THE MACHINERY OF OUR CITY GOVERNMENT IS ANTIQUATED"

The big issue of the 1950s was not corruption but reform in city government. Reform was the outgrowth of efforts of business leaders to plan and implement infrastructure improvements that they deemed essential. By the early twentieth century some of these leaders in urban America were interested in establishing city-planning mechanisms within municipal government. Such planning contemplated a more structured and orderly development of cities than had occurred in the past. In Omaha there were business leaders, especially realtors, who saw the need for a planning structure for their community, and in 1915 the Nebraska legislature had mandated that Omaha establish a city-planning commission. The commission began its work the following year and engaged nationally prominent experts to assist in developing a city plan. However, within the next few years the early hopes of the planning commission gradually withered. The elected city commissioners did not provide adequate funds for planning and the coming of World War I and the immediate postwar problems further undercut planning efforts. Moreover, projects emerging from city planning typically reflected the interests of the business elite, and elected officials were disinclined to move forward with large projects that might arouse the ire of a tax-conscious citizenry. In 1933 Mayor Roy Towl advocated the development of public housing. He viewed such a program as a dimension of city planning that would help to eliminate slums. Federal aid led to construction of the Logan Fontenelle and South Side Terrace public-housing projects in the late 1930s, but planning as a function of Omaha city government would remain a relatively minor activity for the next generation.

Despite the lethargy of city government in moving in new directions, the availability of federal funds, particularly for large projects, did much to keep alive the idea of city planning in the 1930s. A creative step from the private sector came in 1935 when a Chamber of Commerce committee took the initiative in forming the Carter Lake Development Society to channel federal funds into the redevelopment of what had been one of Greater Omaha's most popular recreational places years earlier. The fact that the lake straddled the state line posed a problem in securing federal money. In representing local, county, and state governments in the funding quest, the Carter Lake Development Society was the catalyst in securing a large Civilian Conservation Corps project, which was supervised by the National Park Service. With WPA assistance, the corps put in a new sand beach, built bathhouses, and developed picnic facilities. In 1937 nearly three decades after having provided money for an Omaha city park at Carter Lake, Selina Carter Cornish, widow of Levi Carter, made a large contribution for further work at the site. Because the Civilian Conservation Corps could no longer carry on the project, the WPA continued the improvements.

From the 1930s through the late 1950s, the private sector, particularly the Chamber of Commerce, assumed the lead in looking at Omaha's infrastructure needs. The first fruit of this private approach would be the building of a municipal stadium, a project contemplated since the 1930s. Through the work of a Municipal Sports Stadium Committee, a proposal for a bond issue to construct a stadium in the southeastern part of the city won easy approval from the city's voters in April 1945.

In the wake of this step toward civic improvement and with other American cities looking toward modernization, Henry Doorly, publisher of the *World-Herald*, promoted the creation of a Mayor's City-Wide Planning Committee. In July 1945 Mayor Charles Leeman created such a committee chaired by Russell Hopley, president of Northwestern Bell Telephone Company. The Chamber of Commerce funded the work of the City-Wide Planning Committee, a body of 168 persons from the business community. In the next few months the committee, dividing its labors and using a good bit of information already amassed by private studies and the work of the city-planning director, put forward an array of possible civic improvements. A finance committee then pared this list to what it deemed the most urgent and most financially feasible projects. In November 1946 Omaha's voters approved eleven of the seventeen bond issues proposed in the Blue Book Plan, which derived its name from the cover of the Mayor's City-Wide Planning Committee report. Among the measures approved were bond issues for arterial highways, airport upgrading, a city auditorium, parks, sewers, fire stations, and river-port facilities.

The voters also approved the establishment of four permanent commissions and one nonpermanent commission to oversee the expenditure of the bonds. Each of the four permanent commissions would be responsible for specific topics: the airport; the auditorium, parks, and sanitation, while the fifth body, charged with overall supervision of the Blue Book Plan expenditures, would dissolve when the bond funds were expended. The members of the five commissions were to be nominated by the mayor and confirmed by the city council. These commissions were significant additions to the existing structure of Omaha's municipal government. Presumably the business people who devised the Blue Book Plan proposed these additions to the voters because they doubted that the elected city officials would handle some $20 million in bond funds properly. Rather than suggesting dishonesty, the doubts seemed to question the administrative capacity of the elected council members who as commissioners doubled as the city government's top executive officers. The addition of the five special commissions may not have been a vote of no confidence in the commission form of government that Omahans had implemented in 1912, but it was a notable indicator that the system was not providing the sort of leadership needed in the postwar years.

A more immediate problem faced city hall in 1946. Constrained by a state-imposed tax limit and an inadequate system for assessing taxes, Omaha's municipal government could not meet a pay-raise commitment to firemen and policemen. The problem intensified when a court directed the city to fund the pay raises notwithstanding the lack of revenue. Through the initiative of Robert Storz, vice president of the Storz Brewing Company, local business leaders contributed $160,000 to bail the city out of its predicament.

In Omaha and Council Bluffs the late 1940s brought discussion of whether to replace their existing structures of municipal government with the city-manager system. Like Omaha's commission system, the city-manager plan was a product of the progressive reform thrust that had brought innovations to all levels of the American political system in the first two decades of the twentieth century. Unlike the commission form of municipal government that combined executive and legislative functions, the city manager form placed only legislative responsibility in the elected city council. The council would hire a city manager who would be the chief administrative officer of the executive branch of government and who would serve at the pleasure of the council. The council would select one of its members as mayor, who would be its presiding officer and the city's ceremonial representative.

In the autumn of 1947, the Omaha Manufacturers Association and the Council Bluffs Chamber of Commerce recommended that their respective communities switch to the city-manager system. Since 1853 Council Bluffs had used the mayor-council system that in its 1940s configuration had a council elected partly by ward and partly at-large. The mayor, elected separately, shared administrative authority with other elected officials. In recommending that Council Bluffs adopt the city-manager plan, a chamber officer showed the business perspective that was driving efforts to reform structures of government in both cities. As he put it, "The machinery of our city government is antiquated, large and unwieldy, and therefore inefficient and uneconomical. . . . This city is an enormous business and should be organized and operated like a business."

Hope for a quick public vote on the city-manager plan met opposition, but the Chamber of Commerce continued to advocate the change. In October 1948 L. Perry Cookingham, city manager of Kansas City, Missouri, addressed the chamber on the virtues of the system under which his community operated. In the summer of 1949, the Junior Chamber of Commerce successfully conducted a petition drive to place a proposal for a city-manager system before the electorate. The Central Labor Union opposed the change, primarily because the new system would replace the city council elected partly by ward with a council entirely elected at-large.

Aside from the publicized virtues that a city-manager system presumably would bring, problems ranging from a feud between two aldermen to the challenge of paying for recent street, sewer, and flood-control work probably bolstered the message that change was in order. In October 1949 Council Bluffs adopted the city-manager plan with the support of 56.8 percent of the voters. In April 1950 following a March city-council election, the city-manager system began operation.

13. Broadway looking east from Sixth Street, Council Bluffs, 1947. *Courtesy Council Bluffs Public Library, Council Bluffs, Iowa.*

By this time the *World-Herald* was pushing for the adoption of the city-manager plan in Omaha. Business supporters of the plan used arguments similar to those presented in Council Bluffs to get a city-manager proposal on the ballot. They encountered a particularly tough adversary in Mayor Glenn Cunningham. He admitted that Omaha needed a revised form of government in order to foster better leadership, but he argued against vesting executive authority in a nonelected city manager. This argument had an anti-elitist ring that appealed to voters in South Omaha, Cunningham's home turf, and to like-minded people in other parts of the city. Enough critics proclaimed that the manager would be an autocrat to prompt the *World-Herald* to run an editorial headed "Council Bluffs—Dictatorship" in which the paper branded this argument as "preposterous." The editor noted that some fourteen million Americans had city-manager governments. Former mayor Roy Towl, who had a solid record as a reform advocate, backed the proposed change, but in November 1950 the conservative argument prevailed when about two-thirds of the electorate rejected the city-manager system.

The essential problems continued. There was an obvious drift in city government. Omaha's seven elected commissioners built their own bases of support, showing little interest in cooperating with business interests in a broad sense. The divisions of responsibility among agencies of city government were sometimes unclear, and the addition of the special nonelective commissions in 1946 compounded this problem. No particular event brought matters to a head, but all candidates in the 1954 municipal-election campaign advocated city-charter revision. After the election, the council, perhaps with little enthusiasm, adopted a resolution calling for a vote of the people on holding a charter convention. In a sparse turnout in August, Omaha voters endorsed the calling of the convention.

Nebraska law stated that a charter convention would be composed of fifteen delegates, but it did not specify their mode of election. After much delay the city council decided upon a process in which the voters would chose the top thirty candidates in March 1956 and the final fifteen in May. By the fall of 1955, Mayor John Rosenblatt was concerned about getting good candidates to run for the charter convention. One day, he encountered Chamber of Commerce president A. V. "Al" Sorensen in front of city hall. After routine greetings both men walked on, but the mayor hailed Sorensen back and asked him to encourage qualified persons to seek election to the convention. Sorensen agreed to do so and in the coming months carried through with his commitment. The Chamber of Commerce helped by circulating petitions for eighteen persons, nine of whom subsequently became delegates. Sorensen was one of the sixty persons who entered the two-stage electoral process and was among the thirteen men and two women who were ultimately elected to the convention.

Axel Vergman Sorensen was a fifty-year-old native of Denmark who had come to Omaha as the Westinghouse sales representative for electrical equipment. In 1934 he resigned his position and established his own firm, eventually known as Midwest Equipment Company, selling electrical products to wholesalers and contractors in Nebraska and neighboring states. A hardworking salesman, he was especially successful in supplying rural electrification projects and during the war obtained a contract for providing electrical systems for landing craft. With his financial security assured, Sorensen became active in civic affairs. As vice president of the Chamber of Commerce in 1954, he played an important part in obtaining a AAA professional baseball franchise for Omaha, a development that dovetailed with the recently built municipal stadium.

The charter convention members were for the most part upper-middle-class persons. Ten of the delegates, including Sorensen, lived in the prosperous west-central part of the city. The two women were experienced in civic activities, and most of the men were middle-aged business leaders. Two exceptions were a South Omahan who headed an insurance agency, and a tavern owner. The delegates received no pay and met through the ensuing summer in a room without air conditioning on the top floor of the city hall. Sorensen recalled: "It was the worst job I ever had. The law said we had only 120 days to complete the job. Fifteen people had to come to a meeting of the minds, and we finished on the 119th day. It was a very difficult assignment. We worked morning, noon and night sometimes. We just rolled up our sleeves and got wet." To make the work manageable, city attorney Edward F. Fogarty assisted the convention, and its executive committee engaged Professor William T. Utley, head of the Department of History and Government at the Municipal University of Omaha, as coordinator. Very importantly, the convention hired a Chicago consulting firm, Public Administration Services, which provided expert advisors as needed. In retrospect, this willingness to seek professional assistance from outside the city symbolized the start of a new direction in the conduct of civic affairs.

The resulting document separated the legislative and administrative branches, established full-time personnel and planning departments, and called for a return to a mayor and council form of government. It placed day-by-day administrative responsibility in the hands of the mayor. "We put the mayor up like a sitting duck," a convention delegate told a group, "so that he'll have to answer to the people at the polls." All department heads except the city attorney would serve at the pleasure of the mayor. In a notable commitment to administrative expertise, the document stipulated that department heads other than the city attorney would have at least five years of professional experience relevant to their administrative responsibilities. The council remained a seven-member body and like the mayor would be elected on a nonpartisan ballot. This official nonpartisanship continued the practice established with council elections under the commission system. The new plan also continued the at-large election of council members, but elections would be held every four years as opposed to every three under the existing system. Because of the influence of the local chapters of the NAACP and the Urban League plus the predisposition of some of the convention delegates, the charter included provisions barring racial discrimination in city employment and in contracts with the city. The document also provided for a Human Relations Board that would make recommendations to the mayor and council on civil-rights matters.

A POLARIZED CITY: "HOW MANY PACKINGHOUSE WORKERS WANT TO FLY?"

The charter, which required majority approval, was submitted to the voters in the fall of 1956. Despite a drive mounted by John J. Cavanaugh, the only convention delegate to vote against the proposed charter, arguing that a change would hurt South Omaha, 56 percent of the voters approved the document. In a clearly sectional decision, the three wards in South Omaha turned down the charter by a 63 to 37 percent margin, while the three affluent western wards approved it by the same ratio. The result in the western wards was especially significant for its long-term implications because the total vote in that area was nearly double that in South Omaha.

This cleavage between the south and the west would loom large in the next decade as the people of the city confronted the pressures of modernization. Because Omaha's long-term physical growth was primarily from east to west, the eastern area of the city, including the once separate South Omaha has been described as "old Omaha" in contrast to the newer, western area or "new Omaha." This division can be traced to the late nineteenth and early twentieth centuries as people who achieved varying degrees of material success moved into the newer housing being built away from the old core of the city. Residents of newer, more affluent areas normally voted Republican in contrast to the Democratic voting pattern in the older parts of the city, including South Omaha.

Party identities aside, Omahans were divided by two sharply different outlooks on local government. Sorensen, who was elected to the city council in 1957 and became its president or presiding officer, was an outstanding exponent a business-professional perspective that emphasized the desirability of "business-like" handling of public affairs, including the use of experts in top administrative positions. Vital to this approach was the assumption that when business leaders—the Chamber of Commerce "brass list" as Sorensen put it—rallied behind a shared goal, civic progress would result. This concept of a positive, dynamic municipal government was most common in Omaha's affluent western neighborhoods.

On the other hand, an anti-elitist outlook was traditionally centered in the more modest socioeconomic environs of the older, eastern parts of town. This was especially true in South Omaha, where a residual community identity probably fostered distrust of Omaha's power structure. Likewise, many South Omahans were blue-collar people of central and eastern European background who through years of hard work had achieved some economic security. Election returns from South Omaha that sometimes indicated an unwillingness to follow the leadership of Omaha's civic elite reflected a conservatism that held that city officials should be close to the people and sympathetic to their views. Put another way, the city should stick to basic services, such as fixing potholes and clearing snow from the streets.

Such citizens were comfortable with the commission government whose department heads were elected council members in contrast to the appointed department heads under the new strong-mayor system. As to experts in city government, they would have commended longtime park commissioner Joseph "Joe" Hummel who on leaving office in 1939 remarked, "I tried to save money. Instead of hiring expensive experts, I did the work myself—10 to 16 hours a day I put in."

When the charter went into operation in May 1957, civic leaders proclaimed that the new government would cope with change and that it had the necessary machinery to deal successfully with social needs. Many thought the dawning of an age of harmony at hand. The National Municipal League gave Omaha a 1957 All America Cities Award. Despite the community differences that the adoption of the new charter masked, civic leaders had reason to believe that their city had taken a huge step in the right direction.

Undoubtedly inspired by voter approval of the new charter, a 225-member Mayor's Planning and Development Committee, chaired by A. F. Jacobson, president of Northwestern Bell Telephone Company, proposed a huge program of public improvements in the spring of 1957. In its final form, this program, called the Omaha Plan, included thirteen projects costing a total of $68,180,000. They included a new airport terminal; a new main library; obtaining land for a cultural center; a new police department headquarters;

fire department facilities; highway, sewer, and street construction; and an urban-renewal program for an area north of the central business district. The
business leaders promoting the Omaha Plan contemplated that federal and
state funds would cover over $12,000,000 of the cost and that the Plan would
increase the tax bill of the homeowner by a mere $12.00 to $15.00 dollars annually and a $4.80 per year hike in the sewer-use fee.

For Rosenblatt, who was the last mayor under the commission system
and who had been elected the first mayor under the new charter, and for
city council president Sorensen, this massive spending program was, as Sorensen recalled years later, "too much, too soon." The business leaders who
were advancing the Omaha Plan were not receptive to this message. Sorensen
believed that it would be counterproductive to refuse to back the package
of worthy projects that, if approved, would be less costly than if deferred.
Accordingly, Rosenblatt and Sorensen supported the Omaha Plan. The city
council vote of five to two in favor of submitting the Omaha Plan reflected
polarity of local attitudes, for it was the council members from South Omaha,
James Dworak and Albert L. Veys, who opposed the action.

Heading the campaign for the Omaha Plan in the spring of 1958 was W.
Dale Clark, a highly respected banker. Organized opposition was meager,
centering in groups known as the Taxpayers Plan Committee and the Associated Civic Clubs of Omaha and Douglas County. They reflected the conservative view that looked askance at elitist-driven government. As M. J. Stefacek, president of the Associated Civic Clubs asked, "What a few executives
think the people of Omaha can afford is not the proper way to sell good government to the voters." Railroads and their unions, ignoring the public assistance that contributed to their development in the previous century, denounced the bond issues proposed for airport improvements. A wild card
entered the picture just before voters went to the polls when state senator
Terry Carpenter, a political maverick from Scottsbluff, four hundred miles
away from Omaha, delivered two television addresses urging Omahans to re-
ject the package on grounds that homeowners would pay a disproportionate
share of the plan's costs.

On June 17, 1958, voters handily rejected the entire Omaha Plan. This was,
as Sorensen said, "a taxpayers' revolt, pure and simple." What Sorensen later
called the "South Omaha-Omaha problem" was evident in the debacle as
South Omahans and other eastern areas returned the greatest margins against

the package. The sheer magnitude of the defeat transcended this sectionalism and reflected a failure of business leaders to look beyond their own circle and reckon with the sensibilities of the rank and file of the voters throughout the city.

The rejection of the two Omaha Plan bond issues for airport improvements followed similar rejections in 1950 and 1952. Omaha faced an immediate challenge to keep pace with other cities in aviation services; adding to the urgency was the fact that airlines would soon introduce jet aircraft. Accordingly, the city council placed a proposal on the ballot in the November 1958 election that provided that airport revenue bonds—bonds redeemed without taxes—could be issued without voter approval. When this measure was overwhelmingly defeated it became clear that a new approach was needed.

In the next few months city officials considered various methods for airport development. Council president Sorensen was especially active in this quest for funding, particularly in contacting federal agencies. By February 1959 it was evident that the only option was to divorce the airport from the municipal government and place it under an airport authority that would function without the use of tax money. The new charter stipulated that no authority or other entity having control over public property could be created without voter approval. However, Mayor Rosenblatt obtained opinions from the city attorney and the attorney general of Nebraska that a state law allowing the establishment of airport authorities took precedence over Omaha's charter.

Action became even more pressing when city officials learned in early March that federal funds to cover one-half the cost of a new airport terminal building probably would be available only until June 30. When the city council considered the establishment of an airport authority, the polarity between new Omaha and old Omaha was again evident. The Chamber of Commerce backed the creation of the Airport Authority, and A. F. Jacobson, the leading figure in the formulation of the Omaha Plan told the council that when he looked at Omaha's current airport, "[I]t is not with a feeling of pride." At a time when commercial air travel had not entirely lost its elitist image, M. J. Stefacek, who had been one of the critics of the Omaha Plan, asked, "How many packinghouse workers want to fly?"

In a four to three vote, Sorensen and the other activists on the council voted to establish an Omaha Airport Authority while three members, including South Omahans James Dworak and Al Veys, representing a more traditional perspective, insisted that the voters should decide the question. Because Mayor Rosenblatt was ill and out of town, Sorensen as acting mayor nominated and the council confirmed the initial members of the Airport Authority board of directors. Sorensen, mindful that the authority would need to raise private capital and having already ascertained a source of such money, remarked that he had "sought out five men of this community . . . men who will attract the support of investment bankers."

The creation of the Omaha Airport Authority was timely. The Federal Aviation Agency quickly granted $885,000 for the building of a new terminal, and Omaha's Eugene C. Eppley Foundation gave the Authority $1,000,000. As a result of the Eppley grant, the Airport Authority in 1960 floated a $2,500,000 revenue bond, a figure well above the initial projection. In September 1961 the new Eppley Air Passenger Terminal, nearly three times the size of the old facility, formally opened. Commercial jet service to Omaha began in August 1960, and in 1962 runway improvement was finished. The use of what was now known as Eppley Airfield grew rapidly, and in 1968 the Airport Authority started a new expansion program.

A MOMENT OF UNITY AND TRIUMPH

Council Bluffs occasionally experienced an internal division between the blue-collar residents of flat lands in the western part of the city and the white-collar people who lived in the bluffs on the east side. This had been especially evident in votes leading to the construction of a high school in the western part of town. Such sensibilities were quickly subordinated when Council Bluffs and Omaha faced a massive flood threat from the Missouri River in April 1952. The area of Council Bluffs on the flood plain was home to nearly two-thirds of the city's residents, who were ordered to leave their homes; many spent the duration of the emergency with friends, relatives, or other families who lived on higher ground. Outside the urban area the Missouri overflowed across many miles of farmland, and the people of Council Bluffs and Omaha had the enormous task of constraining the river within a 1500-foot channel. This meant reinforcing some thirty-six miles of levee with millions of sandbags and raising the levee at key points with additions of flashboard and other materials. In the process thousands of volunteers on both sides of the river labored for days amid occasional rain and wet snow. Local government and civil-defense authorities coordinated relief work.

National Guard and other military personnel assisted in the successful effort. The magnitude of the emergency produced a unity and purposefulness among the people of Council Bluffs and Omaha that would endure as their special moment of shared triumph.

AN ODYSSEY OF THREE DECADES

Omaha had entered the 1930s searching for an identity. The events of the decade dashed immediate hopes, overturning illusions about how individuals could cope with bad times. Necessity spawned changed attitudes; the New Deal saw the promotion of a spirit of joint action that carried into the 1940s. Whatever their specific attitudes, depression and war had accustomed Omahans and their neighbors to the prominence of government in society.

The passing of the Tom Dennison machine had not brought the end of traditional vice. Instead, widespread gambling merely vindicated Dennison's observation that "laws that people don't believe in can't be enforced if whole armies tried it." Not only were there no "whole armies" to suppress gambling, law enforcement seemed sporadic and judges could be sticklers for proper evidence in the prosecution of bookies. Moreover, the state line was a boon for the operators and patrons of gambling enterprises. The incongruity that Jack Lait and Lee Mortimer found in the cab driver who informed his patrons about local bookie places while taxis carried ads that urged people to "Visit your church on Sunday" hardly attested to any exceptional hypocrisy on the part of Omahans. Instead, the two messages merely pointed to the diverse realities that historically typify urban life.

In the postwar years the goal of Americans was security. As the Depression passed, the Omaha business community prepared to assume its traditional role in local affairs. Clearly the business leadership surpassed elected officials in setting Omaha's course into the second half of the twentieth century. For this leadership elite, infrastructure improvements, changes in the structure of government, and professionalism at city hall were the keys to building a better city. In both Omaha and Council Bluffs, the chambers of commerce were in the vanguard of successful efforts to modernize municipal government. Elite-driven proposals generally met with favor among the white-collar residents of the more affluent parts of Omaha, but met enough resistance in the older, blue-collar areas to polarize the city. If less evident, such a division existed in Council Bluffs.

Although Omahans still overlooked serious social imperfections, the 1940s and 1950s brought a growing challenge to racial discrimination. Social problems notwithstanding, the metropolitan area's traditional economy was functioning well. For Omahans, as with other Americans, the Cold War brought apprehension, yet Offutt Air Force Base was a strong contributor to the local economy and urban expansion. By 1960 the people of Greater Omaha partook of a precarious peace, had mixed feelings about some dimensions of progress, and generally experienced prosperity. Peace, progress, and prosperity would endure, but the next generation would bring tremendous change.

[Part VI]   Since 1960

[10] Redirections

The generation after 1950 brought a massive shift in the geographical patterns of life in the nation's urban centers. With the Depression and war in the past and prosperity at hand, the automobile became increasingly fundamental to the lifestyle of Americans. Affluence and mobility brought a new thrust toward suburban development and with it a great decentralization in urban life. Life in the Omaha area would conform to this national pattern as automobile registration in Douglas County doubled between 1945 and 1959, and a new westward push of the city began that would continue to the present. In 1956 Congress provided for the construction of an interstate highway system, and in October 1957 the *World-Herald* published a map showing the basic routes that the new superhighways would take through the Greater Omaha area. The building of Interstate Highway 80 would greatly promote the spread and decentralization of residential areas and business activity.

The advent of shopping centers both reflected and stimulated this territorial growth. The first such enterprise in Omaha was The Center at Forty-second and Center streets in the south-central part of the city, which opened in October 1955, and by 1960 the Crossroads at Seventy-second and Dodge streets was in business. Both of these malls had been built on important thoroughfares. In keeping with this sound commercial logic, John A. Wiebe, the developer of The Center, in 1959 announced plans for a huge "regional shopping center" to be called the "Westroads" that would be located near 102nd and Dodge streets just northeast of the prospective interchange of Dodge with a branch of Interstate Highway 80 that would skirt Omaha's western periphery. This would be a $25 million retail complex that would employ 2,500 to 3,000 persons, but the site was zoned residential, and the owners of some expensive homes nearby battled Wiebe's efforts to secure commercial zoning. The city planning board twice rejected his rezoning request, and in the summer of 1960, the question of sustaining or reversing its judgment went to the city council.

Competing business interests were also part of the Westroads controversy. A foe of Wiebe's project was the Brandeis Investment Company, developer of the soon-to-open $10 million Crossroads mall, thirty blocks to the east. The Crossroads included a department store of J. L. Brandeis and Sons, one of the city's most prominent retailers, and Brandeis obviously wanted no new competition for this investment. By contrast, another prominent local firm, Thomas Kilpatrick and Company, a prospective Westroads tenant, ran a full-page newspaper ad noting the large payroll that the complex would have and describing a buffer zone with trees and other landscape features that would protect the ambiance of the residential property owners.

To reach an informed decision on the Westroads issue, city council president A. V. Sorensen used his own money to engage a prominent St. Louis planning firm, Harland Bartholomew and Associates, to study the question and submit its findings. Sorensen recognized that the controversy had generated much ill feeling, and he hoped that the judgment of a respected outside firm would help avert further animosity. The Bartholomew report recommended that the Westroads project be approved subject to the developer establishing a buffer to screen the residential property and providing for traffic control.

In October 1960 after the Westroads promoters had added appropriate covenants to their rezoning proposal, the city council reversed the planning board and approved the project. Although the owners of the nearby homes won a suit to block the Westroads development, the Nebraska Supreme Court in 1963 overturned this decision and sustained the city council's action. Work began on the project in 1965, and a large department store opened in May 1967. Many openings followed in the next three years, and in 1970 the 120 businesses at Westroads employed about 3,500 persons. Ironically, the Crossroads survived the competition, and Brandeis became a major tenant at Westroads.

As Omaha expanded, its downtown area, in keeping with the national pattern, slowly declined as the focal point for entertainment, services, and shopping. The *World-Herald* found that downtown drew 50 percent of women shoppers in 1956 but only 29 percent in 1967. Even more to the point, as sales increased dramatically for the city and metropolitan area, sales figures for downtown dropped markedly.

Few subjects aroused more controversy in Omaha in the mid-twentieth century than the federal urban-renewal program. The program was rooted in the recognition that as cities age, parts of a community often deteriorate, a process that reflected or contributed to economic and social problems. The Housing Act of 1949 and particularly the Housing Act of 1954 provided federal money for cities that devised plans for combating such blight. The essential concept of this program was that cities would use their power of eminent domain to acquire deteriorated buildings. These structures would be razed, and private enterprise would redevelop the property according to a preestablished urban-renewal plan that would benefit the community.

There was little new residential and commercial construction in Omaha during the Depression and World War II, a time when the city experienced significant physical changes. Downtown, particularly in the blocks around the center core, showed signs of decay. Large numbers of blacks remained confined to a blighted district on the Near North Side; older housing predominated in South Omaha's ethnic neighborhoods. After the war, most new building was on the west side and in the growing suburban ring.

In 1946 a Housing and Slum Elimination Committee, part of the Mayor's City-Wide Planning Committee, identified seriously deteriorated housing on the Near North Side and to a lesser extent in South Omaha. Because "slum clearance" was commonly associated with public-housing projects, it was anathema to many people in the city, especially realtors. Therefore, the committee recommended less-drastic remedies such as property condemnation and zoning modifications. Not surprisingly, the leaders who established the priorities for the City-Wide Improvement Plan placed a lower priority upon an assault upon housing blight than improving the airport, parks, streets, and sewers. Despite its need, no remedial program for substandard housing or other blight was presented to the voters in November 1946. By 1951 the prospect of federal funds to cope with urban blight drew the attention of the city government and realtors, and in that year the legislature established procedures for slum clearance. For a time the city council had no interest in authorizing such projects, but the passage of the federal Housing Act in 1954 stimulated local interest in urban renewal. By 1955 a city Urban Renewal Office was ascertaining procedures in redevelopment projects, and in 1956 the city council adopted a minimum housing standards ordinance. That year, Mayor

John Rosenblatt's Area Redevelopment Committee reported on changes in slum conditions since the 1946 report and urged the city to adopt policies that would meet federal urban renewal standards.

In 1958 voters had rejected urban-renewal proposals along with the rest of the Omaha Plan. Future consideration of the subject would reflect the polarization between civic leaders who favored such measures and the anti-elite group that was leery of significant innovations in municipal government. A key champion of urban renewal was city council president A. V. Sorensen who firmly believed that it offered hope for easing a serious problem of substandard and dilapidated housing. Opponents charged that urban renewal would serve special interests and use the power of eminent domain to violate property rights. Leading the battle against renewal and housing-code enforcement was the Small Property Owners' Association (SPOA). The SPOA—whose members Sorensen called "slum lords"—brought a lengthy legal delay in the enforcement of the Minimum Housing Standards Ordinance and successfully lobbied the legislature in 1957 to require a vote of the people to create an urban-renewal agency. While urban-renewal advocates such as Sorensen believed that it would help many black people by reducing blighted housing, some black groups opposed such a proposal, saying there were no provisions to aid persons displaced from existing housing.

In the 1961 mayoral election, James J. Dworak, a South Omaha mortician who had firmly established his credentials as a leading adversary of the big business elite and as a foe of urban renewal, eked out a victory over James Green, the candidate of the established civic leadership. During the campaign, urban renewal was a hot topic in the Nebraska legislature. The Chamber of Commerce lobbied to repeal the 1957 requirement that there be a vote of the people in order to establish an urban-renewal authority; the SPOA sought to retain the popular vote as a bulwark against urban renewal. The bill passed by a wide margin, easing the process by which urban renewal could be adopted, even though the Omaha delegation was closely divided on the issue.

In 1963 Mayor Dworak vetoed an ordinance to create an urban-renewal authority that the council had passed by a four to three vote, and the prorenewal council members could not secure the one vote needed for an override. In 1965 and 1970, Omaha voters rejected urban-renewal proposals. The polarization between the civic leadership and those who distrusted the downtown elite does not fully explain the failure to adopt urban renewal. Part of the problem lay in the fact that its advocates generally did not develop a specific program of projects. This probably reflected a division between the Chamber of Commerce, which was oriented toward urban renewal as a means of rejuvenating downtown, and those persons who were intent upon renewal as a way of eliminating blighted housing. Moreover, as time passed critics of urban renewal could point to problems with such programs in other cities. The struggle over urban renewal in Omaha suggests that the traditional images evoked in the use of the terms "conservative" and "liberal" as used in national and state politics do not always fit well at the municipal level. In Omaha, solidly Republican business leaders who backed urban renewal showed their willingness to use federal programs and eminent domain thereby implicitly forsaking traditional conservative dogma about limited government and property rights. Equally practical, representatives of the black community were divided as to whether urban renewal would improve housing. By contrast, white opponents of urban renewal, often South Omaha Democrats and those typically less affluent than the business elite who supported it, took a staunchly conservative stand on limited government and property rights.

In contrast to Omaha, Council Bluffs did undertake an urban-renewal program. In 1961 the Leo A. Daly Company of Omaha, following a two-year study, made a report to the Council Bluffs City Planning Commission that proposed a variety of civic improvements including closing portions of two downtown streets to motor vehicles and transforming them into shopping malls. New public buildings including a civic auditorium would be constructed nearby. The Daly recommendations, which included redeveloping city schools and reconfiguring railroad tracks to improve neighborhoods, projected that Council Bluffs and its immediate environs would have a population of 88,000 by 1980. Although the development of the city in the next two decades would not follow most of Daly's recommendations and the study proved to be far too optimistic about the growth of Council Bluffs, the report would be the background for a downtown urban-renewal project. This would be the Midlands Mall shopping center, a bold alternative to the normal practice of developing such facilities in areas well removed from central business districts.

In the mid-1960s the city obtained a planning grant for an urban-renewal program, hired an urban renewal director, and the city council designated the downtown area in which a project would be undertaken. Even though voters in 1967 turned down a land-acquisition bond issue, $9,340,574 in federal loans and grants was committed to the project in 1969. Site clearance began the following year, and in 1972 the city council selected a local firm, Midlands-Northern Joint Venture as the shopping-mall developer. Midlands-Northern (later Midlands Corporation) would purchase the land from the city, and the city would fund the construction of a parking garage to serve the shopping center.

The leading figure in the mall project was Midlands president Dale Ball, who owned the First National Bank of Council Bluffs. When Ball came to Council Bluffs from nearby Fremont, Nebraska, in 1964, he quickly recognized that his adopted hometown needed to take a new direction. A decade later he recalled, "I was very depressed by the community. There was a perpetual defeatism. There wasn't a place to have a high-school graduation, so it was held in Omaha. It was the Appalachia of Iowa. . . . We had to do something so dramatic it would change the way people felt."

As the project awaited final approval from the federal Department of Housing and Urban Development and other details were worked out, serious opposition to the undertaking arose from the Gendler Land Investment Company of Omaha that had purchased land for a large shopping-center development on the south outskirts of the city at a point close to Interstate Highways 29 and 80. Although Gendler Investment had been accumulating land at the proposed site since 1966, this announcement left Ball thunderstruck. He declared,

> I don't know any of the details, but if the project can be built as described, it will mean the $9½ million invested in urban renewal by the federal government and Council Bluffs would all be wasted money.
>
> The heart of downtown Council Bluffs would be devoid of buildings and tax base and of very little value.

What emerged was a nasty high-stakes rivalry between competing entrepreneurs similar to the earlier Crossroads-Westroads clash in Omaha plus the prospect that its outcome would decide the fate of downtown Council Bluffs. Public debate centered on a $4.5 million city bond issue to finance the garage for the prospective downtown mall. A petition drive forced a vote on the bond issue, and as the January 1973 referendum approached, opponents of the proposal argued that the shopping-center trade would not produce enough revenue for the parking garage to redeem the bonds and that the taxpayers would be burdened with this debt. A cartoon-illustrated flyer from the All Bluffs Committee to Stop the Bonds depicted Dale Ball as a circus ringmaster cracking a whip, trying to make the taxpayers support his enterprise. According to this conspiratorial scenario, Ball had the backing of "CERTAIN *Elected* CITY OFFICIALS *and* OTHERS WHO MAY HAVE VESTED INTERESTS & STAND TO MAKE A 'KILLING' AT YOUR EXPENSE!"

Supporters of the bond issue, speaking through the Save Our City Committee, said that under the urban-renewal agreement with the U.S. government the city was obligated to provide parking for the shopping mall but that tax revenue from the mall would redeem the bonds. As to the shopping center itself, the committee argued that the development would increase employment, add to the tax base, and "add new life and a new look to downtown Council Bluffs." Its campaign flyer asked, "Who is paying for the opposition to the new downtown shopping center?" The answer: "A private developer who stands to profit if the downtown shopping center is delayed." The *Nonpareil* staunchly supported the bond issue. Reflecting upon the long-term plight of Council Bluffs, the editor observed, "It is time concerned people help make this city the magnetic center of Southwest Iowa and not just a shadow of Omaha."

In December 1972 J. L. Brandeis declared that it would establish a store in the downtown shopping center, and in the week before the bond issue vote, Sears, Roebuck and Company and six Omaha firms followed suit. A Nebraska firm announced that it would construct a hotel and convention center adjacent to the shopping center. These commitments, which noted the employment they would bring, were contingent upon the approval of the parking proposal. Three days before the vote, Omaha city planning director Alden Aust linked the shopping center and parking facility to the prospect of a personalized rapid transit system (PRT), a futuristic scheme in which computer-controlled cars running on an elevated line would link Broadway with its Omaha counterpart, Dodge Street. The planning departments of the two cities had prepared an initial concept for the PRT that would extend from the prospective downtown Council Bluffs shopping mall to the Westroads shopping center. "Defeat of the Urban Renewal bond issue," said Aust, "would seriously jeopardize the feasibility and operation of [the] PRT." The *Nonpareil* pulled all the stops in boosting the bond proposal. In its Sunday edition two days before the special election, the paper ran a front-page editorial hailing the vote on an otherwise prosaic measure as the key to bringing about urban renewal, the elixir that would give the city a new dynamism. The duty of the voters was clear:

> NOW is their chance of a lifetime to chart the future of their city, to see it develop into an attractive, prosperous, proud community—and to give it 'shopping independence' from Omaha.

The *World-Herald*, widely read in Council Bluffs, endorsed the bond issue with some interesting hyperbole:

> The opportunity which is ahead for Council Bluffs is the envy of thousands of the citizens of the metro area on this side of the river.
> Council Bluffs has used urban renewal to move toward the revitalization of downtown while Omaha has not. . . .
> It may be ironical that the smaller city should lead the big city, but it is the fact.

Undeterred by the January cold, a large number of Council Bluffs residents went to the polls, and 70.3 percent of them supported the bond issue, assuring that the downtown urban renewal project would go forward. The *Nonpareil* exclaimed "'Sleeping Giant' Awakens," and noted, "There was no sectionalism in the voting. No east vs. west."

In February 1976 the $35 million Midlands Mall was completed, and in the next two months many stores opened. By the summer of 1977, the occupancy level reached 85 percent and a four-screen movie theater established the mall as an entertainment center. That the urban-renewal project was a boon to downtown Council Bluffs was suggested in a report that 10 percent of the cars in the city-funded garage were from Nebraska and an additional 15 percent were Iowa vehicles from outside Pottawattamie County.

Nevertheless, it was soon evident that Midlands Mall and, by implication its role in the rejuvenation of downtown Council Bluffs, faced challenges. The prospect of one or two malls being built on the outskirts of the city may have discouraged prospective tenants from leasing mall space, and some firms did not deem Midlands Mall large enough to meet their needs. Ball and other persons associated with the Midlands management remained publicly optimistic about its future, but two years after the mall's opening, he observed, "Retailers nationally are still not convinced a downtown area can survive. Even if a downtown development is successful—as we appear to be—some retailers are still skeptical." He also emphasized that the mall constituted only a part of what needed to be done in revitalizing the city's center.

Soon Ball sold the mall, exclusive of the portions that big retailers owned. Over eleven years later, he recalled that he had incurred heavy monthly losses on the mall and that he had lost more than $2 million in the sale. In the meantime, the city and Midlands had sued each other to recover certain costs associated with the project's construction. The litigation dragged on for nearly five years before being decided in the city's favor. Tax squabbles were an added problem in the relationship between Midlands and local government.

In 1980 Ball, pointing to recent downtown construction, said that the Midlands Mall had helped revitalize the central business district of Council Bluffs. Although he said that the absence of interstate highway signs directing travelers to the mall had impaired its development, the enterprise seemed to do well through the mid-1980s. That the urban-renewal project still divided the community was evident when the *Nonpareil* noted, "We have consistently defended the mall against critics who wish the downtown area would return to its pre-mall days and we have accepted our share of criticism from those same critics for our support of the mall."

Parking and other traffic problems in downtown Council Bluffs were alleviated with the building of a bypass for through traffic, later named Kanesville Boulevard, which paralleled Broadway and passed the Midlands Mall to the north. But by 1983 it was apparent that the mall had not triggered downtown redevelopment, and a study found that found that the business district was "more than 50 percent underutilized."

For the champions of downtown, the old specter of a shopping mall on the outskirts of the city near the junction of Interstate Highways 29 and 80 became a reality in 1986 with the opening of the Mall of the Bluffs, a development considerably larger than the Midlands Mall. By then, the Midlands Mall was again up for sale, and early in 1987 a department store that had been one of its anchors closed. Other vacancies followed, and by later that year it was evident that the mall was failing. Looking back to the inception of the project, Ball, who had left Council Bluffs, remarked, "At that time . . . there was a feeling, not only in Council Bluffs but in other cities, that if you moved early enough, before shopping centers were established in outlying areas, and it did well enough, you could hold the people in the downtown area." He added, "It turned out to be a mistake. . . . I don't think that's really worked any place in the country. But at that time we didn't know that."

The Midlands Mall was finally sold in 1988 for a paltry $3 million to a Wisconsin firm, Dhaliwal Enterprises, but the downward spiral continued as bills for desultory renovation work were unpaid and back taxes accumulated. Other aspects of the thirteen-acre urban-renewal program left much to be desired: plans for a hotel and convention center announced shortly before the January 1973 bond-issue vote did not materialize, and the personalized rapid transit system remained a pipe dream.

In 1991 Darshan S. Dhaliwal donated the Midlands Mall and two adjoining office buildings to Western Iowa Educational Endeavors, an organization established to hold the gift in behalf of Iowa Western Community College. The junior college, with operations in several southwestern Iowa towns, had developed an important presence in Council Bluffs since its founding in 1966, and the failed mall offered the school ample space for its local mission. Funding development had been an uphill struggle for Iowa Western, and in recent years voters in its service area had twice rejected bond issues for the school. The gift of the mall was an incentive for Iowa Western to go to the voters again, and the result was the scheduling of a $27,500,000 bond issue in a special election in February 1992. The proposal included improvements across the school's service area, but the largest component was $10,250,000 to refurbish the mall for the college's use. The *Nonpareil*, civic leaders, and other advocates of the proposal saw it as a needed investment in higher education and as a continuing hope for the revitalization of downtown, but critics condemned the proposal as a taxpayer-funded "bail-out" of the ill-fated Midlands project. The measure needed 60 percent of the ballots cast to be adopted but was defeated.

With no other source of funds for redevelopment, Western Iowa Educational Endeavors closed the Midlands Mall on June 30, 1992. Soon the project that was to have been the catalyst in rejuvenating downtown lay forlorn behind boards and fence, occasionally falling prey to vandals. Finally in 1994, John Tabor, an Omaha realtor, paid Western Iowa Educational Endeavors $150,000 for the mall that had once been touted as a $35 million property. Tabor planned to convert the mall into an office park, and to assist him, Mayor Thomas P. Hanafan spearheaded the development of incentives worth up to $500,000, a city commitment to financially guarantee the leasing of some mall space, plus a long-term lease and ultimate ownership of the city-owned parking structure. The city council approved this package; Council Bluffs banks provided a loan for refurbishing the mall, and the property reopened as the Omni Centre Business Park. By 1997 a number of businesses and government agencies occupied a large portion of the renovated space in the Omni Centre, and the value of the property had risen significantly.

In retrospect, the use of the urban-renewal program failed to live up to its expectations in revitalizing downtown Council Bluffs and did nothing to suggest that Omahans had erred in not using this tool. In both cities urban renewal had been divisive. The anti-elitism common amongst Omaha opponents of urban renewal was also evident in some of the opposition to the 1973 bond issue that was part of the Council Bluffs urban-renewal package. Following the failure of the Midlands Mall, Mayor Hanafan and other thoughtful persons recalled that from its inception the project had divided the people of Council Bluffs. As one observer said, "We tend to divide in Council Bluffs. We don't pull together—work as a team—unless there's a crisis." Foes of urban renewal lamented the clearing of old buildings and the passing of downtown as they had known it. On both sides of the river the opponents of urban renewal saw the program as something that was more drastic and intrusive than the circumstances warranted.

DEBATING URBAN GROWTH

An elaborate brochure issued in the mid-1960s by the Omaha Chamber of Commerce contained the usual rosy predictions. It called Omaha "a vital and growing city," citing census returns, a traditional measurement of progress. And there was no doubt that Omaha had added a great many people as part of a trend that would generally continue. In 1960 Omaha had 301,598 residents, and ten years later 346,939 persons lived inside the expanded city limits. Even more dramatic was the advance of the population of the Omaha metropolitan area that included Douglas, Sarpy, and Pottawattamie counties from 457,873 in 1960 to 540,142 in 1970. Because of postwar urban sprawl, it was no longer possible to consider the extent of an urbanized area purely in terms of the central city. Despite different governmental structures, they were part of a whole. The Omaha Standard Metropolitan Statistical Area, which ranked sixty-ninth nationally at the start of the 1970s, continued to grow at a moderate rate. This appeared impressive; but there was not unqualified approval. For the first time in the history of Omaha, observers questioned the need and the desirability of further urban growth.

In 1966 thoughtful critics argued that continued rapid expansion might adversely affect the quality of urban life. They stood aghast at Omaha Chamber of Commerce predictions of over one million people in the metropolitan area by the year 2000. The prospect of adding an additional ten thousand persons every year held little appeal, although several experts gave qualified approval to some future population increase. They saw it as desirable if newcomers were not unskilled laborers, elderly "non-producers," or individuals with little earning power. H. W. Reynolds, director of the Urban Studies Center at the University of Omaha, said, "I don't think the City of Omaha should grow appreciably bigger than it is. Any city that gets to be over a half a million in population begins to get into increasingly insoluble situations—in traffic, health, welfare, for instance." Reynolds believed population growth is good "provided it doesn't take out more than it puts in terms of net worth of the economy." A colleague, sociologist Phil Vogt, stressed the quality of life rather than any financial factors as a reason to support population limits. Vogt believed that cities had "become unmanageable, unfit for human habitation."

Advocates of rapid enlargement, somewhat taken aback by any attack upon an established and generally accepted way to determine urban success in America, responded by claiming that Omaha must move ahead. Alden Aust, city planning director, argued that when a city stopped growing it started to die. He contended that while rapid growth brought problems, it also brought the resources necessary to reach solutions. A fundamental consideration was that Omaha must avoid being surrounded by separate communities that would stop the development of its tax base through expansion. Aust pointed to Cleveland, Detroit, and St. Louis as cities where this had happened. Another incentive for annexation was the fact that population was an important consideration for state and federal spending in urban areas. E. J. Steele, chairman of the University of Omaha Economics Department, claimed that a city would lose population if it made no effort to advance. None of the growth advocates agreed with the critic who remarked, "If quantity would do it, China would be the place to go."

Arguments over how many people should live in the Omaha area continued into the 1970s and came to emphasize environmental considerations. Private organizations, especially the Quality Environmental Council and Zero Population Growth, stressed that Omaha's quality of life was slipping. Crowds, more cars, pollution, and stress from urban life pointed to this conclusion. James Malkowski, director of the Fontenelle Forest on the edge of Bellevue, raised the specter of radiation from nuclear power plants. He sought a systematic study of Omaha's size and observed, "We seem to be entrenched in the philosophy that bigger is better. The Chamber of Commerce attitude prevails—let's get more and more." He cited problems with sewage treatment, pollution, and mass transit as the start of permanent growing pains.

To some extent, the replies to the critics of growth were routine. Aust responded, "Suppose we build a big wall around Omaha; that wouldn't improve the quality of life a bit. I'm not impressed with the arguments that at a certain size, a city's costs go up or that it's bad to be big. We certainly haven't reached that point." Aust added that places had to attain "a certain critical mass" in order to offer extensive cultural, employment, and recreational opportunities. As he said, "There's no playhouse in Weeping Water." Although one Chamber of Commerce official remarked that antigrowth arguments "didn't make a ripple around here," James Monroe, the chamber's manager of economic development in defending growth indicated that his organization was not averse to studying possible limits. The passing of time was bringing a subtle change that suggested that environmental and business perspectives were not necessarily incompatible.

In the meantime, Omaha had pursued an active annexation program through the late 1960s into the early 1970s. Under Nebraska's liberal annexation law, many kinds of areas could be annexed by city council action. On the outskirts of Omaha, real-estate interests had become accustomed to creating legal entities called sanitary improvement districts. While these districts had full government authority except for police powers, they usually were covers for either housing developments or apartment complexes. After these districts incurred ballooning debts for such items as sewer lines, sidewalks, streets, parks, and in some cases even apartment swimming pools, annexation by Omaha had followed as a matter of course, hurting the overall debt ratio.

Efforts to annex the town of Millard on the city's southwestern outskirts generated exceptional controversy. In 1950 Millard had 391 residents, but the construction of a Western Electric plant just to its north brought immediate growth, and by 1965 the community had a population of 5,240. Aust and other city officials were mindful that state law limited Omaha's unilateral annexation power to communities with populations under 10,000. Wishing to avoid the long-term possibility of having Omaha's growth halted by separate communities to its west, the administration of Mayor A. V. Sorensen moved to annex Millard. Residents of that town staunchly resisted this action, legal challenges ensued, and not until 1971, when the U.S. Supreme Court declined to hear Millard's case, did Omaha triumph. In the meantime, following litigation and a negotiated settlement of taxes and other details, Omaha annexed the huge Western Electric plant. To the east of Millard, the town of Ralston, surrounded by Omaha on three sides and Sarpy County to the south, presented no great challenge to Omaha's growth and survived as a separate municipality. In 1965 Omaha made a southward annexation probe into Sarpy County that predictably brought a court challenge. The following year the Nebraska Supreme Court ruled that Omaha could not annex across the county line.

After taking office as mayor in 1973, Edward Zorinsky halted the active annexation program. The key reason for this change was the increase in the city's bonded indebtedness as a result of assuming the debts of annexed areas. Between 1969 and 1971 annexations added $34.7 million to the city's debt, necessitating an increase in the debt levy in 1973. Zorinsky believed that annexing sanitary improvement districts discriminated against Omaha taxpayers and led to unsavory relations between realtors and politicians. In 1976 the Omaha planning department devised a policy to use incentives and "disincentives" to promote development within the city and discourage growth in outer areas. Supporters of this change claimed that 25 percent of every tax dollar spent in Omaha went to expand city services into new western neighborhoods and that 17 percent of land in recently developed areas remained overlooked for residential purposes. They concluded that restraining development west and north would lead to better community-wide services, raise the tax base in the inner city, and revitalize the older parts of town. In a lead editorial, the *World-Herald* raised questions about the potential impact of a new expansion policy. The paper concluded, "There is a critical difference between limiting growth reasonably and strangling needed expansion."

Omaha adopted this restrictive policy in 1977, and despite Aust's desire to see annexations resume as the 1980 census approached, city finance director George Richardson was a strong voice in retaining a conservative approach to territorial growth. Unfortunately, the 1977 development procedures, updated in 1980, did not solve the fundamental challenge of how to control growth in Omaha. The city continued some expansion on its fringes while leaving new sanitary improvement districts outside its boundaries unannexed. This had the effect of leaving mill levies in Omaha artificially depressed and at the same time keeping valuable land off the tax rolls. A direct impact of curtailing annexations was a rather dramatic population loss. The 1980 census showed Omaha with 313,939 people, down almost 33,000 from 1970. In the same period the metropolitan area as a whole added over 29,000 inhabitants, for a total population of 569,614.

In 1981 under the administration of Mayor Mike Boyle, Omaha returned to an active annexation program that by 1983 brought 13,643 people into the city. Bellevue followed a similar pattern. After having made no annexations for thirteen years, Bellevue in 1983 annexed territory that was home to 10,332 persons. Omaha ranked sixth and Bellevue ninth among American cities in numbers of persons added by annexation between 1980 and 1983.

Using annexation as a tool for urban growth in Council Bluffs was far more difficult than doing so in Omaha. Unlike Nebraska's law that made it relatively simple for Omaha to add territory, Iowa law required Council Bluffs voters to approve contested annexation proposals. If they approved such a measure, property owners in the area to be annexed, who were not permitted to vote on the issue, could force the city to demonstrate that it could provide essential services. This meant that litigation was routine. In the 1950s the city did not make any annexations, and a 1967 study showed that since 1940 the population of areas in Pottawattamie County on the outskirts of Council Bluffs had a higher growth rate than that of the city.

The problem of formal expansion was demonstrated in 1967 when Council

Bluffs, with an area of about 21 square miles, considered annexing 34.9 square miles of territory with a population of about nine thousand surrounding the city on the north, east, and south. Opponents raised the usual objections to such measures: residents of the area to be annexed did not wish to be taken in to the city, extending city services would be costly, and the city was ill-prepared to provide such services. Advocates took a positive view on the financial impact of annexation. "Cities must think big," said the *Nonpareil* in advising voters that the huge annexation proposal was essential to orderly long-term development. In a telling comment, the paper declared, "The city of Council Bluffs must provide the leadership for not only this immediate community and Pottawattamie County but for all of Southwest Iowa if we are to fight our way out of the economic doldrums with which we have been troubled for many years."

When the voters overwhelmingly defeated the annexation measure, the *Nonpareil* admitted that the public had seen the proposal "as the brainchild of the elected and appointed officials of the city." In failing to develop popular support for a very important action, the result was similar to the plight of the Omaha Plan ten years earlier. Perhaps, as with the Omaha Plan, the magnitude of the proposal and fear of tax hikes contributed significantly to its defeat. A year later, Council Bluffs voters handily approved a package of annexation measures that totaled 16.8 square miles, less than half the size of the previous proposal. This would prove to be the city's last large annexation in the twentieth century.

THE "TWENTY INFLUENTIALS"

Events that led to an increased dependency on the federal government had a complicated impact on Omaha's power structure. Even though the Knights of Ak-Sar-Ben installed a king and queen every year regardless of depression or war, no individual or group inside Omaha dictated community policy; those decisions seemed to lie elsewhere. The times were not right for another Dennison, Dahlman, or Wattles. Contrary to the apparent vision of most its framers in 1956, Omaha's new form of government had not brought the election of officials who held an implicit consensus that the public welfare and the welfare of business were similar. The emergence of a block of voters in moderate and low-income areas who tended to vote against what they perceived as the initiatives of the local elite hardly encouraged business leaders to stand in the vanguard of civic change.

In 1966 Paul Williams, former managing editor of the weekly *Omaha Sun*, made an influential study of the city's leadership. He focused on the problem stated in his first sentence: "There is a gap about twenty years wide and three elections deep in Omaha's power structure." He found the most powerful men in town, those who had "the money, prestige, time and a desire to do good works," had stopped trying to frame a comprehensive community policy. Instead, they continued to serve on each other's boards and to raise funds for each other's pet civic projects without much thought to a larger policy. What evolved was what one source, experienced in civic and political leadership, called "a sort of power vacuum."

Noting endless variations within the power structure, Williams identified "Twenty Influentials," all business leaders. Insiders claimed that physicians and lawyers were primarily important only in their fields. It went without saying that labor leaders were excluded from the upper levels of community affairs except when their presence could not be ignored or when they accepted invitations to support certain projects such as charter reform. Wealthy women showed little inclination to exercise community power on a grand scale or to play major philanthropic roles. No new Sarah Joslyn had come to the fore.

Williams believed that little more than 1/20 of 1 percent of Omaha's population had the desire, the skills, and the resources to move the city ahead. He thought part of the problem was that many of the Twenty Influentials had been in command positions for too long, some for as many as thirty years. It made little difference that they held considerable power if they had no inclination or way to use it effectively. Moreover, new men found it much more difficult to gain entrance than had been the case prior to the 1930s. Under the selection process that prevailed in the 1960s, aspiring civic leaders were at least ten years away from entering the inner power structure. Newcomers were expected as a first step to win the support of the hierarchy for a "good" community project, one that would be measured against prevailing conservative business standards. "Even if a young aspirant 'makes it' as a campaign fund-raiser and moves up to general chairmanship of a charitable group, he may not consider himself an insider until the majority of 'power elite' people nod at mention of his name, or insist on his presence on their boards and committees," Williams asserted. "The senior executives continuously test the aspirant for willingness to work hard at recruiting and organizing people, for recognition and protection of the diverse interests of persons involved, for ability to 'put together' a project." Those desiring to advance into the upper strata of the power structure accepted the long and tough screening process as a necessity. Was it worth it, given the virtual impossibility of exercising real leadership and the endless possibilities for criticism? Aside from career advantages and a sense of fulfillment from public service, there was the ultimate social reward: selection and coronation as King of Ak-Sar-Ben.

The Twenty Influentials, as was to be expected, had impressive credentials. They carried the titles associated with power in American commercial and industrial life; among them were presidents, chairmen and executive vice presidents, and secretary-treasurers. Some exercised influence as a result of family connections; others had climbed up the corporate ladder in the city's major commercial, industrial, and financial enterprises. Probably the best known was Peter Kiewit, president of the large construction firm Peter Kiewit Sons Company; owner of the *Omaha World-Herald;* and philanthropist. Among the others were John F. Davis, president of the First National Bank; Leo A. Daly, who headed the Leo A. Daly Company, an architectural concern; insurance executive V. J. Skutt of Mutual of Omaha; John F. Merriam, chairman of the board of Northern Natural Gas Company; and Willis Strauss, Northern Natural's president. Gilbert C. Swanson, president of Swanson Enterprises, reflected the importance of the food-processing industry. John F. Diesing was secretary-treasurer of J. L. Brandeis and Sons, and Morris E. Jacobs served Bozell and Jacobs Advertising as chairman of the board.

It was arguable whether all twenty men belonged to a "power elite." They were not the only leaders in Omaha with impeccable credentials; and some of them doubtless felt their inclusion unfair, feeling they had been singled out as responsible for an alleged lack of community leadership. Yet there was no argument about one other name: Edd H. Bailey, president of the Union Pacific. As had been the case for over a hundred years, the chief operating officer of the Union Pacific automatically wielded power in Omaha. In any event, the power structure was amorphous, its members, if they may be called such, were mortal, and their businesses were subject to the unceasing changes of capitalism. As one scholar wrote, "Of the twenty men whose names appeared on the *Omaha Sun Newspapers* leadership list in 1966, five had retired and two had died by 1971. Another was promoted to an out-of-town job, and five others faded from prominence as their companies moved elsewhere or decreased in local importance."

By the early 1980s internal authority seemed to rest in the hands of a small group whom knowledgeable sources called the "Big Five." Three had been members of the Twenty Influentials of 1966: architect Daly, insurance executive V. J. Skutt, and Northern Natural Gas board chairman Willis Strauss. Two newcomers were John C. Kenefick, president of the Union Pacific, and Jack McAllister, president of Northwestern Bell Telephone. Although it was wrong to assume that these men formed a cabal that manipulated Ak-Sar-Ben and ran the city over lunch at the elite Omaha Club, they did represent a rationalizing of community decision making. They all had interests far beyond Omaha; they all had experience dealing with the federal government; and they all had ideas of what was best for Omaha. Following in the tradition of earlier city builders, they appeared to have control over affairs.

THE MAYORS

Local politicians hovered on the edge of the power structure, heeded or ignored in direct relationship to the extent that their policies and actions pleased the business community. Members of the city council had small power bases that were usually associated with neighborhood needs or a specific interest group and only in rare instances had access to large amounts of private money. Given the constraints, about all they could do was to concentrate on winning support for pet issues, serving the needs of constituents, and making an occasional headline to remain in the public eye. This was a predictable result of a return to a mayor and council system. So was the switch to an elected mayor. Despite the aims of the framers of the new charter, the holder of the office was not in a position to chart a course for Omaha. Getting elected and maintaining a political base required the building of support throughout town. This necessitated the making of various commitments that by their nature acted as restraints. Holding the mayor accountable for day-by-day administration did not help much either. The natural inclination was to force the mayor to pay attention to a great number of minor matters if only for protection against possible charges of official misconduct. The biggest problem of all was money. No mayor had the kind of economic power necessary to exercise wide control over events.

The mayors were either from outside the power structure or on the fringes.

The second mayor elected under the new charter was James Dworak, two-term city council member. Charges of corruption ruined his administration. A Chicago builder, John Coleman, claimed that Dworak and others had solicited bribes from him in return for the rezoning of land for townhouses. Ultimately, two city councilmen and a real-estate man were convicted for accepting bribes; a member of the planning board pleaded no contest to a misdemeanor charge of malfeasance in public office, and Dworak won an acquittal after an eight-day jury trial. To say the least, this was inauspicious for charter government. Embittered by his experiences, Dworak left Omaha and moved to California. In a 1975 interview he lashed out at one of Omaha's most prestigious institutions, stating, "If the people of Omaha think Chicago has a political machine, they should try to look at the internal workings of the governors of Ak-Sar-Ben. They control millions of dollars that no one has authority to investigate." Dworak claimed that his administration had many accomplishments: housing for the aged, golf-course construction, revamping of the police communications system, and "cooling" of racial unrest. He failed to mention that during his term many Omaha leaders severed connections with city hall.

None of the mayors who followed Dworak had to face a jury. However, they did have to restore the prestige of the office in the eyes of the business community, and that was not easily accomplished. A. V. Sorensen served ably as mayor from 1965 to 1969, declining to seek reelection. Sorensen, as a result of his contribution as head of the charter convention, had emerged as a civic leader with access to the inner circle of the local establishment. As his highly successful term on the city council drew to a close, he considered running for mayor in 1961, but decided not to do so when business leaders did not come to his support. Perhaps to the chagrin of the city's elite, this paved the way for a surprise triumph by Dworak, who was openly hostile to the local establishment. After four years in private life Sorensen entered the 1965 mayoral campaign against Dworak, who was under indictment in the Coleman episode. Curiously, Sorensen gained business backing for his mayoral campaign only after he had won the primary election. In his campaign, he contended that Omaha's economy had lagged and that its image had suffered under Dworak.

Sorensen knew that he was on the periphery of the city's power structure but seemed content simply to be able to work with this group. An "insider" of "means and influence" said, "He does not have the power in terms of dollars or people of his own to put on a project." Another person acquainted with the ways of power in Omaha explained: "He can deal with them, but he doesn't get entangled with them. He stays apart." Sorensen summed up his own term when he said, "When I took office, we had an administration which was . . . well, less than the people had a right to expect. My job was building a good staff, fostering a favorable climate for new industry and developing pride of people in their community. I think we got that done."

Omaha had four mayors in the decade after Sorensen left office. Eugene Leahy, first in line, was a former Iowa farm boy and Marine Corps staff sergeant. After leaving service, he worked his way through Creighton University, graduating from law school in 1960. He entered politics and soon became a municipal judge. Displaying a dynamic personality, he gave hundreds of speeches in which he attacked drug abuse and "dirty books." Gaining the support of over four hundred different groups, he won a surprisingly easy victory in 1969. As mayor he rode elephants, read Sunday funnies on television, gave several hundred speeches in one four-month period, and delivered tirades against the city council. He gained a reputation as a "people's mayor," a "City Hall jester," and "Omaha's Harry Truman." He stressed a traditional version of "progress"—a larger city through annexation, an increase in public services made possible by an increase in federal funding and a broader local tax base, and a stepping up of efforts to attract new industry. In the first three years of his administration the city budget rose from $42 million to $70 million, primarily at his urging; and he obtained a $4.8 million grant from the Economic Development Administration to help develop the South Omaha Industrial Park. At times Leahy sounded like a conservative Republican, at others like a liberal Democrat. He had no establishment credentials but in general followed policies favorable to business.

By the late 1960s city planning and Chamber of Commerce promotional activity was shifting from an emphasis upon the traditional infrastructure needs of business and industry toward developing a pleasant downtown environment. The conjunction of several elements brought this change. With the decentralization of urban life, the downtown area needed a new attractiveness if it were to survive as the heart of the community. The decline of the meat-packing industry, the growth of white-collar employment, rising educational levels, and an increasing emphasis upon environmental awareness and leisure all contributed to a new perception of what downtown should become. Likewise, the role of city government in urban planning, long over-shadowed by business, was becoming more prominent. In 1967 largely to facilitate securing federal funds, the municipal and county governments of Greater Omaha established the Metropolitan Area Planning Agency (MAPA). As its name suggested, MAPA broadened the role of the public sector in urban planning. The new thrust toward improving the quality of life in downtown and other parts of the city through such devices as preservation of historic buildings and developing green areas to provide relief from the maze of concrete and steel was evident in planning director Alden Aust's Beautification Master Plan of 1968.

These influences came into focus between 1969 and 1973 when Leahy was in office. In 1970 he formed a Mayor's Riverfront Development Committee with members from various parts of the metro area that eventually proposed a park extending for many miles along the Missouri River. This visionary idea did not come to pass, but at the committee's request local architects volunteering their services devised a plan for redeveloping an area from the downtown business district eastward to the river. This 1971 initiative led to an eventual plan for a park running from downtown to the river that was part of a Central Business District Plan completed by the planning department and MAPA in 1973. That year, the city hired Lawrence Halprin, a renowned architect and planner to design this park. Leahy had not initiated the new thrust in city planning or the schemes for river-front development, but he vigorously promoted them. For its time the Riverfront Development Committee's ideas were grandiose, but part of its work gave rise to the plan for a Central Park Mall. Integral to that plan was the construction of new buildings that would frame the mall. In sum, the early 1970s brought a conjunction of influences that would soon begin a massive redevelopment of downtown Omaha.

Leahy's immediate successors were Edward Zorinsky, Robert Cunningham, and Al Veys. All three faced rising inflation and taxpayer hostility. Zorinsky was forty-three years old at his election in 1973. A chemistry and zoology major in college, he had run the H. Z. Vending Company for over twenty years and had served for fourteen years in the military police reserve. He had gained stature as a member of the board of directors of the Omaha Public Power District by questioning the method of distributing engineering contracts without competitive bidding. As mayor, he established a controversial office of management and budget to keep track of what was going on in city departments. Even though he sometimes criticized the business community—he said the Union Pacific had unloaded a "white elephant" on the city when it donated its Omaha station for a museum—he took credit for projects designed to further historical preservation, extend freeways, and build libraries. He followed an "open door" policy and tried to broaden his political base. In 1975 his administration capably met the emergencies resulting from a great January blizzard and a May tornado, which probably boosted his political appeal. After a sudden switch of party allegiance, he was elected in 1976 as a Democrat to the U.S. Senate. Completing Zorinsky's mayoral term, Cunningham allowed the budget office to fall into disuse and ran a caretaker administration.

Al Veys, who had extensive experience on the city council, operated Veys Foodland grocery store in South Omaha. In the spring of 1977, following a write-in campaign, he won nomination to the mayoral general election. In the runoff race he defeated veteran city council member Betty Abbott in an election that showed that some Omahans were "not ready for a woman" as mayor. One of his early moves was to abolish the office of management and budget. "I don't need a middle man to go between me and my department heads," he explained. Veys liked to meet in an informal gathering at the end of every working day with his top advisors to discuss policy and thrash out differences. His whole approach was less frenetic than that of either Leahy or Zorinsky. An assistant allowed, "A lot of people look at style rather than substance. Al's not a flashy guy. Al's not a spell-binding public speaker. Al's just a helluva administrator." Mayor Veys sought to hold down spending while at the same time promoting the growth of Omaha. So, no matter what his style, he followed traditional policies.

In 1981 Veys, seeking reelection, lost to Michael Boyle, a lawyer and former Douglas County election commissioner. Differences on issues were minimal, but the thirty-seven-year-old Boyle gave a more dynamic, "progressive" image than the sixty-two-year-old Veys. Mike Boyle and his wife, Anne, had strong family ties to the Democratic Party, and his bright political future was illustrated as he easily won reelection in 1985.

But in 1986 Mayor Boyle's fortunes plummeted, and by year's end he faced a recall vote. Police problems—often nettlesome for Omaha's political leaders—were central to Boyle's difficulty. As early as 1981 Boyle and the police

clashed when the mayor objected to the 1:00 a.m. presence of off-duty officers outside a bar. In October 1985 Boyle's brother-in-law, John Howell, was
charged with driving while intoxicated. The significance of the incident rose
after allegations that Howell's arrest resulted from improper police surveillance. An investigation led to discharge or other penalties for four police officers, but Chief Robert Wadman refused to approve sanctions against three
of them. In October 1986 the mayor fired Wadman, contending that the chief
had sought to block the probe in the Howell affair. Boyle had also objected
to traffic and other citations against his sons and reportedly told a deputy
police chief that no parking tickets were to be given to his family.

Boyle's firing of Wadman convinced many Omahans that the mayor was
unfit to remain in office. By November a group known as Citizens for Mature Leadership had enough signatures to bring about a recall election, later
scheduled for January 13, 1987. Although Boyle admitted to "excesses," he defended his dismissal of Wadman. The episode revealed the tensions within
the Police Division, for the Omaha Police Union and Fraternal Order of Police vigorously backed the mayor.

"Whirlwind from West Blew Boyle Away" read a *World-Herald* headline
following the recall vote, which by a margin of 56 to 44 percent expelled the
mayor from office. Omaha's western areas strongly supported recall, while
eastern areas generally gave strong support to Boyle. Although the recall was
unprecedented in Omaha's history and a political oddity for an American
city, the vote reflected the longstanding east-west political split. Partisan-
ship did not seem crucial in the recall vote, but Boyle's difficulties may have
been particularly offensive to the city's more elite areas. The recall defies easy
explanation, for Boyle's public policies and the services of city government
during his tenure were not issues. A Boyle loyalist, labor leader Terry Moore,
perhaps best explained the mayor's plight, saying, "Here in Omaha there is a
real sense of a need for politeness and respect for others."

The city council elected one of its members, fifty-nine-year-old Bernie Simon, to complete Boyle's term. Simon, a retired Northwestern Bell marketing manager, had been on the council since 1981. Soon after taking office, the
popular Simon began a struggle with cancer that ended in his death in April
1988. From its own membership the council chose forty-eight-year-old attorney and former University of Nebraska at Omaha professor Walt Calinger,
who had served as school-board president to finish the term Boyle started in
1985.

In the 1989 mayoral primary election, a resurgent Mike Boyle finished first among six major candidates. Facing him in the runoff election was P. J. Morgan, who operated a major real-estate management business and had been a state legislator and county commissioner. Morgan, a Republican, had backed Democrat Boyle in the 1981 mayoral campaign.

For Mike Boyle the pattern of balloting in the runoff election in May replicated the east-west split in the 1987 recall vote. "W. Omaha Boyle's Downfall" read the headline of the story relating Morgan's triumph over Boyle. This contest brought the highest number of votes cast in a mayoral election and in defeat Boyle won more ballots than he had in any previous race.

THE CHANGING ECONOMY

The prolonged debate over the quality of urban life in Omaha and the creation of a development plan came during the general prosperity of the 1960s and 1970s. Despite the phasing out of passenger business and the advent of Amtrak, the Union Pacific Railroad continued as it had for over a century, to lead the way over the Plains and on to the West Coast. The firm's media advertisements—emphasizing its role in building the West, its status as a "great big rolling railroad," and its future—served as indication of its continued importance in Omaha. A survey by *Fortune* magazine showed that in 1975 the Union Pacific, with sales of $1.7 billion, ranked as the nation's fourth-largest transportation company. The railroad's headquarters building in downtown Omaha was an obvious symbol of its role in constructing the city.

Trucks and planes further enhanced Omaha's position as a transportation hub. It was a center of long-haul trucking business, functioning both as a national and regional terminal. This activity had roots in the overland freighting of the 1850s that during the gold rush in Colorado had brought Omaha its first prosperity. Air transport added another element as the number of passengers arriving or departing from Eppley Airfield increased from 677,750 in 1962 to some 1,000,000 in 1965. Three years later, the Omaha Airport Authority announced a $10 million expansion program. With the end of most rail passenger service and the popularization of commercial air travel, Eppley Airfield served travelers in an extensive area around Omaha.

Developments in the meat-packing industry contrasted to what happened in the transportation sector. Neither the promise of incentives by the city government nor appeals to tradition by South Omaha leaders prevented the large companies from pulling important operations out of Omaha; they came because of self interest and left for the same reason. Three of the Big Four moved away within two years of each other in the late sixties: Cudahy in 1967, Armour in 1968, and Swift in 1969. Wilson curtailed operations in 1976. These dreaded developments cost Omaha more than ten thousand jobs, plus an estimated $500 million annually in wages, services, purchases, and taxes. Several causes led to the closings. The largest were age and obsolescence. The prime components of the Omaha plants had all been built prior to World War I, and some dated back to the previous century. By 1966 seventeen modern slaughterhouses operated in small towns and rural areas in eastern Nebraska and western Iowa. A plant in Dakota City, Nebraska, which had fewer than five hundred employees, slaughtered twenty-five thousand head of cattle a week. An Omaha establishment required the services of two thousand men to kill the same number in a similar period. The owners had experienced frequent labor problems in the late 1950s and 1960s when they tried to introduce automated systems. Union officials claimed the companies deliberately made impossible demands that they used as excuses to close down. Responding to federal directives to stop Missouri River pollution, the city government worked with the packers to establish a packing-waste treatment plant. The plant, using a prototype system, opened in 1969 but never worked properly, and the city lost much money in this attempt to help preserve the local packing industry.

Direct stock buying was the final blow to Omaha's chances of remaining a packing center. Buyers went directly to producers, bypassing terminal markets; and small towns offered inducements to packers to build plants much as Omaha interests had done decades earlier. Another attraction was a non-union work force. Omaha lost its number-one position as a livestock market, and in 1973 a New York firm bought the stockyards company, ending ninety years of local ownership. Statistics illustrated the downward course. In 1960 the yard handled 6.2 million cattle, calves, hogs, and sheep. By 1975 receipts amounted to 2.5 million, mostly for 1.2 million cattle and 1.2 million hogs. By then, after being the world's largest livestock market from 1955 until 1973, Omaha had fallen to third. While the stockyards remained important, the glory days had ended. The Big Four left not only Omaha but also Chicago and Kansas City, diversifying operations throughout the central states and bringing an abrupt halt to a colorful and important period in metropolitan industrial development.

Dire warnings that the curtailment of Big Four operations would bring an economic catastrophe failed to materialize. Cheery predictions by Omaha politicians that turning the old packing-house area into an industrial park— demolition experts flattened the huge Armour plant in eight seconds in 1971—had little impact. The attracting of new business to the park, such as the Mid-Continent Refrigerated Service Company, that employed fewer than thirty persons was cosmetic. What was important was that the general prosperity of the American economy in the 1970s overrode the closing of obsolete facilities. Most of the senior unskilled packing-house workers were near the ends of their careers. Retirement benefits and unemployment insurance softened the blow as did other job opportunities. National recessions in 1971 and 1974–75 had only a short-term impact on Omaha. By then, the packing-house workers had retired or been absorbed into the greater local economy. Throughout the boom years that characterized the 1970s, Omaha continued to add to its industrial work force. In 1979 over 25,000 people, more than double the number engaged at the end of the Great Depression, worked in Omaha industry. Meat packing still occupied the services of almost 4,000. Added to that were another 6,900 individuals in general food processing. While more than 14,000 employees held additional manufacturing positions—3,000 in metals, 3,250 in printing, and 8,400 in a host of other classifications—foodstuffs continued to be basic to the Omaha employment market. The comparative ease with which the city absorbed those thrown out of work by Big Four closings suggested its ability to cope with a sharp downturn of the nation's economy in 1980.

The further rise of Omaha as an insurance center was another positive economic sign. In the 1960s and 1970s Omaha emerged as a possible rival to such older established northeastern insurance centers as Hartford, Boston, and Philadelphia. By 1967 Omaha insurance companies employed over 8,500 men and women in white-collar jobs with an annual payroll of $34 million. In seventeen years yearly premiums had increased from $190 million to $600 million. The Omaha-based companies dealt in three broad categories of insurance: life, casualty and liability, and accident and health. During the 1970s, new construction by the leading businesses gave evidence of progress. The Woodmen of the World completed an imposing clean-lined thirty-story skyscraper in the heart of downtown in 1969. Mutual of Omaha, the best known nationally of the city's insurance concerns, twice added to its gigantic office complex located several blocks west of the business district. Even though Omaha had not become the "Midwest Hartford" as proclaimed in booster brochures, excellent management and aggressive advertising had combined to create a growing, profitable, and formidable insurance industry.

The federal government continued to play a very visible role in Omaha's economy. City officials, battling mountains of paperwork required by authorities in Washington and inundated with overly detailed and in many cases incomprehensive directives, voiced bitter frustration. What they wanted was federal money with few strings attached. It made little difference who was president; the message was the same. The course had been set in the 1930s in the middle of economic calamity, and there seemed no turning back. Ronald Reagan hoped to drastically cut federal aid to cities, but his emphasis on defense spending ensured a continuing flow of money from Washington.

Many federal activities helped Omaha. Offutt Air Force Base continued to pump great sums of money into the local economy. Several Strategic Air Command bases closed in the 1960s, but there was never any question of that happening to Offutt, which remained SAC headquarters. SAC's role changed and broadened in accordance with the development of new weapons-delivery systems. With the advent of guided missiles with nuclear warheads, Offutt remained an important American defense component. In 1968 at the height of the war in Vietnam, the installation's population numbered thirty-six thousand airmen and their dependents, plus two thousand civilian workers.

Another military organization, the United States Army Corps of Engineers, with its Missouri River Division headquarters in Omaha, continued to develop plans for local flood control–recreation projects. During the middle 1970s the corps ran into much criticism from citizens' groups when it proposed the construction of a series of dams around Omaha in the Papillion Creek (Papio) watershed. The opposition was part of an adverse national reaction to corps policies; countless critics claimed it had become a bureaucratic monster that built dams for the sake of building dams. In Omaha, following political pressure and revelations of what appeared to be inflated payments for land at dam sites, the corps dropped plans for several dams. Even so, its Omaha office, as it had for a long time, spent considerable money every year in the city and its environs. Most of the funds went for Missouri River improvements, and as Omaha's city leaders devised plans for beautification of the river-front in the late 1960s and early 1970s, the corps provided valuable assistance.

More spectacular was the tremendous amount of money expended as result of the Interstate Highway Act of 1956, the poverty programs of President Lyndon Johnson's administration, and revenue sharing. Two great links in the interstate system passed through the Omaha Standard Metropolitan Statistical Area: east-west I-80 and on the Iowa side, north-south I-29. Another two roads completed the local net. I-680 was a belt route that semicircled Omaha to the west and north; I-480 ran through the center of town. The total cost came to over $140 million; 90 percent was from the federal government. Much of the money came in routine bid openings that received little publicity.

Other projects received more notice. Johnson's Great Society programs, reminiscent of the New Deal and designed to bring social equality for blacks and the urban poor in general, brought in millions. So did allocations in the 1970s. The city's ability to gain government favors, plus more equitable distribution under revenue-sharing and other measures, served well even if the programs were not always welcome. The freeway system broke up or destroyed old neighborhoods. The placing of a Women's Job Corps center downtown with its concentration of many black young people from poverty backgrounds frightened shoppers. Despite the center's close in 1969, it had contributed to a lingering negative perception of downtown. Too much revenue-sharing money went for projects for which it was hard to see a tangible return. Critics especially attacked Great Society measures, noting that the Omaha programs failed to prevent the racial trouble of the 1960s.

"A CITY DESPERATE FOR DEVELOPMENT"

If a knowledgeable Omahan were asked in the early 1980s to name a large locally headquartered business that was noted for its civic contributions, that person might well have mentioned Northern Natural Gas Company. Operating in Omaha since 1930, Northern Natural Gas emerged under the leadership of John Merriam in the 1950s as an important pipeline and gas marketing firm. Merriam was strongly committed to Omaha's cultural life and was a vigorous advocate of the quality of life in the northern Plains. Northern Natural's civic leadership continued under Merriam's successor, Willis Strauss; and in 1985 the firm, by then known as InterNorth, employed 2,209 persons locally.

In early 1985 the price of InterNorth stock rose sharply as a result of purchases by a corporate raider. A calculated expansion of InterNorth's debt could dissuade a takeover; accordingly, the firm determined to pursue a major acquisition that also would be an appropriate business addition. InterNorth thus acquired Houston Natural Gas (HNG), a large energy company. The $2.4 billion transaction placed a premium price upon Houston Natural Gas stock and assured HNG a strong position on the InterNorth board of directors. Particularly noteworthy was the agreement that Kenneth Lay, HNG's chief executive officer would ultimately become chief executive officer at InterNorth.

The details of the acquisition, especially the arrangements with Kenneth Lay, estranged some InterNorth board members and chief executive officer Sam F. Segnar. As a result, Lay became CEO in November 1985—well before the previously arranged time. Because Houston was the premier city in the oil and gas industry, a shift to a Houston-oriented HNG/InterNorth operation was in motion. InterNorth had just built a $36 million headquarters on the western edge of downtown, but Omaha's champions on the board of directors could not prevent this redirection. In November 1985 the board decided that Omaha would remain the firm's corporate headquarters while Houston would become the operational center. However, in May 1986 the HNG/InterNorth board voted to move the headquarters of the company—renamed Enron Corporation—to Houston. By 1991 Enron had only 250 employees in Omaha, and its corporate donation to local charities fell from $2 million in 1985 to $484,000 in 1990. InterNorth's acquisition of Houston Natural Gas led to a serious blow to the city, and as a *World-Herald* headline put it, "Tail Wagged Dog, and Omaha Lost."

The loss of the Enron headquarters and its many well-paid professionals was a challenge to Omaha's civic leaders not soon forgotten. In retrospect Omaha attorney and former legislator Vard Johnson said, "There was a genuine erosion of the spirit." Indeed, a *New York Times* article called Omaha "a city desperate for development." Incentives for economic development seemed essential, and as 1987 began, the administration of Nebraska's newly elected governor, Kay Orr, would take vigorous action. The principal result was the legislature's passage that year of LB 775, a business-incentive statute that strongly reflected the wishes of Charles M. "Mike" Harper, CEO of ConAgra.

ConAgra symbolized the emergence of the new Omaha. Known as Nebraska Consolidated Mills until 1971, the company had evolved from primarily a milling operation into producing a cornucopia of livestock feed and grocery products. But for a time ConAgra struggled with debt and commodity market setbacks, and new leadership was essential. The new leader would be Mike Harper, who came to ConAgra from Pillsbury Company, and brought ConAgra from a $11.4 million loss in 1974 to a $4.1 million profit in 1975. Over the next six years, ConAgra became an ever-bigger presence in the food industry, and Harper rose to the chairmanship of the board. By 1985 ConAgra's earnings exceeded $90 million, and the following year the company began to consider a new headquarters. Particularly ominous for Omaha was ConAgra's discovery that eighteen cities might be cheaper in terms of corporate overhead.

Given the Orr administration's desire to stimulate economic growth in view of the farm crisis of the 1980s and Omaha's anxiety after Enron's departure, Harper and ConAgra did much to shape a revision of state law to favor corporate investment. At the heart of this 1987 legislation were the Employment and Investment Growth Act, commonly known by its bill number, LB 775, and the Employment Expansion and Investment Incentive Act, LB 270, both of which granted tax concessions to companies that invested in the state and expanded employment. When the legislature balked at making corporate aircraft and computers tax-exempt, ConAgra said that it would relocate. Hence, the tax package that became law reflected ConAgra's wishes. Even though Governor Orr and her administration saw the business incentive as partly their handiwork, Harper was the moving force in the tax revision.

The new tax laws assured that ConAgra would stay in Omaha, but the company had a prospective site on the city's northern outskirts that did not square with the downtown redevelopment thrust. To get ConAgra to build downtown required that the city permit the demolition of Jobbers' Canyon, the buildings of Omaha's traditional wholesale district. These structures at the eastern edge of downtown had been nominated for the National Register of Historic Places in 1986, but Harper saw the "big, ugly, red brick buildings" as an impediment to building a river-front ConAgra headquarters. It would not have been necessary to raze the majority of the Jobbers' Canyon structures to make way for the ConAgra headquarters, but when civic leaders saw that ConAgra would not yield on the issue, Mayor Bernie Simon's administration fell into line to satisfy the company. In 1988 demolition in Jobbers' Canyon began, and ground was broken for ConAgra's campus, an $80 million project completed in 1990. Although ConAgra funded development of its thirty-acre campus, the city contributed to street and sewer redevelopment and the project received tax subsidization.

A NEW DOWNTOWN TAKES SHAPE

An important goal of Omaha's city government and important segments of the business community was to obtain funds to revitalize downtown and the river front. When Eugene Leahy had declined to seek reelection, he became the chief executive officer of the Riverfront Development Foundation. He helped to establish the foundation, formed by business interests in 1971, as a vehicle ostensibly intended to secure private and public funding to revitalize a roughly two-hundred-square mile "project area" along the river, mostly in the Omaha vicinity.

Funding for Riverfront Development Program planning and construction flowed from four different sources: federal grants for specific park and recreation programs, matching local and federal monies, state contributions, and private assets. Heralded as a "Return to the River" concept, the Central Park Mall remained the key feature of the program. The plan called for a great green mall a block wide and close to a mile long running through the heart of the central business district west to east toward the Missouri River. In the river valley would be a housing development of over a thousand units called Marina City. The project was very popular with business interests that owned property within the proposed mall. Dozens of buildings inside the limits were old and dilapidated structures that had long since outlived their usefulness. In 1975 the Central Park Mall started to become a reality. A year later most of the site had been cleared at an estimated cost of $15 million, almost entirely in federal funds. By decade's end, the great mounds of dirt and the signs of destruction that marked progress called to mind havoc wrought by World War II bombing raids on urban areas. The mall promised to provide Omaha with a central core park, a small version of Central Park in New York. The project gave evidence of affording Omaha a unique symbol, one of historical significance cut from the city's original design.

In 1982 the first segment of the Central Park Mall, largely funded from federal grants, was completed from Fourteenth to Tenth Street between Douglas and Farnam streets. It included plazas, a landscaped embankment, and

14. Panoramic view of downtown Omaha looking northwest. ConAgra campus is in foreground, 2005. *Courtesy Timothy M. Fitzgerald.*

a lagoon that symbolized Omaha's ties to the Missouri River. In 1992 it was renamed the Gene Leahy Mall in honor of the former mayor. A city bond issue funded the mall's completion from Tenth to Eighth Street in 1994.

The Return to the River came closer to reality in 1990 with the completion of the Heartland of America Park. Adjoining the east end of Leahy Mall, this Douglas County project linked to the ConAgra headquarters, was basic to the new image for downtown. The centerpieces of the Heartland of America Park/ConAgra campus were computer-controlled fountains and a lake. Early plans for the Marina City were too expensive to implement, but Omaha had a "new front door" that county board chairman Mike Albert likened to St. Louis's Gateway Arch.

Starting in the mid-1960s Samuel Mercer, who owned several of the buildings, led the way in turning a four-block section of the declining wholesale and jobbing district into a fashionable, quaint shopping and restaurant area. The successful efforts demonstrated the possibilities for rejuvenating older structures by changing their original functions. By the 1980s the Old Market District had become a tourist attraction and had been nominated as a National Historic District. It was complemented by a significant preservation project. The city-sponsored nonprofit Omaha Performing Arts Center Corporation restored the Orpheum Theater to the splendor it had enjoyed in 1927 when it opened as one of the nation's leading movie palaces. Gala ceremonies in 1975 transcended many controversies over the structure. The former movie theater soon attained eminence as Omaha's performing-arts center, drawing renewed attention to the central business district.

During the 1970s, the construction of gigantic edifices was a crucial element in the rejuvenation of Omaha's business district. The multimillion-dollar W. Dale Clark Public Library graced the western edge of the prospective Central Park Mall. The city and county shifted many administrative offices to the new Omaha Douglas Civic Center, partly financed by a grant from the Eppley Foundation. Both private and public funds contributed to the construction of a combined University of Nebraska at Omaha (formerly the Municipal University of Omaha) downtown educational center–state office building. The Union Pacific Railroad added a large addition to its headquarters, and the Northwestern Bell Telephone Company spent $25 million for an office building. The new Woodmen Tower was the tallest building on the upper Plains. A campaign for a new first-class hotel to serve prospective convention trade culminated in the erection of a Hilton Hotel combined with an office building, the First National Center. Just to the northwest of downtown, Creighton University added a number of buildings. The largest was the gigantic new St. Joseph Hospital, a 784,000-square-foot facility that cost in excess of $65 million. "For several years now, people have been reading and hearing about the redevelopment plans for downtown Omaha and wondering when it was going to happen," a booster article proclaimed. "Guess What? It's happening now." However, there was a setback. In the fall of 1980 J. L. Brandeis and Sons, despite a longstanding commitment, closed its downtown store.

A few observers questioned the need for massive downtown redevelopment or the motives that lay behind some of the activities. The large amounts of public money spent in the district caused concern. People wondered if it might have gone for better purposes, and there was a suspicion that while malls, preservation projects, and up-to-date public buildings were all to the good, a main result was to line the pockets of powerful Omaha businessmen. Even the building of the Hilton Hotel had controversial implications. Shortly after it opened, the Fontenelle Hotel closed its doors, raising the possibility that Omaha had not needed two large hotels and that the existing one could have been renovated for a lot less money than it cost to build a new one. Environmentalists worried about erecting large hotels and offices in an already congested part of town. Other groups, most notably Omaha Landmarks, deplored the destruction of some old buildings. Landmarks lost a battle to preserve part of the old Romanesque main post office when it was razed to make way for the First National Center–Hilton Hotel. The city's original skyscraper, the old Woodmen of the World Building, made way for the smaller University of Nebraska at Omaha educational center and state office building. To some, there was a sinister conspiracy of architects and builders. The Leo A. Daly Company designed many of the new structures, and the Peter Kiewit Sons Company erected several of them. Of course, there were those who just did not think the buildings looked good. Leo Daly, when asked about that in 1977, observed, "Some feel that our architecture in Omaha lacks the appeal . . . of other parts of the country. It might be a shade more conservative than, say architecture in Los Angeles, Las Vegas or Florida, but, all in all, I would think we have a good quality of architecture in Nebraska." No one denied that, for better or for worse, there had been a great deal of construction in Omaha.

The mall was basic to the new planning vision to make downtown a center of "people-oriented amenities," and it was fulfilling another key purpose: the redevelopment of eastern downtown. In 1982 a Chamber of Commerce representative speaking of the nearby area noted, "The Central Park Mall has stimulated $3.77 of private investment for each dollar spent." This construction was part of a pattern that between the mid-1970s and mid-1980s brought some $470 million in redevelopment to downtown. What was happening in Omaha paralleled efforts in other American cities to redevelop their central business districts.

THE DYNAMICS OF THIRTY YEARS

Omaha's population rose from 313,939 in 1980 to 335,795 in 1990, an increase of just under 7 percent, and the number of people residing in the metro area grew from 569,818 to 639,580, an increase of over 12 percent. The continuing development of the southern and southwestern suburban area explains much of this growth. In 1980 Sarpy County had 86,561 residents, and in 1990 the figure was 102,583. During the 1980s, Bellevue's population grew from 21,813 to 30,982, a 42 percent rise that made it Nebraska's fourth-largest city. Papillion had 6,399 residents in 1980 and 10,302 residents in 1990, a growth rate of nearly 61 percent.

In the 110 years from 1860 to 1970, with the exception of a slight population decrease during the 1930s, Council Bluffs had grown each decade. The years from 1970 to 1990 represented a break from this pattern. From a 1970 count of 60,343 persons, the city's population fell to 56,449 in 1980 and 53,222 in 1990. Nevertheless, these decreases and the drop in Omaha's population between 1970 and 1980 were mere glitches in the development of the metro area as it grew by over 31 percent from 1960 to 1990. The most dramatic component of this pattern was Sarpy County where there was an increase of nearly 328 percent from its 1960 population of 31,281. This growth reflected one very basic fact: the continuing urbanization of American life.

The new housing and businesses that marked this growth were both a boon to the economy and a reflection of economic growth. The critics of physical expansion were destined to fail; nevertheless, this growth devoured farmland and cast a shadow over the future of older parts of Omaha. Between 1960 and 1990 Omaha's population east of Forty-second Street fell from almost 200,000 to 113,000. In the area from Forty-second Street to Seventy-second Street, population reached 105,000 by 1970, but by 1990 only about 90,000 persons dwelt in this midcity area.

The period from 1960 to 1990 was one of general prosperity for the people of the metropolitan area despite drastic changes in the local economy. In 1960 Omaha had recently emerged as the premier city in the meat-packing industry, but before the decade was over, this bulwark of the local economy since the 1880s had been greatly weakened. For an even longer period Omaha and Council Bluffs were great railroad centers, but this identity was fading, particularly in Council Bluffs. This change was far less dramatic than the closing of packing houses, but the decline of railroad employment and the crisis in the agricultural economy probably contributed to the economic lethargy and lack of civic confidence that marked Council Bluffs into the 1980s.

Principal types of employment do much to shape community direction, identity, and the image that a place projects to outsiders. Changing economic realities would challenge the people of Omaha and Council Bluffs to rethink where their communities should be headed. Despite socioeconomic polarization, the closing of the packing houses, and the anxiety arising from the departure of HNG/InterNorth, by 1990 Omahans were building a new sense of community direction, if not a community identity and image. Omaha was much more of a white-collar town than it had been in 1960, and the redevelopment of downtown that was taking shape attested to this transition.

Finding a new direction and the identity and image that would emerge from it was intrinsically more difficult for Council Bluffs. Since the nineteenth century, proximity to Omaha had been a two-edged sword. Council Bluffs businesses found it hard to compete with Omaha stores, although the opening of the Mall of the Bluffs in 1986 provided the Iowa side of the metro with a shopping center as impressive as some of the important Omaha outlets. Because so many of its residents were employed across the river, Council Bluffs was to some extent a bedroom community for Omaha. This was perhaps galling to persons who knew that Council Bluffs was Omaha's parent and that Council Bluffs had a history of development that made it a real city as opposed to a typical suburb. On the other hand, whatever the problems of image and substance that bedeviled Council Bluffs, the size and diversity of the Omaha job market provided a strong measure of economic security.

This period provided ample evidence of the power of corporate leaders in shaping the future of Omaha—and by implication the plight of most other cities. Like most places, Omaha was at the mercy of corporate leaders based elsewhere who made decisions to close packing plants or to bring new enterprises to town. Outsider Kenneth Lay sent Omaha reeling when he moved HNG/InterNorth to Houston. Fifteen years later, many Omahans must have experienced a sense of déjà vu when Enron with Lay at its helm became a symbol of corporate irresponsibility. On the positive side, the redevelopment of downtown provided tangible evidence of the value of corporate leaders who were motivated to set the city on a course that embraced the great changes in the economy and lifestyle that appealed to white-collar urban Americans. The city planning department and the Metropolitan Area Planning Agency made important contributions to this process, and elected officials were supportive, but business executives, sometimes with new tax incentives, made the decisions that determined whether the city advanced or stagnated. Certainly by the late 1980s no one would have denied that ConAgra's Mike Harper, not a longtime resident of the city, wielded tremendous power in Omaha.

The importance of federal money that became so evident in the New Deal and World War II years became a durable part of the American scene in the balance of the twentieth century. Whether they realized it or not, residents of the Greater Omaha area benefited from federal spending for purposes as diverse as agricultural programs, Offutt Air Force Base, interstate highway construction, and the development of the Central Park Mall.

[11] Troubled Times, Quieter Times

During the 1960s the cities of America came under severe attack. Presidential aspirants spent campaign time talking about sick cities and how they intended to heal them. No previous major party candidates, with the possible exception of Franklin D. Roosevelt in 1932 and 1936 when he cloaked matters in terms of relief and recovery, had even discussed what they would do about urban areas in such direct ways. By the 1960s, however, cities not only mirrored the society, they were the society. Any serious problem either had an impact or roots in urban centers. Time-honored agrarian values of Jeffersonian democracy no longer seemed relevant. The United States had become a nation of cities.

The urban crisis came to Omaha in the form of racial unrest. In 1960 according to the census, the city had 25,212 blacks: 12,332 males and 12,880 females. By 1970 there were 34,431 blacks, the increase coming primarily as a result of the last stages of the general black migration from the South to northern cities. Although there were fewer blacks in Omaha than in many other metropolises, the grievances of the city's black community were much the same as elsewhere. The 1964 Civil Rights Act had little local impact, except for ending covert discrimination in certain public accommodations. Omaha never had a formal segregation system; denial of rights took subtle forms. Most of Omaha blacks still lived in a jammed-in district on the Near North Side. Few black youths went to college or finished high school. Job opportunities had not improved measurably since the Great Depression. A 1965 report by a Creighton University political science professor, Rene Beauchesne, concluded that for Omaha blacks educational levels had little effect on upward employment. "Being a Negro," Beauchesne's report contended, "in a white man's society apparently disqualified many people and made the 'American Dream' hardly more than something for the 'white folks.'" Militancy spread among blacks in Omaha. Ernest Chambers, a Creighton graduate, barber-shop operator, and emerging black leader, gained a following and received media coverage for his anti-establishment views. He headed a committee of the Near North Side Police–Community Relations Council, which presented to city officials a long list of complaints against Omaha police practices. All this was perplexing to whites used to having the Omaha Urban League and the local chapter of the National Association for the Advancement of Colored People claim to speak for blacks at large.

Mayor A. V. Sorensen said that he felt that blacks would make more rapid progress if they got together and agreed upon what they wanted. In a well-meaning comment, Sorensen declared that Omaha blacks needed a "leadership which [could] speak in a united voice for the Negro community like the Chamber of Commerce [did] for the business community or B'nai Brith [did] for the Jewish community." He indicated his respect for several Omaha African American leaders including Lawrence W. M. McVoy, president of the NAACP, and Douglas Stewart, Urban League executive director. Sorensen said he had met with Chambers, "although he . . . heaped a lot of abuse on" him. The mayor said that he would "be perfectly glad" to call a top-level conference to discuss minority complaints against policemen. This was in March 1966, eight months after the bloody Watts civil disorder in Los Angeles had focused national attention on the plight of urban blacks. Few whites in Omaha envisioned such a thing happening in their city. After all, Nebraska was not California, and unusual things always seemed to happen on the West Coast. Omaha African Americans were "reasonable," or so whites thought when Sorensen claimed his administration was "maintaining communication" on race matters. It turned out that was not enough.

To ease racial tension, Sorensen early in 1966 secured the establishment of the office of coordinator of police-community relations, a senior position in the Police Division. The creation of this post was timely in another sense. In 1964 Mayor James Dworak's public safety director, Chris Gugas, who had administrative authority over the fire and police departments, had demoted police chief C. Harold Ostler. His replacement, L. K. Smith, was chief when Sorensen became mayor, but through litigation Ostler regained his old position. To avoid having two police chiefs at once, Sorensen appointed L. K. Smith as coordinator of police-community relations.

The summer of 1966 brought two disturbances to Omaha with the first occurring during an early July heat wave. For three straight nights there were confrontations between black teenagers and the police. Trouble developed after youths gathered late at night in a Near North Side parking lot at Twenty-fourth and Lake streets serving a Safeway grocery store and a Skaggs Drug Center. One person observed that this was a place to go in lieu of recreational facilities. When police were unable to disperse the gathering, some persons threw rocks and bottles, smashed windows, looted several stores, and damaged a few vehicles. Most of the action occurred along North Twenty-fourth Street. The police concentrated on containing the mobs and holding down violence. On the third night the police had trouble with a milling and rock-throwing crowd of around 150 people, and authorities called in a small contingent of steel-helmeted Nebraska National Guardsmen to restore order. They cleared the streets without violence, ending Omaha's first wave of racial trouble. It was one thing to taunt the police and another to face troops carrying guns and bayonets. There had been only nine minor injuries and minimal damage. There were no fires or sniping. The only gunfire came when police fired a couple of warning shots into the air. Of the 122 persons arrested, one-third were under eighteen years old and only sixteen were over thirty. At another time the affair might have been written off as a product of teenagers letting off steam during a period of very hot weather, but times were not "normal" in 1966. Any clash involving urban blacks assumed grave implications.

A consensus that the rioters acted spontaneously and received no direction failed to prevent instant observations about the causes. Chambers and young blacks who met with Mayor Sorensen on the last day of the disorders attacked the police response, giving no specific reasons beyond suggesting that arrests the first two nights had inflamed the crowd. In addition, they complained about unemployment and a lack of recreational opportunities. Sorensen said, "I can't say that they were happy with me but they had a good chance to tell their grievances." Initially he said that he did not believe the incidents to be racial in character, but after the National Guard had been deployed, he remarked, "Last night, it was racial all the way." Other comments showed sharply differing perspectives. A member of the City Human Relations Board claimed that both police and blacks involved in the fracas appeared "edgy" and that lawmen ordered "people around like animals." Gov. Frank Morrison of Nebraska, at a Los Angeles governors' conference, told a *World-Herald* reporter in a telephone interview that he saw "an environment that is unfit for human habitation in many areas" as the background of the trouble. The governor rejected force as a solution and expressed faith in the ability of Sorensen and "the Negro leadership of Omaha." By contrast, Omaha public safety director Francis Lynch perceived a disturbing evolution in the rioters' animosity. As he put it, "The first night it was just the cops. The second night it was the damn white cops and the third night it was all the white S.O.B.'s."

Following the July trouble, the city and the Nebraska Department of Labor took steps to help young people on the Near North Side find employment, and the federal Neighborhood Youth Corps eventually provided money for such jobs. The city also rented a hall that was used for dances, and the United Community Services, Omaha's umbrella charitable body, provided services to the ghetto youth.

Another step toward heading off more disturbances came when Sorensen quietly approved the creation of a "Mayor's Patrol" composed of young people who had been part of the group gathering at the parking lot where the trouble had begun. The members of the Mayor's Patrol, which were chosen by their cohorts, were monitors who would be in the vanguard of averting disturbances. Near North Side businessmen reportedly paid the Mayor's Patrol, and Sorensen stated that neither public money nor his own personal funds were going to the group. Nevertheless, two members of the city council objected to the patrol, one saying, "It smells of the old protection racket." When Mayor Richard Daley of Chicago called Sorensen and asked him how he had managed Omaha's disturbance, Sorensen praised the "monitor" approach, noting that Dr. Martin Luther King had recommended it. Thirteen years later, Sorensen declared, "In brief, I put the ring leaders of the rioting on my personal payroll at a nominal salary. . . . Their personal knowledge of each other and every member contributing to the chaos, urging the citizens to go home was the real ingredient that worked."

Nevertheless, the inner city exploded again for three nights in a row in early August. The outbreak was similar to that of the previous month. Again, there was no special pattern, although the mayor said that unlike what had been done after the earlier upheaval, the city would not confer with "the hoodlum element." As before, groups of black teenagers milled around on North Twenty-fourth Street in the late evening and early hours of the morning. Rocks were thrown, and there were several arrests. Roving groups smashed windows and looted stores. There were some fire bombings as un-identified individuals, responding to shotgun blasts fired skyward by police to scatter a crowd of 150, hurled Molotov cocktails through several display windows. While few of the fires caused extensive damage, one destroyed the interior of a cleaning establishment, burning a large quantity of clothing. Several places hit during the July rioting were targets a second time. Sorensen visited businessmen in the stricken area. He discounted rumors linking the violence to the death of a black youth suspected of burglary who had been shot a few days earlier by the police. Taking a hard line, he said, "We simply are not going to tolerate this lawlessness, whether it is teenagers or young adults." Urging African American parents to keep closer track of their chil-dren, he warned, "Many whites wish to help the Negro achieve first-class citi-zenship, but this lawlessness stiffens attitudes and makes it difficult to help." The vandalism ended, but the Skaggs Drug Center at Twenty-fourth and Lake closed permanently.

Seemingly unfazed by the trouble, the city council responded by cutting the budget of the Human Relations Board from $5,000 to $1,750. An aide to Mayor Sorensen confided, "This city is conservative in any case, and there seems to be a lot of suggestions that someone stirred up trouble. For some of these men in the Council it is a natural conclusion that any trouble stirred up would be stirred up by those fellows from the Federal government and the Human Relations Board." This approach was hardly calculated to bring racial progress. Obviously the recent addition of recreational facilities and the promotion of job opportunities for black youths had not been enough to prevent more violence. There were still thousands of unemployed black teenagers, all part of a larger problem. In addition to a lack of opportunity, African Americans complained about the drabness of their surroundings, the failure of authorities to enact open housing legislation, the virtually segre-gated nature of the school system, and police brutality. None of these points of dispute appeared ripe for early change, and the same was true of prevail-ing racial attitudes. "We must remember," the chairman of the Human Rela-tions Board reminded city officials, "that no man, black or white, can truly believe he is equal unless the majority of society around him treats him as an equal. And, as long as the majority persists in treating the Negro as a sec-ond-class citizen, we will have angry outbursts against the double standards of American democracy."

In August Sorensen was one of a number of mayors who testified before a U.S. Senate subcommittee studying the causes of urban violence. He had strongly supported efforts to secure an urban-renewal program in Omaha and noted that "slum lords" had contributed to the defeat of urban renewal. But the mayor contended that most responsibility rested with the people of Omaha for simply having neglected community problems. As he put it,

> The desire for a decent place to live plus the opportunity for a decent job at a decent wage is at the very core and heart of the Negro discontent.
>
> Deplorable living conditions and social unrest go hand in hand. Substandard housing, high levels of unemployment and poverty incomes make family breakdown and social disorder predictable.

Sorensen argued that to address these problems properly much more public funding was needed. In Nebraska part of the problem, he believed, rested at the state level where a "rural legislature" had not distributed tax revenue fairly. His comments revealed a classic problem in American city-state relations when he declared, "The State of Nebraska must accept partial responsibility for the attitudes of our minority citizens, having shown no interest down through the years in the problems of minorities and precious little concern for any of the problems of the cities of Nebraska."

Mayor Sorensen urged that the federal government make a commitment to correcting the problems of urban America that equaled its foreign-aid expenditures. More specifically, he recommended the creation of a "Federal municipal bank" that would provide forty-year low-interest loans to cities. With ample reason he saw Omaha's problems as exemplifying the experiences of cities across the nation.

In the autumn of 1966, the challenge of alleviating racial tension while enforcing the law became a heated public issue. Sorensen said that he had requested the police "to accept abuse during the riot period without retaliation except in self-defense," a practice that he said "is no longer effective." Soon, James Harris, a local NAACP official, voiced concern about "the apparent lack of police protection in known danger areas." Meanwhile, there had been evidence of friction between Sorensen and public safety director Francis Lynch. The matter came to a head on November 3 when a *World-Herald* headline declared, "Lynch Blames Mayor for North Side 'Jungle.'" The ensuing story was based upon a letter that Lynch had sent Sorensen contending that the mayor had mismanaged the city's response to the July troubles. He criticized the creation of the Mayor's Patrol and generally argued that Sorensen was inhibiting vigorous law enforcement on the Near North Side. He was also critical of Chief Ostler, who he said was absent from the "front lines" during the July upheaval. In Lynch's words, "Police action, so-called law enforcement on the Near North Side of Omaha, has been at a standstill since July 4, 1966. Mr. Harris, the NAACP, as well as persons who make their homes and conduct their businesses in this area are well justified to fear for their safety. It is a jungle." As Lynch saw it, some two to three hundred hoodlums were the source of the trouble. He concluded, "They are not an 'employment' problem, nor a 'housing' problem—but a police problem."

Sorensen immediately sought and received Lynch's resignation. Predictably, Lynch's hardline stand on law enforcement gained much more public support than did Sorensen's view, and three city council members supported Lynch's perspective as did officers of fire and police unions. Lynch quickly went on to a good private sector position in New York, and Sorensen named L. K. Smith, who was coordinator of police-community relations, to the office of public safety director. Sorensen later recalled that Chief Ostler and Lynch had clashed from the time Lynch assumed his position. He supported Lynch's contention that Ostler had been a poor leader during the rioting, and he retained respect for Lynch's professional stature. Although the former public safety director gave no evidence of being racially prejudiced, he conveyed the image of the tough cop that reflected Omaha's division in 1966. As Sorensen recalled, "Lynch had an uncanny way of getting black citizens angry with him without saying a thing!" Police matters, always a lightning rod for controversy in city government, would attain a new sensitivity as racial tension rose.

Except for some comparatively minor trouble in September, there was no further violence in 1966. Nor did any serious disturbances happen the following year. A variety of social programs seemed to improve matters to the point that the chair of the Human Relations Board thought Omaha on the road to racial harmony. In the fall of 1966, Sorensen had engaged St. Louis Cardinal pitcher Bob Gibson of Omaha to promote constructive behavior among young people on the Near North Side. In 1967 Gibson, a future Hall of Fame member, pitched three winning games for the Cardinals as they defeated the Boston Red Sox in the World Series. At a large Chamber of Commerce luncheon in Omaha later in October, Sorensen extolled Gibson's efforts on the Near North Side. In his words, "We have had a peaceful summer and we must give some credit to Gibson." A few black militants and white social activists pointed out that all the fundamental problems remained, but no one took them very seriously. Despite some inflammatory "black power" rhetoric, serious racial turmoil appeared over in the city. Unfortunately, it was only a lull.

In March 1968 a week of assaults, vandalism, fire bombings, and fear followed a disturbance at a rally in the City Auditorium for presidential hopeful George Wallace, former governor of Alabama. When the controversial Wallace appeared to address a crowd of 5,400 persons, a group of less than forty sign-carrying black and white demonstrators, strategically situated in front of the podium, booed and jeered, throwing sticks and pieces of wood at him. The obviously agitated Wallace denounced his tormentors, bellowing, "These are the free-speech folks you know. And these are the kind of folks the people of this country are sick and tired of." When many of the blacks sat down after being asked to clear the aisles, Wallace continued, "Those responsible for a breakdown of law and order are not the majority of American people, but a group of activists, militants, and communists." There was renewed disorder— more jeering and thrown sticks—and Wallace stood back, asking the police to clear the aisles. Officers who had quickly lined up in front of the speakers' stand did just that, forming a wedge after a black youth apparently swung a fist at a police captain. The lawmen swept the dissenters from the building. A journalist for the *World-Herald* described the scene: "Folding chairs flew, nightsticks cracked down on heads, and some police used a chemical spray designed for crowd control. Some of the audience jumped in with fists and boots. . . . It was over inside the hall within five minutes. But outside, nine windows were broken and here and there a fight between opposing forces."

Comments made afterward were predictable. Black leaders charged that the police used excessive force and that the demonstrators had in effect been led into a trap, guided by Wallace's supporters to a conspicuous place in front of the hall. Mayor Sorensen contended the police acted "superbly" in what he called a clash in an "emotional environment" between "black power advocates and white bigots." He added that he hoped Wallace would not return to Omaha.

The days of black rage that followed the Wallace disturbances caused less destruction than those of 1966. An off-duty policeman armed with a riot gun shot and killed a sixteen-year-old black male after he refused to halt on command, but it was unclear whether his death was related to an attempted jewelry store robbery or to racial strife. Only a few other persons required hospitalization, and there were not many arrests. Yet the trouble had a more direct impact on white Omahans because it spilled out of the Near North Side. There were numerous incidents at Omaha schools, including the large downtown Central High School. Black students chanted "Black Power" slogans in the study halls and frightened teachers and white pupils. African American teenagers broke windows at several schools; at predominantly black North High School, there was trouble in the parking lot as roving gangs of blacks taunted the police. Fear swept through the white community. People temporarily kept their children at home. At almost entirely white schools, there were disruptions caused by rumors that "they"—meaning blacks—were on the way to spark violence. As quickly as it had come, the trouble passed. There was no new outbreak even after the murder of Martin Luther King Jr., which touched off severe civil disorders in many large American cities.

The primary result of the Omaha disturbances was to at least temporarily polarize sides. Inner-city opinion crystallized around charges of "unresponsiveness." City officials warned of the consequences of violent acts by members of both races. "Why don't they do what every minority did?" a white housewife from the west side of town asked. "Why don't they pick themselves up by their bootstraps?" A black laborer informed of the remark replied, "They tell me to pick myself up by my bootstraps. Why, hell, they've taken away my boots."

The Near North Side remained peaceful following an early-hour incident on Memorial Day 1968 when a police officer shot and killed a black youth who ignored a command to stop when fleeing from a car after a high-speed chase. The Safeway parking lot again became the focal point for trouble shortly after 2:30 on a Sunday morning in July following trouble at the city-operated Near North Side recreational center. For some forty-five minutes police encountered sniper fire. No snipers were caught, but one person was injured while being arrested. Soon, the Safeway store followed the example of its former neighbor Skaggs Drug Center and went out of business. Violence, if sporadic, was taking its toll on the economy of that part of the city and Sorensen said, it "is a rare day when I don't get a call from a Near North Side businessman saying that his insurance has been cancelled." By the mid-1960s, the Near North Side was experiencing business decline, and the troubles of 1966 and after aggravated the problem.

Looking back, 1968 rivals 1919 as probably the worst year in the history of twentieth-century America from the standpoint of violence and internal tension. The Martin Luther King Jr. and Robert Kennedy assassinations, the upheaval at the Democratic National Convention in Chicago, and the tumult in Omaha and other cities, like the racial violence of 1919, boded ill for the nation's future. Then, in 1969 three nights of rioting and burning swept over the Near North Side in response to the shooting and killing of a fourteen-year-old black girl by a police officer. The following year, a policeman called to a Near North Side residence to investigate a reported assault, walked into an apparent trap and was killed when he came upon a suitcase bomb that exploded. Two men affiliated with the Black Panther Party, known for its hatred of the police, received sentences of life imprisonment. Throughout the 1970s race continued in the forefront as an Omaha problem, but after the 1969 upheaval no major outbreaks occurred in the inner city. In a sense the riots served a purpose; they conclusively demonstrated the gulf that existed between blacks and whites. As an outgrowth, there were genuine efforts to open lines of communication and to solve Near North Side problems. Upon reflection, the gap between the West Omaha matron and the black laborer did not appear insurmountable.

CALMER TIMES

In the meantime the law had become a much more powerful tool for ending discrimination in housing. Starting in 1963, state senator Edward Danner, an African American from the Near North Side, had worked unsuccessfully in the Nebraska legislature to bar discrimination in real-state transactions. Foes saw such legislation as an intrusion upon property rights. Realtors, favoring a voluntary approach to ending discrimination, saw it as a potential burden to their business. Critics also took issue with other details of the proposed bills. Matters began to change in 1968 when Congress enacted a law banning racial discrimination in housing, and the U.S. Supreme Court held that racial discrimination in housing violated an 1866 federal statute. With federal policy clear and the strong support of Gov. Norbert T. Tiemann, Senator Danner secured the adoption of the Nebraska Civil Rights Act of 1969 that barred ethnic, racial, and religious discrimination in housing transactions.

There were other reasons for the relative calm. The police became more skilled at riot control and came under pressure to be fairer in dealings with blacks. Militants lost favor and either moderated their stands or gave way to others with a milder message. Chambers became a state senator who earned a reputation as a steadfast and effective champion of his Near North Side constituents. While much diversity remained in the black community—one thing whites learned from the confrontations was that blacks did not speak with one voice—there was a reestablishment of Urban League and NAACP leadership along with that of the African American churches. Of paramount importance was the channeling of money into the city core for jobs and social-action programs. Increased efforts to aid black teenagers in the summer months helped prevent a recurrence of what had happened in 1966. While some of the funds came from city, county, and state sources, the greatest amounts flowed from the largesse of the federal government, even under Republican administrations. Any opposition stemmed from charges of waste and corruption in the running of specific projects; the influx of Washington monies was taken for granted. So was government involvement in the school system. A shrill but limited outcry was heard in the fall of 1976 when the Omaha Public Schools started busing students as mandated by the United States Eighth Circuit Court of Appeals. The school board worked closely with the court to work out a plan. An interracial committee, Concerned Citizens for Omaha, which had strong business backing, helped to prepare citizens for the transition, as did the local media. Even though there had been no millennium, the Omaha racial climate appeared better on the surface in 1980 than in 1970.

In the 1960s the black population had expanded westward from its core east of North Thirtieth Street, and from 1970 to 1985 advanced well to the north and northwest. In the meantime, the core—from Cuming Street to Ames Avenue and Sixteenth to Thirtieth streets—steadily lost residents and business. Between 1960 and 1990 the area's population fell from 29,655 to 9,190. Memories of the rioting of the late 1960s and a continuing perception that the Near North Side was a hotbed of crime undoubtedly hindered revitalization. The completion of the controlled access North Freeway in the late 1980s meant uprooted families and disrupted neighborhoods—an experience for African Americans similar to the building of I-480 through a working-class white neighborhood a generation earlier.

Deteriorated housing remained a severe problem in areas of North Omaha, and a common answer was city-imposed demolition. In 1986 city planning director Marty Shukert said that there were between three and five thousand vacant lots in the Near North Side. However, the administrations of Mayor Al Veys and his successor in 1981, Mike Boyle, shifted toward an "urban homestead" program by which federal block-grant money was used to renovate deteriorated dwellings and to assist eligible individuals in purchasing these houses. Such funds came to be used for programs for home renovation and repair and, in conjunction with private investment, expanding the supply of rental dwellings. Between 1986 and 1991 $21 million in federal money was channeled into housing redevelopment in Omaha.

Related to racial disharmony was a quickening of white movement to the suburbs. This process, which started after World War II with the building of the first tract subdivisions in Omaha, had a dramatic impact on housing patterns. Many older neighborhoods underwent fundamental changes. South Omaha progressively deteriorated. While many of the older foreign-born continued to live in the old Magic City, it had lost much of its ethnic flavor even though most of the members of Omaha's Hispanic community lived there. There was little in the way of new construction; many houses had fallen into varying states of disrepair; I-80 divided the community; and the commercial district had badly decayed. Although many second- and third-generation Omahans, usually of modest means, resided in South Omaha, many had moved away. "We don't visit South Omaha much, partly because it isn't the same," a former resident wrote. "Oh from time to time a group of us will drive into near-downtown South Omaha for lunch in the original steakhouse territory, and I still get a kick out of negotiating those narrow, steep hills and admiring those small, peak-roof houses. South Omaha has character." South Omaha's problems mirrored those of other older parts of town.

An area of West Omaha called New Rockbrook, which in 1970 contained many winding roads and numerous stylish homes, served as a prime example of the kind of new neighborhood in which Omahans aspired to live. Census statistics indicated that 80 percent of the houses had been built since 1960. Of the 8,854 residents, 44 percent were under eighteen years of age and 2 percent more than sixty-five years old. Over 99 percent of the people were white, and 58 percent had attended college. The median income of $16,638 was higher than other parts of town. By the 1980s there was a great deal of talk, much of it related to a national energy crisis and rising housing costs, about a return of the middle class to the inner city. Still, statistics showed that the outward march had not stopped and that its racial character remained unchanged. Suburban blacks remained relatively few in number.

Contrasting to New Rockbrook's affluence, the 1970 census delineated a belt of territory in the eastern part of the city where there were many low-income people. It included the inner city and adjoining sections in north and east Omaha and ran through downtown and the east central part of the city including a narrow strip in the far south. Among its 49,297 residents aged sixteen and older were 11,651 persons whose incomes were "below the poverty level." That poverty transcended race was evident in the fact that 6,824 of these persons were white and 4,602 were black. The median family income of the area was $6,499, and of the 28,025 black or white persons aged sixteen and older who were in the work force, 3,668 or slightly over 13 percent had one year or more of college education.

The strong sense of European ethnicity that had once characterized Omaha had disappeared by the later years of the twentieth century. Indeed, the 1990 census indicated that only 14,615 persons in the Omaha Metropolitan Statistical Area were foreign-born. Nevertheless, the census revealed multiple ethnic backgrounds, and this information, albeit based upon sampling, showed that the traditional European heritage of the people of the Greater Omaha area was intact.

In 1990 the metropolitan area was home to 618,262 people. Of this number 82,628 resided in Pottawattamie County, Iowa, and 535,634 lived in the Nebraska portion that now included Washington County, north of Omaha, as well as Douglas and Sarpy counties. The metro had 15,274 persons of Hispanic extraction, primarily with Mexican roots. Heralding future growth, Omaha's 1990 Hispanic population of 9,703 was up from 7,319 in 1980. Council Bluffs had 1,167 persons of Hispanic background in 1990. Blacks, numbering 51,036, remained the urban area's principal ethnic minority. Omaha had 43,829 African American residents, up from 37,864 in 1980, but only 409 blacks lived in Council Bluffs. Particularly noteworthy was the fact that the census showed 6,798 blacks "not in [the] central city"—which meant that they resided in Bellevue and other parts of suburbia.

A generation after the full thrust of the civil-rights movement came to northern cities and two generations after the notable civil rights efforts in post–World War II Omaha, census data starkly reflected a continuing black disadvantage. In Omaha, median income for black households in 1989 was $15,341 compared to $28,965 for white households. Omaha's black unemployment level in 1990 was 13.4 percent, while the figure for whites was 3.5 percent. Education levels revealed another sharp contrast. In Omaha, 9.4 percent of blacks who were at least twenty-five years of age held baccalaureate or advanced degrees, while 24.7 percent of white Omahans had similar credentials.

The measurable plight of the 6,798 blacks not residing in the central city was far better. They had a median household income of $32,068, and their unemployment rate was 5.8 percent. These suburban blacks possessed an educational level slightly higher than that of whites not residing in the central city. Although 66.2 percent of the whites and 58.9 percent of the blacks living in Omaha proper were Nebraska natives, 56.8 percent of the whites and only 25.3 percent of the blacks residing in the metro outside the central city were natives. This suggested that Omaha was attracting African American professionals from outside the area but that many upwardly mobile native blacks were seeking opportunities elsewhere. In any event, life was materially better for the comparatively few blacks living in the suburbs as opposed to the Near North Side or "North Omaha" as it, perhaps euphemistically, had come to be called.

OMAHA AND COUNCIL BLUFFS

As in the past, Omaha surpassed Council Bluffs in some key socioeconomic indicators. In 1970 geographer Joseph W. Preusser pointed to a serious problem of blighted residential areas in Council Bluffs. Identifying twenty-one residential sections or "neighborhoods," he concluded that on the basis of property upkeep, education, income, and other socioeconomic data, one was a "slum," four were "excessively blighted," and only four of the remaining sixteen had "minimal blight." The railroads, Preusser noted, had been the "driving force" in the development of Council Bluffs, but their massive physical presence dissuaded improvements in land use. As he put it, "Railroads tend to be among the most inflexible elements in an urban pattern owing to the capital investment they represent." Adding to the problem was inadequate local tax revenue from the railroads and their recent decline as providers of jobs. Additionally, he pointed to division between the "business and professional people" who resided in the eastern part of town and the working class who resided "west of the tracks"; negative attitudes toward Omaha, especially in the east; and inadequate civic leadership as some of the realities that had thwarted the development of Council Bluffs. The result was an image of a "dirty" place, a city lacking "progressive enthusiasm" that was not keeping up with Omaha.

Nearly two decades later, basic data still showed a disparity between the cities. Per capita income in 1989 was $13,957 in Omaha and $11,318 in Council Bluffs. In Omaha 27.1 percent of employed persons over sixteen years of age held managerial or professional positions in contrast to 17.8 percent in Council Bluffs. Similarly, Omaha households had a median income of $26,927 compared to $25,014 in the Iowa community. The figures for both cities were well below the median household income of $30,323 for the entire Metropolitan Statistical Area, a number that probably bespoke the relative affluence of suburban Douglas and Sarpy counties. Data on education showed that 24.7 percent of Omaha's white residents at least twenty-five years old held a bachelor's or graduate degree in contrast to 10.1 percent of such persons in Council Bluffs.

HIGHER EDUCATION

Omaha benefited from other developments that did much to solve long-standing problems in higher education. At the start of the 1960s, college education opportunities for Omaha high-school graduates were somewhat limited. The closest large public institution was the University of Nebraska–Lincoln. It had evolved over many decades into a respectable university with a broad range of undergraduate and graduate programs. Its strong emphasis on agriculture reflected its land-grant status. The many students from Omaha tended to major in the liberal arts, business, and engineering. The 1960s marked a resurgence to national stature of the Nebraska football team, and the Big Red had a large and enthusiastic following in Omaha. In Omaha, the University of Nebraska College of Medicine brought an ever-increasing amount of money into the community. Even so, it was more of a hospital than a school, and its educational components had small enrollments. It was inaccessible to all except a few fortunate and talented Omaha students.

That left two local principal choices, one private and the other public. Jesuit-operated Creighton University had a large endowment, rigorous entrance requirements, and relatively high tuition. In addition to a liberal arts college, Creighton had several professional schools including medicine, pharmacy, dentistry, and law. The nationally recognized Catholic university was the alma mater of many of Omaha's leaders. In the 1960s school officials began a modernization program, building new dormitories, classrooms, a library, and massive medical facilities. Creighton, which had fewer than five thousand students, was not designed to serve the educational needs of all segments of Omaha life.

The alternative was the University of Omaha, in the early 1960s one of the few remaining municipal universities in the United States. Established by local Protestant leaders as a private institution in 1908, it gained municipal status—and a much-needed city tax levy—in 1931. The school attracted many fine young faculty but was unable to keep most of them. Critics, probably as an expression of snobbery rather than actual knowledge of the institution, referred to it as "West Dodge High." The library was small. Faculty members had heavy teaching loads and little time for research and writing. By the mid-1960s the University of Omaha had some six thousand students and ample evidence of promise, but a highly inflexible financial base derived from its property tax jeopardized its future.

In three years the university changed drastically. Milo Bail, its president since 1948, retired in 1965. He had ably managed OU's finances and had boosted the school's public stature, but his authoritarian mode of leadership was increasingly ill-suited to academe. His successor, Leland Traywick, allowed more faculty involvement in decision making, but the regents were displeased with his leadership and soon ousted him. In the meantime, in 1963 and 1966 the voters of Omaha had rejected proposals to raise the university's tax levy. For years, the University of Omaha had promoted itself as a higher-education option for persons of modest means, but in four ballot proposals between 1930 and 1966 its maximum support had come from the more affluent parts of the city. OU found itself in a paradox: its sizeable full- and part-time enrollment attested to its popularity in the community, but most voters were unwilling to raise its tax support. The solution was the same as in other states—a merger, almost always with a larger university in a smaller town—and the creation of a "system." After a publicity campaign, lengthy negotiations, and legislative action, in late 1967 the Omaha electorate approved merging OU with the University of Nebraska. While much remained to be done, the opportunity and resources appeared at hand to build a better public university in Omaha.

The new University of Nebraska at Omaha, formally established in 1968, aspired to become an "urban university." This apparently meant that it hoped to offer quality education and to marshal the necessary resources to solve a wide range of urban concerns. President Kirk Naylor, who had had a major role in engineering the merger, said, "We're virtually building a new university. . . . We are changing the image of the university to that of a great urban institution. We hope to have the same relationship to the city that land grant universities have had historically to the agricultural areas." He planned to measure success in terms of the impact of UNO on the community, rather than in regard to scholarly papers written or doctoral degrees awarded.

Over the next two decades the university added many faculty members and a number of programs. New buildings and careful landscaping gave the campus an evermore impressive and attractive appearance. By the end of the 1970s, the campus boasted fifteen thousand full- and part-time students, but the urban university concept took different turns than expected. Although a Center for Applied Urban Research and a number of new programs and courses focused upon the city, much of UNO's development followed traditional lines or moved into new areas, most notably computer science. A geography professor pioneered an Afghanistan-studies program that developed into broader activities in international studies. The Omaha campus attracted many foreign students. When Afghanistan came to be a point of conflict in the Cold War and after, the United States Agency for International Development contracted with UNO to educate Afghan teachers and prepare textbooks for their nation's schools.

As to be expected, there was a tendency on the Lincoln campus to see the merger with UNO as the classic shotgun marriage and to view UNO as a rival for state tax funds. Such ill feelings were reciprocated: after an administrator referred to Lincoln as the "flagship campus," the term was used sneeringly at UNO. Intercampus rivalries were durable, but they eased as a generation passed. In the meantime, a clash between the UNO faculty and administration over "merit" salary increases culminated in unionization. Following merger, expectations for faculty research and publication at UNO became typical of the norms for medium-sized public universities. Whatever the problems of adjustment that it produced, merger brought financial resources to UNO that were demonstrably beneficial to its development.

Large donations from Charles and Margre Durham and Willis and Janet Strauss were among the contributions from local business leaders that fostered a dramatic expansion of the UNO campus in the generation after merger. A short distance across town, the University of Nebraska Medical Center would also benefit from such gifts. Fifteen million dollars of the $61.3 million cost of the Lied Transplant Center, which opened in 1998, came from the Lied Foundation Trust, and other donors contributed a similar sum for the structure that did much to enhance UNMC's work in organ transplantation. In 2003 UNMC completed the Durham Research Center with an undisclosed contribution from Charles W. "Chuck" Durham, former CEO of HDR, a large architectural and engineering company, and money from other local business and medical leaders. Given the reality that the success of research institutions was measured largely by their ability to acquire grants, UNMC leaders anticipated that the Durham Research Center would attract scholars who would do much to improve the flow of such funds to UNMC. In 2004 Durham made a contribution for the construction of a companion building.

By this time, Creighton University was modernizing its medical-education facilities. The Hixson-Lied Science Building, completed in 2003, represented an effort to advance undergraduate and medical instruction. Like UNMC, the Creighton Medical Center recognized the need to achieve greater external funding for research. On another front, Creighton, near the northwestern edge of downtown Omaha, gained valuable space with the purchase and demolition in 2002–3 of what had been a fifteen-story public-housing apartment building. The redevelopment of this land would be consistent with a host of projects reshaping the area immediately northeast of downtown.

Bellevue's rapid growth led business leaders in that community to establish Bellevue College in 1966, a secular private institution bearing the same name as a Presbyterian-affiliated school that had functioned between 1884 and 1919. The new Bellevue College experienced problems usually associated with embryonic institutions, but its proximity to Offutt Air Force Base and

Omaha facilitated the hiring of faculty and recruitment of students. Richard Winchell, the school's third president, was an effective leader and a good fund raiser. In time, Bellevue College, now Bellevue University, won academic accreditation, developed an array of programs, and emerged as an important provider of higher education to students in the metropolitan area.

Meanwhile, the College of St. Mary, a Catholic institution, offered a variety of programs suited to the needs of an urban student body. Clarkson College and Nebraska Methodist College, growing out of nursing schools, offered degrees in health-related programs. Grace University, formerly Grace Bible College, granted baccalaureate and master's degrees. By the start of the twenty-first century, the tax-supported Metropolitan Community College, from its four campuses, offered many two-year associate programs.

BUILDING THE CULTURAL BASE

Other Omaha cultural agencies experienced vicissitudes. Many of the difficulties related to the change of Omaha into a white-collar town. For the first time in the city's history, there was a broad interest in cultural pursuits. However, this had not as yet translated into more comprehensive funding of institutions. The Joslyn Art Museum, long considered the city's most prestigious institution, had a succession of problems, with conditions reaching serious proportions in the 1970s. Lagging contributions and rising costs forced financial retrenchment and public requests for funds. The museum cut back on educational programs and drastically curtailed art purchases. Before anonymous donors came to the rescue, it appeared at one point that the Joslyn would have to sell off around $1 million in art works from its collections as a temporary measure to solve a growing deficit. Some critics contended that the troubles were a direct result of the Joslyn's elitist orientation. They argued that the building had a "stuffy" atmosphere, that it rejected twentieth-century art, and that its permanent exhibits, especially the parts that emphasized nineteenth-century Americana, had little general appeal. Less than 150,000 persons visited the museum annually; and many of those came to view special temporary shows—the art of Norman Rockwell, the photographs of Lord Snowdon, and paintings of University of Nebraska Big Red football players. A Jamie Wyeth exhibition drew six thousand patrons in a week.

Other events in the city included the rock group Chicago, which attracted eleven thousand people in a single-night concert. Creighton University's basketball team, which played in the Missouri Valley Conference, had over nine thousand spectators for many games. The Kansas City Kings of the National Basketball Association drew well for the games they played in Omaha during much of the 1970s. A minor-league American Association baseball team, the Omaha Royals, averaged over two hundred thousand fans annually during the course of the decade.

The art gallery appeared stagnant by contrast. In 1975 the Joslyn management tried to generate interest through an energetic advertising campaign. It featured such slogans as "Joslyn—Your Friendly Neighborhood Art Museum" and "A Little Culture Never Hurt Anybody." The effort, which temporarily sharply increased attendance and attracted some new members, alienated the Joslyn's traditional constituents, the advocates of art for art's sake and the affluent contributors. "Public relations is all right," said a critic, "but the Joslyn needs to do more for art." Some felt the "selling" of the Joslyn undignified and uncalled for, cheapening the end product. In response, the director claimed that museums throughout the country were all trying similar methods to curry favor. Manya Nogg, chairman of the drive, said, "A lot of people are intimidated by the Joslyn before they ever go in. My big crusade is to let people know we're not that stuffy and we do care." The prospect of a large gift did not materialize, and changes in directors accomplished little. By 1980 hopes for a renaissance rested upon a change in policy that would see to a phasing out of Americana that seemed to have little relationship to art.

The prelude to major change was a report by the well-known local architectural firm, Leo A. Daly Company, that Joslyn had far too little space for galleries. Sarah Joslyn, who had donated the money for the building, was primarily interested in music, and the visual arts were a secondary consideration in the configuration of the building. In 1987 the Joslyn board was reconstituted to include Omaha's top business leaders, and in 1989 a new director was hired. Such was the prelude to a fund drive that in the 1990s would bring an extensive addition to the museum. As with the revitalization of the eastern part of downtown then in progress and virtually any large civic undertaking, it was Omaha's executive elite who would get the job done.

Raising operating money was the biggest problem faced by Omaha's many and varied cultural institutions. One reason for the Joslyn's troubles was that inflation forced it to look for additional finances; its endowment, which had seemed large fifty years earlier, was no longer enough. By the 1970s Omaha had a number of small performing-arts companies that added to the richness of community life. Most lived hand-to-mouth existences, hoping that some-day a benefactor would come along and put them on their feet. In addition, there were larger and better-publicized organizations such as the Omaha Symphony Orchestra, the Omaha Civic Opera, the Omaha Community Play-house, the Henry Doorly Zoo, the Orpheum Theater, and the Western Her-itage Museum. Their funds came from several sources. The orchestra and opera relied on ticket sales, foundation grants, a close working relationship with UNO, and federal aid. The zoo, operated by a nonprofit organization, received several hundred thousand dollars annually from city coffers. The Orpheum Theater, donated by Ak-Sar-Ben to the city, received an annual public appropriation. The Western Heritage Museum, founded in 1973 by a nonprofit organization, had its headquarters in the former Union Station, given to Omaha by the Union Pacific Railroad. A proliferation of cultural institutions was a relatively recent phenomenon. Few had roots more than a decade old. Even the symphony, by local standards a long-established insti-tution, had evolved from the work of the Women's Division of the Chamber of Commerce in the 1920s.

While there seemed to be general agreement that the Western Heritage Museum, which planned to emphasize area history, was a good idea, its estab-lishment illustrated the difficulties. The building needed work, and it would take several years to develop exhibits that would make the operation self-sup-porting. Mayor Edward Zorinsky, after he had alienated the biggest potential donor, the Union Pacific, by raising questions about why it gave the building to the city in the first place, tried to cut off a direct cash subsidy by the city to the museum. As he observed, "The key to a AAA credit rating isn't to say yes to everyone who asks for money." Nevertheless, the city provided timely financial help, and with effective fund raising Western Heritage survived. Di-rector Michael Kinzel believed that there were many potential donors in the city who were not interested in Joslyn or the symphony who would support a regional history museum. Attorney Ron Hunter, president of Western Heri-tage, worked energetically to advance the project. By 1980 there seemed to be a growing recognition by civic leaders, the city government, and the public that a city the size of Omaha needed a well-rounded cultural mix. Western Heritage benefited from this perception, and in the 1980s the Union Station

15. Interior of Western Heritage Museum, Omaha, 1979. *Courtesy Niel M. Johnson.*

was refurbished, a process greatly assisted by a matching grant of $2.7 million from Omaha's Kiewit Foundation. Professional development of exhibits made the museum an increasingly interesting place to visit.

A BRIEF EMBARRASSMENT OF RICHES

A venerable Omaha institution, Boys Town, came in for criticism for supposedly having too much money. From a modest start in 1917 in an old Omaha mansion that housed twenty-five wayward boys, it became by the 1970s the best-known child-care home in the country. Boys Town's 1,500-acre campus, then just west of Omaha, was an incorporated village with its own mailing address. The seven hundred boys, who lived in what a publicity brochure called a "home-school-city," received an education through high school and learned vocational skills. The founder of Boys Town was Father Edward J. Flanagan, an Irish-born Roman Catholic priest. When he had first visited Omaha in 1912 on his way to an assignment in rural Nebraska, he became so concerned about the plight of the poor that he soon returned to the city. Under his leadership Boys Town, originally named Father Flanagan's Boys' Home, struggled along for many years, narrowly overcoming recurrent financial adversities. An excellent publicist, Flanagan had little financial talent, but he tended to think in grandiose terms. Before his sudden death in 1948 while on a mission to Europe to study youth problems for the White House, he believed his dream of a "city of little men" approached realization.

The turning point had come in 1937 when a Hollywood studio produced the immensely popular film *Boys Town*, featuring Spencer Tracy as Father Flanagan and Mickey Rooney as a homeless youth. Through ingenious direct-mail campaigns, Boys Town accumulated an ever-larger amount of money, most of which went into profitable investments. The managing board, under the jurisdiction of the archbishop of Omaha, included many local business leaders and a few social workers. As the years passed, there was a nagging feeling that Boys Town had lost a sense of purpose, that it had not kept up with the times, and that business considerations superseded helping boys. On March 30, 1972, a special report that was to win a Pulitzer Prize in journalism for the weekly *Omaha Sun* newspapers showed that Boys Town had a net worth of $200 million and that the amount increased every year by around $25 million. The "liquid endowment" of $176 million was larger than that of any other of the nation's Roman Catholic schools. By way of comparison,

Creighton's was $6.8 million and the University of Notre Dame's was $64.8 million. Even though the endowment had risen to approximately $250,000 per boy, aggressive fund raising continued. A downtown Omaha office operated by Boys Town solicited donations by sending out thirty-four million letters annually, which contained heartrending appeals. The editor of *Sun* newspapers charged:

> Though millions of Americans have sent in checks and cash—most of widow's mite proportions—Boys Town has never felt it necessary to tell them where the money was going. Rather than relating its successes and reporting its accumulation of stocks, bonds, and mortgages, Boys Town has continued to plead as if it had the sheriff at the door and an empty coal bin. This approach bordered on institutional arrogance.

Although the money continued to roll in, the directors initiated new programs. By 1977 a Boys Town National Research Hospital, specializing in hearing, speech, and other learning problems in children, was part of the Creighton University campus. In 1979 the acceptance of five girls at Boys Town was another indication of an expansion of the organization's mission. Through the next decade Boys Town's principal operations remained in Omaha, but by 1989 it was spending 43 percent of its budget in other places. In 2005 the organization, now known as Girls and Boys Town, served over 46,000 youngsters across the country, and the following year opened long-planned homes in Washington DC.

TROUBLES WITH NATURE

During its first 140 years, Omaha had experienced only a few natural disasters. Long hot summers and cold winters were a matter of course on the edge of the Great Plains. A Missouri River flood in 1881, considered "great" in retrospect, hurt Council Bluffs more than Omaha. A 1943 flood inundated the Municipal Airport, and the 1952 flood, although precariously contained, was an important inspiration for business leaders to establish the Omaha Industrial Foundation, which effectively assisted firms in acquiring factory sites well removed from the river valley. In a few years Corps of Engineers dams on the upper Missouri made the flood plain safe for development, but as one scholar noted, "the [Omaha Industrial Foundation]'s activities facilitated the decentralization of industry in the city."

The Easter Sunday tornado of March 23, 1913, was Omaha's worst disaster. Just before 6:00 p.m., a tornado entered the southwestern part of the city and ripped a quarter-mile-wide swath of devastation on a six-mile northeastward path. In all, 140 persons died from storm-related causes; about 1,800 dwellings were damaged or wrecked, displacing upwards of 2,500 people. The estimated damage came to $5 million, the equivalent of over $92 million in 2003. The death toll was especially high in the heart of the African American community along North Twenty-fourth Street. In and around Council Bluffs, the storm claimed eleven lives and wrought damages of three hundred thousand dollars.

Mayor Dahlman, heeding the Commercial Club's anxiety about Omaha's image, declared that the city did not need external aid but soon changed his stance. American Red Cross assistance was especially helpful, and money came from across the nation and abroad. Meanwhile, Maj. Carl Hartmann, who commanded the Army Signal Corps unit at Fort Omaha, quickly sent troops to render aid. Fortunately, Hartmann and a subordinate had disaster-relief experience in San Francisco after that city's 1906 earthquake. The Nebraska National Guard was soon on hand. Business and civic leaders, school-teachers, and the Commercial Club did much to achieve a well-planned relief and recovery effort. In July 1914 Omaha voters, apparently satisfied with the pace of recovery, rejected a bond issue for further work.

In January 1975 a two-day blizzard, called the "Century Storm," hit the city. Not quite four months later, on May 6, a mammoth tornado with three tails struck the west-central part of Omaha just before 5:00 p.m. The worst impact area was along Seventy-second Street, a main commercial thorough-fare. A great finger of the storm touched down and stayed on the ground for several miles, racing south to north along the street, smashing buildings in all directions before eventually rising and vanishing into the atmosphere. A stunned survivor recounted, "It was like being in a rainstorm of bottles, plaster, and everything else." Three persons died—many more would have if there had not been some advance warning—and property damage amounted to an estimated $100 million. A large motel complex was almost completely flattened. In the aftermath of the disaster, rebuilding proceeded quickly, helped by federal funds.

In the three decades from 1960 to 1990, as had so often been true in the past, life in metropolitan Omaha exemplified life in urban America. Legislation and court action brought an end to de facto racial segregation, but for many black Omahans achieving success as normally perceived in late-twentieth-century America remained disturbingly elusive. In Omaha, as across the land, social and economic changes during these three decades brought more women into the workplace. Women made up about one-third of the Greater Omaha work force in 1960 and almost one-half in 1990. Reflecting the traditional employment pattern, in 1990 many women filled "administrative support," cashier, clerical, sales, and "service occupations." As in the past, most elementary and secondary teachers were women, and they continued to fill many health-care positions. In addition, women now held over 41 percent of what the census termed "executive, administrative, and managerial positions." Public-safety positions remained male-dominated, but by 1990, 64 of the 1,382 police officers and firefighters in the metropolitan area were female. Race- and gender-based pay and other employment issues remained important, but metropolitan Omaha had changed a great deal between 1960 and 1990.

But by most measures and perceptions the extremes were muted: the problems of the Near North Side, while serious, did not loom as large as those of Los Angeles or many other cities. The sharp decline of the packing industry, while serious, did not leave the city's economy in shambles. Omaha grew significantly, but its growth did not rival that of Sun Belt cities such as Dallas, Houston, Phoenix, Tucson, and San Diego, all of which had begun the twentieth century as far smaller places. Political leaders emphasized Omaha's AAA municipal credit rating—the top level in such matters—but the city's AAA professional baseball team, one level below the major leagues, probably was an accurate reflection of Omaha's stature in urban America. Omahans seemed tacitly mindful of this and like other Midwesterners seemed to accept and often were pleased with the reality that Nebraska and Iowa were not in the vanguard of new social trends.

Indeed, the term "Midwest" and the increasingly popular one "Heartland" implied a muting of extremes, including the pace of change. This had its positive aspects: less social unrest, less traffic, less pollution. It also fostered implications of inferiority—that Omaha and the region had less to offer than better-known places. Indeed, this was often an explanation for the fantastic devotion of the people of the city and the state to University of Nebraska Cornhusker football. In a state without mountains, seashore, salubrious winters, or major-league sports, chants of "Go Big Red" on Saturday afternoons in the autumn bespoke a desire to be foremost in something. This exception aside, Omahans shared a Midwestern diffidence that may have masked a sense of inferiority. More likely, it reflected a trepidation that people on both coasts or in glitzier urban centers might deem their way of life inferior or their city dull.

Joseph Levine, conductor of the Omaha Symphony Orchestra, noted this trepidation in a 1960 article, "Omaha, I Love You," which appeared in the *Saturday Evening Post.* The maestro, an easterner tired of worldwide touring, wrote, "It seemed to me that Midwesterners wavered between intense pride in their accomplishments and a feeling of deep inferiority. They took an almost masochistic delight in running themselves down in front of me, perhaps to watch me defend the considerable strides I thought were being made. . . . I sensed a restlessness, an invigorating sense of excitement in the air, where good music and art are still adventures. It was a marked change from the East, where there is a surfeit of artistic events. There was no apathy, no boredom here."

A decade later, Kenneth Woodward, the religious editor of *Newsweek* and a former Omahan, claimed the city suffered from a massive inferiority complex. As the 1970s progressed, Omahans remained defensive about their community. The attitude was, as a resident observed, "What in the hell ever happened in Omaha?" However, a 1974 study in *Harper's* by Arthur M. Lewis concluded that Omaha ranked tenth in quality among large places in which to live in the United States. Chicago, St. Louis, Kansas City, Denver, and Minneapolis–St. Paul were larger; but that did not dim the accomplishments on the edge of the Nebraska plains. By the 1980s the continuing development of higher education in Omaha, the improvement of the city's cultural institutions, and the extensive downtown redevelopment reflected a common desire to build an even better quality of life.

[12] Reviving Council Bluffs

After the sharp decline of the meat-packing industry and the stunning depar-ture of HNG/InterNorth, Omaha adjusted to new circumstances. Coping with economic change in the mid to late twentieth century was more difficult for Council Bluffs. As the *Nonpareil* had lamented in 1967, the city had been in "the economic doldrums . . . for many years," and the situation remained es-sentially the same through the next decade. In the late 1970s and early 1980s inflation and rapidly rising property taxes encouraged local and state leaders in Iowa to search for new sources of revenue. In 1978 Mayor Ronald Cleve-land of Council Bluffs recommended that the state permit the establishment in his city of a dog-racing track with pari-mutuel betting. Indeed, in the 1940s a dog track had flourished there until the foes of gambling prevailed. By the late 1970s "adult" bookstores and movies of the same genre, plus an atmosphere that suggested that the city had not kept pace with the times, impaired the image of Council Bluffs. Given a huge jump in the county tax levy and other realities, Mayor Cleveland said, "I am confident that a pari-mutuel dog track will help our city significantly meet these spiraling costs. I certainly feel that pari-mutuel betting would be a much healthier activity to generate revenue from our community than the porno shops and the prob-lems we are having with alcohol."

In 1983 the Iowa legislature, with the backing of Gov. Terry Branstad ad-opted a statute permitting the establishment of pari-mutuel betting at dog- and horse-racing tracks. Such tracks were to be operated by nonprofit or-ganizations under the governance of a State Racing Commission. The state would receive 5 percent of the "handle" and an additional 1 percent of this sum would be equally divided between the county and city in which a track was located. The leaders in promoting a dog track at Council Bluffs were officials of Westfair, the county fair organization, and the Chamber of Commerce. With the blessing of the city council, an Iowa West Racing Association, structured along the lines of Ak-Sar-Ben, which ran the horse-racing track in Omaha, was created to bring a dog track to fruition.

Next came the related challenges of securing a license from the State Racing Commission and the millions of dollars needed for the development of a track and related facilities. A loan from the Council Bluffs Industrial Foundation permitted Iowa West Racing Association to start planning work, and by the spring of 1984 that organization had narrowed its search for a prospective track site to an area near the intersection of Interstate Highways 29 and 80. The location offered easy access to Omaha, the prime market for the track. To help finance the project, Iowa West gained city-council permission to issue $12 million in industrial development revenue bonds. Such bonds would not become a municipal liability, and their tax-exempt status was intended to make them attractive to a bank.

The process of securing a track moved relatively slowly due to necessary changes in the racing law and a problem in securing a firm that would handle financing and later manage the operation. Finally, in August 1984 Iowa West Racing Association got its license, and by December a firm known as Alabama-Iowa Management (AIM), headed by Paul W. Bryant Jr., son of a famous University of Alabama football coach, had been established to secure financing, construct, and manage the track. Although AIM got three banks in Council Bluffs to buy $2 million in bonds for the track, the remaining $10 million of the authorized issue was sold to a Montgomery firm. According to John Nelson, president of Iowa West Racing Association, a protective "bias" in support of Omaha's Ak-Sar-Ben track hampered local financing. He also noted that advocates of a proposed horse track near Des Moines and Sioux City businesses that benefited from an existing dog track at North Sioux City, South Dakota, did not want competition from Council Bluffs.

In April 1985 ground was broken for the track in the southwestern part of the city. As the project, which cost $18 million, neared completion the following winter, there were forecasts that the track, named Bluffs Run, would emerge as one of the nation's leading dog-racing facilities. Moreover, Iowa West would soon become a big contributor to local charities, something John Nelson noted that Council Bluffs had always lacked. Stan Duysen, Iowa West's executive-secretary, noted, "This (track) is in many ways better than bringing high-tech jobs in. What we're able to do is employ people, and for many of them it'll be a second job." Duysen and Nelson, who had provided the local leadership in making the track a reality, emphasized the role of the track and its donations to charities flowing from its proceeds in improving the image of Council Bluffs. In the euphoric atmosphere of a gathering in the well-appointed Bluffs Run clubhouse before the track's February 1986 opening, Governor Branstad saw that event as the harbinger of economic development. Reflecting deep-seated local feelings, state senator Mike Gronstal said, "It will be great to have some of that Nebraska money coming this way instead of Iowa money going that way." Equally revealing, Mayor Bill Venard remarked, "Everybody is in a positive mood. A lot of people couldn't believe we were in Council Bluffs tonight."

Opening night brought some 6,100 persons, and the track, which employed 550 persons, continued to draw large crowds whose bets ran well above expectations. Soon the *Nonpareil* spoke of the racecourse as "the talk of the metropolitan area" and "the jewel of Council Bluffs." A parking lot survey showed that 55 percent of the vehicles were from Nebraska and an additional 6 percent were from Missouri and Kansas. By the time the racing season ended in December, Bluffs Run had drawn over 1.1 million patrons. This figure placed Bluffs Run third among the nation's dog-racing tracks in attendance, and its handle was fifth nationally. The state, county, and city made a rich harvest of revenue from the track, and Iowa West Racing Association began donations to local charities. Sharp declines in betting and patronage at the Ak-Sar-Ben track suggested the realities of competing for the gambling dollar but did not dampen the enthusiasm of Council Bluffs boosters. Larry Mankin, a Chamber of Commerce official, concluded that the track had bolstered the statewide stature of Council Bluffs and had given his community self-confidence. He added, "There's no more of these comments that no intelligent life exists west of Des Moines."

"A PRETTY STAGNANT COMMUNITY"

The highly successful beginning of dog racing in Council Bluffs in 1986 seemed to promise better days for a community that had been struggling to keep pace with the economic development of the rest of the metropolitan Omaha area. The next two years brought continuing success to Bluffs Run, albeit that attendance and the handle plateaued. The track ended the 1988 season ranked fifth in patronage and sixth in handle among the country's fifty-two greyhound racecourses. Because of the vulnerability of racetracks to regional competition, a Bluffs Run official blamed the opening of a Kansas City, Kansas, greyhound track for a significant drop in attendance and wagering in 1989. This decline became more pronounced in 1990 by which time Bluffs Run faced the more daunting prospect that a casino-hotel might become part of the local scene.

In 1989 Iowa approved casino gambling, and a well-known Nevada firm, Harveys Casino Resorts, in association with the Santee Sioux Indian Tribe of Nebraska, planned a combined casino, hotel, and convention facility in Council Bluffs. President John Nelson of the Iowa West Racing Association, Bluffs Run's nonprofit sponsor, declared, "I personally don't believe the majority of the people in Iowa in any way, shape or form want casino gambling." More to the point, Iowa West admitted that such competition could bring the end of dog racing at Bluffs Run. Across the river, an Ak-Sar-Ben official said that the planned casino might bring the demise of horse racing in Omaha. Iowa West launched a public relations campaign to bolster attendance at Bluffs Run and to battle local support for a casino. The Greater Council Bluffs Board of Realtors endorsed the project, and a Harveys publicist from Omaha gained tacit approval when he told a meeting of real-estate agents, "Council Bluffs is a pretty stagnant community. It needs something like this to get it going, or it is going to be left behind." The casino project met with a hostile response from the state and was scrapped in 1993 after the U.S. Department of the Interior did not approve tribal land acquisition. In the meantime Bluffs Run's attendance and handle had continued to decline.

In addition to the competition from the Kansas City dog track, Bluffs Run competed with keno gambling in Omaha and Ak-Sar-Ben's efforts to recoup its fortunes through "simulcast" betting on races at other horse tracks. New casinos operated by the Omaha and Winnebago Indians easily accessible from Interstate 29 about an hour to an hour-and-fifteen-minute drive north of the city posed additional challenges. To recover, Bluffs Run gained regulatory concessions on its handle and betting options, relief from a long dispute over paying property taxes, and income from simulcast horse races as well as races at other dog tracks.

Whatever the long-term plight of dog racing, gambling had emerged as an important part of the local economy. For the eight years from 1986 through

1993, Council Bluffs and Pottawattamie County had each received over $3.6 million from pari-mutuel taxes from Bluffs Run while the State of Iowa had gained $35 million from this source. Total taxes amounted to almost $51.2 million while Iowa West's grants, primarily in Council Bluffs, southwestern Iowa, and the Nebraska part of the metro area came to $1.46 million. The track ranked eighth in size among Council Bluffs employers, and had paid $29.4 million to its staff.

THE COMING OF THE CASINOS

By 1994 Iowa West Racing Association had changed its position on casino gambling when state legislation permitted Pottawattamie County voters to decide whether to allow riverboat casinos and the addition of slot machines at Bluffs Run. Harveys Casino Resorts, by now a familiar name locally, was the prime contender for the operation of a riverboat casino, and under Iowa law would need a nonprofit organization to hold its gambling license. Iowa West was the logical organization. Accordingly, Iowa West created a campaign organization, Citizens for Pottawattamie County, to sell separate proposals to allow slot machines at Bluffs Run and riverboat casino gambling to the electorate. Not surprisingly, the advocates of these changes obtained far more money to publicize their cause than did GamBusters, the Council Bluffs Ministerial Association's group that opposed expanded gambling. Attorney Charles Smith, an officer of Iowa West who chaired the Citizens for Pottawattamie County campaign, noted that legal gambling was already the reality, adding, "What we're deciding is whether we're going to have additional money for governmental purposes." Most voters shared this viewpoint, for in May 1994 they approved both measures by substantial margins.

With costs split between Iowa West and Alabama-Iowa Management, the private managerial firm, construction of a casino addition to Bluffs Run and related renovation was in progress by late summer. The result of the $19 million project was the opening in March 1995 of a casino, which was open around the clock, housing over one thousand slot machines. Dog racing continued at what was renamed Bluffs Run Casino after the introduction of this new form of legal gambling in the metro area. A total of 94,084 persons entered Bluffs Run Casino during one week in April 1995, leaving gross revenue of over $2.7 million and tax flow reminiscent of the early days of dog racing.

In the meantime, Harveys and five other firms vied for riverboat casino licenses in Pottawattamie County. In addition to Harveys, three other firms contemplated riverboat casinos and onshore enterprises such as restaurants and convention facilities. All proposals but one included hotels. In each of these proposals, Iowa West Racing Association would be the local sponsor needed to meet the nonprofit provision in the state gaming regulations. Two businesses, one of which was in partnership with the Omaha tribe, developed plans for riverboat casinos that would be docked on the far side of the Missouri River on the enclave of Iowa land leading to Carter Lake. Neither of these would have hotels, and both shared a prospective nonprofit sponsor.

Given market considerations, there was a common expectation that the regulatory body, now known as the Iowa Racing and Gaming Commission, would approve only one or two riverboat casinos in Pottawattamie County. Anticipating that Nebraska might eventually allow casinos that would compete for local gambling dollars, a study sponsored by the Racing and Gaming Commission concluded that Pottawattamie County's market could properly sustain about one and one-half riverboat casinos in addition to land-based Bluffs Run. Whatever the number, local support for prospective operators would be a consideration in the Racing and Gaming Commission's decision. Mayor Thomas Hanafan, on the advice of a special committee, recommended that Harveys receive a license. The city council after much debate eventually endorsed this recommendation. The *Nonpareil* recognized that Harveys was the local favorite but contended that enough licenses should be awarded "to ensure [that] Iowa casinos establish a dominant position in the regional market. That would mean future Nebraska casinos would find it difficult to break in, other than marginally." The *Nonpareil* also stressed the need for casino firms to make huge capital outlays for hotels and other attractions. In a cautionary comment appropriate in light of Council Bluffs' recent history, the paper concluded, "The more they build means the more companies have to lose, making it less likely that they will float away when times are tough—a not uncommon occurrence in the business."

In January 1995 the Iowa Racing and Gaming Commission granted licenses to Harveys and another Nevada firm, Ameristar Casinos. Harveys's project featured a riverboat, an adjoining pavilion with restaurants, and a hotel with a convention center. The project would be built on park land, located a short distance south of the Interstate 480 bridge to downtown Omaha that the firm would purchase from the city of Council Bluffs. Harveys would also commit $1.5 million to the development of softball and soccer facilities on nearby city-owned land. Ameristar's complex included a riverboat casino, dining and entertainment facilities, and two hotels. The Ameristar development would be built immediately south of Harveys on land purchased from a private holder, and the casino firm agreed to make $1 million in charitable donations when the casino opened. The eastern approach to the Union Pacific Railroad bridge ran between Ameristar and Harveys. Just as the bridge once had been the symbol that both united and divided Council Bluffs and Omaha, the casinos would again unite and divide the cities.

"Casinos to bring 3,000 jobs" declared a *Nonpareil* headline following the announcement that Ameristar and Harveys were coming to town. Still, the paper cautioned, "[W]e are concerned that, over time, the industry may mature and tax income stabilize or decline." Moreover, the recent riverboat casino business in Iowa was not noted for its integrity. Three of the five such casinos that began on the Mississippi River in 1991 within two years had abandoned their bases without meeting their commitments. The land-based facilities that would adjoin riverboat casinos were essential to building a convention and tourism business. Council Bluffs and Pottawattamie County authorities with the backing of the Iowa Racing and Gaming Commission went to considerable lengths to ensure that Ameristar and Harveys would fulfill their onshore contractual obligations. Council Bluffs probably benefited from the experience of the Mississippi River cities in the early 1990s. The 1994 revision of Iowa law governing riverboat casinos ended betting limits and hence was an incentive for gaming firms to put more capital into hotels and other facilities on land. Indeed, the Ameristar and Harveys developments at Council Bluffs were high-cost operations from their inception, and the capital commitment to these undertakings increased as construction progressed. Likewise, to give stability and respectability to the casinos, the Council Bluffs city council adopted zoning measures barring adult movie theaters, massage parlors, and other enterprises with seamy reputations from the casino area.

Mayor Hanafan and other supporters of the new direction of gambling contended that the riverboat casinos and their land-based facilities would make Council Bluffs a tourist destination, thus contributing to the patronage of Omaha's Old Market and other west-bank attractions. Many Nebraskans looked forward to the opening of the casinos, but some leaders were highly critical of more gambling opportunities on the state's border. The *World-Herald* was a consistent foe of casinos, and in Lincoln, Gov. Ben Nelson and Attorney General Don Stenberg had said that they would be alert lest any Iowa-based casino vessel venture into Nebraska waters. Mayor Hal Daub of Omaha feared that hotels adjacent to the casinos would draw business away from his city's accommodations. He also declared, "Crime always follows along with gambling." The fact that Council Bluffs had gambling and adult movie theaters led the combative Daub to brand Iowa as a "triple-X-rated state," a well-publicized comment for which he eventually apologized.

The opening of Bluffs Run Casino in 1995 and Ameristar and Harveys in 1996 created almost 2,400 jobs. Although Bluffs Run was not then permitted to establish table games, all three establishments flourished, and in 1998 some 9.1 million persons lost $293 million in slot machines or other casino betting. Council Bluffs had not had a new hotel since the long-closed Chieftain opened in 1927, but the hotels, completed first at Harveys and then at Ameristar, did a good business and subsequently expanded. In the process, Council Bluffs' convention business boomed.

The expansion of gambling in Council Bluffs in 1995–96 not only contributed to the demise of horse racing at the Ak-Sar-Ben track, but also brought a huge decline in the patronage of keno parlors in the Omaha area. Despite Mayor Daub's admonitions against gambling, keno had generated significant revenue for the cities of Omaha and Ralston, but these streams of money quickly declined. Patronage at the Indian casinos north of the metro area fell sharply, and problems related to excessive gambling, such as bankruptcy, increased markedly. John Nelson of the Iowa West Racing Association took a realistic view of the casinos. On balance, he saw the innovation as beneficial for Council Bluffs, "But for those people who can't stop (gambling), it's catastrophic."

In 1999 Harveys purchased Bluffs Run for $165 million. Fifty million dollars of this sum was spent to buy out the contract of Alabama-Iowa Management, and the remaining $115 million went to the Iowa West Foundation, the charitable arm of Iowa West Racing Association. Harveys would operate Bluffs Run, but to comply with the state law requiring ownership by a nonprofit organization, the property would be leased to Iowa West Racing Association. The transaction soon placed Harveys's Council Bluffs enterprises

16. Harrah's, one of the Council Bluffs casinos, 2005. *Courtesy Timothy M. Fitzgerald.*

in the vanguard of that firm's operations. The importance of these Council Bluffs casinos was highlighted in 2001 when Harrah's Casinos purchased Harveys. The $625 million deal included a casino in Colorado, one in Nevada, and the two in Council Bluffs. As Gary Loveman, chief executive of Harrah's said, "The Iowa properties are what really made this deal magical for us."

As the twenty-first century began, gambling in Council Bluffs continued to flourish, a reality that probably was in part due to the convenient proximity of hotels and other entertainment facilities. Over ten million patrons visited the casinos in 2000. In the year ending June 30, 2002, slot machine and table game betting losses at Council Bluffs came to $377 million. The casinos were a bonanza for state and local government. That year the Council Bluffs casinos brought $85.8 million to the treasury of the State of Iowa, while Pottawattamie County collected almost $1.9 million and the city of Council Bluffs garnered over $4.4 million in tax revenue. Local property taxes added substantially to these figures. For all Iowa casinos, payouts to gamblers were about 93 per cent of money wagered.

Iowa law stipulated that every eight years Pottawattamie County and the ten other counties with casinos would ask their voters to decide if such gambling would continue. In 2002 over 79 percent of the people voting in Pottawattamie County backed the retention of casinos, and the electorate in the other counties with state-licensed casinos gave strong approval to continuing these establishments. In 2004 Ameristar gained approval for a significant expansion, and the following year, a large expansion program began at Bluffs Run, which was to be renamed the Horseshoe Casino. The new facilities at the Horseshoe, in keeping with a revision of state law, would include table games.

In the meantime, the *World-Herald* remained vigorously opposed to expanding gambling in the Cornhusker State, but advocates pointed to the majority of Nebraska vehicles in the parking lots of the Council Bluffs casinos as evidence of a tremendous outflow of cash. Casinos in Nebraska, they argued, would keep this money at home, an argument bolstered by growing stringencies in tax revenues. In the general election of November 2004, Nebraskans rejected two major gambling proposals, one of which specified that Omaha could have two casinos. Differing Nevada gambling interests had heavily backed each measure. Among those who joined the battle against the measures were Warren Buffett, chairman of the board of Berkshire Hathaway, who normally stayed aloof from state and local issues; Congressman Tom Osborne, former Cornhusker head football coach who was probably the most popular person in the state; and Omaha's outspoken state senator Ernie Chambers. A majority of the voters in Douglas and Sarpy counties supported the proposal to allow two casinos in Omaha, but the balloting revealed the socioeconomic differences basic to Omaha's old east-west division. Support for casinos in the city's eastern areas may have been based in part upon the prospect that such establishments would bring jobs, while opposition in the western part of the city reflected that area's higher income and educational levels. In any event, it seemed probable that the casino issue in Nebraska had not been resolved; in the meantime, Council Bluffs remained free from competition.

Despite arguments that casino gambling fostered bankruptcy and other problems, other evidence cast a more positive light on the impact of the Council Bluffs casinos on Nebraska. About one-half of the casino employees were Nebraska residents, and in 2002 the casinos spent $18.8 million in purchases of at least $50,000 from individual Nebraska businesses, including $1.84 million in *World-Herald* advertising as the paper itself noted. The $18.8 million spent in Nebraska equaled 22 percent of the total purchases of at least $50,000 from single firms, while $28.4 million or 33 percent of such buying went to Iowa businesses. Nevada vendors received $24.6 million or 28 percent of such spending, while businesses elsewhere gained $14.7 million or 17 percent of this trade.

IOWA WEST FOUNDATION

The start of casino gambling in Council Bluffs in 1995 had a major impact on Iowa West's charitable and public-service contributions. For the Iowa West Foundation, the sale of Bluffs Run brought a tremendous infusion of capital essential to its long-term mission. Before 1996 Iowa West had distributed some $3.6 million in grants, but starting that year annual grants rose sharply and reached a cumulative total of more than $106 million by 2002–3.

By the 1990s Council Bluffs had long outgrown its Carnegie Library, a fixture of downtown since 1905. Voters had twice rejected bond issues for a new library, but individual donations to a library foundation, coupled with large contributions from the Iowa West Foundation and the Lied Foundation

17. Council Bluffs Public Library, 2005. *Photo by Kay Dalstrom.*

Trust, led to the completion of a spacious and highly attractive prairie-style structure in 1998. The library's appearance and its advanced technology made it a key component in efforts to revitalize downtown and build the image of a progressive community.

Since 1921 the Union Pacific Railroad's operational headquarters building in downtown Omaha had included a small museum commemorating the company's history, but space needs led the firm to close the museum in 1996. With financial help from the Iowa Department of Economic Development, the Iowa West Foundation, the Lied Foundation Trust, and a group known as the Friends of the Carnegie Cultural Museum, the former Council Bluffs library building was converted into a new Union Pacific Railroad Museum. Aside from exhibits, the museum would house a huge photograph collection. Its opening on May 10, 2003, the anniversary of the driving of the golden spike, also recalled Council Bluffs' earlier status as the eastern terminus of the Union Pacific. In 1991 the city's former Rock Island depot, dating from 1899, had been converted into the RailsWest Museum, and both old structures were now monuments to the glory days when "railroads" and "Council Bluffs" were almost synonymous.

The Iowa West Foundation played a critical role in building a convention center–arena that would serve the entertainment needs of the metro area and foster the further development of the hospitality industry in Council Bluffs. In 1999 the foundation purchased land for this project at the junction of Interstate Highways 29 and 80 just west of Bluffs Run and close to the other two casinos. The $74 million arena would seat 7,500 persons and would be home ice for the popular Omaha Lancers hockey team. Boosters of the project contemplated that private firms would develop entertainment, lodging, and other businesses adjacent to the convention center–arena. Omaha's Mayor Daub, who had strained intercity relations with his strident opposition to casinos and other features of the Council Bluffs entertainment scene, commended the project, saying that it would complement a much larger convention center–arena that his city was building.

Aside from the land, the Iowa West Foundation provided over $25 million for what was known as the Mid-America Center. Harveys Casino committed $7.5 million, and the city of Council Bluffs agreed to provide a similar sum in sewer and street work. A critical source of money was the Vision Iowa Fund, a development mechanism provided by the state legislature. When Brent

Siegrist of Council Bluffs, who was speaker of the Iowa House of Representatives, addressed the Vision Iowa board on the advantages of a convention center–arena, he said, "My personal favorite here is the professional hockey team from Nebraska moving to Council Bluffs. . . . Needless to say, I'm giddy about that. Anything we can take from Nebraska . . . I'm always for that." In any event, Vision Iowa granted and loaned a total of $31 million for the project. The *World-Herald*, praising Vision Iowa for its contribution, emphasized the proximity of the projected arena–convention center to other attractions on both sides of the river. In October 2002 the Omaha Lancers — temporarily renamed the River City Lancers—were playing in the Mid-America Center, and the convention portion of the structure soon would be completed.

Just south of the Mid-America Center, the Western Historic Trails Center opened in 1997. Built by the National Park Service with the help of the Lied Foundation Trust, the Iowa West Foundation, and other contributors and operated by the State Historical Society of Iowa, the center's exhibits commemorated the nineteenth-century overland travelers who passed through the Council Bluffs area and the routes that they followed. A low-slung building— "quiet architecture" as one historian put it—set in the serenity of tallgrass prairie on the Missouri River bottoms gave the Western Historic Trails Center an atmosphere that belied its proximity to the interstate highways and the casinos. The Iowa West Foundation also contributed to the building of the Southwest Iowa Performing Arts Center, completed in 2001 on the campus of Iowa Western Community College.

From its inception Iowa West was interested in improving the physical attractiveness of Council Bluffs. By 2000 the foundation had made a number of contributions to the beautification of downtown, such as sidewalk murals portraying aspects of Council Bluffs history. In 1999 Marty Shukert, former Omaha planning director who had been professionally active in Council Bluffs, set forth a new plan known as "CB-21," a guide for community development into the twenty-first century. One feature of CB-21 was improving the image of the far-western portion of Broadway, historically the city's leading thoroughfare and gateway from Omaha. In 2001 the Council Bluffs Convention and Visitors Bureau adopted a publicity slogan that termed their community "Iowa's Leading Edge." This was an obvious incentive to eliminate negative images of the city and fit well with CB-21 and Iowa West's interest in community beautification. "There's no way around it: West Broadway in

Council Bluffs is an ugly street," began a *World-Herald* editorial commending the civic leaders who were trying to tackle this problem. An important step came when the Iowa West Foundation funded the building of four decorative towers with variable lighting features and landscaping that symbolized the area's loess hills. As Mayor Hanafan said when the towers were completed and illuminated in 2002, "It really cleans up the area. . . . You really feel good coming through here."

A NEW FORM OF GOVERNMENT

In the meantime, Council Bluffs sharply revised its governmental structure. In 1956 and 1958 voters rejected proposals to end the city-manager form of government that had been in place since 1950 and restore the mayor-council system. A petition campaign brought the proposal before the voters again in the autumn of 1985 in a special election. The issue seemed to draw relatively little public interest as proponents of the change contended that the city needed a strong chief executive who was popularly elected, while opponents argued that the city-manager system was satisfactory. Advocates of retaining the city-manager form of government included seventeen persons who had served on the five-member city council and whose colleagues had been chosen in annual elections to the largely ceremonial position of mayor. Tom Hanafan, a council member since 1981 and then current mayor, was one of this group. The *Nonpareil* backed the retention of the city-manager form, and although the Chamber of Commerce did not campaign on the issue, its governing body supported the status quo. By contrast, Ronald Cleveland, who had served as mayor in 1978, advocated the adoption of the strong-mayor plan, charging that there had been irresponsible use of city funds under the manager system. "For the most part," he contended, "city managers used our city as a stepping stone in their professional careers and could care less about our city," and he said that a popularly elected local person would be more likely to render better service to the community. In a comment that reflected a serious local malaise, Cleveland declared, "I say open your eyes. Business and population have gone down under the city manager, not up. Look at the cities that have grown since the 1950s: Omaha, Lincoln and Bellevue all have strong-mayor forms of government."

On a cold early December day, only about 18 percent of the registered electorate cast ballots. They adopted the change to the strong-mayor form of municipal government by a margin of 54 to 46 percent in a vote that revealed a continuing division between the eastern and western parts of the city. In the western precincts, the heart of the blue-collar residential area, 69.7 percent of the votes were in favor of the change. In the eastern bluff area, 62.2 percent of the ballots supported keeping city-manager government. Tight budgets in recent years that resulted in the discharge of some city employees, and cuts in municipal services may have contributed to dissatisfaction with the city-manager system. Cleveland asserted that the outcome reflected opposition to "smart alecks" in city government who did not manage tax money well and a desire to get rid of city manager Michael Miller. In any event, the vote reflected a socioeconomic split within the city similar to that prevailing in Omaha.

CONTINUITY IN LEADERSHIP

A person who symbolized both continuity and change as Council Bluffs entered a new century was Mayor Thomas P. Hanafan. Ironically, while serving as a council member and mayor in 1985 he wanted to keep the municipal administrative system that vested executive power in a city manager. After the voters terminated that system in favor of a strong mayor as the city's chief executive, Hanafan won a close election in 1987 to a two-year term as the first popularly elected mayor in two generations. In 1989 he was elected to a four-year mayoral term and reelected in 1993, 1997, 2001 and 2005. By the last date his eighteen years of continuous service as mayor easily made him at age fifty-eight the city's longest-serving chief executive. Indeed, although Jim Dahlman had gained renown as Omaha's "perpetual mayor" for his nearly twenty-one years in office, his maximum time of uninterrupted tenure was twelve years.

Hanafan, a Council Bluffs native, had played varsity football in high school and at the University of South Dakota where he graduated with a major in history. Returning home, he found enough satisfaction working in sales to abandon teaching and law as career options. His sales experience and volunteer service as a YMCA basketball coach reflected a pleasure in working with people and served the community well as he helped shape the great changes of the 1990s. As mayor he was mindful of the need to improve both the image and the cultural and economic well-being of the city. Under the strong-mayor system he was an important figure in dealing with the many business interests responsible for the great changes that came to Council Bluffs. In 1994 he had played an important part in devising the incentives that brought about the launching of the Omni Centre Business Park that ended the nightmarish legacy of the failed Midlands Mall. He continued to work on the difficult problem of downtown rejuvenation and was a key figure in making the Mid-America Center a reality.

Hanafan's personal popularity, perhaps enhanced by his disinclination to move up the political ladder, did not always translate into voter support for specific proposals. A tendency of the Council Bluffs electorate to oppose measures that might raise taxes gave a negative cast to public affairs in the late twentieth century. As with the building of a new public library, progress sometimes came without the commitment of a majority of local voters. Hanafan was a vital cog in that progress, but after his reelection in 1997, he praised the people of the city for having moved away from what he termed "kind of a can't-do attitude. . . . We can't do that because we're Council Bluffs" to a perception that they could shape their community's future. His positive outlook was also evident in his enthusiasm for the development of the entire metro area.

THE "COUNCIL BLUFFS REVIVAL"

Aside from the economic impact of casino gambling, the 1990s brought other developments that contributed to what a *World-Herald* headline termed the "Council Bluffs Revival." New home building was an essential to this revival and also began an eastward thrust in the growth of the metro area. As the decade began, Council Bluffs was well behind the Nebraska side of the river in home construction. As Mayor Hanafan said in 1991, "We have about 10 percent of the metropolitan area population but only about 2 or 3 percent of the housing starts."

The opening of the Mall of the Bluffs in 1986 in the southeastern part of the city, its subsequent expansion and the development of nearby businesses probably stimulated and certainly benefited from residential housing construction in that area. While there was significant variation in the annual number of subdivisions constructed, the general pattern was significantly upward. As Omaha sprawled ever farther to the west, the option of living in or around Council Bluffs became more attractive. As one Council Bluffs contractor said in 1997, "It's a quicker commute to (downtown) Omaha, 5 to

10 minutes, than from a lot of areas of Omaha. And the perception that this was an armpit of the world over here is changing." From 1995 to 2001 the city granted some four thousand housing permits. The more expensive subdivisions were generally east of I-80, and in a five-year period the number of homes in Pottawattamie County worth at least two hundred thousand dollars approximately doubled. Loess hills lots often provided excellent views, particularly to the west. "Starter" dwellings were less expensive in the Nebraska part of the metro, but "upscale" homes tended to be cheaper in the Council Bluffs area than similar houses in Omaha.

Still, there were peculiar man-made and natural challenges to the physical expansion and internal development of Council Bluffs. Iowa law continued to make annexation difficult. In 2001 voters, now including residents of the area to be annexed as well as the city's electorate, rejected an expansion measure that Council Bluffs' leaders maintained was essential to the proper growth of their community. Unlike Omaha, much of Council Bluffs lay on Missouri River bottomland where drainage was a problem. The loess hills added to the volume of water while the landward side of the Missouri River levee impeded its dissipation. Developing a storm-sewer system in this area was particularly costly, requiring pumping stations and larger pipe than would be used elsewhere; hence, the cost of bringing storm sewers to neighborhoods with vacant lots was prohibitive. Nevertheless, following a ten-inch rainfall in 1999, the city soon added six pumping stations to help prevent flooding. In an effort that took five years, the city council in 2001 approved a loess hills preservation plan that identified five locales where conservation efforts were especially needed. The plan fostered proper land development and management within the rugged erosion-prone bluffs.

Speaking of the economic development of Council Bluffs since the opening of the casinos, Hanafan in 2002 said, "We've come a long way in a relatively short period of time." Ameristar, Harrah's, and Bluffs Run Casino ranked respectively as his community's first-, second-, and fourth-leading employers. Naturally, these enterprises overshadowed other aspects of the city's economy, but in recent years, employment in manufacturing had grown markedly. For example, IBP, a meat packer, was the third-largest employer in Council Bluffs. Retail employment grew steadily through the 1990s, and many persons from Nebraska found it convenient to shop at the Mall of the Bluffs or other stores on the southern edge of town. At the beginning of the twenty-first century, a continuing decentralization of retailing within the metropolitan area brought proportionately much greater increases in sales outside Omaha's borders. Between 1998 and 2002, taxable sales in Omaha rose by 10.3 percent, compared to 27.5 percent in Council Bluffs and 34.9 percent in Sarpy County. Of course, in total dollar volume, Omaha's preeminence within the metro was unassailable, but Council Bluffs had become far more competitive in retail business than had been the case in the past.

Nevertheless, the 2000 census showed that Council Bluffs continued to trail Omaha in some respects. The percentage of Council Bluffs residents holding baccalaureate or advanced degrees, while rising, was just over one-half the figure for Omaha and significantly below the number for Iowa as a whole. In 1990 the median income of Council Bluffs residents was slightly under 93 percent of the median figure for Omahans, but despite a sharp increase in the following decade, the figure for Council Bluffs slipped to 90.53 percent of the median income of people living in Omaha. As it had been in 1990, the Council Bluffs median income figure in 2000 remained below that of the rest of Iowa. The median price of homes in Council Bluffs rose from 81.5 percent of the Omaha figure in 1990 to 83 percent in 2000.

Many upscale homes on both sides of the river were outside city limits, but the percentage of houses worth at least two hundred thousand dollars rose far more sharply in Pottawattamie than in Douglas County. This strongly illustrated the recent appeal of real estate in the Iowa part of the metro. If Iowa law had made it easier for Council Bluffs to annex, figures on the city's housing values might have been higher. Likewise, as Iowa's second-ranking county in area, Pottawattamie County was much larger and had far more rural land and more small towns than Douglas County. Indeed, merger between Omaha and Douglas County, discussed sporadically for many years was becoming a real, if not imminent, possibility by 2005.

THE STATE LINE AND URBAN REALITIES

As the twenty-first century began, the state line dividing the metro area remained a meaningful division. The Greater Omaha Convention and Visitors Bureau would not mention the proximity of the Council Bluffs casinos unless asked. As a representative of that body said, "[W]e want people to stay in Omaha-area hotel rooms and to spend money in Omaha. We don't want them taking expendable money to casinos." From an official of the Council

Bluffs Chamber of Commerce came a similar message: "We always market Council Bluffs as an important, vital part of the metropolitan-area mix. . . . But we are two separate communities with two separate governmental bodies, so there are some things we don't work on hand in hand." The boundary was an obstacle for metro-area Iowans who wished to attend a state university offering baccalaureate and graduate degrees. Unlike other Midwestern states, Iowa never created a system of four-year public institutions located in each of its principal regions; instead, it developed major baccalaureate-graduate institutions in Iowa City, Ames, and Cedar Falls—all between 160 and 250 miles from Council Bluffs. By contrast, the University of Nebraska–Lincoln was about sixty-five miles away and the University of Nebraska at Omaha was eight miles from downtown Council Bluffs. Although the latter institution made an effort to provide scholarships to cover the nonresident portion of tuition for qualified students from Iowa, the fact that Iowa and Nebraska lacked formal reciprocity attested to the significance of the state boundary. Yet, as was the case with gambling at the Chez Paree, the Dodge Park Kennel Club, and the Stork Club in the 1940s, the advent of legal dog racing and casino gaming two generations later demonstrated that many people found the state line convenient. Taverns open for an hour longer than in Nebraska and cheaper gasoline in Council Bluffs also appealed to Omahans.

By 2000 influences uniting the Iowa and Nebraska portions of the urban area loomed far larger than the points of division. Since 1965, outside interests had owned the *Council Bluffs Daily Nonpareil*, the oldest newspaper in the cities. In 2000 a group composed of the Iowa West Foundation, an Omaha investment firm known as the McCarthy Group, and Southwest Iowa Newspapers, the last owned by the *Omaha World-Herald*, purchased the *Nonpareil*. Two years later, John P. Nelson, the chief executive of an Omaha insurance brokerage firm and a resident of Council Bluffs, was chosen to be the 106th King of Ak-Sar-Ben and the first from Council Bluffs. He had been a leading figure in bringing greyhound racing to the area, the creation of the Iowa West Foundation, the development of the Western Historic Trails Center, and other civic activities. In any event, recent history pointed to a new importance of Council Bluffs within the metropolitan area.

[13] Groundbreaking Changes

In the period 1990 to 2000 Omaha's population grew from 335,795 to 390,007, an increase of slightly over 16 percent. At the start of the new century Omaha ranked forty-second in population among the cities of the United States. Bellevue continued to boom, growing from 30,982 to 44,382, surpassing Grand Island as the Nebraska's third-largest community. Papillion, Sarpy County's seat, had 10,302 residents in 1990 and 16,383 a decade later, and its northern neighbor, La Vista, grew from 9,840 to 11,699. Chalco, an unincorporated area in Sarpy County, had 7,337 residents in 1990 and 10,736 in 2000. Council Bluffs reversed its two-decade decline as its population rose from 53,222 in 1990 to 58,268 in 2000. The 1990 population of 639,580 for the metro, which since 1993 had included Cass County, Nebraska, reached 716,998 in 2000, an increase of more than 12 percent. In the latter year metropolitan Omaha ranked sixtieth in population among the nation's metro areas.

At the start of the new century, it was evident that Omaha lacked national recognition. When Omaha was founded, American cities, particularly within a given region, rivaled one another in their quests for economic development. Even though the time when a local editor praised his own presumptive metropolis in florid terms while bombastically proclaiming the utter disadvantages of its competitors was long gone, the rivalries nonetheless endured. Accordingly, Omaha's boosters were on the lookout for something that would bring their city national recognition. Over a generation earlier in 1968, with the packing industry in decline and Omaha moving beyond the economic foundations that had propelled it to prominence, Mayor A. V. Sorensen asked the public to propose a symbol for the city. Just as the Gateway Arch had become the hallmark of St. Louis, Omaha needed a symbol to proclaim its role as "Nebraska's largest city, the gateway to the West." But Sorensen looked away from Omaha's past when he said, "We don't want a bull on a pedestal."

He named a committee to select a winning symbol, and when the effort came to naught, he proposed touting Omaha as "The City of Fountains," only to discover that Kansas City had taken that image.

Over the years various symbols or attractions were conceived, but probably the most interesting was that of Robert Hogenmiller Jr., a commercial artist, who in 1997 proposed a 610-foot-high stainless-steel structure called "Vortex, the Tornado Tower," built in the form of a stylized tornado with an elevator to an observation deck and featuring a nightly laser light display. About four years later, a local marketing firm came up with a simple logo for advertising the city. Below a large, boldface "OMAHA" was, in smaller format, "RARE, WELL DONE." However, in 2003 the Greater Omaha Convention and Visitors Bureau dropped this slogan. The Greater Omaha Chamber of Commerce then launched a series of *Wall Street Journal* ads aimed at drawing the attention of corporate leaders to Omaha as a good place for major operations. These ads entailed plays upon words to link historical images of the city and region to modern realities, for example, against a view of a cow captioned "Livestock," were juxtaposed the words "Live Stock," used in reference to the stock prices of the securities of the five Omaha-headquartered firms that were on the Fortune 500 list.

Despite these promotional efforts, there was little at the beginning of the twenty-first century to suggest that despite highly positive comments of some visitors Americans were on the verge of placing Omaha in the ranks of the nation's great cities. For that matter, a survey revealed that Omahans typically deemed their city "just average," and fewer residents rated their community as "the best possible city to live in" compared to the average figure for how residents of other places viewed the desirability of their hometowns. By contrast, 88 percent of the people responding to a survey concluded that the Greater Omaha area was an "ideal" place to rear children, although the same study pointed to specific problems.

World-Herald columnist Michael Kelly faithfully responded to slighting remarks about Omaha such as when Sid Hartman of the *Minneapolis Star-Tribune* paraphrased Hubert Humphrey's 1976 comment that "Without professional sports, the Twin Cities would be just a cold Omaha." Motion picture producer Alexander Payne, an Omaha native, in using his hometown as the setting for such films as *Election* (1999) and *About Schmidt* (2002), conveyed images that movie reviewers and undoubtedly many other persons took to be stark depictions of life in the Midwest. Kelly noted that references to Omaha in reviews of *About Schmidt* included such expressions as a "mundane metropolis" and "a sterile city," but he correctly observed that the film, which he praised, was "about Schmidt. . . . not about Omaha." Rainbow Rowell, his colleague at the *World-Herald*, reached a similar conclusion, saying, "I'd rather he made good movies in Omaha than movies that make Omaha look good."

Around the turn of the twenty-first century, there was at least one spring weekend each year when Omahans took absolute pride in their image. The scenario was simple: two men in their seventies sitting on a stage behind a table. In front of them were some eleven to fifteen thousand people from across the country and abroad. The event was the festive annual meeting of the shareholders of Berkshire Hathaway, sometimes called "the Woodstock of capitalism." Many attending had waited cheerfully outside the auditorium in the chill spring air for some time before the doors opened at 7:00 a.m. One of the men on the stage was Warren Buffett, an Omaha native, a resident of the Dundee section of the city, and Berkshire Hathaway's guiding figure. Frequently called "the oracle of Omaha," he was the second-wealthiest person on the planet. Sharing the stage with Buffett was his principal associate, Charles Munger, a former Omahan residing in Los Angeles. The national media covered the meeting, and as Buffett and Munger responded to questions, some highly sophisticated, Omaha was briefly a financial capital of the world. Warren Buffett, who maintained a low profile in civic affairs, had done far more than any individual to bring outside attention to Omaha.

Even though Omaha had no official symbol, by the 1990s the redeveloped part of downtown with its new high-rise buildings, the Leahy Mall, the Heartland of America Park, and the ConAgra campus formed an impressive panorama at the city's eastern gateway. The completion in 1991 of U.S. West's data-processing facility and Landmark Center office building on the south side of Leahy Mall typified the redevelopment of eastern downtown and the city's adaptation to corporate change. U.S. West originated in the court-ordered reorganization of the Bell Telephone System in the 1980s and became the parent of Omaha-based Northwestern Bell Telephone Company, the principal provider of telephone service in a five-state region. Although U.S. West established its headquarters in the Denver area and eliminated

Northwestern Bell, the firm, renamed Qwest, remained one of Omaha's large employers.

Just south of Leahy Mall and its rejuvenated surroundings was the Old Market area of shops and restaurants that had emerged since the late 1960s as an entertainment area drawing over 1,200,000 visitors annually. The new Embassy Suites Hotel on South Tenth Street adjacent to the Old Market and ConAgra was another mark of the vitality of the eastern downtown area. But with some exceptions such as the Orpheum Theater and the Westin Aquila Hotel, downtown west of Thirteenth Street lacked vitality. Sixteenth Street had a pleasing appearance, but its heated bus stop shelters attracted panhandlers and other street people whose presence gave this part of downtown a bad image. As the *World-Herald*'s Kenneth Freed wrote in mid-1996, "Downtown Omaha is full of 'vacancy' and 'for rent' signs. Empty or barely occupied buildings abound, and there is no major convention center, a feature experts agree would attract other significant development."

The first years of the twenty-first century brought massive change to the northeastern section of downtown. This was the outcome of specific business decisions, but it fit a plan. In 1996 the mayor and city council designated a thirty-three-block area of northeastern downtown to be a zone wherein the city could use eminent domain to foster redevelopment. Of course, other methods were available. For example, at Tenth and Dodge streets, tax increment financing was used in redeveloping two warehouses into a Marriott Courtyard Hotel. To the west, at Fourteenth and Capitol streets, the *World-Herald* made a huge investment in a new plant, called the Freedom Center, which housed new presses while at Seventeenth and Dodge the Hruska United States Courthouse, named after Roman Hruska, longtime Republican U.S. senator from Omaha, was finished.

While transportation no longer occupied its old prominence in Omaha's economy, the Union Pacific Railroad remained an important force in the city. The 1980s witnessed the incorporation of the Western Pacific and the Missouri Pacific into the Union Pacific system. Through the Missouri Pacific, the Union Pacific acquired the KATY system and the Chicago and North Western gradually became part of the UP. In 1996 federal regulators approved the merger of the Union Pacific and Southern Pacific lines thereby fulfilling Edward H. Harriman's early twentieth-century ambition.

Following its massive acquisitions, the Union Pacific, with thirty-three thousand miles of track and forty-seven thousand employees in 2002 was the largest of North America's six biggest railroads. Over four thousand of its employees worked at its Omaha headquarters. However, the changes initially had a mixed impact upon Omaha. Just south of the ConAgra campus, the railroad renovated its 1891 freight house into the Harriman Dispatching Center, which the company heralded as the world's most advanced rail control system when it opened in 1989. This operation centralized dispatching in Omaha and fit in well with the revitalization of the river-front area and the city's emergence as an information technology center. But system expansion, particularly the acquisition of the Missouri Pacific, led to a 1988 decision to close the UP shops just north of downtown and move shop work to North Little Rock, Arkansas. Accompanying the loss of the shops that employed some eight hundred persons was the pulling up of most of the adjoining tracks. Soon, much of the area where the Union Pacific's groundbreaking ceremony had taken place in 1863 was a weed-strewn expanse of unused land along the highway between downtown and the airport.

In 1999 Union Pacific's corporate headquarters, historically located elsewhere, were moved to Omaha from Dallas. Given the few employees involved, the impact was miniscule, but the action was an important symbolic augmentation of the city's business stature. Far more significant was the possibility that five hundred or more employees would be moved from St. Louis to Omaha, but the company's twelve-story headquarters building, dating from 1915, was inadequate for existing local operations that were spread over eighteen additional sites. For many years, the Union Pacific had contemplated constructing a new headquarters, but the firm did not act until it got its desired incentives. The package that brought about the railroad's decision in 2001 to construct a new building was an extension of a state investment tax-incentive law and the city's contribution of a building site in the block south of the company's current headquarters between Fourteenth and Fifteenth and Dodge streets. The Chamber of Commerce would obtain this land and give it to the city, which would then pay to clear the site. The property would then be given to the Union Pacific, and the railroad would give its old headquarters to the city. The city would also build a parking garage to serve the new nineteen-story building. By the spring of 2002, work was in progress on the $260 million structure and was completed in 2004. The state tax incentives available to the railroad were reported to be worth between $30 million and $82.5 million. Omaha's identity as a railroad center had faded, but the Union Pacific still had tremendous clout in Nebraska.

"TO GROW AND PROSPER WE CANNOT LET OTHER CITIES PASS US BY."

By the 1980s and 1990s it was increasingly evident that if Omaha were to attract top-billed mass-audience live entertainment and develop its convention business, it would need to replace or greatly enlarge the city-owned Civic Auditorium, which had opened in 1955. Between 1985 and 1993 there were several such recommendations, one of which resulted in the completion in 1997 of a $26 million modernization of the Civic Auditorium. One important feature of this improvement was an ice rink for the University of Nebraska at Omaha's new Division 1 hockey team, but the venue was still inadequate for large conventions and other events typically associated with major cities. Indeed, in the long run, hockey would be a key to the future of the Civic Auditorium. In 2005 after a thirty-year absence of professional hockey in Omaha, the National Hockey League Calgary Flames, with the Knights of Ak-Sar-Ben as the local partner, brought an American Hockey League franchise to the city. The Omaha Ak-Sar-Ben Knights, would play at the Civic Auditorium.

In 1997 two consultants engaged by the Chamber of Commerce advised civic leaders that Omaha should build a $200 million arena and convention center that would seat from eighteen to twenty thousand persons. Mayor Hal Daub, long a booster of the undertaking, saw a combination of revenue bonds and private money as the way to bring the project to fruition without hiking taxes. The Chamber of Commerce enlisted youthful David Sokol, a native Omahan and chief executive officer of CalEnergy, to chair a planning group for an arena–convention center. In November 1997 the Sokol commission reported that Omaha needed a sixteen-thousand-seat arena, nearly twice the capacity of the existing Civic Auditorium. The commission considered two prime sites: an area just northeast of downtown that until 1988 had been the location of the Union Pacific shops and yards, and an old area of apartments, small businesses, and warehouses in the southeastern part of downtown adjoining the Old Market. The fine restaurants, shops, and quaint atmosphere of the Old Market and easy access to hotels led Sokol's group to recommend that an arena–convention center be built on the southeastern site, despite Mayor Daub's preference for the Union Pacific property.

Some Old Market businesses supported the Sokol commission's recommendation, but many proprietors saw the potential traffic and arena crowds as incompatible with their area's ambience and the fact that it had some two thousand residents. Moreover, the southeastern location was within the Omaha Rail and Commerce District that in 1996 had been added to the National Register of Historic Places because of its association with Omaha's development. The ultimate undoing of the proposal rested in the fact that it contemplated a one-half-cent hike in the city sales tax, an increase that first required the approval of the state legislature and then the sanction of Omaha's voters. The Chamber of Commerce, then gearing up for an ultimately unsuccessful attempt to secure a statewide restriction on tax increases, obviously opposed this mode of funding. Without the support of most Omaha legislators, the proposal died in committee in the 1998 session of the Nebraska legislature.

Mayor Daub turned his attention back to his preferred site and the Union Pacific agreed to give the city time to put together a proposal to purchase its property northeast of downtown. Des Moines was moving ahead with plans for an arena–convention center and the specter of Omaha not keeping pace with other places reemerged. As Daub said, "To grow and prosper we cannot let other cities pass us by." What emerged by the fall of 1998 was a plan for a new arena–convention center that had been shorn of a tax increase but that continued to include a huge contribution from the private sector. The next year, the legislature, recognizing that more convention business would bring tax revenue into Nebraska, adopted a law that permitted up to $75 million in state sales tax receipts to be used to defray the costs of the convention center portion of the project. The legislation stipulated that Omaha voters would absolve the state from financial liability if the tax revenue were not generated.

As the arena–convention center proponents planned for a bond issue vote in May 2000, it became clear that if private contributors were to donate some $75 million, the project would have to be under the control of a Metropolitan Entertainment and Convention Authority (MECA), separate from the city government. Sokol, speaking of the corporate view of city hall, said, "This isn't an issue of distrust," but he noted that potential donors saw a need to utilize business talent and minimize bureaucracy. The result was the creation of a five-member planning body made up of one member named by the city

18. Qwest Center, Omaha, 2005. *Courtesy Timothy M. Fitzgerald.*

council, another by the mayor, and three members chosen by the private sector. It would have an executive director, and its funds would come from the city and private contributors. Mayor Daub and the city council approved this arrangement. When the voters went to the polls to decide upon a bond issue for the arena–convention center, they would also decide on making this body permanent. The permanent MECA would be modeled after the Omaha Airport Authority and would not have taxing power. What was emerging looked much like the genesis of the five nonelective special commissions that implemented the large spending program contemplated in the Mayor's City-Wide Planning Committee program of 1946.

In January 2000 the city council approved the placing of a $198 million arena–convention center bond issue before the voters in May. The following month, the city and the Union Pacific Railroad agreed on purchase terms for 104.1 acres of land, subject to approval of the bond issue. Four days before the voters went to the polls, the leader of the private fund drive, Ken Stinson, CEO of Peter Kiewit Sons, announced that the $75 million private fund-raising goal had been met. One-third of this sum came from the Peter Kiewit Foundation, an entity separate from the Kiewit firm.

On election day Omahans approved both the arena–convention center bond issue by a 63 to 37 percent margin and the permanent MECA. The strongest support came from western areas of the city, although it generally carried in the east. Most of the opposition was in parts of North Omaha where there was a perception that the project would detract from city services to that area. By March 2001 construction was under way and the huge complex, named the Qwest Center Omaha, opened in 2003. In addition to hosting a variety of special events, the arena became the new home of the Creighton University basketball team and the University of Nebraska at Omaha hockey team, both of which moved from the Civic Auditorium. Work related to the building of the convention center and arena included an extensive reconfiguration of Abbott Drive, the artery linking downtown to Eppley Airfield, and other streets northeast of downtown. Meanwhile, along Abbott Drive a new lighting system called the "string of pearls" did much to enhance the approach to the city from the airport.

Although the arena–convention center was close to downtown, the construction of a hotel adjoining the convention center was essential. By the spring of 2001, it was evident that prospective private developers of a suitable hotel would require a subsidy. In May, Hal Daub was defeated for reelection, but shortly before he left office and without waiting for a consultant's report, he selected a proposal for a twenty-eight-story, 528-room Marriott Hotel. When the new mayor, Mike Fahey, took office, he immediately suspended Daub's decision, and a month later decided in favor of an eight-story, 400-room Hilton Hotel. What had become the city's premier downtown hotel in the 1970s no longer carried the Hilton name, but a Hilton Garden Inn soon would open near the Old Market area. The Hilton adjoining the convention center would cost less than the Marriott, and because in either case the city would have to issue bonds for financing the structure, Fahey concluded that financial prudence warranted selection of the Hilton.

A stalemate soon developed when a majority of the city council, which had to approve financing arrangements stood firmly behind Daub's choice. These council members, like many boosters of Omaha's convention business, believed that the larger Marriott would make the city more attractive in recruiting conventions than the smaller Hilton. They also felt that the tall, ultramodern style of the Marriott fit better with the arena–convention center than did the lower, traditional design of the Hilton. A way out of the imbroglio finally came when Chamber of Commerce officials met with Mayor Fahey who agreed to consider a 450-room hotel. When he learned that the city could afford to back the needed bonds, he agreed to the project and appointed a committee to work with the architect in finding a design more compatible with the arena–convention center than the original Hilton proposal. By early in 2002 the details were settled, and at the groundbreaking ceremony, Fahey declared that the Hilton Omaha Hotel would be part of "a bright, vibrant new future on our riverfront."

Whether this was only the rhetoric usually associated with groundbreakings or an accurate prediction was of course uncertain. When the people of Omaha approved the arena–convention center bond issue there had been some recognition that the venture was risky. This became far more apparent as a national economic recession and the fear of terrorism brought a marked decrease in air travel. A spate of convention center construction was in progress across the country, which highlighted the competition that Omaha would face. As Joe Mysak of Bloomberg News Service wrote, "It may be a long time before people choose Omaha over New Orleans. Or Chicago. Or Kansas City. Or Memphis. Or Savannah."

In the meantime, other developments were fast transforming the nearby river-front area. In the 1870s smelting had become one of Omaha's early industries, and over a century later the American Smelting and Refining Company (Asarco) plant on the Missouri River just north of the Interstate 480 bridge was a remnant of the city's early industrial development. Into the 1990s this plant employed some 225 people, but the company was losing environmental litigation, including a local case arising from Missouri River pollution that brought a large fine and a big payout for environmental improvements. The prospect of expending some $40 million to reduce pollution at its plant at the foot of Douglas Street led the firm to shut down its Omaha operations. Asarco worked out a plan that fit nicely with Mayor Daub's emphasis upon river-front rejuvenation. The company would remove its plant and seal off the contaminated soil on the site in order to stop the further spread of lead and other pollutants. Uncontaminated soil would be placed above the capped material, and the twenty-three-acre tract would become a city park. As long as the city kept the cap intact, Asarco would remain liable for the containment of the polluted soil.

Critics found this solution unsatisfactory, but it passed muster with the Nebraska Department of Environmental Quality and a federal judge. The Asarco plant closed in 1997, and the following year the city council with minor modifications approved the plan for converting the company's property into a park. When the work was completed, a brief squabble arose over the naming of the unusual new park. Just before the municipal election in May 2001, the city council named it Union Labor Plaza, but the newly elected council quickly renamed it Lewis and Clark Landing. By 2004 a Martin Luther King Jr. footbridge connected the Qwest Arena with the Landing, and a similar Heartland bridge, passing under I-480, tied Lewis and Clark Landing to the Heartland of America Park. A restaurant at the Landing added to the park's ambience, but the location's past was not forgotten. A large monument, *Labor*, sculpted by Matthew Placzek, paid tribute to the role of working people in Omaha's development. Where in the early twentieth century the fires in the smelter furnaces symbolized industrial America and where fourteen languages of immigrant workers could be heard, postindustrial Omahans could enjoy their leisure.

On the riverbank immediately upstream from the smelter site was the Port of Omaha, used primarily for outbound barge shipments of grain and inbound loads of steel and asphalt. Upstream from the port was the scrap-metal yard of Aaron Ferer and Sons. For persons traveling on Abbott Drive to or from the airport or who might be present at the new convention center, the dingy old storage tanks at the port and the heap of scrap metal did not convey the image that Omaha's boosters desired. An odd circumstance presented an ideal remedy.

In 1969 two entrepreneurs in Lincoln had established a consulting firm, Selection Research, which in 1988 purchased the Gallup Organization of Princeton, New Jersey, and assumed the Gallup name. Though the public associated Gallup with political polling, the company's business was much more diverse, including market research, consulting, and executive leadership training. Lincoln became the seat of Gallup's American operations, and by 2000 the company employed six hundred persons there. Conducting training seminars for rising business executives was a key element of Gallup's future, but Lincoln lacked suitable commercial air service and the telecommunications options that the firm desired. Because Gallup reportedly preferred to stay in Nebraska, it initiated an investigation of sites in Omaha. It soon became apparent that the Aaron Ferer land and adjoining property, close to Eppley Airfield, would make a fine location for what would be known as Gallup University, the company's executive-training enterprise. The city and county governments and the Chamber of Commerce quickly arranged a package of inducements that resulted in Gallup deciding to build a campus on this river-front site. In 2002 construction began on the $75 million project, which was projected to bring some five thousand executives to Gallup University's seminars each year and which would also serve as Gallup's operational head-quarters.

Bringing in many executives, including high-ranking corporate officials, probably would boost Omaha's image in the long run. Nevertheless, one of the firm's vice presidents, Debby Anstine, told a local business gathering that her company had asked its clients where they wanted to send executives for seminars. As she said, "They picked Omaha because there isn't a lot more going on here." She added, "Pretty much the perspective of business [executives] was that people would learn, grow, focus on what they need to here in Omaha." In any event, the completion of the Gallup campus in 2003 was a key element of the city's river-front redevelopment.

Shortly after the plans for the Gallup move to Omaha took form, the National Park Service announced plans to move its thirteen-state Midwest headquarters from an old building in the southern part of downtown to a site on the river just north of Lewis and Clark Landing. The structure, known formally as the Carl T. Curtis National Park Headquarters, was designed and landscaped according to advanced environmental standards and was completed in 2004.

In the meantime, plans went ahead for the development of Riverfront Place, two towers of expensive condominiums to be erected between the National Park Headquarters and Gallup University. In selecting a group of out-of-town developers over two local firms to build the project on six acres purchased from the city, Mayor Fahey declared that Riverfront Place would help show that "a downtown succeeds when it becomes not just a place to work or visit, but a place to live." However, on the Council Bluffs side of the river opposite the Gallup campus, plans for the building of two expensive high-rise condominiums and two apartment buildings stalled when developers could not secure financing.

From the standpoint of visual and recreational appeal in the river-front redevelopment, easily the most dramatic innovation was a projected pedestrian bridge linking Omaha and Council Bluffs from a point just north of the National Park Service building. Most of the some $22.6 million for this project would come from the federal government as a result of the efforts of Robert Kerry near the end of his service as a Democratic U.S. senator from Nebraska. How the structure was designed was all-important, for it might mark the identity of a new Metro Gateway. The *World-Herald* ably caught the symbolism:

> The bridge . . . will be one of two things. It will either be good enough, a pleasant way to stroll across the river, a nice picture postcard to send home to Mom and Dad in Montana, ho-hum, zzzzzzz.
>
> Or it will be an exciting addition to Omaha's public facilities, a centerpiece of the community, part bridge and all art, something so striking that people will gawk and take pleasure in the vista and remember Omaha because of what they saw. . . .
>
> Omaha is no longer a concrete-and-chain-link city, no matter how much some people might like it to remain one. What was *good enough*

19. Looking west from the Missouri River. Eugene Leahy Mall is in foreground, and the tallest building is First National Center, Omaha, 2005. *Courtesy Timothy M. Fitzgerald.*

for Omaha in the past isn't adequate for the future, where high-tech jobs and high-tech businesses—and high-tech people—thrive.

A design competition followed, and the result was a bridge and its approaches that featured a sweeping curved appearance with interesting suspension pylons. It would be, as Mayor Fahey and Mayor Hanafan of Council Bluffs saw it, a symbol comparable to the St. Louis Gateway Arch. However, when the low bid for the project was about twice the available funds, altering costs delayed the start of construction until 2006.

If the pedestrian bridge were to become the great landmark of the river front, the new century's architectural landmark for downtown was the graceful First National Tower, completed in 2002. This office building was the result of the tremendous recent growth of the First National Bank, a closely held pioneer Omaha firm. Aside from having avoided being swept up in the corporate acquisitions common to the banking industry, First National had been a leader in the processing of credit card transactions. The firm also constructed a large data-processing building downtown.

The 632-foot, forty-story First National Tower at Sixteenth and Dodge streets, built at a cost of $208 million, became the tallest building between Chicago and Denver. In keeping with the emphasis upon making downtown attractive, First National, inspired by developments in Charlotte and Dallas, built a small park near the tower that featured a computer-controlled fountain and sculptured Canada geese. The new skyscraper fit well with the nearby Woodmen Tower, and with both visible for many miles, especially up and down I-29 in Iowa, Omaha had a visibility that trumpeted the urban Midwest. The nighttime illumination of both buildings further attested to the city's importance.

The massive redevelopment of the river front and eastern downtown drew attention to the fact that other areas of the city needed revitalization. By 2003 an organization called Destination Midtown was engaged in a comprehensive study on how to improve the area extending west from Twenty-fourth Street to Saddle Creek Road and south from Cuming to Center Street. The participants in Destination Midtown included large employers in the area, such as Peter Kiewit Sons, Mutual of Omaha, Creighton University, and the University of Nebraska Medical Center, small businesses, and neighborhood organizations, plus the Omaha City Council and the city planning department. Among their goals was improving the environment, physical appearance, and traffic flow in order to make this older part of Omaha an attractive place.

The first years of the new century brought some business revival on North Twenty-fourth Street in the old heart of black Omaha. A city-funded "streetscape beautification" for North Twenty-fourth Street contemplated a better image for the thoroughfare. Two innovations highlighted part of the heritage of this part of the city. At Twenty-fourth and Erskine streets, the Dreamland Plaza with its sculpture, *Jazz Trio*, by Littleton Alston, commemorated the old Dreamland Ballroom and at Twenty-fourth and Lake, the North Omaha Love's Jazz and Arts Center was a tribute to Preston Love's musical career. Elsewhere, there were other bright spots in the old Near North Side, such as the homes in the Concord Square area around Twenty-fourth and Hamilton streets.

Just north of the shining new buildings of eastern downtown and west of the attractive new river front was an eighty-block area in desperate need of renovation. In 2005 Mayor Fahey announced plans for redeveloping the area labeled "North Downtown" or "No Do," in geographic sectors that featured entertainment and the arts, business headquarters, light industry, and residential and retail land uses. The city was prepared to give land in a core area to entrepreneurs who would undertake projects that would stimulate the overall redevelopment of North Downtown.

Beyond North Downtown, much remained to be done to improve social and economic conditions in North Omaha. Some problems transcended race and reached beyond the black community to include much of the northeast quadrant of the city. Symbolic of this point was the announcement in April 2005 that a locally popular Target store on Saddle Creek Road would close and move west to the Crossroads Mall on North Seventy-second Street. Two other general merchandise or "big box" retailers had previously left the northeastern section of the city, leaving only one such establishment east of Seventy-second Street, and that at Fiftieth and L streets in Omaha's southeastern area. As a *World-Herald* editorial noted, "The problem is that lip service has long been paid to the idea of boosting business in north Omaha without the development of a solid plan." Whatever their race or economic circumstances, Omahans residing in the eastern part of the city increasingly found themselves having to go west—sometimes far west—for shopping and services. Indeed, *World-Herald* columnist Rainbow Rowell, noting shopping and entertainment options on the east side of the river, asserted that "Council Bluffs just gets more and more appealing. . . . And driving to Council Bluffs is rarely as stressful as driving to west Omaha."

An organization known as Omaha by Design, a creative amalgam of business, professional, and other persons in the private and public sectors, played a significant part in developing and fostering a broad-gauged approach to neighborhood improvement. The purpose of the organization, which had a strong environmental emphasis, was "to extend the benefits of quality urban design throughout Omaha," and it devised specific goals that were incorporated into the city's master plan. In any event, the purposes of Omaha by Design, Destination Midtown, and the North Downtown initiative transcended economic objectives and sought to make the concept of a pleasant, livable environment that had been basic to downtown and river-front redevelopment a reality in other parts of the city.

ECONOMIC CHANGE

In the last two decades of the twentieth century Omaha embraced the rapid change in the telecommunications industry and in information-age technology, making high-tech enterprise a tremendous force in the local economy. The new competitive era in telecommunications brought the rise of MCI as a big name in long-distance telephone service and in the mid-1990s the company built a $100 million World Communications Park in northwest Omaha. A leader in building Omaha's position in telecommunications was MFS Communications Company, founded by Peter Kiewit Sons construction company in 1986. The value of MFS skyrocketed, and in a $14.12 billion stock transaction in December 1996, the company became a subsidiary of WorldCom, a Jackson, Mississippi, firm.

Omaha became the nation's chief center for telemarketing, and by 1991 over twice the number of people worked in telecommunications as in the packing industry. In 1995 the *New York Times* noted, "There are at least 30 telemarketing companies currently operating in this former corn-and-cattle town, and 20,000 or so Omahans—about 5 percent of the resident population—work for them dialing out more than one million quality calls per week."

A great telecommunications capacity arising from the presence of the Strategic Air Command at nearby Offutt Air Force Base, early availability of fiber-optic telephone lines, and excellent service from Northwestern Bell contributed to Omaha's leap to primacy as a telemarketing center in the 1980s. Phone marketing from the Central time zone was an advantage as were the relatively unaccented speech of the telephone sales representatives, the Midwestern work ethic, and reasonable real-estate and operating expenses.

Telemarketing was often stressful with scant chance of career development, yet it served the needs of many, particularly those wishing temporary employment with flexible working hours. Indeed, other telecommunications jobs mushroomed as Omaha became the reservations center for a number of hotel chains and other firms using long-distance telephone service to reach a customer base.

The linkage between telecommunications, information-age technology, and the service sector of the economy was demonstrated in the dramatic rise of Omaha-based First Data Resources (FDR). In 1969 some local banks cooperatively established the nonprofit Mid-America Bank Card Association to process their credit card business. The nonprofit status of Mid-America Bank Card ended in 1971 with its transformation into First Data Resources. Through the 1970s First Data grew and in 1980 was purchased by American Express. The business later reemerged as a separate firm, First Data Corporation, which grew into a Fortune 500 firm with many subsidiaries. Omaha was headquarters for a major unit, First Data Resources, which in 1996 employed some 6,250 persons in the city and was the metro area's largest private employer. By then, FDR electronically processed one-third of the nation's credit card business and handled other credit card functions. FDR generated 35 percent of the first-class mail in metropolitan Omaha. In 2002 the company and its Denver-based parent had some 7,000 employees in Omaha, ranking second to Alegent Health, a hospital system, as the metro area's largest private-sector employer.

Whatever the apprehensions about Omaha's economy in the mid-1980s, the 1990s brought economic growth to the metro area. In 2001 there were 93,634 more jobs on the average in the Omaha Metropolitan Statistical Area than there had been in 1990. This represented an increase of 28.3 percent, contrasted with the national job growth increase of 20.1 percent. While the service sector provided the highest employment growth rate in the country during the years 1990 to 2001, the construction and mining sector was the fastest growing component of employment in the Omaha MSA, increasing 74.3 percent, in contrast to a 3 percent decrease in this category nationally. By the mid-1990s Omaha had a building boom, and in 2001 there were 22,741 jobs in this sector in the Omaha MSA, but mining accounted for only about 200 of this figure.

In 2001 the service sector accounted for 33.7 percent of the jobs in the Omaha MSA in contrast to 29.9 percent in 1990 and 16 percent in 1970. More than forty-four thousand service-sector jobs had been added to the Omaha MSA work force between 1990 and 2001. Data processing was a big part of this sector as were health-related positions, the latter showing Omaha's continuing prominence as a medical center.

The second largest area of employment was trade, which comprised 23.8 percent of the metro area jobs in 2001, down slightly from its 1990 figure, but up significantly in total number of persons in such occupations. However, within the trade sector there was a significant distinction between retail and wholesale occupations. Seventy-five percent of the trade-sector jobs in the Omaha MSA in 2001 were in retailing and 25 percent were in wholesaling, and between 1990 and 2001 the number of jobs in retailing had risen steadily, while the number in wholesaling had fluctuated with no overall rise.

Transportation, communication, and utilities employed 7.4 percent of the local work force in 2001 in contrast to 5.3 percent nationally. Thus, Omaha retained part of its traditional identity, for more persons were employed by these industries in 2001 than in 1955, albeit the percentage of local people employed in this sector was significantly below midcentury levels. Omaha's Werner Enterprises, founded in Council Bluffs in 1956, benefited from deregulation in the 1980s to become a large trucking firm.

Between 1990 and 2001 the number of Omaha-area jobs in manufacturing rose 5.7 percent, but in the last year this sector composed 9.0 percent of the local work force in contrast to 17 percent in 1970. There were 38,152 persons employed in manufacturing in 2001; of this total, 15,441 worked in durable-goods production, most notably industrial equipment and metal fabrication, and the remaining 22,711 produced nondurable goods. The fact that over half of these jobs in nondurable production were in food and related commodities showed that this traditional base of the local economy, although diminished from its earlier stature, remained significant. However, the relative decline of manufacturing and transportation and the growth of the service sector indicated the long-term transition from a blue-collar to a white-collar economy.

From the frontier era through the Cold War, military spending had contributed to the economic well-being of the Omaha area. Reorganization of the command structure of United States' nuclear forces following the Cold War brought the end in 1992 of the Strategic Air Command, whose headquarters had been at Offutt Air Force Base since 1948, and the establishment of U.S. Strategic Command (StratCom). This and other changes brought a significant decline in personnel at Offutt, but the base remained a major air force installation. Moreover, the prospect that defense restructuring would deal a hard blow to Bellevue did not materialize. As the twenty-first century began, Offutt Air Force Base, with some ten thousand military and civilian personnel, down about twenty-six thousand from the Vietnam War era, was still the metro's biggest employer.

Unemployment in Omaha, as in Nebraska as a whole, remained low, averaging about 3 percent, well under national averages. This fact had a downside. With a small population and some out-migration of persons between ages eighteen and forty-four, Nebraska in the mid-1990s had a labor shortage that tended to force up entry-level wages. In the mid-1990s some one thousand new jobs were being added in Omaha each month. The small labor pool may have contributed to Omaha's failure to induce Micron, an electronic technology corporation, and motorcycle manufacturer Harley Davidson to establish operations in the city.

The period between 2000 and 2004 brought an economic slowdown, reflecting national conditions. The result was a much slower rate of employment growth in the metro area than had been the case in the 1990s, and in 2003 unemployment reached 4.4 percent, a figure that remained under the national average. There were gainers and losers among the several economic sectors with the notable change being a 20 percent drop in information-technology jobs, largely attributable to the failure of one firm, Inacom Corporation.

ETHNIC AND GENDER REALITIES: OLD AND NEW

Overall employment figures obscured economic problems for some minorities. From 1990 to 2000 the black population of Omaha rose from 43,829 to

51,917 and constituted 13.3 percent of the city's population. In the metropolitan area the black population of 59,447 made up 8.3 percent of the total population in 2000. In these years the number of Hispanics in Omaha grew from 9,703 to 29,397, and in 2000 was just over 7.5 percent of the city's total population, while the 39,735 persons of Hispanic extraction constituted slightly over 5.5 percent of the metro area residents. In 2000 there were 19,294 persons of Asian origin and 3,759 American Indians who respectively totaled 1.7 percent and 0.6 percent of the Omaha MSA's population. A 1998 University of Nebraska at Omaha study found an unemployment rate of 2.9 percent for white non-Hispanic persons, 7.2 percent for blacks, 6.0 percent for Hispanics, and 3.0 percent for other groups. North Omaha and South Omaha had significantly higher unemployment rates than the 3.3 percent overall figure for the metro area, and age and educational levels were among the variables that complicated unemployment data. Likewise, underemployment—people desiring more hours of work or currently working in jobs for which they were overqualified—was a significant problem. The 1998 UNO study concluded that some 83,970 persons or about 21.6 percent of the Omaha MSA work force was underemployed. Minority persons were more apt to be underemployed than white non-Hispanics.

Even though some blacks attained managerial positions and the number of black-owned local firms rose markedly, the economic plight of many African Americans, including some entrepreneurs, remained bleak. In 1996 Omaha's black male unemployment was fourfold greater than that of the whole work force, while black female unemployment was twice the overall rate.

A primary pattern of northwestward expansion of the black population continued, but by 1995 black families were dispersed through the newer areas of the western and southwestern parts of the city as well. Nevertheless, according to 1996 data, 41,951 black persons lived east of Seventy-second Street, but only 2,415 resided to the west.

By the late 1980s gangs and drugs were a problem in Omaha as in other cities. Violence accompanying gangs and drug dealing became a particular burden for the Near North Side and adjoining areas. Gang rivalry and drug-related crime continued through the mid-1990s, and a *World-Herald* article headlined "Bullets Rain as Gangs Duel; Two Men Hurt" symbolized the worst social problems of Omaha and urban America. This situation led to the formation in 1989 of a group known as "Mad Dads," which sought to create a strong presence of adult black men on the streets in order to counteract gang influence. The organization spread to other cities and won praise from President George H. W. Bush.

In the 1990s as in the 1960s, police relations with the black community were controversial. Black persons made up about 13 percent of Omaha's population, but African Americans numbered 43.3 percent of arrests made by Omaha police in 1994. According to state senator Ernie Chambers, this was evidence of "out-and-out racism and discrimination." An approach to crime prevention known as "community policing," which emphasized youth programs and other elements of police-community liaison, did not find favor with officers and other persons who held a more traditional view of police work. In any event, law enforcement was on the cusp of critical social problems, and a study indicated that white and nonwhite persons tended to have significantly different attitudes toward the police.

As in the past, specific episodes highlighted this reality. After a white police officer shot and killed an armed black man in October 1997, a grand jury investigated the incident in accord with a 1988 law authored by Senator Chambers that required such a probe when a person died while in custody. The grand jury returned a manslaughter indictment against the officer, but a judge threw out the charge on grounds that an alternate juror had prejudiced the proceedings. A second grand jury did not return an indictment.

The case suggested the chasm between the black community and the police as blacks showed public support for the dead man's family and the police union made clear its support for the officer. These passions resulted in a confrontation in January 1998 between a white police officer who was the vice president of the police union and a black officer who had been president of the Brotherhood of Midwest Guardians, an African American police group. The dispute reflected division within the police department over perceptions of how sensitive white officers were to minorities. Affirmative-action hiring and promotion of blacks, effective under a consent decree from 1980 to 1993, had rankled some white officers who believed that blacks received unfair advantages.

The family of the slain man and leaders of the black community denounced what they deemed to be insensitivity on the part of the police, and the episode left enough bitterness to bring the city council in 2000 to create the office of police auditor, overriding Mayor Daub's veto. The auditor would have authority to review grievances about law enforcement and recommend changes, and as Marc Kraft, president of the city council, said, "It's like having a chaperone. . . . It helps prevent inappropriate actions."

In July 2000 while the creation of the position of police auditor was still being debated, a high-speed police chase of a stolen vehicle ended with a white officer fatally shooting the black driver who proved to be unarmed. As might be expected, some blacks saw the incident as another manifestation of police racism, while persons, apparently white, found radio talk shows and e-mail responses to newspaper stories handy ways to defend the police. The police department handled this incident better than it did the 1997 case, but the grand jury did not indict the officer. With grand-jury testimony sealed and an inconclusive investigation within the police department, the details of the episode remained unclear.

During his tenure as chief of police between 1998 and 2003, Donald L. Carey, who came to Omaha from Independence, Missouri, made better relations between the police and minorities a high priority. Following the July 2000 incident, the department began training officers on how to avoid violent situations after vehicle chases. The department implemented an "early warning system" to remedy problems of job performance of officers, including difficulties in dealing with the public. Whatever consolation it may have provided, data showed that Omaha ranked low among the nation's cities in fatalities resulting from police gunfire. Despite Mayor Daub's dislike for the term, "community policing," Omaha's police force was working with citizens at the neighborhood level to combat crime. Community policing became an accepted policy under Mayor Fahey, who named a black officer, Capt. Thomas H. Warren Sr., to succeed Donald Carey as chief of police. Warren, the first African American to attain this position and brother of former mayoral candidate Brenda Council, was a twenty-year veteran of the Omaha police force with a record of community service.

The 1980s brought a move away from large public-housing projects as the Omaha Housing Authority (OHA) adopted a "scattered site" approach. Between 1991 and 1995 the units of OHA's Logan Fontenelle project, which dated from the New Deal era, were razed, and in 1996 two other North Side OHA housing projects were demolished. Giving a refreshed look to the Logan Fontenelle area were the single-family units of Conestoga Place, erected by the nonprofit Greater Omaha Corporation. Persons displaced from OHA projects either went to scattered site dwellings or received subsidies to lease housing. As OHA director Robert Armstrong put it, "Social problems are magnified when you have large concentrations of low-income people in a small geographic area." Dispersion, he felt, "allows people to move into neighborhoods and not be identified as poor because of where they live." While implementation of the scattered site program occasionally aroused racism, it is noteworthy that in 1995, 22 percent of the heads of household in scattered site dwellings were white.

The Omaha Public Schools retained a key role in shaping race relations, but court-mandated busing of white and black children to achieve racial integration remained controversial. White enrollment in the Omaha Public Schools plummeted in the 1970s, and largely because of this decline, black enrollment rose from 21 to 30 percent of the OPS total in the two decades after the start of busing in 1976. Although 10.4 percent of the Bellevue Public School students in 1995–96 were black, no other suburban district in the Nebraska portion of Greater Omaha had a black enrollment exceeding 3.5 percent. The extent to which white flight contributed to this disparity could not be measured, but clearly the burdens and benefits of racial integration through busing were unevenly distributed through the metro area.

Whatever the impact of busing on improving race relations and learning opportunities, passing time and demographic changes brought calls for modification or elimination of the program. In 1984 court oversight of busing in Omaha had ceased, but reappraisal of busing was complicated by the fact that as a group black students in the mid-1990s—as a decade earlier—trailed white students in the reading, language, and mathematics scores of the California Achievement Test. In 1999 under the leadership of Superintendent John Mackiel, OPS proposed a $254 million bond issue for modernizing the system's physical facilities. Although the massive proposal transcended the issue of racial equity and provided for improvements to schools in predominantly white areas, most of the money would be used for improving old schools and building some new schools in eastern and southeastern parts of the city where blacks and Hispanics resided. Compulsory busing would end if the measure passed. Students generally would attend neighborhood schools, and OPS deemed it essential that the old facilities in minority areas be on a par with schools in the more affluent, white sections. In May fewer than 52 percent of the voters approved the package with primary support from voters in the white central and western areas. A slight majority of voters in the predominantly black area of northeast Omaha opposed the proposal, as did a larger majority in the southeastern part of the district's service area. Doubts about promised improvements and trepidations about a tax increase may have inspired many negative votes.

Following the end of busing, OPS established twenty-two academies in Omaha's poverty areas. These elementary schools, with a higher ratio of teachers to students, sought to improve learning on the part of minority pupils. Magnet schools, most of which predated the end of busing, emphasized certain subjects and served both minority and nonminority students. But just as busing had been no panacea in improving the educational status of blacks, standardized test scores in the first few years after the return to neighborhood schools showed that the disparity between the overall educational achievements of white and black students would be extremely difficult to overcome. With the start of the 2002–3 school year, minority students comprised 50.9 percent of the enrollment in the Omaha Public Schools. Although blacks accounted for 31.2 percent of the total, the proportion of Hispanic students had risen from 2.7 percent of the total enrollment in 1984–85 to 16.6 percent in 2002–3. A 1989 Nebraska law permitting youngsters to enroll in schools in districts in which they did not reside was another challenge to OPS as it competed with suburban school systems to enroll high-achieving students. In any event, data from both Omaha and Council Bluffs suggested that poverty transcended race as a problem in academic expectations and achievements.

This era brought institutional changes that did much to give blacks political influence. The key figure in bringing about these changes was Senator Chambers, who since 1971 had been the voice of blacks at the state level. Because of the configuration of legislative districts, Omaha blacks had often served in the legislature, but blacks had never been able to build political bases large enough to win at-large elections for county and local offices. Through Chambers's efforts, the mode of selecting the Omaha Board of Education was changed from at-large to district elections in 1975. Four years later, he secured legislation requiring that Omaha city council members, chosen at-large since 1912, be elected by district. In 1991 he brought about district election of the Douglas County board of commissioners. In 1981 computer programmer Fred Conley became the first black elected to the city council; in the subsequent decade and a half, other blacks won election to offices chosen by district.

Other ethnic realities were visible in the city. Starting in February 2001, motorists driving on Dodge Street past Thirty-fifth Avenue would have noticed that a red, white, and green flag flew in front of a building that formerly housed a florist business. Prominently marked "Consulado de Mexico," this was the Mexican diplomatic office for Iowa, Nebraska, and the Dakotas. The opening of the consulate reflected the rapidly increasing numbers of people in the region who were of Hispanic, especially Mexican, background. Although specific population figures were questionable, the Hispanic population of the metropolitan area reportedly increased by 139.9 percent between 1990 and 2000. The huge increase in Hispanic population was concentrated in the southeastern part of Omaha. Traditionally Czech, Polish, and Lithuanian neighborhoods that had given an east European image to South Omaha were now home to many Mexican Americans, persons newly arrived from Mexico, and other Hispanics. This was also true of the census tract including Little Italy. Jobs in Omaha's remaining packing plants drew many of the newcomers who faced hardships reminiscent of the experiences of immigrants generations earlier.

Hispanic-oriented businesses flourished in South Omaha, but the area had a significant gang problem. The fact that many Hispanic persons who came to the Omaha area were in the United States illegally was merely the local manifestation of a national reality. In 2003 outstanding *World-Herald* feature stories described the process by which layers of subcontractors and labor brokers hired immigrant workers with forged papers for construction projects while avoiding difficulties with the Immigration and Naturalization Service. The legal vulnerability of the workers led to their exploitation, while the federal and state governments were defrauded of tax revenue. A number of these workers were employed as drywall installers in the construction of the new arena and convention center. The influx of Hispanic people was a big challenge to the Catholic Archdiocese of Omaha. Only a few priests and nuns were fluent in Spanish, and the church lacked the financial resources to extend social services to this growing constituency. Even though the newcomers were from Catholic countries, evangelical Protestant groups attracted many Hispanics.

Women as a group continued to earn less than men, yet they were increasingly evident in professional and managerial positions. A survey done under the auspices of the Women's Fund of Greater Omaha found that between 1995 and 2000 the number of women in Omaha serving as chief executive officers increased from 12 percent to 22 percent of such positions in the city. Despite this evidence of increasing opportunity, men still possessed the lion's share of high-paying positions, even though 57 percent of the people employed in Omaha were women. Firms with programs for developing managerial talent were more apt to have women in their senior ranks. The National Foundation for Women Business Owners estimated that between 1987 and 1996, the number of Nebraska businesses owned by women had risen 63 percent with a corresponding employment increase of 229 percent and a sales growth of 359 percent. In 1997 there were 52,157 businesses in the Greater Omaha area of which 13,408 were owned by women. The metro area then had 15,018 firms with paid employees, and women owned 1,925 of these enterprises.

"WHO'S BUYING THOSE FANCY NEW HOUSES?"

In 1978 the city of Omaha had an area of 91.54 square miles, but with a return to a more active annexation policy in 1982, grew to 118.26 square miles by 2002. As Omaha physically expanded, the city's population density fell from 5,933 persons per square mile in 1960 to 3,179 in 1996. Omaha continued its westward growth, which was only partly the result of annexations. By 1990 more Omaha–Douglas County people resided west of 120th Street than in old Omaha east of Forty-second Street. During the 1990s the countryside west of I-680 between West Dodge and West Maple and northward was the prime area of upscale residential development.

In the 1980s the construction of new houses outpaced population growth in Douglas and Sarpy counties by nearly a two-to-one margin. A 1993 *World-Herald* headline, "Who's Buying Those Fancy New Houses?" undoubtedly posed a question in the minds of many Omahans. In that year, the city planning department noted, "This increase in sales activity is primarily due to low interest rates which make it more affordable to buy a home. Homeowners are also taking advantage of low interest rates to 'trade up,' enabling them to buy more house for the same amount of money." Part of the answer to the newspaper's question lay in trends in late-twentieth-century American life. Omahans of the post–World War II baby boom generation were a significant part of the new-home market. Fewer children per household, more divorce, and increased longevity contributed to a housing-market boom. Corporate executives moving to the city and affluent professionals composed a market for expensive houses. A diversified, prosperous local economy undergirded this impressive growth.

As the western areas came to symbolize newness and affluence in contrast to the image of a large part of the older section, C. David Kotok of the *World-Herald* noted, "Omaha may be becoming, in effect, two cities—one east of 72nd Street and one west." The newspaper clearly showed in a 1997 series of feature stories that incomes and housing values in the newer, western sections of the city were on the whole much higher than those in Omaha's older, eastern districts. Moreover, new employment was heavily concentrated in the west. While suburban growth meant more tax revenue, it brought added demands for municipal services. The increasing distance and the sharp social and economic differences between the newer and older parts of the city had disturbing implications for the future.

Urban sprawl eroded Omaha's 1970s-era status as a "20-minute city"—the normal time needed for driving between home and work or most crosstown trips. Increasing traffic volume—the result of social and economic trends—brought congestion, and arterial street and highway construction inevitably produced bottlenecks. Efforts such as the 1989–94 project to extend the Kennedy Freeway to Bellevue, eased the situation. Paradoxically, the completion of the Kennedy Freeway contributed to suburban growth in Bellevue. More auto traffic brought declining use of public transportation; between 1988 and 1996 passenger volume on Metro Area Transit buses fell by about 30 percent.

COMMUTING

Figures on job commuting between Douglas, Sarpy, and Pottawattamie counties in 2000 showed the interdependence of the various parts of the metro area and the economic dominance of Omaha. Slightly over 40 percent of the employed residents of Pottawattamie County worked in Douglas and Sarpy counties. Just over 2 percent of the work force of Douglas and Sarpy counties held jobs in Pottawattamie County. As any driver on the Kennedy Freeway between Omaha and Bellevue could verify, there was heavy commuting between Douglas and Sarpy counties. While slightly less than 5 percent of Douglas County's employed persons worked in Sarpy County, 54 percent of Sarpy County's workers made their livings in Douglas County. The livelihood of Bellevue and vicinity had diversified well beyond an overwhelming dependence upon Offutt Air Base. At the far southern end of the metro, less than 34 percent of the employed people of Cass County had jobs there; just over 32 percent worked in Douglas County and 13.5 percent in Sarpy County. From Washington County, at the north end of the metro, in 2000 the pattern was similar: 47.3 percent of its employed residents worked there, and nearly 41.6 percent worked in Douglas County.

At the beginning of the twenty-first century the traditional pattern of traveling between a home in the western suburbs and a downtown or midcity job marked the routine of most Omaha area commuters. Nevertheless, as many businesses located in the western part of the metropolitan area, a significant trend toward "reverse" commuting became evident. Of course, Iowa residents working in the Nebraska part of Greater Omaha had always been reverse commuters, but now many people were making the daily trek between homes in older residential areas of Bellevue and Omaha and offices in the outlying areas. Heading west in the morning and east in the evening, the reverse commuters experienced much easier traffic conditions, and as one of them remarked, "I always have the sun at my back."

Some 2,611 persons made an even longer commute between their homes in Douglas, Sarpy, Washington, and Pottawattamie counties and their jobs in Lancaster County (Lincoln). Even more Lancaster County residents (3,507) went the other direction on I-80 to jobs in the Greater Omaha area. Cass County, although part of the metro Omaha area, is close to Lincoln, and 13.5 percent of its work force was employed in Lancaster County.

In 2003 the White House Office of Management and Budget added three counties—Harrison and Mills in Iowa and Saunders County in Nebraska—to the Omaha Metropolitan Statistical Area. This expansion reflected the growth in commuting between these counties and Omaha and brought the population of what became the eight-county Omaha MSA to 767,041, a figure that reached an estimated 813,170 in 2005. The new definition highlighted the growing significance of the Iowa portion of the metro while the addition of Saunders County, which does not border the Missouri River, attested to Greater Omaha's westward thrust. Over forty miles of farmland still separated the southwestern outskirts of the Omaha metro from Lincoln's northeastern outskirts, and there was no likelihood that an urban strip would link the two cities in the foreseeable future. Nevertheless, Saunders County, bordering Lancaster County to the north, further emphasized the proximity of the Omaha and Lincoln metropolitan areas. The Office of Management and Budget also expanded the Lincoln metro to include Seward County, adjoining Lancaster County to the west. This gave metropolitan Lincoln a 2003 population of 266,787. The Omaha and Lincoln metropolitan areas now comprised ten continuous counties, and by deemphasizing the open spaces within this area, one could speak of a combined urban complex of more than 1,000,000 persons.

If an ever-larger population had positive booster implications, suburban growth in Omaha as elsewhere suggested a host of potential long-term problems. In 2003 Omaha's continuing expansion led assistant city planning director Steve Jensen to remark, "If we're not careful, we'll have the very same problems that everybody in the country has." There were other people who shared Jensen's concern as there had been over a generation earlier, but there was not much evidence that the people of metropolitan Omaha or their leaders were looking beyond such immediate realities as traffic congestion and gasoline prices.

Between 2000 and 2005 suburbs in Douglas and Sarpy counties continued to grow rapidly. Census estimates in 2005 indicated that Gretna in Sarpy County was home to some 4,680 persons, a 106.4 percent increase in the first five years of the new century. Although Douglas County's 5 percent growth brought the largest numerical addition of people to the metropolitan area, Sarpy County's 14 percent increase reflected its longstanding dynamism. Population in the remaining six metro counties rose by about 1 to 6 percent. In any event, growth in the Greater Omaha area contrasted bluntly to the continuing population decline in small towns and rural counties in the west central region.

POLITICS

Following his election in 1989, Mayor P. J. Morgan established a solid record and in 1993 was easily reelected. Like Boyle a decade earlier, Morgan appeared upward bound in politics, but in September 1994 he resigned to take the presidency of Lincoln's Duncan Aviation Company. Councilman Subby Anzaldo became interim mayor and was a candidate in a special mayoral election held in November 1994. In a three-way race, attorney and former

Republican congressman Hal Daub came out on top with Democrat Brenda Council, a Union Pacific attorney and city council member, in second place, and Anzaldo third. The runoff contest between Council and Daub the following month symbolized two sharply different perspectives on urban America in the 1990s.

In 1992 after eleven years on the Omaha Public School Board, Brenda Council won election as the first black woman to serve on the city council. But 1994 was a year of conservative political resurgence, which favored Daub's candidacy. Indeed, a poll showed that local voters saw crime as the state's top issue, and Daub portrayed himself as a tougher foe of criminals than his opponent. On an issue of dubious relevance to municipal policy, he vigorously supported the death penalty, which Council opposed. Not surprisingly, Daub had the support of the police union.

On election day he won handily, carrying six city council districts. Whatever the role of race and gender in this special mayoral election, *World-Herald* columnist Michael Kelly quoted an older female as having said, "I ain't ready for a woman." Kelly added, "A few probably ain't ready for a black."

In 1997 Omaha returned to its normal four-year cycle of mayoral elections with Brenda Council running close behind Daub in the primary vote. For the most part the general election campaign was a rerun of the 1994 contest with Daub emphasizing his hardline stand against crime. Daub went on to eke out a 735-vote victory over Brenda Council with particular help from South Omaha in addition to his West Omaha base. This close vote seemed to belie the excellent local economy and Daub's good record of accomplishments during his short period in office, but his manner, which he personally termed "hard-charging," clearly alienated many voters.

The next four years brought a continuation of the good economic times and the further redevelopment of downtown Omaha. With over six years in the mayor's office, Daub sought a second full term. Creighton University law professor Richard Shugrue put it well when he said, "Hal gets to take credit for an awful lot of good things that have happened in this town on his watch." Of course, there were problems: the police shooting of two black men underscored the issue of race relations, and frequent bickering between the mayor and the city council had become wearisome.

Daub's opponent would be Michael Fahey, an Omaha businessman who had served on the Omaha planning board and the Democratic National

Committee and had been a good fund raiser for his party. Fahey's father had been a precinct captain in Kansas City's Pendergast organization. Speaking of Fahey, Marty Shukert, who had been Omaha city planning director, said, "He's a very good consensus builder, a unifying sort of personality."

The *World-Herald* recommended the replacement of a number of city council members and the election of Fahey as mayor. The paper praised Daub, saying, "[I]n terms of managing the city bureaucracy, keeping a rein on city spending and moving forward on the development of the riverfront, Daub may very well go down as one of the best mayors Omaha had in the 20th century." On the other hand, it noted, "Daub operates with a perceived inflexibility and forcefulness that, although periodically necessary, also creates resentments." The paper said, "A new, cooperative, collegial, respectful tone coming out of city government should help overcome the perception that Omaha is divided by geography, race and income."

When the votes were cast, Mike Fahey won by only 1,074 votes. Omaha's east-west political split endured and continued to divide the city roughly along Seventy-second Street. West of that line Republican Daub won by sizeable margins while to the east, Fahey prevailed. Good support from South Omaha had been critical in Daub's 1997 victory over Brenda Council but did not materialize against Fahey in 2001.

A notable result of the 2001 municipal election suggested a changing attitude towards race in Omaha politics. Franklin Thompson, a University of Nebraska at Omaha professor who had served on the Douglas County Republican Committee and the city personnel board, won a west Omaha council seat, becoming the first black person on the city council from outside North Omaha. Moreover, his constituency, which led the city in support for Daub, had fewer persons of minority origin than any other council district. With the easy reelection of Frank Brown, the black incumbent from North Omaha, two of the seven city council members were African Americans.

The Fahey administration and the city council faced a few controversial issues such as the size of the hotel adjoining the new convention center and arena and the handling of serious revenue problems during a downturn of the economy, but the "cooperative, collegial, respectful tone" that the *World-Herald* desired at city hall was the order of the day. Accordingly, the 2005 city election was the least contentious campaign in twenty years as Fahey took 61 percent of ballots in defeating Dave Friend, a recently retired police captain. A low voter turnout and the fact that six of the seven council members were reelected attested to the calmer time.

CULTURE AND ENTERTAINMENT

The years after 1990 brought advances in Omaha's cultural life. Long-contemplated expansion of the Joslyn Art Museum became a reality with the completion of a new building designed by Sir Norman Foster and Partners of London, and the existing structure was renovated. Old Union Station, now known as the Durham Western Heritage Museum in honor of benefactor Charles Durham, was extensively refurbished and the exhibit area greatly expanded, including the addition of trackside exhibit capacity. To help re-create the atmosphere in the waiting room during the heyday of rail travel, Omaha sculptor John Lajba produced lifelike figures of travelers and station personnel that contained audio presentation devices. Adding to the distinction of the renowned Henry Doorly Zoo were the Lied Jungle, the Durham Tree Top Restaurant and educational center, the Walter and Suzanne Scott Kingdoms of the Sea Aquarium, an IMAX theater, and the Desert Dome. The two-acre Hubbard Gorilla Valley was the latest addition. A short distance to the northeast, across I-80, the Omaha Botanical Gardens opened on the site of a onetime city refuse fill. The completion of a visitor center at what was renamed the Lauritzen Gardens made this an increasingly important attraction. Not far to the south, on the eastern edge of Bellevue, the Fontenelle Forest, with its newly built Katherine and Fred Buffett Forest Learning Center, remained an outstanding reminder of the region's environmental diversity.

Starting in 1950, Omaha was the annual host of the College World Series. By the 1970s this early June event at Rosenblatt Stadium, adjacent to the Henry Doorly Zoo, was giving the city national exposure. Given this popularity, the National Collegiate Athletic Association insisted upon improved facilities if the College World Series were to remain in the Omaha, and after 1987 the city expended $33 million in improvements at the old ballpark, which also was the home of the city's AAA minor league team. Although maintaining adequate support for minor league baseball became a challenge, this problem did not diminish the popularity of the annual playoffs that determined the NCAA national championship. In 1995 Mark Purdy, a columnist for the *San Jose Mercury News*, commenting upon the play of the college baseball teams and atmosphere of the event, remarked, "The College World Series is nothing at all like the real World Series. It's much better."

Old buildings that were refurbished for cultural uses reminded local people and visitors of Omaha's past. A structure at Twentieth and Howard streets became the Omaha Children's Museum and the long unused Astro Theater found new life as the Rose Blumkin Performing Arts Center. This architecturally prominent building dating from 1927 houses the Omaha Theater Company for Young People. In 1997 the Bemis Center for Contemporary Arts, established in 1985, moved into a refurbished warehouse at Thirteenth and Leavenworth streets, near the Old Market. In the new century, construction went forward on the Holland Performing Arts Center, which replaced a Campbell's Soup plant on two blocks immediately north of the Leahy Mall. The Holland Center, which opened in 2005, includes a performance hall seating two thousand persons, a smaller recital hall, and an outdoor amphitheater. The moving force in the undertaking was the Omaha Performing Arts Society, led by John Gottschalk, publisher of the *World-Herald*. Most of the money came from private donors, such as retired Omaha businessman Richard Holland and his wife Mary, with the city contributing some funds, including the cost of reworking streets and sidewalks. The Performing Arts Society, using some of the city money, completed further renovation of the Orpheum Theater that it now operates.

A highly publicized controversy over historic preservation on a small portion of the Performing Arts Center site obscured two important points. First, when the business leaders, including the Chamber of Commerce, reached a consensus on a civic project, city government followed their leadership. Secondly, by the 1990s the process of corporate fund raising had been systematized, largely through the work of Walter Scott, chairman emeritus of Peter Kiewit Sons.

In the meantime, in the bluffs above the Platte River valley in Cass County, the 1990s brought the opening of Mahoney State Park and the adjoining Strategic Air and Space Museum. The nearby Lee G. Simmons Conservation Park and Wildlife Safari, under the operation of the Henry Doorly Zoo, offered visitors the opportunity to see bison, antelope, wolves, and other creatures in their natural setting. These developments, about halfway between Omaha and Lincoln, were popular attractions for residents of both urban areas.

On Friday, May 3, 1996, residents of the Ak-Sar-Ben neighborhood in south central Omaha did not hear a familiar sound: the bugle call to the post at the Ak-Sar-Ben racetrack. This rainy spring day would have opened the racing season, but for the first time in fifty-two years there would be no horse racing at Ak-Sar-Ben. In 1978 daily attendance at the track had averaged 16,018 persons, and in 1984 Ak-Sar-Ben recorded the sixth-highest patronage of any horse track in the nation. But in 1986 with the opening of the dog track in Council Bluffs, Ak-Sar-Ben's attendance plummeted. New racetracks in other cities and the two new Indian-owned casinos in Iowa undoubtedly took their toll. In 1992 the Knights of Ak-Sar-Ben sold the 350-acre Ak-Sar-Ben property to Douglas County, but the track's decline continued. The many buses filled with racing fans from around the region no longer pulled into the Ak-Sar-Ben parking lot, and local people had other wagering options, particularly with the addition of slot machines at Bluffs Run in 1995. That season, Ak-Sar-Ben's daily attendance averaged only 3,524. The financial survival of the track seemed to require the addition of casino gambling at Ak-Sar-Ben, but Nebraska had not followed Iowa in allowing a massive expansion of gaming. With two riverboat casinos with their lodging and dining facilities about to open at Council Bluffs, the Douglas County Racing Board canceled the 1996 Ak-Sar-Ben racing meet.

The plight of the racetrack was a symbol of changing times, for First Data Resources, Ak-Sar-Ben's neighbor to the west, soon announced a plan to convert the northern part of the Ak-Sar-Ben property into an information technology center that would employ about two thousand persons. FDR would purchase 140 acres from Douglas County and donate part of this former Ak-Sar-Ben property to the University of Nebraska at Omaha, which would develop a south campus to house information science, technology, and engineering programs. The adjoining business and educational facilities would have a cooperative relationship, which would enhance Omaha's emergence as an information technology center. The FDR–UNO proposal quickly won the support of Omaha's civic leadership, and despite the efforts of racing interests to revive the Ak-Sar-Ben track, the Douglas County commissioners approved the plan. Private donors contributed $47 million for the development of an information science and technology center, and the state provided $23 million for this venture in higher education. The opening of the Peter Kiewit Institute of Information Science, Technology and Engineering on the former Ak-Sar-Ben grounds in August 1999 brought a sharp increase in the enrollment in the information science and technology programs in Omaha, which were jointly administered by UNO and the University of Nebraska–Lincoln.

At the beginning of the twenty-first century, Omaha remained a city with vital regional ties as its many telephone directory entries under "Midwest" and related headings suggested. Agriculturally related businesses and food processing remained important; horses still clopped through downtown streets each September in celebration of River City Roundup, and by its very name the Durham Western Heritage Museum suggested how Omahans saw their tradition. Likewise, the Union Pacific Railroad Museum and the Western Historic Trails Center in Council Bluffs attested to the importance of the Greater Omaha area in America's westward expansion. The Union Pacific's Platte valley route and Interstate 80 were heavily traveled transcontinental thoroughfares that signified that Omaha was still a Gate City. A bucolic stereotype of Omaha persisted: a 1995 *Money* magazine article on multibillionaire Warren Buffett, who ran Berkshire Hathaway from Kiewit Plaza on Farnam Street, included a fanciful image of Buffett holding an ear of corn with a cornfield and barn in the background.

Yet much of old Omaha was gone. By 1983 Omaha's packing industry had experienced its principal decline, but between 1983 and 1993 receipts of salable livestock fell from 1,245,300 head to 469,500. If there were any lingering doubts, the 1999 closing of the stockyards clearly showed that a "bull on a pedestal" was not a fit symbol for the new Omaha. Another casualty of change was the Omaha Grain Exchange. When the railroads, faced with barge traffic competition in the 1960s, stopped using the Missouri River as a break point for freight rates on grain, a reason for maintaining the exchange ended. Railroad deregulation and computerized quotations of grain prices further reduced the need for the exchange which closed in 1985. Because the Union Pacific Railroad now had a network extending from Chicago to Los Angeles and Seattle and from Duluth to Laredo, Omaha was no longer the great jumping-off point to the West. The Gate City was giving way to a new Omaha, a city of the information age with national and global ties but with no new identity to distinguish it from other urban centers. The new Omaha with all the paraphernalia of the information age seemed unrelated to its historical roots.

Or was it? Omaha was born amid the technology of the telegraph—the first thrust of the electronic age—and steam power. The technological and capitalistic synergies of the nineteenth century produced what one person of that age termed "almost an annihilation of distance." Historian James C. Malin, one of the most analytical commentators on the development of the central Plains, observed that the opening to settlement of the region from the Missouri River to the Rockies occurred within a global context of transportation and communication. Farsighted promoters of the settlement of the Plains, he noted, contemplated building a railroad that not only would be a gateway to America's Far West but would serve the nation's interests in the Pacific basin. Technology linked to a "global perspective" influenced creative thought in the mid-nineteenth century. Omaha was born in a restless age, and as a western Missouri editor said in January 1854, "Old things, old ideas, old ways are giving way, and nothing will satisfy the people but rapidity." In the words of Senator Stephen Douglas, a key figure in the birth of Nebraska and a national leader in the 1850s, "No man can keep up with the spirit of this age who travels on anything slower than the locomotive, and fails to receive intelligence by lightning [telegraph]." Douglas, whose name would grace an important Omaha street, clearly saw the role of technology in freeing humanity from the constraints of space and time.

One hundred and fifty years after its founding, Omaha was in the vanguard of the electronic information age, which had begun with the telegraph and was part of a national and global infrastructure that had fulfilled the vision of Stephen Douglas. In helping to shape a new era, Omahans retained the ambitious, creative, and restless spirit that marked their city's birth.

Beyond the bright indicators of progress was the challenge of whether Omahans would alleviate the social and economic disparities polarizing their community. Likewise, whether they would be able to reconcile continuing physical growth of their city with a high quality of life was open to question. Omaha's problems, like its achievements, made it a representative American community. Indeed, this typicality probably contributed to the city's low profile that its boosters sought to overcome. While distant forces and massive trends had shaped the city's development, its people had done much to mold their own destiny within patterns familiar to other Americans.

Timely economic diversification had been important to Omaha's development, but this had been less evident in the history of Council Bluffs. As the twenty-first century began, casino gambling provided much money for civic projects and other valuable undertakings, particularly on the Iowa side of the river. However, three big questions remained. Would the casinos remain a major part of the local economy? Would the quality of civic leadership, money from gambling, and external realities beyond local control bring about economic diversification and development that had been elusive in the past? Would population growth and urban expansion in the Iowa part of the metropolitan area continue to emerge as a practical alternative to the westward thrust on the Nebraska side? Whatever the future, there was a new relevance to the name, "the Council Bluffs," which had first described the area on both sides of the Missouri where the Upstream Metropolis now stood.

Sometime in 1853 an obscure ferry operator and small-time promoter, William Brown, stood on the Iowa side of the Missouri River and gazed across to the bluffs that would soon be part of Nebraska Territory. He decided it a good place for a town; and, as events proved, he was right.

[For Further Reading]

There is a great variety of material available on Omaha, but comparatively little on Council Bluffs. This bibliographic essay is not intended to be exhaustive. Although it indicates the sources used in writing this book, a primary purpose is to call attention to items that should be useful to students who wish to pursue further study of the history of the Council Bluffs–Omaha area. This essay often mentions the *Omaha World-Herald* with varying titles for the evening, morning, and Sunday editions; hence, the abbreviations, WH, OWH, EWH, MWH, and SWH are used. *Nebraska History*, the quarterly publication of the Nebraska State Historical Society, is the single-most important outlet for scholarship on Omaha. It is cited as NH. Much local history has been written as master of arts theses, particularly at the Municipal University of Omaha and its successor, the University of Nebraska at Omaha, indicated respectively as "OU" and "UNO." The main Omaha Public Library (W. Dale Clark Library), the Council Bluffs Public Library, and the Douglas County Historical Society Library are cited respectively as "OPL," "CBPL," and "DCHS."

GENERAL SUGGESTIONS

An excellent introduction to Omaha's development are two videos, *If These Walls Could Speak* (1994), covering from the frontier period to World War II, and its sequel, *Omaha Since World War II: The Changing Face of the City* (2004), both produced by University of Nebraska at Omaha Television. Turning to written works, a number of local histories explore the Omaha experience. They vary greatly in content and quality. These books, some of which have accompanying biographical volumes commonly called "Mug Books," are unstructured and uncritical. Most of the authors were local residents who, despite no formal training in historical methodology, did thorough jobs of collecting data. They borrowed from each other without attribution; so a user has to be careful and start with the earliest work that deals with a particular subject. The same pattern holds for local histories done on other American cities. Some are very long, and few have ever been read from cover to cover. However, they contain information not readily available elsewhere on dominant groups, urban services, industrial progress, and social life. Used with care, they become valuable research tools.

Some local histories are old enough to be considered primary sources in their own right. Alfred Sorenson, a local journalist, wrote *Early History of Omaha, or Walks and Talks among the Old Settlers* (1876), *Omaha Illustrated: A History of the Pioneer Period and the Omaha of Today* (1888), and *History of Omaha from the Pioneer Days to the Present Time* (1889). The last is among the best summaries of early Omaha. Sorenson moved away for several decades but returned to write his valedictory, *The Story of Omaha from the Pioneer Days to the Present Time* (1923). There is a long section on Omaha and Douglas County in A. T. Andreas, *History of the State of Nebraska*, vol. 1 (1882, reprint 1975). Two long and very detailed tomes were authored by James W. Savage and John T. Bell, *History of the City of Omaha Nebraska and South Omaha* (1894) and Arthur C. Wakely, ed., *Omaha: The Gate City and Douglas County Nebraska: A Record of Settlement, Organization, Progress and Achievement*, 2 vols. (1917). A combination history and reminiscence, Edward F. Morearty, *Omaha Memories: Recollections of Events, Men and Affairs in Omaha, Nebraska, from 1879 to 1917* (1917) contains excellent economic, political, and promotional material. Pioneer days are covered in Frank J. Burkley, *The Faded Frontier* (1935). Of much less value are two old settlers' accounts: John T. Bell, *Omaha and Omaha Men: Reminiscences* (1917) and John Rush, *A Pioneer's Reminiscences* (1928). Potboilers include Fred Carey, *Romance of Omaha* (1929); Byron Reed Company, *The Story of Omaha* (1946); Richard Hewitt, *The History of Omaha, 1854–1954* (1954); and Margaret Killian, *Born Rich: A Historical Book of Omaha* (1978).

The *Omaha World-Herald* commissioned a centennial history of Omaha by Walter H. Rawley Jr. of the University of Nebraska, published in the paper in eight parts from April 18 through June 6, 1954. See also the paper's sesquicentennial publication, "Omaha . . . 150 . . . and counting," accompanying the June 13, 2004, edition. Dorothy Devereux Dustin, *Omaha and Douglas County: A Panoramic History* (1980) emphasizes nineteenth-century developments, has many pictures, and an extensive bibliography. Bob (Robert T.) Reilly, Hugh Reilly, and Pegeen Reilly, *Historic Omaha: An Illustrated History of Omaha and Douglas County* (2003) is also a popular history. Robert T. Reilly, *The Omaha Experience* (1990) and Eileen Wirth, *Omaha: The Omaha Experience* (1996) are extensively illustrated Greater Omaha Chamber of Commerce booster works that contain helpful material. Two of the present authors, Lawrence H. Larsen and Barbara J. Cottrell, in *The Gate City: A History of Omaha* (1982) treated the city's development from its founding through the late twentieth century and placed that evolution in regional and national contexts. A 1997 revised edition of this work with a concluding chapter by Harl A. Dalstrom carried Omaha's story to the 1990s. Particularly useful for Bellevue is Jerold L. Simmons, ed., *"La Belle Vue": Studies in the History of Bellevue, Nebraska* (1976). For Bennington, see Bennington Centennial Book Committee, *Bennington, Nebraska: 1892–1992* (1992). *Memories of the Jewish Midwest*, a periodical published by the Nebraska Jewish Historical Society, has articles on the Jewish experience in the metropolitan area. Nebraska Press Association, *Who's Who in Nebraska* (1940) is useful for biographical data.

The following booklets published in 1989 from the Douglas County Historical Society's Dr. C. C. Criss and Mabel Criss Memorial Lecture Series cover the span of Omaha history: Jerry E. Clark, *The Indians of Eastern Nebraska at the Time of White Settlement: An Anthropology of the Pawnee and Omaha;* Charles W. Martin, *Early Pioneer Trails and Their Impact upon the Omaha Area;* Richard E. Bennett, *The Mormon Experiment at the Missouri;* Lawrence H. Larsen, *Frontier Omaha and Its Relationship to Other Urban Centers;* Garneth O. Peterson, *Urban Settlement and Growth in Douglas County;* Janet Daly, *Urban Visions: City Planning in Twentieth Century Omaha;* and Harl A. Dalstrom, *A. V. Sorensen and the New Omaha.*

Similar to the pioneer histories of Omaha is *History of Pottawattamie County, Iowa* (1883, reprint undated). This volume compiled by a Chicago firm has useful material on the early development of Council Bluffs including biographies. With no author indicated, its preface acknowledges the contributions of John H. Keatley, D. C. Bloomer, and unnamed residents of Pottawattamie County to the work of W. T. Giles and Frank M. Wright, the project's historians. In the same vein, also including biographies, is Homer H. Field and Joseph R. Reed, *History of Pottawattamie County, Iowa, From the Earliest Times to 1907*, 2 vols. (1907). See also Pottawattamie County History Book Committee, *Pottawattamie County Iowa, A Collection of Historical Sketches and Family Histories* (1978). Charles H. Babbitt, *Early Days at Council Bluffs* (1916, reprint 1975) has good material on the presettlement period, the Pottawattamie Indian interlude in the area, and the Mormon sojourn. Genevieve Powlison Mauck, "The Council Bluffs Story through the *Nonpareil's* Eyes," *The Palimpsest* 42, September 1961, although light on twentieth-century developments, is the first work to trace the history of Council Bluffs beyond the frontier period. William E. Ramsey and Betty Dineen Shrier, *Silent Hills Speak: A History of Council Bluffs, Iowa* (2002) is topically organized with numerous photos, citations, and biographical information. This book is episodic, but readers will find it interesting and useful. See the *Newsletter* of the Historical Society of Pottawattamie County, CBPL, for short essays on many topics.

Some topical works transcend time periods. Robert L. Miller, *A Selected History of the Council Bluffs Police, 1853–2003: From Frontier Justice to a Modern Municipal Police Department* (2003) is a well-done chronological treatment. Arvid E. Nelson Jr., *The Ak-Sar-Ben Story: A Seventy-Year History of the Knights of Ak-Sar-Ben* (1967) ably discusses Omaha's best-known civic organization. Stephen Szmrecsanyi, *History of the Catholic Church in Northeast Nebraska: Phenomenal Growth from Scannel to Bergan (1891–1969)* (1983) is a balanced account of the development of the Diocese (later Archdiocese) of Omaha. Deborah C. O'Donnell, "The League of Women Voters of Greater Omaha 1920–1995," master's thesis, UNO (1996) and Sharen Rotolo, "The Women's Division of the Omaha Chamber of Commerce, 1922–1976," master's thesis, UNO (2001) show the evolution of gender roles in their portrayals of the histories of two organizations. Val J. Goodman, "Vinton Street: Evolution of an Ethnic Retail Ribbon, 1889 to 1989," master's thesis, UNO (1993), treats a century of business and ethnic change along an important Omaha street. Harry B. Otis with Donald H. Erickson, *E. Pluribus Omaha: Immigrants All* (2000) surveys the city's ethnic groups using biographical sketches. A summary of railroad passenger service that emphasizes local depots is John Peterson, "Omaha and Council Bluffs: Gateway Cities to the West," *Passenger Train Journal* 20, September 1989. Carla Johnson, *Union Pacific and Omaha's Union Station: A History of the Union Pacific Railroad Passenger Stations in Omaha, Nebraska, 1866–1971* (2001) is a valuable contribution. William Kratville, *Images of Rail: Railroads of Omaha and Council Bluffs* (2002), although primarily a photographic work, has a brief local history of each line. Richard Orr, *O&CB: Streetcars of Omaha and Council Bluffs* (1996) is a detailed, well-illustrated treatment of the history of the horse-car, cable-car, and electric street railways in the metropolitan area. Bus transportation in the metropolitan area is thoroughly discussed in G. Mac Sebree, "Omaha and Council Bluffs," *Motor Coach Age* 47, January–March 1996 and 47, October–December 1996. Louise Gilmore Donahue's booklet, *Pathways to Prosperity: A History of the Greater Omaha Chamber of Commerce* (1993) has much useful information on the work of the Chamber of Commerce and its predecessor, the Omaha Commercial Club. Garneth Oldenkamp Peterson, "The Omaha City Council and Commission: A Profile, 1858–1930," master's thesis, UNO (1980) analyzes the evolution of background characteristics of these elected figures. Peterson's historical narrative in Landmarks Heritage Preservation Commission, *A Comprehensive Program for Historical Preservation in Omaha* (1980) discusses the city's history through 1940 with emphasis upon neighborhoods. She relates the nineteenth- and twentieth-century development of what has been called the Near North Side in her narrative in Landmark Heritage Preservation Commission, *Patterns on the Landscape: Heritage Conservation in North Omaha* (1984). The last two works are available through the Omaha City Planning Department. Peterson's "Who's in Charge? A Framework for Examining Community Leadership in Omaha over the Past Century," NH 72, Summer 1991 discusses the changing patterns of civic leadership in Omaha from the founding of the city to 1990.

Three books, plus several unpublished drafts and working papers, are essential to the study of Omaha. The Federal Writers Project of the Works Progress Administration in Nebraska planned to publish a general history of Omaha, along with studies on specialized subjects. Following the termination of the WPA in 1943, the Nebraska State Historical Society gained custody of the Omaha Federal Writers Project records. They cover many aspects of the life of the city up to World War II. The collection is complemented by one of the best volumes in the American Guide Series, Federal Writers Project, *Nebraska: A Guide to the Cornhusker State* (1939). It has excellent material on Omaha. Another valuable source is James C. Olson and Ronald C. Naugle, *History of Nebraska*, 3rd ed. (1997). This standard history of the Cornhusker

State provides the framework for studying the economic, social, and political development of Omaha and its hinterland. Although there are other histories of Nebraska, Olson and Naugle is analytical and comprehensive. In a class by itself is the chapter on Omaha in George Leighton, *Five Cities: The Story of Their Youth and Old Age* (1939). This material appeared originally as "Omaha, Nebraska: The Glory has Departed," *Harper's Magazine* 177, July–August 1938 and was reprinted in condensed form in NH 19, October – December 1938. Leighton produced a thematic history that emphasized a clash of wills between labor and management. His unflattering portraits of prominent civic leaders made his work controversial in Omaha. Useful in establishing the Iowa context of the development of Council Bluffs are William J. Petersen, *The Story of Iowa: Progress of an American State*, 2 vols. (1952); Leland L. Sage, *A History of Iowa* (1974); and Dorothy Schwieder, *Iowa: The Middle Land* (1996). Federal Writers Project, *Iowa: A Guide to the Hawkeye State* (1938), reprinted as *The WPA Guide to 1930s Iowa* (1986), has good material on Council Bluffs.

Several indexes deal with the history of the Greater Omaha area. These include Nebraska Press Association, *Who's Who in Nebraska* (1940); Carol Gendler, comp., *Index to the Jewish Press (1920–1977) Including Omaha Jewish Bulletin (1919–1927)* (1978); Raymond Wilson, comp., "Nebraska History in Graduate Theses at the University of Nebraska-Omaha," NH 56, Summer 1975; and "One Hundred Years of Growing: An Omaha Bibliography, 1854–1954," found in the OPL. Especially valuable are Frederick W. Adrian, comp., *Theses and Dissertations Dealing with Nebraska and Nebraskans* (1975); Michael L. Tate, comp., *Nebraska History: An Annotated Bibliography* (1995); William Petersen, comp., *Iowa History Reference Guide* (1952); and Patricia Dawson and David Hudson, comps., *Iowa History and Culture: A Bibliography of Materials Published between 1952 and 1986* (1989). These indispensable volumes include references to articles, books, theses, and dissertations. The Dawson and Hudson bibliography is supplemented in Patricia Dawson's "Iowa History and Culture: A Bibliography of Materials Published from 1987 through 1991," which appeared serially in *Annals of Iowa* 52, Spring, Summer, and Fall 1993. Annual and long-term indexes of NH and *Annals of Iowa*, the latter a publication of the State Historical Society of Iowa, are also helpful.

There is a wealth of information about Omaha in local newspapers. The most extensive holdings, usually on microfilm, are in the Nebraska State Historical Society and at major Omaha libraries. See Anne P. Diffendal, comp., *A Guide to the Newspaper Collection of the State Archives: Nebraska State Historical Society* (1977). The *Bee*, published from 1872 to 1927, is of special value during its first decades when editor and publisher Edward Rosewater took a direct interest in all aspects of the paper's operation. The *News*, in print from 1899 to 1927, tended toward sensationalism. The amalgamation of the two papers, the *Bee-News*, lasted from 1927 to 1937. The *World-Herald*, created by a merger in 1889, has the longest continuous publication record of any Omaha paper. In many ways the *World-Herald* is the "manuscript of the city," and its use is essential for important events. The weekly *Sun* publications are especially valuable for the 1960s because of excellent investigative reporting, but the paper ceased publication in 1983. Early papers—most short-lived—include the *Arrow* (actually published in Council Bluffs), the *Nebraskian*, the *Tri-Weekly Nebraska Republican*, the *Times*, the *Nebraskian and Times*, the *Weekly Herald*, the *Telegram*, the *Union*, and the *Dispatch*. Among South Omaha journals were the *Globe-Citizen*, the *Tribune*, the *Nebraska Daily Democrat*, the *Daily Stockman*, and the *Magic City Hoof and Horn*. The *Examiner* covered Omaha Society from 1884 to 1921. The leading black journal, the *Star*, started publication in 1938. There have been few other black papers: the *New Era*, the *Guide*, the *AfroAmerican Sentinel*, and the *Monitor*. The *Jewish Bulletin* is available for two years after World War I. Since then, the primary Jewish paper has been the *Jewish Press*. Omaha has had a rich ethnic press: *Den Danske Pioneer*, *Freie Presse* and *Wochentliche Tribune*, *Volkszeitung-Tribune*, *Denni Pokrok*, *Gwiazda Zachodu*, *Narodni Pokrok*, *Nova Doba*, *Posten*, *Osveta Americke*, *Pokrok Zapadu*, and *Public Ledger* (Italian). These publications sought regional audiences and did not concentrate on local news developments. Taken collectively and used selectively, the papers of Omaha, both big and small, mirror the life of the city and its people.

The earliest newspaper in what became the Omaha metropolitan area was the *Frontier Guardian*, published at Kanesville, (Council Bluffs)Iowa, from 1849 to 1852 and briefly thereafter as the *Frontier Guardian and Iowa Sentinel*. The *Frontier Guardian* is especially valuable for information on the Mormon presence at Kanesville and for the role of that settlement as a jumping-off place for overland travel. Other Council Bluffs papers include the *Chronotype* (1855–56); the *Western Bugle*, which appeared under variants of this name until 1870; the *Daily Telegraph* (1861–72); and the *Council Bluffs Globe* (1883–97).

One 1888 issue of the *Council Bluffs Reflector* is available as is the *Pottawat-tamie Journal* (1905–6), the Council Bluffs *Jeffersonian* (1933–34), and the *Labor News* (1931–32). The *Farmer Labor Press* continued from 1933 to 1982. The oldest newspaper remaining in publication in the metropolitan area is the *Council Bluffs Nonpareil*, dating from 1857. It is one of the best sources for information on the history of the city. As might be expected, the Omaha newspapers provide some coverage of Council Bluffs events.

The Decennial Census of the United States is the foundation for writing an urban biography of an American city or metropolitan area. The census is more tedious and difficult to use than many other sources. In particular, confusing tables and indexes coupled with small print vex scholars. Still, while much of the data extracted is by necessity background information that does not show up directly in final published form, it is absolutely necessary to gain a firm grasp of demographic, social, and economic characteristics. There is an ever-increasing amount of data on Omaha from the 1860 census onward. For example, the 1860 census has no information on housing; the 1970 census has an entire volume on the subject. Special federal censuses such as *Street and Electric Railways* (1910), *Religious Bodies: 1906* (1910), *Religious Bodies: 1936* (1941), and *1997 Economic Census: Minority and Women-Owned Business Enterprises—Omaha*, NE-IA MSA, (the last available at http://www.census. gov/epcd/mwb97/metro/M5920html) are basic to the study of urban history and, with other components of the U.S. Census, fundamental to our narrative. Additionally, the Iowa state censuses between 1856 and 1925 have good information on Council Bluffs and Pottawattamie County.

CHAPTER 1

Physical geography of localities and regions may contribute significantly to urban development. The first chapter treats the environment, the prehistoric and historic native peoples, and the coming of traders and other European-Americans to what became the Greater Omaha area. The focus is on the early and especially the middle years of the nineteenth century. By the late 1840s, the Mormon sojourn at Kanesville produced what would become Council Bluffs in 1853, the remote western Iowa settlement whose entrepreneurs would give birth to Omaha the following year.

Olson and Naugle, *History of Nebraska* has excellent background material on the Omaha area prior to the creation of Nebraska Territory and the opening of the area to settlement in 1854. A helpful work on a key feature of the area's natural environment is Cornelia F. Mutel, *Fragile Giants: A Natural History of the Loess Hills* (1989). Because the Missouri River played a critical part in the development of Omaha and the region, readers will find Hiram M. Chittenden's classic two-volume work, *History of Early Steamboat Navigation on the Missouri River* (1903) useful. In addition to comments on the Pottawattamie Indian presence in the area, Chittenden and Alfred Talbot Richardson, *Life, Letters and Travels of Father Pierre-Jean De Smet, s.j., 1801–1873* (1905, reprint 1969) provides valuable glimpses of early steamboat travel on the Missouri and the presettlement environment of what became Council Bluffs, Iowa. Robert Kelley Schneiders, *Unruly River: Two Centuries of Change along the Missouri* (1999) is an excellent work that emphasizes environmental considerations. See also William J. Orr, trans. and ed., and Joseph C. Porter, ed., "A Journey through the Nebraska Region in 1833 and 1834; From the Diaries of Prince Maximillian of Wied," NH 64, Fall 1983. David L. Bristow, *A Dirty, Wicked Town: Tales of 19th Century Omaha* (2000), drawing from Erastus Beadle, *To Nebraska in 1857: A Diary of Erastus Beadle* (1923), provides an image of the tallgrass prairie on the eve of settlement. William Cronon, *Nature's Metropolis: Chicago and the Great West* (1991) shows how the nineteenth-century development of the Midwest and Great Plains depended upon lumber from the forests of the upper Great Lakes country. Because the area known as the Council Bluffs was dependent upon St. Louis for its early development, James Neal Primm, *Lion of the Valley: St. Louis, Missouri* (1981) and William E. Foley, *A History of Missouri, Volume I, 1673 to 1820* (1971, reprint 1999) help establish a regional context for understanding the history of the Missouri River valley in the eighteenth and early nineteenth centuries.

A good summary treatment of the area's prehistoric people is found in James H. Gunnerson, "The Ancient Ones," in *The First Voices* special issue of NEBRASKAland *Magazine* 62, January–February 1984, but see also Lynn Marie Alex, "Prehistoric and Early Historic Farming and Settlement Patterns," *South Dakota History* 13, Spring–Summer 1983. The classic work on the Omaha Indians is Alice C. Fletcher and Francis La Flesche's two-volume anthropological study, *The Omaha Tribe* (1911, reprint 1972). The essay by Michael L. Tate and Niel M. Johnson, "Travelers from the Great Waters: Indian Peoples of the Middle Missouri," in Simmons, "*La Belle Vue*" gives an excellent introduction to the historic tribes of the Omaha area and their plight in the nineteenth century. Dennis Hastings, "An Omaha Chronology," in *The First Voices* special issue of NEBRASKA*land Magazine* is also useful. The plight of the native peoples is indicated in the titles of two fine books essential to this chapter: Judith A. Boughter, *Betraying the Omaha Nation, 1790–1916* (1998) and David J. Wishart, *An Unspeakable Sadness: The Dispossession of the Nebraska Indians* (1994). James A. Clifton, *The Prairie People: Change and Continuity in Potawatomi Culture 1665–1965* (1977) and the Reverend Joseph Murphy, O.S.B., *Potawatomi of the West: Origins of the Citizen Band*, ed. Patricia Sulcer Barrett (1988) discuss the Potawatomi sojourn in southwestern Iowa in the context of the tribe's broader experience. Narrower in scope but still valuable are Frank Anthony Mullin, "Father De Smet and the Pottawattomie Indian Mission," *The Iowa Journal of History and Politics* 23, April 1925; William Lyle Davis, S.J., "Peter John De Smet: Missionary to the Potawatomi, 1837–1840," *Pacific Northwest Quarterly* 33, April 1942; Robert C. Carriker, *Father Peter John De Smet, Jesuit in the West* (1995); and Jeanne P. Leader, "The Pottawattomies and Alcohol: An Illustration of Illegal Trade," *Kansas History* 2, Autumn 1979.

Especially valuable works on the early white presence are Charles H. Babbitt, *Early Days at Council Bluffs* (1916, reprint 1975), including the quotation from the St. Louis superintendent of Indian affairs; David J. Wishart, *The Fur Trade of the American West, 1807–1840: A Geographical Synthesis* (1979); and Richard E. Jensen, *The Fontenelle and Cabanné Trading Posts: The History and Archeology of Two Missouri River Sites, 1822–1838* (1998). See also two articles by Jensen: "Bellevue: The First Twenty Years," NH 56, Fall 1975, reprinted in Simmons, "*La Belle Vue*" and "The Pawnee Mission, 1834–1846," NH 75, Winter 1994. Other works dealing with Indian-white contact include Samuel Allis, "Forty Years among the Indians and on the Eastern Borders of Nebraska," *Transactions and Reports of the Nebraska State Historical Society* 2 (1887); Gail De Buse Potter, "A Note on the Samuel Allis Family: Missionaries to the Pawnee, 1834–46," NH 67, Spring 1986; David Lavender, *The Fist in the Wilderness* (1998); and Charles Preuss, *Exploring with Frémont: The Private Diaries of Charles Preuss, Cartographer for John C. Frémont on His First, Second, and Fourth Expeditions to the Far West*, trans. and ed. Edwin G. Gudde and Elizabeth K. Gudde (1958). See also Ramsey and Shrier, *Silent Hills Speak*, including sidebar by Gail George Holmes on Capt. Billy Caldwell. Thomas F. Schilz and Jodye L. D. Schilz, "Beads, Bangles, and Buffalo Robes: The Rise and Fall of the Indian Fur Trade along the Missouri and Des Moines Rivers, 1700–1820," *Annals of Iowa* 49, Summer–Fall 1987 and W. Raymond Wood, *Prologue to Lewis and Clark: The Mackay and Evans Expedition* (2003) are valuable for their discussions of white commerce with native people, particularly trade with the Omaha Indians at the peak of that tribe's power. The larger context of the Platte Purchase, in part the result of an Indian treaty negotiated at Bellevue, is discussed in Christopher M. Paine, "The Platte Earth Controversy: What Didn't Happen in 1836," *Missouri Historical Review*, 91 October 1996.

The most notable works on individual traders who were active in the area are Walter B. Douglas and Abraham P. Nasatir, *Manuel Lisa* (1964); Richard Edward Oglesby, *Manuel Lisa and the Opening of the Missouri Fur Trade* (1963); and John E. Sunder, *Joshua Pilcher: Fur Trader and Indian Agent* (1968). The following essays in a multivolume work, LeRoy R. Hafen, ed., *The Mountain Men and the Fur Trade of the Far West*, summarize the careers of key figures in the fur trade of the Omaha area: Ray A. Mattison, "John Pierre Cabanne, Sr.," vol.2 (1965); Mattison, "Joshua Pilcher," vol. 4 (1966); Nasatir, "James Mackay," vol. 4; Oglesby, "Manuel Lisa," vol. 5 (1968); John E. Wickman, "Peter A. Sarpy," vol. 5; John E. Wickman, "Peter A. Sarpy," vol. 4; and Alan C. Trottman, "Lucien Fontenelle," vol. 5, reprinted in Simmons, "*La Belle Vue.*" See also Edward F. Sterba, "Peter Sarpy 1805–1865" in Simmons, "*La Belle Vue,*" and Kathryn M. French, "Manuel Lisa," *South Dakota Historical Collections* 4 (1908).

An excellent discussion of the Mormon presence in what became the Omaha–Council Bluffs area is Richard E. Bennett, *Mormons at the Missouri, 1846–1852: "And Should We Die . . . "* (1987). See also Robert Trennert Jr., "The Mormons and the Office of Indian Affairs: The Conflict over Winter Quarters, 1846–1848," *NH* 53, Fall 1972 and E. Widtsoe Sumway, "Winter Quarters, 1846–1848," *NH* 35, June 1954; 36, March 1955. William G. Hartley, "Mormons and Early Iowa History (1838 to 1858): Eight Distinct Connections," *Annals of Iowa* 59, Summer 2000 is especially noteworthy because of its account of the final decision of the Mormons to head toward the Council Bluffs. An authoritative treatment of the development of Kanesville until it was renamed "Council Bluffs" in 1853 is Phillip L. Cooper, "The Antecedents of Council

Bluffs, Iowa: From Exploration to Town Charter," master's thesis, UNO (1973). Other particularly helpful works are Jean Trumbo, "Orson Hyde's *Frontier Guardian*: A Mormon Editor Chronicles the Westward Movement through Kanesville, Iowa," *Iowa Heritage Illustrated* 77, Summer 1996 and Kami Wilson, "Stability and Transition: Kanesville, Iowa and *The Frontier Guardian*, February 1849–February 1852," graduate seminar paper, Department of History, UNO. On early planning for the Mississippi and Missouri Rail Road route to Council Bluffs, see Maury Klein, *Union Pacific: Birth of a Railroad: 1862–1893* (1987).

CHAPTER 2

This chapter covers early prospects, the settlement of Omaha, the capital fight, the outfitting trade, the formation of the business community, and the construction of the Union Pacific Railroad. These subjects are discussed in detail in the local histories. Many of the quotations and anecdotes originally appeared in Sorenson, *History of Omaha*. Integral to this story was continued development of Council Bluffs. The completion of railroads reaching Council Bluffs from the north, south, and east did much to establish what later scholars would call the "Omaha Gateway" in the nation's transportation system.

Wishart, *An Unspeakable Sadness* details the movement to reservations of the Otoe-Missouria and Omaha peoples. Olson and Naugle, *History of Nebraska* has excellent material on early town promotion and politics in Nebraska Territory. Ella Bartlett Knight, "Geographic Influence in the Location and Growth of Omaha," master's thesis, Clark University (1924) argues that Omaha defeated its immediate rivals for geographic reasons. John W. Reps, *Cities of the American West: A History of Frontier Urban Planning* (1979) has a section on Omaha. For data on surrounding settlements see Simmons, *"La Belle Vue"*; Niel M. Johnson, ed., *Portal to the Plains: A History of Washington County, Nebraska* (1974); Marian G. Miles, "The Founding of Florence, 1854–1860," master's thesis, UNO 1970; Edward F. Kearns, "History of Papillion, Nebraska," master's thesis, OU (1962); Norman Graebner, "Nebraska's Missouri River Frontier, 1854–1860," NH 42, December 1961; Donald F. Danker, "The Nebraska Winter Quarters Company and Florence," NH 37, March 1956; Michael W. Homer, "After Winter Quarters and Council Bluffs: The Mormons in Nebraska Territory, 1854–1867," NH 65, Winter 1984; and for material on Bellevue, Michelle C. Gullett, "'If Even a Few Souls are Reclaimed, the Labor is not Lost': William Hamilton's Life among the Iowa and Omaha Indians, 1837–1891," master's thesis, UNO (1994). Dorothy Devereux Dustin, "Plotting and Platting North of the Platte," *Omaha* 3, August 1978 is a short popular account of promotional activities. Harl A. Dalstrom, "Bess Streeter Aldrich's Frontier Omaha, 1866–1868," *Heritage of the Great Plains* 28, Fall–Winter 1995 also emphasizes this theme. The general subject of promoters and their methods is developed in Charles N. Glaab and A. Theodore Brown (revised by Charles N. Glaab), *A History of Urban America* (1976).

There are a number of valuable studies on Omaha's initial economic development. The best thesis on the subject is Bertie Bennett Hoag, "The Early History of Omaha from 1853 to 1873," master's thesis, OU (1939). Two *NH* articles deal with freighting: Walker Wyman, "Omaha: Frontier Depot and Prodigy of Council Bluffs," 17, July–September 1936 and Carol Gendler, "Territorial Omaha as a Staging and Freighting Center," 49, Summer 1968. There is considerable information that touches on Omaha in two books by William E. Lass. They are *A History of Steamboating on the Upper Missouri River* (1962) and *From the Missouri to the Great Salt Lake: An Account of Overland Freighting* (1972). Clarence Bagley, "Nebraska in 1852," *NH* 5, January–March 1922 recalled crossing the Missouri on the steam ferry. Burkley, *The Faded Frontier* has interesting material on the issuance of scrip by the city government as does a *SWH* article, May 9, 1954. Nan Viergutz Carson, "Thomas Barnes Cuming, Jr. and the Location of Nebraska's Territorial Capitol," master's thesis, OU (1961) is a fine study of an important topic. There are biographical sketches of Kountze and Creighton family members in the local histories. The activities of the Kountze family in Denver are analyzed in Lyle W. Dorsett, *The Queen City: A History of Denver* (1977). For biographical sketches of the Creightons see P. A. Mullens, *Creighton* (1901).

Klein, *Union Pacific: Birth*; Burkley, *The Faded Frontier*; and J. R. Perkins, *Trails, Rails and War: The Life of General G.M. Dodge* (1929, reprint 1981) have good accounts of the possible significance of Abraham Lincoln's 1859 visit to Council Bluffs in the subsequent location of the Union Pacific terminus. Stanley P. Hirshson, *Grenville M. Dodge: Soldier, Politician, Railroad Pioneer* (1967) takes a more critical view of Dodge's career, as does David Haward Bain's *Empire Express: Building the First Transcontinental Railroad* (1999).

The decision-making process that led to Omaha becoming the starting point for the first transcontinental railroad was complex. Because of political and economic machinations, students of the subject have been forced to piece the story together from many different places. Bain's outstanding *Empire Express* tells the stories of the building of the Union Pacific and Central Pacific railroads and the leaders who shaped this process in the context of national development. Two monographs, both done many years ago, are still essential: John P. Davis, *The Union Pacific Railway: A Study in Railway Politics, History, and Economics* (1894) and Nelson Trottman, *History of the Union Pacific: A Financial and Economic Survey* (1966). A more recent study is Charles Edgar Ames, *Pioneering the Union Pacific: A Reappraisal of the Builders of the Railroad* (1969). It has an excellent bibliography. The author, a direct descendant of Union Pacific railroad builder Oakes Ames, applied the skills of a professional investment analyst to the question of the railroad's financing and its corporate structure. He reached conclusions somewhat similar to those in Robert W. Fogel, *The Union Pacific Railroad—A Case in Premature Enterprise* (1960). A very helpful book on an operational level is Grenville Dodge, *How We Built the Union Pacific Railway and Other Railway Papers and Addresses* (1910, reprint 1965). Of major value is Wallace D. Farnham, "The Pacific Railroad Act of 1862," *NH* 43, September 1962. A particularly useful essay is Barry B. Combs, "The Bellevue Scare," in Simmons, *"La Belle Vue."* Don Snoddy, Barry Combs, Bob Marks, and Del Weber, eds., *Their Man in Omaha*, vol. 1 of *The Barker Letters 1860–1868* (2004) shows the anxiety of some Omahans over the prospect of a Union Pacific terminus at Bellevue. The congressional investigation of the Union Pacific in the 1870s concentrated on larger questions than the terminal selection. The voluminous Union Pacific Railroad Papers at the Nebraska State Historical Society deal with later railroad operations and policies. The railroad builders are viewed in a harsh light in Leighton, *Five Cities*. Klein's *Union Pacific: Birth* is a critical but fair treatment of the road's leaders from its inception to its 1893 bankruptcy and has important operational details. Stephen E. Ambrose's highly readable *Nothing Like It in the World: The Men Who Built the Transcontinental Railroad, 1863–1869* (2000), like Klein, has material on such matters as the "burnettizing" process for tie preservation.

George Francis Train was among the most colorful of Omaha promoters. There is an interesting character analysis of Train in Sorenson, *History of Omaha*. Train's 1863 speech on the destiny of Omaha is printed in full in the *Nebraska Republican*, December 4, 1863, an issue that covered the Union

Pacific groundbreaking ceremony in detail. See also *Council Bluffs Nonpareil*, December 5, 1863. Train praised himself in his autobiography, *My Life in Many States and Foreign Lands* (1902). For a summary of his uncommon and controversial life see the *Dictionary of American Biography*, "Train, George Francis." For the last two quotes describing Train, see Davis Britton, "George Francis Train and Brigham Young," *Brigham Young University Studies* 18, Spring 1978 and J. R. Johnson, *Representative Nebraskans* (1954).

Mauck, "The Council Bluffs Story" highlights the development of Council Bluffs during the period covered in this chapter. Three persons who made their homes in Council Bluffs—Amelia Bloomer, William H. Kinsman, and Grenville M. Dodge—typified the dynamics of life in mid-nineteenth-century America. For Bloomer, see Louise R. Noun, "Amelia Bloomer, A Biography," part 1, "The Lily of Seneca Falls" and part 2, "The Suffragist of Council Bluffs," *Annals of Iowa* 47, Winter 1985; 47, Spring 1985. See also Noun, *Strong-Minded Women: The Emergence of the Woman-Suffrage Movement in Iowa* (1969). Kinsman's brief career is treated in Raymond A. Smith, "Yours in Haste: W. H. Kinsman" and Richard W. Peterson, "Tell the Boys I Die Happy," both in *Palimpsest* 66, November–December 1985. For Dodge, who became Council Bluffs's most renowned citizen, see Perkins, *Trails, Rails and War* and Hirshson, *Grenville M. Dodge.*

For the convergence of railroads upon Council Bluffs in the period 1867 to 1869, see Sidney Halma, "Railroad Promotion and Economic Expansion at Council Bluffs, Iowa, 1857–1869," *Annals of Iowa* 42, Summer 1974. The following essays by E. Douglas Branch: "Council Bluffs in 1865"; "The C.B. and St. Joe"; "The North Western"; "The Rock Island"; and "The Final Ties," all in *Palimpsest* 10, June 1929 provide more information. See also Richard C. Overton, *Burlington Route: A History of the Burlington Lines* (1965, reprint 1976). H. Roger Grant, *The North Western: A History of the Chicago and North Western Railway System* (1996) and William H. Thompson, *Transportation in Iowa: A Historical Summary* (1989) also treat the building of railroads into Council Bluffs immediately after the Civil War. Schwieder, *Iowa*, has summary material on the lines reaching Council Bluffs.

CHAPTER 3

In this chapter the people of Omaha engage in community building, found a claim association, move toward law and order, and establish social and religious institutions. Council Bluffs, though older, still exhibited the rough characteristics of a frontier community but also took important steps toward refinement and stability. All the local histories contain material on the subjects covered. Short biographies of settlers who left or stayed can be found in Sorenson, *History of Omaha;* Wakely, *The Gate City;* and Andreas, *Nebraska.* Of the discussions of the claim associations, Sorenson's is the easiest to follow. He has a readable account of the fight for law and order, although there is more detailed information about the same incidents in Wakely. His book is also valuable for its data on the formation of institutions. Burkley, *The Faded Frontier* discusses the experiences of the Burkley family and the establishment of the claim association. Olson and Naugle, *History of Nebraska* has a good quotation by J. Sterling Morton on the expectations of the pioneers, plus information on land policy. See Roy Robbins, *Our Landed Heritage: The Public Domain, 1776–1936* (1942, 1962, and rev. ed., 1976) for a standard account of American land policy. What happened in Nebraska is sketched in Addison Sheldon, *Land Systems and Land Policies in Nebraska* (1936).

A number of sources treat Omaha's social development. Charles W. Martin, ed., "Omaha in 1868–1869: Selections from the Letters of Joseph Barker," *NH* 59, Winter 1978 and Snoddy, Combs, Marks, and Weber, *Their Man in Omaha* are especially valuable in showing facets of Omaha's evolution. See also Don Snoddy, Barry Combs, Del Weber, Bob Marks, and Pat Kennedy, eds., *Their Man in Omaha,* vol. 2 of *The Barker Letters 1869–1876* (2006). Josie McCague McCulloch, who grew up in pioneer Omaha, wrote what she called "scrappy notes" in "Memories of Omaha: A Reminiscence," *NH* 35, December 1954. Extralegal attempts at bringing law and order are analyzed in Olive Goss, "Vigilantes of Eastern Nebraska," *NH* 13, January–March 1932. The punishment for horse stealing in Nebraska Territory was codified in the territorial statutes adopted from Iowa's criminal code. Philip A. Kalisch, "High Culture on the Frontier: The Omaha Library Association," *NH* 52, Winter 1971 is a valuable account of an early attempt at bringing social niceties. See also Robert D. Harper, "Theatrical Entertainment in Early Omaha," *NH* 36, June 1955. As noted in Dalstrom, "Bess Streeter Aldrich's Omaha," the first part of Aldrich's novel, *The Lieutenant's Lady* (1942) has a historically sound portrayal of life in Omaha between 1866 and 1868. Her images are confirmed in the contemporary accounts cited in Dalstrom's article and quoted in this chapter. R. McLaren Sawyer, "Samuel Dewitt Beals: Frontier Educator," *NH* 50,

Summer 1969 explores the career of an influential Omaha educational figure. The best material on early city government is in Irene Zika, "Some Aspects of Territorial and State Legislative Control of the Municipal Government of Omaha (1857–1875)," master's thesis, OU (1946). The quote from Charles N. Glaab at the end of the chapter is from the preface of his book, *Kansas City and the Railroads: Community Policy in the Growth of a Regional Metropolis* (1962).

For the material on Council Bluffs, chapter 3 relies upon Mauck, "The Council Bluffs Story" and *History of Pottawattamie County, Iowa* (1883). Miller, *A Selected History of the Council Bluffs Police* was helpful for its treatment of vigilante activity. The quote on the McGuire lynching is from Field and Reed, *History of Pottawattamie County*, vol. 1.

CHAPTER 4

Here, the leaders of Omaha and Council Bluffs seek a solid economic base. Subjects dealt with include Omaha's position in the nation's urban system, the problems created by Union Pacific policies, the fortunes of Nebraska, the coming of stockyards and packing plants, the founding of South Omaha, the expansion of trade and commerce, the growth of the railroad net, the depression of the 1890s, the Populist crusade, and the Trans-Mississippi Exposition. Although the local histories have a great deal of information on Omaha's economy, there is uncritical acceptance of the doctrine of progress, with the Panic of 1893 viewed as a temporary setback. The building of a hinterland is a key element in the Omaha story for this period, and Olson and Naugle, *History of Nebraska* provides much information on the subject.

By 1900 Omaha, together with South Omaha and Council Bluffs, had become an American regional center. The tendency of people to live in cities and the construction of interior urban systems in the last half of the century was noted by many observers. A classic account is Adna Weber, *The Growth of Cities in the Nineteenth Century* (1899, reprint 1963). Arthur Schlesinger, *The Rise of the City* (1933) saw urbanization as a central theme in the late-nineteenth-century United States. Lawrence H. Larsen, *The Urban West at the End of the Frontier* (1978) places Omaha within the context of an urban system that served the Great Plains. He summarizes the reasons why Chicago won the battle for economic domination of the Midwest in "Chicago's Midwest Rivals: Cincinnati, St. Louis, and Milwaukee," *Chicago History* 5, Fall 1976.

See also Primm, *Lion of the Valley*. The appropriate sections of three surveys are helpful starting points in understanding urban geopolitical relationships: Glaab and Brown, *Urban America*; Bayrd Still, *Urban America: A History with Documents* (1974); and Blake McKelvey, *The Urbanization of America: 1860–1915* (1963). The policies followed by three of Omaha's rivals are examined in Dorsett, *The Queen City*; A. Theodore Brown and Lyle W. Dorsett, *KC: A History of Kansas City, Missouri* (1978); and Robert James Willoughby, "Unfulfilled Promise: St. Joseph, Missouri's Nineteenth-Century Competition to Become the Regional Metropolis of the Great Plains," PhD diss., University of Missouri-Kansas City (1997).

Railroad building and policy remained central to the Omaha–Council Bluffs experience. Wakely, *The Gate City*; Savage and Bell, *History of the City of Omaha*; and Sorenson, *The Story of Omaha* all hailed the obtaining of the "High Bridge" as a community triumph. The bridge opened in 1872, partially fell during a tornado in 1877, was rebuilt and used until a new bridge opened nearby in 1887. That bridge remained in operation until the present span was completed in 1916. See *SWH*, *Magazine of the Midlands*, October 9, 1977; Klein, *Union Pacific: Birth*; Wallace Brown, "George L. Miller and the Boosting of Omaha," *NH* 50, Fall 1969; and Gary W. Garabrandt, "A Brief Look into the Life of Charles Childs, a Bellevue Pioneer," in Simmons, *"La Belle Vue."* Orr, *O&CB* details the early importance of the bridge in the development of local transportation. The completion of the bridge brought about the legal contest that led to the U.S. Supreme Court decision that Council Bluffs was the official eastern terminus of the Union Pacific. The *Council Bluffs Nonpareil*, May 15, 1875, published the federal circuit court decision in favor of Council Bluffs, and the subsequent 1876 U.S. Supreme Court decision is *Union Pacific Railroad Company v. Hall et al*, 91 U.S. 343 (1875 U.S. Lexis 1372). The *Nonpareil*, *Omaha Herald*, and *Omaha Republican* show the contrasting responses on opposite sides of the river to this decision.

Davis, *The Union Pacific Railway*; Trottman, *History of the Union Pacific*; Ames, *Pioneering the Union Pacific*; and Klein, *Union Pacific: Birth* all stress the road's management problems and deteriorating financial position. Gene R. Pugh, "The Consolidation of the Union Pacific and Kansas Pacific Railroads in 1880," master's thesis, OU (1963) examines a short-run success that caused long-run problems. On the receivership sale of the Union Pacific, see Maury Klein, *Union Pacific: The Rebirth 1894–1969* (1990). The building of the Union Pacific stations, viaducts, and improvements at the line's Omaha shops are treated respectively in Carla Johnson, *Union Pacific and Omaha Union Station;* Savage and Bell, *History of the City of Omaha;* and Klein, *Union Pacific: Birth.* For the Chicago, Burlington and Quincy Railroad, see Overton, *Burlington Route;* Thomas M. Davis, "Building the Burlington through Nebraska—A Summary View," NH 30, December 1949. Rod "Bat" Masterson's article, "Plattsmouth, Nebraska," in *Burlington Bulletin* 16, June 1986 has valuable details on the history of the Burlington in Plattsmouth, a town that became part of the Omaha metropolitan area. Leighton, *Five Cities* called the railroads Omaha's "glory." Larsen, *The Urban West* contains information on the extent of Omaha's railroad net in 1880.

Overton, *Burlington Route* and Cronon, *Nature's Metropolis* have material on the inauguration of the Burlington *Fast Mail* train from Chicago to Council Bluffs. Frank P. Donovan, "The Wabash Reaches Omaha," *Palimpsest* 45, October 1964; August William Derleth, *The Milwaukee Road: Its First Hundred Years* (1948, reprint 2002); H. Roger Grant, *The Cornbelt Route: A History of the Chicago Great Western Railroad Company* (1984); and John F. Stover, *History of the Illinois Central Railroad* (1975) have useful details on the lines that came to Council Bluffs and Omaha after the initial period of railroad development. Julius Grodinsky, *Transcontinental Railway Strategy, 1869–1893: A Study of Businessmen* (1962) includes excellent material on corporate policies that governed railroad operations in the regions served through Council Bluffs and Omaha.

Mauck, "The Council Bluffs Story" plus two booster publications, F. L. Hayden, ed., *The Council Bluffs of 1889* (1889) and the transportation supplement in the *Nonpareil*, October 28, 1900, have helpful information on a variety of topics on the late-nineteenth-century development of Omaha's eastern neighbor. Andrew McMillen's description of the bottomlands on the Iowa side of the river west of the early Council Bluffs and other *Nonpareil* articles containing his recollections are found in vol. 3, "History," vertical files, CBPL. For summary comments on the ague, or fever, in midcontinent bottomlands, see R. Carlisle Buley, *The Old Northwest: Pioneer Period,* vol. 1 (1950, reprint 1978) and John Madson, *Where the Sky Began: Land of the Tallgrass Prairie* (1982). Carlos A. Schwantes, "Soldiers of Misfortune, Part I: Iowa Railroads versus Kelly's Army of Unemployed, 1894," and "Soldiers of Misfortune, Part II: Jack London, Kelly's Army and the Struggle for Survival in Iowa," *Annals of Iowa* 46, Winter 1983; Spring 1983 relate an important episode of the 1890s that unfolded partly in Council Bluffs.

The advantages of Nebraska are extolled in L. D. Burch, *Nebraska as It Is: A Comprehensive Summary of the Resources, Advantages and Drawbacks of the Great Prairie State* (1878). Everett Dick, *The Sod House Frontier* (1937) contains valuable data on Nebraska settlement patterns. So do Olson and Naugle, *History of Nebraska* and Richard C. Overton, *Burlington West: A Colonization History of the Burlington Railroad* (1941). Herbert L. Glynn, "The Urban Real Estate Boom in Nebraska during the '80's," master's thesis, University of Nebraska (1927) examines the economic aspects of the settlement boom. Samuel Aughey, *Sketches of the Physical Geography and Geology of Nebraska* (1880) and C. D. Wilber, *The Great Valleys and Prairies of Nebraska* (1881) claimed that Nebraska's annual rainfall was increasing. The promotional activities of an important Nebraska leader are discussed in James C. Olson, *J. Sterling Morton* (1942). For a problem not mentioned by the promoters see Gary D. Olson, ed., "Relief for Nebraska Grasshopper Victims: The Official Journal of Lt. Theodore E. True," *NH* 48, Summer 1967.

Basic to the rise of the packing industry are the Omaha Livestock Market, Incorporated, Papers, Nebraska State Historical Society. Of special value are the incorporation papers, the corporate minutes, and the financial statements. See also an undated document in the papers, "Extracts from the 'History of the City of Omaha' by James W. Savage and John T. Bell, published, October 21, 1893." John A. McShane's account of how he convinced packers to move to South Omaha is in Sorenson, *The Story of Omaha*. This book also has good material on William Paxton. *South Omaha Stock Yards and Packing House Interests Illustrated* (1898) is an informative promotional pamphlet. Consul W. Butterfield's chapters in the section, "History of South Omaha" in Savage and Bell, *History of the City of Omaha* have valuable data on the emergence of South Omaha as a stockyards and packing center as well as a community. The *OWH*, April 23, 1976, ran a "Special Report" on South Omaha. An outstanding treatment of the early history of local meat packing is Gail Lorna DiDonato, "Building the Meat Packing Industry in South Omaha, 1883–1898," master's thesis, UNO (1989). There is considerable information on the rise of the cattle industry in Nebraska in Louis Atherton, *The Cattle Kings* (1961); Edward Everett Dale, *The Range Cattle Industry* (1930); and Mari Sandoz, *The Cattlemen* (1958).

Omaha's commercial and industrial life won approval in G. H. Brown, *The Industries of Omaha, Nebraska* (1887); *Omaha Illustrated: A History of the Pioneer Period and the Omaha of Today* (1888); and *Historical and Descriptive Review of Omaha: Her Leading Business Houses and Enterprising Men* (1892). Conditions in Omaha after the economic collapse are elaborated upon in Morearty, *Omaha Memories*. Much usable data is contained in W. N. Nason, *Fifteenth Annual Report of the Trade and Commerce of Omaha for the Fiscal Year Ending December 31, 1891* (1892). Mark D. Budka, "The White Lead Industry in Omaha, Nebraska," *NH* 73, Summer 1992 is a fine treatment of an early industry, and Janet R. Daly-Bednarek, *The Changing Image of the City: Planning for Downtown Omaha, 1945–1973* (1992) has background information on the Carter Lake area. For Omaha as a military center, see Walter C. Sharp Jr., "Fort Omaha and the Winning of the West," master's thesis, OU (1967). Omaha newspapers gave extensive coverage to the 1892 Populist convention, printing the texts of many speeches. Gurdon W. Wattles explained the tactics he used to enter Omaha society in *Autobiography of Gurdon W. Wattles: Genealogy* (1922).

For the great event that symbolized the passing of the frontier and Omaha's stature as a city of regional prominence, the basic account is James B. Haynes, *History of the Trans-Mississippi and International Exposition of 1898* (1910). A useful promotional booklet from the time is John C. Small, *The City of Council Bluffs, Iowa, Pottawattamie County, Iowa, and the Trans-Mississippi and International Exposition* (1898). Good historical treatments include Kenneth G. Alfers, "Triumph of the West: The Trans-Mississippi Exposition," *NH* 53, Fall 1972; Patrice Kay Beam, "The Last Victorian Fair: The Trans-Mississippi [and] International Exposition," *Journal of the West* 33, January 1994; and a UNO videotape, *Westward the Empire: Omaha's World's Fair of 1898* (1998).

CHAPTER 5

Social and political developments in the last three decades of the nineteenth century dominate this chapter: vice and crime, politics, community leaders, urban services, religious institutions, voluntary associations, architectural forms, and ethnic groups. Albert Shaw equated the Trans-Mississippi Exposition to the march of civilization in "The Trans-Mississippians and their Fair at Omaha," *Century Magazine* 56, December 1898; Sorenson, *The Story of*

Omaha attributes the 1869 poem about conditions in the city to a local journalist. Although his evidence appears conclusive, some other local historians claim the author was a well-known poet, John G. Saxe.

Valuable material on the issue of the sale of alcoholic beverages in Omaha and Council Bluffs is found in F. S. Spence, comp., *The Facts of the Case: A Summary of the Most Important Evidence and Argument[s] Presented for Prohibition in the Report of the Royal Commission on the Liquor Traffic Compiled under the Direction of the Dominion Alliance for the Total Suppression of the Liquor Traffic* (1896, reprint 1973). On the legal and political contexts, see Schwieder, *Iowa;* Mauck, "The Council Bluffs Story"; Richard J. Jensen, *The Winning of the Midwest: Social and Political Conflict, 1888–1896* (1971); and Paulo E. Colletta, *William Jennings Bryan,* vol. 1 of *Political Evangelist, 1860–1908* (1964). All the local histories have considerable sections on Omaha as a wide-open town. Burkley, *The Faded Frontier* examines Canada Bill and his gang. Sorenson, *The Story of Omaha,* contains a good narrative account of vice activities. Josie Washburn, *Underworld Sewer: A Prostitute Reflects on the Trade, 1871–1909* (1909, reprint 1997) is helpful. Morearty, *Omaha Memories,* examined conditions firsthand and made some perceptive comments. He also has helpful data on politics, the administration of justice, and influential leaders.

Bristow, *A Dirty, Wicked Town* covers various topics from this period, not all of them sordid; but crime, race, and the 1891 lynching are discussed in Bristow and Savage and Bell, *History of the City of Omaha.* Bristow's extensive treatment of the lynching is excellent; our quote on public sentiment respecting George Smith's fate is from Savage and Bell. This chapter relies upon Miller, *A Selected History of the Council Bluffs Police* for the proposed solution to the transient problem and the threatened lynching in 1894. H. H. Field's report of arrests in 1883–84 is found in the Council Bluffs *Globe,* March 17, 1884. Clare V. McKanna Jr., *Homicide, Race and Justice in the American West, 1880–1920* (1997) has a chapter on Omaha. See also the two following articles by McKanna: "Alcohol, Handguns, and Homicide in the American West: A Tale of Three Counties, 1880–1920," *Western Historical Quarterly* 26, Winter 1995 and "Seeds of Destruction: Homicide, Race, and Justice in Omaha, 1880–1920," *Journal of American Ethnic History* 14, Fall 1994. Kathleen Louise Fimple, "Midwestern Mosaic: A Study of the Homogeneity of Ethnic Populations in Omaha, Nebraska, 1880," master's thesis, South Dakota State University (1978) has maps that show Omaha's ethnic geography. Sherrill F. Daniels, ed., "'So Different from Country Life': The 1888 Omaha Letters of Frisby L. Rasp," *NH* 71, Summer 1990 gives interesting vignettes of city life. Brown, "George L. Miller and the Boosting of Omaha" analyzes the activities of an important Omahan. There is much primary material on Edward Rosewater in the Rosewater Family Papers in the Nebraska State Historical Society.

Information on urban services and institutions is available in a number of places including Wakely, *The Gate City* and in Dustin, *Omaha and Douglas County*. In addition to Orr, *O&CB*, the following discuss street transportation for this period: Street Railway Department of Omaha, *History of Street Railways in the City of Omaha, 1867–1928* (n.d.); E. Bryant Phillips, "Interurban Projects in and around Omaha," *NH* 29, March 1948; and "Horse Car Days and Ways in Nebraska," *NH* 30, September 1949; Dennis Thavenet, "A History of Omaha Public Transportation," master's thesis, OU (1960); and the Gurdon W. Wattles Papers in the UNO Library. For other services see Metropolitan Utilities District, *Water Supply: The Story of Omaha's Municipal Water Supply* (1942); Ronald W. Hunter, "Grand Central Hotel, Three-Alarm Pyre," *Omaha* 4, June 1979; Harry Edward Dice, "The History of the Omaha Fire Department: 1860–1960," master's thesis, OU (1965); Michael Joseph Harkins, "Public Health in Early Omaha, 1857–1900," master's thesis, UNO (1973) and his "Public Health Nuisances in Omaha, 1870–1900," *NH* 56, Winter 1975; Jacqueline Johnson, "A History of Health and Safety Conditions in the Omaha Public Schools from 1872 to 1908," master's thesis, UNO (1968); Board of Trade, *Trade and Commerce* (1892); and *Ninth Annual Report of the Board of Park Commissioners of Omaha, Nebraska, for the Year 1898*. See also Daly-Bednarek, *The Changing Image of the City* and Savage and Bell, *History of the City of Omaha*; Mauck, "The Council Bluffs Story"; Hayden, *The Council Bluffs of 1889*; Field and Reed, *History of Pottawattamie County*; Transportation supplement, *Nonpareil*, October 28, 1900; and Lawrence H. Larsen, "Urban Iowa One Hundred Years Ago," *Annals of Iowa* 49, Fall 1988.

Religious surveys include Carol Gendler, "The Jews of Omaha: The First Sixty Years," master's thesis, OU (1968); Szmrecsanyi, *The Catholic Church in Northeast Nebraska*; Henry Casper, *History of the Catholic Church in Nebraska: The Church on the Fading Frontier, 1864–1910* (1966); Alonzo DeLarme, *History of the First Baptist Church of Omaha* (1925); Carol Gendler, "The First Synagogue in Nebraska: The Early History of the Congregation of Israel of

Omaha," NH 58, Fall 1977; Everett Jackman, *The Nebraska Methodist Story: 1854–1954* (1954); and James Robbins, "A History of The Episcopal Church in Omaha from 1856 to 1964," master's thesis, OU (1965). Good material on ethnicity and the question of cultural retention versus Americanization is found in Sister Marilyn Graskowiak, "Parochial Education in a Czech Community: The School Sisters of Notre Dame in Elementary Education in Omaha 1920–1960," master's thesis, UNO (1977). Cary De Cordova Wintz, "Social Response to Ethnic Groups in Omaha, Nebraska: 1892–1910, master's thesis, Kansas State University (1968) shows that the level of ethnic tensions reflected other social and economic conditions. In tracing ethnicity within the city, maps of Omaha ward boundaries in 1894 and 1905, courtesy of Garneth O. Peterson, were valuable.

Three fine essays are in the Federal Writers Project Papers: Anne Frank, "Metropolitan Utilities District," August 10, 1938; Carl Uhlarik, "Education," August 30, 1939; and Ellen Bishop, "Religion," August 30, 1939. See also Robert S. Kittell, "The Omaha Ice Trust, 1899–1900: An Urban Monopoly," NH 54, Winter 1973. Welfare activities are covered in Dustin, *Omaha and Douglas County.* McCulloch, "Memories"; and Victor Rosewater, *School Days in Early Omaha* (1912) have information on social affairs. Howard P. Chudacoff, *Mobile Americans: Residential and Social Mobility in Omaha, 1880–1920* (1972) demonstrates that Omahans often moved. See also his article, "A Look at Ethnic Neighborhoods: Residential Dispersion and the Concept of Visibility in a Medium-Sized City," *Journal of American History* 60, June 1973. Census statistics are questioned in Edgar Z. Palmer, "The Correctness of the 1890 Census of Population for Nebraska Cities," NH 32, December 1951.

There is excellent data on Omaha architecture in *Standard Blue Presents Buildings of the 80's in Omaha* (1976); Landmarks Incorporated and Junior League of Omaha, *Omaha City Architecture* (1977); and Landmarks, Inc. [Kristine Gerber and Jeffrey S. Spencer], Building for the Ages: Omaha's Architectural Landmarks (2003). Leonard K. Eaton, *Gateway Cities and Other Essays* (1989) has a chapter on the Jobbers' Canyon wholesale district. Two works done under the auspices of Landmarks Heritage Preservation Commission: *A Comprehensive Program for Historic Preservation in Omaha* and *Patterns on the Landscape: Historic Conservation in North Omaha* contribute to an understanding of what is sometimes called the city's "built environment." Garneth Peterson's historical narratives in the Landmarks Heritage Preservation Commission books are valuable discussions of Omaha's history during this period. See also Penelope Chatfield, "Old Market Historic District," National Register of Historic Places Inventory-Nomination Form, December 1977, in the State Historic Preservation Office of the Nebraska State Historical Society.

CHAPTER 6

Key themes in this chapter are agricultural progress, the resurgence of the Union Pacific Railroad, the rise of Gurdon W. Wattles, labor troubles, the development of community economic goals, industrial and transportation advances, the impact of World War I, the role of James E. Davidson in the electric power business, and the prosperity of the 1920s. Trottman, *History of the Union Pacific* and Klein, *Union Pacific: Rebirth* have good analyses of how E. H. Harriman improved the Union Pacific's fortunes. There is rich material on economic matters in Olson and Naugle, *History of Nebraska* and Schwieder, *Iowa*. Details on Omaha can be found in Wakely, *The Gate City*; Sorenson, *The Story of Omaha*, and Morearty, *Omaha Memories*. Judy Horan's essay on early medicine in Omaha in the *World-Herald*'s sesquicentennial publication, "Omaha . . . 150 . . . and counting" briefly treats the development of the University of Nebraska College of Medicine. The Chamber of Commerce ad touting Omaha hospitals appeared in the *Nonpareil*, August 16, 1921. A published 1941 talk by Sanford R. Gifford, MD, "Garlic and Old Horse Blankets," copy in OPL, centering on the career of his father, Harold Gifford Sr., MD, gives a vivid perspective of a medical practice that drew patients from across the region.

Details on Council Bluffs topics are found in Ramsey and Shrier, *Silent Hills Speak;* Publicity Committee [Council Bluffs] Chamber of Commerce, comp., *Council Bluffs, Iowa* (n.d.); New Homes Edition supplement in *Nonpareil*, May 9, 1926; *Nonpareil*, January 11, 1932, obituary of Donald Macrae Jr., MD; and *Nonpareil* articles in the historical clipping file, CBPL. See Helen Ruth Montague, comp., "The Water Supply of Council Bluffs, Iowa" (1934), an unpublished manuscript, CBPL, for the quotation on the muddy tap water. The quotation on truck traffic is from the *Nonpareil*, January 29, 1919.

Leighton, *Five Cities* attacks Wattles's handling of the 1909 transit strike and takes a dim view of Davidson's motives. Wattles defended his role in the transit strike in *A Crime against Labor: A Brief History of the Omaha and Council Bluffs Street Railroad Strike* (n.d.). His papers show that he did not consider himself antiunion. There were strikes in Omaha before Wattles: see

Ronald Gephart, "Politicians, Soldiers and Strikers: The Reorganization of the Nebraska Militia and the Omaha Strike of 1882," NH 46, June 1965. For aspects of Omaha's labor history, see the following works by William C. Pratt: his booklet *Omaha in the Making of Nebraska Labor History* (1981); "The Omaha Businessmen's Association and the Open Shop, 1903–1909," NH 70, Summer 1989; "Advancing Packinghouse Unionism in South Omaha, 1917–1920," *Journal of the West* 35, April 1996; "Divided Workers, Divided Communities: The 1921–22 Packinghouse Strike in Omaha and Nebraska City," *Labor's Heritage* 5, Winter 1994; and "'Union Maids' in Omaha Labor History," in Nebraska Department of Education and Nebraska State Council for the Social Studies, *Perspectives: Women in Nebraska History* (June 1984). See also Oliver B. Pollak, "The Workman's Circle and Labor Lyceum in Omaha, 1907–1977," NH 76, Spring 1995. Inez Whitehead, "Fort Omaha Balloon School: Its Role in World War I," NH, 69 Spring 1988 covers an interesting aspect of local wartime activity. A fine work on a topic of local, national, and international importance is Gary Gernhart, "A Forgotten Enemy: Omaha Encounters the 1918 Influenza Pandemic," master's thesis, UNO (1998).

The Omaha Livestock Market, Incorporated papers reveal the continued growth of the livestock industry. A promotional pamphlet, *Union Stock Yards Company of Omaha, Limited* (1926) has valuable data. So does the *Official Souvenir Book: Omaha Grain Exchange* (1909). The experiences of a suburban area are analyzed in Dorothy Ruth Mutz, "Benson: A Residential Suburban Community," master's thesis, OU (1935). Emmet C. Hoctor, "Tom Hoctor and the Magic City: The South Omaha Annexation Fight, 1890–1915" NH 64, Summer 1983 details the long struggle over South Omaha's municipal status. The physical expansion of Omaha is examined in Garneth Peterson's historical narrative in *A Comprehensive Program for Historic Preservation*. Victor Rosewater, "Omaha, the Transcontinental Gateway," in L. P. Powell, *Historic Towns of the Western States* (1901) painted a rosy picture of the future, as did George Craig, *Omaha's Financial, Commercial, and Manufacturing Resources Epitomized* (1912). Two essays treat the history of an important Omaha retailer: "The Brandeis Story," WH April 10, 1974; The Brandeis Stores, *Down through the Years* (1936) discusses the physical characteristics of the downtown store. Optimistic predictions are made in *Omaha—Gate City of the West: The Growth of a City* (1929). Tommy R. Thompson, *A History of the University of Nebraska at Omaha, 1908–1983* (1983) shows another dimension of how some Omahans sought to advance their community. Leslie R. Valentine, "Boosting 'Omaha the Market Town': The 1906 Trade Excursion across Northern Kansas," *Kansas History* 15, Summer 1992 illustrates the work of the Omaha Commercial Club, the predecessor of the Chamber of Commerce, in building Omaha's business links to the region.

The story of the Ford Motor Company assembly plant is briefly treated in DCHS clipping files on that firm and in Folder #46, WPA files, University Archives, UNO. The impact of motor vehicles is discussed in Clinton Warne, "The Acceptance of the Automobile in Nebraska," *NH* 37, Summer 1956; Tommy R. Thompson, "The Devil Wagon Comes to Omaha: The First Decade of the Automobile, 1900–1910," *NH* 61, Summer 1980; Orr, *O&CB*; the first part of Sebree, "Omaha and Council Bluffs" on bus service; and William Thompson, *Transportation in Iowa*. *SWH*, April 27, 1919 has a good story on the role of trucking in linking Omaha to the surrounding area. *Nonpareil* articles in the historical clipping files of the CBPL are helpful. *Langwith's Motor Trails Map [of] Missouri* (1930), published for Phillips Petroleum, and the *Texaco Road Map [of] Kansas and Nebraska* (1933) show some of the early highways serving Omaha–Council Bluffs and the status of their development. Gary D. Dixon, "Harrison County, Iowa: Aspects of Life from 1920 to 1930," master's thesis, UNO (1997) shows how the automobile made Omaha–Council Bluffs increasingly important in the lives of rural and small-town people. The building of a new Union Station is discussed in Johnson, *Union Pacific and Omaha Union Station*. For early aviation, see Leslie R. Valentine, "The Development of the Omaha Municipal Airfield, 1924–1930," master's thesis, UNO (1980) and his article of the same title, *NH* 61, Winter 1980. Valentine's "The First All Nebraska Air Tour, 1929: 'One Big Family in the Air or on the Ground,'" *NH* 66, Spring 1985 treats Omahans and aviation boosting. Janet R. Daly-Bednarek, *America's Airports: Airfield Development, 1918–1947* (2001) places Omaha's early airport development in a national context. The coming of another technological advance to Omaha is discussed in Katherine F. Wyatt, "The Beginnings of Broadcast Radio in Omaha, Nebraska, 1919 to 1923" master's thesis, UNO (1992).

CHAPTER 7

Among things considered in this chapter are the character of the population, the persistence of interracial violence, the traditions associated with a wide-open town, the imperfections of machine politics, and the search for cultural refinement. Sorenson, *The Story of Omaha* has a section on the 1919 riot. The best general account of Omaha social life in the first three decades of the twentieth century is "Omaha Guide, Part 1, History of City," in the FWP Papers.

Material on women in the work force is based upon U.S. Census, 1900, *Statistics of Women At Work* (1907); U.S. Census, 1910, vol. 4, *Population 1910 Occupation Statistics* (1914, reprint 1999); *SWH*, July 1, 1900, "Help Wanted-Female" listings; and the essays by William C. Pratt, "'Union Maids' in Omaha Labor History 1887–1945"; Marjorie Sobotka, "Rose Rosicky"; and Vicki L. Bagrowski, "Bess Furman 1894–1969" in Susan Pierce, ed., *Perspectives: Women in Nebraska History* (1984). See also Liz Watts, "Bess Furman: Nebraska's Front Page Girl," *NH* 74, Summer 1993; and Susanne George Bloomfield, ed., *Impertinences: Selected Writings of Elia Peattie, a Journalist in the Gilded Age* (2005). Bloomfield's presentation of the OWH career of a notable woman writer offers insights into life in Omaha and its region in the 1890s.

The immigrant experience, which involved South Omaha as well as Omaha proper, has been chronicled in a number of places. Special Federal Writers Project reports include J. H. Norris, "Russians in Omaha," October 4, 1937; Rose Michael, "Russian Recreation in Omaha," December 10, 1936; Ray Cunningham, "Chinese in Omaha," September 14, 1936; and "Japanese of Omaha," September 14, 1936; Robert Curran, "Syrians in Omaha," December 30, 1936; and Marie Donohue, "Sheeley Town," August 8, 1938. The Sons of Italy sponsored the publication of a Federal Writers Project manuscript, *The Italians of Omaha* (1941). For other studies of immigrants see Rose Rosicky, *A History of Czechs in Nebraska* (1929); Jeronimus Cicenas, *Omahos Lietuviai Lithuanians of Omaha* (1955); Jonathan P. Herzog, "Our Sacred Lithuanian Word: St. Anthony's Thirst for Cultural Homogeneity," *NH* 84, Fall 2003; T. Earl Sullenger, *The Immigrant in Omaha* (1934); and Tommy R. Thompson, "Wearin' of the Green: The Irish and St. Patrick's Day in Omaha," *NH* 81, Winter 2000. Graskowiak, "Parochial Education in a Czech Community"; Szmrecsanyi, *The Catholic Church in Northeast Nebraska;* and an article by Elizabeth Sears, *SWH*, April 16, 1905 are helpful. See also "'Twas a 'Melting Pot,'" *South Omaha Sun*, June 10, 1971.

Contemporary local papers treated the 1905 anti-Japanese episode as did the *New York Times*, April 18, 1905. Resentment against an ethnic group resulted in violence in 1909. Two works by John G. Bitzes cover this incident: "The Anti-Greek Riot of 1909—South Omaha," master's thesis, OU (1964) and his subsequent article that has the same title, NH 51, Summer 1970. For information on Mexican immigrants and a tragic episode that began in Omaha and ended near Scribner, Nebraska, see Michael De La Garza, "The Lynching of Juan Gonzalez," NH 85, Spring 2004.

The WH, the *Bee*, and the *News* all afforded extensive coverage of the 1919 riot. An editorial in the *Monitor*, October 2, 1919, expressed the view of a black editor. Especially good are Orville D. Menard, "Tom Dennison, the Omaha Bee, and the 1919 Omaha Race Riot," NH 66, Winter 1987 and Clayton D. Laurie, "The U.S. Army and the Omaha Race Riot of 1919," NH 72, Fall 1991. *Omaha's Riot in Stories and Pictures* (1919) is a straightforward account. An excellent summary in the Federal Writers Project reports is D. K. Bukin, "Omaha Race Riot." Orville Menard, searching the 1920 census, discovered the correct spelling of the maiden name of the woman who was allegedly assaulted prior to the 1919 riot. For background on the riot, see Michael L. Lawson, "Omaha, A City in Ferment: Summer of 1919," NH 58, Fall 1977 and Federal Writers Project monograph sponsored by the Omaha Urban League Community Center, *The Negroes of Nebraska* (1940). The admonition "Look at what happened in Omaha" is found in Michael Fedo, *The Lynchings in Duluth* (1979, reprint 2000). Willard B. Gatewood Jr., "The Perils of Passing: The McCary's of Omaha," NH 71, Summer 1990 has good material on racial attitudes in Omaha. Hardships notwithstanding, African Americans developed organizations that fostered and reflected community stability as shown in Dennis N. Mihelich, "The Origins of the Prince Hall Mason Master Grand Lodge of Nebraska," NH 76, Spring 1995. The first chapter of Harry Haywood's *Black Bolshevik: Autobiography of an Afro-American Communist* (1978) has a valuable perspective on blacks in South Omaha.

Miller, *A Selected History of the Council Bluffs Police* provides basic details on the 1903 racial episode and the plight in 1910 of Chief Richmond. The *Nonpareil*, February 23, 24, 1909, relates the repercussions in Council Bluffs of the anti-Greek riot in South Omaha, and its issues between May 28 and July 15, 1913, plus articles on March 18, 1914, and June 23, 1915, cover the Jones murder and the ensuing troubles. See also the *Glenwood (IA) Opinion*, June 26 to July 3, 1913, and December 20 to 30, 1915, for the trials of Francesco Guidice.

The *Nonpareil*, September 29, 30 and October 1, 4, 1919, describes the impact of Omaha's 1919 riot upon Council Bluffs.

Political reform efforts failed to change conditions in Omaha. Newspaper reaction to the commission plan is analyzed in William F. Schmidt, "Municipal Reform in Omaha from 1906 to 1914 as Seen through the Eyes of the Omaha Press," master's thesis, OU (1963). Mayor Edward Smith's ill-fated administration is examined in Louise E. Rickard, "The Politics of Reform in Omaha, 1918–1921," NH 53, Winter 1972. An excellent discussion of the city's political dynamics is Richard K. Wilson, "Business Progressivism in Omaha, 1900–1917," master's thesis, Creighton University (1977). The best account of machine government is Orville D. Menard, *Political Bossism in Mid-America: Tom Dennison's Omaha, 1900–1933* (1989). See also Menard, "Tom Dennison: The Rogue Who Ruled Omaha," *Omaha* 3, March 1978 and John Kyle Davis, "The Gray Wolf: Tom Dennison of Omaha," NH 58, Spring 1977. A researcher, Alan Jacobsen, theorized that Dennison played a role in the 1919 riot: WH, February 10, 1979; *Gateway* (UNO student newspaper), February 2, 1979. H. W. Becker's article in the *Sun* papers on September 20, 1979, said the 1892 death of a South Omaha mayor, Charles P. Miller, sounded like a "Tom Dennison gang frameup." On William E. Nesselhous, see also *Nonpareil*, January 3, 1937. Josie Washburn exposed vice practices in *The First Drink Saloon and Dance Hall* (1914). A dramatic spiritual reform effort is portrayed in Leslie R. Valentine, "Evangelist Billy Sunday's Clean-Up Campaign in Omaha: Local Reaction to His 50–Day Revival," NH 64, Summer 1983. The scrapbooks in the James Dahlman Papers in the Nebraska State Historical Society (on microfilm, OPL) shed some light on his career. See also R. K. De Arment, "Omaha's Cowboy Mayor," *True West* 42, March 1995 and Fred Carey, *Mayor Jim: An Epic of the West* (1930). For gambling and prostitution in Council Bluffs, see Raymond A. Smith Jr., "John C. Mabray: A Con Artist in the Corn Belt," *Palimpsest* 64, July–August 1983; Frank W. Smetana, *A History of Lake Manawa 1881–1981* (1981); Ramsey and Shrier, *Silent Hills Speak;* and the obituary of Ben Marks, *Nonpareil*, April 26, 1919.

Interesting accounts of Omaha's elite are found in Killian, *Born Rich* and Oliver B. Pollak, "Capitalism, Culture, and Philanthropy: Charles N. and Nettie Fowler Dietz of Omaha, 1881–1939," NH 79, Spring 1998. Two NH articles by Dennis N. Mihelich, "George Joslyn: America's First Media Mogul," 82, Spring 2001 and "The Joslyns of Omaha: Opulence and Philanthropy," 83, Spring

2003 provide fine treatment of the lives of George and Sarah Joslyn. There is an excellent description of the Joslyn Memorial in The American Guide Series, *Nebraska*.

CHAPTER 8

The central concerns of this chapter are depression, war, and prosperity. Topics include William Randolph Hearst's temporary entry into Omaha, the collapse of the economy, the frustrations of the Omaha business community, the role of the New Deal, the traction strike, the impact of World War II, the plans for postwar consolidation, the acquisition of the Strategic Air Command headquarters, and the prosperity of the 1950s. Lawrence H. Larsen and Barbara J. Cottrell, "Omaha and the Great Depression: Progress in the Face of Adversity," *Journal of the West* 24, October 1985 and Dustin, *Omaha and Douglas County* survey the period. Much valuable material can be found as well in Rawley's centennial history in *WH*. Olson and Naugle, *History of Nebraska* and Schwieder, *Iowa* detail the economic fortunes of their states during this era. For an important social service, see Mary Lyons-Barrett, "The Omaha Visiting Nurses Association during the 1920s and 1930s," *NH* 70, Winter 1989.

Mauck, "The Council Bluffs Story" has some information on this period, and Ramsey and Shrier, *Silent Hills Speak* treats the building of the South Omaha Bridge and the Council Bluffs City Building. For the most part, this chapter relies upon the *Nonpareil* for information on Council Bluffs during the Great Depression, but the short-lived weekly *Council Bluffs Jeffersonian* is useful. Smetana, *A History of Lake Manawa*, details work in the 1930s and after to save that body of water. Basic to the Farmers' Holiday movement are John L. Shover's book, *Cornbelt Rebellion: The Farmers' Holiday Association* (1965) and his articles, "The Farmers' Holiday Association Strike, August 1932," *Agricultural History* 39, October 1965 and "The Farm Holiday Movement in Nebraska," *NH* 43, March 1962. Albert Noyes, "Council Bluffs: The Blue Denim City," *Iowan* 1 August–September 1953 is a good portrayal of that city at midcentury. Information on the Broadway viaduct is from City Manager folder, historical clippings, CBPL.

A spokesman predicted great things for Omaha in "Hearst Has Faith" in Fred Carey, *Romance of Omaha* (1929). The plight of Omaha's Ford Motor plant is treated in the Ford Motor clipping files, DCHS. For the transit strike of 1935, see Mary Cochran Grimes, "The Governor and the Guard in the Omaha Tram Strike of 1935," *NH* 69, Fall 1988; Larsen and Cottrell, "Omaha and the Great Depression"; and Leighton, *Five Cities*. There is an account of the strike in "Omaha Guide, Part 1, History of City," in the Federal Writers Project Papers. Scrapbooks in the Roy Nathan Towl Papers in the Nebraska State Historical Society contain clippings concerning the strike. For a chronology of the strike see the *EWH*, June 21, 1935. For the Sealock tragedy and later developments at the Municipal University, see Thompson, *History of the University of Nebraska at Omaha*. Press reaction to events of the 1930s is analyzed in Ira Jones, "A Study of the Editorial Policy of the Omaha *Bee-News* and the Omaha *World-Herald* with Regard to Social Problems," master's thesis, OU (1937). Business and political trends in the late 1930s are portrayed in Walter L. Pierpoint, as told to O. K. Armstrong, "Omaha Taxpayers Point the Way," *Saturday Evening Post* 210, July–September 1937; Jerold L. Hohndorf, "The White Spot Campaign and Collectibles" (1989) (a collector's newsletter in the possession of Harl A. Dalstrom), and Harl A. Dalstrom, "'We have redeemed Nebraska': Kenneth S. Wherry and Republican Resurgence in the Cornhusker State, 1937–1940," *Journal of the West* 41, Fall 2002. The Omaha Chamber of Commerce Industrial Bureau, *Omaha* (1936) aimed at attracting new industries. A "confidential" report, U.S. Department of Labor, Nebraska State Employment Service, Affiliated with Social Security Board, "A Survey of the Employment Situation in Omaha, Nebraska" (1941), in the Nebraska State Historical Society summarized the labor situation on the eve of World War II. For a later time, see William C. Pratt, "Employer Offensive in Nebraska Politics, 1946–1949," in *Politics in the Postwar American West*, ed. Richard Lowitt (1995); William C. Pratt, "Workers, Bosses, and Public Officials: Omaha's 1948 Packinghouse Strike," *NH* 66, Fall 1985; and Wilson J. Warren, "The Impasse of Radicalism and Race: Omaha's Meatpacking Unionism, 1945–1955," *Journal of the West* 35, April 1996.

Nebraska politicians helped the Omaha area gain wartime and postwar facilities. Richard Lowitt, *George W. Norris: The Triumph of a Progressive* (1978) has valuable material on George Norris's role in obtaining an aircraft assembly plant. See also the George Norris Papers in the Manuscript Division of the Library of Congress; the Chester Davis Papers in the joint collection of the University of Missouri Western Manuscript Collection and the State Historical Society of Missouri Manuscripts, PPF880, and "Davis, Hon. Chester,

Member, Advisory Com. to council of Ngt. Defense, November 30, 1940," in the Franklin D. Roosevelt Library. The following publications provide valuable material on Bellevue's rise in the 1940s: Willie Browning, "Mules to Missiles: A Brief History of Old Fort Crook," in Simmons, *"La Belle Vue"*; George A. Larson, "Nebraska's World War II Bomber Plant: The Glenn L. Martin–Nebraska Company," NH 74, Spring 1993; Jerold L. Simmons, "Public Leadership in a World War II Boom Town: Bellevue, Nebraska," NH 65 Winter 1984; and Jacqueline McGlade, "The Zoning of Fort Crook: Urban Expansionism vs. County Home Rule," NH 64, Spring 1983. The SAC Historian's Office at Offutt Air Force Base has some unclassified material on the move of SAC headquarters to Nebraska. Kenneth S. Wherry's role is detailed and analyzed in Harl Adams Dalstrom, "Kenneth S. Wherry," PhD diss., University of Nebraska (1965). The SAC commander at the time of the move to Omaha said he played no part in the decision: Curtis E. LeMay with MacKinlay Kantor, *Mission with LeMay* (1965). A summary of a facet of air defense is found in Stephen Harris, "Early-Warning Radar," *The Canadian Encyclopedia*, 1 (1985). Carl Abbott, *The Metropolitan Frontier: Cities in the Modern American West* (1993), places the impact of World War II and the cold war upon the Omaha area in broad context.

Public policy on Missouri River development is vital to Greater Omaha and a vast drainage area. See Robert L. Branyan, *Taming the Mighty Missouri: A History of the Kansas City District Corps of Engineers, 1907–1971* (1974); Marion Ridgeway, *The Missouri Basin's Pick-Sloan Plan: A Case Study in Congressional Policy Determination* (1955); Henry C. Hart, *The Dark Missouri* (1957); and Schneiders, *Unruly River.*

Reports produced by the Omaha City Planning Department either helped to set or explain policy: *Omaha, Nebraska, City Plan* (1945); *Housing* (1946); *Housing Plan* (1977); and *Future Land Use* (1977). Dustin, *Omaha and Douglas County* has good material on the rise of the insurance industry. For the story of a remarkable local enterprise see Robert C. Phipps, *The Swanson Story: When the Chicken Flew the Coup* (1976). For another side see David Harris, "Swanson Saga: End of a Dream," *New York Times Magazine*, September 9, 1979. See also articles by Kris Mullen, SWH, April 3, 1994, and John Taylor, OWH, April 1, 1999. The Swanson TV advertising jingle is the recollection of Harl A. Dalstrom. Background material on Woodmen of the World is from Daly-Bednarek, *The Changing Image of the City* and Sorenson, *The Story of*

Omaha. The changing fortunes of the power industry are examined in Martin Pennock, "The Formation of the Omaha Public Power District," master's thesis, UNO (1971). A valuable factual summary of statistics about Omaha in the late 1950s is Omaha Chamber of Commerce, *This Is Omaha* (1958).

CHAPTER 9

Featured in this chapter are the realities of the Great Depression, the effect of New Deal social programs, the changes wrought by World War II, the gradual shift of Omaha from a blue- to white-collar town, and the quest for political reform. For events involving A. V. Sorensen, this chapter uses Harl A. Dalstrom, *A. V. Sorensen and the New Omaha* (1988). Janet R. Daly, "Early City Planning Efforts in Omaha, 1914–1920," NH 66, Spring 1985 covers the beginnings of a key function of municipal government. Daly-Bednarek's book, *The Changing Image of the City*, though centering on the period 1945 to 1973, has good material on pre-1945 planning efforts.

The 1930s were harsh years for the people of Greater Omaha. Blacks experienced very hard times as illustrated by T. Earl Sullenger and J. Harvey Kerns, *The Negro in Omaha* (1931); J. Harvey Kerns, *Industrial and Business Life of Negroes in Omaha* (1932); and Francis Y. Knapple, "The Negro High School Student: A Study of the Negro Students in Omaha Central High School (1935–1941)," master's thesis, OU (1952). Peterson in *Patterns on the Landscape* has essential details on the development of the black community. Preston Love, *A Thousand Honey Creeks Later: My Life in Music from Basie to Motown* (1997) has good material of an important aspect of the culture of the black community. Harl A. and Kay Calamé Dalstrom, "'Back by Popular Demand!': Dancing in Small-Town South Dakota," *South Dakota History* 32, Winter 2002 notes the importance of Omaha as a booking center for black and white dance bands. Dennis N. Mihelich, "World War II and the Transformation of the Omaha Urban League," NH 60, Fall 1979 discusses the league's emerging leadership in advancing civil rights. Kathleen M. Davis, "Fighting Jim Crow in Post World War II Omaha, 1945–1956," master's thesis, UNO (2002) is an outstanding contribution to the history of the civil-rights movement. In the same vein are Jeffrey H. Smith, "The Omaha De Porres Club," *Negro History Bulletin* 33, December 1970, and his 1967 Creighton University master's thesis of the same title. Szmrecsanyi, *The Catholic Church in Northeast Nebraska* also treats racism within the church. The late Professor Paul L.

Beck told Harl A. Dalstrom that he had advised black secondary-education students at the University of Omaha to consider seeking positions in Minneapolis. On the life of "Denny" Holland, see obituary by Julia McCord, OWH, January 15, 2003. For European ethnicity, see DCHS clipping file on Latvians and Lithuanians and Cicenas, *Lithuanians of Omaha* and *Mes Lietuvai We Lithuanians* (1984). Herzog, "Our Sacred Lithuanian Word" is also useful for this period.

The Federal Writers Project Papers contain invaluable "Life Histories": R. F. Worley, "Peter Christensen," May 1, 1941; Joseph Glarizo, "Sam Piccioni," March 28, 1941; A. E. Finch, "James Breezee," August 22, 1941; and Louis B. Adams, "Wesley J. Cook," November 26, 1941. WPA and PWA final reports for Nebraska, such as "Nebraska, Division of Women's and Professional Projects," Part 1 (1938) in the National Archives Building, NARS, Washington, DC are of great value. John Vachon's Farm Security Administration photos, held by the Prints and Photographs Division, Library of Congress, may be viewed online at http://lcweb2.loc.gov/ammem/fsahtml/fachap02.html. For Tillie Olsen and Omaha, see her *Yonnondio: From the Thirties* (1974). Linda Ray Pratt, "Tillie Olsen: Author, Organizer, Feminist," in Pierce, *Perspectives* is an excellent summary of Olsen's career and the themes of her writings.

Folders in the clipping files of the DCHS and Menard, *Political Bossism in Mid-America* have helpful material on Dan Butler, Richard Metcalfe, and Roy Towl. Apparent local efforts to control Omaha relief programs are mentioned in an article from the *Columbus (NE) Telegram*, reprinted in *Lincoln Star*, October 11, 1938. A useful compendium of newspaper clippings on gambling in the Omaha area in the late 1930s is found in the "Bookies" War folder and the Carter Lake folder, WPA files, University Archives, UNO Library. WH stories on October 21 and November 6, 1950 illustrate the persistence of gambling. Miller, *A Selected History of the Council Bluffs Police* notes arrests for gambling in Council Bluffs between 1944 and 1956. Gary Newman's SWH feature article (January 21, 1990) discusses gambling in the Omaha area into the 1950s and Robert Dorr's February 9, 1997, feature story in that paper treats the career of Jackie Gaughan. Nelson, *The Ak-Sar-Ben Story* relates that organization's sponsorship of horse racing.

For a survey of wartime trends see Dorothy May Cathers, "Civilian War Activities in Omaha During World War II," master's thesis, University of Nebraska (1952). A connection between the home front and the war is shown in Douglas R. Hartman, "Lawrence W. Youngman: War Correspondent for the *Omaha World-Herald*," NH 76, Summer–Fall 1995.

A 1944 report of the Omaha City Planning Commission, *Land Use and Zoning*, contains valuable data. There is interesting information on postwar social conditions in *Report of a Community Survey of Omaha, Nebraska* (1946). The Young Men's Christian Association and Young Women's Christian Association Committee for Program Planning in Omaha prepared the report. Grandiose hopes for Omaha's postwar plan are discussed in "An American City's Dream," *Life* 23 July 7, 1947. Daly-Bednarek, *The Changing Image of the City* and Donahue, *Pathways to Prosperity* treat the private funding of the pay increases for fire and police personnel. Generalizations on women in the Greater Omaha work force are based upon U.S. Census, *Census of Population: 1960*, vol. 1, *Characteristics of the Population*, part 29, *Nebraska*.

Midcentury brought the adoption of new forms of city government in Council Bluffs and Omaha. For Council Bluffs, see city manager clipping folder, CBPL, and for Omaha, see Daly-Bednarek, *The Changing Image of the City*, and the WH coverage prior to the November 1950 vote rejecting the change. Omaha's successful effort to adopt a strong-mayor system received massive newspaper coverage and is analyzed in an excellent work: Harold T. Muir, "The Formation and Adoption of the 1956 Omaha Home Rule Charter, 1954–1956," master's thesis, UNO (1969). Daly-Bednarek, *The Changing Image of the City* and Dalstrom's *A. V. Sorensen and the New Omaha* and his "Omaha's East-West Voting Division" paper presented at the Missouri Valley Historical Conference, March 8, 1990, treat the "old" and "new" Omaha polarity in public affairs during this period. See also Rene R. Beauchesne, "The Political Impact of the Omaha Home Rule Charter (1956)," typed manuscript, Alumni Memorial Library, Creighton University. Commissioner Hummel's comment about not hiring "expensive experts" is found in OWH, May 10, 1939, copy courtesy Orville Menard. That Omaha's improvement initiatives in the generation after World War II approximated those in other western cities is evident in Abbott, *Metropolitan Frontier*.

Conflicting views of city life are presented by the Omaha Chamber of Commerce, *This Is Omaha* and Jack Lait and Lee Mortimer, *U.S.A. Confidential* (1952). Omaha received good national publicity when it gained an award: Ben Kocivar, "The National Municipal League and *Look* Salute the All American Cities," *Look* 22 February 4, 1958. An OWH article by John Whitesides, February 25, 1985, and an accompanying map are valuable to an understanding of the boundaries of Benson, Dundee, Florence, and South Omaha. The clipping file index, History and Social Sciences Department, OPL, leads to data from the Omaha Council of Churches, Church Census, October 1950. For this informal enumeration in Council Bluffs, see *Nonpareil*, November 2, 5, 1950. For the successful battle against the 1952 flood, see Ramsey and Shrier, *Silent Hills Speak* and B. F. Sylvester, "Omaha's Flood, 1952," NH 35, March 1954. The reference to the east-west split over constructing a high school for the western part of Council Bluffs is exemplified in a vote reported in the *Nonpareil*, March 9, 1920. Joseph W. Preusser, "A Hierarchy of Residential Neighborhoods Determined by Blight Conditions: The Case of Council Bluffs, Iowa," master's thesis, UNO (1970) addresses the east-west split. For the later development of Omaha's airport, see Kevin Glenn Huey, "The Development and Growth of Eppley Airfield: 1925–1984; From the Early Days of the Omaha Airfield to the Silver Anniversary of the Airport Authority," master's thesis, UNO (1988).

There are many excellent aerial photographs of the Omaha area in a *World-Herald* project, *Omaha from the Air: Magic Carpet Photo Series* (1947). See also J. J. Hanighen Company, *Omaha Skyline, A History: 75 Years of Building* (1961).

CHAPTER 10

Subjects covered in this chapter include the development of shopping centers, the differing plights of urban renewal in Omaha and Council Bluffs, debates over urban growth including annexation, and Omaha's leadership. Other topics include the continuation of federal involvement, the dramatic changes in Omaha's economy, and the start of downtown redevelopment. Daly-Bednarek, *The Changing Image of the City* has essential material on Omaha's downtown development and related topics from the postwar period to 1973. For urban renewal, see Donald Louis Stevens's excellent master's thesis, "The Urban Renewal Movement in Omaha, 1954–1979," UNO (1981) and his "Government, Interest Groups and the People: Urban Renewal in Omaha, 1954–1970," NH 67, Summer 1986. Dalstrom, *A. V. Sorensen and the New Omaha* (1988) discusses the early development of shopping centers in Omaha and other matters in which A. V. Sorensen was involved. Eaton, *Gateway Cities* and Jim Schwab, "Omaha Held Hostage," *The Progressive* 53, May

1989 treat the plight of Jobbers' Canyon. Samuel Mercer, *The Old Market and Omaha* (1994) gives the perspective of someone who played a crucial part in preserving and reanimating this distinctive commercial area. Because there are few historical works on the period since 1960s, historians have to construct their own conceptual framework and act as "instant sociologists." Excellent articles in the *wh* and the *Sun* publications make it possible to build a synthesis. The Central Park Mall and ConAgra clipping files at the *opl* provide important details on the redevelopment of the eastern part of downtown, and other files have material on individuals. The *wh* clipping files at the *dchs* have extensive material on Council Bluffs, while the *Nonpareil* and the clipping files at the *cbpl* are essential. *New York Times* articles sometimes provided summary perspectives on Omaha. The quotation from Terry Moore following the recall of Mayor Boyle is from a January 15, 1987, *Times* article by William Robbins. See also *Chicago Tribune* articles by Rogers Worthington, January 14, 15, 1987.

Journalistic accounts about the quality of life are augmented by John P. Zipay, *The Changing Population of the Omaha smsa 1960–1967 with Estimates for 1970* (1967); Lawrence A. Danton, *The Economic Structure of the Omaha smsa* (1967); and Keith Nollen, "An Inventory of Land Uses: Northwest Omaha," master's thesis, *uno* (1972). Of special value is the Omaha City Planning Department, *The Urban Development Policy* (1977, updated March 1980). The role of the Eppley Foundation in improving Omaha's airport is discussed in Harl Adams Dalstrom, *Eugene C. Eppley: His Life and Legacy* (1969). South Omaha's triumphs and tragedies are summarized in Niel M. Johnson, *South Omaha: A Brief History* (1977); "South Omaha—Centennial City," *Sun* papers, April 13, 1967, and "South Omaha: A Special Report," *owh*, April 23, 1976. There is interesting material in Downtown Omaha, Incorporated, *The Downtowner*, advertising supplement, *owh*, March 8, 1976. *Orpheum* (1975) treats a major restoration project. Dalstrom, A. V. *Sorensen and the New Omaha* (1988) treats the development of shopping centers.

Analyzing a community power structure is a difficult task. One of the best studies ever produced on the dominant groups in an American city is Paul Williams, "Twenty Top Omaha's Power Structure," *Sun* papers, April 7, 1966. The quotation on changes in the "Twenty Influentials" from 1966 to 1971 is from Daly-Bednarek, *The Changing Image of the City*. See also Paul Hammel, "Who Wields the Power in Omaha?" *Sun* papers, July 22, 1981. For Peter

Kiewit and his firm, see Hollis Limprecht, *The Kiewit Story: Remarkable Man, Remarkable Company* (1981).

CHAPTER 11

This chapter contains material on social unrest, housing patterns, higher education, cultural trends, Boys Town's financial condition, vice matters, natural disasters, and the quality of life. Much of the story has been pieced together from the *WH*, the *Sun* papers, and the *Star* and draws from Dalstrom, *A. V. Sorensen and the New Omaha* (1988). The 1990 U.S. Census of Population, *Social and Economic Characteristics: Metropolitan Areas* (1993) provides much information. The quotation on the OIF's stimulation of industrial decentralization is from Daly-Bednarek, *The Changing Image of the City.* Data on blight in Council Bluffs and related points are from Preusser, "A Hierarchy of Residential Neighborhoods Determined by Blight Conditions." See also Roger L. Pearson, "The Power Structure of Council Bluffs: A Methodological and Descriptive Analysis," master's thesis, UNO (1968).

There is valuable background information on the urban crisis in Marion Taylor, "A Survey of Employer Attitudes toward the Employment of Qualified Negroes in White Collar Positions in Omaha," master's thesis, OU (1954) and Mihelich, "World War II and the Transformation of the Urban League." Paul A. Jensen, "The Nebraska Civil Rights Act of 1969," a UNO graduate-student paper done under the direction of Professor William C. Pratt was helpful. Retrospective material on the Near North Side troubles are found in *OWH*, April 5, 2000 (article by Rick Ruggles); *SWH*, January 19, 2000 (article by Robert Dorr and Tanya Eiserer); and *SWH*, August 27, 2000 (article by Leslie Reed). Ashley Howard, "The Omaha Riots of the 1960s and the Economic Decline of the Near North Side," a paper presented at the Missouri Valley Historical Conference, March 4, 2005, presents evidence showing that, contrary to common belief, the riots of the 1960s exacerbated rather than caused the economic decline of the Near North Side. For the changing aspects of Omaha living patterns see George W. Barger, *Social Cohesion in Omaha: A Preliminary Study* (1968) and Al Pagel, "Two Lifestyles in the City—the Old and the New," *SWH*, *Magazine of the Midlands*, October 16, 1977.

The development of Creighton University is covered in an article in the same publication on February 12, 1978, authored by Gary Johansen, titled, "The School Was Too Far Out." Dennis Mihelich, *The History of Creighton*

University, 1878–2003 (2006), is a valuable addition to historical scholarship on Omaha and the history of higher education. In addition to Thompson, *History of the University of Nebraska at Omaha*, two useful sources on that institution are Lillian Henderson Campen, "The Early History of the University of Omaha," master's thesis, OU (1951) and Martha Helligso, "The Administrative Development of Graduate Education at the University of Omaha, 1909–1968, master's thesis, UNO (1971). Dalstrom, "Omaha's East-West Voting Division" traces the strong support from the affluent parts of the city for the University of Omaha. For the early development of the Omaha Symphony, see Rotolo, "The Women's Division of the Omaha Chamber of Commerce, 1922–1976." Good summary material on the development of the Joslyn Art Museum is found in Kyle MacMillan's OWH stories of May 10, 11, 1993 and SWH, November 13, 1994. Jim Delmont's stories, SWH, June 16, 1996, provide similar material on the Western Heritage Museum.

"Boys Town: America's Wealthiest City," *Sun* papers, March 30, 1972, received a Pulitzer Prize. See also Paul Goodsell's article, SWH, March 9, 1997, and stories by Christopher Burbach, OWH, August 24, 2000, and Joseph Morton, October 5, 2006. Summary data on Girls and Boys Town is found in http://www.girlsandboystown.org/aboutus/locations/index.asp. Investigative accounts on sin include "Call Girls Tell Their Story," *Sun* papers, September 10, 1970 and "Prostitution in Omaha: Business Is Brisk," WH, June 23, 1971. Sally Torpy, "The 1913 Omaha Tornado: A Calamity Overcome," *Heritage of the Great Plains* 26, Summer 1993 treats the city's greatest disaster in terms of lives lost. Miller, *A Selected History of the Council Bluffs Police* has summary material on the storm. Dustin, *Omaha and Douglas County* briefly discusses this and other weather-related events. A work by the Omaha City Planning Department, *Disaster Response: The 1975 Omaha Tornado* (1977) is useful as is Howard Silber, ed., *The Omaha Tornado May 6, 1975* (1975). A new Omahan praised the city in Joseph Levine, "Omaha, I Love You," *Look* 24 July 30, 1960. Omaha is compared with other cities in Arthur M. Lewis, "The Worst in the U.S. and Omaha's Standing," WH, January 29, 1975.

CHAPTER 12

The period from 1985 to the start of the twenty-first century brought great changes to Council Bluffs. This chapter discusses the principal developments of these years: the introduction of dog racing and later casino gambling and related attractions that were intended to invigorate a lethargic economy, the role of the Iowa West Foundation in community betterment, the establishment a new form of municipal government, and the role of the state line in shaping life in the Council Bluffs–Omaha area. Essential to telling the story of dog racing and casino gambling are the gambling folders in the vertical files of the Council Bluffs Public Library. These contain clippings from the *Nonpareil*, the *World-Herald*, and the *Des Moines Register* plus two reports from the Iowa West Racing Association. A search of the *Nonpareil* in the period leading to the 1985 vote on the switch to the strong-mayor system provided information on that topic. For 1997 onward, the narrative relied primarily upon stories in the *OWH* and *SWH*, supplemented by *Nonpareil* articles and the Iowa West Foundation 2002 Annual Report. Ramsey and Shrier, *Silent Hills Speak*, was helpful. The term, "Council Bluffs Revival," comes from Patrick Strawbridge's article, *OWH*, April 25, 2000. Gail Holmes used the words "quiet architecture" to describe the Western Historic Trails Center, article by Dave Moratz, *OWH*, April 23, 2002. Particularly useful were the following feature stories on Tom Hanafan, all in the *OWH*: Interview by Bob McMorris, April 30, 1988; articles by Gary Newman, January 3, 1997; Stephen Buttry, November 5, 1997; Patrick Strawbridge, August 8, 2001; editorial, November 1, 2001; and Michael Kelly column, November 13, 2001.

CHAPTER 13

This chapter treats the history of Omaha from 1990 to 2005, a time of continuing rebuilding downtown and a massive redevelopment immediately to the northeast. Mindful of Omaha's low profile in urban America, civic leaders used these changes and other improvements to highlight the quality of life in the city. The reconfiguration of Omaha's economy toward a service orientation continued and information-age enterprises became fundamental to the city's vitality. A vigorous local economy marked this period, but the socioeconomic problems that exploded in the 1960s were largely unresolved. The rapid growth of the Hispanic population brought a new ethnic dimension to the metropolitan area.

The principal sources for this chapter were articles in the *WH* and *SWH*. Feature stories, such as the eight-part series, "Omaha: A Community Profile," published April 6–14, 1997, and Michael O'Connor's "Commuting in 'reverse,'" October 4, 2003, were particularly helpful. Articles by C. David Kotok

(March 21, 2006) and Henry J. Cordes (June 24, 2006) on the 2005 population estimate are examples of timely *WH* and *SWH* stories on demographic trends shaping the urban area and region. A five-part series on the public schools, April 20–24, 1997, and its May 12, 1999 treatment of the outcome of the OPS school-bond vote exemplify the paper's fine coverage of education issues. For important summary information on employment in Greater Omaha, 2000 to 2004, see the article by Steve Jordon and C. David Kotok, *SWH*, March 27, 2005, and sidebar to article by Chris Clayton, *WH*, July 30, 2005. An article by Ron Suskind, *Wall Street Journal*, November 8, 1991, had useful information on Warren Buffett. See also Andrew Kilpatrick, *Of Permanent Value: The Story of Warren Buffett* (1994) and Roger Lowenstein, *Buffett: The Making of an American Capitalist* (1995). Stories in the *Lincoln Star-Journal*, August 11 and 21, 2001, treated the subject of tax incentives for a new Union Pacific headquarters. Some statistical data is from Daly-Bednarek, *The Changing Image of the City*. A Greater Omaha Chamber of Commerce publication, *Trends in the Omaha Economy 1990–2001* (May 2002) and *Trends, 1990–2003* (n.d.) were essential, and the following chamber publications were used: *In Brief* (February 2003); *Top 100 Employers Omaha Metropolitan Area* (March 2003); and *Indicators for the Minority Community* (June 2001). The last-mentioned work and E. David Fifer, *Omaha Conditions Survey: 1998* (1998), a publication of the Center for Public Affairs Research, UNO, provided information on "underemployed" persons. Indeed, the many publications of the Center for Public Affairs Research have valuable material on a variety of socioeconomic trends in the recent history of Greater Omaha. Abbott, *Metropolitan Frontier*, although not mentioning Omaha's switch from at-large to district elections, stresses the importance of this phenomenon in enhancing the voting power of America's urban minorities.

The National Foundation for Women Business Owners, "Women-Owned Businesses in Nebraska: 1996 A Fact Sheet" was useful. See Pottawattamie County Growth Alliance, *Council Bluffs: Iowa's Leading Edge* (n.d.) for a variety of statistics. Dale Swenson and Liesl Earthington, Department of Economics, Iowa State University, *An Iowa Economic Atlas* (n.d.)—Adobe PDF copies available through dswenson@iastate.edu or leathing@iastate.edu— places the Council Bluffs–Omaha trade area in the context of the rest of Iowa. Copy, courtesy of Mark Norman of the Council Bluffs Chamber of Commerce. A Metropolitan Area Planning Agency document, "Major Commuting Patterns 2000," courtesy of Mark Norman, gives essential data on commuting. See also OWH articles by Paul Goodsell, February 8, 2003, and Michael O'Connor, August 27, 2003. An unpublished Omaha Planning Department document, "Omaha Corporate Limits by Annexation," details Omaha's territorial growth. Mark Purdy's *San Jose Mercury* column on the College World Series was reprinted in the *Las Vegas Review-Journal*, June 5, 1995, copy courtesy of the late Col. Don E. Kahley, USAF. On Omaha as a grain-marketing point in the period 1960 to 1965, see John T. Wilhelm, "Delimitation of the Omaha Wheat Source Supply Region," master's thesis, UNO (1968). *A Visit to the Omaha Grain Exchange* (1967), Omaha Grain Exchange clipping file, vertical files, OPL, briefly explains the functioning of that organization. For the demise of the exchange, see article by Alan Gersten, OWH, September 19, 1987, same file. The purposes of Omaha by Design are found in a WH advertisement supplement by that organization and on its website, www.omahabydesign.org.

The Historian's Office, U.S. Strategic Command, Offutt Air Force Base, provided information about changes at Offutt in the 1990s. Michael Peterson's "72nd St. a Critical Boundary for Candidates," *Nebraska Observer*, April 26, 1989, is a brief but good discussion of Omaha's political geography. Cronon, *Nature's Metropolis* and especially James C. Malin, *The Nebraska Question, 1852–1854* (1953) were valuable in relating contemporary Omaha to the city's nineteenth-century origins.

[Index]